The Daily Telegraph
Schools Guide

The Daily Telegraph
Schools Guide

Over 400 of the best independent and state schools

Edited by **John Clare**

HEINEMANN : LONDON

First published in Great Britain 1992 by
William Heinemann Ltd
an imprint of Reed Consumer Books Ltd
Michelin House, 81 Fulham Road, London SW3 6RB
and Auckland, Melbourne, Singapore and Toronto

ISBN 0 434 13548 8

A CIP catalogue for this title
is available from the British Library

Typeset by Wakefield Associates, Derby
Printed in Great Britain by Clays Ltd, St Ives plc

Contents

Introduction

All the schools in this guide are good – but in a variety of ways to suit children of different abilities and aptitudes. Some are highly selective: they have rigorous entry requirements and admit only the cleverest children. Others are less selective but tend to admit only the academically able with the potential to achieve at least 2 good A-levels and go on to university.

The rest of the schools – nearly half the total – accept children of all (or nearly all) abilities. Depending on their catchment areas, some achieve better exam results than schools which are openly selective. Many specialise in meeting the needs of the less academically able and those with learning difficulties, such as dyslexia.

The best school for any child is the one which suits him or her best: the one, in other words, that offers a challenging but not overwhelming environment. The aim of this guide is to provide a sufficiently detailed portrait of each school – including its admission requirements – to enable parents to decide whether it is likely to suit their child and is therefore worth investigating further.

The guide contains descriptions of 430 schools: 310 independent (i.e. fee-paying) and 120 state. The independent schools are divided between 60 preparatory schools and 250 senior schools. The prep schools take children at the age of 7 but many have pre-prep departments admitting those as young as $3^1/_2$. Traditionally, girls move on to senior school at 11 while boys transfer at 13. Many of the senior schools have their own junior departments, from which promotion is more or less automatic; all have sixth forms offering A-levels. The state schools – all secondary – comprise 35 grammar schools, which are academically selective,

and 85 comprehensives, which are not; all but a handful have sixth forms. Both the independent and state schools offer a choice between single sex and co-education, and between day and boarding.

I chose the schools in a variety of ways. For those that are academically selective, the most important criteria were their exam results. The guide therefore includes virtually all the top 250 independent and state schools as measured by their A-level subject entries graded A or B. In 1992 the national average was 29%. No school which admits only the ablest children should score less than 40%, though results do vary from year to year. The entries also recorded the proportion of GCSE pupils who achieved at least 5 passes at grades A to C (either for the year stated or averaged over the past 3 years). In 1991 the national average was 37%. No academically selective school should score less than 85%.

Although there are no such simple criteria for schools which admit children of a wide range of abilities, exam results are still a vital measure of effectiveness. A school which claims to have a comprehensive intake but consistently scores below the national average at GCSE or A-level is unlikely to offer its pupils a stimulating educational environment. Those with favoured, middle-class catchment areas – like many of the schools in the guide – should score considerably above the national average.

Results apart, I relied for information on a network of contacts built up over nearly 10 years of reporting on education. The good independent schools are relatively easy to identify: those who run them are accustomed to the idea of parental choice and are generally willing to offer well-informed (if off-the-record) judgements about their competitors. Sadly, the state sector is often characterised by a conspiracy of silence. Many state school heads still maintain that one school is as good as another (despite Her Majesty's Inspectors' reporting year after year that a third of state school pupils 'get a raw deal'), and that all any parent needs to know is which one is nearest. Such heads find the idea of a consumer guide abhorrent. Indeed, the Secondary Heads Association strongly advised its members to boycott this one (advice which most of them ignored).

Each of the chosen schools was visited by one of a team of 34 inspectors, all experienced educationists. Many are recently-retired heads (of both state and independent schools); the rest included former members of Her Majesty's Inspectorate, local authority chief inspectors, senior Government advisers and teachers. They worked to a common pro-forma, which meant they were all looking at the same things and asking the same questions; I edited their reports to ensure consistency. Eight of the schools inspected were not thought worthy of inclusion.

There is no suggestion that these are the only good schools in Britain. Such a claim would be absurd. However, this guide does offer parents a benchmark: here is what a good school of its type is like. How does the one you may be considering for your child compare?

Note
If you have any comments about the schools in this guide or any suggestions for other schools to be included in the next edition, please write to John Clare, Education Editor, Daily Telegraph, 1 Canada Square, Canary Wharf, London E14 5DT.

Glossary of Terms

A-levels and AS-levels Taken usually in 3 (but sometimes 2) subjects by about 30% of pupils after 2 years' study post-GCSE, they are the main qualification for entry to higher education. They are graded A–E and grades A–C are required for admission to courses at the more established universities. AS-levels are equivalent to half an A-level. They were designed to give pupils an opportunity to broaden their studies; however, the take-up so far has been low.

Assisted places Awarded to bright children from disadvantaged homes to enable them to attend selected independent schools. The Government pays all or part of the tuition (but not boarding) fees on a sliding scale dependent on parental income. About 30,000 places are held at any one time. Further information from: ISIS (the Independent Schools Information Service), 56 Buckingham Gate, London, SW1E 6AG (tel:071-630 8793/4).

BTEC A qualification awarded by the Business and Technician Education Council. A vocational alternative to A-levels, it can lead on to higher education.

Bursaries and scholarships Bursaries are awarded by independent schools to children who meet their academic requirements but whose parents cannot afford the full fees; they are usually means-tested. Scholarships (of varying value) are awarded to children who are academically outstanding or excel in music, art or, sometimes, sport; they may be means-tested.

'Chalk and talk' Shorthand for traditional, didactic instruction: the whole class is taught by a teacher who stands in front of a blackboard and does most of the talking. Now often replaced (or, at least, supplemented) by 'active learning': classes are divided into small groups of pupils who work together at 'projects'.

Common Entrance The exam taken by prep school pupils (usually at 11+ by girls and 13+ by boys) before they transfer to senior school. The chosen senior school marks the papers and decides the minimum standard it requires: the most severely selective demand an average mark of 65%; the least selective, 45%.

City Technology Colleges State-funded comprehensive schools which teach the national curriculum but concentrate heavily on maths, science and technology; they were established as an experiment in collaboration with industry and commerce and are exceptionally well resourced.

Day boarders Sleep at home but are otherwise as fully involved in school life as boarders.

Direct Grant status Given under the 1944 Education Act to independent schools which offered up to half of their places to children from state schools; the cost was borne by the Government and local education authorities. The Labour Government abolished it in 1975; in 1981 the Conservative Government introduced the assisted places scheme *(qv)* as a replacement.

Dual-award science Instead of taking science as three separate subjects – physics, chemistry and biology – a growing number of pupils are being taught it as an integrated subject for which two grades are awarded at GCSE.

'First-time buyers' Parents of independent school pupils who were not themselves educated at independent schools. They now comprise about 40% of those who are paying for their children's education; many are seeking the grammar-school education they themselves received but which is now rarely available in the state sector.

'Gap year' A break between A-levels and

higher education. Both schools and universities are increasingly encouraging young people to take a year off to travel, read and broaden their minds.

GCSE The General Certificate of Secondary Education; taken in up to 10 subjects (sometimes more) by virtually all 16-year-olds at the end of their compulsory education. It is graded A–G, and grades A–C are reckoned to be equivalent to a pass at O-level, the exam that GCSE replaced in 1988.

Girls Public Day School Trust An estimable institution founded in 1872 to set up schools that would provide girls with 'a fine academic education at comparatively modest cost' – something which the trust's 26 member schools still do (most are included in this guide).

Grammar schools State schools which select pupils by academic ability as measured by their performance in tests at 11+. They were largely abolished in the drive for comprehensive education during the late 1960s and early 1970s; only about 150 survived (a quarter of them are included in this guide).

Grant maintained State schools that have voted to opt out of local education authority control: they run themselves and are directly funded by the Government.

Highers Taken in Scotland 1 year after Standard Grade *(qv)* and not, therefore, the equivalent of A-levels, which are taken 2 years after GCSE.

International Baccalaureate A broader-based and generally more demanding alternative to A-levels which requires pupils to keep up their study of both the arts and the sciences. It is offered by a growing number of independent schools but by only a handful in the state sector.

Opting out See grant-maintained.

Oxbridge Shorthand for Oxford and Cambridge universities. Because they are the hardest to get into for most subjects, academically selective schools tend to keep a careful tally of how many of their pupils are admitted each year.

Standard Grade The Scottish equivalent to GCSE.

Streaming and setting Two methods of dividing children by ability to ensure that those at the same stage are taught at the same pace. Streaming involves sorting the children into broad ability bands (generally below average, average and above average); setting is further refinement which recognises that a child who is, say, below average in maths may be above average in English. Both are opposed by most advocates of comprehensive education, who argue that children of all abilities should be taught in the same class.

Voluntary-controlled/aided Schools that were originally built by voluntary bodies, usually churches but sometimes trusts. They are now largely funded by local education authorities but retain a good deal of autonomy.

NB Unless otherwise stated, fees are for 1991-92. They are expected to rise by an average of 7% in 1992-93.

The Schools

Preparatory Schools

ABBERLEY HALL
Worcester WR6 6DD
Tel (0299) 896275

Boys • Boarding and some day • Ages 8-13 (plus small junior department) • 212 pupils (88% boarding) • Fees, £6,990 boarding; £1,995-£5,250 day
Head: Michael Haggard, mid-50s, appointed 1974.

Good all round; admits boys of all abilities and sends them on to most of the leading independent schools.

Background Slightly forbidding, mid-Victorian mansion (in urgent need of refurbishment) on ancient hilltop site near the Severn Valley. (Moved here from London in 1916 'to escape the Zeppelins'.)

Atmosphere Genuine warmth belies the gaunt exterior; air of relaxed but dignified informality. Boys dress casually for lessons (but no jeans or trainers); some staff happy to be called by their nicknames. Pleasant dormitories (8 beds on average) carpeted, curtained and clean.

The head Old Boy of Abberley Hall; went on to Winchester and Cambridge, returned here briefly to teach, finally came back as head. Conforms to the popular image of a good prep-school head: kindly, caring, steeped in tradition. Married with 2 sons; hobbies include philately and tapestry.

The teaching Varies from desks in rows to informal small-group work. All subjects taught to a high standard but especially classics, history, 3 sciences, computer-aided design and technology. Setting by ability in maths, French; brightest boys spend 2 years in scholarship form; average class size 10-12. Nearly all staff appointed by present head; mostly well-qualified graduates (80% male); 2 special-needs teachers. Good drama and music (75% learn an instrument); bright, large room for art and pottery.

The pupils Well-mannered boys who converse confidently with visitors. Mostly from business, professional and farming backgrounds; many have strong family connections with the school. Most live within 1$^1/_2$ hours' drive and go home every other weekend. Recruitment by word of mouth; no formal selection procedures; IQs range from 80 to 145. 3 scholarships, 5 bursaries a year.

Results Head boasts no boy has failed to get into his (guided) first-choice school for 7 years.

Destinations Mostly to leading independent schools, including Eton, Harrow, Shrewsbury, Winchester.

Sport Extensive playing fields; all major games compulsory; school performs well in competition with the best. Fine new sports hall; all-weather pitch; heated outdoor pool. Wide range of options include golf, archery, fencing, judo, trampolining (prep schools champions).

Remarks Happy, successful school. Buildings need rescuing by English Heritage.

ABERLOUR HOUSE

Aberlour,
Banffshire AB38 9LJ
Tel (0340) 871267

Co-educational • Boarding and day •
Ages 7-13 • 126 pupils (61% boys; 90%
boarding) • Fees (1992-93), £7,455
boarding; £5,100 day
Head: John Caithness, 49, appointed
January 1992.

---

*Small, happy prep school principally
serving Gordonstoun* (qv) *whose ethos it
shares; lots of outdoor activities*

Background Founded 1937; elegant Georgian country house plus extensive purpose-built additions in idyllic Spey Valley setting (peacocks and peahens roam the grounds). Co-educational since the early 1970s.

Atmosphere Homely, happy; emphasis on developing self-reliance. School is well-resourced; everything bright, tidy, clean. Cosy dormitories (6-10 beds); some rather crowded.

The head Educated at Merchiston Castle and St Andrews; taught in New Zealand for 5 years; formerly head of Catteral Hall. Teaches Latin and scripture. Married, 2 children (both educated at Gordonstoun); wife much involved on the pastoral side.

The teaching First-rate; very committed staff. Full Common Entrance curriculum; half take Latin (but Greek is no more); good technology. Setting by ability in maths, French; average class size 16; extra help for those who need it. Good music: 70% learn an instrument; small orchestra, choir. Lots of weekend expeditions (and a refreshing readiness to interrupt the timetable for other worthwhile activities). Pupils encouraged to develop interests and pursue projects. Annual summer school for gifted and talented children.

The pupils Enthusiastic, cheerful. Parents mainly from professions and industry; more than half from Scotland, a quarter from the rest of the UK. Admission by interview; not severely selective; entry to Gordonstoun is not guaranteed. Parents may assess themselves above or below the standard fee; if below, the child will be accepted only if the shortfall is made up by an award from the Gordonstoun Foundation.

Results Good Common Entrance record.

Destinations 87% transfer to Gordonstoun; 12% to Rannoch.

Sport Chiefly rugby, hockey, cricket for the boys; netball, hockey, rounders for the girls; all do athletics; riding is popular. Facilities include extensive playing fields, sports hall, small heated pool, 4 all-weather tennis courts.

Remarks Education not confined to the classroom: a school that develops free spirits and contributing citizens.

ARDVREK

Gwydyr Road,
Crieff,
Perthshire PH7 4EX
Tel (0764) 3112

Co-educational • Boarding and day •
Ages 4½-13 • 155 pupils (62% boys, 77%
boarding) • Fees (1992-93),
£7,050-£7,425 boarding; £4,350-£4,500
day
Head: Jerry Bridgeland, 43, appointed
1990.

---

*Pleasant, thriving school; good academic
and sporting record.*

Background Founded 1883; moved to present purpose-built premises (Scottish baronial style) 1885; later additions include fine music school. Some accommodation rather cramped; further building in progress. Co-educational since 1976.

Atmosphere Busy, happy, well-ordered community; strong boarding ethos. Junior dormitories attractive but crowded; seniors in 6- to 8-bed rooms; some space for private study.

The head Quiet, confident; pupils find him very approachable. Read chemistry at Oxford

(Blues in swimming, pentathlon, water polo); taught at Gordonstoun and Shrewsbury. Married, 2 children (1 was a pupil here); wife closely involved in the school and helps those with learning difficulties.

The teaching Form teaching in pre-prep department, subject specialist thereafter; French from age 10, Latin from 11. Small classes; pupils streamed by ability into Trojans and Greeks. Most learn a musical instrument; 36-strong orchestra, 2 mixed choirs; Gilbert & Sullivan every other year. Frequent outings, visiting speakers. Sometimes the whole school spends the day in the hills, walking and fishing.

The pupils Confident, secure; smartly turned-out. Parents mostly from professions and industry; 75% Scottish. Admission by interview; fairly wide ability range.

Results Common Entrance failures unheard of; average of 6 scholarships or exhibitions a year.

Destinations Mainly Strathallan, Glenalmond, Gordonstoun; significant minority south of the border to Eton, Radley etc.

Sport Chiefly rugby, cricket for the boys; hockey, netball, rounders for the girls; full inter-school fixture lists (and a good record). All do athletics and swimming; cross-country, golf, skiing, shooting also on offer. Facilities include 5 acres of playing fields and enclosed, all-weather pitch.

Remarks Successful school apparently surprised by its popularity; accommodation needs extending.

ARNOLD HOUSE

8 Loudon Road,
St John's Wood,
London NW8 OLH
Tel (071) 286 1100

Boys • Day • Ages 5-13 • 227 pupils •
Fees, £4,755
Head: Jonathan Clegg, 61, appointed 1977.

Well-established; good results.
Old-fashioned but enlightened approach.

Background Founded 1905. 2 amply-proportioned houses in quiet, tree-lined street; gardens back and front; double-asphalt playground.

Atmosphere Kindly; feels like a family. Space at a premium but uncramped by London standards; plenty of cheerful art on the walls. Compulsory religious assembly with C of E vicar once a week; Onward Christian Soldiers-type hymns.

The head Educated at Shrewsbury and Oxford. Relaxed, approachable; much liked by parents. Has appointed all 23 staff. Keen to ensure every boy receives the encouragement he needs: values effort above achievement. Attaches much importance to interviewing parents and children; evident harmony of the school is the result.

The teaching Lively. Both experience and enthusiasm are evident; parents can be confident their sons will receive a thorough grounding, and enjoy it too. Classroom arrangements vary from informal groups to front-facing rows; maximum size 14-15; extra help for dyslexics. (Reasonable conformity expected but great efforts made to accommodate individual needs.) Well-designed new science laboratory; 10 computers and more on the way. Up to 1 hour's homework a night. Good art room; lots of music (70% learn an instrument); annual play produced to a high standard. Extra-curricular activities include chess, cooking, bicycle maintenance.

The pupils Well-mannered; enjoy friendly relations with staff. Fairly wide range of abilities but nearly all capable of coping with Common Entrance; 20% Jewish. Admission on first-come basis; apply before first birthday.

Results Good Common Entrance passes to most major independent schools; 12 scholarships since 1987. (Not a crammer but boys who merit scholarships tend to get them.)

Destinations Many to Westminister; also Charterhouse, Eton, Haileybury, Harrow, Highgate, King's Canterbury, Malvern, Millfield, Rugby, University College School.

Sport 2 afternoons a week devoted to traditional games at nearby sites; swimming at Swiss Cottage; cricket coaching at Lord's. Gymnastics taught to a high standard. Fully equipped sports hall.

Remarks Well-ordered, happy school with a deservedly good reputation.

ARNOLD LODGE
Kenilworth Road,
Leamington Spa,
Warwickshire CV32 5TW
Tel (0926) 424737

Co-educational • Day, (some weekly boarding) • Ages 3-13 • 350 pupils (75% boys) • Fees, £1,575-£3,432 (£5,052 weekly boarding)
Head: Andrew Reekes, early-40s, appointed 1991.

Highly-regarded, well-resourced prep school; good scholarship record; strong sport.

Background Founded 1864 by a master from Rugby (and named after the great Dr Arnold). Attractive, solidly reassuring 1830s brick frontage plus later additions. Co-educational since 1979.

Atmosphere Well-ordered, friendly, secure community in bright, cheerful surroundings. Big emphasis on social accomplishments (importance of good spoken English stressed –

results apparent); civilised dining room; good food. Weekly boarding accommodation pleasantly furnished and homely. Long tradition of helping others (current aim is to raise £10,000 for a fibrillator at the Birmingham Children's Hospital).

The head Oxford history scholar; formerly director of studies at Cheltenham. Good communicator (letters to parents are models of clarity); brisk, direct management style (lectures for the Industrial Society and is director of a firm specialising in interview techniques). Close, amicable relations with staff and pupils alike. Married, 2 children.

The teaching Styles range from formal (regarded as 'indispensable') to more modern approachs; all equally successful with highly responsive pupils. Experienced, well-qualified staff of 31 (half women); average age late 30s. All national curriculum subjects taught, including promising work in technology. Some setting by ability in maths, English; maximum class size 16. Homework set daily, scrupulously corrected; effort and attainment reports to parents 3 times a term. Music plays central role (flourishing orchestra, music club and choir) but premises cramped. Good art; elegant dance studio; excellent library. 30-plus clubs and societies; French exchanges; Outward Bound.

The pupils Mainly from business and professional families; 12% ethnic minority. Admission at 3 or 4 by interview with parents; at 7 or 8 by tests in English, maths, verbal reasoning.

Results Head claims 100% success at Common Entrance: i.e. all pupils go on to their (negotiated) choice of independent school. Scholarships over the past two years to Warwick, Malvern, Repton, Oakham, Clifton, Wrekin, Oundle, Uppingham, Bromsgrove, Ellesmere.

Destinations Most girls move at 11 to King's High (Warwick), Kingsley (Leamington Spa), King Henry VIII (Coventry). At 13, 40% of boys go to Warwick, another 40% to Malvern/Rugby/Clifton/Cheltenham.

Sport Strong in football, rugby, cricket, netball. 12 acres of playing fields 1 mile away; leased swimming pool adjoining school.

Remarks High-achieving, happy, well-run school. Good value for money.

ASHDELL
266 Fulwood Road,
Sheffield,
South Yorkshire S10 3BL
Tel (0742) 663835

Girls • Day • Ages 4-11 • 125 pupils • Fees, £2,760-£3,120
Head: Mrs Jane Upton, 48, appointed 1984.

First-rate, traditional education for bright girls.

Background Founded in its present form in 1949 (previously a dame school). Delightful premises: 2 large, dignifed, Victorian houses plus coach house surrounded by pleasant gardens in attractive residential area close to the city centre.

Atmosphere Busy, intimate community. Happy, smiley faces (staff and children); bright, cheerful classrooms; neat, attractive uniforms. Everything maintained to a high order of good taste and style; big emphasis on good manners, consideration for others, self-discipline.

The head Warm, direct, humorous; totally absorbed in the school; has very strong convictions. Demands high standards from girls, parents and staff. Formerly taught French and German in large Sheffield comprehensives (her husband is deputy head of one).

The teaching Well-qualified, devoted staff (they voluntarily gave up their pay rise in 1991 to help to keep costs down); formal, structured methods; small classes. Great stress from the start on the basic skills of reading (parents required to play their part), writing (uniform style taught), spelling and arithmetic. Full curriculum ('a busy child is a happy child')

includes science (handsome new lab), French, Latin; all required to do ballet, speech and drama and learn a musical intrument. Extra help for those in difficulty (including dyslexia); enrichment groups for the very able. Regular homework, carefully marked. Extra-curricular activities include Brownies, cookery, gymnastics.

The pupils Bright, confident. Entry at 4 by interview: child needs to demonstrate academic potential; parents must show willingness to be actively involved. Head says: 'I want to be sure they support what we're aiming for rather than just buying what we do.'

Results Regular scholarships; virtually all win a place at their first-choice school.

Destinations About half to Sheffield High; most of the rest to boarding schools such as Cheltenham Ladies', Oakham, St Anne's (Windermere).

Sport Netball, rounders on nearby sports field; swimming in university pool, half a mile away.

Remarks Excellent value for money; highly recommended.

ASHDOWN HOUSE
Forest Row,
East Sussex RH18 5JY
Tel (034282) 2574

Co-educational • Boarding and some day • Ages 8-13 • 175 pupils (75% boys; 94% boarding) • Fees, £7,500 boarding; £6,000 day
Head: Clive Williams, 47, appointed 1975.

Traditional prep school keeping up to date; good languages, music, art; owns a chateau in France.

Background Founded 1886. Georgian mansion (grade-2 listed) in 40 acres; classical Greek pillared entrance at the end of a long drive; extensive views across the games fields to Ashdown Forest. Co-educational since 1976.

Atmosphere High expectations lead to a sense of purposefulness in games and lessons alike. Polite, friendly children (stand aside for staff, open doors for visitors). Pretty dormitories, wall-papered with matching curtains, carpets, continental quilts.

The head Old Boy of Ashdown House; returned here to teach after Eton and Cambridge. Still teaches part-time: scripture, scholarship Latin and Greek. Pleasant, relaxed manner; pupils find him approachable. Wife, Rowena, teaches history and art, oversees the care side (with 3 qualified nurses).

The teaching Styles range from the didactic to a lively, more dynamic approach. Mixed-ability classes for first 2 years, streaming thereafter, including scholarship form. Good French: pupils spend a fortnight at school's own chateau in Normandy, attend lessons with local children. Wait-and-see attitude to the national curriculum; all but a handful do Latin. Some classrooms in rather ramshackle buildings but accommodation generally adequate; average class size 15. Staff of 18 (a third women); most live with their families on site. Qualified remedial teacher for those with learning difficulties (though the school claims no special expertise). Good music: two-thirds learn an instrument; 33-strong orchestra plus various mixed ensembles, 3 choirs. 250-seat arts centre used for musical and stage productions, also morning assemblies. Good library; tatty books gradually being discarded.

The pupils Mostly from middle, upper-middle-class backgrounds; half from London, a quarter expatriate. Most of average or above-average ability; no written admission tests but head interviews every child prior to entry.

Results Scholarships in 1991 to King's (Canterbury), Sherborne, Gordonstoun, Blundell's.

Destinations Eton, Charterhouse, King's (Canterbury), Wycombe Abbey, Winchester, Harrow, Roedean, Marlborough, Woldingham etc.

Sport Chiefly soccer, rugby, cricket for the boys; netball, rounders for the girls; long list of fixtures against other schools. Hockey, tennis riding, golf also on offer. Neighbouring farmer's barn converted into large sports hall for badminton, judo etc. Heated outdoor pool.

Remarks Solid school; good all round.

AYSGARTH
Bedale,
North Yorkshire DL8 1TF
Tel (0677) 50240

Boys • Boarding • Ages 8-13 • 117 pupils
• Fees, £6,900
Head: John Hodgkinson, late 40s,
appointed 1988.

Traditional prep school, keeping up to date; wide range of abilities; good sport.

Background Founded 1877 at Aysgarth; moved to its present site in Wensleydale 1890. Purpose-built red-brick premises, externally graceless but redeemed by tranquil 50-acre woodland setting; later additions include well-equipped labs, music rooms, games/assembly hall.

Atmosphere Purposeful, cheerful – quintessential prep school. Careful pastoral care system (friendly matron, domestic staff); fairly formal discipline. Good home-cooked food (in rather noisy dining room); pleasant dormitories.

The head Pragmatic, laid-back style; formerly a housemaster at Uppingham. His wife keeps a close eye on dormitories and domestic arrangements.

The teaching Claims to be unrepentantly traditionalist but succeeds in keeping up to date. National curriculum largely followed; good computing, electronics, design/technology; all do Latin. Specialist teaching after first year; average class size 11-12; good remedial provision for the less able. The art room, to quote the head, is 'a magic grotto'; musical and dramatic standards are high.

The pupils Mainly from the North of England, with a substantial Scottish clan. Entry by interview, predominantly at age 8; pupils of a wide range of abilities accepted. Some financial help for families in difficulty.

Results Good Common Entrance record; recent scholarships/exhibitions to Loretto, Glenalmond, Harrow, Sedbergh.

Destinations Particularly Eton (17 places since 1989); also Ampleforth, Harrow, Radley, Sedbergh, Uppingham, Winchester. Less academically able boys proceed to suitable schools.

Sport Main games: soccer, rugby and cricket (wicket would grace a county ground, First XI undefeated in 5 years). Facilities include indoor pool, rifle range, courts for squash, tennis, fives.

Remarks Well-run school; prepares boys thoroughly for Common Entrance. Good value for money.

BEAUDESERT PARK
Minchinhampton,
Gloucestershire GL6 9AF
Tel (0453) 832072

Co-educational • Day and boarding •
Ages 8-13 (plus pre-prep department) •
171 pupils (65% boys; 55% day) • Fees,
£4,572-£5,142 day; £6,987 boarding
Head: John Keyte, mid-50s, appointed
1970.

Much sought-after; strong all round.

Background Founded 1908; moved to attractive 10-acre site on the edge of Minchinhampton Common 1918; became co-educational 1981. Elegant, late-Victorian timbered building (country-house feel); later additions blend in.

Atmosphere Well-ordered, busy; firm discipline in a warm, supportive community; emphasis on purposeful involvement. Classrooms carpeted and curtained; boarding becoming increasingly popular.

The head Graduate of Trinity College, Dublin; here nearly 30 years. He and his wife both teach; their 2 sons were pupils. Keen to ensure all-round, balanced education: 'We don't specialise but we do want every child to find something he or she is good at'.

The teaching Lively, stimulating; children encouraged to aim high. National curriculum-plus; French from age 7, Latin from 10. Some subject setting according to ability; potential scholars streamed and work in groups of 8-10; other classes 15; extra help for 'those who need a leg up'. Well-equipped science labs; lots of art on display. Experienced teachers (60% men); half live on site.

The pupils Bright, responsive; from supportive, middle-class homes. 80% of boarders live within 40-mile radius; day children from up to 10 miles away. About half enter from (oversubscribed) pre-prep department; admission for the rest by tests and observation. 'We are a competitive school,' says head. 'We do not select those who would be unhappy here.'

Results About 6 scholarships a year (Malvern, Cheltenham, St Mary's Calne, Wycombe Abbey etc); all go on to schools of their (negotiated) choice.

Destinations Mostly to: Cheltenham, Cheltenham Ladies', Clifton, Eton, Harrow, Marlborough, Malvern, Malvern Girls', Radley, Rugby, St Mary's Calne, Sherborne, Winchester, Wycombe Abbey.

Sport Traditionally strong; soccer, rugby, hockey, cross-country for boys; hockey, netball for girls. Cricket, tennis (6 courts), swimming (impresive indoor pool), athletics also on offer. Badminton, basketball, gymnastics etc in sports hall.

Remarks Lively school; achievement encouraged; childhood enjoyed.

BELHAVEN HILL

Dunbar,
East Lothian EH42 1NN
Tel (0368)62785

Boys • Boarding (some day) • Ages 7 1/2
-13 • 90 pupils (10 day) • Fees, £7,005 (
£4,530 day) (books extra)
Head: Michael Osborne, 47, appointed
1987.

*Most traditional of Scottish preps; good
academic record; well-geared to serving
leading English senior schools.*

Background Founded 1923, since when its
character has changed remarkably little. (Co-
education, introduced in 1975, was not well
supported; abandoned in 1989.) Almost entire
school contained in mid-18th century mansion
(plus later additions) in 18-acre wooded estate
on the outskirts of Dunbar, 30 miles east of
Edinburgh.

Atmosphere Happy, disciplined, civilised
community; busy without being boisterous;
staff-pupil relations friendly yet respectful.
Dormitories sound and serviceable but far
from luxurious; no claim to be home-from-
home, though some signs of new paintwork
and furniture. Classrooms scattered around
the grounds, some in prefabricated huts and
many less than inviting (bare walls and scarred
desks).

The head Former Belhaven pupil (1952-
1958) and teacher (1973-81); went to Radley
and Cambridge. Well versed in, and keen to
preserve, the traditions and character of the
school. Wants to give greater prominence to
music but otherwise sees little reason to
tamper with well-tried, successful formula.
Leads a dedicated team and teaches a full
timetable. Married with a young family.

The teaching Predominantly traditional chalk-
and-talk; subject-based throughout. French
introduced from the start, Latin a year later
and Greek when required. Apart from half-
days for games on Wednesdays and Saturdays,
a completely timetabled day from Bible reading after breakfast to end of lessons at 7 p.m.

10 full-time staff (3 women); half graduates,
half with teaching diplomas; all equally committed and versatile; good blend of experience
and youth. (Most live on campus and are
much involved out of the classroom.) Junior
classes of 17-18; seniors streamed by ability in
groups of 8-12. Oral French traditionally
strong (French speaking at lunch twice a
week). Design and technology not yet seen to
justify investment of time and money; carpentry preferred. All juniors learn the recorder;
lessons also available in piano, violin, brass,
woodwind and bagpipes; 3 choirs. Low-key
drama. Rationed television favours the survival
of archetypal boarding prep-school hobbies:
stamps, chess and other board games, model-
making, gardening, table-tennis, model railway.

The pupils Bright, cheerful, socially polished;
small community fosters independence, self-
reliance. Most from land-owning classes,
farming, professional backgrounds (96% from
Scotland). Entry by interview; selection by
early registration rather than ability (word-of-
mouth the only advertising).

Results Regular handful of scholarships to
schools on both sides of the Border.

Destinations Most boys registered for major
English public schools (especially Eton, Harrow) but targets revised after careful assessment of a pupil's ability to face the competition. Approximately half transfer to Scottish
schools; Glenalmond the most popular.

Sport Strong rugby, hockey and cricket; good,
well-drained pitches. Regular fixtures with
other prep schools. Squash court and heated,
outdoor pool date from 1930s; sports hall more
recent. Also golf, tennis and dry-slope skiing.

Remarks A school that adjusts slowly to
change and continues to proclaim the value of
academic rigour. Unlikely to appeal to progressive parents but clearly fulfilling its aims.

BILTON GRANGE
Dunchurch,
Rugby,
Warwickshire CV22 6QU
Tel (0788) 810217

Boys (and some girls) • Boarding and day
• Ages 8-13 (girls 11-13) • 197 pupils (185
boys; equal numbers day and boarding) •
Fees, £6,825 boarding; £5,118-£5,802
day (reductions for Service children,
clergy and teachers)
Head: Hon. Tim Fisher, late 50s,
appointed 1969.

*Spirited, purposeful school; good
scholarship record; exceptional grounds
and facilities.*

Background Founded 1873; moved to present 180-acre parkland site 1887. Regal Pugin mansion joined to 18th-century farmhouse; elegant late-Victorian chapel; many later additions (science labs, technology block, theatre etc).

Atmosphere Secure, happy; pupils clearly feel at home. Good discipline: 'Any breach of common sense is a breach of the school rules'. Spacious classrooms (some rather bare); labyrinthine corridors (lots of nooks and crannies); girls' dormitories comfortable, well-furnished; boys' accommodation could scarcely be described as homely – serried ranks of baths and wash-basins (no partitions) will need attention. Meals, taken in the original dining hall (with minstrel gallery), are sociable occasions; good-quality food.

The head Warm, approachable (but claims to be an autocrat). Sixth son of the former Archbishop of Canterbury; choral scholar at King's College, Cambridge; 16 years at Repton, the last 6 as housemaster. Epitome of a prep-school head.

The teaching Broadly traditional in style; painstakingly thorough with meticulous attention to individual needs. Streaming by ability; setting in maths in top 2 years. All do French; most take Latin; scholarship pupils add German/Greek/Spanish. Lots of computing; outstanding design and technology. Well-qualified staff of 18 (1 woman), nearly all appointed by present head. Maximum class size 16. Flourishing music: three-quarters learn an instrument (17 practice rooms); chapel choir, orchestra, wind band, various ensembles. Lively drama. Extra-curricular activities range from tree-houses to stocks and shares.

The pupils Eager, responsive, well-mannered; from fairly wide social spectrum. 'Each boy,' says the prospectus, 'comes to the school to blossom.' Non-competitive entry; evidence sought of ability to cope with the work. Admission on first-come basis; registration 2 years ahead recommended.

Results Up to 10 scholarships a year – academic, art, music.

Destinations About half go on to Uppingham, Oundle, Rugby, Stowe; rest to Malvern, Marlborough, Oakham, Repton and (mainly) other independent schools.

Sport Major games: rugby, hockey, cricket (tours to Zimbabwe). Others include athletics, tennis, swimming (heated indoor pool), squash, shooting, golf, gymnastics, sailing, adventure training.

Remarks Successful, cheerful school; traditional values.

BRAMBLETYE
East Grinstead,
Sussex RH19 3PD
Tel (0342) 321004

Boys • Boarding and day • Ages 8-13 •
224 pupils (80% boarding) • Fees, £7,200
boarding; £2,250 day
Head: Donald Fowler-Watt, 55, appointed
1969.

*Much admired; good academic and
sporting record; strong on the arts;
science and technology not neglected;
wide range of extra-curricular activities.*

Background Founded 1919 by a clergyman;
moved from Sidcup to its present 140-acre site
in 1932.

Atmosphere Imposing Victorian country
mansion approached by a long drive (cricket
field and pavilion to the left, superb views of
Weir Wood reservoir and Ashdown Forest to
the right). Well-tended gounds and playing
fields (6-hole golf course; small lake for
fishing). Dormitories gradually being upgraded; most have a homely feel.

The head In post 22 years (during which time
the school has doubled in size). Has a good
rapport with the pupils; teaches every class 1
period a week; takes older boys for scholarship
English. Also runs soccer and cricket teams;
helps with drama and music. His wife, Sheila
(SRN), looks after health and welfare; keeps in
close touch with parents.

The teaching 22 qualified, full-time staff (a
third women). Pupils streamed by ability
(setting in maths and French after first year).
Class sizes range from 12 to 18. Bright boys
who reach the top of the school at 11 are
prepared for scholarships in smaller groups.
Improved science and technology (thanks to
influence of national curriculum); lots of
computers; Latin from the third year. Special
help for dyslexics. Fine new arts centre (seats
270) with computerised stage lighting, good
acoustics, orchestra pit, music practice rooms.
Opportunity to learn most instruments (including bagpipes and classical guitar); orchestra, swing band, junior and senior choirs. Lots
of art, craft and pottery. Choice of 24 extra-
curricular activities: bridge, chess, fencing,
cookery, stamp collecting, video-film making
etc. Regular worship in school chapel.

The pupils All abilities admitted; first-come-
first-served; no entry test but detailed report
requested from current school. Most come
from within a 50-mile radius, mainly from
south London.

Results 1991: 3 scholarships to Winchester,
Charterhouse, Cranleigh.

Destinations Mostly to Ampleforth, Caterham, Charterhouse, Cranleigh, Eastbourne,
Eton, Haileybury, Harrow.

Sport Excellent facilities including gym,
heated indoor swimming pool, squash and
tennis courts. Main games: soccer, rugby,
cricket. Also on offer (visiting coaches): golf,
athletics, volleyball, badminton, judo, fencing,
shooting (.22 range), fishing, hockey. Lots of
fixtures against other prep schools.

Remarks School turns out confident, happy,
well-rounded boys.

BRAMCOTE
Filey Road,
Scarborough,
North Yorkshire YO11 2TT
Tel (0753) 373086

Boys • Boarding • Ages 8-13 • 95 pupils •
Fees, £5,985
Head: John Gerrard, 52, appointed 1990.

*First-rate traditional prep school; broad
range of abilities; good teaching; lots of
extra-curricular activities.*

Background Founded 1893; 4 spacious
Victorian houses near the sea-front.

Atmosphere Pupils and staff are under no
illusions: this is a demanding academic environment; boys are here to work hard in order
to gain entry to good independent boarding

schools. The emphasis, however, is on a broad education, with plenty of music and sport and a multitude of other activities. Boarding accommodation is rather spartan (an indestructible bed and a chair for each boy) but no one seems to mind. Long-weekend exeats every 3 weeks.

The head Read classics at Cambridge and has taught in prep schools ever since. Here since 1973; deputy head 1985. Married; wife teaches maths and undertakes a host of other duties.

The teaching Could hardly be more traditional; regular testing, mark orders, staff meetings to assess progress and register weaknesses. Curriculum geared almost exclusively to the demands of Common Entrance and scholarship exams; teaching groups never larger than 16 (leading to quite uninhibited class discussion). Extra help for those with special needs; boys diagnosed as dyslexic do not take Latin; specially gifted promoted to a higher form. First-years (age 8 upwards) taught maths, English by their form teacher but other subjects taught by specialists. Thereafter subject teachers predominate and exam considerations are never far from the thoughts of staff or boys. English and classics are particularly strong; good science and computing. Long-serving staff of 12 (2 women) who work long hours to provide a wide range of evening and weekend activities. All but 10 boys learn a musical instrument and are required to practise for a set period after breakfast. There appear to be very few idle moments.

The pupils Mainly from upper-middle-class families; 70% from Yorkshire, rest widely scattered. Entry is non-selective; many boys would not have passed the 11+.

Results Virtually all go to the school of their first choice, though parental wishes have sometimes to be tempered.

Destinations Most able aim for scholarships to Eton and Winchester; others to Harrow, Oundle, Repton, Sedbergh, Shrewsbury.

Sport Soccer, rugby, cricket – a profusion of teams in each, despite limited numbers. Hockey, tennis, squash, golf, swimming, arch-ery also popular. Fine playing field the size of a large county cricket ground.

Remarks Well-run school; one of the few left of its kind.

CALDICOTT
Farnham Royal,
Buckinghamshire SL2 3SL
Tel (0753) 646214

Boys • Boarding and day • Ages 7-13 •
250 pupils (66% boarding) • Fees, £7,470
boarding; £5,475 day
Head: Peter Wright, 64, appointed 1968
(retires July 1993).

Successful school; good academic and sporting record; old-fashioned values retained.

Background Founded 1904; moved to present 20-acre site on the edge of the Burnham Beeches 1938; large Victorian house with purpose-built later additions in attractive, well-maintained grounds.

Atmosphere Friendly, competitive, perhaps a little over-serious; boys made well aware of the importance of hard work, good results; big emphasis on social graces; strong Christian ethos (daily worship in delightful chapel). Many staff are resident and fully committed to extra-curricular and weekend activities. All boys must board for their last 2 years; homely, comfortable dormitories. School inspires much loyalty among parents and former pupils.

The head Old Boy of the school; joined the staff in 1952 to teach French and rugby and has done so ever since; his personality is all-pervasive (and likely to remain so – he is retiring to a house just outside the gate). Successor (from September 1993): Mike Spens, 43; scientist (science not at present one of the school's strengths); housemaster at Radley; married.

The teaching Keen, competent, if old-fashioned in some areas; steadily directed at scholarships and Common Entrance; good standards expected and achieved. Pupils streamed by ability from the start; taught by subject specialists from age 10. All do French from first year, Latin from second year, computing from third year (letters home on a word processor). Teaching areas bright, carpeted, well-equipped; good provision for technology; class sizes 14 to 18. Good music; all first-years learn recorder and violin; 50% have individual lessons; orchestra, string and wind groups, choirs. Lots of art (in rather cramped room) and drama. Plenty of extra-curricular activities; boys kept purposefully occupied in their free time.

The pupils Well-mannered, courteous. Most from London and within 20 miles of the school; 40 from abroad, including Hong Kong, Thailand. Entry, mostly at age 8, by simple maths test, reasonable reading age and report from previous head.

Results Good scholarship and Common Entrance record; regular music awards.

Destinations Chiefly to Eton, Harrow, Radley, Rugby, St Edward's (Oxford), Wellington; a few to Buckinghamshire grammar schools.

Sport Very strong rugby (thanks to present head); well-coached cricket and hockey; athletics, tennis, shooting and swimming also on offer. Facilities include splendid playing fields, fine sports hall, 3 hard tennis courts. Ideal for a boy keen on games.

Remarks Good all round.

CARGILFIELD
Barnton Avenue West,
Edinburgh EH4 6HU
Tel (031) 336 2207

Co-educational • Day and boarding •
Ages 3-13 • 182 pupils (60% boys; 65% day) • Fees (main school) £5,175 day;
£7,290 boarding
Head: Alan Bateman, 50, appointed 1991.

Friendly school catering for a broad ability range; good academic and sporting record. Small enough to offer individual attention but large enough to cater for variety.

Background Scotland's oldest prep school; founded 1873, moved to present 20-acre, semi-rural site 5 miles from Edinburgh 1899. Day boys admitted 1976; girls 1978; pre-prep department opened 1979; nursery 1982. Elegant, mock-Tudor, red-roofed buildings (with some less attractive modern additions). Charming chapel, which, with 180-degree turn of seating, becomes a theatre or dance hall.

Atmosphere Happy, well-ordered (but not regimented) community. Boys' dormitories spacious but uninviting: high ceilings, drab wallpaper, few personal pictures or posters (no source of discontent, however). Girls' dormitories smaller, cosier, perhaps a trifle cramped.

The head Here since 1986; promoted after previous head's 13-year reign; popular choice with staff and pupils alike. Educated at Blundell's and Trinity College, Dublin; taught in Canada and at Colet Court. Open to new ideas but careful to conserve inherited strengths and traditional values. Close partnership with wife, Suzanne. Pupils notice a gentler, more relaxed regime.

The teaching Healthy blend of experience and youthful vigour; relations with pupils friendly but not over-familiar. Nursery oversubscribed; bright, lively, well-staffed. Adjoining pre-prep department offers gentle but increasingly structured approach to learning; early emphasis on English and maths. Thereafter, full Common Entrance syllabus; Latin for the more able; Greek for the chosen few; computer studies and technology (show-piece studio) for all. Classrooms generally bright (class sizes average 12) but some prefabs and temporary huts (one housing rabbits, guinea pigs, hamsters, gerbils etc). Music particularly strong; time-tabled lessons plus private tuition; half learning instruments; small orchestra and jazz band.

The pupils Confident, well-mannered, happy. Parents primarily from the professions and industry but also a significant number from the Services. Entry by interview but not particularly selective; 85% come from Scotland. Every effort made to maintain boarding atmosphere (lots of weekend trips etc); day pupils encouraged to participate.

Results Regular consultation with parents ensures appropriate senior school targets and, therefore, 100% Common Entrance success.

Destinations Most to Scottish independent schools: Strathallan, Fettes, Glenalmond, Loretto etc; south of the Border to Oundle, Sedbergh, Eton, Winchester.

Sport Daily games for all: rugby, hockey, cricket for boys; hockey, rounders, netball for girls. Good facilities: well-tended cricket square; 3 flood-lit, all-weather tennis courts; also archery, badminton, gymnastics, swimming. Busy fixture list; creditable record all round.

Remarks Happy school; secure environment; sound education; wide variety of activities and sports.

CLIFTON
Clifton,
Bristol BS8 3HE
Tel (0272) 737264

Co-educational • Day and boarding •
Ages 6-13 years • 535 pupils (75% boys,
55% day) • Fees, £3,870-£5,610 day;
£7,740 boarding
Head: Roger Trafford, 53, appointed 1982
(leaving March 1993).

Large, lively prep school; good teaching; excellent facilities.

Background Part of Clifton College *(qv)* and proud of it; established as a separate entity 1937; run separately but shares governing body. Well-maintained Victorian buildings in pleasant residential area close to the Downs. Co-educational since 1987, now aiming for equal numbers of girls and boys.

Atmosphere Open, friendly. Careful pastoral care system helps break down the size and create a manageable, warm community; close relationships between staff and pupils ensure every child is well known by someone. Boarding accommodation (8-bed dormitories) cheerful, clean, homely; good food.

The head Able, charming, accessible. Educated at Oxford; formerly head of King's (Taunton) Prep; 1992 chairman of Incorporated Association of Preparatory Schools (which represents nearly all the prep schools in this guide); leaves March 1993 to take over The Dragon *(qv)*. Likes to quote St Benedict's advice to an abbot on how to run a monastery: 'He must so arrange everything that the strong have something to yearn for and the weak nothing to run from'. Married; wife teaches history here.

The teaching Styles vary from formal to progressive: juniors learn tables, grammar, spelling, handwriting; elsewhere the emphasis is on team teaching and cross-curricular collaboration; first-rate staff of 50, half appointed by present head. National curriculum introduced 1991; all do Latin, French from age 9; German, Greek on offer from 11; Portuguese,

Spanish available. Good facilities for design/technology. Setting by ability from age 8 upwards; extra help for slow learners and dyslexics; class sizes 16-20. High standards of presentation expected; homework compulsory, becoming progressively more taxing. Strong drama – in well-equipped theatre and music; two-thirds learn an instrument (free tuition in any instrument for 1 term); orchestras, wind bands, recorder groups, choirs. Big range of extra-curricular activities. Regular language exchanges with French schools; plans to establish links with Italy, Germany and Spain.

The pupils Well-mannered, highly motivated, neatly uniformed; mostly from middle-class backgrounds but 30% receive some help with fees; significant Jewish minority; 10% foreign. 60% of parents are 'first-time buyers' of independent education. Fairly wide ability range; no entry exam at 6, 7, 8.

Results Regular scholarships to a variety of schools.

Destinations Most to Clifton College (85% of the college's intake); rest to other Bristol schools and Eton, Malvern, Sevenoaks, Sherborne, Winchester.

Sport Excellent facilities shared with the college include 80 acres of playing fields, all-weather hockey pitch and tennis courts, well-equipped gym, indoor pool. Rugby especially strong.

Remarks. Happy children, caring staff; academic success high on the agenda but not paramount.

COTHILL HOUSE
Frilford Heath,
Abingdon,
Oxford OX13 6J L
Tel (0865) 390800

Boys • Boarding, some day • Ages 8-13 • 222 pupils • Fees, £7,800 boarding; £5,220 day
Head: Adrian Richardson, mid-40s, appointed 1976.

Friendly, happy school; academically sound. Derives much benefit from chateau in France.

Background Founded 1870. Dominates village 6 miles south of Oxford. Extensive, well-kept grounds; main building a beautiful old house with fine views; classrooms in battered (and chilly) 20-year-old 'temporary' huts.

Atmosphere Cheerful, good-humoured. Strong sense of community; no 'them-and-us' feeling between staff and boys. Dormitories (mostly in main house) centrally heated, carpeted, pleasantly furnished; partitions afford degree of privacy. Excellent food (in overcrowded dining room).

The head Gentle, but keeps firm discipline. Worked first for a shipping line (travelled extensively) and then in the City where he 'lost a lot of money and decided to become a schoolmaster'. Went to Oxford as a mature student; taught in a tough comprehensive.Believes time spent away from education is a good thing and bears this in mind when appointing staff. Teaches boys to be aware of their privileges while deriving maximum satisfaction from them. His wife, Rachel, shares responsibility for pupils' welfare. Their front door always open; boys in and out all day.

The teaching Academically respectable but this is not a hot-house. Most staff have degrees and teaching qualifications; good balance of age and sex. Mixed-ability classes for first 2 years (average size 16), streaming thereafter. Ablest taught with older boys; individual tuition for those with reading and writing problems.Particularly good French thanks to recent purchase of Chateau de Sauveterre, 16-bedroom, 19th-century mansion 40 miles south of Toulouse. All 11- and 12-year-olds get a term's total immersion in French life and language. They attend schools in Sauveterre (on exchange basis), explore the French countryside (camping in the Pyrenees), and spend weekends with French families. (Only extra for parents is the air fares). Boys unanimous in their approval.

The pupils Friendly, articulate, high-spirited (but well within the bounds of good manners). Mainly upper and upper-middle-class backgrounds; predominantly from London and the South East. Most of average intelligence but some significantly below and a few significantly above. No entrance exam but boys are assessed during a visit to the school in the term prior to entry. Head looks for ability to shine in 1 or more of: academic work, sport, social skills.

Results Most get into the senior school chosen for them by their parents in careful consultation with the head.

Destinations Mainly Eton, Radley, Harrow but many others of similar ilk.

Sport Daily games for all; facilities generally good (9-hole golf course, shooting range). All boys can swim by the time they leave.

Remarks Well-run school; greatest strength is its concern for the boys' welfare and happiness.

CRAIGCLOWAN
Edinburgh Road,
Perth PH2 8PS
Tel (0738) 26310

Co-educational • Day • Ages 5-13 (plus nursery) • 265 pupils (equal numbers of boys and girls) • Fees, £3,210
Head: Michael Beale, 44, appointed 1979.

Lively, successful school; small classes; wide range of activities.

Background Founded 1952; nearly closed in late 1970s but has grown steadily under the present head. Set in 13 acres on the southern outskirts of Perth; splendid views of the surrounding countryside. Large Victorian mansion; less substantial additions include ageing wooden classroom block.

Atmosphere Busy, purposeful; secure environment with a strong sense of identity.

The head Energetic; expects equal commitment from staff and pupils; very much in charge (wife acts as bursar). Has a genuinely paternal, affectionate relationship with pupils; gets on well with parents.

The teaching Unashamedly traditional (grammar analysed on the blackboard); Scottish emphasis on the 3Rs; also much project work (crowded, lively wall displays). Subject-based specialist teaching for top 3 years; classes streamed by ability. Some Latin, lots of rigorously taught French, good technology. Small teaching groups (average size 13); plenty of individual attention; accelerated promotion for academically gifted. Long school day plus homework for all; termly exams. Lots of dance, drama (in make-shift theatre) and music; nearly two-thirds learn an instrument. Extra-curricular activities include debating, bird club, model-making etc.

The pupils Confident, courteous, cheerful. Parental occupations mainly professional/business. Two-thirds live within 15 miles. Entry at 5, 7, 8, 9 by interview and previous school report; fairly wide ability range.

Results Nearly all do well enough in Common Entrance to proceed to the senior school of their (carefully guided) choice.

Destinations Mostly to Scottish independent schools: Fettes, Glenalmond, Gordonstoun, Loretto, Merchiston, St Leonard's, Strathallan; some to similar south of the Border.

Sport Rugby, hockey, cricket for the boys; hockey, rounders, netball for the girls. All do athletics, swimming. 8 acres of playing fields (not all level), 3 asphalt tennis courts. Saturday ski trips in season.

Remarks Excellent preparation for senior school, whether boarding or day. Good value for money.

CROFTINLOAN
Pitlochry,
Perthshire PH16 5JR
Tel (0796) 472057

Co-educational ● Boarding and day ●
Ages 7$^1/_2$-13$^1/_2$ ● 98 pupils (60% boys;
87% boarding) ● Fees, £6,900 boarding;
£5,100 day
Head: Nicholas Heuvel, 35, appointed
September 1992.

Sound academic school; lots of outdoor activities.

Background Founded 1936; attractive 60-acre estate among the woods and farmland that surround the town; elegant early-Victorian shooting lodge and purpose-built additions of varying quality (no heavy investment in buildings here); some accommodation rather cramped. Girls first admitted 1976. School's reputation has risen steadily over past 10 years.

Atmosphere Happy, secure, homely. Committed, caring staff: warm, easy relationships with pupils. Comfortable dormitories (6-8 beds); fairly crowded dining hall.

The head New appointment; has taught science here for the past 10 years; popular with the pupils. Read religious studies at Lancaster.

Married, 2 young children; wife was matron here.

The teaching Geared to Common Entrance and scholarship exams. Early emphasis on literacy and numeracy; French introduced from second year, science from third year, Latin from fourth year. Mixed-ability classes (average size 14); extra help for those in difficulty. Well-equipped computer room (in a Nissen hut). Lots of music; two-thirds learn an instrument; small orchestra, 2 choirs. Full programme of hobbies and activities, including modelling, cooking, chess, woodwork, shooting etc.

The pupils Confident, courteous, cheerful; mostly from farming and professional backgrounds; 92% from Scotland. Entry by interview.

Results Good Common Entrance record; 2-3 scholarships a year.

Destinations Most to Scottish schools, particularly Glenalmond, Loretto, Strathallan; 30% go south of the Border (Downe House, Winchester, Radley, Eton etc).

Sport Chiefly rugby, hockey, cricket for the boys; netball, hockey, rounders for the girls; cross-country, soccer, tennis, golf, athletics, skiing also on offer. Lots of opportunities for outdoor pursuits such as climbing, canoeing, orienteering. Facilities include 6 acres of (level) playing fields, 2 all-weather tennis courts, small heated pool.

Remarks Busy, successful school.

THE DOWNS
Colwall,
Malvern,
Worcestershire WR13 6EY
Tel (0684) 40277

Co-educational • Day and boarding •
Ages 4-13 (plus kindergarten) • 196 pupils
(55% boys; 55% day) • Fees,
£2,001-£5,160 day; £6,852 boarding
Head: Andrew Auster, mid-30s, appointed
1989.

*Busy, successful school; strong music;
wide range of extra-curricular activities.*

Background Founded by Quakers in 1900 as
'primarily a society, not an institution for
instruction'. Pleasant, well-maintained red-
brick buildings set in 55 acres of playing fields
and gardens at the foot of the Malvern Hills.
Co-educational since 1977. Numbers had
dropped prior to present head's appointment
but are now increasing.

Atmosphere Warm, welcoming; strong sense
of community and purpose. Friendly, open
relations between staff and pupils. Light, airy
classrooms; homely boarding accommodation
(boys' bathrooms yet to be modernised).

The head Enthusiastic; leads from the front.
Accomplished musician (bassoon, piano,
trombone, tuba); keen on promoting international awareness (visiting pupils from Madrid,
St Petersburg).

The teaching Stimulating; styles range from
Socratic questioning to practical project work.
Form teachers for younger pupils; subject
specialisation thereafter. Some streaming by
ability; scholarship class; extra help for dyslexics. NB: average class size 11. Library needs
up-dating. All encouraged to take part in full
programme of extra-curricular activities, including drama, art, craft, cookery, technology,
sculpture, photography, computers, wildlife,
needlework, textiles, pottery, skiing, horse-
riding, squash, ballet, carpentry, etc. Music
particularly strong; aim is to nurture the
talented and encourage a love of music in all.

The pupils Courteous, lively, responsive.

Reasonable academic mix: some highly able,
few below average. Home backgrounds mainly
professional/managerial; some farming, Services, multi-nationals; nationwide catchment
area. Admission by interview and previous
school report (if any).

Results All proceed to senior school of their
(negotiated) choice. Scholarships in 1991 to
King Edward's (Birmingham), Millfield,
Shrewsbury.

Destinations To 47 schools in the past 6
years, including Ampleforth, Bryanston, Dean
Close, Downside, Eton, Harrow, Headington,
King's (Worcester), Malvern, Malvern Girls',
Milton Abbey, Taunton.

Sport Good facilities, including all-weather
hockey pitch, tennis courts, heated outdoor
pool.

Remarks Distinctive school with plenty to
offer.

THE DRAGON
Bardwell Road,
Oxford OX2 6SS
Tel (0865) 310054

Co-educational • Day and boarding •
Ages 7-13 • 665 pupils (85% boys; 60%
day) • Fees, £3,795-£4,959 day; £7,755
boarding
Head: Hugh Woodcock, mid-60s,
appointed as a 'caretaker' September
1992; to be succeeded by Roger Trafford
in April 1993.

*Famously eccentric prep school;
academically outstanding.*

Background Founded 1877 in leafy North
Oxford; run for much of its idiosyncratic
history by members of the Lynam family or
their confidants. Conservation area makes it
hard to obtain planning permission for new
buildings, which are sorely needed. Site strad-
dles busy road (but council refuses pedestrian
crossing).

Atmosphere Informal, slightly anarchic (more like a college than a prep school). Children call younger teachers by their first names; older women answer to 'Ma', older men to 'Pa'; all treat each other as equals. Staff wear casual dress (jeans and sweatshirts), relax in their own well-used bar. Most classrooms depressingly tatty and untidy (features which appear to endear the school to teachers and pupils alike). Fairly homely boarding houses (no school work allowed); linoleum floors said to be justified by the propensity of small boys to be sick at night.

The head Appointed *pro tem* following the sudden resignation of the previous head who was the first 'outsider' to hold the job and failed to fit in. Woodcock (one of this guide's inspectors) was a pupil, teacher and governor here and confesses to having a love affair with the place; recently retired after 20 years as head of Dulwich College Prep. His successor, Roger Trafford, currently head of Clifton Prep *(qv)*, faces a tough assignment: quirky North Oxford parents; powerful Old Boys; combative governors. Can be relied on to keep them all in order.

The teaching Overall quality excellent. 64 staff (a third women) all highly qualified and committed. General style lively, informal; mixture of front-of-class and group teaching. Pupils unashamedly streamed from age 9; setting in maths, modern languages from 10; form positions calculated 4 times a term. Bright children stretched hard; extra help for those in difficulties, including dyslexics. Outstanding classics; lots of computing but technology and science (cramped labs) less well served. Class sizes range from 10-21. Average 1 hour's prep a night. Excellent library. Strong music tradition. Lots of clubs and societies.

The pupils Academic ability varies from astronomical to fairly modest. Most from professional homes; quite a few are the children of academics. School's large size mitigated by restrictions on the area with which the younger ones have to cope. Bullying, of which there is said to be 'thankfully little', attracts a letter home and can lead to suspension. Corduroy uniform for everyday wear: engagingly scruffy.

Girls – first admitted 'when the Sex Discrimination Act made it necessary' – used to be referred to as 'Honorary Dragons' but are now, so the school insists, full Dragons (but some staff still refer to the pupils as 'the boys'). Admission by interview and performance on assessment days; registration any time after birth; lists closed for 1997 (day), 1998 (boarding).

Results Excellent. Average of 20 scholarships a year (24 in 1992). Unlikely any child will fail to get into school of first choice.

Destinations To more than 100 senior schools; Eton takes the largest number.

Sport Usual games (cricket team tours Australia, Zimbabwe) plus fencing, judo, ballet, canoeing etc. Facilities include sports hall, outdoor pool, squash court, 9 hard tennis courts and 'lots of room for roller skating'.

Remarks Hard to beat. Children treated as adults and respond accordingly.

DULWICH COLLEGE PREP
42 Alleyn Park,
London SE21 7AA
Tel (081) 670 3217

Boys • Day and some weekly boarding •
Ages 7-13 (plus associated pre-prep) •
526 pupils (40 weekly boarders) • Fees
(1992-93), £4,560-£5,115 day; £7,485
boarding
Head: George Marsh, 48, appointed 1991.

First-rate academic school; boys thoroughly prepared for the best independent schools.

Background Founded 1885; shares governing body with Dulwich College Prep School, Cranbrook *(qv)*. Victorian premises with numerous later additions including, most recently, a music school and concert hall.

Atmosphere Bustling, enthusiastic; eager, competitive boys enjoying what they are doing, anxious not to miss anything. Friendly staff-pupil relations; highly supportive parents. Strong Christian ethos.

The head Read geography at Oxford; taught at The Dragon (where he was a pupil), followed by 2 comprehensives and Millfield; formerly head of Edgarley Hall. Keen that pupils should find school exciting and stimulating. Married, 2 children.

The teaching A mixture of class, group and individual work; maximum pupil involvement encouraged. National curriculum-plus; French from 8+, Latin from 9+, Greek on offer; all follow a full programme of art, drama, music, PE and games. Specialist teaching from third year; pupils streamed by ability into 3 bands; further setting in some subjects. Average class size 20-22, reducing to 16-18. Reports to parents 4 times a year. Lots of extra-curricular activities, including pottery, weaving, debating, bridge, chess; 3 orchestras and numerous smaller ensembles, 2 choirs; regular expeditions, educational cruises, overseas visits.

The pupils Articulate, self-assured, keen to learn and do well. Top 15-20% of the ability range from a wide catchment area; some have an hour's journey to school. Parents mostly in the professions, business, the City; many make considerable sacrifices (few bursaries). School heavily over-subscribed. Admission at age 7 by interview and tests in English, maths, verbal reasoning; automatic entry from pre-prep department (whose pupils will have been similarly screened at 5).

Results Good. 25% win scholarships; proportion would be much higher but parents tend to prefer paying for a place at a major school to accepting a scholarship to a minor one.

Destinations Most to Dulwich College (a completely separate institution); rest to all the leading public schools, including Winchester, Eton, Harrow.

Sport Chiefly rugby, soccer, cricket, athletics; judo, fencing, gymnastics, swimming, trampolining also on offer. 10 acres of playing fields, indoor pool.

Remarks Very good all round.

DULWICH COLLEGE PREP (Cranbrook)

Coursehorn,
Cranbrook,
Kent TN17 3NP
Tel (0580) 712179

Co-educational • Day and some boarding • Ages 3-13 • 540 pupils (equal numbers of girls and boys; 85% day) • Fees, £1,440-£4,425 day; £6,660-£6,795 boarding
Head: Michael Wagstaffe, 46, appointed 1990.

Large for a prep school but well-organised. Mixed-ability intake up to the age of 7. Pupils proceed to state and independent schools in equal numbers. Good music, drama, art and PE.

Background Founded 1885 at the suggestion of Dulwich College; evacuated 1939 to Tudor manor house in Cranbrook. One of 2 prep schools of the same name (shared governing body); completely separate from Dulwich College. 3 autonomous sections: Nash House, 3-6; Lower School, 6-9; Upper School, 9-13.

Atmosphere 40 acres of gardens and playing fields surrounded by farmland in the Weald of Kent. Some classrooms in temporary huts. Dormitories bright and cheerful.

The head Formerly a housemaster at Bryanston. Teaches history and current affairs to older pupils, also games. Lives on site with his wife, who helps with pastoral side.

The teaching Mixed-ability up to age 7, when teaching becomes more formal. French from 8+; Spanish and Latin optional. 50 staff (majority women). Well-resourced classrooms (plenty of computers); average size 20. Specialised help for dyslexics and others with learning difficulties. Scholarship class from 11+. Good music (80% learn an instrument);

also art, drama, PE (all leading on occasion to scholarships); excellent facilities. Choice of more than 80 extra-curricular activities: chess, ballet, bridge, photography, sewing etc.

The pupils Polite, lively. Admitted from 3-7 on first-come-first-served basis; selective entry thereafter; tests in verbal reasoning, spelling and maths to ensure they will be able to cope with Common Entrance. Most from within 20-mile radius: Maidstone, Tenterden, Rye, Wadhurst, Brenchley, Marden.

Results (1991) Scholarships to Ardingly, King's Canterbury, Roedean, Tonbridge; also to Cranbrook *(qv)* – a state school which charges only for boarding (and is very popular with DCPS parents).

Destinations As well as the above: Bryanston, Eastbourne, Hurstpierpoint, Lancing, Sevenoaks, Sutton Valence; approximately 50% to state schools.

Sport All major boys' and girls' games; good facilities; emphasis on teaching skills.

Remarks Good all-round education for pupils of all abilities.

EDGARLEY HALL
Glastonbury,
Somerset BA6 8LD
Tel (0458) 832446

Co-educational • Boarding and day •
Ages 8-13 (plus pre-prep department) •
483 pupils (68% boys; 57% boarding) •
Fees (1992-93), £8,640 boarding; £5,625 day
Head: Richard Smyth, 44, appointed 1991.

Distinctive school; comprehensive intake (dyslexia a speciality). First-rate music and sport.

Background Founded 1946 as a junior school for Millfield *(qv)*. Attractive 90-acre rural estate on lower slopes of Glastonbury Tor.

Atmosphere Happy, stimulating; an ordered but caring environment; considerable freedom allowed. Scattered boarding houses, some in converted farmhouses (parents can choose).

The head Recent appointment (previously head of a prep school in Cheshire); no plans for radical change but wants to put more emphasis on art and drama (school has always been strong in music and sport). Modern, managerial style. Married, with young children.

The teaching Generally good; lots of individual help in small classes (average size 12). Some streaming by ability; setting in maths, languages. Weak technology. 140 children – many with learning difficulties, including dyslexia – are withdrawn from mainstream classes for some periods each week to be given specialist help in the school's language development centre (one of its great strengths). Magnificent music block; 40 learn at least 1 instrument.

The pupils Deliberately wide ability range; admission on the basis of interview and previous school report; lots of scholarships and bursaries (fees set so that wealthy parents subsidise the less well-off).

Destinations 90% transfer to Millfield (15% with a scholarship).

Sport Strong (many national honours); excellent facilities.

Remarks Lively, busy school; excels at getting the best from children of all abilities and aptitudes.

THE HALL

23 Crossfield Road,
Hampstead,
London NW3 4NU
Tel (071) 722 1700

Boys • Day • Ages 5-13 • 375 pupils •
Fees, £4,560
Head: Richard Dawe, 60s (from
September 1992 to August 1993).

*One of London's leading prep schools.
Stimulating environment; fairly wide
ability range; good results.*

Background Founded 1889; main school in
purpose-built premises on somewhat cramped
site; impressive facilities include sports hall
and technology centre.

Atmosphere Lively, energetic. A traditional,
rather formal school – not unfriendly but
certainly not cosy. After teaching here, Edward Blishen wondered, 'How could one be at
ease ever with a male person of prep school
age?'

The head Caretaker appointment following
the sudden resignation of the previous head,
who fell out with staff, parents and governors
and left after 1 year. Dawe has just retired after
15 years as head of Westminster Under School.
Experienced, well liked, widely respected;
regarded as an admirable solution to an
awkward problem.

The teaching Varied styles; thoroughly competent. Spelling, handwriting taught formally
and firmly; imaginative science; lots of computing and technology. No streaming by
ability in the junior school; setting in English,
French, Latin, maths starts at age 10. No
classes larger than 18. Twice-yearly exams but
no form orders; head emphasises the value of
effort ('better at does not mean better than').
No special provision for dyslexia but extra help
for anyone struggling; scholarship class for the
ablest. Homework builds up to 2 hours a day.
Timetabled drama and music; many take
individual instrumental lessons. Interests of all
kinds fostered; dozens of prizes awarded
annually for art, public speaking, poetry,
computing, classics, singing, cricket, snooker
etc.

The pupils Fairly broad mix. School is heavily over-subscribed (120 apply for 50 places a
year) and entry is deliberately non-selective:
names pulled out of a hat – with a little social
engineering to ensure not all are the sons of
Hampstead lawyers. Registration advised by
age of 3.

Results Variable but good overall; Common
Entrance passes to most major independent
schools. Scholarships in 1991 to: King's (Canterbury), Millfield, Oundle, Westminster.

Destinations In addition to the above:
Bedales, Bryanston, City of London, Clifton,
Eton, Harrow, Highgate, Marlborough, Mill
Hill, Radley, Rugby, St Paul's, Sherborne,
University College School, Winchester etc.

Sport Played twice a week, mostly at Hampstead Cricket Club, 7 minutes' walk away.
Playground areas used for organised games
(staggered breaks because of lack of space).

Remarks Good school for those who can
cope; more tender plants may not thrive.

HALSTEAD

Woodham Rise,
Woking,
Surrey GU21 4EE
Tel (0483) 772682

Girls • Day • Ages 3-11 • 205 pupils •
Fees, £3,240
Head: Mrs Annabelle Hancock, 51,
appointed 1987.

*Uncompetitive, non-selective school;
good teaching; impressive results.*

Background Founded 1927 in Kent; moved
to Devizes during the war; re-opened on
present 4-acre site 1947. Comfortable
Edwardian villa (feels more like a house than a
school) in a leafy part of Woking. Later
additions include handsome new art block.

Atmosphere Gentle, nurturing; every girl encouraged to explore her strengths and capabilities. Extra help available as needed; no such thing as failure. Competitiveness discouraged (to the initial dismay of some parents).

The head Able, determined. Aims to produce 'an embryo young lady, with charm and poise and courtesy, but with foundations and aspirations to climb any mountain and master any challenge'. Does no teaching but knows the children well and is about the school constantly. Staff say she has created an atmosphere in which individual talents can flourish.

The teaching High-quality. Basic skills developed from the start (in bright, cheerful nursery); junior classes (of 22) work more formally in small groups; classes of 16 from age 7. Much cross-curricular teaching and project work; high standards of accuracy and presentation expected; computing integrated into the curriculum. Science taught to a high standard in custom-built lab. Excellent art and design includes pottery, textiles, drawing, painting (some work would do credit to GCSE pupils). Senior schools praise the quality of the girls' maths. No streaming or setting by ability; no form orders or grading – but progress constantly monitored. Extra help for those with dyslexia or similar learning difficulties. Lots of music; piano lessons; 2 choirs.

The pupils Well-mannered, friendly (art of conversation encouraged); mainly from City, professional backgrounds. Discipline no problem: 'One expects them to behave decently, and therefore they do'. Traditional uniform (hats with turned-up rim, but cloaks being phased out). Admission strictly on first-come basis (no selection); registration at birth advised.

Results Excellent. All pass Common Entrance to chosen school.

Destinations Mainly local day schools: Sir William Perkins's, Guildford High, St Catherine's (Bramley) etc.

Sport Not a particular strength; 2 games periods a week; swimming at local indoor pool.

Remarks Happy, creative school; produces articulate, balanced children.

HAWTREYS
Tottenham House,
Savernake Forest,
Marlborough,
Wiltshire SN8 3BA
Tel (0672) 870331

Boys • Boarding • Ages 8-13 • 112 pupils • Fees, £8,100
Head: Graham Fenner, 41, appointed September 1992.

Heavily traditional; socially exclusive; academically comprehensive.

Background Founded 1869 in Slough by the Revd John Hawtrey, a housemaster at Eton; moved 1846 to elegant 18th-century mansion (grade-1 listed) in Savernake Forest; 50 acres of grounds (Italianate gardens) with adjoining 200-acre deer park.

Atmosphere Buttoned-up, formal, institutional. Wooden, 2-seater desks in large, chilly classrooms (ornate ceilings, carved doors); stark dormitories, bathrooms; tatty prefects' room (and no other communal areas); extraordinarily noisy dining room. A highly ordered, structured routine.

The head New appointment. Determined to change much of the above ('You've got to listen to the customer'). Formerly head of a prep school in Kent. Enthusiastic, dynamic, direct; determined to create a warmer, more homely feel. Wife is French (and keen to contribute).

The teaching Traditional, didactic (desks in rows); lively lessons – but few concessions made to the less able. Big emphasis from the start on spelling and tables; separate sciences in reasonably equipped labs; at least 20 minutes of daily French for all. Little computing or technology. Boys streamed by general ability; setting in maths; brightest spend 2 years preparing for scholarships; extra help for dyslexics. Average class size 11. First-rate teaching in art, music; 80% learn at least 1 instrument; orchestra, choir. Most of the library is given over to antique books, which the boys are not allowed to use.

The pupils Confident, articulate, responsive. Most from highly privileged backgrounds; many with fathers and grandfathers who were pupils here. Non-selective entry; lists used to close years ahead but not currently (numbers have fallen).

Results Variable; usually some scholarships.

Destinations Up to a third go to Eton; rest mainly to Marlborough, Radley, Sherbourne, Stowe, Winchester etc.

Sport Good facilities; respectable record in rugby, soccer, cricket. Also on offer: cross-country, fly fishing, clay-pigeon shooting, riding, gardening.

Remarks Ripe for revival.

HILL HOUSE
Hans Place,
London SW1X 0EP
Tel (071) 584 1331

Co-educational • Day • Ages 3-14 • 1,050 pupils (57% boys) • Fees (1992-93), £3,200-4,300
Head: Col. Stuart Townend, 83, appointed 1951 (!)

Vast, eccentrically run, distinctive school; generally good results.

Background Founded 1951 by Col. Stuart Townend and his wife, who still own it; their son, Richard, is the heir-apparent. A warren of buildings scattered around Knightsbridge. Most famous Old Boy is Prince Charles ('a school fit for a prince', claims the prospectus). Co-educational since 1981 (but the Colonel still refers to the pupils as 'the boys').

Atmosphere Busy, businesslike (run 'on

Army lines', says the Colonel); discipline firm but kind; good manners emphasised. Strong international flavour: embassy children never refused a place; 50 nations currently represented. Crocodiles of pupils in their unmistakable uniform of gold sweaters and rust-coloured knee-breeches ('knickerbockers in Knightsbridge') wind along the pavements on their way to and from twice-daily games in Hyde Park and elsewhere. From the age of 8, all spend at least 4 weeks a year at the school's boarding house in Switzerland.

The head Autocratic, shamelessly élitist, fiercely individual and forthright; thrives on publicity. Strongly disapproves of civil servants who prevent him doing things, of people who do not try and of anyone who is unkind to children. Read science and maths at Oxford; was a formidable sportsman (hockey, football, athletics, skiing); had a distinguished Army career. Great believer in physical fitness ('it gives you happiness'); refuses to hire any teacher who arrives breathless in his top-floor office; imposes a £40-a-day fine on staff who take time off for illness (and paid up himself when he broke a leg). Runs the London end from Monday to Thursday (without secretaries, bursars or any other administrative help); spends the weekends in Switzerland (teaches skiing). Has an excellent rapport with the pupils ('If you find a child's talent, his whole character changes'); commands the loyalty and respect of staff and parents.

The teaching Staff of about 115 (hired and fired at whim); most are young; 70% are women ('In general, men can't teach children under the age of 7'); many come from Australia and South Africa (all, the Colonel insists, are fully qualified); all take turns cooking school lunches. 80 forms divided into 20 divisions in: Small School (ages 3-5), pre-prep (5-7), Transitus (6-8), Glion Lower and Middle (8-11), Glion Upper and Exam (10-14 – boys and girls taught separately). Small classes; average size 12-15. Broad curriculum: Latin, biology, computer programming, carpentry, ballet (in addition to the basics). Lots of music: 20 teachers.

The pupils Bright, lively; the sons and daughters of fashionable London – Cabinet Ministers, Middle-Eastern royals, pop stars, bankers, doctors, media folk; most live within walking distance. Entry by queuing outside the Colonel's door – and hope he takes a liking to you.

Results Generally good Common Entrance record: most go on to their first-choice school (although the schools complain they cannot make head or tail of the reports they receive from Hill House).

Destinations Eton, Harrow, St Paul's, Westminster etc.

Sport Outstanding. Children taught the basic principles of up to 27 sports so they can discover which suits them; all learn to swim. Use made of the best facilities London has to offer.

Remarks Unique institution ('It's my school so they must do what I say'); extroverts thrive best.

HORRIS HILL
Newtown,
Newbury,
Berkshire RG15 9DJ
Tel (0635) 40594

Boys • Boarding • Ages 8-13 • 155 pupils • Fees, £7,530.
Head: Malcolm Innes, 52, appointed 1978.

Long-established, traditional prep school; high academic standards; first-rate sport.

Background Founded 1888 by A H Evans, previously a master at Winchester, to train boys for the college's high academic standards. Large red-brick Victorian villa in 70 acres of beautiful grounds and woodland just south of Newbury; extensive later additions, including science labs, music block, large sports hall/theatre.

Atmosphere Purposeful, business-like, slightly austere; every boy expected to do his best and not to let himself down; relations with staff are respectful. Grace before meals (food is good and plentiful); senior boys shake head's hand after evening prayers. Cheerful dormitories; own duvets; classical music played for ½ hour each evening; functional communal bathrooms.

The head Courteous, reserved, dedicated; hopes to 'make the weak ones strong and the strong ones gentle'. Educated at Haileybury and Cambridge; taught here before university and came back immediately afterwards (in 1962). Teaches 12 periods a week; maths to the junior form, English to the top form. A bachelor (as are many of the masters – who work 7 days a week, live on the job and tend to stay).

The teaching Traditional in style and content. Major subjects are English (emphasis on grammar, spelling, accuracy), maths, Latin, French; science is expanding; computing restricted to the lower school; Greek, German offered in the top year. No streaming by ability; each boy goes up the school at his own pace (giving him the time, says the head, to discover his strengths); average class size 12-14 (some classrooms rather dilapidated). Very little use of text-books; teachers set their own exercises; plenty of prep. Fortnightly form orders; full reports to parents each term. Some remedial help available (but this is not a school for the severely dyslexic). Lots of music: two-thirds learn an instrument (new practice rooms badly needed); orchestra, 2 choirs. Rooms for hobbies (including ambitious model railway) manned by masters, open every day between tea and prep, all day Sundays.

The pupils Polite, friendly; mainly from professional backgrounds; extensive catchment area. Sensible uniform (no badges or paraphernalia); school provides all sports kit. Wide ability range; no entry test; boys required only to be able to read, write and use the multiplication tables. 'On the whole I leave it to parents,' says the head. 'I ask them if they think their sons will be happy here. When I do select, it's the parents I choose rather than the boys.'

Results Good; most go to the public school of their choice; about 3 scholarships a year.

Destinations A third to Winchester, a third to Eton and the rest to various public schools, including Harrow, Milton Abbey, Radley, Sherborne.

Sport A strong suit; good record against other schools, particularly in soccer and cricket (in 1992 the captains of the First XIs at Winchester, Eton and Harrow were all former pupils). Also on offer: hockey, squash, fives, athletics, cross-country, tennis, swimming, badminton, basketball. Facilities include 9 football pitches, splendid sports hall, 9-hole golf course, heated outdoor pool. 'We're keen on competitive games,' explains head.

Remarks Very successful school; strong all round; best suited to outgoing boys.

KING'S COLLEGE SCHOOL
West Road,
Cambridge CB3 9DN
Tel (0223) 65814

Co-educational • Day and boarding •
Ages 7-13 (plus pre-prep department) •
225 pupils (72% boys; 76% day) • Fees
(1992-93), £4,725 day; £7,290 boarding;
£2,448 choristers
Head: Gerald Peacocke, 61, appointed
1977 (retires August 1993).

Attractive school; strong musically and academically; fairly wide ability range. Provides boy choristers for King's College.

Background Founded 1878, though roots go back to the foundation of the college in 1441; Victorian premises plus later additions. Girls first admitted 1976.

Atmosphere Friendly, liberal, informal. Close-knit community; strong religious ethos, commitment to Christian values. Good boarding facilities. Lessons on Saturday mornings.

The head Kindly, approachable. Took a First in modern languages at Oxford. Married, 4 grown-up children. Successor: Andrew Corbett, head of history at Port Regis.

The teaching Well-qualified, long-serving staff (deputy head has been here 30 years). Specialist subject teaching from age 9; streaming by ability from 11; scholarship form for most able pupils; good help for dyslexics. Broadly national curriculum; all do Latin; Greek, German on offer. Average class size 18. First-rate music: 85 learn at least 1 instrument (22 visiting teachers); 2 orchestras, 3 choirs (tours to USA, France, Italy, Switzerland).

The pupils Mostly from middle-class/professional/farming backgrounds; many mothers work to pay the fees. Entry for non-choristers by tests of attainment and potential; fairly wide ability range; minimum IQ 105. 16 choristers and 8 probationers (all boys and full boarders) selected by voice trials between 7 and $9^{1}/_{2}$; scholarships cover two-thirds of boarding and tuition fees.

Results Good Common Entrance record; virtually all gain admission to their (negotiated) first-choice schools. Regular academic and music scholarships to Ampleforth, Charterhouse, Eton, Marlborough, Sevenoaks, Uppingham, Winchester, Wycombe Abbey.

Destinations Apart from the above: Harrow, Oakham, Oundle, The Leys, The Perse, St Mary's (Cambridge) etc.

Sport Played with enthusiasm; good results in tennis, squash; rugby, soccer, hockey also on offer. Facilities include ample playing fields, heated pool.

Remarks Successful school; informal, friendly atmosphere.

LLANDAFF CATHEDRAL SCHOOL

Llandaff,
Cardiff CF5 2YH
Tel (0222) 563179

Co-educational • Day and some boarding
• Ages 3½-13 • 400 pupils (78% boys;
90% day) • Fees, £2,403-£3,474 day;
£5,088-£5,253 boarding (choristers pay
one-third fees)
Head: John Knapp, early-50s, appointed
1983.

*Traditional prep school; good teaching
and results; strong music.*

Background Re-founded 1880 (roots go back
to the 9th century); housed in the former
Bishop's Palace in attractive grounds close to
the cathedral (monkey-puzzle trees in the
garden). Roald Dahl was a pupil here in the
1920s (until his mother removed him because
he was caned so viciously). Governed by the
Woodard Corporation (founded by a Victorian cleric who wanted to blanket the country
with Christian schools for the irreligious
middle classes).

Atmosphere Strong Anglican ethos (day
starts in chapel); firm discipline ('Corporal
punishment is occasionally used if it is deemed
absolutely necessary'). Mock-Tudor boarding
house: bunk beds, teddy bears; spartan washing facilities. Very good food.

The head Shy, austere but kindly; once contemplated going into the Church. Formerly
head of Leeds Grammar junior school. Married, 2 children (1 was a pupil here).

The teaching Bright, busy pre-prep department; extra help for dyslexics. Traditional
teaching and curriculum in junior and senior
schools: Greek, Latin, history essays on what it
would be like to be a medieval pope; maximum
class size 20. Homework carefully monitored.
Music of prime importance (orchestra re-
hearses almost daily); choir is the hub (frequent public performances).

The pupils School is non-selective but choristers are required to 'satisfy the organist as to
voice and ear; the headmaster in English,
arithmetic, fluent reading and intelligence; the
school medical officer as to fitness'. Choristers, who rise at 6.45 a.m. and rehearse for 2
hours a day, are required to board but voice
trials have been offered recently to day boys.

Results Good Common Entrance record;
regular scholarships.

Destinations Chiefly: Malvern, Monmouth,
King's (Taunton) and similar.

Sport Main games: rugby, cricket, tennis;
football, netball, cross-country, swimming
also on offer. Facilities include 12-acre playing
field, outdoor pool.

Remarks Good all round.

LUDGROVE

Wokingham,
Berkshire RG11 3AB
Tel (0734) 789881

Boys • Boarding • Ages 8-13 • 187 pupils
• Fees £7,575
Joint heads: Gerald Barber, 49, Nichol
Marston, 51; appointed 1973.

*Fine, long-established school; spacious,
rural setting; civilised atmosphere;
excellent sporting record; strong links
with Eton.*

Background Founded 1892 in Cockfosters;
moved to present Victorian mock-Tudor
premises (originally built as a school) 1937.
Beautifully tended grounds, huge stately trees,
views over fields and woods; 130 acres in all
(limitless space for small boys to make camps
and dens). Princes William and Harry are
pupils.

Atmosphere Settled, family air and a certain
timeless quality: Old Boys, returning as adults,
might feel little had changed. School aims to
create a happy environment, while insisting on
good manners, consideration for others, re-

spect for the environment (decent behaviour worked on constantly). Very high standard of pastoral care; boys relaxed, happy; parents encouraged to visit often. Boarding accommodation comfortable, if functional; iron bedsteads, communal bathrooms.

The heads Both educated at Eton and Oxford and both born to the profession: Barber is the third generation of his family to run Ludgrove; Marston's father was head of Summer Fields. Both love teaching and have heavy timetables: Barber takes Latin and scripture for 22 hours a week, Marston maths for a daunting 37 hours. Barber is married with teenage children (his wife oversees all domestic arrangements, and much else besides – her father was also a prep-school head); Marston a bachelor. Barber puts great emphasis on traditional academic standards: 'Important to get the framework firmly established'.

The teaching Traditional; desks (often ancient and ink-stained) in rows; no moving around by subject except for French, science, (no smart new facilities here!) and computing (16 computers linked to a network). Well-qualified, long-serving staff. Emphasis on grammar, spelling, 'discipline in thought' (Latin grammar from second year); particular strengths in maths, classics. Streaming by ability in third year; potential scholars moved on to fast track; extra help for those with mild dyslexia. Average class ('division') of 15. Fortnightly 'orders' – boys given their place in division and grades for effort; reports to parents every 3 weeks. Excellent facilities for art, pottery, carpentry; design/technology not a particular strength. Music, previously rather weak, now thriving: two-thirds learn an instrument; orchestra, good choir. Annual Shakespeare and pantomime in superb sports-hall-cum-theatre.

The pupils Naturally polite, courteous – without being unduly deferential (females, though, are all addressed as 'ma'am'); overwhelmingly from upper-class homes. Entry is non-selective (but severe learning difficulties cannot be catered for); application at birth essential; lists full until 2000.

Results Most proceed to school of first choice; roughly 2 scholarships a year.

Destinations 55% to Eton; Harrow, Radley also popular.

Sport First-class record, particularly in cricket; also soccer, rugby, hockey. Facilities include extensive playing fields, superb sports hall, tennis, fives and squash courts, 9-hole golf course, snooker tables. Indoor swimming pool is a period piece.

Remarks Very traditional school; turns out well-mannered, confident boys well prepared for public-school life.

MAIDWELL HALL
Maidwell,
Northampton NN6 9JG
Tel (060 128) 234

Boys • Boarding (plus a few day places) • Ages 8-13 • 96 pupils • Fees, £7,500 (£4,250 day)
Head: John Paul, 54, appointed 1978.

Costly, miniaturised version of a top public school; sends privileged boys to Eton and Harrow.

Background Founded 1932. Setting almost a cliché: glimpse of turreted splendour among the trees; long drive flanked by rhododendrons; lawns (carpeted with snowdrops) running down to a lake; sweep of gravel to the front door. Medieval mullioned windows; endless corridors of polished wood.

Atmosphere School's aim to give boys 'a full education with a wide range of accomplishments' achieved with dignity and style.

The head Teaches regularly (as does his wife, who is also responsible for pupils' happiness and welfare). Expects high standards of behaviour: when boys are told off in measured terms they are not inclined to argue. (His greatest pride is the climbing wall which occupies the whole of one end of the gym: he designed it.)

The teaching A modernised traditional education: Latin at one end of the spectrum, computer studies at the other all in classes of not more than 12. Reception class somewhat unimpressive (only one 8-year-old knew his tables and none of the rest could work out 6 x 6) but progress accelerates thereafter. As they work their way up the school, boys master their Latin verbs, do their sums neatly, and learn to describe electrical circuits with evident understanding. Exceptionally able may skip a form; remedial teachers come in twice a week. Fortnightly reports to parents with marks for effort and achievement. Lots of drama and music: orchestra, choir, half learn an instrument. Several staff changes recently; some who remain have served 20 years or more. (School owns 9 houses in the village.)

The pupils Mostly upper-middle-class; some parents presumably make awesome sacrifices (a few scholarships available). Matrons lay out the boys' clothes. Each has his own washbasin with his name on it.

Results Nobody fails Common Entrance; top boys work for scholarships and achieve their fair share.

Destinations 4 out of 5 go on to Eton, Harrow, Radley, Stowe, Uppingham and Oundle.

Sport Organised games 5 days a week – just about everything on offer (3 large playing fields, 2 tennis courts, squash court). Boys are free once a week to choose their own activity: sailing, fishing (well-stocked lake), riding, rock-climbing etc. Evening options include snooker, chess, table tennis.

Remarks Expanding despite the recession; parents must know what they are buying.

MALSIS
Cross Hills,
North Yorkshire BD20 8DT
Tel (0535) 633027

Boys • Boarding and some day • Ages 7-13 • 190 pupils • Fees, £6,300
Head: John Clark, early-50s, appointed 1975.

Fine school; wide ability range; first-rate teaching; excellent facilities.

Background Founded 1920 as a prep school for Giggleswick. Grand 19th-century manor house (ceilings lovingly restored) set in 40 acres (peacocks and game birds reared on site); later additions include splendid chapel; well-equipped technology department in converted stables.

Atmosphere This really is a family: parents play an active part in the life of the school; staff includes 7 married couples (who all live near by); head and his wife always on hand. Warm, friendly dormitories (6-12 beds); food ample and nourishing. Mud-encrusted, over-ambitious ditch jumpers taken in matron's stride without recrimination. Tangible pride in everything achieved.

The head Inspired leader, clearly capable of attracting highly qualified staff from widely differing backgrounds who gel together as a team. Believes strongly in the value of boarding. Interests include farming (and rearing game birds).

The teaching Formal without being dull; pupils acquire sound grounding in grammar and real love of reading. Youngest spend 40% of their time with 1 teacher to encourage feeling of security; specialised teaching thereafter and setting by ability; small classes. National curriculum followed; outstanding classics course ensures a sound base in Latin and a life-long love of Greece and Rome; technology achieves a nice balance between traditional skills and computer-aided design. Dyslexia unit provides extra support for 16 pupils. Very strong music: more than two-thirds learn an instrument; excellent concert band; choir often heard on radio and TV. Extra-curricular activities include chess, bridge, table tennis, model railways, photography – even wine making.

The pupils Lively, easy to talk to, enthusiastic about all the school has to offer (exeats are generous but many prefer to stay). Most live within a radius of 100 miles, including the conurbations of South Yorkshire and Lancashire and the rural counties of the North. Entrance by interview: intake genuinely comprehensive but with a bias towards the more able; average IQ about 107.

Results Good Common Entrance record; most go on to their first-choice boarding school; some to independent day schools.

Destinations Total of 60 schools but chiefly Shrewsbury, Oundle, Sedbergh, Uppingham, Harrow, Cheltenham.

Sport Strong; particularly rugby, cricket; also swimming, athletics. Others include golf, fishing, canoeing, sailing. Well-equipped sports hall; superb indoor pool.

Remarks The best in boarding education. Highly recommended.

THE MANOR
Faringdon Road
Abingdon,
Oxford OX13 6LN
Tel (0235) 523789

Girls (3-11) and boys (3-7) • Day • 355 pupils (58 boys) • Fees, £1,302 (nursery)-£3,117
Head: Mrs Jo Hearnden, early 50s, appointed 1985.

Lively, cheerful school. Family atmosphere in exceptionally attractive surroundings.

Background Founded 1947; pleasant site 6 miles from Oxford. Converted 12th-century barn for dancing (and playing in when it rains).

2 new classroom blocks, large multi-purpose hall.

Atmosphere Strong sense of family (nearly three-quarters of the staff have, or have had, children here). Delightful classrooms, all with huge windows set low enough for even the smallest child (and tallest adult) to enjoy the splendid views. Walls covered in children's work and their photographs (marked with coloured spots showing how many books they have read during the term). No peeling paint, scuffed skirting boards or any other sign of neglect.

The head Northern Ireland-born; Froebel-trained; irresistibly enthusiastic. Taught here 10 years (producing 3 children of her own); left for promotion; returned as head. Still teaches each class 1 period a week. Extravagant with praise for staff who, in turn, clearly admire her.

The teaching Challenging, stimulating ('They must understand, not learn like parrots'); lots of individual attention. Style changes as pupils move up the school: project work, group activities, disciplined play in the nursery; increasingly front-of-class and subject-based thereafter. Responsive children quick to volunteer answers and opinions. Specialist science teaching from 7; French from 9 (emphasis on conversation); all girls take English Speaking Board exams; head supervises regular handwriting practice. Class sizes average 22 (each with teacher plus assistant); smaller groups for older children. Scholarship and remedial needs catered for. Detailed (9-page) marking policy deems negative comments unacceptable: mistakes marked with a small dot to be turned into a tick as soon the correction has been made. All-woman staff (not intentional, says head) aged 40-55; their cheerfulness and high morale pervade the school.

The pupils Lively, interested, interesting; hard to believe any child could be unhappy here. Mostly from professional, middle-class homes. Some registered before birth but school suggests 2 years prior to entry is best. Biggest intake at 3; rest join at 4 and 7 on the basis of assessments. Head stresses entry is not selective and that the school is prepared to cope with a wide range of difficulties.

Results All go on to their first-choice schools though care is taken to ensure the choice is 'wise'.

Destinations Oxford High, Headington, St Helen & St Katharine etc.

Sport All the normal games plus gym, ballet, country dancing, judo. Swimming at Radley once a week.

Remarks Delightful, happy, well-run school.

MILBOURNE LODGE
43 Arbrook Lane,
Esher,
Surrey KT10 9EG
Tel (0372) 462737

Boys (and some girls) • Day • Ages 7-13 (plus pre-prep department) • 195 pupils (15 girls) • Fees, £3,900
Head: Norman Hale, 60s, appointed 1949.

Outstanding academic school; first-class results; keen sport.

Background Founded 1912 (by Woodrow Wyatt's father); moved to present site 1948 (leaving pre-prep department in the original building); attractive Victorian villa in 7 acres plus access to limitless woodland.

Atmosphere Vibrant, happy. Hard work taken for granted; discipline, obedience assumed. School exudes a family feel – with a strong competitive edge.

The head Larger-than-life; bursting with energy and enthusiasm; believes passionately in the pursuit of excellence. Educated at Shrewsbury, where he gained his love of classics, and Oxford, where he read modern history. Teaches 17 periods a week: Latin to the youngest, Latin and Greek to the top set. No plans to retire in the foreseeable future: school is his life (and very much his creation).

The teaching Lively, sometimes idiosyncratic, all of a high standard. Big emphasis on traditional curriculum (no computers or cross-curricular projects here) and solid grounding (work marked rigorously for grammar and spelling – corrections obligatory). Latin from the outset (declensions learnt in less than 2 terms); history taught without textbooks by inspired raconteur; imaginative science, lively maths; no design/technology until exams are safely out of the way. All pupils streamed by ability (top stream prepared for scholarships); plus and minus marks for effort and performance (very few minus marks); grades sent to parents every 3 weeks. Average class size 20; nightly homework. Lots of music; all encouraged to learn an instrument; orchestra, choirs, string band. Thriving chess club; numerous trips to London theatres etc.

The pupils Bright, keen, well-mannered (all leap to their feet when adults enter the room) and clearly well-taught. Mainly from commuter-belt professional homes in Esher, Woking, Weybridge, Walton etc; supportive/ambitious parents. Entry by written tests (selection ensures B+ material); early registration advised. Financial help available for above-average children: head regards this as more important than building sports halls etc.

Results Very good; high Common Entrance standards achieved. Average of 8 academic scholarships a year to top schools, plus regular music scholarships.

Destinations Chiefly Bradfield, Epsom, Eton, Harrow, Wellington, Winchester.

Sport Football, rugby, cricket, tennis (1 hard court in constant use), netball; athletics taken seriously (like everything else). Head believes keenly in sport and exercise: all play something for at least 1 hour a day. Good playing fields; heated outdoor pool; no gym (but school routinely wins local competitions).

Remarks Single-minded pursuit of excellence produces fine results from bright children. Highly recommended.

MOOR PARK

Ludlow,
Shropshire SY8 4EA
Tel (0584) 872342

Roman Catholic (but most pupils are non-Catholics) • Co-educational • Boarding and day • Ages 7½-13 (plus associated pre-prep) • 150 pupils (60% boys; 60% boarding) • Fees, £6,510 boarding; £4,725 day
Head: John Badham, 44, appointed 1988.

Attractive, happy school; first-rate teaching; strong sport.

Background Founded 1964 as a Catholic boys' boarding school with a national catchment area; has become – in response to market forces – increasingly non-Catholic, co-educational and local. Magnificent 83-acre estate with woods, bogs, meadows, lakes and hidden dells – a wondrous fantasy land for any child's imaginings. Main building was originally Queen Anne but has been much messed about and was the inspiration for Tom Sharpe's *Blott on the Landscape*; modern classroom block; prefabs scheduled for demolition.

Atmosphere Liberal, Christian ethos; carefree, unabashed children who respect authority and each other. All – whatever their faith – are treated as Catholics: no one opts out of mass. Well-organised pastoral care system. Girls accommodated in beautifully decorated 8-bed dormitories (murals, fresh flowers); boys' accommodation being refurbished; parents have free access. Day pupils stay until 6.30 p.m.

The head Charming, kindly, humorous. Catholic convert; keen to preserve the Catholicism that gives the school its identity; formerly head of a Catholic prep school in London.

The teaching Youthful, enthusiastic staff (average age 35); equal numbers of women and men. National curriculum followed. Relaxed atmosphere in pre-prep department: learning through fun. Pupils set by ability in maths, English, French from age 7½; specialist help for slow learners, including dyslexics. First-

rate art and music; more than half learn an instrument. Lots of charitable work.

The pupils Confident, not overly disciplined; fairly wide social mix (not a snob school), most from within a radius of 30 miles. A third of parents are 'first-time buyers' of independent education; 35 % of pupils are Catholics. Entry is non-selective; automatic entry from pre-prep department.

Results Regular scholarships to Downside, Eton, King's (Worcester), Marlborough, Shrewsbury, Winchester.

Destinations As well as the above: Ampleforth, Charterhouse, Malvern, Monmouth, Radley.

Sport Taken seriously. Good record in netball, soccer, cricket, rugby, hockey, squash, tennis. There is also an assault course and a 9-hole golf course in the grounds; fishing and canoeing on the lakes; camping in the woods; an outdoor climbing wall; large outdoor pool; cross-country running.

Remarks Latin motto translates as 'To God who gives joy to my youth': a school that can offer joy to any child.

MOUNT HOUSE

Tavistock,
Devon PL19 9JL
Tel (0822) 612244

Boys • Boarding and day • Ages 7-13 • 190 pupils (80% boarding) • Fees, £6,750 boarding; £4,890 day
Head: Charles Price, 49, appointed 1984.

Friendly school in idyllic surroundings on the slopes of Dartmoor. Good Common Entrance record.

Background Founded 1881 in Plymouth; moved 1941 to lovely 19th-century house overlooking Tavistock. Beautiful, well-maintained grounds bordered by the river Tavy.

Atmosphere Warm, welcoming; everyone held in respect and affection; everything neat and spotless. Large bedrooms converted into dormitories (4-10 beds or bunks in each) curtained, carpeted; boys bring own duvet covers; lots of cuddly toys. Good, plain cooking.

The head Approachable, liked by his staff (no departures in 4 years). Married, 2 children.

The teaching Fairly formal; high standards of work expected and achieved. Mixed-ability classes (15 in each) for first 2 years; streaming thereafter; extra help as needed, especially in English. Scholarship class for the 2 years before Common Entrance. Well-qualified staff of 21: know their subjects and their pupils. Good facilities for computing, technology, art, music.

The pupils Lively, well-mannered; sons of doctors, naval officers, farmers etc. 60% from Devon and Cornwall; many have family connections with the school. Fairly wide range of ability; admission by (reasonably simple) tests in reading, writing, maths taken 6 months before entry. 2 free places for boys whose parents would not otherwise be able to consider an independent school; some minor bursaries.

Results 100% Common Entrance success for past few years: i.e. all have gone to (negotiated) first-choice school. Half-a-dozen scholarships annually.

Destinations Most popular: Blundell's, King's (Taunton), Sherborne. Others include Wellington, Winchester, Eton.

Sport Big emphasis on teaching skills (games every afternoon). Good record in rugby, soccer, cricket. Facilities include swimming pool, superb sports hall (walls of shire horse stable adapted for rock climbing).

Remarks Happy school; provides a solid foundation. Boys work hard, play hard, sleep well.

MOWDEN HALL
Newton,
Stocksfield,
Northumberland NE43 7TP
Tel (0661) 842147

Co-educational • Boarding and some day • Ages 8-14 • 155 pupils (75% boys) • Fees, £6,420 boarding; £4,290 day
Head: Andrew Lewis, 40s, appointed 1991.

Effective, friendly school; wide range of abilities; small classes.

Background Founded 1935; ageing country mansion with some later additions in magnificent wooded setting. Croquet lawn overlooks the lake.

Atmosphere Lively, bustling school; discipline gentle, based on mutual regard; appropriate degree of freedom allowed (if they want to fall out of trees they can); staff and pupils eat together (no complaints about the food). Weekends are family occasions: campfires are lit, sausages sizzled, gardens hoed. Dormitories stark (up to 20 beds in each) and in urgent need of upgrading.

The head Informal, approachable; he and his wife always on hand (their own children are pupils). Spent 21 years at Repton, the last 5 as a housemaster.

The teaching Thorough and practical; high standards achieved. All streamed by ability from second year (movement between streams as pupils develop). Teaching increasingly based on national curriculum but all do Latin and French from second year; imaginative maths (it really is fun); good computing across a range of subjects. Average class size 9; impressive amount of extra help for the less able. Lots of music: two-thirds learn an instrument. Good theatre.

The pupils Hard-working (but given plenty of time to be children); delightful to talk to – even the youngest have a point of view. Most enter in the September nearest their 8th birthday; no entrance exam; intake spans the full ability range. Catchment area extends from north of the Border to London but most come from the North East; many are siblings of existing or former pupils.

Results Good Common Entrance record; head makes great efforts to ensure 'horses for courses'. 33 scholarships/exhibitions over the past 10 years.

Destinations More able pupils to Ampleforth, Eton, Harrow, Loretto, Oundle, Repton, Sedbergh, Uppingham, Winchester; less able placed in specialist schools.

Sport Good rugby, hockey; athletics, swimming, squash, golf also on offer. Fine playing fields and all-weather tennis courts but both sports hall and outdoor pool are unheated.

Remarks Not a wealthy institution (and it does not stand on ceremony); offers children of all abilities a good all-round education.

ORWELL PARK

Nacton,
Ipswich,
Suffolk IP10 OER
Tel (0473) 659225

Co-educational (girls admitted from September 1992) • Boarding and some day• Ages 7-13 • 200 pupils (90% boarding) • Fees, £7,725 boarding; £5,775 day
Head: Ian Angus, 49, appointed 1979.

Outstanding, well-run prep school; first-rate teaching; strong music; wide range of extra-curricular activities.

Background Founded by a clergyman in 1867; moved to present spectacular 90-acre site overlooking the estuary of the River Orwell in 1937; fine 18th-century mansion with many later additions. Resources concentrated on essentials rather than frills; fine science labs and technology workshops.

Atmosphere Wide range of games, hobbies and extra-curricular pursuits makes this an all-rounders' paradise; at the same time there is a strong commitment to the traditional prep-school values of discipline (shirt-tails tucked in, hands out of pockets), polite behaviour and academic excellence. All pupils help with the washing up and take part in a daily 'charring' routine. Well-organised pastoral care system. Parents invited to visit frequently. Dormitories carpeted and tidy but often very crowded; the new girls' wing is admirable.

The head Dynamic; full of restless energy and new ideas; moves round the school at a breathtaking pace; shakes every senior pupil's hand after evening prayers. Educated at Harrow and Trinity College, Dublin; has spent nearly all his career here. Wife was formerly head of St Felix, Southwold.

The teaching Designed to meet the needs of Common Entrance, scholarship exams and the national curriculum; particular stress on spelling, tables and reading skills. Some streaming by ability at the junior level; setting in major academic subjects thereafter; lots of extra help for slower learners; class sizes vary from 8 to 20. School is lavishly staffed and turnover is low (80% have been here more than 5 years); part-timers teach hobbies and leisure pursuits, on which there is a big emphasis. Outstanding art studios; strong music (15 visiting teachers, more than 40 practice rooms). Observatory with 10-inch refractor telescope and radio station enables pupils to talk to astronauts and track their passage overhead.

The pupils Most live within a 2-hour journey; 10% from abroad. Non-competitive entry by informal interview with the child and extensive meeting with the parents. School is fairly full. Some bursaries and scholarships available.

Results Virtually all pass Common Entrance to their first-choice school; regular academic and music scholarships.

Destinations More than 60 senior schools in the past 10 years. Most popular, apart from East Anglian schools, are Harrow, Oundle and Uppingham.

Sport Strong tradition in team sports and individual pursuits; games played daily. Facilities include extensive playing fields, splendid new sports hall with 3 squash courts, outdoor heated pool, 5 hard tennis courts, 9-hole golf course and Army-built assault course.

Remarks Hums with activity from before breakfast to past bedtime; it would be very hard to be bored here. Highly recommended.

PACKWOOD HAUGH
Ruyton-XI-Towns,
Shrewsbury,
Shropshire SY4 1HX
Tel (0939) 260217

Co-educational • Boarding and day •
Ages 7-13 • 300 pupils (65% boarding,
65% boys) • Fees, £6,480 boarding;
£5,025 day
Head: Patrick Jordan, 50, appointed 1988.

Impressive scholarship record; good sport.

Background Founded 1892; moved from Packwood, Warwickshire, in 1941 to present site on the edge of a north Shropshire village. Much building in the past 5 years.

Atmosphere Good humour in the classrooms; cuddly toys in the bedrooms. Friendly encouragement for children to reach high academic and sporting standards.

The head Won a choral scholarship to St John's College, Cambridge; read law and economics. Previously deputy head of a prep school in Dorset. Has introduced a more relaxed regime: greater emphasis on participation in sport, less on winning; more art and music, less Latin (which he teaches). Removed alarming Star Wars wallpaper in boys' dormitories. Wife teaches reception class.

The teaching 'Very serious notice' taken of national curriculum but technology and computing rather rudimentary. (Reduced Latin still occupies 6 out of 42 periods a week.)

Classes (average size 15) streamed to help match pupil to senior school destination. Good art, music (choir, two-thirds learn an instrument). Lots of encouragement for recreational reading (specialist help for those with reading difficulties). Model railways, stamps, chess in the evenings ('We don't have time to watch TV, but we don't miss it').

The pupils Most boarders come from within 50-mile radius (exeats limited to 2 weekends a term); day pupils mainly from Shrewsbury. All kept busy but not hounded or harried. ('We want the children to clear hurdles, but also land safely on the other side.')

Results Between 6 and 12 scholarships a year to Cheltenham, Cheltenham Ladies', Harrow, Oundle, Rugby, Shrewsbury, Wycombe Abbey etc. No Common Entrance failures but great care taken to match pupil to school.

Destinations Commonly, Shrewsbury for the boys, Moreton Hall for the girls; school also well represented at Eton, Ellesmere, Harrow, Malvern, Wrekin, Wycombe Abbey.

Sport All main games. All-weather, floodlit hockey pitch; tennis and squash courts; open-air swimming pool has solar heating panels; grounds big enough for a 2-mile cross-country; canoeing on the River Perry.

Remarks Good results all round; emphasis also on good manners, consideration for others, ability to use spare time.

PAPPLEWICK

Windsor Road,
Ascot,
Berkshire SL5 7LH
Tel (0344) 21488

Boys • Boarding and day • Ages 7-13 •
202 pupils (75% boarding) • Fees, £7,830
boarding; £5,550 day
Head: Rhidian Llewellyn, 34, appointed
January 1992.

*Traditional prep school; lively teaching;
friendly atmosphere; strong sport.*

Background Founded 1949; Edwardian
mansion with later additions in 8 acres beside
Windsor Great Park.

Atmosphere Cheerful, kindly, busy; boys
fully occupied but no feeling of pressure.
Christian values fostered (daily chapel service); discipline based on thoughtfulness for
others rather than on rigid rules; good manners, courtesy expected. Pastoral care clearly
good; boys happy and relaxed. Inter-connect-
ing dormitories under the eaves: cosy but
rather crowded. Meals are self-service; head
queues like everyone else (no high table here).
Parents can visit on half days and most
weekends.

The head Educated at Pangbourne (captain
of cricket, his great love) and took a history
degree at School of Slavonic and East European Studies. Formerly a housemaster at The
Dragon. Believes a principal function of
boarding schools is to introduce children to as
wide a range of activities as possible – and is
utterly opposed, therefore, to weekly boarding.
(Weekends are packed with activities: all staff
come in on Sunday and boys have a huge
choice.) 'But,' the head adds firmly, 'a boy
must leave feeling work is more important than
rugby.'

The teaching Ranges from the traditional
(rows of old-fashioned desks) to innovative
projects of all kinds. Lively English (importance of grammar and spelling emphasised);
compulsory Latin; lots of computing (excellent facilities); inspired teaching in art, de-
sign/technology. All streamed by ability (to
enable them to go at their own pace); setting
in most subjects for the last 3 years; average
class size 12. Scholarship boys spend 2 years at
the top of the school; extra help available for
dyslexics, slow learners. Grades for achievement and effort, but no form orders; reports to
parents every 3 weeks. Good music with strong
choral tradition (1 choir sings at outside
services, and has been on tour); orchestra and
individual instrumentalists taught in slightly
dilapidated music block. Wide range of hobbies and clubs.

The pupils Well-mannered, confident; mostly
from middle-class, professional families in
London and Home Counties (strong local
presence); 20% of parents live abroad. Entry is
non-selective; apply well in advance of 6th
birthday; £250 deposit secures a place.

Results Good Common Entrance standard;
4-5 scholarships a year.

Destinations Wide range of independent
schools, especially Wellington, Charterhouse,
Harrow, Eton.

Sport A strong tradition: daily participation;
good record against other schools, particularly
in rugby. Hockey, football, cricket, tennis,
athletics also on offer; judo a particular
strength. Facilities include all-weather pitch, 3
hard tennis courts, squash courts, small outdoor unheated pool. Playing fields adequate
but on the small side.

Remarks Good all-round preparation for
public schools.

PILGRIMS'
3 The Close,
Winchester,
Hampshire SO23 9LT
Tel (0962) 854189

Boys • Day and boarding • Ages 8-13 •
180 pupils (53% day) • Fees, £4,800 day;
£6,555 boarding
Head: Michael Kefford, 50s, appointed
1983.

---

*Traditional prep school; serves also as a
choir school for Winchester Cathedral
and Winchester College. Outstanding
music; all boys expected to reach high
academic standards; atmosphere of
Christian commitment.*

Background Founded 1931 as a prep school
for the cathedral choristers; college quirister
joined 1961. (Serving 2 greater institutions has
caused tensions in the past.)

Atmosphere Exceptionally beautiful setting.
Main building in cathedral close rebuilt in
1687 (and possibly designed by Sir Christopher Wren). Medieval Pilgrims' Hall (inspiring but cold) used for morning assembly; new
teaching block (warm, well-equipped) echoes
the surrounding architecture (in a way that
would delight the Prince of Wales). Elegant
playing fields beside the city wall; cricket and
football in the dean's garden.

The head Cambridge graduate; has spent a
lifetime in schools and is modestly proud of
this one; does not claim to be a musician but is
eloquent in his admiration of the boys' singing
and playing. Wife very much involved; looks
after catering and health.

The teaching Fairly intense; high standards
achieved in many subjects; 20 well-qualified
staff. Demanding curriculum: French and
computing from 8; Latin, Greek, technology
from 10. Mixed-ability classes in first year;
streaming thereafter. Largest class 18; average
size 13. Basic talents developed in a disciplined
and caring community but much more than
basic knowledge is the goal. Reports to parents
every 3 weeks. Musical opportunities excep-

tional (choir scholars travel abroad, work with
famous musicians); 2 orchestras, band, 2
'commoners' choirs. 150 out of 180 play 1 or
more musical instruments. Time also for
railway and stamp clubs, natural history society.

The pupils Nearly all from professional or
business families, often with 2 working parents. Many live in and around Winchester.
Entry at 8 by test and interview; several
applicants for each place. Voice trials for 38
choral scholars (including 16 quiristers).

Results Good scholarship record.

Destinations Many to Winchester; others to
Charterhouse, Marlborough, Bryanston and
other major schools.

Sport Lots of team games; some golf. Floodlit
sports area and use of college swimming pool.

Remarks Fine school; feels like an extended
family.

PORT REGIS
Motcombe Park,
Shaftesbury,
Dorset SP7 9QA
Tel (0747) 52566

Co-educational • Boarding and day •
Ages 7-13 • 275 pupils (65% boys; 80%
boarding) • Fees (1992-93), £8,700
boarding; £6,348 day
Head: David Prichard, late-50s, appointed
1969.

---

*Impressive school; fine head;
outstanding facilities.*

Background Founded in Harley Street, London 1881; moved to Motcombe Park 1947;
late-Victorian mansion in 150 rolling Dorset
acres. Recent additions include luxurious
boarding house, superb new science/techno-
logy/computing centre.

Atmosphere Happy, busy, well-ordered.
Children carefully looked after. ('This is a

home not an institution,' says the head. 'I'm the *paterfamilias*. I insist every child brings a teddy and I say goodnight to all of them at least twice a week.')

The head Took over a school that had few pupils and less money and turned it into a booming enterprise (one of the most expensive in the country, as he proudly acknowledges). An enthusiastic (and hard-headed) visionary whose zest is undiminished; completely dedicated to the happiness and all-round success of his pupils. Educated at Radley and Oxford (read history and rowed); taught for 14 years at Monkton Combe. Recently married to Elizabeth Major, head of Warwick Prep *(qv)*.

The teaching Challenging. Broad curriculum; pupils streamed by ability; all take French from age 9; more able add Latin; everyone does lots of reading. Extra help for gifted and slow learners alike. Plenty of drama and music; more than half learn an instrument. Hobbies of every kind.

The pupils Spontaneous, friendly; mostly from upper-middle and upper-class backgrounds (the Princess Royal is a parent). Wide catchment area; mainly southern England, London to Cornwall. Entry is non-selective.

Results Good but not outstanding; head says there is too much going on to leave time for scholarship cramming. Virtually all pass Common Entrance and enter the public school of their (negotiated) choice.

Destinations Mostly Bryanston, Sherborne, Sherborne Girls', Millfield, Milton Abbey, Marlborough.

Sport First-rate coaching (particularly in gymnastics); excellent facilities.

Remarks Very attractive, well-run school; a fully-rounded education.

RIDDLESWORTH HALL
Diss,
Norfolk IP22 2TA
Tel (095381) 246

Girls • Boarding and some day • Ages 7-13 (plus pre-prep department) • 120 pupils (85% boarding) • Fees (1992-93), £7,755-£7,920 boarding; £4,350-£5,940 day
Head: Miss Susan Smith, 41, appointed 1991.

Sound teaching; good creative arts and sport; beautiful surroundings.

Background Founded 1946; grand Georgian mansion (substantially re-built in the 1900s after a disastrous fire) on a spacious, wooded estate 15 miles south-west of Norwich; long-overdue refurbishment now in hand. Bright, clean classrooms in converted stable block; fine art/pottery workshops; science and technology facilities barely adequate. Striking new pre-prep department opened by the Princess of Wales, who was a pupil here.

Atmosphere Happy, secure, businesslike; girls trained to be polite, self-possessed and do as they are told. Strong family feel (fresh flowers in reception rooms, log fires in winter). Dormitories being upgraded (curtains, wall-to-wall carpets); 19th-century bathrooms next on the agenda. Good food in formal dining room (no cafeteria feeding or casual table manners here). Substantial accommodation for small pets.

The head Cheerful, friendly, enthusiastic; liked and respected by staff and pupils. Read music at Bristol; has taught in state and independent schools; formerly director of music at a girls' school in Malvern. New to the prep-school world, and clearly loving it; keen to raise academic standards ('Girls must be prepared to enter a very competitive world').

The teaching Formal in style. Well-qualified, long-serving staff, mostly women. French from 6+, Latin from 9+; pupils set by ability in English, French, maths; some remedial help for those who need it (but school does not specialise in this area); English as a foreign language for overseas pupils; class sizes 12-15. Big emphasis on creative arts, taught by visiting staff: music, speech & drama, puppetry, ballet. Wide range of extra-curricular activities, including pets, lace-making, Brownies. Lots of trips and expeditions.

The pupils Mostly from East Anglian middle-class/professional backgrounds (some landed gentry); 15 expatriates; regular recruitment from Spain. Fairly wide range of abilities; entry by academic and verbal reasoning tests; applicants and parents interviewed to assess suitability. Some scholarships, bursaries.

Results Good Common Entrance record; virtually all go at 11 or 12 to independent senior school of first choice.

Destinations Mostly to single-sex boarding schools: Benenden, Queenswood, St Mary's (Calne), St Felix (Southwold), Wycombe Abbey. Increasing numbers to co-educational boarding schools: Gresham's (Holt), Oundle etc.

Sport Wide choice: strong swimming (in fine indoor heated pool); netball, tennis, rounders, hockey, athletics also on offer. Lots of rural pursuits: riding, clay-pigeon shooting, fishing, archery.

Remarks Good school for girls willing to 'have a go'.

SALISBURY CATHEDRAL SCHOOL
1 The Close,
Salisbury,
Wiltshire SP1 2EQ
Tel (0722) 322652

Co-educational • Day and boarding •
Ages 8-13 (plus pre-prep department) •
154 pupils (73% boys; 63% day) • Fees
(1992-93), £4,794 day; £6,432 boarding
(half-fees for choristers)
Head: Christopher Helyer, 47, appointed
1991.

Small, happy school; fine music; beautiful setting.

Background Founded 1091 by St Osmund, nephew of William the Conqueror, as a choir school for the new cathedral at Old Sarum; became a prep school in the 1920s; housed since 1947 in the Bishop's Palace, parts of which date from 1220; many later additions in 27 acres of the cathedral close. The first (and, so far, only) cathedral school to admit girl choristers (they sing in a separate choir). £1-million appeal launched for sports hall and technology centre.

Atmosphere Friendly, hard-working; emphasis on good manners, unobtrusive discipline; each pupil's birthday marked with a chocolate bar. Boarding accommodation adequate but slightly down-at-heel.

The head Educated in Australia; taught at King's, Peterborough; formerly head of the choir schools at Grimsby and Exeter. Teaches maths, coaches junior cricket, takes non-rugby players running; interests include (not surprisingly) church music. Married; wife looks after the domestic side of the boarding house.

The teaching Emphasis on basic skills, careful marking of written work, close monitoring of progress. Form teachers for first 2 years; subject specialists thereafter. Pupils set by ability in maths, languages; scholarship and Common Entrance streams from age of 11; small classes. Very strong music: all introduced to brass, woodwind and strings before deciding to specialise; 16 visiting teachers. Lots of drama.

The pupils Most join from pre-prep department; voice trials for choristers in January.

Results Good Common Entrance record; recent music scholarships to Sherborne, Charterhouse, Marlborough.

Destinations In addition to the above: Blundell's, Bryanston, Canford, Cheltenham, King's (Canterbury), Lancing, Winchester. Some leave at 11 for state grammar schools.

Sport Strong rugby; hockey, cricket, swimming, cross-country, netball, basketball, golf also on offer. Facilities include extensive playing fields, all-weather pitch, tennis courts, outdoor heated pool.

Remarks Good all round.

SANDROYD
Rushmore,
Tollard Royal,
Near Salisbury,
Wiltshire SP5 5QD
Tel (0705) 516264

Boys • Boarding • Ages 8-13 • 148 pupils
• Fees, £7,425
Head: David Cann, late-40s, appointed 1982.

Happy, purposeful school; good all round.

Background Founded 1888; moved to present premises 1939; 18th-century mansion in 400-acre deer park on Cranborne Chase.

Atmosphere Family-run school with a genuine family atmosphere – a sense of unostentatious courtesy and caring. Excellent staff-pupil relations; healthy competition and purposeful use of free time encouraged. Pleasant dormitories; boys moved termly to avoid cliques, widen friendships.

The head Read history at Cambridge; for-

merly joint head of Copthorne, Sussex. Teaches French and scripture, produces plays. Married, 3 sons (all were pupils here); wife responsible for the domestic side.

The teaching Traditional, in stressing the value of learning (10 minutes a day devoted to memorising basic factual information in all subjects); progressive, in encouraging spontaneity and lots of pupil participation in lessons. Well-qualified, committed staff of 20, three-quarters appointed by present head. Arts subjects are strong – good Latin, French – but there is growing emphasis on science, technology and computing. Streaming by ability to meet the needs of high-fliers and slow learners; average class size 12. First-rate music; 2 orchestras, 3 choirs. Head believes boys learn best by doing and is rightly proud of the wide variety of practical activities (many of them outdoor) which the school provides.

The pupils Happy, outgoing, disciplined; predominantly from upper-middle-class backgrounds. Entry by interview and informal assessment; fairly wide ability range; early registration advised.

Results Good Common Entrance record; 21 awards to independent schools in past 8 years.

Destinations Twice as many go to Sherborne as any other school, followed by Eton, Radley, Milton Abbey.

Sport Team games and individual sports 7 days a week; rugby particularly strong; hockey, soccer, cricket, athletics, tennis etc all coached. Facilities include indoor heated pool, .22 rifle range.

Remarks 'Happy preparatory school days,' says the prospectus, 'should be well-fed, exciting and full of peaks which can just be climbed – with higher ones tomorrow.' Aspiration realised.

ST ANDREW'S

Meads,
Eastbourne,
Sussex BN20 7RP
Tel (0323) 33203

Co-educational • Day and boarding •
Ages 8-13 (plus pre-prep department, 3-8)
• 320 pupils (79% boys; 60% day) • Fees,
£4,485 day; £6,930 boarding
Head: Hugh Davies Jones, 48, appointed
1984.

First-rate school. High academic standards; good scholarship record; strong on arts and games.

Background Founded 1877 as a boarding school for boys (curriculum consisted of Latin and cricket); co-educational since 1977. 19-acre site at the foot of the South Downs; original Victorian buildings modernised and extended.

Atmosphere Still very much a boarding school, despite the preponderance of day pupils: lessons on Saturday mornings, supervised prep for all in the evenings. Pleasant environment: lots of work displayed in classrooms and corridors; well-furnished boarding houses (1 each for boys and girls); double-glazed, centrally heated; single rooms for seniors. Day begins with a chapel service led by the school chaplain (Anglican but all faiths welcomed). Meals served by members of staff.

The head Good with staff, pupils and parents (has been a head for 20 years). Teaches scripture to the juniors, general studies to the scholarship class. Wife, Sarah, teaches maths, takes Brownies and Cubs, runs clothes shop, helps out in the kitchen.

The teaching Mixed-ability for first 2 years (form teachers); streaming thereafter (subject teachers) and setting for maths. Children moved up on stage-rather-than-age principle; scholarship class for the brightest; extra help for those with learning difficulties. National curriculum followed (school helped pilot national tests for 7-year-olds) but senior work dominated by demands of Common Entrance.

All do French and Latin, some add Greek and German. Attractive, well-resourced classrooms; average class size 16. 32 teachers, a third women. Children assessed weekly on effort, attitude, achievement, behaviour; outstanding work shown to the head and entered in honours book. Attractive, well-stocked library (plus bean bags). Excellent facilities for art, pottery, craft, technology. Good music centre (6 practice rooms); several choirs; 60% learn an instrument. Lots of drama. Regular French exchanges (pupils stay with French families, attend local school). Vast range of evening hobbies: astronomy, bridge, computers, tapestry, woodwork etc.

The pupils Lively, happy, pleased to talk about their work. Mostly from business and professional families. Day pupils drawn from 20-mile radius (school mini-buses); half the boarders live abroad. Entry tests a term prior to admission. (National test scores in English, maths and science showed approximately two-thirds were at Level 3, i.e. above-average ability.)

Results (1991) 12 gained scholarships: Ardingly, Benenden, Eastbourne, Lancing, Eastbourne, Sevenoaks, Queenswood etc. All gained places at first-choice schools.

Destinations Mostly Eastbourne and Moira House; also Bethany, Bryanston, Charterhouse, Cranbrook, Eton, Harrow, Malvern, Marlborough, Millfield, Oakham, Oundle, Radley, Roedean, Rugby, St Bede's, Seaford, Sherborne, Stowe.

Sport Huge range; good facilities; long fixture list. Main games: football, rugby, cricket (boys); netball, hockey, rounders (girls). Gym, heated indoor pool, 2 floodlit tennis courts (plus part-time professional).

Remarks Good all round; highly recommended.

ST AUBYNS
Rottingdean,
Brighton,
East Sussex BN2 7JN
Tel (0273) 302170

Boys • Boarding and day • Ages 8-13 •
115 pupils (75% boarding) • Fees, £6,900
boarding; £5,280 day
Head: Julian James, 52, appointed 1974.

---

*Small, old-fashioned prep school with a
strong family atmosphere. Good sporting
record; lots of music.*

Background Founded 1895. Main building
Regency/Georgian (grade-2 listed) in centre of
village; many recent additions.

Atmosphere Exceptionally happy; no bullying; not a school where one needs 'best friends'
to cling on to; head and his wife always on
hand to sort out any problems. Well-
supported by parents (many fathers were
pupils here). Pleasant dormitories (but not all
carpeted, and iron bedsteads still being phased
out). Bible reading and prayers before lights
out.

The head Former pupil here (1947-52); went
to Charterhouse, trained as a teacher and then
came back. Teaches French; has something
positive to say about every child. Wife, Hilary,
helps out on the pastoral side; meets with boys'
food committee to plan the menus.

The teaching Boys divided on entry into
scholarship and Common Entrance streams;
setting in some subjects. Wait-and-see attitude
to national curriculum (how does it fit in with
Common Entrance? national testing at 14?).
Latin and Greek on offer; French exchange (8
days in St Malo, staying with French families,
attending local school). Extra help for those
with special needs, including dyslexia; foreign
children (16 in total) taught English as a
second language. Good library; lots of computers. Strong art (including pottery, sculpture) and music: 70 boys learning 80 instruments; drum and bugle band, choir etc.

The pupils New boys carefully nurtured:
head and his wife meet them at Victoria

station; all arrive at school together, have tea,
meet Perkins (Golden Retriever), watch video
before bed. Entry by assessment and tests in
English, maths; all current pupils have IQ of
110+. Most from London and Sussex. Day
boys work a full day: 8.10 a.m. to end of
supervised prep at 6.25 p.m.; lessons on
Saturday mornings.

Results Regular scholarships to Eton, Harrow, Radley, Winchester (but none in 1991).

Destinations Most common (apart from the
above): Cranleigh, Eastbourne, Lancing, Milton Abbey, St Bede's, Stowe.

Sport Soccer, rugby, cricket (indoor nets);
full fixture lists. Also on offer: badminton,
basketball, judo, fencing. Facilities include
sports hall, shooting range, heated outdoor
pool, all-weather tennis and squash courts.

Remarks Successful school; deliberately kept
small to preserve its traditional, homely ethos.

ST JOHN'S COLLEGE SCHOOL
73 Grange Road,
Cambridge CB3 9AB
Tel (0223) 353532

Co-educational (but boys and girls taught
separately) • Day and some boys'
boarding • Ages 4-13 (girls 4-11) • 440
pupils (68% boys; 90% day) • Fees
(1992-93), £2,367-£4,734 day; £7,344
boarding; £2,448 choristers
Head: Kevin Jones, 40s, appointed 1990.

---

*Strongly academic choir school; first-rate
teaching and results; very good music.*

Background Founded 1660 as a choir school
for the college, which still owns it (two-thirds
of the governors are college Fellows). Moved
to present Edwardian premises 1955; many
later additions; girls and pre-prep department
200 yards away. Supportive parents raise
£4,000 a year.

Atmosphere Traditional,   well-ordered,

purposeful; strong Christian ethos; choristers add a special dimension. Boarding restricted to 55 boys (including 20 choristers). Pleasant dormitories; good food.

The head Educated at Cambridge; formerly deputy head of the Yehudi Menuhin music school. Teaches English and drama.

The teaching Formal; basic skills rigorously taught from the start; extra help for those with special needs, including dyslexics. High quality staff of 40 (both French teachers are native speakers); average class size 20. National curriculum-plus; all do Latin for at least 1 year; first-rate design/technology; good art (techniques of the Old Masters carefully studied). Outstanding music: 85% learn at least 1 instrument; frequent trips abroad.

The pupils Mostly from professional and business families in a county-wide catchment area. Entry to kindergarten (after 4th birthday) by registration within a few months of birth (automatic progress through the school thereafter); at 7 by informal assessment; voice trials for choristers. Average IQs 110-120. School is over-subscribed.

Results Good Common Entrance record; nearly all go on to their first-choice school. Regular scholarships to Benenden, Eton, The Leys, Oakham, The Perse, St Mary's (Cambridge).

Destinations Most to independent senior schools; a few to local state schools.

Sport Rugby, cricket for the boys; netball, rounders for the girls. School has use of the college playing fields.

Remarks Very good all round.

ST PAUL'S (Colet Court)
Lonsdale Road,
London SW13 9JT
Tel (081) 748 3461

Boys • Day (and some boarding) • Ages 8-13 • 420 pupils (95% day) • Fees (1992-93), £5,520 (£8,790 boarding) Head: Geoffrey Thompson, 46, appointed 1992.

A flying start for clever young Paulines: élite entry; excellent teaching.

Background Founded 1881; functional 1960s buildings adjoining St Paul's *(qv)*; amenities shared with the senior school include spacious dining hall, chapel, technology workshops, sports centre and playing fields.

Atmosphere Little chattering figures playing with balls and bats almost redeem the anonymous, dreary buildings, all grey pebble and utility slab. Inside, by contrast, seems almost cosy. Classrooms are a good size and bright with decoration; the large day room is set up for chess and bridge; in the hall 2 boys are practising their juggling routines for a Victorian music hall concert; a solitary bagpiper tunes up in the corner. The boarding house has friendly dormitories and a large games room; it also houses the computer room and the library, so there is a constant flow of day boys through the passages.

The head New appointment but was once head of science here, and already looks an old hand. Has a calm, easy authority; conversations do not stop when he comes into the room. Keen on discipline, order, clear guidelines: hands out of pockets and no litter. Married; lives next to the school.

The teaching Intensive, structured, largely traditional in style. Some staff also teach in the senior school; most are graduates. All the usual subjects; emphasis on Latin, science, technology. This is a good place for friendly, dedicated teachers who do not have to be home too early: there are dozens of out-of-classroom activities, nearly all generated by the enthusiasm of the staff; many take place at the weekend or in the holidays (cycling in Brittany, walking in Switzerland, rugby in Australia, chess at Pontins). Boys are treated as rational, likeable creatures; sports days, concerts and parents' evenings are amusing challenges rather than bores. Some staff believe the boys read less than they did, thanks to computer games and TV, but the library is well stocked and well used. Half learn an instrument; 50-strong orchestra, 2 choirs.

The pupils Robust, keenly competitive (these are Paulines in the making); they argue the question confidently, with good vocabulary and individual view-points. Waiting lists limited to 500 for each year (lists now closed until 2000); in the end, about 150 compete for 72 places; tests (held on the same day as those for King's College Junior School and Westminster Under School to reduce multiple applications) in maths, English, verbal reasoning; most candidates interviewed by 3 separate masters. NB: a boy entered for Colet Court is automatically entered for St Paul's, and will only be accepted on the understanding that the senior school is his first choice. Some assisted places and music scholarships.

Results Boys are not specifically prepared for Common Entrance or for scholarships to senior schools other than St Paul's; nonetheless, some win scholarships to Eton and Winchester.

Destinations 90% proceed to St Paul's.

Sport Rugby and cricket are both keenly played but there are many alternatives. Excellent facilities shared with the senior school.

Remarks Fine school for bright boys with plenty of potential.

STORMONT
The Causeway,
Potters Bar,
Hertfordshire EN6 5HA
Tel (0707) 54037

Girls ● Day ● Ages 4-11 ● 175 pupils ● Fees £2,935-£3,345
Head: Miss Fenella Pearson, 60s, appointed 1964 (retires August 1993).

First-rate, happy school. Lively, enthusiastic pupils; talented, capable staff.

Background Founded 1944 in elegantly converted Victorian mansion.

Atmosphere Purposeful, industrious, with an intimate family feeling. Children's art decorates classrooms and corridors. Parents raise up to £7,000 a year for books, electronic keyboards, microscopes, playground equipment etc.

The head Soon to retire after nearly 30 years in the job. Held in great affection; has devoted her life to fashioning a fine school.

The teaching Head wishes pupils to be stretched but not pressurised; good standards of neatness and presentation expected. National curriculum followed; national tests taken in English, maths, science (4 lessons a week). Nearly all read fluently by age of 7 (extra help for those with learning difficulties). Form teachers up to 8+; subject teaching thereafter. French taught from 9; final-year girls spend a week in France. 17 staff (all women). Bright, spacious classrooms; splendid library; excellent facilities for art, pottery (wheel and kiln), design/technology (lots of computers). Music in former coach house; all 7- and 8-year-olds learn recorder; more than a quarter have individual music tuition; 2 orchestras; choir.

The pupils Happy, responsive; mostly from middle-class homes with high expectations. Admission on first-come basis after 4th birthday; early registration advisable (lists closed for 1994 and 1995).

Destinations Mostly to highly competitive day schools: St Albans High, City of London Girls, Haberdashers' Aske's etc. All pupils happily accommodated with the head's advice in a school suitable to their temperament and ability.

Sport Multi-purpose hall for PE and games; tennis court; playing field for rounders, athletics. Every girl swims once a week at nearby Queenswood School.

Remarks Well-run, exceptionally well-equipped school.

SUMMER FIELDS
Banbury Road,
Oxford OX2 7EN
Tel (0865) 54433

Boys • Boarding and day • Ages 8-13 •
245 pupils (15 day) • Fees, £7,800
boarding; £4,890 day
Head: Nigel Talbot-Rice, mid-50s,
appointed 1975.

Outstanding, lively school in North Oxford's Summertown; exceptionally good facilities.

Background Founded 1864. Elegant golden brick buildings surrounded by 60 acres of gardens, playing fields and farmland.

Atmosphere Whole school buzzes with activity and enthusiasm. Competition is the mainspring of life: boys divided into leagues; points for conduct, work and games. Classrooms mainly new, large, light, attractively furnished; dining hall (complete with high table and portraits) is imposingly panelled and echoes accordingly. Boarding houses carpeted, centrally-heated, comfortable; profusion of soft toys, garish posters, photographs.

The head Energetically committed to the pursuit of excellence – by which he means hard work, hard play, good manners. Busily involved in every aspect of school life; well-liked by boys and staff. Here since 1965.

The teaching Varied in style but uniformly excellent. (In a maths lesson, the desks were ignored as boys crowded excitedly around one who was playing the part of a decimal point: they acted as fractions or whole numbers while additions and subtractions were made. In Latin, they seemed just as happy sitting behind desks translating from a text, any stumbling being dealt with humorously by a teacher who would clearly brook no nonsense.) Able, enthusiastic staff have high expectations (suggested reading list for a 9-year-old runs to 44 titles) and offer constant encouragement; they make the boys want to learn. Average class size officially 16 but most seem much smaller. Streaming by ability in last 3 years; all except first-years do $1^1/_4$ hours of prep every week night. 'Tests,' the boys complain engagingly, 'happen all the time'. Very strong music: 70% learn an instrument; 2 full-time, 25 part-time teachers; 30 practice rooms; orchestras, choirs etc.

The pupils Delightful manners; highly articulate; a captivating eagerness to tell all (biggest complaint is the sandals the younger ones have to wear). Each classroom displays a poster headed 'Are you unhappy?' listing all possible sources of aid (including telephone helplines). Some boys very clever indeed but most of average intelligence; mainly from upper- and upper-middle-class families in London and the South East. Entry by tests in English and maths and observation during a day at the school (to see whether they will fit in). Places cannot be guaranteed until 1999; names can, however, be placed on a waiting list.

Results Excellent; 12 scholarships to Eton in 1992. On the whole, boys get into the schools for which their parents have entered them.

Destinations Mainly Eton and Radley; others include Ampleforth, Downside, Harrow, Marlborough, St Edward's (Oxford), Stowe, Winchester.

Sport Superb facilities (2 large swimming pools, adventure playground); respectable match record; but not a sporty school. Those who are not keen are allowed to opt out.

Remarks An excellent – if very traditional –

school. Boys receive a solid grounding in the sciences and the arts in an atmosphere that encourages them to see learning as a pleasure.

SUNNINGDALE

Sunningdale,
Berkshire SL5 9PY
Tel (0344) 20159

Boys • Boarding • Ages 8-13 • 124 pupils • Fees (1992-93), £6,225
Joint heads: Nick and Tim Dawson, 58, appointed 1967.

Small, privately owned school; solid, all-round education for boys of a wide range of abilities; strong sport.

Background Founded 1874; red-brick Victorian villa in 27 acres of playing fields and woods close to Windsor Great Park; rather dilapidated in appearance (yellowing paint, faded school photos, untended flower beds); strongly reminiscent of a bygone age.

Atmosphere Informal, slightly eccentric (no front door bell or other means of drawing attention to a visitor's presence). Cheerful, friendly boys on easy but respectful terms with the masters; good manners *de rigueur* (swearing or hands in pockets definitely not on). Strong Christian tradition, daily chapel service, grace at meals. Senior boys housed in wooden cubicles in 2 large dormitories, private but spartan; ancient communal bathing facilities; no showers. Matron has been here more than 30 years. Sweets twice a week; ice cream van on Sundays.

The heads Twins; educated at Cothill House and Eton (where they decided that their ambition was to run a prep school). Both have been here since 1958; they bought the school in 1967 and still own it. Both teach 28 periods a week – between them, they teach every boy each day – and are involved in every aspect of the school, from mowing the cricket pitches to entertaining parents: a remarkable double act (small boys constantly running between them

bearing messages). N D is a bachelor; T D is married with 4 children (one a pupil here); both are courteous, amusing and completely dedicated. They do not aim to attract the real high-fliers but to give the average boy a solid preparation for his public school (principally Eton).

The teaching Traditional in style and – largely – in content; emphasis on good grounding, grammar, spelling, punctuation. Particular strengths in maths and French; science well taught (in a somewhat basic hut); remedial English on offer throughout. Not a forcing house; boys go at their own pace. Weekly grades for effort and peformance (discussed individually with N D); fortnightly form orders; termly reports to parents. Good music: inspired teaching; any boy with even minimal aptitude encouraged to try an instrument; lively singing.

The pupils Most have parents who were themselves privately educated (some at Sunningdale); many in the professions or the City. Entry is non-selective; register at birth.

Results Good Common Entrance record; average of 1 academic scholarship a year.

Destinations 65% to Eton; rest mainly to Harrow, Stowe, Radley.

Sport Strong tradition. Cricket, tennis, athletics, swimming, soccer, squash, fives all taken seriously. Facilities include sports hall (large, converted barn), outdoor pool, 6-hole golf course.

Remarks Old-fashioned, happy school.

TOCKINGTON MANOR
Tockington,
Near Bristol BS12 4NY
Tel (0454) 613229

Co-educational • Boarding and day •
Ages 7-13 • 160 pupils (roughly equal
numbers of girls and boys, 56% boarding)
• Fees, £7,959 boarding; £5,550 day
Head: Richard Tovey, 43, appointed 1975.

Well-run school; wide range of abilities; idyllic surroundings.

Background Opened by the present head's father in 1946; converted Queen Anne manor farmhouse plus careful additions; 28 acres of beautiful grounds including an arboretum. Co-educational since 1975.

Atmosphere A real family feel. Relaxed staff, happy children; informal, caring discipline. Cheerful 8-bed dormitories. Lessons on Saturday mornings; day pupils stay until 5.45 p.m.

The head Enthusiastic, committed. Educated at Clifton; taught in the state sector; keen on cricket and rugby. Teaches for half the timetable, infecting all with his ebullient *joie de vivre*. Wife oversees catering and health care.

The teaching Sound overall; all staff properly qualified; pupils set by ability from age 8. Largely formal approach in maths and English; big emphasis on mastering basic skills; aim is never to lose sight of Common Entrance at 13. French introduced from age 9; two-thirds start Latin at 10+. Cross-curricular work encouraged: for example, project on flight embraces Daedalus and Icarus plus a visiting engineer from British Aerospace. Extra help for slow learners/dyslexics. Lots of time for reading (well-stocked library); frequent visits to Stratford, regular school plays; half learn a musical instrument; ballet taken seriously.

The pupils Happy, confident, well-balanced. Mostly from well-off homes (fees are high, no assistance); majority of parents are 'first-time buyers' of independent education; no landed gentry; 10-15 from abroad, particularly Spain and the Far East (children often come without

English and return home fluent). Fairly broad spectrum of ability; no entrance exam.

Results Good Common Entrance record; great care taken to find the right senior school. Regular scholarships to Malvern, Monmouth, Shrewsbury etc.

Destinations Not a feeder for anywhere in particular; 42 children went on to 28 schools in 1991.

Sport 6 specialist staff; all usual games offered; particularly strong cross-country. Fencing, archery, croquet, horse-riding also on offer. Facilities include 2 large games fields, heated outdoor pool, 5 tennis courts.

Remarks Good all round, with a growing reputation.

WARWICK
Bridge Field,
Banbury Road,
Warwick CV34 6PL
Tel (0926) 491545

Day • Girls (3-11) and boys (3-7) • 420
pupils (100 boys) • Fees, £1,125-£3,300
Head: Mrs Elizabeth Prichard, 45,
appointed 1981.

Sparkling school on the southern edge of Warwick; provides a stimulating environment from an early age.

Background Founded as part of King's High, Warwick in 1879; separated 1944; moved to present attractive 5-acre site adjoining Warwick School *(qv)* 1971. Spruce, modern buildings; spacious, airy classrooms.

Atmosphere Friendly, well-ordered; bubbling with activity; emphasis on courtesy and consideration for others.

The head Vigorous organiser and innovator (keen on 'brain storming'); school has doubled in size under her leadership. First woman to head the Incorporated Association of Preparatory Schools (to which nearly all the prep schools in this guide belong). Taught biology for 11 years at Bedford Modern; plays the oboe; coaches badminton. Married to David Prichard, head of Port Regis *(qv)*.

The teaching Indisputably good. 30 teachers (all women, nearly all appointed by present head) give painstaking attention to preparing, explaining, marking, recording – and are readily accessible to parents. Full national curriculum; French from age of 8; speech and drama for all. Setting by ability in English and maths from 8. Special needs (both for the gifted and those with learning difficulties) taken seriously. Average class size 22 but many teaching groups number 10 or fewer; 13 nursery nurses and other assistants. Homework increases from 20 minutes nightly at age 7 to 40 minutes at 10. 2 libraries plus full-time librarian. Strong music; two-thirds learn an instrument; orchestra and choir.

The pupils Eager, responsive; broad social mix. Well looked after by form mistresses. Enthusiastically competitive house system. Applications by 1st birthday for entry at 3 or 4 (clear indication of the school's reputation). Entry at 7 or after by informal assessment.

Results Occasional scholarships (top award to Millfield, 1991).

Destinations At 7, virtually all boys move to the junior department of Warwick School; at 11, more than half girls go to King's High, rest to Kingsley (Leamington Spa), Malvern Girls', Cheltenham Ladies' etc.

Sport Very good facilities. Football (boys), netball and hockey (girls) in winter; rounders, tennis and athletics in summer. Local and national successes in swimming.

Remarks Happy, effective school; a model of its kind. Good value for money.

WELLESLEY HOUSE

Broadstairs,
Kent CT10 2DG
Tel (0843) 62991

Co-educational • Boarding (and some day) • Ages 7½-14 • 197 pupils (73% boys; 92% boarding) • Fees, £7,800-£8,100 (£6,900 day)
Head: Richard Steel, 43, appointed 1990.

Good, traditional school.

Background Founded 1869; moved to present purpose-built premises 1900; pleasant 16-acre site in a densely populated area on the outskirts of the town, 1 mile from the sea. Girls first admitted 1977.

Atmosphere Friendly; well-mannered pupils proud of their school. High standards of cleaning and maintenance. Boarding accommodation adequate if a little cramped (dormitory sizes range from 4 to 19); some being upgraded and refurnished. Children complimentary about the food; dining room noisy.

The head Previously head of a prep school in Hertfordshire; teaches English, scripture and current affairs for nearly half the timetable. Married, 3 children (one a boarder here); wife runs the domestic side. Both have a good rapport with staff and pupils.

The teaching Good, particularly in classics, maths, French, science. Pupils placed by ability in one of 3 streams – scholarship, Common Entrance or average Common Entrance; curriculum varies accordingly (bottom group do not take Latin or Greek). Wait-and-see attitude to the national curriculum; computing not currently timetabled. Average class size 13. Extra help for dyslexics (who must have an IQ of 112+). Good drama; first-rate facilities for art (including pottery kiln and wheel); lots of music – more than three-quarters learn an instrument. Wide range of extra-curricular activities; all learn carpentry.

The pupils Mostly from London and the South East; many have family connections. Interview but no testing prior to entry. Head says: 'The parents choose the school, we don't select the children. After we've been together for a couple of hours we'll both know whether the child is suitable for the school.' Some bursaries for clergy and Service children.

Results Generally good; usually some scholarships (top award to Charterhouse in 1992).

Destinations 40% of boys to Eton and Harrow; remainder to Haileybury, King's (Canterbury), Stowe, Tonbridge, Winchester etc. Girls to Benenden, Cheltenham Ladies', Roedean etc.

Sport Chiefly cricket, football, rugby for the boys; netball, rounders, hockey for the girls. Also on offer: athletics, cross-country, basketball, badminton, golf, swimming, shooting. First-rate facilities include sports hall, squash and tennis courts, covered pool, putting green.

Remarks Pupils are well educated and cared for.

WESTBOURNE
50-54 Westbourne Road,
Sheffield S10 2QQ
Tel (0742) 660374

Boys • Day • Ages 4-13 • 165 pupils • Fees, £2,055-£3,525
Head: Colin Wilmshurst, early-50s, appointed 1984.

Well-established reputation for hard work and achievement.

Background Founded 1885; large house on a small site in an attractive Victorian residential area close to the city centre. Much ingenuity in the use of premises.

Atmosphere Relaxed, informal – but discipline, good order and standards apply. Hardworking classes; boisterous playtime release.

The head Came here as deputy in 1981. Parents find him encouraging, helpful, reassuring. Lives at the school with his wife; children are grown-up.

The teaching Sound. Keen, well-qualified staff; national curriculum-plus. Science taught as 3 separate subjects; all do Latin, French, design/technology, computing; German on offer. Setting by ability in some subjects; maximum class size 20 (6 in scholarship class). Specialist help for dyslexics. Good music and drama.

The pupils Cheerful, lively; talk with confidence and poise. Mostly from professional families; wide catchment area. Entry at any age. No admission tests; first come, first served.

Results Strong record of scholarships to The Leys, Malvern, Shrewsbury etc.

Destinations Wide variety of independent schools, including Gordonstoun, Malvern, Oakham, Repton, Rugby, Uppingham; some to local state schools.

Sport Soccer, rugby, cricket, athletics and tennis played against other prep schools with notable success.

Remarks Deservedly popular school; sound education in a happy environment.

WESTMINSTER CATHEDRAL CHOIR
Ambrosden Avenue,
London SW1P 1QH
Tel (071) 834 9247

Boys • Roman Catholic (some non-Catholics) • Day and boarding • Ages 8-13 • 90 pupils (one-third boarding, all choristers) • Fees, £4,980 day; £2,460 choristers
Head: Peter Hannigan, 59, appointed 1977.

Small, exceptional school; good teaching; outstanding musical training.

Background Founded 1901 by Cardinal Vaughan to provide 30 choristers for the new cathedral at Westminster; saved from closure in 1976 by Cardinal Hume, who reconstituted it with 60 places for fee-paying day boys and appointed the present head. Cramped premises in the shadow of the cathedral, overlooked by neighbouring blocks of flats; large asphalt playground put to maximum use.

Atmosphere Dedication to the life of the cathedral and devotion to the Roman Catholic faith are central. School pulsates with energy and purpose, yet has a noticeably kindly and nurturing feel. Pianos in odd corners, window ledges piled high with art work; the sound of someone practising a musical instrument always in the background. A high degree of self-discipline is implicit in the lives of the choristers, whose days are extraordinarily busy and demanding. No formal rules but decent behaviour and kindliness to others expected. All choristers board in 1 room: austere but homely.

The head Enthusiastic, totally committed; has built up the school and established its fine reputation. Married, 4 grown-up children; wife oversees the pastoral care of the boys (mother to all the choristers) and is crucial to the functioning of the school.

The teaching Imaginative and at times inspired (despite some rather dark and poky classrooms with rows of ancient desks); highly qualified staff (half women), all appointed by present head. Pupils set by ability in each subject; academic standards are high; extra help available for dyslexia or other problems. French is outstanding; computers widely used; design/technology not neglected. The music, not surprisingly, is superb; choristers all learn 2 instruments (they practise twice a day, once before breakfast, in addition to 2 choir rehearsals); most of the day boys learn at least 1. Not much time for hobbies (or writing home).

The pupils Healthy social mix: many choristers come from homes where private education was never previously contemplated; day boys from mainly professional and wealthy backgrounds. Annual intake of 6 choristers, 12 day boys. Choristers selected after voice trials in March, June, November; head is looking not just for voice potential and musicality but for the ability to fit into the community and a special, indefinable quality that signals a potential chorister (stamina essential). Parents of prospective day boys should apply 2 years before entry; admission by tests and interview. Generous scholarships for choristers.

Results Most go on to the school of their choice; choristers virtually certain of a music scholarship somewhere.

Destinations Chiefly Catholic public schools – Ampleforth, Stonyhurst, Oratory; also Westminster, St Paul's, Eton, Harrow.

Sport Not a particular strength. Apart from the playground (used extensively for roller skating), school has no facilities of its own. Pupils have access to Westminster's playing fields for football and tennis; swimming and badminton in nearby sports centre; indoor cricket at the Oval.

Remarks Energetic pursuit of excellence combined with an almost family feel. Highly recommended.

WINDLESHAM HOUSE
Washington,
Pulborough,
West Sussex RH20 4AY
Tel (0903) 873207

Co-educational • Boarding • Ages 7-13 • 355 pupils (64% boys) • Fees, £7,200
Heads: Mr and Mrs Charles Malden, appointed 1958.

First-rate prep school; high academic standards; wide range of hobbies and activities.

Background Founded 1837 and has remained in the same family ever since; claims to have been the first prep school and the first to admit girls (in 1967). Moved to present premises 1934; early 18th-century house plus numerous later additions in 60-acre country estate.

Atmosphere Strong family feel; big emphasis

on all-round achievement. 'Children,' says the Windlesham Charter, 'should be happy first and foremost...a naughty child is an unhappy child.' Two basic rules: politeness and punctuality; chief sanction is loss of free time. No uniform; regimentation avoided as much as possible; parents regard the school as sensible and down-to-earth. Largish dormitories found to be happier than small ones; bedtime stories broadcast nightly; always an adult around for the children to talk to.

The heads Elizabeth-Anne and Charles Malden exemplify the school's Christian family spirit. Both are Cambridge classicists with a wide and cultured appreciation of the arts. They are proud to have had the opportunity to fulfil their aims together for more than 30 years.

The teaching Broad curriculum; all do Latin, French (40 add Greek), design/technology, computing, cooking, needlework. Setting by ability in maths, French, Latin; no class more than 20; extra help for those with specific needs including dyslexia and English as a second language. First-rate art, drama; lots of music; full orchestra; any instrument taught.

Activities and hobbies for all tastes, including calligraphy, clock-making, enamelling, pistol shooting, robotics; boys and girls still find time to read (most popular authors Dahl, Blyton, Tolkien).

The pupils Half have parents working abroad, mostly in the Diplomatic Service; two-thirds have, or have had, siblings here. Admission by interview; no selection tests (but average IQ about 115); register names as early as possible.

Results Good Common Entrance record; regular scholarships.

Destinations Most to co-educational independent schools such as Bedales, Bryanston, Marlborough, Stowe; others to Eton, Harrow, Wycombe Abbey.

Sport Games compulsory twice a week; wide range on offer, including tennis, squash, fencing, judo, gymnastics; standards in the team games are high. Fine sports hall; heated pool.

Remarks A happy and demanding school. Highly recommended.

Secondary Schools

THE ABBEY
17 Kendrick Road,
Reading,
Berkshire RG1 2DZ
Tel (0734) 872256

Independent • Girls • Day • Ages 11-18
(plus associated junior school) • 764
pupils • 177 in sixth form • Fees (1992-93),
£3,630
Head: Miss Barbara Sheldon, late-40s,
appointed 1991.

---

*Strong, traditional academic school;
first-rate results.*

Background Founded 1887; red-brick buildings on 6-acre site in quiet, tree-lined road;
later additions include good science labs, fine
assembly hall, vast sixth-form centre reminiscent of an airport lounge (acres of curved,
caramel-coloured sofas and little tables).

Atmosphere Christian foundation (portraits
of bishops line the stairs); reassuringly timeless
(change for change's sake avoided under
31-year reign of previous head). Warm heart of
a proud, provincial grammar school still beats
here: sensible green skirts and jerseys; rows of
solid desks with lids (to whisper behind and
bang down hard when cross); happy, chattering groups at the bus stop hung about with
shapeless bundles and violin cases.

The head Read English at Birmingham;
taught in state and independent schools before
becoming deputy head of King Edward VI
Handsworth. Strong believer in single-sex
education; keen to reduce the proportion who
leave after GCSE for co-educational sixth
forms. Accessible, firm (but, say the girls, she
listens).

The teaching Stable, happy staff; thorough,

sensible teaching. Rigorous curriculum; big
emphasis on sciences (taught as 3 separate
subjects), computing (starts at age 4, compulsory up to GCSE); all do French, Latin from
first year and can add Spanish or German.
Most do 10-11 GCSEs; more than half take
science A-levels. Some classrooms rather
crowded. Well-used art room; music, speech
and drama available.

The pupils Mostly from professional backgrounds; wide catchment area (parents organise special buses). Entry by competitive tests
at 11 (grammar-school standard required);
virtually all junior school applicants admitted
(and make up half the intake). Assisted places,
scholarships, bursaries.

Results GCSE: 99% gain at least 5 grades
A-C. A-level (1992): creditable 62% of entries
graded A or B.

Destinations 75% stay on for A-levels; nearly
all proceed to higher education, many after a
'gap year' (20% to Oxbridge).

Sport Lots available; hockey, netball, tennis
all played to a high standard. Facilities include
excellent indoor pool.

Remarks Solid, well-run, purposeful school.

ABBOTSHOLME
Rocester,
Uttoxeter,
Staffordshire ST14 5BS
Tel (0889) 590217

Independent • Co-educational • Boarding
and some day • Ages 11-18 • 247 pupils
(65% boys; 85% boarding) • 62 in sixth
form • Fees, £9,207 boarding; £6,138 day
Head: Darrell Farrant, mid-50s, appointed
1984.

---

*Small, distinctive school; wide range of
abilities admitted; self-confidence
promoted.*

Background Founded 1889 by Dr Cecil

Reddie, the eccentric father of English progressive education. Handsome Victorian country house plus later additions in 130 idyllic acres (including 70-acre working farm – founder believed in the 'dignity of labour') on the edge of the Peak District. Co-educational since 1969.

Atmosphere Homely, informal, unpretentious. Strong sense of community; big emphasis on the physical and mental challenges of outdoor life (another of Reddie's legacies); parental involvement encouraged. Daily service in splendid chapel.

The head Relaxed, unobtrusive; effective leader. Was head of English at Merchiston Castle then head of a boarding school in British Columbia. Married, 2 children (one was a pupil here).

The teaching Small classes (maximum size 20); enthusiastic teachers; broad curriculum (all do technology, music, art, home economics, religious studies); Japanese, Chinese, Russian also on offer. Pupils go at their own pace; aim is to discover what each is good at; progress closely monitored. Extra help for those with dyslexia, language difficulties. Choice of 22 subjects at A-level, including compulsory general studies. Outdoor education built into the timetable: growing vegetables, looking after cattle, sheep, pigs etc (some pupils study agricultural science); lots of rugged expeditions (Everest, Arctic). Community service ranges from running cub pack for local children to working in Indian hill villages.

The pupils Cosmopolitan; broad range of abilities (those joining from prep schools – which three-quarters do – require only 45% at Common Entrance). Scholarships, bursaries available.

Results GCSE (1991): 69% gained at least 5 grades A-C. A-level (1992): modest 21% of entries graded A or B.

Destinations About half go on to higher education (2 to Oxbridge in 1991).

Sport Facilities include 20 acres of playing fields, splendid sports hall, heated pool, grass tennis courts. School is not competitively minded but rugby, soccer, hockey, rounders, netball, squash, badminton, cross-country are all on offer. Also: camping, canoeing, caving, rock-climbing, mountaineering, fishing, windsurfing, clay-pigeon shooting, horse riding.

Remarks Opportunity for everyone to shine at something; good choice for the right child.

ABERDARE BOYS'
Cwmdare Road,
Aberdare,
Mid Glamorgan CF44 8SS
Tel (0685) 872642

Comprehensive • Boys • Ages 11-18 • 740 pupils • 90 in sixth form
Head: Dr Geoffrey Abbott, 45, appointed 1991.

Comprehensive catering for children of a wide range of abilities in an area of high unemployment.

Background 1978 amalgamation of grammar school and 2 secondary moderns; depressing concrete-clad, flat-roof buildings on a bleak site; entrance serves as a bus turning area and a place to keep the dustbins; some classrooms in huts.

Atmosphere Well-ordered, caring: dedicated staff; smartly dressed, hard-working pupils; hopeful parents. School's aims include: 'to give pupils a sense of wonder at what mankind can achieve, and encourage their ambitions'.

The head Welsh-born; PhD in maths from Aberystwyth; came here to teach maths in 1971 and has no plans to leave. Unmarried.

The teaching Standard national curriculum; all do Welsh for first 3 years; French and Welsh the only languages on offer for GCSE. Pupils divided on entry into A and B streams (the latter accounts for 30% of the intake and includes pupils with official statements of special needs); further setting in maths, English, science; average class size 25. Choice of

16 subjects at A-level (good results in English, maths, sciences, economics); vocational alternatives include BTEC courses in conjunction with local further education college.

The pupils Drawn from an area of high unemployment; more than a third entitled to free school meals. 'Many pupils here have been no further than Merthyr and some have never been to Merthyr.' School never sees a quarter of the parents.

Results (1991) GCSE: very modest 27% gained 5 or more grades A–C (18% passed none – 'invariably long-term truants whose absence was condoned by their parents', says the prospectus). A-levels: 42% of entries graded A or B (an exceptionally good year).

Destinations 38% continue into the sixth form; about 65% of these take A-levels; a few proceed to higher education.

Sport Quite strong rugby, even though the pitch is a mud bath in the winter. Children bussed to local sports centre and swimming pools 1½ miles away.

Remarks School struggling against heavy odds.

ABINGDON

Park Road,
Abingdon,
Oxfordshire OX14 1DE
Tel (0235) 531755

Independent • Boys • Day and boarding •
Ages 11-18 • 750 pupils (80% day) • 240
in sixth form • Fees, £4,290 day; £8,082
boarding
Head: Michael St John Parker, 51,
appointed 1975.

Strong academic school; broad curriculum; high-quality teaching.

Background Known to exist in 1256 but re-endowed in 1563 by John Roysse, a London mercer: Mercers' Company maintain a lively (and generous) interest. Moved to present site 6 miles south of Oxford in 1870; beautiful grounds; attractive Victorian red-brick buildings; later additions blend in; new sixth-form centre for 1994.

Atmosphere Fizzing: intelligent, lively, unpretentious boys; able, hard-working teachers. Some classrooms gloomy and tatty; varying standards of maintenance. Pleasant, spacious boarding houses ('bullet-proof' carpeting); day boys' rooms scruffy.

The head Read history at Cambridge; taught at King's (Canterbury) and Winchester. Still enthusiastic after 17 years in post; currently planning to 'set off in deliberate pursuit of excellence'. Describes his management style as 'pragmatic' – 'high-handed' say some. Liked by the boys, who joke about his being a stickler for traditional standards (hates loud noise, bans parties). Teaches occasionally. Married, 4 children.

The teaching Well-prepared, well-managed, interesting lessons; quieter boys drawn in by judicious questioning and gentle humour. All-graduate staff of 64 (6 women), 16 of whom have been here even longer than the head. Largest class size 27. First-year curriculum includes compulsory Latin, technology, computing; choice of French, German, Russian. Setting by ability from age 13 in science, maths, French. Particular strengths in science, languages (ancient and modern), computing (gifted teaching, excellent facilities – no boy could leave here computer-illiterate). All take up to 11 GCSEs; sixth-formers do 3-4 A-levels plus broad general studies course. Excellent library (14,000 volumes). Good music (some with girls' school). Lots of foreign exchanges; extensive post-GCSE work experience programme. Extra-curricular activities include cadet force, Duke of Edinburgh award scheme, community service.

The pupils Most from business, professional, Service families. Entry by school's own exam: written papers in English, composition, maths, reasoning – designed to test potential rather than attainment. (Those joining from prep school need an average of 60% at Common Entrance.) 15-20 a year join the sixth form:

minimum of 7 GCSEs grade A-C plus previous head's reports. Assisted places, scholarships (including music), bursaries.

Results Nearly all gain at least 5 grades A-C (and most achieve 10). A-level (1992): 54% of entries graded A or B.

Destinations Nearly all proceed to higher education (13 to Oxbridge in 1991). Many take a 'gap year'.

Sport All main games; everyone expected to participate at least twice a week; fencing, sailing, aerobics etc also on offer. Excellent facilities include extensive playing fields, modern sports hall (shared with the community), boathouse on the Thames (one of the strongest rowing schools in the country), heated outdoor pool, 8 tennis courts, shooting range.

Remarks Good all round; aiming to be even better.

ALICE OTTLEY
Upper Tything,
Worcester WR1 1HW
Tel (0905) 27061

Independent • Girls • Day • Ages 4-18 • 710 pupils • 118 in sixth form • Fees, £4,074
Head: Miss Christine Sibbit, early-50s, appointed 1986.

Good academic school; high standards all round.

Background Founded 1883 as Worcester High School for Girls; renamed after the first head in 1914. Elegant Georgian buildings on attractive city-centre site; later additions include high-tech science/art block, fine sports hall. Whole school clean, tidy, impeccably decorated.

Atmosphere Friendly, vibrant, well-ordered; high standards of behaviour based on expectations rather than rules; no problems of discipline, attendance or timekeeping. Brisk daily

assemblies: Church of England tradition but all welcome. Strong belief in merits of single-sex education. Highly competitive house system.

The head Eminently approachable; popular with staff and girls. Read geography at Leicester; formerly deputy head of Tunbridge Wells Girls' Grammar. Teaches geography to all 12-year-olds.

The teaching High quality; successful mix of traditional and modern methods geared to the needs of able girls; bright, cheery classooms. National curriculum-plus; emphasis in junior school on basic skills; French, Latin from age 11; second modern language (German or Spanish) from 13; science taught as 3 separate subjects. Pupils streamed by ability from 12; further setting in maths, French; maximum class size 22 in senior school, reducing to 15 in sixth form. Progress carefully monitored; homework meticulously marked. Most do 9 GCSEs and 3 A-levels (from choice of 20) plus general studies. Particularly good results in science and languages; first-rate work in art and textiles. Lots of drama and music (Elgar taught here); half seniors learn an instrument; 2 orchestras. Wide variety of extra-curricular activities, including Duke of Edinburgh award scheme. Ample opportunities for foreign travel, language exchanges; all do 2 weeks' work experience.

The pupils Confident, articulate; all academically able. Fairly broad social mix (86 assisted places) but few from ethnic minorities; catchment area has 25-mile radius. Admission from ages 4-7 by informal assessment, from 8 by tests in English, maths, verbal reasoning; automatic promotion from junior school at 10. Up to 5 apply for each place; application advised 1 year ahead.

Results GCSE: nearly all gain at least 5 grades A-C. A-level (1992): 51% of entries graded A or B.

Destinations 75% stay on for A-levels; 90% of these proceed to higher education (6 a year to Oxbridge).

Sport Chiefly lacrosse (many county and national honours), netball, athletics, rounders (but no hockey). Badminton, cross-country, rowing, gymnastics also on offer. Facilities include hard tennis and netball courts on main site; lacrosse, athletics on nearby sports field.

Remarks Good school for able girls.

ALLEYN'S
Townley Road,
Dulwich,
London SE22 8SU
Tel (081) 693 3422

Independent • Co-educational • Day •
Ages 11-18 • 930 pupils (equal number of
boys and girls) • 250 in sixth form • Fees,
£4,905
Head: Dr Colin Niven, appointed
September 1992.

Respectable results; strong in music,
drama, art, sport.

Background Founded 1619 by Edward Alleyn, the Elizabethan actor-manager; moved to present 26-acre site 1882; fine Victorian Gothic buildings with many later additions. Became fully independent (and co-educational) when Direct Grant status was abolished in 1975.

Atmosphere Grammar-school ethos but less academically selective than either Dulwich College or James Allen's Girls', its partners in the Alleyn's Foundation.

The head New appointment. Previously head of the Island School, Hong Kong and St George's School, Rome. Doctorate from Lille University.

The teaching Broad curriculum: choice of 23 subjects at GCSE, 25 at A-level. Mixed-ability teaching in first year; setting in maths and Latin thereafter; upper and lower band from third year; all take 9 GCSEs (but not all do a foreign language). Most take 3 A-levels plus choice of extras. 84 staff (35 women); class sizes range from 27 in lower school to an average of 10 in the sixth form. Strong music;

two-thirds participate; 30 performing groups (several public concerts a year); superb facilities include 10 practice rooms, 2 recital rooms, recording studio. 6 major drama productions a year; high-quality drawing, painting, sculpture, pottery.

The pupils Polite, well-motivated; expected to work hard and take responsibility for their own learning. Drawn from across the social spectrum: business, professional, working-class; wide catchment area. Most come from (up to 100) state primary schools; admission based on entry tests, interview and school reports. 25 assisted places and 6 scholarships a year.

Results GCSE: 84% gain 5 or more grades A-C. A-level (1992): 45% of entries graded A or B.

Destinations Most stay on to do A-levels and proceed to higher education (4 a year to Oxbridge).

Sport Good facilities; netball, hockey, tennis, swimming, athletics, for girls; football, hockey, cricket, athletics, swimming (indoor pool) for boys.

Remarks Rather old-fashioned; poised for change under a new head.

AMPLEFORTH
York YO6 4ER
Tel (04393) 224

Independent • Roman Catholic • Boys •
Boarding (and some day) • Ages 10-18
(plus associated prep school) • 670 pupils
(97% boarding) • 240 in sixth form • Fees,
£7,656-£9,570 (£6,243-£7,917 day)
Head: Father Dominic Milroy, 60,
appointed 1980 (retires December 1992).

Britain's largest monastic boarding
school; wide ability range; good teaching
and results; strong sport.

Background Founded 1802 by Benedictine

monks; run by the Abbot and Community of Ampleforth Abbey, the largest Benedictine community in Europe. Splendid 1,000-acre site on the edge of the North Yorkshire moors; austere Victorian-Gothic buildings plus 1920s additions by Sir Giles Gilbert Scott, dominated – spiritually and visually – by the abbey church. Fine new design/technology centre; some classrooms in ageing wooden huts.

Atmosphere Powerful Liberal Catholic tradition; 'an education rooted in the priorities of Christian life'; compulsory religious studies, mass twice a week, house prayers twice a day. Resolutely single-sex and boarding (when the trend is the other way); a certain tendency to other-worldliness. 'On the one hand,' says the head of the sixth form, 'we're telling the boys they have to work hard for their GCSEs and A-levels so they can get on in the world; on the other, we're saying none of this is what really matters.' Boys say they are taught to think for themselves, not dragooned into Catholicism. Big emphasis on house system (9 out of 10 are run by monks) and learning to live in a closely knit community. Some houses less homely than others (cramped dormitories, broken-down study cubicles, long trek through the physics lab to reach the showers). No uniform: the scruffiness is legendary.

The head Urbane, kindly, highly regarded; 1992 chairman of the Headmasters' Conference (representing 230 of the top independent schools). Came here as an 11-year-old in 1943; joined the monastery at 18 'in a fit of romantic idealism'; read modern languages at Oxford; returned to be ordained and to teach. Ever conscious of living with one foot in Babylon, the other in Jerusalem: 'the barbarians are always at the gate'. Successor is Father Leo Chamberlain, 52, who was also a pupil here; read history at Oxford then joined the monastery; has been a housemaster since 1972.

The teaching Traditional in style; greatest strengths in English, history, classics, modern languages ('The science labs,' observes the head, 'have needed up-dating for 30 years'). Staff of 79, including 6 women, 27 monks; average class size 20, reducing to 15 for A-levels. National curriculum-plus; science taught as 3 separate subjects; nearly all do Latin, some take Greek; German, Spanish on offer. Boys take 7-11 GCSEs, depending on ability. Wide choice of 25 subjects at A-level, including ancient history, business studies, electronics; most do 3, plus religious studies. Good music: a third learn an instrument; orchestra, wind band, choir; full cycle of medieval Mystery plays performed once every 5 years. Cadet force compulsory for 2 years. Annual pilgrimage to Lourdes; regular language exchanges with schools in France, Germany and Spain.

The pupils Half enter the junior house at 10+ from the state sector; rest join at 13 from 40 prep schools, including nearby Gilling Castle. Formal entry requirement of 60% at Common Entrance; however 'the headmaster is willing to consider boys who may have difficulty achieving this mark, but whose qualities in other fields or whose family circumstances make them eligible for entry'. In practice, the intake is comprehensive ('We're better at valuing the weaker than schools where success is dominant'); some boys have IQs of less than 100. Applications from those who are not Catholics 'receive careful and sympathetic consideration'; currently 3% from non-Catholic families.

Results GCSE: most gain at least 5 grades A-C. A-level (1992): modest 39% of entries graded A or B. 'The aspirations of a Benedictine school do not lend themselves easily to the jargon of the market place,' observes the head.

Destinations 98% stay on for A-levels; 80% of these proceed to higher education (17 to Oxbridge in 1991).

Sport Very strong, especially rugby and cricket. Facilities include unlimited playing fields, 9-hole golf course, 3 artificial lakes for fly-fishing. Beagle pack is one of the finest in the country.

Remarks Benedictines have been successfully educating Catholic boys for nearly 1,500 years and, despite the materialist pressures, confidently expect to continue doing so. The sternly monastic life is not universally popular among the boys.

ARNOLD
Lytham Road,
Blackpool FY4 1JG
Tel (0253) 46391

Independent • Co-educational • Day (and some boarding) • Ages 11-18 (plus associated junior school) • 823 pupils (55% boys; 95% day) • 194 in sixth form • Fees, £2,196-£3,018 (£6,054 boarding) Head: John Kelsall, 48, appointed 1987 (leaving August 1993).

Lively, successful school; good all round.

Background Founded 1870; Direct Grant from 1938 to 1975; then became fully independent and co-educational. On a slightly cramped site but constantly expanding and updating its facilities; superb new design centre opened 1990.

Atmosphere Lively yet orderly; full of ideas and energy; striking sense of enterprise (sixth-formers run 2 profit-making businesses). Spiritual dimension taken seriously; traditional virtues respected. Pleasant boarding house; attractive junior school near by.

The head Dynamic, optimistic, radiates good cheer; determined to provide the best for his pupils. Read economics at Cambridge; taught in both the independent and state sectors (previously head of a grammar school). Clearly liked and respected by staff. Takes over as head of Brentwood in September 1993.

The teaching Methods range from computerised, instructional technology to chalk, talk and text book. Classroom atmosphere controlled yet friendly; pupils encouraged to participate and think. Full and varied curriculum; particular strengths in design/technology, English, science (outstanding chemistry under departmental head who has a PhD). Average class size 25; 8-14 in the sixth form. Good

music and drama; much-used dance studio. Design centre provides outstanding facilities for painting, pottery, photography, fashion and fabrics, food technology, silk screen printing, hot metalwork. Thriving Duke of Edinburgh award scheme; cadet force popular, not least with the girls. Plenty of international exchanges, visits, sporting tours. Highlight of the school's extra-curricular activities is its village aid programme: pupils have adopted a village in Tanzania and raise funds to enable the villagers to help themselves; they visit in groups so know the problems at first hand and can see how the money is being spent.

The pupils Lively, cheerful, well-mannered, from wide social backgrounds; 10 on assisted places; some parents struggle to cope. All in uniform, from kindergarten upwards; sixth-formers choose their own smart grey suits; prefects wear undergraduate gowns. Discipline rarely a problem (no trouble with drugs, despite Blackpool's reputation) but head would not hesitate to invite hopeless cases to leave. Entry into senior school via tests in English, maths and verbal reasoning but no minimum IQ level. Entry to sixth form requires at least 5 GCSEs at grades A-C plus right attitude and motivation. Pretty well all aim for a professional career.

Results GCSE: 90% gain at least 5 grades A-C. A-level (1992): 47% of entries graded A or B.

Destinations 85% go on to the sixth form (about 20 join from other schools); 80% of these proceed to higher education (12 a year to Oxbridge).

Sport Good reputation; top-class rugby (coached by former Welsh international and British Lion) and cricket (coach played for Lancashire). Girls play hockey, netball, tennis. Swimming, golf, badminton and squash also on offer. New sports hall and off-site, greatly expanded playing fields planned.

Remarks Delightful school with a strong belief in itself; going from strength to strength. Committed, hard-working staff; outstanding head.

ASHFORD
East Hill,
Ashford,
Kent TN24 8PB
Tel (0233) 625171

Independent • Girls • Day and boarding • Ages 5-18 (plus nursery) • 650 pupils (500 in senior school; 78% day) • 121 in sixth form • Fees, £3,273-£4,465 day; £6,369-£7,569 boarding.
Head: Mrs Patricia Metham, 47, appointed September 1992.

Traditional, academic school; generally good results.

Background Founded 1898; moved 1910 to pleasant 23-acre town-centre site (bordering the Stour). Mixture of purpose-built and period buildings, including 16th-century Alfred House.

Atmosphere Active, well-ordered. Boarding houses basic but adequate.

The head New appointment. Teaches English, theatre studies. Wants to extend connections with local industry and develop links with Europe (well placed for the Channel Tunnel). Married, 2 daughters at university.

The teaching Good. All start 3 languages (French, German, Spanish) plus at least 1 year's Latin; choice of separate sciences or combined course (school recently won a national competition to put a classroom science experiment into space). First-year seniors streamed by ability; setting in maths, English, French. All take 8-10 GCSEs; some do English and maths a year early. Choice of 19 subjects at A-level; English and chemistry the most popular. Low staff turnover (few young teachers). Biggest problem with homework is persuading girls not to overdo it. Active art, drama (8 plays a year), music (choirs, 2 orchestras, a third learn an instrument). Popular community service and Duke of Edinburgh award scheme.

The pupils Confident, responsive. Most from solid professional backgrounds – doctors, businessmen, farmers; 10% from overseas.

Firm discipline; smart uniform strictly adhered to; sixth-formers allowed to wear 'anything within reason'. Nearly all juniors enter the senior school; admission at 11 by tests in English, maths, verbal reasoning (to identify those who can be expected to go on to higher education). Some scholarships and assisted places.

Results GCSE (1991): 98% gained at least 5 grades A-C. A-level (1992): disappointing 41% of entries graded A or B (has been much higher).

Destinations 75% stay on for A-levels; most of these proceed to higher education (6 a year to Oxbridge).

Sport Good facilities; usual games played well; wide range of options also available.

Remarks Effective, no-nonsense school; aims to give girls confidence in themselves and their abilities.

AYLESBURY GRAMMAR
Walton Road,
Aylesbury,
Buckinghamshire HP21 7RP
Tel (0296) 84545

Grammar (voluntary-controlled) • Boys • Ages 11-18 • 1,100 pupils • 400 in sixth form
Head: Ian Roe, 50s, appointed September 1992.

Successful academic school; strong science and computing; good sport.

Background Founded 1598; moved to present purpose-built premises 1907. Later additions include first-rate science and technology blocks. Supportive parents engaged in constant fund-raising.

Atmosphere First impression is of a traditional grammar school run on public-school lines: blazers and flannels, rather formal relations between staff and boys, 'firm but positive' discipline. However, this is a warm, lively innovative institution preparing boys for the 21st century in a thoroughly enlightened way.

The head New appointment. Previously deputy head; has taught modern languages here for 30 years.

The teaching High-quality, challenging. Good languages (but classics being squeezed by the national curriculum); outstanding sciences (all do physics, chemistry for GCSE); excellent computing (software written to professional standards). Work in many areas goes well beyond exam requirements. Mixed-ability classes (within a fairly narrow range); setting in French (boys choose their own sets); average class size 28. Good choice of 23 subjects at A-level, including geology, sociology, art history, Greek; many take 4 including general studies; a few take 5. Wide variety of extracurricular activities: public speaking, war gaming, monitoring worldwide radio activity by satellite etc. Popular Duke of Edinburgh award scheme; community service (links with a hospital in Malawi).

The pupils Able, articulate, confident. Most from middle-class backgrounds (parents move house to get their sons in here – and send them to crammers); entry by strongly competitive 12+ test administered by Buckinghamshire County Council.

Results (1992) GCSE: 95% gained at least 5 grades A-C. A-level: 39% of entries graded A or B.

Destinations 95% stay for A-levels; 90% of these proceed to higher education (20-25 a year to Oxbridge).

Sport Very strong rugby, cricket, squash, tennis. Facilities include heated pool, 4 squash courts.

Remarks Prestigious grammar school.

BABLAKE

Coundon Road,
Coventry CV1 4AU
Tel (0203) 228388

Independent • Co-educational • Day • Ages 11-18 • 840 pupils (equal numbers of boys and girls) • 213 in sixth form (60% boys) • Fees, £2,883
Head: Dr Stuart Nuttall, mid-40s, appointed 1991.

Good results; strong sporting record; lots of help with fees.

Background Founded 1344 by Queen Isabella (grandmother of the Black Prince); re-founded by the City of Coventry in 1560 after the dissolution of the monasteries. Moved to present 11-acre site and distinguished red-brick buildings in 1890. Shares governing body with nearby King Henry VIII *(qv)*; the 2 schools give away nearly £400,000 a year in scholarships and bursaries.

Atmosphere Purposeful, well-ordered (though slightly hectic at change-over times). Convivial staff room; civilised dining room; good food. Some classrooms cramped by modern standards. Standing-room only in twice-weekly whole-school assemblies.

The head Bridge-player with a First in chemistry from Salford and a PhD from Bristol; formerly deputy head of Royal Grammar, Guildford. Infectiously enthusiastic; brimming with ideas for development; direct, uncomplicated management style. Married, 3 children.

The teaching Challenging, high-quality; commendable attention to individual needs. Experienced, all-graduate staff of 69 (30 women); average age 45-50 (result of low turnover); 98% match of teachers' specialisms to subjects taught. No streaming (within narrow ability band); class sizes vary from 20-24 in early years, 10-12 in sixth form. Most take 10 GCSEs and 3-4 A-levels (from choice of 15); extra courses for lower-sixth in astronomy, meteorology, theatre arts, Spanish. Superlative new language centre; satellite dishes offer access to all European languages at the touch of a button. Bablake Weather Station markets forecasts to the media. Strong art and pottery. Lots of clubs, societies, foreign visits. School owns a residential field centre in mid-Wales and a house in Normandy.

The pupils All academically able (top 10%); wide social backgrounds; 10% ethnic minority. No problems of discipline or attendance; staff-pupil relations open and relaxed. Entry tests in English, maths, verbal reasoning; admission to sixth form requires minimum of 5 GCSEs at grades A or B with As in A-level options.

Results GCSE: 95% gain at least 5 grades A-C. A-level (1992): 51% of entries graded A or B.

Destinations 90% continue into the sixth form; nearly 90% of these proceed to higher education (15% to Oxbridge).

Sport 27-acre playing fields and large pavilion 1 mile away: 4 rugby pitches, 5 hockey pitches (2 all-weather and floodlit), 30 tennis courts, 4 netball courts, athletics track, swimming pool, games hall and fitness room. Strong in rugby, hockey, netball, cricket; tennis, squash, also on offer.

Remarks Effective school, successfully preparing young people for higher education. Deservedly respected in Coventry and beyond.

BACKWELL

Backwell,
Bristol BS19 3PB
Tel (0275) 463371

Comprehensive • Co-educational • Ages 11-18 • 1,400 pupils (equal numbers of girls and boys) • 290 in sixth form
Head: Richard Nosowski, 49, appointed 1988.

Large, well-run comprehensive; good teaching and results.

Background Opened in the 1950s and has grown steadily since; mainly 1960s flat-roofed buildings on a pleasant, 260-acre semi-rural site.

Atmosphere Purposeful, well-disciplined (loudest noise is the hum of the all-pervasive computers). A real sense of freedom and belonging (unlocked classrooms, ready access to the computers at break); pupils' work widely and colourfully displayed. Sixth-formers help juniors with reading and maths. Strongly supportive parents.

The head Clear-headed, serious, unflappable. Educated at Oxford; has 27 years' teaching experience. Consults and listens but makes the decisions; seen by the pupils as a relaxed if somewhat remote authority figure whom they respect.

The teaching Well-qualified, hard-working staff. Broad curriculum underpinned by large computing presence. Good English (80 grades A-C at GCSE), strong art (a third take it at A-level). Lots of drama and music; 15% learn an instrument, 2 orchestras, choirs. Most who stay on into the sixth form take 2 or 3 A-levels; popular options include psychology, sociology. All do 2 weeks' work experience.

The pupils Well-motivated, pleasant; mostly (but not exclusively) from middle-class homes; 40% come from outside the official catchment area.

Results (1992) GCSE: 63% gained at least 5 grades A-C. A-level: 32% of entries graded A or B.

Destinations 60% continue into the sixth form; many of these proceed to higher education.

Sport Long-distance running is a particular strength; good football; netball, hockey for the girls. Facilities include 20 acres of playing fields, sports hall; local authority swimming pool and squash courts on site.

Remarks Popular school: worth moving house for (and many parents do).

BADMINTON
Westbury-on-Trym,
Bristol BS9 3BA
Tel (0272) 623141

Independent • Girls • Boarding and day • Ages 7-18 • 360 pupils (75% boarding) • 90 in sixth form • Fees, £6,930-£9,225 boarding; £3,465-£5,040 day
Head: Clifford Gould, 45, appointed 1981.

Strong school; good results; fine facilities; first-rate art, music, drama; socially privileged pupils.

Background Founded 1858; moved to present premises 1900; Georgian house plus later additions – including library and music school designed by Sir Hugh Casson, president of the governors – on a delightful 50-acre site (decorative gardens, mature trees).

Atmosphere Civilised, privileged; a school small enough for familiarity and warmth. Few overt reminders of its 'progressive' history (popular in the 1920s with middle-class Fabians – Iris Murdoch and Indira Gandhi were pupils); these days high spirits are contained within a tighter framework. However, the development of critical, questioning minds is still said to be at the heart of the school's philosophy. Excellent boarding accommodation; 8 to a dormitory; sixth-formers choose between single and double rooms.

The head A decisive, public-relations-oriented chief executive (the school makes an annual 20% profit which is ploughed back into renovation and building); one of a handful of male heads of independent girls' schools (no sign yet of the reverse). Read English at Trinity College, Dublin; much influenced in his youth by teaching at Bedales and Frensham Heights, both progressive schools. His matured philosophical position is a marriage of progressive thinking and disciplined behaviour under strong control and leadership from the top. Hugely proud of his pupils' artistic, musical and debating skills.

The teaching Able staff (only 4 men) employing a mix of traditional and more innovative styles. Good science (high-flying but not exam-bound); big emphasis on languages – French (from age 7), German, Spanish; tentative interest in the national curriculum; all have the opportunity to become computer-literate. Exceptionally high standards of art, drama (long list of productions) and music; more than 80% learn an instrument (81 girls on grades 7 or 8); numerous concerts and choral evenings. Language exchanges with schools in France and Spain; art trips to Portugal; musical links with St Petersburg.

The pupils Confident, energetic; daughters of medical consultants, GPs, lawyers, headteachers and the occasional West Country landed gentry; 20% of parents are expatriates (Foreign Office, British Council, Armed Forces). Head feels children from less favoured backgrounds do not fit in easily; he has also sharply reduced the proportion of foreigners. Automatic entry from junior to senior school at 11; rest admitted either by Common Entrance (minimum 55% mark required) or tests in English, maths, non-verbal reasoning (minimum IQ of 110 required); 2 applications for every place. Some academic and music scholarships.

Results GCSE: virtually all gain at least 5 grades A-C. A-level (1992): impressive 65% of entries graded A or B.

Destinations 85% proceed to higher education (3 or 4 a year to Oxbridge).

Sport All the usual games offered. Facilities include 20 acres of playing fields, indoor pool, courts for tennis, squash, badminton. Fencing, riding, golf also on offer.

Remarks Behind the traditional and somewhat exclusive facade the old aim of nurturing the free spirit struggles to survive.

BALERNO HIGH
5 Bridge Road
Balerno,
Mid Lothian EH14 7AQ
Tel (031) 449 5833

Comprehensive • Co-educational • Ages 12-18 • 810 pupils (equal numbers of girls and boys) • 80 in sixth year
Head: Ian Nicol, mid-50s, appointed 1982.

Outstanding comprehensive; strong academic record; brings the best out of every child.

Background Established 1982 to serve the growing communities of Balerno, Kirknewton, Ratho and surrounding areas. Modern, functional buildings in a sylvan setting beside the River Leith; facilities are excellent.

Atmosphere Not just a community school but a school in its community. Age range extends from toddlers to pensioners: some 4,500 attend leisure classes and clubs and join the fifth- and sixth-year pupils for Highers. The heart of the school is a vast, covered social area with intimacy provided by partitions and informal seating; everything is immaculate, including an inviting cafeteria where pupils dine in harmony with adults and visitors (food is tasty and well presented). The discipline is that of a community rather than a school: there is an air of consideration, tolerance and industry. There is no doubt that the main purpose is education and academic excellence but this is as far from an ivory tower as one could get (and all the better for it).

The head Deceptively self-effacing: an excellent manager and the school is very much his creation. Takes refuge from education in fly

fishing, old cars, rugby (was a superb scrum-half in his youth) and cricket.

The teaching First-rate. Emphasis is on informality and individual learning; classrooms are effervescent; all abilities nurtured and strengthened (outstanding help for dyslexics). Broad curriculum; setting by ability from third year; average class size 25. All take 7 subjects for Standard Grade from choice of 20 in addition to a wide range of non-examined courses; fifth-years choose between Highers and vocational modules; 13 subjects on offer in sixth year; greatest strengths in maths, science, modern languages.

The pupils Take evident pride in their school. Virtually all drawn from the official catchment area; furious competition for the remaining few places. The whole ability range is represented but with a large bulge at the upper end.

Results Highers (1991): 42% gained at least 5 grades A-C, which put the school at the top of the league table of more than 300 Scottish comprehensives.

Destinations 84% stay on for Highers; 80% of these remain for a sixth year; 45% of all leavers proceed to higher education (1 or 2 a year to Oxbridge).

Sport Strong at team games: accent is on sampling and finding the ones that will endure beyond school. Good facilities, including sports hall, gymnasia, swimming pool, adjacent rugby and hockey pitches.

Remarks Scottish schooling at its best: academic achievement combined with a broad liberal education. Highly recommended.

BANCROFT'S
Woodford Green,
Essex IG8 ORF
Tel (081) 505 4821

Independent • Co-educational • Day •
Ages 11-19 (plus associated junior
school) • 717 pupils (52% girls) • 200 in
sixth form • Fees (1992-93), £4,920
Head: Dr Peter Southern, 45, appointed
1985.

*Attractive, well-resourced school; good
teaching; broad curriculum; wide range
of extra-curricular activities.*

Background Founded 1737 under the will of
Francis Bancroft, who left his estate to the
Drapers' Company; moved to present site on
the edge of Epping Forest 1880s; handsome
Victorian buildings plus many sympathetic
additions. Well-equipped classrooms, first-
rate library, fine creative-activities centre.
Drapers' Company still provides most of the
governors and gives generous financial assistance.

Atmosphere Diverse social, ethnic and religious mix – Christians, Jews, Muslims, Sikhs –
successfully fused into a well-ordered, friendly
community. Full-time (Christian) chaplain.

The head Read history at Oxford, Edinburgh
and London; taught at Dulwich; formerly
head of history at Westminster. Still teaches
history to 12-year-olds and sixth-formers.
Married, 2 sons.

The teaching Good quality; diverse styles.
Well-qualified staff of 60 (40% women), half
appointed by present head; average age 35.
Broad curriculum includes strong creative and
practical elements: art, ceramics, design/tech-
nology, computing, electronics. Pupils set by
ability; average class size 25, smaller for
GCSE, 10-15 in sixth form. Most take 8-10
GCSEs and 3 A-levels plus general studies.
Lots of music: 2 orchestras, 100-strong choir
(has visited China); ambitious drama in 700-
seat hall. Flourishing cadet force, Sea Scouts,
Duke of Edinburgh award scheme; good
debating. Regular language exchanges with

schools in France and Germany; classical
tours to Italy, Greece, Egypt, Turkey and
Israel.

The pupils Confident, friendly. Big social
mix from a 15-mile radius; 25% receive help
with fees through assisted places, scholarships,
bursaries. Admission by interview and school's
own tests in English, maths; grammar-school
standard. Up to 7 apply for each place (but
many apply to more than 1 school).

Results GCSE: virtually all gain at least 5
grades A-C. A-level (1992): 48% of entries
graded A or B.

Destinations 85% stay on for A-levels; 70%
of these proceed to higher education (up to 6
a year to Oxbridge).

Sport Chiefly rugby, hockey, cricket, squash,
golf, netball, tennis, athletics, swimming; good
record; many individual successes. Facilities
include 21 acres of playing fields, all-weather
hockey pitch, sports hall, indoor pool.

Remarks Sound school; good all round.

BARKING ABBEY
Sandringham Road,
Barking IG11 9AG
Tel (081) 594 3541

Comprehensive • Co-educational • Ages
11-18 • 1,542 pupils (53% boys) • 205 in
sixth form
Head: Tony Maxwell, early-50s, appointed
1983.

*Well-run comprehensive; wide range of
backgrounds and abilities.*

Background 1970 amalgamation of a grammar school and 2 secondary moderns; functional 1930s buildings on 2 sites nearly 1 mile
apart; premises well maintained and being
upgraded.

Atmosphere Well-ordered; strong sense of
purpose and commitment. High academic
standards but equal attention paid to the least

able; sixth-formers help juniors with learning difficulties. Good pastoral care system: great trouble taken to ensure every child is well-known by some members of staff; progress through the school carefully monitored. Parents kept well informed.

The head Good leader; delegates extensively to 4 deputies; formerly head of another comprehensive in the borough. Married, 2 children.

The teaching Enthusiastic staff of 92, 60% appointed by present head. Big emphasis on reading (20% are poor readers at 11+). All do French; German, Urdu and Punjabi also on offer; computers used across the curriculum; all take 2-year course in business information; good educational video library. Homework taken seriously. Good choice of 23 subjects at A-level (sixth-form shared with neighbouring school); vocational alternatives include BTEC. Lots of music; orchestra, brass band, 2 choirs.

The pupils Enthusiastic about the school and their teachers. Wide social and racial mix; two-thirds from working-class homes; 30% Asian. School is heavily over-subscribed; 400 apply annually for 270 places; priority to siblings and those living nearest.

Results (1991) GCSE: 34% gained at least 5 grades A-C. A-level: 24% of entries graded A or B (below the national average).

Destinations 60% continue into the sixth form (more than half to do 1-year vocational courses); half of those who take A-levels proceed to higher education.

Sport Chiefly: football, cricket (regular county honours), netball, hockey, tennis, athletics. Both sites have extensive playing fields; sports hall planned.

Remarks Good all round.

BATH HIGH

Hope House,
Lansdown,
Bath BA1 5ES
Tel (0225) 422931

Independent • Girls • Day • Ages 4-18 • 625 pupils (390 in senior school) • 94 in sixth form • Fees, £2,424-£3,156
Head: Miss Margaret Winfield, 50s, appointed 1985.

Successful school; equally good results in modern languages and sciences.

Background Founded 1875 (Girls' Public Day School Trust); moved to present hill-side site (fine terraced gardens with views over the city) 1924. Georgian premises restored after 1942 bombing; later additions functional but not unpleasant. Space at a premium (some non-science classes taught in labs); junior school moving in spring 1993, allowing senior school to expand.

Atmosphere Welcoming; purposeful. Good working relations between pupils and staff; girls respond to teachers' high expectations.

The head History graduate, Leicester University; previously head of an independent girls' school in Oldham. Lively, enthusiastic; staff welcome her clear leadership and open style. Believes in 'pushing every girl as far as she can go – but I never want them to lose their sense of fun'. Teaches all first-years.

The teaching 56 highly qualified, committed staff (few men). National curriculum-plus; all take French and German from first year, many continuing to GCSE; half take Latin and Greek to GCSE, some to A-level; strong sciences, particularly physics (the most popular subject at A-level). 2 parallel groups of 30 in first year; setting by ability in maths and languages thereafter; classes of 20 for GCSE. Good careers education.

The pupils Highly motivated, responsive, appreciative of their teachers ('They make things interesting and they're fairly strict'). Largely from professional middle classes (many daughters of Old Girls); catchment area up to a radius of 15 miles (fleets of buses). Entry at 11+ by exams in English, maths, verbal and non-verbal reasoning plus interviews and head teachers' reports. 18 assisted places.

Results GCSE: 97% gain at least 5 grades A-C. A-level (1992): 56% of entries graded A or B.

Destinations Most continue into the sixth form and proceed to higher education (6 a year to Oxbridge).

Sport Involvement in a wide range of sport and physical activity encouraged; less of the traditional emphasis on hockey and netball (which, nonetheless, are strong). Netball and tennis courts on site but main playing fields 1 mile away. Sports hall planned.

Remarks Happy, high-achieving school.

BAY HOUSE
Gomer Lane,
Alverstoke,
Gosport,
Hampshire PO12 2QP
Tel (0705) 587931

Comprehensive • Co-educational • Ages 11-16 • 1,600 pupils (equal numbers of boys and girls)
Head: Richard Cootes, early-50s, appointed 1981.

Large, successful, well-run school. Good GCSE results; strong music and art.

Background Result of a 1972 merger between a grammar school and a secondary modern; lost its sixth form in 1987 when secondary education in the area was re-organised. Based on the Bay House, built in 1848 by Decimus Burton for the Baring family; 1960 addition blends well but more recent buildings (including some temporary huts) do not. Attractive site overlooking the Solent and the Isle of Wight.

Atmosphere Dedicated staff; supportive, well-behaved pupils. No sign of vandalism or defacement; litter solely attributable to sea-gulls and squirrels (who remove it from the bins). Large school on a relatively small campus – but does not feel like it.

The head Read history at Nottingham and did an MA in the philosophy of education at London. Taught in grammar, secondary modern and comprehensive schools and trained teachers at Oxford. Doubles his salary by writing history text books.

The teaching Enthusiastic; varied styles. Teachers (nearly all appointed by present head) not afraid to teach or explore hard concepts; plenty of scope for pupil participation, projects, small-group work. 330 enter every year, divided into 3 mixed-ability streams; setting by ability in maths, science, foreign languages, English. Broad, rigorous curriculum; all do French, music, art, drama; German, Spanish, Latin on offer; technology provision being updated. Extra help for those with special needs; enrichment programme for the most able. Big emphasis on homework. Excellent music: choir of pupils, staff and parents; 70-strong junior band, senior concert band, string quintet, recorder consort – all feed into main orchestra.

The pupils Average urban intake, socially and academically: this is not a middle-class ghetto. Strict uniform (no jewellery); effective, responsible school council. Excellent staff-pupil relations.

Results (1991) GCSE: 44% gained at least 5 grades A-C.

Destinations 72% of leavers continue in full-time further education.

Sport Strong soccer, athletics, netball, gymnastics.

Remarks Provides equally well for pupils of all abilities. First-rate head; enthusiastic, young staff. Highly recommended.

BEACONHURST GRANGE
Bridge of Allan,
Stirling,
Stirlingshire FK9 4RR
Tel (0786) 832146

Independent • Co-educational • Day
(boarding being phased out) • Ages 3-18
(from September 1992) • 237 pupils
(equal numbers of boys and girls) • Fees,
£1,125-£3,645
Head: Roger Clegg, 42, appointed 1984.

*Successful, well-run prep school now
planning to admit all ages; strong
modern languages.*

Background Result of 1975 amalgamation
between 2 single-sex prep schools; embarked
September 1992 on staged development to a
550-pupil all-age school. Large Victorian
house on a hill-top on the outskirts of Stirling;
unattractive flat-roofed prefab classrooms (but
carpeted and warm within); new classrooms
and science labs under construction; more
planned.

Atmosphere Happy, well-ordered community; friendly relations between staff and pupils
and between pupils of different ages; family
atmosphere may be difficult to maintain as
numbers increase.

The head Music graduate of Edinburgh University; taught at Gordonstoun, Edinburgh
Academy. Personable, confident, energetic;
has nearly doubled numbers since he came
here by establishing an excellent local reputation; his planning for the projected expansion
has been meticulous. Married, 2 children.

The teaching No streaming by ability; average class size 13. Full range of Common
Entrance subjects; strong commitment to
modern languages – German from age 7,
French from 9; computing from 10; timetabled
art, music, religious education, PE, games. All
will do 8 Standard Grades, including German
and French. Busy extra-curricular programme
includes drama, concerts, needlework, carpentry, Writers' Workshop, Spanish Club (for

those wanting to tackle a third modern language).

The pupils Animated, courteous; parents
mainly in industry, professions, farming within
a 15-mile radius. Entry to nursery and pre-prep
by interview; thereafter by tests, interview,
previous school report. Some scholarships
available.

Results Most have gone on to their first-
choice senior schools; 1-2 scholarships a year.

Destinations Previously, Dollar, Strathallan,
Morrison's; now virtually all will stay.

Sport School's own facilities are limited but it
has negotiated full use of Stirling University's,
next door. Major games: rugby, football,
cricket (boys); hockey, netball, rounders, tennis (girls). Athletics, skiing, swimming,
windsurfing, badminton, horse riding also on
offer.

Remarks Facing expansion with confidence.

BEDALES
Steep,
Petersfield,
Hampshire GU32 2DG
Tel (0730) 263286

Independent • Co-educational • Boarding
and day • Ages 3-18 • 661 pupils (406 in
senior school; roughly equal numbers of
boys and girls; two-thirds boarding) • 152
in sixth form • Fees (senior school),
£10,455 boarding; £7,494 day
Head: Ian Newton, 40s, appointed
September 1992.

*Progressive, well-equipped school with
many distinctive features; noted for its
strengths in the arts.*

Background Founded 1893 by J H Badley,
Fabian socialist committed to the equality of
the sexes (co-educational since 1898) and the
outdoor life (cold baths, earth closets and hard

labour); moved to beautiful, rural 120-acre site (includes a small farm) in 1900.

Atmosphere Unusually happy, friendly community; pupils and staff on unselfconscious first-name terms; mingle naturally in their joint activities. All faiths respected: religious, moral and ethical questions approached through the 'exploration of the spirit and not by insisting on the centrality of doctrine and belief'.

The head New appointment. Physicist; educated at Dulwich College and Oxford; taught at Rugby, where he was the first girls' housemaster. Married with 2 children.

The teaching Methods vary to match the task in hand: some lessons formal (desks in rows, hands in the air), others based on discussions, projects, joint tasks in small groups. Aim is to avoid early specialisation so the range of work is wide. Music, art, design compulsory in the first year; at least 1 continued to age 16. Latin offered from 13; German and Spanish from 14. Final GCSE choices delayed until 15. Setting by ability in French and maths only. Most take 3 A-levels (from choice of 17); extra courses range from history of jazz to the psychopathology of everyday life. Arts, crafts, drama, music enjoy high esteem as a natural part of everyone's life, not just for the most talented; exceptional standards achieved (£2-million theatre planned). Outdoor work includes pig- and sheep-farming, recycling tools for the Third World (working forge), building barns, baking bread. Twice-termly assessments in each subject for achievement and effort.

The pupils Live closely together and form strong friendships with both sexes and all ages. Casual dress; most in jeans, shirts and sweaters (sometimes with hats, scarves, bracelets and earrings). Ways of living worked out by school council and staff, according to what seems to work well; privacy, though, can be hard to find (probably deliberately). Most boarders from middle-class families living within 2 hours' drive; some from Scotland; 20% from abroad. Half senior school pupils enter from the junior school; rest admited at 13 after tests in English, maths, verbal reasoning and assessment during a 48-hour visit (likened by the school to a junior selection board). Sixth-form entrants need at least 6 GCSE passes. Some assisted places.

Results GCSE: 93% gain at least 5 grades A-C. A-level (1992): 52% of entries graded A or B.

Destinations All but a few stay for A-levels; most of these proceed to higher education (10 a year to Oxbridge) after taking a 'gap year'.

Sport Compulsory but need not loom large in pupils' lives. Chiefly hockey, football (for both sexes), tennis. All-weather pitch; excellent sports hall.

Remarks Exceptional school; recommended for bright, motivated children with unusual or hidden talents.

BEDFORD
Burnaby Road,
Bedford MK40 2TU
Tel (0234) 340444

Independent • Boys • Day and boarding • Ages 7-18 • 1,100 pupils (700 in senior school; two-thirds day) • 300 in sixth form • Fees, £4,000-£5,505 day; £6,300-£8,170 boarding
Head: Dr Philip Evans, early-40s, appointed 1990.

Good, unashamedly academic education for top 15% of the ability range. Relatively low cost; no frills; a quarter receive help with fees.

Background Granted letters patent by Edward VI in 1552 'for education and instruction of boys and youths in grammatical learning and good manners'. One of 4 Harpur Trust schools endowed by William Harpur, Bedford man who became Master of the Merchant Taylors and Lord Mayor of London. Substantial Victorian buildings on prime site in the heart of town; well-groomed playing fields.

Atmosphere Confident, assured. Senior staff

wear gowns, adding gravitas and authority. Urban setting and the large number of day boys mean the school has to find the right balance between trust and coercion: relies on pupils' good sense and self-discipline.

The head Top-rank scholar and educationist (member of the Government's School Examinations and Assessment Council). Took a First in natural sciences at Cambridge; PhD from Imperial College; taught at St Paul's for 15 years. Charming, quick-minded, boyishly enthusiastic; hard to imagine him reading the Riot Act (he was appointed after an unhappy period in which there were 3 heads in 2 years), but has clearly won the respect of the older hands. Teaches religious education; plays the organ in the school chapel; keen on cricket and Welsh poetry. Married to a chemist (who is also an organist).

The teaching Traditional (but not lacking in variety or imagination); streaming by ability throughout. Science taught as 3 separate subjects; Latin and Greek offered to the most able; little sign, however, of art. Of the 19 subjects offered at A-level best results are in maths, physics, chemistry and biology. Nearly all staff male (distinctly masculine air) but some women teachers in the prep school and sixth form. Reports to parents 4 times a year show how each boy is doing in relation to form average. Religion taken seriously (but chapel accommodates only half the school). Vast range of out-of-school activities; strong drama; lots of music (nearly half learn an instrument); enthusiastic cadet force.

The pupils Selected by interview and written exam from a strong field; bright, confident, articulate (reading age in prep school commonly 2 years ahead of chronological age). Mostly from business, professional and academic families; 15% ethnic minority; nearly 100 assisted places; Harpur bursaries available to those living in the county. Day boys assigned to boarding houses for tutorials etc, giving them a sense of belonging. (Shy boys could feel overwhelmed by so much going on but there are plenty of quiet corners for those who just want to settle down with a book.)

Results GCSE: 95 gain at least 5 grades A-C.

A-level (1992): 49% of entries graded A or B (has been higher).

Destinations 80% to higher education (10% to Oxbridge); rest into jobs or other forms of training.

Sport All expected to take part. Particularly strong rugby; also hockey, cricket, rowing. Excellent facilities include gym, indoor pool, all-weather pitch, 16 tennis courts.

Remarks Good all-round education; everything done whole-heartedly, but without pomposity. 'We don't believe in ivory towers,' says head.

BEDFORD MODERN
Manton Lane,
Bedford MK41 7NT
Tel (0234) 364331

Independent • Boys • Day and some boarding • Ages 7-18 • 1,150 pupils (93% day) • 257 in sixth form • Fees, £2,772-£3,804 day; £6,087-£7,119 boarding
Head: Peter Squire, 55, appointed 1977.

Solid school; strong in sciences and technology; generous bursaries (nearly half receive help with fees).

Background Founded 1566, one of 4 Harpur Trust schools; moved 1974 to purpose-built premises on attractive, 45-acre hilltop site; reverted to full independence with the abolition of Direct Grant status 1976.

Atmosphere Busy, self-confident; notably open-minded ethos. Lessons on Saturday mornings.

The head Read modern history at Oxford. Married, 2 grown-up children.

The teaching Generally traditional in approach; all written work neat, carefully corrected. Particular strengths (and first-rate facilities) in science (taught as 3 separate subjects), computing, design/technology. All do at least 1 year each of French, German, Latin. Setting by ability in maths, French. Solid GCSE results; few tailenders. A-level entries dominated by sciences, maths, economics. Active drama and music. Regular language exchanges with France and Germany.

The pupils Pour in from near and far (including 85 who arrive daily by coach from Milton Keynes). Wide social mix; 300 have Harpur Trust bursaries; 140 on assisted places. Head says 'finances are never a bar' to any boy living in the county who has the required ability. School is over-subscribed – $2^1/_2$ applicants for every place – but less selective than a traditional grammar (approximately top 30% of the ability range).

Results GCSE (1991): 91% gained at least 5 grades A–C. A-level (1992): rather modest 43% of entries graded A or B.

Destinations Most stay on for A-levels and proceed to higher education (9 to Oxbridge in 1991).

Sport Strong rugby (recent tour to Australia); hockey, rowing, tennis, squash, fives and athletics all pursued to high standards. Facilities include cathedral-sized gym, hangar-like indoor pool.

Remarks Good all round.

BEECHEN CLIFF
Alexandra Park,
Bath BA2 4RE
Tel (0225) 420366

Comprehensive (grant-maintained) •
Boys (plus girls in sixth form) • Ages 11-18
• 800 pupils • 166 in sixth form (10 girls)
Head: Roy Ludlow, 40s, appointed 1990.

Good academic reputation; high standards of work and behaviour; strong sport.

Background Formerly City of Bath Boys', a prestigious grammar school; amalgamated with a secondary modern in 1972 and became a comprehensive, taking its name from the hill on which it stands. Local authority wanted to close it and open a sixth-form college on the site. Parents opted for grant-maintained status – finally approved in 1990 after a High Court battle.

Atmosphere Massive rather than elegant building of Bath stone with fine views over the city; high-ceilinged corridors and classrooms create spacious if somewhat stark effect. Unattractive, utilitarian 1960s additions plus temporary huts; school currently resembles a building site (new technology block etc). Smart uniform; emphasis on courtesy and discipline.

The head Energetic, experienced; determined to preserve the school's academic and sporting traditions. Linguist, francophile, married with a son at the school.

The teaching Mostly formal; big emphasis on achievement in a generally friendly and positive atmosphere. (2 cardinal sins: disruption of classes and defiance of authority; 10 boys a term suspended.) Mixed-ability teaching in the first year, setting thereafter except in technology. Extra provision for those with special needs (sixth-formers and parents help, too) but only *ad hoc* assistance for the gifted. Well-qualified staff of 64, many long-serving; number of women being increased. English and modern languages particularly strong; computer proficiency for all. Class sizes average 26; sixth-form groups of 12. Choice of 20 A-level courses (all take general studies) plus pre-vocational qualifications (but no coherent programme of work experience). Music being rebuilt after years of neglect; ditto drama and art.

The pupils Wide range of social backgrounds with professional classes disproportionately represented. All abilities admitted but intake (from 32 primary schools) skewed towards the top of the range. No truancy problems.

Results GCSE: 46% gain at least 5 grades A–C. A-level (1992): 31% of entries graded A or B.

Destinations 65% continue into sixth form; 75% of these proceed to higher education (some to Oxbridge).

Sport Exceptionally strong in cricket, rugby, soccer, hockey and athletics – a source of much pride among the pupils. Tennis 'jogs along'; little swimming. Long tradition of outdoor pursuits: mountaineering, rock climbing, orienteering, caving, canoeing. Winter survival course in Snowdonia; trips to the Alps and Kenya; cottage in the Brecon Beacons.

Remarks School sets great store by its ethos – traditional values, discipline, encouragement of high standards. Undoubtedly a good school; with a bit more imagination (less looking backwards) it could be an outstanding one.

BENENDEN

Benenden,
Cranbrook,
Kent TN17 4AA
Tel (0580) 240592

Independent • Girls • Boarding • Ages 11-18 • 420 pupils • 127 in sixth form • Fees, £10,500
Head: Mrs Gillian duCharme, 54, appointed 1985.

Strong academic school; first-rate teaching and results; excellent facilities.

Background Founded 1923 by 3 mistresses from Wycombe Abbey; impressive Victorian mansion set in more than 200 acres of farm and parkland; £1 million a year spent on refurbishment and new facilities, including fine design/technology centre, luxury indoor pool, campus-wide computer network. Princess Anne was a pupil here.

Atmosphere Traditional, élitist, isolated (sixth-formers amazed to hear that local state schools could not match Benenden's facilities). Hierarchical structure; junior girls do favours for seniors in return for small gifts. Discipline through 'discussion and agreeing punishments together'. All boarding houses ('dormies') have been upgraded and refurnished to an exceptionally high standard; £2-million sixth-form house under construction.

The head Read modern languages at Cambridge; worked for the British Council; taught in several schools in the USA; formerly head of a fashionable independent school in New York.

The teaching High quality. Variety of styles; relatively small groups (maximum class size 20); a third of the staff are men. National curriculum-plus; Latin compulsory for first 3 years; all do 2 languages – French, German, Spanish, (modern) Greek on offer; science taught as a combined subject; most take 8 or 9 GCSEs. Setting by ability in maths, French, Latin. Choice of 20 subjects at A-level; theatre studies popular. Facilities for art, drama and music are excellent; nearly half learn an instrument; full symphony orchestra, 4 choirs.

The pupils Largely from professional backgrounds in the south of England; 10% from abroad. Admission by Common Entrance or school's own tests plus weekend assessment; register 3 years before entry. Some scholarships.

Results GCSE: virtually all gain at least 5 grades A-C. A-level (1992): disappointing 49% of entries graded A or B (has been much higher).

Destinations Nearly all stay on for A-levels; more than 90% proceed to higher education (8 a year to Oxbridge).

Sport Compulsory. Wide choice; lacrosse, swimming, tennis particularly strong. Fine facilities, including sports hall, 9 lacrosse pitches, 15 tennis courts, 2 squash courts.

Remarks Posh, successful, old-fashioned.

BENTON PARK
Harrogate Road,
Rawdon,
Leeds LS19 6LX
Tel (0532) 502330

Comprehensive • Co-educational • Ages
11-18 • 1,400 pupils • 213 in sixth form
Head: Jeffrey Smith, 56, appointed 1976.

---

*Well-run, popular school; wide
curriculum; good facilities. General level
of achievement is good; the best is
outstanding.*

Background Opened 1960 as a secondary
modern; became a grammar school 1970; went
comprehensive 1974. Set in 15 pleasant acres
on the north-western edge of Leeds in a mainly
affluent residential area. Flat-roofed, 2-storey
building with later additions; 4 classrooms in
prefab donated by local company; school hall
can accommodate only a third of pupils.

Atmosphere Not unlike a grammar school;
highly professional staff; confident, smartly
dressed pupils. Most classrooms spacious,
well-furnished, newly painted (school controls
its own £2.5-million budget).

The head Well respected by staff and pupils;
30 years in the profession; teaches A-level
Latin. School takes up most of his life but he
finds time to play squash and pursue his
interests in classical music and jazz.

The teaching Enthusiastic. 2 ability bands
from the start (based on primary school
reports) and setting in some subjects. Broad
curriculum to suit all aptitudes; academic
subjects complemented by media studies,
child-care etc. Plenty of computers; satellite
tracking to record foreign language TV programmes; geography department receives
weather pictures direct from Telstar; down-to-
earth design and technology; good electronics.
Regular trips abroad: art pupils to Amsterdam,
geographers to Isle of Arran, foreign linguists
gain work experience in Germany. Extra help
for those with special needs. Lots of music:
bands, orchestras, early music group, choirs
(regular concerts for charity).

The pupils Mostly from the immediate
neighbourhood but about 300 come by bus.
Sixth-formers have big influence on general
behaviour; act as guides and mentors for
younger pupils (and volunteer to hear them
read). School uniform worn throughout.

Results (1992) GCSE: 45% gained at least 5
grades A-C. A level: disappointing 27% of
entries graded A or B (has been much higher).

Destinations About 40% stay on for A-levels;
two-thirds of these proceed to higher education (4 a year to Oxbridge); remainder to
training or jobs.

Sport Very strong, especially netball and tennis; regional and national honours. Main
games (5 teams fielded at all ages): rugby,
soccer, cricket, hockey; also basketball, badminton, athletics, cross-country. Good PE; all
follow a basic fitness and healthy-living course.

Remarks Successful comprehensive; all expected to give of their best.

BERKHAMSTED
Castle Street,
Berkhamsted,
Hertfordshire HP4 2BB
Tel (0442) 863236

Independent • Boys • Day and boarding •
Ages 10-18 (plus associated prep school)
• 700 pupils (80% day) • 200 in sixth form •
Fees (1992-93), £2,624-£3,140 day;
£7,872-£9,420 boarding
Head: Rev Keith Wilkinson, 44, appointed
1989.

---

*Solid, traditional school; good results;
strong sport.*

Background Founded 1541 (original Tudor
hall survives); dignified, town-centre site;
mainly Victorian buildings (some subject to
preservation orders). Shares board of governors with Berkhamsted Girls' *(qv)*.

Atmosphere Day begins with bells and

hymns. Big emphasis on hard work, hard play; lessons on Saturday mornings. Rebels thin on the ground. Good pastoral care system; cheerful boarding accommodation (boys graduate from one house to another as they progress up the school).

The head Modest, engaging, very approachable; sets great store by good manners. Graduate of Hull, taught at Eton; has worked as a parish priest.

The teaching Long-serving staff; grammar-school curriculum; setting by ability in most subjects. Compulsory Latin; able boys take 3 separate sciences to GCSE (rest do a less demanding 'balanced' course); emphasis on facts in history (contrary to fashionable trends); first-rate English; impressive design/technology; lots of computing. GCSE options include classical civilisation, business studies. Good A-level results in maths, sciences, languages, economics (shared with girls' school). All do helpful study-skills course in exam technique, revision, note-taking, work presentation etc. Strict homework, promptly and constructively marked (in red ink). Art department aims to inculcate genuine skills as well as giving opportunities for free expression. Good drama, music; orchestras, bands, choirs etc. Head lays great stress on service to others: pupils participate in Riding for the Disabled, club for handicapped children, help for the housebound.

The pupils Fairly wide spread of abilities; less selective than a grammar school. Head says he is glad to accept any boy capable of making good use of what the school has to offer.

Results GCSE: virtually all gain at least 5 grades A-C. A-level (1992): 45% of entries graded A or B.

Destinations Nearly all stay on for A-levels and proceed to higher education.

Sport Good record in rugby, hockey, cricket (main playing fields half a mile away); swimming, tennis, badminton, squash etc in the town sports centre. Athletics, cross-country, rowing, shooting, fencing also popular (awesome quantity of muscular energy expended in a bewildering variety of ways). Every boy

expected to take part in physical activity of some kind, even if it is just a long walk in the countryside.

Remarks Good all round; boys stretched – and seem to thrive on it.

BERKHAMSTED GIRLS'
King's Road,
Berkhamsted,
Hertfordshire HP4 3BG
Tel (0442) 862168

Independent • Girls • Day and boarding • Ages 3-18 • 580 pupils (480 in senior school; 80% day) • 110 in sixth form • Fees, (1992-93) £2,625-£4,329 day; £6,198-£7,902 boarding
Head: Miss Valerie Shepherd, 50s, appointed 1980.

Good all-round education in the best public school tradition.

Background Founded 1888; shares board of governors with Berkhamsted (*qv*). Agreeable buildings in attractive 30-acre setting on the edge of the Chilterns.

Atmosphere Calm, harmonious; no furrowed brows or wringing hands. Daily prayers and hymns in splendid Centenary Hall.

The head Modest, reticent style; knows all her pupils well. Has a science degree from Southampton.

The teaching Top-quality staff (nearly all appointed by present head). Juniors receive a solid grounding in the basic skills; taught by specialist teachers in bright surroundings. ('We hope to foster a love of learning,' says the prospectus.) Traditional curriculum in senior school; compulsory Latin (stoutly defended by the girls as a mental discipline); good English (remarkably high standard of writing in the school magazine); separate sciences (first-class results in human biology). A-level strengths include economics (biggest entry – taught in collaboration with boys' school), maths, science, geography. 2 excellent libraries. Impressive art; strong music (2 orchestras, 3 choirs); flourishing drama. All do at least 1 week's work experience.

The pupils Remarkably articulate; all determined to make something worthwhile of their lives. Entry by oral and written tests in language and maths; school currently oversubscribed. Assisted places; some scholarships.

Results GCSE (1991): 98% gained at least 5 grades A-C. A-level: creditable 55% of entries graded A or B.

Destinations 90% stay on for A-levels; 80% of these proceed to higher education (4 to Oxbridge in 1991).

Sport Good lacrosse, netball, tennis, rounders, athletics, swimming. Compulsory PE throughout the school. Facilities include heated outdoor pool; some playing fields 10 minutes' walk away.

Remarks Attractive, solid school.

BIRKENHEAD
58 Beresford Road,
Birkenhead,
Merseyside L43 2JD
Tel (051) 652 4014

Independent • Boys • Day • Ages 5-18 • 1,077 pupils (866 in senior school) • 195 in sixth form • Fees, £2,070-£2,865
Head: Stuart Haggett, 45, appointed 1988.

Traditional, academic ethos; highly selective; excellent exam results. Spiritual dimension taken seriously.

Background Founded 1860 on 50-acre site in respectable, Victorian suburb; Direct Grant from 1935 to 1975, then fully independent. Formidable governing body headed by High Court judge and including Sir Graham Day, the business tycoon, whose son was a pupil.

Atmosphere Quiet, workmanlike; strong

sense of order (arising not so much from rules and regulations as from tradition and high expectations); prefects in undergraduate gowns. Pupil-teacher relations relaxed without being matey.

The head Committed Christian; clear educational philosophy; stresses the need to cater equally for pupils' academic development and character formation. Not a martinet but will have no nonsense; obviously liked and respected by staff. Modern linguist; teaches German and French (many friends in France with whom he exchanges homes in the holidays.) Married, 2 daughters.

The teaching Formal rather than permissive (desks in rows). Mixed-ability classes in first year of senior school, streaming thereafter. Spacious science labs; modern technology and computer centres; attractive art rooms. Class sizes, 25-30. Broadly grammar school curriculum (Latin, Greek); all take 8 GCSEs, of which 4 – English, French, maths, physics – are compulsory. 3 A-levels the rule, plus general studies. Nearly half of the staff have Oxbridge degrees; 3 PhDs. Definite recognition of pupils' spiritual needs: young, full-time chaplain eager to give RE greater academic status. Wide selection of extra-curricular activities; successful cadet force; concert hall (fine acoustics) attracts musicians and singers of international repute. Prep school has visiting elocution teachers.

The pupils Courteous but by no means cowed. All, including sixth-formers, in strict school uniform. Most from professional homes, though many have modest backgrounds (a third of each year group benefit from assisted-places scheme). Wide catchment area: Wirral, Chester, North Wales; parents run a service of 14 buses. Entry to prep school by interview plus tests of word and number recognition, fine motor skills, conversational fluency; to senior school by tests in English, maths, verbal reasoning; average IQ 120.

Results GCSE: 99% gain at least 5 grades A-C. A-level (1992): 53% of entries graded A or B.

Destinations Most juniors admitted to the senior school – and constitute about half its intake. Nearly all stay on for A-levels; 90% of these to higher education.

Sport All major games played; strong rugby and hockey.

Remarks A fine school; combines concern for pupils' welfare with notable academic success; warm but challenging atmosphere. Ideal for boys wishing to proceed to higher education and the learned professions.

BIRKENHEAD HIGH
86 Devonshire Place,
Birkenhead,
Merseyside L43 1TY
Tel (051) 652 5777

Independent • Girls • Day • Ages 5-18 • 930 pupils (750 in senior school) • 180 in sixth form • Fees, £2,424-£3,156
Head: Mrs Kathleen Irving, 40s, appointed 1986.

Happy school; consistently impressive exam results; strongly committed to work and all-round character development.

Background Founded 1885; member of Girls' Public Day School Trust; moved to present site in pleasant residential district 1905. Senior school recently enlarged by modern extensions; linked by footbridge to attractive, rapidly expanding junior school.

Atmosphere Sparkles with optimism and energy; everyone cheerful yet serious and hard working (from kindergarten upwards). Every girl expected to accept a measure of responsibility; strong sense of family (sixth-formers look after younger girls); pupils and staff working together in a common cause.

The head Formerly a pupil here; zoology graduate; became deputy head of large comprehensive at 28. Open, down-to-earth manner; go-ahead without being trendy; combines respect for tradition with support for critically

assessed innovation. Married, 1 child in the school. Hobbies: fell walking, gardening, industrial archaeology and attending Liverpool Philharmonic.

The teaching Dedicated, enthusiastic staff; strong sense of accountability to pupils and parents. (Delightful atmosphere in junior school classrooms, all with high-quality displays.) Methods range from traditional chalk-and-talk to informal group discussions. Broad curriculum, with rich offering in languages: French, German, Spanish, Russian, Latin and Greek, even Dutch. A-level options include computing, business studies, geology, theatre studies. Unusually high proportion opt for, and do well in, maths. Class sizes range from 27 to between 5 and 12 in the sixth form. Homework set daily and systematically marked. Disapproval the chief sanction if expectations not met. Excellent library; full-time chartered librarian. Wide range of extra-curricular activities includes imaginative drama, 2 orchestras, Renaissance wind band, keep-fit classes; clubs and societies for virtually every subject in the curriculum. 200 girls involved in Duke of Edinburgh award scheme. Much charitable activity, including a club for mentally handicapped adults run with local boys' grammar school.

The pupils Lively but basically serious-minded: they work hard and play hard. Few discipline problems. Wide social background (a third on assisted places). Entry at 4-plus by individual assessment; at 7-plus girls should be able to read, write a simple essay and do a page of sums; at 11-plus school sets own tests in maths, English and verbal reasoning. Minimum IQ level not specified. Nearly all juniors proceed to senior school (which also draws from 40 primary schools). Older girls impress visitors by their courtesy, maturity and keen interest in public affairs; all expect to have a professional career. No prefects but elected school captain and 3 deputies. Smart black uniform with white trimmings (sixth formers allowed freedom of dress within limits).

Results GCSE: nearly all gain at least 5 grades A-C (30 out of 112 achieved As in 8 or more subjects in 1991). A-level (1992): 54% of entries graded A or B. (In music, 9 girls achieved Grade 8, 5 gaining distinctions.)

Destinations 90% proceed from GCSE to A-level; 90% of these go on to degree courses (15 a year to Oxbridge).

Sport Major games: netball, hockey, lacrosse, volley ball, tennis and badminton; competitive swimming in excellent pool, shared (like the tennis courts) with the local community.

Remarks Happy, hard-working school doing a first-class job.

BISHOP GORE
Delabeche Road,
Sketty,
Swansea SA2 9AP
Tel (0792) 202983

Comprehensive • Co-educational • Ages 11-18 • 1,285 pupils (roughly equal numbers of girls and boys) • 220 in sixth form
Head: Charles Suff, 58, appointed 1982.

First-rate, well-run comprehensive; good teaching and results.

Background Founded 1682 by Bishop Hugh Gore 'for the sons of poor burghers to be educated in virtue and good literature'; still the school's motto, still pertinent. Moved to present spacious parkland setting overlooking the sea in 1952; red-brick buildings ranged around 2 courtyards plus flat-roofed 1970s additions. Most famous Old Boy: Dylan Thomas (his father taught English here). Special unit for children with Down's syndrome.

Atmosphere Happy, purposeful, disciplined (the impact of the place is immediate); high standards set and achieved.

The head Large, kindly; much liked and respected. Read history at Swansea and spent 5 years teaching it here early in his career; senior lecturer in history at Carmarthen; formerly head of a grammar school in Aberystwyth. Still teaches 'if there is a gap' (currently sociology in the sixth form); does bus duty twice daily (says he has liked buses since he worked as a conductor during his student days). Married, 2 grown-up sons (1 was a pupil here).

The teaching Standard national curriculum; German, Spanish on offer in addition to French and Welsh (compulsory for first 3 years). Setting by ability in maths, science from second year and in other subjects thereafter; extra help for those with special needs, including the gifted; average class size 25-26. Choice of 22 subjects at A-level, including economics, theatre studies, sociology, German; vocational alternatives include secretarial qualifications; monthly grades for effort, attitude and attainment. Thriving drama and music; 2 orchestras, brass band, 3 choirs; regular concerts. Work experience on the Continent; geography field trips to the French Alps.

The pupils From all over Swansea and beyond.

Results (1992) GCSE: 45% gained 5 or more grades A-C. A-levels: 38% of entries graded A or B.

Destinations 40% continue into the sixth form; 90% of these proceed to higher education (3 or 4 a year to Oxbridge)

Sport Good rugby, cricket; netball, hockey, athletics, tennis also on offer. Facilities include extensive playing fields, indoor pool.

Remarks Good school: a fine place to be, whether as pupil or teacher.

BISHOPSHALT
Royal Lane,
Hillingdon,
London UB8 3RF
Tel (0895) 233909

Comprehensive (grant-maintained) •
Co-educational • Ages 11-18 • 1,000
pupils (slightly more boys than girls) • 158
in sixth form
Head: Dr Leslie Bather, 61, appointed
1970.

*Good record in exams, sport, community
involvement; heavily over-subscribed;
strong parental support in north-west
London suburbia.*

Background Opened as a grammar school
1907; moved to present site 1928; went comprehensive (under present head) 1977; opted
out 1990. Utilitarian buildings centred on
Victorian mansion (conservatory much
admired by John Betjeman); ornate plaster
ceilings and stained glass. Well-kept grounds
with ornamental garden, arboretum, sunken
croquet lawn. Cash advantages of grant-maintained status have led to structural improvements and much needed redecoration.

Atmosphere Orderly and industrious, thanks
to high expectations and frequent use of praise.
Visitors treated with friendly courtesy.

The head Still hugely enthusiastic after more
than 20 years in post; determined to exploit the
opportunities of grant-maintained status to the
full (usefully, first degree and doctorate were
in economics and politics). Keeps in touch
with pupils by teaching RE to all first-years.
Committed to maintaining grammar school
standards (wears gown for assembly) but
without neglecting the needs of the less able:
parents duly appreciative. Attaches greatest
importance to securing and supporting high-calibre staff.

The teaching Nearly all graduates; equal
numbers of men and women; all but 6 (out of
68) appointed by present head. Pupils and
parents alike praise teachers' skill and commitment. Classroom performance, work displays
and exam results all testify to high-quality
tuition. Strong support for those with special
needs (a third of annual intake are between 2
and 3 years behind in reading); care also taken
to identify and provide for the gifted. 20
subjects offered at A-level. Lots of music
(50-strong orchestra, 2 choirs); subsidised
trips to theatres etc; full programme of foreign
exchanges.

The pupils Varying backgrounds: middle-income professional families to wage-earning
council tenants; growing ethnic mix. Uniform
willingly worn; even sixth form smartly turned-out. Admission (400 apply annually for 180
places) without reference to pupils' ability or
aptitude; priority to siblings and those living
nearest the school. Open entry to sixth form.

Results (1991) GCSE: 48% gained at least 5
grades A to C. A-level: 47% of entries graded
A or B.

Destinations 55% continue into the sixth
form (others to further education colleges) and
most of these go on to higher education.

Sport Extensive playing fields; well-equipped
gym; pupils regularly selected for borough,
county and even national teams.

Remarks Lively, hard-working, neighbourhood comprehensive; strong sense of community; cheerful determination to succeed.

BISHOP'S STORTFORD

Maze Green Road,
Bishop's Stortford,
Hertfordshire CM23 2QZ
Tel (0279) 758575

Independent • Boys (plus girls in sixth form) • Day and boarding • Ages 13-18 (plus associated junior school) • 365 pupils (55% day) • 152 in sixth form (35 girls) • Fees, £6,600 day; £9,120 boarding
Head: Steve Benson, 52, appointed 1984.

Small, sound school; wide ability range; good sport.

Background Founded 1868 to provide a liberal and religious education for the children of Noncomformist families. Pleasant buildings in 34 acres on the outskirts of the town (plus 100 acres of playing fields). Later additions include well-equipped design/technology centre.

Atmosphere Small school; everyone knows (and cares for) everyone else. Boarding accommodation being renovated.

The head Read history at Cambridge (hockey Blue); taught at Gresham's for 18 years; appointed deputy head here 1982. Popular with staff and pupils. Married, 3 children (1 a pupil here).

The teaching Staff of 41 (4 women), half appointed by present head; some have been in post for 20+ years. National curriculum-plus; Latin, German on offer; sciences taught as 3 separate subjects; most take 10 GCSEs. All streamed by broad ability; setting in maths, French. A-level options include business studies, economics, design/technology (but no vocational qualications on offer); all do general studies course. Lots of music (orchestra, choir) and drama. Big variety of extracurricular activities.

The pupils Wide ability range: some pupils have an IQ of 100, others go to Oxbridge. Assisted places, bursaries, scholarships.

Results GCSE (1991): 90% gained at least 5 grades A-C. A-level (1992): 45% of entries graded A or B.

Destinations Most stay on for A-levels and proceed to higher education (6 to Oxbridge in 1991).

Sport Good record in rugby, hockey, cricket (tours to Sri Lanka, Barbados), swimming. Facilities include large sports hall, indoor and outdoor pools, all-weather pitch.

Remarks Safe school; children well cared for.

BISHOP WORDSWORTH'S

The Close,
Salisbury,
Wiltshire SP1 2ED
Tel (0722) 333851

Grammar (voluntary-controlled) • Boys • Ages 11-18 • 638 pupils • 186 in sixth form
Head: Clive Barnett, appointed September 1992.

Traditional boys' grammar; good academic record; strong music and rugby. Cramped accommodation in the cathedral close.

Background Founded 1890 by Bishop John Wordsworth; threat of closure – stoutly resisted by parents – has hung over the school for 20 years. Odd assortment of buildings, including a dozen prefabs.

Atmosphere Orderly, purposeful, academically serious. Almost a time-warp: every boy in blue blazer, flannels, plain shirt, shoes 'of conventional shape and style'; no duffle bags. Christian assemblies; monthly service in the cathedral.

The head New appointment. Read history at Oxford; was deputy head of Portsmouth Grammar. Keen sportsman; has written a musical based on *Nicholas Nickleby*.

The teaching Traditional: desks in rows, chalk-and-talk (works well with boys of this calibre). Always strong in science (taught as 3 separate subjects); other departments, including technology (which is poorly housed) catching up. No streaming but some setting by ability in maths and languages. Most take 9 GCSEs; choice of 14 subjects at A-level. 42 well-qualified staff (8 women). Outstanding music: orchestras, brass ensemble, 60-strong choir (sings evensong in the cathedral). Lots of clubs and societies: debating, war games, orienteering etc.

The pupils Up to 105 admitted annually on basis of county selection test; places for top 25% to 30%. Wide rural catchment area extending into Hampshire.

Results (1992) GCSE: 97% gained at least 5 grades A-C. A-level: 40% of entries graded A or B.

Destinations 90% stay on for A-levels; 90% of these proceed to high education (several a year to Oxbridge).

Sport Cramped campus and limited facilities restrict what can be offered; playing fields within walking distance. Rugby and athletics particularly strong – fixtures against leading independent schools.

Remarks Enjoys strong local support.

BLACKHEATH HIGH
Wemyss Road,
Blackheath,
London SE3 0TF
Tel (081) 852 1537

Independent • Girls • Day • Ages 4-18 •
550 pupils (380 in senior school) • 70 in
sixth form • Fees, £2,844-£3,684
Head: Miss Rosanne Musgrave, 40,
appointed 1989.

Popular, over-subscribed; exam results improving.

Background Purpose-built (1880) by Girls' Public Day School Trust. Balustraded double staircase leads down to sunken hall of classical proportions (complete with plaster busts). Premises (in rather dingy street) now cramped; seniors soon to transfer to new 3-acre site across the heath. Senior school will grow to 450, juniors (on exisiting site) to 300.

Atmosphere Bustling with energy; big emphasis on openness, community involvement.

The head Appointed at 37 (formerly head of English at Haberdashers' Aske's Girls'); full of ideas (curriculum under continuous review); loves headship and responsibility.

The teaching Cross-curricular approach to 'diminish the development of a perception that the lessons are made up of unconnected subjects'; 9-period day makes time for extras such as life-skills course (personal and social education, computer literacy, study and presentation skills etc). 45% take 2 languages; Latin and German on offer, also 3 sciences. GCSE pass rate has significantly improved. Most do 3 A-levels plus non-examined courses in world affairs, contemporary literature, science now, women's studies etc. Strong music; 75% learn an instrument; 2 orchestras and wind band; choirs and choral groups.

The pupils Wide range of backgrounds, including growing number from ethnic minorities. Admission to junior school at 4 after assessment by head; at 7 and 11 by tests in English and maths plus interview. Big catchment area from north and south of the Thames (4 times over-subscribed at 11 – partly a result of multiple applications). Some assisted places.

Results GCSE: all gain at least 5 grades A-C. A-level (1992): creditable 59% of entries graded A or B.

Destinations 90% do A-levels and go on to higher education (several a year to Oxbridge).

Sport Mainly hockey, netball (some play for England Under-16), tennis and athletics (5-acre playing fields 10 minutes away). 40 girls row on the Thames and compete in regattas.

Remarks Successful, expanding school.

BLUE COAT

Church Road,
Liverpool L15 9EE
Tel (051) 733 1407

Comprehensive (voluntary-aided) • Boys
(plus girls in sixth form) • Ages 11-18 • 700
pupils • 220 in sixth form (80% boys)
Head: John Speller, 42, appointed 1989.

*Distinguished school; officially a
comprehensive, in reality selective.*

Background Founded 1708 with the aim of
teaching 'poor children to read, write and cast
accounts' and be instructed in the principles of
the Established Church. Liverpool City
Council's attempts to shut it down in 1985-86
were thwarted by a huge public outcry.
Edwardian buildings in imposing neo-classical
style (clock tower, oak panelling, moulded
ceilings); beautiful domed chapel looks like a
miniature St Paul's (daily Christian worship
with Hymns Ancient and Modern). Internal
maintenance below par: peeling paintwork,
tatty lockers.

Atmosphere Marble floors and long, high-
ceilinged corridors induce a sense of respect
for the school's fine history, as do the innumer-
able photographs of former assembled multi-
tudes and sporting colossi. Pupils move
around in civilised manner; school uniform
worn with pride; prefects in gowns, some with
yellow piping; girls treated with gratifying
respect. Scholarship and hard work plainly
valued; high culture for local children at no
charge (George Orwell would have approved).

The head Read French at Durham; has an
MA from the Open University. Taught
French, Spanish, English at grammar schools
and comprehensives. Youthful, energetic,
shrewd, definitely non-trendy. Married, with 3
children; loves cricket.

The teaching High-quality, versatile; pupils'
imaginations and intellects ignited. Standard
grammar-school curriculum; most take 7
GCSEs but some as many as 10. Sciences
taught as 3 separate subjects; main languages
French and Spanish; Latin, Hindi, Portuguese, Chinese also on offer. No streaming by
ability in first 2 years; setting in maths and
French. Sixth-formers do 3 A-levels plus
general studies; some tutoring for Oxbridge
entrance exams. Class sizes 30, reducing to 22
for GCSE, 15 in sixth form. Committed staff
of 48, including 8 women (recent advertise-
ment for a history teacher attracted 39 applicants). Homework strictly enforced. Strong
musical tradition (Blue Coat brass band);
good drama; lively pottery department; vigorous, imaginative painting. Fine record in
helping worthy causes.

The pupils Evidently proud of their school's
reputation. Exemplary behaviour in class; no
disorder in the corridors; well-mannered in the
dining room; attentive in assembly. From a
wide variety of backgrounds (50 entitled to free
school meals) with a preponderance from
more affluent homes in south Liverpool. No
entry tests; admission after discussion between
each applicant and 2 experienced members of
staff, who are looking for promise and motivation. ('Pure brain power is not the only thing,'
says head.) Heavily over-subscribed: in 1991,
399 applied for 120 places.

Results GCSE: 93% gain at least 5 grades
A-C. A-level (1992): 47% of entries graded A
or B.

Destinations 95% proceed from GCSE to
A-level; 75% of these go on to higher education
(10 a year to Oxbridge).

Sport Outstanding record, particularly in basketball and soccer; many county and national
players. Cricket, athletics also popular; rugby
being introduced. $7^1/_2$ acres of playing fields
near by; large gym (no sports hall), swimming
pool, 2 squash courts.

Remarks School has given generations of
'ordinary' children a first-rate education – and
continues to do so. Deserves to be better
funded.

BLUNDELL'S
Tiverton,
Devon EX16 4DN
Tel (0884) 252543

Independent • Boys (plus girls in sixth form) • Boarding and day • Ages 13-18 • 450 pupils (75% boarding) • 220 in sixth form (85% boys) • Fees, £9,750 boarding; £6,015 day
Head: Jonathan Leigh, 40, appointed September 1992.

Strongly traditional school; admits a fairly wide range of abilities; emphasis on character building.

Background Founded 1604 by Peter Blundell, local clothier; moved to present 100-acre site in a valley near Tiverton 1882. 19th-century buildings of charm and character; fine chapel large enough to accommodate the whole school (each day begins with a short service of dedication).

Atmosphere Dignified, serene: rather like an Oxbridge college (teachers in flowing black gowns). Institutional dormitories gradually being replaced by carpeted study-bedrooms.

The head New appointment. Educated at Eton and Cambridge; taught history at Cranleigh since 1975; became second master. Has a fine tenor voice, plays fives and is fond of horse racing.

The teaching Sound, lively; variety of methods; good inter-action between pupils and staff. All pupils set by ability; most take at least 9 GCSEs (3 separate sciences, compulsory religious studies). Choice of 20 subjects offered at A-level, including sports science, Greek, history of art; most do 3 plus programme of general studies. Some classrooms – especially science – have a rather discouraging turn-of-the-century aura. Computing facilities poor (1 small room with a handful of machines). 48 teachers, half over age of 45 (which, combined with the weight of tradition, sometimes leads to a certain inertia). Excellent new theatre; lots of plays, revues, concerts. About half learn a musical instrument; 35-piece orchestra, band, chamber groups, small ensembles. Regular language exchanges with France and Germany. Community involvement includes caring for elderly and handicapped.

The pupils Pleasantly confident and forthcoming. Most from middle-class/professional families in the South West; drawn from more than 100 prep schools. Flexbile entry standards (i.e. not highly selective); potential, motivation, commitment taken into account. Various scholarships, exhibitions, bursaries. Sixth-form girls reasonably well integrated.

Results GCSE: 85% gain at least 5 grades A-C (90% in 1991). A-levels (1992): rather modest 31% of entries graded A or B.

Destinations Most stay for the sixth form; two-thirds of these proceed to higher education (few to Oxbridge).

Sport Wide range of games on offer; good athletics. First-class facilities (but no indoor pool).

Remarks Something worthwhile for everyone; spiritual values and moral development emphasised.

BOLTON
Chorley New Road,
Bolton BL1 4PA
Tel (0204) 840202

Independent • Boys • Day • Ages 7-18 • 1,000 pupils (850 in senior school) • 250 in sixth form • Fees, £3,000-£3,996
Head: Alan Wright, 49, appointed 1983.

First-rate, hard-working school. Good results; excellent facilities.

Background Founded 1524; re-endowed by Lord Leverhulme in 1913 as a single school with separate boys' and girls' divisions on the same 32-acre campus west of Bolton. Main building (imposing red sandstone) dates from

1897. Linked to Bolton Girls' *(qv)* by battlemented tower.

Atmosphere Deeply serious (the splendidly confident Victorian architecture creates a somewhat severe effect). But this is a warm, happy, bustling school; relations between teachers and boys are excellent; high staff morale helps generate a sense of optimism. No coercion but a definite sense of order; behaviour in lessons is impeccable. Morning assembly in awe-inspiring hall with hammer beam roof; assembled multitude sits on carved, high-backed chairs whilst a musically-gifted third-year plays the huge organ.

The head Personable, good-humoured, extremely shrewd. Went to Manchester Grammar; First in chemistry at Birmingham; taught at King Edward's, Birmingham and Royal Grammar, Newcastle-upon-Tyne. Clearly respected by staff and pupils (his door really is open the whole time). Committed Anglican, lay reader; married, 3 children – the eldest was a pupil here, the youngest still is.

The teaching Formidably well-qualified staff of 70 (6 women); 9 PhDs, 18 with Oxbridge degrees; cheerful, dedicated, have the highest expectations of their pupils. Much of the teaching is properly didactic – chalk, talk and text book – with plenty of pupil involvement; no streaming or setting (within a narrow ability band); heavy homework programme. Standard grammar-school curriculum but all take 2 languages to GCSE (out of Latin, Greek, French, German, Russian); sciences taught separately. Average class size 28, reducing to 22 for GCSE, 12 in the sixth form. Outstanding technology; several boys have patented solutions to industrial problems. Vast range of extra-curricular activities; drama, debating, Christian Union etc shared with girls' school. Regular foreign exchanges and visits, including annual 4-week trek across Europe (staff and boys carry their food in tea chests – eccentric, obviously English).

The pupils Bright, lively, courteous; respond eagerly to the heavy work load their pursuit of excellence requires. All well turned-out instrict school uniform. By no means all come from favoured backgrounds; 270 on assisted places. School heavily over-subscribed (4 applications for each place); entry tests in English, maths, verbal reasoning; interview and previous head's report also important. Nearly all juniors admitted to senior school; others drawn from 80 primary schools.

Results GCSE: 98% gain at least 5 grades A-C. A-level: 57% of entries graded A or B.

Destinations 95% proceed from GCSE to A-level; 90% of these to higher education (about 16 a year to Oxbridge).

Sport All major games played, plus water polo; soccer the main sport but rugby is making rapid advances. Superb, modern sports hall and swimming pool; excellent playing fields and cricket pitch.

Remarks Dedicated staff; manifestly happy and achieving pupils; academic rigour combined with compassion.

BOLTON GIRLS'
Chorley New Road,
Bolton BL1 4PB
Tel (0204) 840201

Independent • Girls • Day • Ages 4-18 • 1,100 pupils (750 in senior school) • 200 in sixth form • Fees, £2,055-£2,937 Head: Mrs Margaret Spurr, 58, appointed 1978.

Lively, academic school; very good results, but not an exam factory. Excellent facilities. 50% of pupils receive help with fees.

Background Girls' (separate but equal) half of Bolton School *(qv)*. Roots go back to boys' grammar (1524) and girls' high (1877). Lord Leverhulme – local lad made good – endowed both in 1913, creating a single foundation. Battlemented entrance links the 2 schools on 32-acre site west of Bolton, close to motorway network. Present Lord Leverhulme is chairman of governors.

Atmosphere Strong sense of continuity and dignity: solid, sandstone building; Great Hall with raised organ; broad corridors; oak fittings and furniture. Fizzing with energy but no suggestion of disorder; importance of courtesy stressed. Conscious effort made to maintain clean, wholesome environment – in strong contrast to surrounding streets defaced by litter and graffiti.

The head Shrewd, decisive but with a relaxed, courteous style. Passionate advocate of all-girls' schools on grounds that they prevent stereotyping, raise attainment levels and encourage feminine qualities without restricting opportunities. Mixes tradition with innovation: insists on Authorised Version of Bible at morning assembly; introduced lunch-time language courses for local businessmen, which raise money and create useful contacts. Married, 2 children. Sought early retirement but governors wisely persuaded her to stay until 1994.

The teaching Generally formal without being oppressive (virtually all staff graduates – 5 Oxbridge, 1 PhD). Standard grammar-school curriculum (including Latin and Greek); no streaming (within narrow ability band); regular homework. Class sizes vary: 26-27 in first year of senior school; 8-10 in sixth form. Lots of sharing with boys' division: they come to the girls for religious education; girls go to them for Russian; joint general studies lessons in sixth form. Strong music (annual music scholarship at 11+). Wide range of extra-curricular activities; study centre in Cumbria.

The pupils Mainly from middle-class homes but others from very modest backgrounds. (Main catchment area: Bolton, Bury, Rochdale, Wigan, Leigh, Chorley, parts of Salford – all served by efficient coach service.) 40% on assisted places; means-tested bursaries also available. Selective entry from the start: kindergarten heavily over-subscribed; admission decided on interview. Tests at 11 in English, maths; no minimum IQ specified; great store set by interview. Admission to sixth form pre-supposes 6 good GCSEs. Sixth-formers expected to 'dress appropriately for school

business – eye make-up, lipstick and nail varnish are not allowed'.

Results GCSE: all gain at least 5 grades A-C. A-level (1992): creditable 59% of entries graded A or B.

Destinations Most junior school pupils pass into the senior school, which also draws from up to 60 primary schools. Most stay on to do A-levels: 80% proceed to degree courses (16 a year to Oxbridge).

Sport All major games; outstanding lacrosse and water polo (fine swimming pool in new sports complex).

Remarks Delightful, challenging, happy school; freedom within a sensible disciplinary framework. Girls enjoy the benefits of single-sex education without being isolated from boys.

BRADFIELD College

Bradfield,
Near Reading,   0118 964450
Berkshire RG7 6AR
Tel (0734) 744203

Independent • Boys (plus girls in sixth form) • Boarding and some day • Ages 13-18 • 577 pupils (94% boarding) • 275 in sixth form (72% boys) • Fees, £10,350 boarding; £7,776 day
Head: Peter Smith, 48, appointed 1986.

Everything on offer in a beautiful setting: splendid facilities; good results.

Background Founded 1850 (for the sons of gentlemen) by Thomas Stevens, Rector and Lord of the Manor of Bradfield. Magnificent 200-acre estate in beautiful countryside; buildings of soft red brick and flintstone centred around a crossroads just outside the village. Recent additions include 2 girls' boarding houses.

Atmosphere Sense of space, calm, timelessness. A friendly, civilised community; staff live on site and give freely of their time; day pupils required to remain until 9 p.m.

The head Educated at Magdalen College School and Oxford; formerly head of history and a housemaster at Rugby. Says his pupils are 'relatively conformist' and believes there is a danger of boarding schools producing 'a kind of caste who don't necessarily find it easy to relate to other young people'. Was an accomplished cricketer. Married, 2 teenage daughters.

The teaching Emphasis on discussion, pupil involvement, practical work. All placed in 1 of 3 broad ability bands; further setting by subject. Most take 10 GCSEs; options include Latin, Greek, German, Spanish, separate sciences, technology, electronics, business studies. Choice of 20 subjects at A-level; most do 3 in addition to non-examined general studies course; extra coaching for Oxbridge. First-rate music: more than half learn an instrument; orchestra, jazz band; chapel choir much in demand (1992 tour of Hungary). Drama includes triennial performance of a Greek play in Greek before an audience of 2,000, followed by a tour of Greece. Good art (2 studios) and extra-curricular technology (hovercraft built here).

The pupils Pleasant, self-confident. Most from business/professional backgrounds. Housemasters do their own recruiting. School is not especially selective; some pupils on grammar-school borderline. Up to 24 scholarships a year; assisted places in sixth form. 'The Bradfield male is extremely insecure about the whole concept of femininity, feminism and female existence,' according to the school magazine's (female) editor. 'Perhaps their insecurity is born from the sudden introduction of the idea of an opposite sex at such a late stage in their development.'

Results GCSE: virtually all gain at least 5 grades A-C. A-level (1992): 43% of entries graded A or B.

Destinations 90% stay on for A-levels; 90% of these proceed to higher education (14 to Oxbridge in 1991).

Sport Chiefly soccer, hockey, cricket, tennis, athletics; other activities include rugby, squash, badminton, fives, fencing, judo, golf, swimming, fishing, sailing. Facilities are excellent.

Remarks All the advantages of a boarding school education exploited to the full.

BRADFORD GIRLS' GRAMMAR
Squire Lane,
Bradford,
West Yorkshire BD9 6RB
Tel (0274) 545395

Independent • Girls • Day • Ages 11-18 • 676 pupils • 180 in sixth form • Fees (1992-93), £3,600
Head: Mrs Lynda Warrington, 43, appointed 1987.

Traditional academic emphasis; good results.

Background Founded 1875 (when it was decided that a 1662 charter for the education of the children of Bradford included girls); moved to 17-acre site 2 miles from the city centre in 1936. Pleasant 3-storey building plus handsome new sixth-form centre.

Atmosphere Happy, hard-working.

The head Joined the staff in 1979 to teach physics; became deputy head 1983.

The teaching Enthusiastic; overhead projectors used as much as blackboards. Setting by ability in maths and French from the start. Latin compulsory for first 3 years; German, Spanish, Russian available from third year; Italian, Greek in the sixth form; well-equipped language laboratory. Good science (9 labs); compulsory introduction to computing; all learn the basic skills of working with wood, metal, acrylics (girls recently assembled a kit car which made a sponsored return journey to Venice). Cookery and needlework, thanks to the national curriculum, have mutated into 'food and textile technology'. Class sizes 30, reducing to 20 for GCSE, 12 for A-levels.

Enthusiastic drama and music (orchestra, choir, madrigals etc); lots of clubs and societies.

The pupils 300 apply for 120 places at 11+; vast catchment area served by fleet of coaches. Assisted places, scholarships, bursaries; 20% pay less than full fees.

Results Good. GCSE: 99% gain at least 5 grades A-C. A-level (1992): 48% of entries graded A or B (has been higher).

Destinations About 80% stay on for A-levels; most of these proceed to higher education (8 to Oxbridge in 1991).

Sport Strong hockey, netball; most other sports available, including synchronised swimming.

Remarks Good school for bright, ambitious girls.

BRADFORD GRAMMAR
Keighley Road,
Bradford ,
West Yorkshire BD9 4JR
Tel (0274) 545461

Independent • Boys (plus girls in sixth form) • Day • Ages 8-18 • 1,150 pupils (1,000 in senior school) • 320 in sixth form (80% boys) • Fees, £3,174
Head: David Smith, mid-50s, appointed 1974.

Grammar school tradition; expects and gives nothing but the best; academic excellence the norm.

Background Charter dates from 1662. 20-acre site; main building 1930s gothic; looks like a stately home. Assembly hall has the proportions and feel of a moderate-sized cathedral. Recent additions (thanks to generous gifts and endowments) include magnificent library, sports hall, theatre.

Atmosphere Highly disciplined; everyone busy; staff under as much pressure as the pupils.

The head Doyen of his profession (former chairman of Headmasters' Conference); appointed head of a comprehensive at 34; affable; generous with his time, especially to young people with problems. Teaches history and religious education for a quarter of the timetable.

The teaching Enthusiastic staff of 75 (12 women). All senior boys follow 3-year foundation course which includes computer technology (lavish facilities), workshop skills and music. Wide range of options at GCSE and A-level (Russian TV by satellite). Sixth-form teaching as near to university style as possible. Good art (David Hockney is an Old Boy) and music; 20% learn an instrument; orchestras, choirs etc. Bewildering variety of extracurricular activities; more than 50 clubs and societies; regular exchanges to France and Germany.

The pupils Academically bright (average IQ 120); mainly from affluent homes but 25% on assisted places. Entry at 8, 9, 10, 11 by tests in English and maths plus, at 13, science and French; half senior school pupils drawn from junior school but entry is not automatic; remaining places over-subscribed by 3:1. Presence of sixth-form girls (entry by interview and GCSE performance) has had a moderating influence on the chauvinistic tendencies of self-confident young men.

Results GCSE: 99% gain at least 5 grades A-C. A-level: 57% of entries graded A or B.

Destinations 85% proceed to degree courses (30 a year to Oxbridge).

Sport Strong rugby (New Zealand tour in 1993); boating club with international-level coaching. Other facilities include swimming pool, running track, squash courts and multi-gym.

Remarks Successful, well-equipped, supremely self-confident school.

BRAYTON HIGH

Doncaster Road,
Selby,
North Yorkshire YO8 9QS
Tel (0757) 707731

Comprehensive • Co-educational • Ages
11-16 • 1,020 pupils (equal numbers of
girls and boys)
Head: Hugh Porter, 40, appointed 1991.

---

*Successful, well-run comprehensive;
good teaching and results.*

Background Opened as a purpose-built comprehensive 1979; lost its sixth form to a tertiary college 1984. Attractive rural setting; mostly single-storey buildings in a good state of repair and decoration.

Atmosphere Calm, purposeful; all seem to know what is expected of them. No sign of graffiti or litter; truancy rate negligible; simple uniform worn by all. Corridors lavishly decorated with pupils' artwork. Lively parents' association.

The head Good manager; gets on well with staff and pupils; emphasises the importance of high academic expectations. Read history at Liverpool; came here as deputy head 1988. Married, 3 young children.

The teaching High-quality; lively, well-planned, well-paced lessons. 61 staff (36 women), average age 35. Maximum class size 26; pupils sit not in rows but groups of 4-8; some setting by ability in maths, English, languages. First-years choose between French, German, Russian; all do 'balanced' science; good computing, design/technology. Extra help for those with special needs, including moderate learning difficulties. Homework regularly set and marked. Music for all in first 3 years; good art; drama concentrates on self-discovery rather than prestige productions. All do 2 weeks' work experience.

The pupils Cheerful, relaxed, responsible. Most from Selby and Brayton; rest from villages to the south and east (some travel up to 15 miles). Local unemployment is high but 90% of parents own their own homes. School admits the full ability range.

Results (1991) GCSE: creditable 44% gained at least 5 grades A-C.

Destinations 68% proceed to further education (including 27% who take A-levels).

Sport Soccer, basketball, athletics for the boys; hockey, netball for the girls; cross-country for both. Extensive playing fields; good sports hall.

Remarks Her Majesty's Inspectors reported (1990): 'Standards of work are generally high. In some areas, for instance science, they are exceptional...A committed staff, well led, is producing positive relationships and high quality education.'

BRIGHTON

Eastern Road,
Brighton BN2 2AL
Tel (0273) 605788

Independent • Co-educational • Boarding and day • Ages 13-18 • 482 pupils (80% boys; 80% boarders) • 198 in sixth form • Fees, £8,640-£9,630 boarding; £6,330 day
Head: John Leach, 53, appointed 1987.

Rather old-fashioned; respectable results.

Background Founded 1845 to provide 'a thoroughly liberal and practical education in conformity with the principles of the Established Church'. Attractive Victorian Gothic buildings (by George Gilbert Scott) around a grass quadrangle; later additions blend in.

Atmosphere Formal to the point of stuffiness; pleasant, polite pupils. School fully co-educational since 1988 but has failed to attract girls in the numbers it would like. Boarding accommodation gradually being upgraded.

The head Previously a housemaster at St Edward's, Oxford; teaches 10 periods of classics a week. Would like to raise the academic level of the intake (minimum mark required at Common Entrance a modest 50%) but without much success to date.

The teaching Good, particularly in science (taught as 3 separate subjects), maths and modern languages. Setting by ability in most subjects; class sizes 17-24; 8-12 in the sixth form. Specialised help for dyslexics. Spacious, well-stocked library. Lots of music; 30% learn an instrument; 70-strong choir. Community service an alternative to cadets; money raised for a shanty town near Bombay – some pupils spend their 'gap year' there.

The pupils Mostly from business and professional backgrounds within an arc drawn from Worthing to Seaford. 60% enter from adjoining junior school; state-school applicants take tests in English, maths. Some assisted places.

Results GCSE: 90% gain 5 or more grades A-C. A-level (1992): 46% of entries graded A or B.

Destinations 80% stay on in the sixth form; 90% of these proceed to higher education (11 to Oxbridge in 1991).

Sport Good record in rugby, cricket (tours to India, Pakistan, West Indies), hockey. Facilities include indoor pool, tennis and squash courts; most playing fields some distance away.

Remarks Middle-of-the road school; some notably good teaching.

BRIGHTON & HOVE HIGH
The Temple,
Montpelier Road,
Brighton BN1 3AT
Tel (0273) 734112

Independent • Girls • Day • Ages 4-18 • 709 pupils (486 in senior school) • 90 in sixth form • Fees, £2,052-£3,156
Head: Miss Rosalind Woodbridge, 40s, appointed 1990.

Highly academic school; first-rate results; good music.

Background Founded 1876; member of Girls' Public Day School Trust. Elegant Regency town house (built for Thomas Kemp, founder of Kemp Town) plus adjoining collection of Victorian houses containing spacious laboratories, 2 well-equipped computer rooms, fine gym.

Atmosphere Calm, purposeful.

The head Historian; formerly deputy head of Croydon High (also a GPDST school).

The teaching Challenging: aim is to train girls to think for themselves. Most take 9 GCSEs (including average of more than 2 sciences); options include classics, third foreign language, computing, home economics. Most popular A-level subjects: maths, economics, history, Latin, religious studies. Plenty of drama, music; more than a third learn an instrument, 2 choirs, 2 orchestras, band. Art and technology confined to Victorian basement where facilities (and light) are restricted. Mathematical and classical societies enjoy big following. Flourishing Duke of Edinburgh's award scheme. Charitable activities embrace senior citizens and Third World children.

The pupils Mixed backgrounds; largely middle-class but a third on assisted places; no flaunted affluence. Girls are individuals in a smallish school. Self-confidence and self-discipline aimed at and achieved. Stiffly competitive entry tests at 4, 7 and 11. Catchment area extends to Lewes, Worthing, Haywards Heath and beyond.

Results GCSE: 95% gain at least five grades A-C. A-level (1992): very impressive 73% of entries graded A or B.

Destinations Half stay for A-levels (remainder to sixth-form colleges etc) and then proceed to higher education (medicine popular) or other professional training.

Sport Netball and tennis on site; other facilities 5 minutes away by coach.

Remarks Good all-round education for able girls.

BRISTOL CATHEDRAL
College Square,
Bristol BS1 5TS
Tel (0272) 291872

Independent • Boys (girls in sixth form) • Day • Ages 11-18 • 460 pupils • 120 in sixth form (three-quarters boys) • Fees, £3,327
Head: Roy Collard, 39, appointed 1990.

Compact city-centre school; strong links with cathedral; gentle, liberal regime; imaginative teaching; generally good exam results.

Background Founded 1140; reconstituted by Henry VIII 1542. Bristol's only royal school. Set in cathedral precincts; buildings span 8 centuries; little hope of further expansion, except possibly upwards. Dr Wesley Carr, cathedral's influential dean, is chairman of governors.

Atmosphere Tension-free; smallness makes for intimacy and warmth. Staff know every child by name; happy, good-humoured relations; no hint of vandalism or alienation; true community feel. Cloisters, winding staircases; cheerfully decorated traditional classrooms.

The head Cambridge-educated geographer; previously director of studies at Oundle. Direct, approachable; good working relationships with senior staff. Determined to main-

tain school's centuries-old liberal ethos. Married, 2 young children.

The teaching Impressive team of 36 graduates (6 women). Setting in maths only, from second year. Go-ahead modern languages department (European awareness fostered through satellite TV, international evenings, French and German exchanges etc). Maths and science popular at A-level. National curriculum selectively implemented: head anxious to maintain classics, music, drama at present levels. Class sizes start at 30 but get smaller. Vibrant music; half play an instrument (recent organ scholarships to Oxbridge); choristers make big contribution. Good pastoral care. Staff meet 3-4 times a term to discuss each child's grades and welfare; termly reports to parents. Lots of genuine charity work (not just Red Nose day); community service an alternative to sport for senior pupils (helping in primary schools, visiting the elderly).

The pupils Natural, open, happy; no hint of snobbishness. Well motivated; few disciplinary problems (third-years and above allowed into the city at lunch-time – a privilege they enjoy and do not abuse). Wide range of social backgrounds; more than a third on assisted places. Selective entry; joint exam with Bristol Grammar and Queen Elizabeth's Hospital; many academic and music scholarships. Sixth-form co-education has worked well but lack of space prevents expansion.

Results GCSE: 97% gain at least 5 grades A-C. A-level (1992): very disappointing 23% of entries graded A or B (has been much higher).

Destinations 15-20% take A-levels elsewhere; replaced by newcomers. Almost all go on to university (5-7 a year to Oxbridge).

Sport Chiefly rugby, soccer, hockey, cricket, badminton, fencing. Playing fields 3 miles away by bus; hired tennis courts and swimming baths.

Remarks Charming school; ideal for the academically able, artistic or musically talented.

BRISTOL GRAMMAR
University Road,
Bristol BS8 1SR
Tel (0272) 736006

Independent • Co-educational • Day •
Ages 11-18 (plus separate junior school) •
984 pupils (70% boys) • 240 in the sixth
form (70% boys) • Fees, £3,288
Head: Charles Martin, 53, appointed 1986.

---

*First-rate, traditional grammar school;
strong academic bias but by no means a
sweat shop.*

Background Founded 1532; moved to present site 1879. Rather overpowering Victorian buildings (including vast dining hall) around pleasant, grassy quad.

Atmosphere Friendly – despite the school's size. Alert, confident pupils; busy staff; co-education working well.

The head Thoughtful, brisk, widely experienced (previously head of a state grammar school in Birmingham). Abolished Saturday morning school as anachronistic; encourages sixth-form leavers to take a 'gap year' preferably in the Third World. Read English at Cambridge.

The teaching High-quality; successful mixture of traditional and progressive styles. Well-qualified, hard-working staff of 80 (48 men, 32 women), nearly a third appointed by present head. Mixed-ability classes in first 2 years; setting thereafter in maths, science, French. First-rate maths (94% pass rate at GCSE) and modern languages (more than 90% pass GCSE French and German, 100% success in Russian A-level); regular exchanges with schools in Bordeaux, Hanover, Moscow. 30 take Greek at GCSE; most A-level classics pupils go to Oxbridge. New technology centre planned for 1994. School library reputed to be the best in the country: 60,000 volumes; space for 100 readers. Wide range of extra-curricular activities (war games to wood sculpture). Big emphasis on community work and fund-raising for causes at home and abroad.

Pupils Confident, articulate; without pretension or snobbery. Well-disciplined (head is *very* anti-bullying); uniform worn throughout (boys allowed long hair as long as it is clean). Most from professional/middle-class homes but a third on assisted places, which helps ensure a social mix. All are academically able (school shares 11+ entrance exam with Bristol Cathedral, *qv*, and Queen Elizabeth's Hospital, *qv*, and tends to take the largest proportion of high-flyers); 2-3 apply for each place. Most pupils from the junior school (on an adjoining site with its own head) proceed to the senior school.

Results GCSE: 95% gain at least 5 grades A-C. A-level: 48% of entries graded A or B.

Destinations 95% stay on for A-levels; nearly all of these proceed to higher education (15 a year to Oxbridge).

Sport Very strong, especially hockey (all-weather pitch), rugby, soccer, cricket; many county players. Impressive new sports hall (squash courts, climbing wall etc); 15 acres of playing fields 15 minutes away by bus.

Remarks Well-run school; highly recommended.

BROMLEY HIGH
Blackbrook Lane,
Bickley,
Bromley,
Kent BR1 2TW
Tel (081) 468 7981

Independent • Girls • Day • Ages 4-18 •
720 pupils (520 in senior school) • 120 in
sixth form • Fees, £2,844-£3,684
Head: Mrs Joy Hancock, 40s, appointed
1988.

---

*Successful school serving much of
south-east London. Good exam results;
strong sporting tradition; wide range of
extra-curricular activities.*

Background Founded 1883 by Girls' Public Day School Trust; moved to superb, purpose-built accommodation 1981. Spacious, well-maintained buildings on 24-acre site adjoining outer-suburban parkland.

Atmosphere Everyone welcoming; air of peaceful industry prevails; strong belief that girls do better in single-sex schools. Corridors celebrate successes in music, drama, art, sport, public speaking.

The head Involved in everything but delegates widely (staff turnover minimal). Emphasises that the school's traditional emphasis on academic success is tempered by a broad extra-curricular programme. (The proportion of girls staying on for the sixth form has risen from 50% to 75% in 3 years). Determined the school should see itself as part of the community.

The teaching Lively, effective. Junior department (ages 4-11 in separate buildings) hums along. Continuity with upper school emphasised; heavily over-subscribed; nearly all move up. (Junior department is soon to be doubled in size, which will make it even harder to get in at 11.) Seniors work in large, bright classrooms (maximum of 26 pupils). Well-equipped workshops, 7 laboratories (all take double science). Choice of 20 subjects at A-level, including political studies, economics and government. Strong music; all juniors and more than 40% of seniors learn an instrument.

The pupils Hard-working, confident (all achievement cherished); well-behaved. 20 assisted places a year.

Results GCSE: 95% gain at least five grades A-C. A-level (1992): 46% of entries graded A or B.

Destinations Most to higher education (including Oxbridge).

Sport Hockey, netball, tennis, athletics; heated indoor swimming pool.

Remarks Happy, effective school; excellent facilities.

BRYANSTON
Blandford,
Dorset DT11 0PX
Tel (0258) 452411

Independent • Co-educational • Boarding and day • Ages 13-18 • 670 pupils (65% boys; 95% boarding) • 253 in sixth form (60% boys) • Fees, £10,920 boarding; £7,281 day
Head: Tom Wheare, 47, appointed 1983.

Successful progressive school. High standard of academic work; good sport, music, drama, art.

Background Founded 1928 to break the 'rigid and outdated' public-school tradition. 400-acre wooded estate by the River Stour. Grand Norman Shaw mansion built in the 1890s for the Portman family dominates the campus; fine new theatre and technology centre; other additions less impressive.

Atmosphere Relaxed, mature, rather like a university campus; emphasis on self-motivation and self-discipline. Progressive educational philosophy retained but tempered to the needs of the 1990s (compulsory shorts now abandoned).

The head Choral scholar at King's College, Cambridge; read history. Taught at Eton then became a housemaster at Shrewsbury. Wholly at ease with the Bryanston ethos; cannot imagine wanting to work anywhere else. Believes in social order rather than discipline; says effective education depends on pupils and teachers inter-acting as equals; describes his aim as the creation of a 'loving community'. Produces plays, conducts.

The teaching No streaming but some setting by ability. Pupils prepared from the start to take full responsibility for their work; each seen individually by a tutor every week to discuss increasingly demanding assignments; grades for achievement and effort. All introduced to French and German; compulsory course in beliefs and values; musical instrument taught free for the first term. Choice of 21 subjects at A-level plus 60 optional courses ranging from catering to philosophy, conservation to media studies. Full-time staff of 67 (half appointed by present head) and more than 50 part-timers. First-rate music and drama; every form of art and craft – ceramics, woodwork, metalwork, sculpture.

The pupils Fairly wide ability range (modest 50% required at Common Entrance); most from London, south and south-west England. Dress informal; boys claim they need wear a tie only once a year, on Speech Day. Sexes at ease with each other (was one of the first boys' schools to admit girls).

Results GCSE (1991): 98% gained at least 5 grades A-C. A-level (1992): 50% of entries graded A or B (has been higher).

Destinations 90% continue into the sixth form; 80% of these (95% in 1990) proceed to higher education (up to 15 a year to Oxbridge); 11% to further education in music, art, drama.

Sport Big range of activities for teams and individuals, including rowing (on the Stour), canoeing, sailing, shooting, girls' hockey and netball, boys' hockey and rugby (both currently outstanding).

Remarks Distinctive school; liberal philosophy; good choice for the right child.

BURFORD

Cheltenham Road,
Burford,
Oxford OX8 4PL
Tel (0993) 823303

Comprehensive • Co-educational • Day and some boarding • Ages 11-18 • 1,203 pupils (54% boys; 93% day) • 206 in sixth form • Boarding fees, £4,530
Head: Robert Back, 42, appointed 1990.

Well-run 'flagship' comprehensive; creditable results.

Background Foundation dates from 1571; effectively a comprehensive since 1949 (the

first in the country). Extensive grounds include a working 48-acre farm; a rural idyll on the edge of the Cotswolds.

Atmosphere Traditional values (and an air of innocence) successfully preserved. Enthusiastic, high-calibre staff (they send their children here); smart, well-behaved pupils; supportive parents; competitive house system (points earned for work and behaviour). Spacious, attractive boarding houses in original town-centre stone buildings.

The head Personifies the ethos of the school: civilised, humane, committed to the highest possible standards. Read English at Sussex; taught extensively in state schools; still teaches A-level English. Starts the day by making routine announcements over the public address system (reassuring to the passengers to know the captain is on the bridge).

The teaching Varied styles; pupils set by ability from second year; extra help for those with special needs. Some take GCSE maths a year early; options include second modern language and Latin. Big emphasis on the world of work; some GCSE and A-level courses centre on the farm, where many pupils enjoy the chance to work with livestock and relate what they are doing to the 'real' world; introduction of National Vocational Qualifications eagerly awaited; traditional skills of woodwork and metalwork still taught. All gain work experience; good links with local farmers.

The pupils Cheerful, alert; from diverse backgrounds (and more than 60 primary schools); 40 qualify for free meals; a third come from outside the official catchment area. School is over-subscribed and expanding.

Results (1991) GCSE: 41% gained at least 5 grades A-C (girls did substantially better than boys). A-level: 29% of entries graded A or B.

Destinations 60% stay on for A-levels; most of these proceed to higher education (a few to Oxbridge).

Sport Wide choice; emphasis on participation. Facilities include vast sports hall shared with neighbouring community college.

Remarks Successful school; high standards all round.

BURGESS HILL
Silverdale Avenue,
Burgess Hill,
West Sussex RH15 0AQ
Tel (0444) 241050

Independent • Girls • Day and some boarding • Ages 4-18 • 528 pupils (90% day) • 60 in sixth form • Fees, £2,220-£4,740 day; £7,140-£7,875 boarding
Head: Mrs Rosemary Lewis, 49, appointed September 1992.

Up-and-coming school; thorough teaching; reliably good results.

Background Founded 1906 on the principles of the Parents' National Educational Union (PNEU) for the then-radical purpose of providing girls with a broad-based liberal education. Well-proportioned Victorian building in 12 acres; later additions include modern, carpeted classrooms and labs. School expanding; space limited.

Atmosphere Calm, organised, secure; even a shy child would find the domestic scale and green setting un-threatening. 2 boarding houses in converted Edwardian villas; homely rather than luxurious. Sixth-formers have separate house and considerable independence.

The head New appointment. Formerly deputy head of Roedean; highly experienced and likely to keep up her predecessor's momentum.

The teaching Sound, straightforward encouragement rather than constant intellectual confrontation; classes orderly but not subdued. Long-serving, committed staff (including 3 men); up-to-date curriculum. All do French from 10+; 13-year-olds get a 'taster' term of German and Spanish, leading to GCSE options. Good science, taught as 3 separate subjects; textiles a speciality for GCSE and A-level; business studies and computing also available. No streaming by ability; setting in maths, French from 12+. Class sizes 25, reducing to 18 or fewer for GCSE. Homework regularly set and marked. Good music: more than half learn an instrument; orchestras, jazz and wind bands, choirs. Duke of Edinburgh award scheme, community service and work experience on offer; careers lessons compulsory. Regular French and German exchanges.

The pupils Well-motivated, from modestly comfortable backgrounds, neither wealthy nor particularly sophisticated. Juniors decorous but lively; seniors polite rather than pushy but prepared to speak up; sixth-formers poised and well turned-out (no uniform, but no jeans either); streetwise non-conformists might not fit in. Most pupils are local, with a sprinkling of Service and out-of-county boarders. Entry at 4+ by oral test and interview; at 7, 11 and 13 by school's own entrance exam, standardised tests (minimum IQ of about 115) and interview (no Common Entrance). Range of ability is quite wide; school not over-subscribed (but not struggling either). Some scholarships and assisted places.

Results GCSE: virtually all gain at least 5 grades A-C. A-level (1992): creditable 61% of entries graded A or B.

Destinations 75% stay on for A-levels; 75% of these proceed to higher education (5 to Oxbridge in 1991).

Sport 2 on-site playing fields and courts for hockey, netball, tennis; athletics, dance, gymnastics also on offer; fencing, judo, aerobics are extra.

Remarks A school with gentle traditions; not a forcing-house but capable of producing academic success for able girls and useful results for others.

BURY GRAMMAR (BOYS)
Tenterden Street,
Bury, Lancashire BL9 0HN
Tel (061) 797 2700

Independent • Boys • Day • Ages 11-18
(plus associated junior school) • 780
pupils • 160 in sixth form • Fees, £2,925
Head: Keith Richards, 44, appointed 1990.

Strong academic school; good results.

Background Founded 1634; moved to present purpose-built premises 1966; impressive new facilities for design/technology; further expansion under way. Became fully independent with the abolition of Direct Grant status in 1976.

Atmosphere Friendly, business-like; good relationships between staff and boys.

The head Determined, enthusiastic; has tightened up on discipline and broadened the curriculum; keen to make the school more open and welcoming. Read classics at Cambridge; has taught widely in both state and independent schools, including Manchester Grammar and King's, Chester. Clearly respected by staff and boys.

The teaching Fairly traditional methods; long-serving staff; strongly academic approach. National curriculum-plus; all do Latin in first year; more than half take 2 modern languages for GCSE (German and Spanish on offer); setting by ability in maths, French (top sets take GCSE a year early). Limited choice of 16 subjects at A-level but more planned. Some music: small orchestra, choir. Well-supported cadet force. Regular language exchange with school in Cologne.

The pupils Bright, hard-working. Entry by interview and school's own tests in English, maths; 3 apply for every place.

Results GCSE (1991): 95% gained 5 or more grades A-C. A-level (1992): disappointing 42% of entries graded A or B (has been higher).

Destinations Nearly all stay on for A-levels;

80% proceed to higher education (5 or 6 a year to Oxbridge).

Sport Compulsory; wide choice; good facilities. Strong soccer, cricket, swimming, cross-country.

Remarks Rather traditional school now moving forward under a new head.

BURY GRAMMAR (GIRLS)
Bridge Road,
Bury,
Lancashire BL9 0HH
Tel (061) 797 2808

Independent • Girls • Day • Ages 11-18
(plus associated junior school) • 840
pupils • 200 in sixth form • Fees, £2,961
Head: Miss Janet Lawley, mid-40s,
appointed 1987.

Lively academic school; good teaching and results; strong sport.

Background Founded 1884; handsome Edwardian buildings with many later additions. Became fully independent with the abolition of Direct Grant status in 1976.

Atmosphere Busy, friendly. Emphasis on good manners, self-discipline; strong (but not overbearing) work ethos.

The head Able, forceful. Read geography at Bristol; taught in girls' grammar schools; formerly vice-principal of a sixth-form college.

The teaching Full range of methods; good mix of experienced and younger staff. National curriculum-plus; science on offer as 3 separate subjects; languages include German, Spanish, Italian. Some setting by ability in maths, French; average class size 30, reducing to 20 for GCSE, 10 in the sixth form. Most do 9 GCSEs and 3 A-levels (half do 4). First-rate art. Lots of drama (in conjunction with boys' school) and music; 25 learn an instrument; orchestra, choir. Regular language exchanges with schools in France and Germany.

The pupils Bright, confident; from a wide range of backgrounds; more than 200 have assisted places. Entry by school's own tests; 2-3 apply for each place.

Results GCSE: all gain at least 5 grades A-C. A-level (1992): 44% of entries graded A or B.

Destinations Almost all stay on for A-levels and proceed to higher education (up to 10 a year to Oxbridge).

Sport Regular county honours in hockey, swimming, badminton, netball.

Remarks Well-run, happy school; good all round.

CAMDEN GIRLS'
Sandall Road,
London NW5 2DB
Tel (071) 485 3414

Comprehensive (voluntary-aided) • Girls (boys in sixth form) • Ages 11-18 • 755 pupils • 215 in sixth form (90% girls) Head: Geoffrey Fallows, 50, appointed 1989.

Egalitarian ethos; feminist emphasis on girls achieving full academic potential (but greatest strengths in art and music). Diverse intake welded into united, harmonious community.

Background Founded 1871 by Frances Mary Buss, pioneer of women's education, as sister school for North London Collegiate *(qv)*, with which it retains links. Became a voluntary-aided grammar under 1944 Act; went comprehensive 1976. Buildings on cramped inner-city site (war damage in the 1940s, cement failure in the 1970s) regularly extended in mix of styles. The result, surprisingly, is a sense of organic growth and continuity (though some areas still need modernising and decorating). Parents invited to pay £10 a term to supplement funds.

Atmosphere No uniform; mixed-ability

teaching; competition played down; minimal supervision. All talents encouraged by supportive staff. Individualism flourishes but in a context of mutual respect: a caring community.

The head Public school (Shrewsbury) followed by classics at Oxford. Taught in the independent sector before deliberately rejecting it. Came here as deputy head in 1975. His management style, despite the egalitarian ethos, is traditional and hierarchical, with the emphasis on consultation rather than consensus. Married, 2 grown-up daughters.

The teaching No streaming or setting before the sixth form; class sizes 26-27 (smaller than in many comprehensives); much teaching on individual or small-group basis. National curriculum-plus: classical studies for all (Latin an alternative); child development, dance, Greek also available. Wide range of A-levels (general studies compulsory) plus technical and vocational qualifications offered in consortium with 4 neighbouring schools. High expectations; pupils encouraged to take responsibility for their own learning and to judge themselves against their own potential, rather than in competition with others (old-style school reports largely replaced by records of achievement). Music and art outstanding; large numbers opt for both at GCSE and A-level. Ambitious programme of concerts for 3 choirs, 2 orchestras, chamber-music ensembles, wind band and recorder group (Mozart Requiem, Haydn Mass and more popular musicals staged with drama groups); regular tour to Germany.

The pupils Widely differing family backgrounds: parents include middle-class professionals, technicians, skilled craftsmen, manual workers and unemployed; relative affluence alongside social deprivation. 40% black or Asian; wide racial, cultural and linguistic mix; all seem to thrive in notably relaxed atmosphere. Some 200 apply annually for 107 places; local authority admission procedure gives priority to siblings, those with medical or social needs, girls living nearest the school. (Admission to sixth form by interview.)

Results GCSE: creditable 60% gain at least 5

grades A-C. A-level (1992): 35% of entries graded A or B.

Destinations 70% continue into sixth form; similar proportion proceed to higher education, including art college.

Sport Emphasis on individual activity rather than team games; limited competition with other schools.

Remarks Feminist tradition maintained in a cultured society which promotes independence and self-motivation.

CAMPION
Kislingbury Road,
Bugbrooke,
Northamptonshire NN7 3QG
Tel (0604) 830677

Comprehensive • Co-educational • Ages 11-18 • 1,240 pupils (equal numbers of boys and girls) • 200 in sixth form
Head: Tim Bartlett, mid-40s, appointed 1988.

Civilised, purposeful school; good results; strong sporting record; enthusiastic parental support.

Background Founded 1967 under Bartlett's predecessor, who remained at his post for 20 years. Functional, workaday buildings (plus 4 battered mobile classrooms) in pleasantly rural setting on the western outskirts of Northampton.

Atmosphere Despite its size, school feels low-key, reassuring, not in the least intimidating; no torrent of pupils hurtling down the corridors. Predominantly secular, but none the worse for that: strong emphasis on good manners, service, sense of duty. (Sixth-formers regularly volunteer to help the younger ones with their work.) School rules well understood and accepted.

The head Read French and German at Oxford; became a bus driver; worked for Oxfam; started teaching at Stantonbury, a progressive (and controversial) comprehensive in Milton Keynes, to which he remains fiercely loyal. Believes firmly in hard work, competition, excellence. Delegates, consults (endlessly), is eminently approachable and still finds time to teach.

The teaching Refreshingly pragmatic, free from educational dogma. Some classrooms almost comically traditional: rows of battered desks facing the teacher who sits on a raised podium with an enormous blackboard behind. Others on the 'child-centred' model: 4-5 pupils working on their own (and quietly) at each of half a dozen small tables. Either way, direct, no-nonsense approach to learning. Even in painting and pottery the emphasis is on mastering techniques and skills rather than on giving rein to pupils' unfettered imaginations. Overall pupil-teacher ratio 17:1 but upper forms favoured. Mixed-ability classes of around 30 in first 2 years, then smaller numbers grouped by ability in maths, science (taught as 3 separate subjects), French, German. Homework at least 5 nights a week; all written work checked for grammar and spelling (corrections to be written out 3 times); high standard of spoken English also expected. Good music (choirs, 46-piece orchestra).

The pupils Bright, open, responsive. Largely from lower-middle and middle-class families; many from rural backgrounds (school boasts its own farm). A few qualify for free school meals. Truancy rate virtually nil. Pleasant uniform carefully adhered to. Sixth-formers, who are allowed to wear what they like, blend in. (No sign of make-up, jewellery, outlandish hair styles or other exotic plumage.) Pastoral care house-based and good; staff-pupil relations excellent.

Results (1992) GCSE: 40% gained at least 5 grades A-C. A-level: 39% of entries graded A or B. Good results also in vocational courses.

Destinations About half leave at 16, equally divided between those who take A-levels or other qualifications elsewhere and those who go straight into a job. Most who take A-levels go on to higher education.

Sport Excellent facilities including fully equipped gym and floodlit, all-weather, multipurpose pitch. Usual team games plus sailing, badminton, table tennis all played to exceptionally high standards. (In 1989-90, 80 pupils represented the county in sporting events.)

Remarks Happy, well-run, effective school; embodies the comprehensive ideal.

CANFORD
Wimborne,
Dorset BH21 3AD
Tel (0202) 882411

Independent • Boys (plus girls in the sixth form) • Boarding and day • Ages 13-18 • 500 pupils (80% boarding) • 224 in sixth form (75% boys) • Fees, £10,375 boarding; £7,575 day
Head: John Lever, 40, appointed September 1992.

Pleasant, solid school; fairly wide ability range. Plenty of sport, drama, music.

Background Founded 1923 by the Martyrs Memorial Trust as a low-church alternative to the loftier ethos of leading public schools – an impulse that remains. Beautiful 300-acre country estate bordered by the River Stour; 19th-century manor house plus fine medieval hall ('John of Gaunt's Kitchen'). Substantial recent additions include science labs, music school, art/design centre.

Atmosphere Civilised, cheerful, disciplined – Christian in the best sense. Prefects have a pastoral rather than an authoritarian role; girls a small minority but well integrated.

The head New appointment. Read geography at Cambridge (rowing blue); taught at St Edward's, Oxford then became head of geography and a housemaster at Winchester. Married, 3 children.

The teaching Able, versatile staff; varied teaching styles; academic achievement emphasised. First-years divided between top

form and 4 mixed-ability classes; setting as appropriate thereafter. All do 3 sciences for GCSE; options include Latin, German, economics; most take 3-4 A-levels (but some struggle to do 2). Strong instrumental and choral music. Voluntary cadet force (lots of adventure training).

The pupils Mostly from middle-class homes in the south of England, including many Service families; 20% from abroad (mainly expatriates). Fairly wide ability range; modest 50% required at Common Entrance. Some assisted places.

Results GCSE: nearly all gain at least 5 grades A-C. A-level (1992): 49% of entries graded A or B.

Destinations 90% stay for A-levels; 80% proceed to higher education (6 a year to Oxbridge).

Sport Choice of 20 team and individual sports; particular strengths in rugby, hockey (all-weather pitches), cricket, squash. Rowing, fishing, sailing on the Stour; 9-hole golf course; real tennis court.

Remarks Good all round.

CANON SLADE
Bradshaw Brow,
Bolton BL2 3BP
Tel (0204) 591441

Comprehensive (voluntary-aided) • Co-educational • Ages 11-18 • 1,478 pupils (55% girls) • 261 in sixth form
Head: Revd Peter Shepherd, 43, appointed 1989.

Exceptional comprehensive; wide, imaginative curriculum; excellent sport.

Background Founded 1855 by a committee chaired by Canon James Slade, vicar of Bolton. Became a Direct Grant grammar school 1946; moved to present 55-acre site 2 miles east of town centre 1956; opted for voluntary-aided status 1976; comprehensive since 1978. Mixture of flat-roofed 1960s buildings and more distinguished 1970s additions; some accommodation cramped, in need of redecoration. New £250,000 sports hall paid for by parents and friends.

Atmosphere Permeated by Christian values (termly communion service conducted in an atmosphere of genuine reverence); staff and pupils clearly share a strong sense of common purpose. Orderly movement between lessons; no evidence of misbehaviour in or out of the classroom; no litter. All pupils below the sixth form in strict school uniform (and they look a treat). 2 large display cases crammed with evidence of sporting successes; impressive artwork adorns the corridors.

The head Lives his faith without advertising the fact. Grammar school boy from modest, working-class background; read history at Reading. First teaching post in a tough, inner-city secondary modern (he is 6'5"); given all the bottom streams and loved it. Later obtained divinity degree and MPhil from London (thesis on Christian-Hindu dialogue); ordained but has not run a parish. First headship at 34. Totally dedicated and very able. Married, 2 daughters – both pupils here. Reads science fiction, brews beer.

The teaching Good. Lively, well-prepared lessons; teachers versatile in their methods. Broad curriculum (no premature specialisation); exceptionally wide choice of 35 subjects at GCSE (including German, Spanish, Latin, separate sciences) and 27 at A-level (including Greek, psychology, fashion, environmental science). Good technology; religious studies *not* a Cinderella subject; special needs taken seriously. Mixed-ability teaching in first year; setting thereafter. Classes on the large side: 30 in the first year, gradually tapering to average of 12 in the sixth form. Homework strictly monitored. Strong drama and music (recent production of *West Side Story* much admired locally); 2 choirs, brass band, orchestra, string ensemble etc. Huge range of clubs and societies (chess, Christian Union, computers, gardening, karate, model railways); regular pupil exchanges with France, Germany, Spain – and one planned with Japan. Generous support for charities.

The pupils Hard-working, courteous; very few disciplinary problems (truancy is rare). Backgrounds range from middle-class to very modest homes; many are children of teachers (always a good sign) and clergy. Good pastoral care system to ensure no one gets 'lost'; school council gives everyone a voice. Increasingly over-subscribed (serves the whole of the borough and beyond); no selection tests; priority to those with allegiance to a Christian church. Admission to the sixth form requires good GCSE grades.

Results GCSE: creditable 57% gain at least 5 grades A-C. A-level: 30% of entries graded A or B (slightly above the national average).

Destinations About 50% proceed from GCSE to A-level; 70% of these go on to higher education (4-6 a year to Oxbridge).

Sport Outstanding record, especially in basketball and soccer; other sports include hockey, netball, cricket, tennis, athletics, cross-country. Extensive playing fields; sports hall, swimming pool etc.

Remarks Impressive school; something for everyone; first-rate head.

CARDINAL VAUGHAN

89 Addison Road,
London W14 8BZ
Tel (071) 603 8478

Comprehensive (grant-maintained) •
Roman Catholic • Boys (plus girls in sixth form) • Ages 11-18 • 630 pupils • 155 in sixth form (68% boys)
Head: Anthony Pellegrini, 51, appointed 1976.

Well-run school catering for a wide range of abilities; strong religious base; high academic standards; good music and art.

Background Founded 1914 as a memorial to

Cardinal Vaughan (who built Westminster Cathedral). Originally fee-paying; became a voluntary-aided grammar school 1948, went comprehensive 1977; grant-maintained since 1990 (following a threat to close the sixth form). Slightly gloomy, dilapidated Victorian building plus functional 1960s block and later additions on a cramped site in leafy Holland Park.

Atmosphere Happy, vibrant, very well disciplined; Roman Catholicism and Christian values absolutely fundamental. School makes no bones about aiming for excellence and gives lots of help to those with special needs. Supportive parents; loyal Old Boys.

The head Here all his working life (after reading history at London School of Economics); head of the lower school 1963; deputy head 1969. Unmarried and clearly dedicated to the school; constantly about the place, knows all the children (on playground duty every lunchtime); teaches liberal studies and religious education. Gentle, mild-mannered, approachable; always wears an academic gown and encourages staff to set the same example. Great music lover: takes credit for building up the school's music to its current high standard.

The teaching Generally formal, traditional, structured; every lesson starts with the sign of the cross, every classroom contains a crucifix, often referred to. Dedicated, well-qualified staff, most appointed by present head. Large, lively classes (some over 30 and crammed); pupils streamed by academic ability; emphasis on foundations, grammar, spelling. More able take Latin from third year and science as 3 separate subjects; newly refurbished labs; numbers taking science at A-level increasing. Greek taught out of school hours; some go on to take classics at university. Well-established design/technology; first-rate art; religious education compulsory throughout. Regular homework, rigorously monitored; excellent library. Very good music: 2 orchestras, 3 choirs, one of which, the Schola Cantorum, regularly tours abroad. Lots of clubs: chess, computers, model railway (popular refuge at lunchtime, particularly for juniors). Regular language trips to France.

The pupils Friendly, responsive; wide range of abilities and social backgrounds; membership of Roman Catholic Church the common factor. Truancy rate negligible; pupils sent home if incorrectly dressed. Catchment area extends to Hillingdon and Richmond; school full to capacity and always over-subscribed.

Results (1992) GCSE: creditable 68% gained at least 5 grades A-C. A-level: 31% of entries graded A or B.

Destinations 65% stay for A-levels (most of the rest go elsewhere to take vocational courses which the school cannot currently offer); most of these proceed to higher education (2 or 3 a year to Oxbridge).

Sport Chiefly soccer, rugby, rowing; regular Saturday-morning matches against other schools. Facilities include good gym for basketball, volleyball; playing fields at Twickenham.

Remarks First-rate comprehensive; highly recommended.

CATERHAM
Harestone Valley,
Caterham,
Surrey CR3 6YA
Tel (0883) 343028

Independent • Boys (plus girls in sixth form) • Day and boarding • Ages 13-18 (plus associated prep school) • 440 pupils (73% day) • 184 in sixth form (73% boys) • Fees, £4,935 day; £9,060-£9,615 boarding Head: Stephen Smith, 57, appointed 1974.

Solid academic school; good results.

Background Founded 1811 in Lewisham for the sons of Congregational ministers; strong links remain with the United Reformed Church. Moved 1884 to present attractive 80-acre site at the foot of the North Downs; 3-storey red-brick Victorian buildings plus many later additions, including fine new library. Became fully independent with the abolition of Direct Grant status in 1976.

Atmosphere Unashamedly academic ('our overall objective is A-level success and higher education entry'); firmly disciplined ('lateness for class, unruly behaviour, poor manners and a poor standard of dress will be punished by the award of lines; the accumulation of 400 lines results in a Housemaster's Detention'). Religious worship compulsory. Dormitories have been reduced in size by partitioning but boarding accommodation is in need of refurbishment.

The head Knows his pupils well, works his staff hard; has a reputation as a perfectionist. Teaches general studies to the sixth form. Was captain of rugby at Cambridge, played for England.

The teaching Fairly traditional in style. National curriculum largely adopted; particular strengths in French, German, Latin, art, design/technology. All pupils streamed by ability; additional setting in most subjects; some extra help for dyslexics. Average class size 20, reducing to 9 in the sixth form. Choice of 19 subjects at A-level. Strong drama and music; orchestras plus many smaller ensembles; a quarter learn an instrument; good facilities for concerts and individual practice. Community service includes visiting a hospice and working with the mentally and physically handicapped. Regular language exchanges to France and Germany.

The pupils Most from professional backgrounds but 25% receive substantial help with fees; 40% of boarders are expatriates or foreign nationals. 85% of senior school's intake comes from the associated prep school; entry by tests in English, maths, verbal reasoning; minimum IQ 110.

Results GCSE: 85% gain at least 5 grades A-C. A-level (1992): 50% of entries graded A or B.

Destinations Virtually all stay on for A-levels and proceed to higher education (3 to Oxbridge in 1991).

Sport Chiefly rugby, hockey, cricket; others include athletics, swimming, golf, shooting, tennis, squash, badminton, cross-country, karate, netball. Good playing fields but heated indoor pool dates from 1889 and the gym is also showing signs of age.

Remarks Good all round.

CAVENDISH
Warners End Road,
Hemel Hempstead,
Hertfordshire HP1 3DW
Tel (0442) 254566

Comprehensive • Co-educational • Ages 11-18 • 1,100 pupils (equal numbers of girls and boys) • 190 in the sixth form Head: Michael Griffin, mid-40s, appointed 1992.

Large, friendly 'flag-ship' comprehensive on northern edge of Hemel Hempstead. Caters for full ability range; respectable results; heavily over-subscribed. Exceptional parental and community involvement.

Background Founded 1959 as a technical grammar school. Mainly 1960s buildings on somewhat crowded site; some new classroom and technology blocks; further (much needed) improvements planned. Spacious sixth-form centre in own grounds.

Atmosphere Enthusiastic, warm, considerate towards others (sixth-formers regularly spend free time helping younger pupils). Meticulous pastoral care combats daunting size; no one need feel lost for long. Lots of humour and spontaneity.

The head Quietly spoken, perceptive, friendly; consults widely; aims to run a genuinely comprehensive school; has a firm hand on the tiller (first headship at 37).

The teaching Stimulating, unashamedly 'pupil-centred'; children encouraged to question and criticise. No streaming by ability; setting only in maths and French. Extra help in small groups for those who need it. Well-qualified staff of 70 (just over half women); low turnover. Well-equipped classrooms; lots of computers. Good music (20 learn an instrument); 2 orchestras, band, smaller instrumental groups. Ambitious programme of visits; field trips to Yorkshire, Loire Valley; pupil exchanges with German school.

The pupils Friendly, polite, articulate. Largely from immediate neighbourhood but many from further afield. Home backgrounds: farming, professional, technical, commercial. Wide ability range but neither least able nor most able lose out. Rules clearly understood and accepted; school uniform insisted upon (except in sixth form, where moderate dress styles are the norm); truancy not a problem. 250 apply annually for 180 places (local authority controls admissions).

Results (1991) GCSE: 45% gained at least 5 grades A-C. A level: 32% of entries graded at A or B. Good results in vocational exams.

Destinations 58% stay on after 16 for 1-year courses or A-levels; rest into jobs or further training.

Sport Excellent facilities (community use encouraged): heated indoor swimming pool, fully equipped gym, all-weather pitches, athletics track, cricket square, tennis courts etc. Plenty of Saturday games. Regular representation at county level in soccer, rugby, netball and, especially, table tennis.

Remarks Hard-working, successful school.

CENTRAL NEWCASTLE HIGH

Eskdale Terrace,
Newcastle-upon-Tyne NE2 4DS
Tel (091) 281 1768

Independent ● Girls ● Day ● Ages 11-18 ●
580 pupils ● 150 in sixth form ● Fees,
£3,444
Head: Mrs Angela Chapman, 50s,
appointed 1984.

Well-deserved reputation for academic excellence; good results; first-rate art.

Background Founded 1895 by Girls' Public Day School Trust; pioneered the entry of women into the professions in the North (Old Girls range from doctors to airline pilots). Rambling Victorian premises in a terraced backwater close to the city centre; first-rate labs, well-equipped language rooms, stately library, pleasant airy classrooms; music block under construction.

Atmosphere Effervescent, bustling; excellent rapport between staff and pupils (who stand when visitors enter the room). An air of confidence bred by success.

The head Shrewd, energetic, decisive. Priorities are academic success and ensuring that girls leave confident, self-disciplined and with a sense of their own worth. Married with a grown-up family; plays tennis; explores the battlefields of the Western Front.

The teaching Thorough; tending to the formal; fair amount of traditional chalk-and-talk, enlivened by discussion and questioning; particularly good classics, modern languages, history, geography, art. Mature, dedicated staff (most appointed by present head). Academic curriculum; all do 2 years' Latin; choice of French or German; Greek, Spanish, Russian also on offer. Technology less well developed. Setting by ability in maths, modern languages; class sizes 24-28. Choice of 19 subjects at A-level (sixth-form entry requires at least 6 GCSEs at grade B); more than half do at least 1 science; art (housed in a converted synagogue) flourishes; 'general interest' course offers philosophy, Arabic, cookery, sports studies etc. Lots of drama and music; busy extra-curricular programme; clubs, debates, rehearsals in every nook and cranny.

The pupils Bright, enthusiastic, unreservedly pleased to be here. Two-thirds enter from associated junior school; rest after tests and interview (head looks for a 'certain spark'). Vast catchment area. Some assisted places and scholarships.

Results GCSE: 95% gain at least 5 grades A–C. A-level (1992): 55% of entries graded A or B.

Destinations Most stay on for A-levels; 90% of these proceed to higher education (10 a year to Oxbridge).

Sport Strong netball, hockey, tennis plus a range of minority sports. Playing fields some distance away.

Remarks Stylish, well-run school for able, ambitious girls; possibly not for shrinking violets. Good value; highly recommended.

CHANNING
Highgate,
London N6 5HF
Tel (081) 340 2328

Independent • Girls • Day • Ages 5-18 • 444 pupils (300 in senior school) • 56 in sixth form • Fees, £2,994-£4,545
Head: Mrs Isabel Raphael, 53, appointed 1984.

Small, effective school; improving academically.

Background Founded 1885 'for the daughters of Unitarian ministers and others' (church links remain). 3½-acre site at the top of Highgate Hill; mixture of attractive 18th-century buildings and 1980s functional; new, well-designed sixth-form centre.

Atmosphere Friendly, business-like; past reputation for turning out 'young ladies'

supplanted by a growing emphasis on academic standards.

The head First-rate; dedicated, professional (with a formal and at times formidable manner). Educated at Cheltenham Ladies' and Cambridge; first taught at Channing 20 years ago. Lived in Vietnam, Paris, New York; formerly head of classics at City of London Girls'. Keen that all should go on to higher education; aims to make the school less remote from the local community.

The teaching Broad curriculum; music, art, design, computing compulsory for first 3 years in senior school; setting by ability in maths and French from third year. English teaching particularly good; science much improved; classical Greek offered to A-level. Class sizes 26, reducing to 20 for GCSE and fewer in the sixth form. High level of individual attention – no one allowed to fall by the wayside. Lots of homework. Specialist help for dyslexics in junior school. Regular pupil exchanges with France, Germany, Spain. Much music and drama in conjunction with Highgate *(qv)*.

The pupils Well-mannered (not a school for the flamboyantly rebellious); varied races and creeds. About half the 11+ entry come from the junior school (but admission is not automatic); rest equally from state and independent sectors. Tests in English and maths; potential and ability to think more important than a polished performance. Utilitarian uniform (below the sixth form) of dark brown skirts and jerseys. No assisted places but some scholarships and bursaries.

Results GCSE (1991): 91% gained at least 5 grades A–C. A-level (1992): remarkable 73% of entries graded A or B (an exceptionally good year).

Destinations Numbers staying on for A-levels fluctuate; two-thirds proceed to higher education.

Sport Not the school's strongest point but there is enough scope for the enthusiastic. 7 tennis courts within the school grounds; playing field near by.

Remarks Small, safe school with an excellent head.

CHARTERHOUSE
Goldalming,
Surrey GU7 2DN
Tel (0483) 426222

Independent • Boys (plus girls in sixth form) • Boarding and some day • Ages 13-18 • 698 pupils (88% boys; 96% boarding) • 330 in sixth form (70% boys) • Fees, £10,800 boarding; £8,900 day Head: Peter Attenborough, late-50s, appointed 1982 (retires August 1993).

First-rate school; excellent teaching and exam results; superb facilities. Music, drama, cricket, football all equally good.

Background Founded in the City in 1611 by Thomas Sutton, money-lender (known to his contemporaries as Croesus); moved to beautiful 200-acre site in Godalming 1872. Regarded by the Victorians as one of the 9 'great' public schools. (Old boys include Addison and Steele, John Wesley, Thackeray, Baden-Powell, Vaughan Williams, Robert Graves.) Girls first admitted to sixth form 20 years ago; no plans to become fully co-educational.

Atmosphere Disciplined but friendly; powerful traditions; strong sense of family and mutual trust. Exuberant Victorian buildings carefully modernised; striking 1970s boarding houses; spacious new design/technology centre; Gothic brick chapel and library worth a cultural detour. Housemasters have a high degree of autonomy: some houses sporty, others musical; most pupils have own study.

The head Classicist; educated at Christ's Hospital and Cambridge. Was head of classics at Uppingham then head of Sedbergh. Grown-up family; wife, Sandy, plays a full part in school life.

The teaching Generally outstanding. Most pupils take 8 or 9 GCSEs (English, maths, French a year early). Broadly based curriculum with plenty of options. Scholars and other bright pupils taught separately from the start. Regular grading system keeps all up to the mark. Choice of 20 subjects at A-level. Departments open 7 days a week for abundant project work (too much, say some parents). 20 plays a year in Ben Travers Theatre; good music (resident composer); fashion shows; charity concerts; annual international poetry festival etc, etc.

The pupils Charming, happy, expect to do well. Most from Home Counties; about 100 live abroad. Sixth-form girls – mostly from single-sex boarding schools – value the 'university-like' freedom. (They belong to boys' houses but live out with teachers' families or friends of the school.) Entry at 13+ by scholarship examination or Common Entrance; lists close 2 years ahead; early registration advised. Up to 12 foundation scholarships a year, assisted places, 7 scholarships in sixth form.

Results GCSE: 100% gain at least 5 grades A-C. A-level (1992): very creditable 66% of entries graded A or B.

Destinations Over 90% proceed to higher education (30 a year to Oxbridge); about half take a 'gap year'.

Sport Every interest catered for; good cricket and football; 9-hole golf course; climbing and pot-holing at residential centre in Derbyshire.

Remarks Traditional public school; fine all-round education.

CHATHAM GIRLS' GRAMMAR
Rainham Road,
Chatham,
Kent ME5 7EH
Tel (0634) 851262

Grammar (grant-maintained) • Girls •
Ages 11-18 • 576 pupils • 118 in sixth form
Head: Mrs Ingeborg Watson, 40,
appointed 1991.

Selective; over-subscribed; long tradition of academic success.

Background Founded 1907; moved to present red-brick site 1913; became a grammar school after the 1944 Education Act.

Atmosphere Situated in a densely populated urban area at the top of Chatham Hill. Facilities modernised over the years but recent expansion has led to a rash of temporary huts. Paintwork sorely neglected inside and out; grant-maintained status (achieved 1992) should lead to improvements.

The head Previously deputy head of a grammar school in Bromley. Teaches 5 periods a week (history, economics, general studies) to the youngest and oldest pupils.

The teaching Full national curriculum; particular strengths in English and maths. No streaming (within fairly narrow ability band). All girls expected to take 9 GCSEs. 3 separate sciences on offer, also German and Latin. Lots of homework; enriched curriculum for exceptionally able; physically handicapped catered for. 40 staff (25 men); class sizes 26-30 (12 in sixth form). Good music; a third learn an instrument. Work experience or work shadowing for lower-sixth (some stay with French families and help at local primary schools). Wide range of extra-curricular activities: chess, debating, Duke of Edinburgh award scheme, community service in children's ward of a local hospital.

The pupils Top 25% of the ability range; mixed social backgrounds. (NB: passing the 11+ does not secure automatic entry; siblings and proximity to school taken into account; volume of parental appeals has led to the recent expansion.) Main catchment area: Gillingham, Chatham; also Rochester and Strood.

Results (1992) GCSE: 84% gained at least 5 grades A-C. A-level: disappointing 26% of entries graded A or B (has been – and ought to be – much higher).

Destinations Over half to higher education (1 or 2 to Oxbridge); rest to further education or jobs.

Sport Hockey, netball plus (unusually for girls) soccer and rugby. Limited on-site facilities (small gym, ageing tennis courts) but swimming, badminton, squash at local sports centre.

Remarks Traditional grammar school; impressive range of extra-curricular activities.

CHEADLE HULME
Claremont Road,
Cheadle Hulme,
Cheshire SK8 6EF
Tel (061) 485 4142

Independent • Co-educational • Day and boarding • Ages 7-18 • 1,100 pupils (equal numbers of boys and girls; 90% day) • 240 in sixth form • Fees, £2,700-£3,360 day; £3,900 boarding Head: Donald Wilkinson, 37, appointed 1990.

Good academically but not obsessed with exams. Everyone expected to participate fully in and out of the classroom.

Background Mid-Victorian founders decreed it should be 'conducted on the most liberal principles and be open for the reception of both sexes'. Direct Grant until 1976. Buildings (set in 80 acres) range from high Victorian to purpose-built modern; slightly battered in parts. Brand-new block for modern languages and computing.

Atmosphere Warm, welcoming; friendly staff-pupil relations but the limits are well understood. Spread of buildings means much to-ing and fro-ing between lessons, but no hint of disorder. Small boarding house plays a vital part: means school is never closed. Boarders may invite day friends for tea; seniors help look after juniors; excellent nursing and medical facilities; spacious rooms, spotless corridors.

The head Historian with an Oxford research degree. Open, modest, courteous style; a thinker but not a pedant; delegates widely. Keen to stress all-round – not just academic – development of pupils. Formerly taught at Manchester Grammar. Married, 2 children; wife, a GP, lives on campus.

The teaching Well-qualified staff of 110 (roughly equal numbers of men and women). Hard work emphasised, but not all traditional chalk-and-talk; teachers invite pupils to question and speculate. Setting in maths and French from third year, otherwise mixed-ability. Class sizes vary from 30 in first year to 7-8 in sixth form. Sensible, no-nonsense approach to discipline, without being threatening. Regular homework. Large, well-stocked, much-used library. Good music; more than 20 learn an instrument (lessons £76 extra a term); 5 choirs, 3 orchestras, 2 wind bands. Astonishing range of extra-curricular activities: mahjong, beekeeping, canoeing, debating, philosophy, Amnesty International. (Only a dedicated staff could sustain such a rich and varied programme.)

The pupils Lively, articulate; mainly from professional, middle-class families but also more modest backgrounds (150 assisted places). Few discipline problems; all wear traditional uniform; sixth-formers set good example. Entry at 7, 8, 9, 11 or 13; school sets own tests; boarders can take Common Entrance at 11; no IQ test. Sixth-form entry requires minimum of 6 GCSE grades C or above.

Results GCSE: 97% gain at least 5 grades A-C. A-level (1992): 56% of entries graded A or B.

Destinations 85% stay on into the sixth form; about 90% of these go on to higher education (12 a year to Oxbridge).

Sport Excellent facilities, including swimming pool, fully-equipped gym, extensive playing fields. Cricket, hockey, rugby, netball (11 teams), lacrosse, tennis.

Remarks Highly regarded school; competitive entry; emphasis on self-reliance, concern for others, giving of one's best. Young, vigorous head likely to lead it on to even better things.

CHELMSFORD COUNTY HIGH
Broomfield Road,
Chelmsford,
Essex CM1 1RW
Tel (0245) 352592

Grammar (grant-maintained) • Girls •
Ages 11-18 • 669 pupils • 200 in sixth form
Head: Mrs Bernice McCabe, late-30s,
appointed 1990.

Successful, highly selective school; excellent music and sport.

Background Founded 1906 'to offer the girls of Essex a broad education'. Solid Victorian buildings plus dilapidated 1950s extension on pleasant 12-acre site near the town centre. Became grant-maintained September 1992.

Atmosphere Cheerful, busy. Big emphasis on encouragement, praise, making everyone feel special. Prospectus's claim that this is 'a forward-looking school which retains a strong belief in traditional values' fairly states the position. Impressive 98% attendance at parents' evenings.

The head Read English at Bristol (and teaches it to first-years and sixth-formers). Keen on democracy (masses of committees and working parties).

The teaching Traditional: chalk-and-talk; desks in rows; emphasis on competition (tests and results are important here); pupils expect

– and are expected – to do well. All do French in first year, add German in second year, Latin in third year. Setting by ability in maths, French, 3 sciences; all expected to take 10 GCSEs; choice of 18 subjects at A-level. Old-fashioned labs due for an overhaul. Long-serving staff of 44 (80 women). Lots of high-quality music; 60 take part in choirs, orchestras, chamber groups. Good art (in cramped accommodation). Regular exchanges with schools in France and Germany; work experience ranges from Paris hospital to North Sea oil rig.

Pupils Bright (top 5% of the ability range); confident; quietly behaved (without being docile); truancy non-existent. Mainly from professional/managerial homes within a radius of 20 miles (lots of school buses). Admission by county's 11+ selection procedure; entry to sixth form requires 7 GCSEs, grade B or above.

Results (1992) GCSE: 99% gained at least 5 grades A–C. A-level: creditable 51% of entries graded A or B.

Destinations All stay on for A-levels; impressive 98% of these to higher education (including 15 a year to Oxbridge).

Sport Good hockey (county and national players), athletics, swimming (heated indoor pool).

Remarks Hard-working school; becoming less old-fashioned.

CHELTENHAM
Bath Road,
Cheltenham,
Gloucestershire GL53 7LD
Tel (0242) 513540

Independent ● Boys (plus girls in sixth form) ● Boarding and day ● Ages 13-18 ● 566 pupils (two-thirds boarding) ● 260 in sixth form (55 girls, rising to up to 100 from September 1992) ● Fees, £10,425 boarding; £7,875 day
Head: Peter Wilkes, 51, appointed 1990.

Stately surroundings; High Church foundation; good all round.

Background Celebrated 150th anniversary in 1991; oldest of the Victorian public schools (founded for the 'sons of gentlemen'); long tradition of scholarship and service. Big building programme under way (technology block, theatre, sports hall, girls' boarding house etc).

Atmosphere Classical English view across the cricket field towards the spires of the Cotswold-stone chapel and hall: sets the tone.

The head Enthusiastic, humorous. Oxford classicist; taught in Zimbabwe and Iran; housemaster at Rugby. Married, 3 children; has a home in the south of France. Keen on European dimension; introduced the International Baccalaureate (September '92) as an alternative to A-levels.

The teaching Wide range of styles but leaning towards the less formal. 65 staff (5 women); all well-qualified graduates (half Oxbridge); average age 33 'and falling'. National curriculum-plus; most boys take 10-11 GCSEs. Particular strengths in maths, science (15 laboratories), technology (headed by successful electronics inventor who comes to school in a Porsche); also English, classics, modern languages (full satellite links). Setting in most subjects; academic progress closely monitored. Class sizes range from 20 in early years to 8-10 in sixth form. Library both imposing and well-stocked. Strong music and drama; plays and concerts throughout the year; excellent singing in chapel. Plenty of extra-curricular activities, including cadet force (used to be one of the leading military schools), community service.

The pupils Broad ability range (IQs 100-140+) but strong competition for day places (scholarships and bursaries available). Largely from professional and business backgrounds; also farming and the Services; many have family ties; most live within 1 hour's drive. Formal but friendly relations with staff. Strongly competitive house system. (8 houses, small dormitories in early years, then study-bedrooms, known as 'pits'.)

Results GCSE (1991): 96% gained at least 5 grades A-C. A-level (1992): 50% of entries graded A or B.

Destinations Over 90% take A-levels; 90% of these proceed to higher education (17-18 a year to Oxbridge, girls doing particularly well).

Sport 3 half-days set aside each week; professional coaching in cricket, hockey, squash, rackets, tennis. College regularly fields 18 rugby XVs, 17 hockey XIs, 12 cricket XIs, 12 rowing VIIIs. Excellent facilities include first-class cricket ground, new indoor pool, all-weather hockey pitches and tennis courts, fully equipped boat house at Tewkesbury.

Remarks Scholarly, orderly school in beautiful buildings and grounds.

CHELTENHAM LADIES'

Cheltenham,
Gloucestershire GL50 3EP
Tel (0242) 520691

Independent ● Girls ● Boarding and day ●
Ages 11-18 ● 850 pupils (80% boarding) ●
260 in sixth form ● Fees, £10,110
boarding; £6,420 day
Principal: Miss Enid Castle, mid-50s,
appointed 1987.

Distinguished school; all-round excellence.

Background Founded 1854 in the belief that the 'education of girls is of no less importance than that of boys'. Anxious to avoid blue-stocking image, founders added that a girl's intellectual powers were to be cultivated to 'fit her as a wife, mother, mistress and friend, the natural companion and helpmeet for man'. Current head puts it differently: 'We assume every girl will have a career. Women who don't have the qualifications and ability to earn a decent living are very vulnerable to being exploited by men.'

Atmosphere Fortress-like Victorian Gothic building: marble corridors, stained glass, high seriousness. Staff and girls welcoming, friendly, unaffected. 11 pleasant boarding houses within walking distance.

The head Historian; part-time magistrate. Taught in state schools (also in Kenya and Bahamas); her third headship. Quick to dispel any notion that the college is posh or élitist ('I'm really not interested in producing young ladies – I want pupils to leave here as capable and assertive young women.'). A spinster like her 8 predecessors (who include the formidable Dorothea Beale, principal for 48 years and founder of St Hilda's College, Oxford). Enthusiastic traveller (has seen the sun rise from the top of Mt Kilimanjaro).

The teaching Generally formal in style; lively lessons; keen class participation. Broad curriculum; strong science (16 laboratories); also classics, modern languges (German, Russian, Spanish, Italian). No streaming but setting in maths, French, Latin. High standards of work throughout; plenty of prep. First-class staff of 94 (a third men – 'The girls need to see that men can work under women'); also 25 part-timers, 40 visiting music teachers and 400 support staff. Class sizes 15-20; 10-12 in sixth form. Music a major feature; almost all play an instrument; several orchestras, wind band, ensembles, choirs. Girls encouraged to participate in wide variety of clubs and societies; community service; Duke of Edinburgh's award scheme. Extensive programme of visits at home and abroad.

The pupils Out-going, well-mannered, self-assured; strong advocates of single-sex education. Distinctive green uniform worn with pride. Most from business and professional backgrounds; many have family ties with the school; 15% from overseas (both expatriate and foreign). All from upper end of the ability range (11-year-olds need to score 70% at Common Entrance); some assisted places.

Results (1991) GCSE: 98% gained at least 5 grades A-C. A-level: impressive 61% of entries graded A or B.

Destinations Over 90% continue into the sixth form; 90% of these proceed to higher education (15-20 a year to Oxbridge).

Sport Extensive playing fields; championship-standard tennis courts; superb new £1.6-million sports centre. Excellent tennis and hockey; also riding, rowing, golf etc.

Remarks Fine school providing a broadly-based, high quality education .

CHENDERIT
Archery Road,
Middleton Cheney,
Banbury OX17 2QR
Tel (0295) 711567

Comprehensive • Co-educational • Ages 11-18 • 946 pupils (equal numbers of girls and boys) • 174 in sixth form
Head: David Martin, 45, appointed 1985.

Effective 'progressive' comprehensive; first-rate teaching.

Background Opened 1979; functional, single-storey, purpose-built premises plus later additions in a pleasant rural setting; buildings rather grim inside.

Atmosphere Emphasis on co-operation and consideration rather than competition; staff bend over backwards to make everyone feel equally valued. To ensure all are stretched, pupils are required to set their own attainment targets, review their performance and draw up individual action plans; relations with staff are excellent. No prefects: pupils expected to accept responsibility for themselves and others at all ages. Parents welcomed at any time; many help out with reading and other activities. Adequate food (but high in fat and sugar).

The head Restless, innovative, strong on educational theory. Studied African history at London; taught at a comprehensive in Hertfordshire, where he rose from probationer to deputy head in 3 years; became head of a failing school in Kettering and saved it from closure. When he came here, miscreants were required to line up with their noses to the gym wall: his vision was of a school in which a 'democratic education' would be the right of every pupil. Staff say he did a 'brilliant job' in turning the school round. Teaches 6 subjects at A-level (including philosophy, sociology, psychology and history) and patrols the lunch queue; pupils seem completely at ease with him. Married, 3 children.

The teaching Lively, well-prepared lessons in a variety of styles. Staff are youthful (average age 30), cheerful and hard-working (15 of the

55 have taken MAs recently). Standard national curriculum; choice between German and French; first-rate art; no child can leave without becoming computer-literate. Some setting by ability in science, languages and maths; extra help for those with special needs (but that does not include the gifted); class sizes average 25-30. Most take 10 GCSEs; sixth-formers choose between A-levels and vocational courses. Very good library. Well-run careers service; all do 2 weeks' work experience. Regular exchanges with schools in France, Germany, Japan and Poland.

The pupils High-spirited, enthusiastic; average attendance rate 93%. Drawn from more than 30 primary schools; 20% have a reading age 2 years below their chronological age. Navy blue and cherry red uniform; school council voted recently to allow girls to wear trousers and all to wear sweatshirts. School is 25% over-subscribed.

Results (1992) GCSE: creditable 51% gained at least 5 grades A-C. A-level: 36% of entries graded A or B.

Destinations 75% continue into the sixth form; 60% of these proceed to higher education (about 2 a year to Oxbridge).

Sport Usual range; participation compulsory. Facilities include playing fields, sports hall, 8 tennis courts, 4 netball courts but no swimming pool.

Remarks Warm, friendly school; no child will feel out of his/her depth (pupils here are very quick to notice the use of 'incorrect' language).

CHETHAM'S
Long Millgate,
Manchester M3 1SB
Tel (061) 834 9644

Independent • Co-educational • Boarding and day • Ages 8-18 • 265 pupils (65% girls; 85% boarding) • 100 in sixth form • Fees, £13,323 boarding; £10,314 day (all qualify for means-tested Education Department grant); £4,125 for choristers (half paid by Manchester Cathedral)
Head: Rev Peter Hullah, 42, appointed September 1992.

Musical power-house with an international reputation; offers excellent all-round education.

Background Founded as a charity school in 1653 by Sir Humphrey Chetham, local merchant; became independent in 1952 and a music school in 1969 (following publication of a report that pointed to the lack of national provision for musically gifted children). Now the biggest of its kind in the country. City-centre site next to the cathedral (for which it is the choir school); 17th-century buildings with many later additions in varying styles ranged around an Oxford-like quadrangle.

Atmosphere Warm, busy; devotion to musical excellence almost religious in its intensity. Powerful sense of tradition (pupils wear Blue Coat dress on founder's day) and common purpose. Excellent boarding accommodation; friendly, relaxed relationships.

The head New appointment. Educated at Bradford Grammar; read theology at King's College, London; taught in Uganda; returned to train for the priesthood; served as chaplain at Sevenoaks and King's, Canterbury. Youthful, enthusiastic; not a musician; keen to stress that Chetham's offers a wide – and not just a musical – education. Married, 2 children.

The teaching Full academic curriculum – even though a third of the timetable is devoted to music. GCSE subjects include Latin, French, German, computer studies, drama, 3 separate sciences; 17 A-level courses, including sociology, Japanese. Dedicated teaching staff of 35 (18 men, 17 women) plus 122 part-time music tutors (many drawn from leading northern orchestras) who teach pretty well every musical instrument known to man on a one-to-one basis (97 practice rooms). School also offers courses in composition, conducting, singing, and Alexander Technique (for reducing tension and stage fright). Extra-curricular activities include regular trips to the countryside, youth hostelling, sailing etc.

The pupils Cheerful, articulate. Wide range of social backgrounds; all musically gifted and academically bright; all seem to accept that a gift means nothing unless nurtured and developed by professional guidance and systematic practice. Natural, spontaneous relationships between boys and girls (no pin-ups in the boys' rooms – perhaps the presence of real girls makes paper ones unnecessary). Entry at 8, 11 or 16; no academic requirements; sole criteria are musical ability and potential; 600 apply annually for 55 places.

Results GCSE: 73% gain at least 5 grades A-C. A-level (1992): creditable 52% of entries graded A or B.

Destinations Nearly all do A-levels; two-thirds of these proceed to music colleges, rest to higher education.

Sport No playing fields and no games against other schools but plenty of PE, indoor sports and swimming.

Remarks Remarkable school; gets the best out of highly gifted children.

CHICHESTER GIRLS' HIGH

Stockbridge Road,
Chichester,
West Sussex PO19 2EB
Tel (0243) 787014

Comprehensive • Girls • Ages 11-19 • 1,250 pupils • 196 in sixth form
Head: Mrs Lyn Parkin, mid-50s, appointed 1980.

Popular, somewhat old-fashioned school; traditional values emphasised.

Background Comprehensive since 1972, when it merged with a former grammar school. Divided between 2 sites, an uncomfortable half mile apart (consolidation plans postponed owing to fall in property values).

Atmosphere Protective, disciplined, good-mannered; appeals to conservative parents seeking single-sex state education.

The head Historian; formerly head of a comprehensive in Sheffield. Efficient, approachable; big emphasis on courtesy. Has a daughter in the school.

The teaching Formal, traditional (demonstration lessons at parents' evenings); most classes streamed by ability; strict homework. Rather distant relations between staff and pupils. Good modern languages (regular exchanges with schools in France, Spain, Germany). Some A-level courses shared with adjacent boys' school (impressive choice of 27 subjects); good vocational courses with local technology college. Fine new drama suite (music block to come); 3 orchestras, several choirs.

The pupils All abilities from all backgrounds. Late developers, socially: sixth-formers (on separate site) noticeably more relaxed, self-sufficient, poised. Main catchment area Chichester and surrounding villages but some from across Hampshire border – an area in which a significant number of girls go to independent schools. Over-subscribed, nonetheless: priority to those living near by and to siblings.

Results (1991) GCSE: 52% gained at least 5 grades A-C. A-level (1992): 42% of entries graded A or B.

Destinations 60% proceed to sixth form (remainder into training or jobs) but only half take A-levels; modest 30% of these go on to higher education (a few each year to Oxbridge).

Sport Extensive playing fields on main site. Good squash, hockey, gymnastics, swimming. All-weather hockey pitch and canoe centre shared with boys' school.

Remarks Safe school; good (and improving) exam results in many subjects.

CHRIST'S HOSPITAL
Horsham,
West Sussex RH13 7LS
Tel (0403) 211293

Independent ● Co-educational ● Boarding ● Ages 11-18 ● 794 pupils (65% boys) ● 189 in sixth form ● Fees, £7,600 (but see below)
Head: Richard Poulton, early-50s, appointed 1987.

Public-school education for the less well-off and those who can demonstrate a boarding need; respectable results; first-rate art, music, drama.

Background Founded 1552 by Edward VI to educate the children of London's poor; the boys' section moved to monumental, red-brick, purpose-built premises on 1,200-acre estate 1902; girls followed 1985. Later additions include first-rate theatre and sports hall. Fees heavily subsidised by endowments and City rents: 'the people's public school'. Old Boys include Coleridge and Lamb.

Atmosphere Encrusted in tradition: pupils wear Tudor uniform (full-length Bluecoats, clerical bands, saffron socks), march into lunch behind military-style band. A strong sense of a community apart (accompanied in

the not-so-distant past by harsh discipline and widespread bullying). 16 boarding houses, many about as homely as station waiting rooms: dormitories vast and bleakly decorated, study areas extremely cramped (physical privations are said to enhance the bonds between pupils).

The head Has done much to break down the old regimented order but acknowledges that change is slow. Read history at Cambridge; taught at Bryanston for 14 years; formerly head of a small independent school in Gloucestershire. Writes history text books; keen on rowing. Married, 3 grown-up children.

The teaching Generally good; particular strengths in (combined) science, languages, English, history. GCSE options include Latin, Greek, Italian. Choice of 22 subjects at A-level; most do 3. Good art (5 artists-in-residence), drama and music; 2 orchestras, 3 bands, 5 choirs. Lots of extra-curricular activities; active cadet force, Duke of Edinburgh award scheme, community service.

The pupils Genuine social cross-section (wider than in most suburban comprehensives); many from London primary schools, ethnic minorities, one-parent families, Services, clergy. Prospectus notes that entrants need a 'certain minimum of self-confidence and a willingness to mix and make friends' and cannot expect the 'sheltered existence found in a small family group'. Complex admission procedures related to boarding need and parental income (which must be below a fixed amount at the time of entry); all candidates required to pass 11+ tests in English, maths, aptitude; places offered to those who perform best; about half are classified as 'well above average'. All fees paid on a means-related sliding scale, re-assessed annually.

Results GCSE: 95% gain at least 5 grades A-C (and most get 8). A-level (1992): creditable 55% of entries graded A or B.

Destinations 85% stay on for A-levels; about 80% of these proceed to higher education.

Sport Something for everyone: rugby, hockey, netball, cricket, tennis, athletics, swimming. Superb sports hall.

Remarks Not for the faint-hearted.

CIRENCESTER DEER PARK
Stroud Road,
Cirencester,
Gloucestershire GL7 1XB
Tel (0285) 653447

Comprehensive • Co-educational • Ages
11-16 • 996 pupils (roughly equal
numbers of girls and boys)
Head: David Crossley, mid-30s,
appointed 1991.

*Effective modern comprehensive; good
GCSE results.*

Background Opened as a comprehensive in
purpose-built premises 1966 (an amalgamation of 3 schools, including a grammar with
roots going back to the 13th century); lost its
sixth form (to a neighbouring tertiary college)
1991. Extensive recent additions on an attractive, well-maintained site.

Atmosphere Stimulating; staff and pupils
jointly committed to high academic standards
and good behaviour.

The head Energetic, enthusiastic. Read history at York; appointed deputy here 1989.
Teaches equivalent of 1 day a week.

The teaching Healthy mixture of didacticism
and 'active learning'. Hard-working staff, half
appointed in past 5 years. Pupils set by ability
in maths, science, languages; extra help for
those with special needs. Good computing,
design/technology (strong links with business
and industry); fine facilities for drama, music.
Regular language trips to France, Germany,
Spain; links with schools in India, Russia.

The pupils Confident, lively; half from Cirencester, rest from small rural primary schools.
School over-subscribed (240 apply for 193
places); priority to those living in the catchment area, siblings, geographical proximity.

Results (1991) GCSE: 49% gained at least 5
grades A-C.

Destinations More than 70% transfer to the
tertiary college to take A-levels or vocational
courses; up to 50% of these proceed to higher
education (3 or 4 a year to Oxbridge).

Sport Strong basketball, rugby, cricket; Saturday matches retained; extensive playing
fields but no sports hall or swimming pool.

Remarks Go-ahead, innovative school.

CITY OF LONDON BOYS'
Queen Victoria Street,
London EC4V 3AL
Tel (071) 489 0291

Independent • Boys • Day • Ages 10-18 •
850 pupils • 230 in sixth form • Fees
(1992-93), £5,349
Head: Bryan Bass, 58, appointed 1990.

*Successful academic school; good
results; strong music; fine facilities.*

Background Medieval foundation but present school dates from 1837; moved to present
superb modern premises 1989; compact
Thameside site with spectacular views of St
Paul's, surprisingly insulated from its busy
surroundings. Major funding by the Corporation of London; all governors are members of
the Common Council.

Atmosphere Orderly, purposeful, no-
nonsense; high energy levels contained by 'old
fashioned' discipline; decent behaviour insisted on. Boys on polite, easy terms with staff.
Good pastoral care system.

The head Has a relaxed, friendly approach –
and clear ideas about what he wants. Educated
at Wells Cathedral School and Oxford (read
English); taught extensively in state and independent schools, including 11 years at Manchester Grammar. Thoroughly committed to
the school's philosophy and character (pursuit
of excellence, good order, hard work) but has

made some changes, including abolishing streaming by ability in first 3 years and widening subject choice. Teaches 4 periods a week. Married, 3 grown-up children.

The teaching Lively, traditional: thorough grounding; regular testing; high standards of grammar, accuracy and presentation in written work. First-class staff of 83 (few women); many here a long time. Fairly broad curriculum for first 3 years; setting by ability in maths, French (some take GCSE a year early); no specific help for dyslexics (in practice, school not suitable). Very good science, taught as 3 separate subjects; all must do at least physics or chemistry. Most take 9 GCSEs; options include business French, electronics, technology. Computing taught only to first-years but widely used in other areas of the curriculum (97 screens). Impressive facilities throughout; average class size 21. Wide choice of A-levels, including 12 subjects at AS-level. Half-termly reports to parents giving grades for effort and achievement; full reports twice a year. Strong musical tradition; 2 choirs, 2 orchestras, chamber groups, wind band; termly drama productions in well-designed theatre; good art studios. Plenty of extra-curricular activities; all boys join cadet force or do community service. Regular language trips to Paris and Hamburg.

The pupils From a wide range of social, racial and religious backgrounds in a catchment area that extends as far as Sevenoaks and Welwyn Garden City. Many parents work in the City; most are 'first-time buyers' of independent education. Entry (predominantly from state primary schools) by competitive tests at 10, 11, 13; interview an important part of the selection process. School over-subscribed by about 4 to 1; ability range quite wide but all are bright. Entry to sixth-form requires a minimum of 6 GCSEs grades A-C and at least a B in intended A-level subjects. Some scholarships, assisted places.

Results GCSE: all gain at least 5 grades A-C. A-level (1992): impressive 67% of entries graded A or B.

Destinations 90 stay on for A-levels; 97% of these proceed to higher education (22 to Oxbridge in 1991).

Sport Wide range of options but not strongly competitive; playing fields 8 miles away. Main games: rugby, football, hockey, cricket, tennis; volleyball, basketball, badminton, swimming, water polo also on offer; cross-country run over Thames bridges. Facilities include fine sports hall and indoor pool.

Remarks Good all round; highly recommended.

CITY OF LONDON GIRLS'
Barbican,
London EC2Y 8BB
Tel (071) 628 0841

Independent • Girls • Day • Ages 7-18 • 646 pupils (542 in senior school) • 151 in sixth form • Fees, £4,473
Head: Lady France, 56, appointed 1986.

Strong academic school; first-rate teaching and results; fine facilities; good music.

Background Founded 1894 by William Ward, a coal merchant, who wanted the school to 'correspond, as near as may be' to City of London Boys' *(qv)*; City Corporation appoints the governing body. Moved to fine purpose-built premises in the heart of the Barbican 1969; later additions include superbly equipped design/technology centre; more building under way.

Atmosphere Busy, purposeful, not at all posh; school's aim is to produce 'mature young women with the confidence to play leading roles in the professions and business'. Facilities are first-rate; the site makes for an unusual and exciting atmosphere. Well-organised pastoral care system.

The head Energetic, charming. Educated at Oxford; taught at North London Collegiate; formerly deputy head of Bromley High. Able administrator; teaches study skills to younger girls. Married to a senior civil servant; 2 grown-up children.

The teaching Very professional; many long-serving staff. National curriculum-plus; 6 languages on offer, including German, Russian, Spanish; very good art (100% gained grade As at GCSE) and design/technology. Setting by ability in maths, science; average class size 26. A-level options include computing, home economics, theatre studies. Strong music: more than half learn an instrument (many of the music staff also teach at the nearby Guildhall School of Music and Drama); orchestra, choirs. Busy extra-curricular programme. Regular language exchanges with schools in France and Germany.

The pupils Bright, robust; a mixture of races and religions, mostly from North London. Entry at 7 and 11 by interview (each girl's application form has to be signed by a member of the Corporation) and tests; competition is severe (350 apply for 50 places at 11; 40% come from state schools). More than 100 assisted places.

Results GCSE: virtually all gain at least 5 grades A-C (60% gain at least 5 grade As). A-level (1992): creditable 64% of entries graded A or B.

Destinations Nearly all stay on for A-levels and proceed to higher education (7 or 8 a year to Oxbridge).

Sport Surprisingly strong. Facilities include magnificent indoor pool and gymnasium; outdoor space for tennis, netball, rounders. Badminton, fencing, football also on offer.

Remarks A school of real quality; highly recommended.

CLIFTON

College Road,
Clifton,
Bristol BS8 3JH
Tel (0272) 739187

Independent • Co-educational • Boarding and day • Ages 13-18 (plus associated prep school, *qv*) • 700 pupils (70% boys; 60% boarding) • 264 in sixth form • Fees, £10,320 boarding; £7,200 day
Head: Hugh Monro, 42, appointed 1990.

Sound school; first-rate teaching; fairly wide range of abilities; good drama and sport.

Background Founded 1862 by a group of distinguished Bristolians; beautiful collection of Victorian-Gothic buildings grouped round the inspiration for Sir Henry Newbolt's famous poem: *'There's a breathless hush in the Close tonight/Ten to make and the match to win/A bumping pitch and a blinding light/An hour to play and the last man in...'.* Fully co-educational since 1987; proportion of girls rising steadily.

Atmosphere Fine traditions live on in an able, friendly, happy community. First-rate boarding accommodation in large Victorian houses; Jewish boys have their own house and synagogue.

The head Confident, outgoing, open-minded. Educated at Rugby and Cambridge; has worked in industry and taught in America; formerly head of Worksop. Keen to widen school's horizons.

The teaching Mix of traditional chalk-and-talk and more progressive, project-based styles; some particularly gifted and charismatic teachers. Very good English (120 take A-levels and complete the course in 1 year); strong maths and science (scientist-in-residence); nearly all who do GCSE French get A grades; German, Spanish, Russian, Italian also on offer. First-rate drama in well-equipped theatre (Old Boys include Sir Michael Redgrave, Trevor Howard, John Cleese). Big emphasis on service and charitable work. Regular language exchanges with French schools.

The pupils Mostly from middle-class/professional backgrounds; fairly wide ability range; about a third are high-fliers. Admission by Common Entrance (minimum 50% mark required, but even that is negotiable); 85% join from the associated prep school, which is non-selective at ages 6-8.

Results GCSE: 95% gain at least 5 grades A-C. A-level (1992): 49% of entries graded A or B.

Destinations 80% stay on for A-levels; 85% of these proceed to higher education (23 to Oxbridge in 1991).

Sport Strong tradition, especially in cricket ('Play up, play up and play the game'). Facilities include 80 acres of playing fields 10 minutes away by bus. Rugby, hockey, tennis, squash, badminton, fencing, rowing also on offer.

Remarks Good all round; energetic new head.

CLIFTON HIGH
College Road,
Clifton,
Bristol BS8 3JD
Tel (0272) 730201

Independent • Girls (boys admitted to junior school from 1993) • Day and some boarding • Ages 3-18 • 836 pupils (92% day) • 112 in sixth form • Fees, £1,650-£4,275 (plus £3,525 boarding) Head: Mrs Joyce Walters, mid-50s, appointed 1985.

Traditional, fairly academic school; good facilities; strong sport.

Background Founded 1877; large Victorian premises in residential area close to the Downs; later additions include sixth-form centre, art and craft block.

Atmosphere Busy, friendly; strongly traditional. Well-organised pastoral care system. Good boarding accommodation: no more than 4 to a dormitory; sixth-formers have own rooms.

The head Read classics at Oxford. Radiates a commitment to academic excellence (still teaches Greek at A-level) and bemoans the anti-intellectualism of a TV-dominated culture. Sees competition as healthy and necessary; wants girls to feel proud of achievement rather than apologise for it. Good communicator; a PR-oriented chief executive.

The teaching Mostly formal in style; national curriculum implemented 'in spirit' (technology a recent innovation); science on offer as 3 separate subjects. Strong history, maths, classics. Good music: a third learn an instrument; lots of choral singing. Fine new facilities for art, including pottery and textiles. Successful Duke of Edinburgh award scheme.

The pupils Contented, unpressured; mostly from middle-class, professional backgrounds. Entry to junior school by interview; at 11 by tests in English, maths, verbal reasoning – similar to Common Entrance but no specific pass mark; not unduly selective. Some assisted places.

Results GCSE: 91% gain at least 5 grades A-C. A-level (1992): 46% of entries graded A or B.

Destinations 80% stay on for A-levels; nearly all of these proceed to higher education (3-6 a year to Oxbridge).

Sport A particular stength, especially tennis; county honours also in swimming, hockey and netball. Facilities include 10 acres of playing fields 5 minutes away by coach.

Remarks Good all round; becoming more competitive.

COLCHESTER COUNTY HIGH

Norman Way,
Colchester,
Essex CO3 3US
Tel (0206) 576973

Grammar • Girls • Ages 11-18 • 655 pupils
• 180 in sixth form
Head: Dr Aline Black, 56, appointed 1987.

Strong academic school; good teaching and results; lots of music.

Background Founded 1909; moved to present site and purpose-built premises 1958; lacks the space needed for more labs and better facilities for technology and music.

Atmosphere Busy, open, friendly; good relations between staff and pupils. Everything clean and in good order.

The head Strong leader. Read physics at Manchester; PhD in chemistry from Birkbeck; taught science at City of London Girls' for 10 years; worked as a local authority inspector; formerly head of a girls' grammar school in Kent. Believes firmly in single-sex education for girls. Married, no children.

The teaching Mainly traditional in style. Long-serving, well-qualified staff (6 have PhDs in science), 20 male. National curriculum-plus; science taught as 3 separate subjects; Latin, German, Spanish on offer. Girls streamed by ability in maths; classes of 20 for GCSE. Nearly all take 9 GCSEs and at least 3 A-levels from a choice of 20; maths, English and science the most popular. Lots of drama and music; a third learn an instrument; orchestra, choir. Regular language exchanges with schools in France and Germany.

The pupils Lively, confident, articulate; mostly from professional/middle-class backgrounds in a wide catchment area. Entry by local authority 11+.

Results (1992) GCSE: all gained at least 5 grades A-C. A-level: impressive 59% of entries graded A or B.

Destinations 80% stay on for A-levels (most of the rest go to sixth-form or further educa-

tion colleges); 85% of these proceed to higher education (about 6 a year to Oxbridge).

Sport Chiefly hockey, tennis, netball, athletics, gymnastics. On-site playing fields and indoor pool.

Remarks Very good all round.

COLFE'S

Horn Park Lane,
London SE12 8AW
Tel (081) 852 2283

Independent • Boys (plus girls in sixth form) • Day • Ages 11-18 (plus associated prep school) • 700 pupils • 200 in sixth form (80% boys) • Fees, £4,245
Head: Dr David Richardson, 46, appointed 1990.

Good all round; strong art, music, drama, sport.

Background Origins can be traced to 1494; re-founded 1652 by Rev Abraham Colfe to provide an education for 'pupils of good wit and capacity and apt to learn'; governors are the Leathersellers' Company, which funds scholarships and bursaries. Moved to present 18-acre site and purpose-built premises 1964; became independent 1977. Recent additions include £2-million sports complex.

Atmosphere Pleasant, relaxed, well-behaved.

The head Good leader; respected by staff. Keen to raise academic standards, particularly in the sixth form.

The teaching Broad curriculum; science taught as 3 separate subjects; choice of German, French, Russian; Latin on offer; computing still fairly rudimentary. Mixed-ability classes for first 2 years; setting in maths from third year; fast stream from fourth year; part-time specialist help for dyslexics. Most take 9 GCSEs, some 10 or 11. Average class size 20, reducing to 12 in sixth form. Choice of

20 subjects at A-level; special coaching for Oxbridge. Good art: large numbers take it for GCSE and A-level. Strong music; a third learn an instrument (24 visiting teachers); many choirs, orchestras, smaller ensembles. Well-supported Air Training Corps. Regular language exchanges to France, Germany, Russia.

The pupils Mostly from middle-class/professional backgrounds in wide south London catchment area. Entry to senior school by tests at 11+ and 13+ (Common Entrance not used); minimum IQ 112. Some scholarships, bursaries, assisted places.

Results GCSE: 85% gain at least 5 grades A-C. A-level (1992): rather modest 36% of entries graded A or B (has been higher).

Destinations Most stay on for A-levels and proceed to higher education (5 to Oxbridge in 1991).

Sport Major games: cricket, rugby, football; other activities include athletics, badminton, basketball, cross-country, golf, hockey, netball, sailing, squash, swimming, tennis. More than 30 acres of playing fields on 2 sites; superb sports hall and indoor pool.

Remarks Sound, well-run school.

COLLINGWOOD
Kingston Road,
Camberley,
Surrey GU15 4AE
Tel (0276) 64048

Comprehensive (grant-maintained) • Co-educational • Ages 12-18 (11-18 from September 1994) • 1,575 pupils (equal numbers of girls and boys) • 340 in sixth form
Head: Peter Halls-Dickerson, 55, appointed 1974.

First-rate, purposeful comprehensive; wide range of abilities and backgrounds; good results.

Background 1971 amalgamation of 2 secondary moderns and a grammar school on adjoining sites in the middle of a (mostly privately-owned) housing estate; 1960s buildings showing signs of considerable wear and tear; some classrooms in wooden huts; grounds somewhat neglected; pitches in a pretty poor state. Grant-maintained status should lead to all-round improvements.

Atmosphere Relaxed, happy, resourceful; a no-nonsense feel. Huge numbers of pupils move around the sprawling campus several times a day in an orderly fashion (but at a considerable cost in time). Good pastoral care system; children soon find their feet.

The head Strong personality; bluff exterior; believes passionately in comprehensive education. Went to a grammar school, read English at Oxford; taught at a succession of secondary moderns. Took over here 3 years after a difficult merger (80% secondary modern, 20% grammar, more than half the staff left) and has created what Her Majesty's Inspectors described in a recent report as a 'popular, successful, well-organised, efficient school achieving high academic standards'. Aims at excellence for all; insists happiness and confidence are fundamental to achievement. Married, 2 grown-up daughters (both were pupils here).

The teaching Varied styles; some formal.

Well-qualified staff, most appointed by present head. All pupils set by ability from the start to enable them to go at their own speed; needs of the most able and those with learning difficulties equally well catered for; progress regularly assessed and setting adjusted accordingly. Broad curriculum; no apparent areas of weakness; good facilities for science and design/technology. GCSE options include business studies, sociology, home economics, computer studies. Small classes (sizes vary from 13 to 18); some rooms freshly decorated, others in a poor state with battered equipment; good library (staff on hand after school). Wide choice of A-, AS-levels and vocational courses, including BTEC. Homework set in all years and rigidly enforced; regular grades for attainment and effort; detention for bad work. Lively expressive arts. Good careers department; work experience in Germany. Extra-curricular activities include very successful Duke of Edinburgh award scheme. Regular trips abroad.

The pupils Broad social mix; very wide ability range. Non-selective: apply to tutor for admissions by mid-November for entry the following year.

Results (1992) GCSE: impressive 63% gained at least 5 grades A-C. A-level: 31% of entries graded A or B.

Destinations 55% continue into the sixth form; 60% of those who take A-levels proceed to higher education (3 or 4 a year to Oxbridge).

Sport Good range on offer: hockey, soccer, rugby, athletics, tennis, squash, badminton, basketball.

Remarks Well-run school; all abilities catered for.

CONYERS
Green Lane,
Yarm,
Cleveland TS15 9ET
Tel (0642) 783253

Comprehensive • Co-educational • Ages 11-18 • 1,100 pupils • 190 in sixth form
Head: Laurie Metcalfe, mid-50s, appointed 1980.

Lively, informal comprehensive; impressive exam results; turns out well-rounded, confident youngsters.

Background Founded as Yarm Grammar School in 1590 by Thomas Conyers, gentleman; became a comprehensive in 1975; moved to present site 1977. Standard, undistinguished local-authority accommodation; no assembly hall; beginning to feel over-crowded.

Atmosphere Enjoys being a comprehensive and is proud of its academic success. Strong work ethic; disciplinary problems rare; social problems few. Noticeably relaxed relations between staff and pupils.

The head Mathematician; strong believer in the comprehensive system; has taught in a wide range of schools – independent and state – in Northumberland and Humberside. Delegates well (wife is one of 3 deputy heads) but provides firm leadership when required. Has appointed nearly all his staff (and claims to have forgotten most of their surnames).

The teaching Wide variety of styles based on an easy informality which seems to bring out the best in able and less able pupils alike. National curriculum-plus; all take a second language in the second and third years; strong emphasis on maths and science (perhaps reflecting the influence of parents, many of whom work in engineering and for ICI). Mixed-ability classes with setting in maths, French, German and – for GCSE – in English and science. Class sizes 25-27, fewer for GCSE, maximum 15 for A-levels. Sixth form largely A-level oriented (choice of 20 subjects); 15 pursue 1-year course. Good provision for art and technology – but emphasis is on the mainstream subjects. Firm homework policy monitored by parents.

The pupils Hard-working, courteous, well-behaved. Catchment area almost entirely middle-class or rural; nearly all pupils drawn from 4 primary schools.

Results (1992) GCSE: impressive 71% gained at least 5 grades A-C. A-level: 33% of entries graded A or B.

Destinations 55% continue into sixth form (80% of the rest undertake some form of further education); 95% of those who take A-levels proceed to higher education.

Sport Strong in rugby, football, netball. Excellent sports hall, good playing fields (but cricket square has suffered badly from lack of maintenance).

Remarks First-rate staff; school makes the most of its catchment area.

COPTHALL
Page Street,
Mill Hill,
London NW7 2EP
Tel (081) 203 1074

Comprehensive • Girls • Ages 11-18 •
1,062 pupils • 157 in sixth form
Head: Mrs Sheila Walden, early-50s,
appointed 1979.

Strongly academic comprehensive; good results.

Background 1973 amalgamation of 1930s grammar school and 1960s secondary modern: two buildings 5 minutes' walk apart, both in very poor state of repair. £7½-million rebuilding programme under discussion.

Atmosphere Quiet, industrious. Strong emphasis on academic attainment; highly developed system of merit awards; extra-curricular programme rather restricted. Staff-pupil relations relaxed without being over-familiar; good pastoral care (some pupils face acute

social problems); genuine racial harmony. Ambitious, supportive parents.

The head Experienced, well-regarded, very much in control.

The teaching High quality; 84 full and part-time staff (12 men), 80% appointed by present head. German, Spanish on offer in addition to French; good science, computing; strong drama, theatre arts, art and design. Mixed-ability classes of 30 in first year; setting and smaller groups thereafter. Choice of 18 subjects at A-level; good results in science, economics. Vocational alternatives include 1-year courses in business studies, shorthand, keyboarding. Lots of music: 2 orchestras, 2 choirs; regular performances. All do 2 weeks' work experience.

The pupils Enthusiastic, articulate, self-confident. Socially mixed intake; 30% Asian; other minorities include Greek, Chinese, Japanese. School heavily over-subscribed; 360 apply for 180 places a year. Admissions handled by Barnet council; priority to sisters and those living nearest.

Results (1991) GCSE: 49% achieved at least 5 grades A-C. A-level impressive 49% of entries graded A or B.

Destinations 60% continue into the sixth form (many of the rest take vocational courses at sixth-form and further education colleges); 45% of these proceed to higher education.

Sport Chiefly hockey, netball, tennis; all take swimming and dance lessons. Ample playing fields; 12 tennis courts.

Remarks Hard-working, effective school.

CORFE HILLS
Higher Blandford Road,
Broadstone,
Dorset BH18 9BG
Tel (0202) 697541

Comprehensive • Co-educational • Ages 13-18 • 1,531 pupils • 456 in sixth form
Head: Andrew Williams, 40s, appointed 1990.

Well-regarded, modern comprehensive; high expectations; good drama and music.

Background Opened in 1976 as the upper school for an educational pyramid of 3 middle schools and 6 first schools: they work closely together to plan the education of pupils of all abilities from 5 to 18. Purpose-built, well-designed, mostly single-storey premises set in beautiful country on the edge of the New Forest. Strongly supported by parents and local industry.

Atmosphere Traditional codes of courtesy, discipline, hard work. An open society with good relations between staff and pupils; rather like a university campus.

The head Read history at Oxford; came here as deputy head in 1986. Thoughtful, approachable; highly regarded by staff, pupils, parents, governors. Married; 2 daughters in the school, 1 son in a feeder middle school.

The teaching Emphasis is on discussion, teamwork, pupils taking responsibility for their own learning, developing study skills. Broad curriculum; all do French plus German or Spanish; combined science. Sixth-formers choose between A-levels (24 subjects on offer, including PE, sociology) and a vocational diploma course in services to business, technical and production services or services to people. Extra help for slow learners and those of exceptional ability. Homework seen as a vital; parents expected to check regularly. Lots of drama and music; orchestras, ensembles, choirs etc; spectacular productions in Towngate Theatre, Poole. Study tours to Belgium, Russia; regular foreign exchanges.

The pupils Confident, purposeful. School always over-subscribed; catchment area covers area around Broadstone, Merley, Corfe Mullen, Sturminster Marshall.

Results (1992) GCSE: creditable 57% achieved at least 5 grades A-C. A-level: 33% of entries graded A or B.

Destinations More than 70% stay on in the sixth form, a quarter to take the 1-year vocational course; 60% of those who do A-levels proceed to higher education.

Sport Programme of 'sport for all' to develop fitness and skills. School well represented in competitive games at county, regional and national level. Adjacent playing fields, good sports hall but no swimming.

Remarks A state school for the 1990s.

CORSHAM
The Tynings,
Corsham,
Wiltshire SN13 9DF
Tel (0249) 713284

Comprehensive • Co-educational • Ages 11-18 • 836 pupils (equal numbers of girls and boys) • 110 in sixth form
Head: Ernest Taylor, 62, appointed 1972 (retiring August 1993).

Sound, well-run school; respectable results.

Background 1973 merger of 2 adjoining secondary moderns; functional buildings in pleasant, semi-rural setting.

Atmosphere Ordered, friendly; good staff-pupil relations; parental involvement encouraged; a strong community feel. 'I've taught in 5 schools,' a member of staff observed, 'and this is the only one I'd send my children to.'

The head Helped create the school 20 years ago. Inspiring teacher; firm leader; keen that his impending retirement should not impose a 'planning blight'.

The teaching Lively, effective. Good-quality staff of 55, nearly all appointed by the present head; responsive, hard-working pupils. Strong languages (French, German) and science. Setting by ability from second year; extra help for those with special needs; classes on the large side. Choice of 21 subjects at GCSE, 18 at A-level. Music and drama are improving.

The pupils Fairly wide range of abilities (but few less able); many from Service families. Catchment area has a 10-mile radius.

Results (1992) GCSE: 44% gained at least 5 grades A-C. A-level: 29% of entries graded A or B (has been higher).

Destinations Only 30% stay on for A-levels; 70% of these proceed to higher education.

Sport Strong football, hockey, tennis. Facilities include extensive playing fields, all-weather games area; community sports centre and pool near by.

Remarks Decent comprehensive with some first-rate teaching.

COTTENHAM
High Street,
Cottenham,
Cambridge, CB4 4UA
Tel (0954) 50444

Comprehensive • Co-educational • Ages 11-16 • 760 pupils
Head: Tony Cooper, 39, appointed 1990.

Successful community school; good results; first-rate art.

Background Opened 1963 – one of a chain of village colleges designed to serve as cultural and recreational centres for scattered rural communities. Pleasant buildings; attractive setting.

Atmosphere Friendly, positive. Great stress on helping others; large sums raised annually for charity. 95% attend parents' evenings.

The head (Warden) Read physics at Imperial College, London; teaches GCSE science. Firmly committed to comprehensive education and the idea of schools serving their communities; speaks highly of his local authority (school receives £2,000 a year per pupil).

The teaching Sound. Setting by ability in all subjects; broad curriculum includes Latin, Spanish, computing. Particularly good results in business studies, art; also English literature, science, geography, maths, history, French. 6 forms of entry, divided into classes of 25-28 pupils (but 30+ for GCSE). Written work neat and clear. Outstanding painting, pottery; first-rate technology. Firm homework policy. Extra help for those with learning difficulties (some quite severe); unit for 8 hearing-impaired children. Plenty of music; regular concerts. All do 2 weeks' work experience (and run a bank on the premises).

The pupils Polite, cheerful, articulate; from compact, homogeneous catchment area. Discipline not a problem; children seem genuinely to want to learn. School not over-subscribed but neither is it short of pupils.

Results (1991) GCSE: 56% gained at least 5 grades A-C (well above the national average for all-ability schools).

Destinations 70% go on to do A-levels, mostly at Cambridge sixth-form colleges; most of these proceed to higher education.

Sport Emphasis on 'health-related fitness'; school not averse to competitive games but not obsessed by them. Facilities include spacious playing fields, floodlit all-weather pitch, gym, outdoor pool.

Remarks Effective school; high academic standards.

CRANBROOK

Cranbrook,
Kent TN17 3JD
Tel (0580) 712163

Grammar (grant-maintained) •
Co-educational • Day and boarding •
Ages 13-18 • 700 pupils (54% boys; 60%
day) • 260 in sixth form • Boarding fees
(1992-93), £4,350
Head: Peter Close, 48, appointed 1988.

---

*Good academic school; fairly wide ability
range; strong sport.*

Background Founded 1518; granted royal
charter by Elizabeth I in 1574 (still proudly
displayed in the library); has occupied the
same fine 70-acre site for more than 450 years.
Main building dates from 1727; Victorian and
later additions. Opted out of council control
January 1992. Local estate agents say the
school's catchment area adds 10% to house
prices.

Atmosphere Happy, hard-working (lessons
on Saturday mornings); boarders and day
pupils mix well. Strong pastoral care system.
Six pleasant boarding houses.

The head Cambridge classicist; has taught in
both the independent and state sectors; finds
himself 'twitching with frustration' at not
being able to provide what children need.
Married, 3 daughters.

The teaching Mix of traditional and modern
methods. National curriculum-plus; all start
Latin, half continue with it; 60 do more than 1
language; 'combined' science being replaced
by 3 separate sciences (against the national
trend). Pupils set by ability in maths, French,
Latin; average class size 28, reducing to 11-16
in the sixth form. Most pupils do 9 GCSEs and
3 A-levels (from choice of 21) plus general
studies. Plans afoot to offer a vocational
alternative. Good art; nearly a third learn at
least 1 musical instrument (orchestra, chamber groups, choir); lots of drama. All first-years
must join the cadet force or do community
service. Regular exchanges with schools in
France, Germany, Spain, Russia and USA.

The pupils Bright, responsive, confident.
Day pupils from within a 5-mile radius;
boarders from London and the South East.
Entry from state schools via 2-year assessment
in collaboration with local heads (top 20%-
25% of the ability range); from prep schools by
Common Entrance (minimum 55% mark
required). Head emphasises the school is not
an academic hot-house: some children are very
bright but other struggle to pass 2 A-levels.

Results (1992) GCSE: 96% gained at least 5
grades A-C. A-level: 39% of entries graded A
or B.

Destinations More than 90% stay on for
A-levels; up to 80% of these proceed to higher
education.

Sport All main sports played, most to county
level; all participate. Good facilities.

Remarks Good all round; very popular with
parents.

CRANLEIGH

Cranleigh,
Surrey GU6 8QQ
Tel (0483) 273997

Independent • Boys (plus girls in sixth
form) • Boarding and day • Ages 13-18
(plus prep school on same site) • 550
pupils (85% boarding) • 255 in sixth form
(70% boys) • Fees, £10,530 boarding;
£7,905 day
Head: Tony Hart, 52, appointed 1984.

---

*Safe, traditional school; good art, drama,
music; excellent sporting facilities.*

Background Founded 1865; imposing Victorian red-brick buildings plus later additions;
attractively set in 200 acres of Surrey farmland.

Atmosphere Relaxed, well-disciplined; sense
of mutual respect betwen staff and pupils;
sound pastoral care system (appreciated by
parents). Adequate dormitories, carpeted,
curtained; some still to be refurbished.

The head Oxford graduate; formerly a Treasury civil servant; teaches A-level economics. Says of his career switch: 'Probably the best decision I have ever made; I wanted to run something myself and not simply be a cog in a machine...Learning what makes the average teenager tick was the most difficult part.' Strongly committed to the boarding life. Staff praise his alert mind and capacity to get things done (he has pushed through a major building programme).

The teaching Pupils streamed by ability from the start; additional setting in maths, French (which some take for GCSE a year early). All do GCSE chemistry; options include 3 sciences, 2 modern languages, Latin. National curriculum not adopted: school watching developments. Choice of 20+ subjects at A-level. Average class size 20, reducing to 12 in sixth form; 67 staff (8 women); all required to live within 10 minutes' cycling distance (!) Mild dyslexia catered for. Good art (painting, ceramics, print-making) and drama (new studio theatre, computerised lighting etc) – school anxious to preserve and build on the traditions established by Sir Michael Redgrave, who taught, acted and directed here in the 1930s. Strong music: more than a third learn an instrument (21 peripatetic teachers); orchestras, wind band, choirs. Sixth-form linguists spend periods in France and Spain living with local families, attending local schools (head keen to develop European links).

The pupils Most from London and Home Counties but nearly 10% are non-British (40 nationalities represented); 20% enter from associated prep school. Minimum of 55% required at Common Entrance; few assisted places; academic, music, art scholarships.

Results GCSE: 93% gain at least 5 grades A-C. A-level (1992): 54% of entries graded A or B.

Destinations Nearly all proceed to higher education (6 to Oxbridge in 1991 but usually more).

Sport Major games: rugby, hockey, cricket, tennis; lacrosse, hockey for the girls. Excellent facilities include 100 acres of playing fields, all-weather pitch, indoor and outdoor pools, 9-hole golf course, riding school, 16 tennis courts, 6 fives courts, 6 squash courts, rifle range etc.

Remarks Good all round. (Intelligent, helpful prospectus.)

CROYDON HIGH
Old Farleigh Road,
Selsdon,
Surrey CR2 8YB
Tel (081) 651 5020

Independent • Girls • Day • Ages 4-18 • 1,050 pupils (700 in senior school) • 170 in sixth form • Fees, £2,844-£3,684
Head: Mrs Pauline Davies, 40s, appointed 1990.

Academic school; high standards; good music and sport.

Background Founded 1874 by the Girls' Public Day School Trust; moved out of central Croydon to present spacious 22-acre site in 1964. Multi-level building with masses of stairs and corridors (showing signs of wear).

Atmosphere Well-ordered; hums with life. Junior department particularly lively and industrious; nothing rigid or stereotyped here.

The head Highly competent; formerly deputy head of King Edward VI, Chelmsford (*qv*); master's degree in science education. Encourages girls to consider careers in science and engineering.

The teaching Good modern languages (more than half do 2 for GCSE); options include Latin, Greek, 3 separate sciences. All take 9 GCSEs; most do 3 A-levels plus 1 AS-level or extra GCSE. Understanding Industry course culminates in 2 weeks' work experience for all. Regular pupil exchanges with France, Germany, Spain. Strong drama and music; 25% learn an instrument; 3 orchestras, 4 choirs, several chamber groups. Busy extra-curricular programme; debating, Duke of Edinburgh award scheme etc.

The pupils From the top 15% of the ability range; wide catchment area; 3 applicants for every place. Admission to the junior school at 4+ by observation of performance in group tasks; at 7 by tests in reading and writing. Entry to senior school at 11 by tests in English, maths, verbal reasoning. Assisted places available.

Results GCSE: all gain at least 5 grades A-C. A-level (1992): 51% of entries graded A or B.

Destinations Most stay on for A-levels and proceed to higher education (6 a year to Oxbridge).

Sport Excellent netball (1991 national champions); good tennis. Facilities include sports hall, indoor pool.

Remarks Good all round; highly respected locally.

DAME ALICE OWEN'S
Dugdale Hill Lane,
Potters Bar,
Hertfordshire EN6 2DU
Tel (0707) 43441

Comprehensive (voluntary-aided –
grant-maintained from April 1993) •
Co-educational • Ages 11-18 • 1,148
pupils (equal numbers of boys and girls) •
224 in sixth form
Head: David Bolton, 56, appointed 1982.

Popular, well-resourced comprehensive; strong academic bias; high standards all round.

Background Founded in Islington in 1613 by Dame Alice Owen (thrice-widowed by a brewer, a mercer and Judge Thomas Owen); girls' school added 1886; became a co-educational comprehensive and moved to present, fine 32-acre site 1973. Trustees of the foundation are the Worshipful Company of Brewers.

(Following Dame Alice's instructions, the governors visit the school once a year to inspect the pupils' progress and present them with 'beer money'.) Buildings well-maintained but some in need of replacement; grand £1.8-million technology centre opened 1991 by Duke of Edinburgh.

The atmosphere Orderly, hard-working, traditional. Pupils immaculately uniformed; staff wear academic gowns to (strongly Christian) assembly. Supportive parents have raised £32,000 in past 4 years; 92 voted in July 1992 to opt out of council control.

The head Read English at Oxford; taught in a wide range of independent and state schools; first headship in 1974. Committed Christian; provides firm leadership (said to indicate disapproval by an expressive silence); held in high regard by pupils, teachers, parents. Married, 3 adult children.

The teaching High-calibre; firmly traditional in style but with a willingness to innovate. Pupils divided into 2 ability bands ('upper' and 'middle'); setting in some subjects; plenty of extra help for those who need it. Particular strengths in maths, geography, modern languages (French and German nationals on staff, regular exchanges with schools in Lyons and Heidelberg). 65 teachers (two-thirds appointed by present head); average age mid-30s; equal numbers of men and women; glad to be here and give freely of their time. Good library (10,000 volumes). Strong music; more than a quarter learn an instrument; orchestras, band, 2 choirs; 3 major concerts a year. Plenty of extra-curricular activities: drama, photography, debating, angling, chess, computing etc. Much fund-raising for charity (£7,000 in 1991).

The pupils Wide range of backgrounds and abilities; most above average but 12% arrive with reading ages significantly below chronological ages. 400 apply for 189 places, allocated by the governors on the basis of: making Owen's first choice, sibling or other family connections, likelihood of child benefiting from the full course of education available (i.e. capable of A-levels), making a contribution to corporate life of the school, fitting into the disciplined (but friendly) ethos. Wide catchment area (extends to Islington); 35% from beyond county boundaries.

Results (1992) GCSE: 72% gained 5 or more grades A-C. A-level: creditable 45% of entries graded A or B.

Destinations 60% stay on for A-levels; others take 1-year vocational courses; 56% proceed to higher education (11 to Oxbridge in 1991).

Sport Superb facilities include 22 acres of playing fields, fully equipped sports hall, 12 tennis courts, 4 squash courts, all-weather pitches for football, hockey. Large programme of inter-school fixtures; regular Saturday matches; rugby and cricket particularly strong.

Remarks First-rate school; traditional values; pupils work and play hard.

DAME ALLAN'S
Fowberry Crescent,
Fenham,
Newcastle-upon-Tyne NE1 9YJ
Tel (091) 271 5910

Independent • Co-educational (but boys and girls taught separately from 11-16) • Day • Ages 9-18 • 940 pupils (equal numbers of boys and girls) • 200 in sixth form • Fees, £2,375-£3,115
Principal: Terry Willcocks, early 50s, appointed 1988.

Long, proud record; combines academic success with a relaxed, friendly approach. Matches up well to the competition.

Background Founded 1705 by the widow of a Newcastle tobacco merchant as a charity school for 10 poor boys and 20 poor girls who were to be taught to 'read, write and cast accompts'. Moved to present purpose-built premises (1 wing for boys, another for girls) in 1935; undistinguished suburbia. Ambitious (and much needed) building programme now in train. (Parents and former pupils raising prodigious sums to upgrade laboratories and classrooms.)

Atmosphere Purposeful, friendly; plenty of Geordie charm. Separate schools create the impression of 2 quite small, well-integrated families. Discipline unobtrusive; rules based on courtesy and kept to a minimum.

The head Approachable; claims not to be authoritarian but is clearly in command. Has taught in independent schools on both sides of the Border. Came here with a brief to combine the sixth forms while the main schools remained separate; believes this arrangement achieves the best of both worlds; parents seem to agree.

The teaching Academic thrust is clear but methods are varied and based on warm staff-pupil relations. Superb, lively teaching in junior school. Senior school subject range a little narrow (partly conditioned by the accommodation): no technology; home economics ('domestic science') for girls only. Mainstream academic subjects soundly taught (imaginatively in the case of English and drama). Excellent grounding in modern languages: all do French and German for first 3 years. Class sizes: 22 (18 for GCSE), 11 in sixth form. Setting only in GCSE maths and French. Good art and music.

The pupils Drawn from a wide area, including Wooler, South Shields, Durham, Alston, Hexham and Otterburn as well as Newcastle. Entry by examination and interview; keen competition; IQs 110+. (Senior school draws equal numbers from the junior school, state primaries and prep schools.)

Results GCSE: 95% of girls and 91% of boys gain at least 5 grades A-C. A-level: 43% of entries graded A or B.

Destination 80% proceed from GCSE to A-levels; same proportion go on to higher education (average of 8 a year to Oxbridge).

Sport Boys' rugby and cricket first class; girls equally strong in hockey and netball. Good on-site playing fields; fine new sports hall.

Remarks Successful, flourishing school; deserves its high reputation in the North East.

DANIEL STEWART'S & MELVILLE
Queensferry Road,
Edinburgh EH4 3EZ
Tel (031) 332 7925

Independent • Boys (plus associated girls' school) • Day (and some boarding) • Ages 12-18 (plus associated co-educational junior school) • 791 pupils (96% day) • 248 in sixth form • Fees (1992-93), £3,666 (£7,116 boarding)
Head: Patrick Tobin, 50s, appointed 1989.

Solid academic school; sound results; strong at games, particularly rugby.

Background 1972 merger of Daniel Stewart's, founded 1855, and Melville, founded 1832; formally twinned – under 1 head and with a shared governing body – in 1978 with Mary Erskine, a girls' school with nearly 600 pupils aged 11-18; the senior schools remain single sex. Main building is a remarkable Victorian extravaganza with towers, turrets and pinnacles; many functional later additions plus fine new technology centre.

Atmosphere Friendly, cheerful, a little boisterous. Homely, comfortable boarding accommodation.

The head Educated at Oxford; taught history and economics at Christ College, Brecon and Tonbridge; formerly head of Prior Park, Bath. Believes 'you can have discipline without freedom, but you cannot have freedom without discipline'.

The teaching Broad curriculum; Latin, German on offer; pupils set by ability in maths only; average class size 23. All do 8 Standard Grades from choice of 19, including Greek, computer studies, technology; nearly all take 5 Highers. Lots of drama and music (in conjunction with girls from Mary Erskine): most learn an instrument; 2 orchestras, various smaller ensembles, including successful jazz band; regular tours abroad. Well-supported cadet force and Duke of Edinburgh award scheme; all third-years in both schools spend 8 days in the Highlands 'learning to appreciate the outdoors'. 'Colours', including a red blazer, awarded for debating, drama, chess etc. Exchanges with pupils in France, Germany, USA and Canada.

The pupils Fairly wide social mix but predominantly from professional and business backgrounds; nearly all live within a 15-mile radius. Automatic promotion from junior school; rest take tests in English, maths, verbal reasoning. School is not unduly selective.

Results Standard Grade: 88% gain at least 5 grades 1-3. Highers: 56% of entries graded A or B.

Destinations 94% stay on for Highers; 77% of these stay on for a sixth year; 80% of these proceed to higher education (3 a year to Oxbridge).

Sport High standard. Chiefly rugby, hockey, cricket, athletics; tennis, badminton, squash, golf, swimming, cross-country also on offer. Facilities include sports hall, indoor pool; main playing fields 2 miles away.

Remarks Good all round; exam results improving steadily.

DARTFORD GIRLS' GRAMMAR
Shepherds Lane,
Dartford,
Kent DA1 2NT
Tel (0322) 223123

Grammar (grant-maintained) • Girls • Ages 11-18 • 750 pupils • 195 in sixth form
Head: Mrs Jillian Hadman, 55, appointed 1986.

Forward-looking grammar school; strengths in modern languages, technology, business studies.

Background Founded 1904; moved to present purpose-built premises (on busy main road) 1912. Imposing, battlemented Kentish ragstone facade; battered, ageing classrooms being refurbished; archaic science labs need modernising; some temporary huts. (Grant-maintained status should help rectify the neglect.)

Atmosphere Busy, purposeful, well-behaved.

The head Energetic; keen to bring the school up to date (while preserving its traditional academic strengths); enthusiastic advocate of links with industry and Europe.

The teaching High-quality; national curriculum-plus; most do second foreign language (choice of French, German, Spanish); setting by ability in maths only. Lots of computing; good technology (emphasis on teamwork, problem-solving) and art and design (works adorn the walls). Sixth-form teaching shared with neighbouring boys' grammar; impressive choice of 32 subjects (including 3 sciences, business studies, theatre arts). Strong music; joint drama with boys. Lots of work experience and links with industry (foreign languages taught to business executives). Community service includes helping with meals on wheels, working in school for handicapped children.

The pupils Backgrounds range from working-class to professional; 34 languages spoken; 8% ethnic minority. Top 25% of the ability range; wide catchment area (pupils drawn from 85 primary schools); entry by Kent 11+, former head's recommendation and samples of work in English and maths (having a brother at the boys' school also helps).

Results (1991) GCSE: 93% gained at least 5 grades A-C. A-level (1992): disappointing 34% of entries graded A or B (has been higher).

Destinations Nearly all continue into the sixth form and proceed to higher education (3 to Oxbridge in 1991).

Sport Usual games plus badminton, tennis (11 grass courts), swimming, rowing, golf.

Remarks Deserves to be better funded and equipped; grant-maintained status should help.

DAUNTSEY'S
West Lavington,
Near Devizes,
Wiltshire SN10 4AE
Tel (0380) 812325

Independent • Co-educational • Day and boarding • Ages 11-18 • 621 pupils (52% boys; 55% day) • 190 in sixth form • Fees (1992-93), £5,784 day; £9,345 boarding Head: Christopher Evans, 54, appointed 1985. 3 5 14

Sound, not unduly selective school; good all-round education for children of average ability.

Background Founded 1542 under the will of William Dauntsey, mercer of the City of London; moved to 100-acre estate in Vale of Pewsey 1895; Victorian premises being refurbished; substantial recent additions include 1,200-seat memorial hall (partly financed by the Mercers' Company). Became fully independent with the abolition of Direct Grant status in 1975 but retains links with the local education authority.

Atmosphere Strong sense of family; no attempt to produce a stereotype. Pleasant boarding houses (boarding increasing, against the trend); day pupils stay until 5.30 p.m.

The head Read English, archaeology, anthropology at Cambridge after National Service in Nigeria. Formerly second master at Taunton. Teaches English; enjoys easy relationship with pupils.

The teaching High-quality; stable staff of 63; good mix of men, women, youth and experience. 60 pupils enter at 11, mostly from state primary schools, and are placed in 3 mixed-ability forms; all do Latin, French; setting in maths from second year. Another 40 enter at 13, mostly from prep schools; setting by ability in maths, foreign languages. All take 3 sciences to GCSE plus non-examined courses in religious education, PE, careers. Strong commitment to breadth in sixth form; all expected to do at least 1 AS-level in addition to A-levels (choice of 17 subjects). Under the Lavington

Link, introduced in 1968, some Dauntsey's staff teach at Lavington comprehensive; in return, Wiltshire County Council pays for 15-20 Lavington pupils to attend Dauntsey's sixth form. (Works well; pity others have not copied.) High standard of music; well-supported orchestras, choirs; lots of drama.

The pupils Polite, orderly (rules kept to a minimum – encapsulated as 'common sense and courtesy'). Most boarders from Wiltshire and neighbouring counties. Modest 50% required at Common Entrance.

Results GCSE (1991): 95% gained at least 5 grades A-C. A level (1992): creditable 53% of entries graded A or B.

Destinations 80% stay on for A-levels; 88% of these proceed to higher education (about 7 a year to Oxbridge).

Sports Good standards in all major team games and individual sports. Facilities include sports hall, all-weather hockey pitches, tennis courts, swimming pool, 9-hole golf course.

Remarks Attractive school; highly recommended.

DAVENANT FOUNDATION
Chester Road,
Loughton,
Essex IG10 2LD
Tel (0992) 812608

Comprehensive (grant-maintained) •
Co-educational • Ages 11-18 • 960 pupils
• 140 in sixth form
Head: David Daniels, 50, appointed 1981.

Impressive comprehensive; good results; high standards all round.

Background Founded in Whitechapel in 1680 by Rev Ralph Davenant; moved to present site in 1965 at the invitation of Essex County Council; changed from boys' grammar to co-educational comprehensive 1976. Davenant Trust contributes £70,000 a year;

supportive parents – they voted for grant-maintained status – and well-wishers raise another £50,000.

Atmosphere Grammar-school ethos carefully preserved. 14 members of staff have children of their own here, including the head.

The head Educated at Cambridge; taught in Chicago. Engaging manner; strongly committed to Christian values and highest possible educational standards; makes no secret of his impatience with fashionable theories ('If I wanted to empty this school I would send a letter round the parents announcing that pupils could wear what they like and we were abandoning competitive sports').

The teaching Traditional, rigorous; all pupils follow clear, written schemes of work. Annual intake of 150 divided into 2 broad ability bands; setting in maths, French from second year; extra help for those with learning difficulties; average class size 27-28. Full national curriculum; strong English, maths, science; good technology. Choice of 13 subjects at A-level plus general studies. First-rate music; more than half learn an instrument (severe shortage of practice rooms – pianos everywhere). Business-like careers department; all fourth-years do work experience. Extra-curricular programme includes well-supported Duke of Edinburgh award scheme; regular expeditions to South Downs, Lake District; frequent trips abroad.

The pupils Smart, purposeful, well-behaved. Strict uniform (detailed regulations take up a sizeable chunk of the prospectus); sixth-formers wear suits. School is heavily over-subscribed: 286 apply for 150 places; no selection by ability; priority to those whose parents are committed Christians.

Results (1992) GCSE: impressive 61% gained 5 or more grades A-C. A-level: disappointing 27% of entries graded A or B (has been much higher).

Destinations About half stay on for A-levels.

Sport Taken seriously. Major games: rugby, soccer, hockey, netball, gymnastics, cricket, athletics, swimming, tennis, badminton, basketball. Facilities include spacious playing fields, 4 hard tennis courts, 4 netball pitches, indoor pool (small for a school of this size – but in constant use).

Remarks Successful, well-run school.

DEAN CLOSE

Cheltenham,
Gloucestershire GL51 6HE
Tel (0242) 522640

Independent • Co-educational • Boarding and day • Ages 12-18 • 452 pupils (57% boys; 60% boarders) • 185 in sixth form • Fees, £9,780 boarding; £6,780 day
Head: Chris Bacon, mid-50s, appointed 1979.

High all-round standards; Christian Evangelical tradition.

Background Founded as a boys' school in 1886 to commemorate Rev Francis Close, Rector of Cheltenham and Dean of Carlisle; became co-educational in 1969, one of the first Headmasters' Conference schools to do so. Red-brick Victorian buildings (plus good recent additions) on impressive 70-acre site. Annual surplus of £500,000 available for improvements.

Atmosphere 'The school is firmly attached by its foundation to the scriptural basis and Articles of the Church of England, and its evangelical tradition is maintained,' says the prospectus. Strong sense of caring and community. Boarding accommodation fairly basic but adequate.

The head Committed Christian; lay reader. Genial, friendly, enthusiastic; greets all he meets by their first names. Oxford chemistry graduate; still teaches A-level. Married, 3 daughters. Tends herd of Herefords on the Welsh Border in the holidays.

The teaching 48 full-time staff; all highly qualified graduates (40% Oxbridge); most appointed by present head. National curricu-

lum-plus: 3 separate sciences and classics retained. Setting by ability in all subjects; pupils respond to high expectations in lively, positive manner. Classrooms range from ancient to modern but all are well-equipped (excellent computer network). Average size: 24 (12 in sixth form). Dyslexia unit (trained staff). Strong music: more than half play an instrument; many orchestras, bands and choirs (50-strong chapel choir regularly sings abroad). Good drama in fine new £2-million performing arts centre. Extra-curricular activities include more than 100 clubs and societies.

The pupils Well-mannered, confident, sociable. Mainly from business and professional homes; boarders largely from expatriate and Service families. Admission policy based on the expectation that 95% will proceed to higher education.

Results (1991) GCSE: 96% gained at least 5 grades A-C. A-level: 52% of entries graded A or B.

Destinations Almost all do A-levels; 95% of these to higher education (average 9 a year to Oxbridge).

Sport Impressive facilities: superb indoor swimming pool; sports hall; all-weather pitches. Outstanding hockey (both boys and girls).

Remarks Fine, strongly led school.

DENMARK ROAD HIGH
Denmark Road,
Gloucester GL1 3JN
Tel (0452) 23335

Grammar • Girls • Ages 11-18 • 510 pupils • 100 in sixth form
Head: Margaret Bainbridge, early 40s, appointed September 1992.

Traditional grammar school; expanding; entry becoming more selective.

Background Founded 1883 in Gloucester;

moved to present purpose-built red-brick buildings (grade-2 listed) 1909. Later additions include science labs, library, gymnasium. Plans for new technology block but no funds; sixth-formers need more space.

Atmosphere Suburban setting; well-maintained grounds. Pleasant, spacious building (wide stone stairways, stained-glass windows, light airy classrooms). Honours boards line the walls. A sense of order and purpose; also warmth and courtesy.

The head New appointment. French graduate (Manchester); spent all her career at a co-educational grammar school in Lincolnshire, rising to deputy head.

The teaching Deliberately academic; highly motivated girls encouraged to value learning, to achieve and admire achievement in others. Discipline apparently effortless. Well-qualified, long-serving staff of 35 (4 men). Strengths in most subjects (maths, science, English, history, theology have all led recently to Oxbridge entry). All pupils do 2 foreign languages; many take GCSE French a year early. Computing, design and technology still at a rather rudimentary stage. Average class size 27 (setting in maths and French). Arts 'brilliant', say pupils. Good music, thriving orchestra.

The pupils Broad social mix. Mainly from suburban Gloucester but increasingly from further afield: Forest of Dean, Tewkesbury etc. Entry by county-administered verbal reasoning tests (average score of successful applicants: 117). Sixth-formers confident, articulate; highly appreciative of hard-working staff.

Results (1991) GCSE: 90% gained at least 5 grades A-C. A-level: 44% of entries graded A or B.

Destinations 70% proceed from GCSE to A-levels; most of these go on to higher education (5 a year to Oxbridge).

Sport Netball, hockey, tennis. Reasonable facilities (on-site playing fields); some form of physical activity compulsory for all. Annual water-sports trip to south of France.

Remarks Good academic school; achievement in a caring environment.

DEVONPORT HIGH GIRLS'
Lyndhurst Road,
Peverell,
Plymouth PL2 3DL
Tel (0752) 705024

Grammar • Girls • Ages 11-18 • 640 pupils • 140 in sixth form
Head: Mrs Janet Dunball, 51, appointed 1991.

Sound academic school.

Background Founded 1911; moved to its present imposing but ageing premises 1939; some classrooms in temporary huts.

Atmosphere Calm, relaxed, cordial. Girls and staff busy, interested in their work. Good pastoral care.

The head Shrewd, perceptive; long experience in both comprehensive and grammar schools.

The teaching Varying styles, all challenging; well-qualified, committed staff (25% men); girls encouraged to take responsibility for their own learning. Broad curriculum; all start second modern language in second year. Good design/technology. All do at least 9 GCSEs; most take 3 A-levels; best results in biology, geography, English, French, economics, maths.

The pupils Fairly wide social range from Plymouth and Devonport. Entry via 11+ administered by Devon County Council; standard grammar school intake.

Results GCSE: virtually all gain at least 5 grades A-C. A-level (1991): 44% of entries graded A or B.

Destinations Most stay on for A-levels; 75% of these proceed to higher education.

Sport Wide choice; particular strengths in

basketball, netball, hockey. Excellent facilities for circuit training, aerobics.

Remarks Happy, hard-working.

DOLLAR ACADEMY
Dollar,
Clackmannanshire FK14 7DU
Tel (0259) 42511

Independent • Co-educational • Day and boarding • Ages 5-18 • 1,115 pupils (764 in senior school; 53% boys; 80% day) • 250 in sixth form • Fees (1992-93), £2,682-£3,459 day; £6,588-£7,869 boarding
Head: Lloyd Harrison, 58, appointed 1984.

Sound academic school; fairly wide range of abilities; strong sport.

Background Founded 1818; handsome (if rather austere) purpose-built premises plus some less distinguished additions (including 'temporary' huts) in a pleasant, spacious setting at the foot of the Ochil Hills. Classrooms are well resourced and attractively furnished; fine new music centre. School has been co-educational from the start.

Atmosphere Calm, purposeful, well-ordered. Boarding houses recently refurbished; accommodation varied but generally quite good.

The head Hard-working (arrives at 6 a.m.); gets on well with staff and pupils. Educated at Bradford Grammar and Oxford; taught classics at Glenalmond, Leeds Grammar and Colne Valley High; formerly head of Northallerton Grammar.

The teaching Emphasis in the junior school on reading, writing and sound numeracy; choice between French and German; no setting by ability; average class size 26-27. Standard curriculum in senior school; all do economics, computing, Latin; pupils set by ability in maths and English; progress closely monitored. All do 7 subjects for Standard Grade (from a choice of 19, including accounts

and finance, graphic communication and Greek); most take at least 1 science and 1 modern language. Virtually all stay for Highers (choice of 24); additional courses available in Spanish, Japanese, biotechnology etc. More than 90 remain for the sixth year: wide choice of subjects; small classes. Strong music: 20% learn an instrument; 2 orchestras, 6 choirs. Well-supported cadet force. Lots of extra-curricular activities. Regular exchanges with schools in Germany and France.

The pupils Courteous, cheerful, well-motivated. Drawn from a fairly wide range of social backgrounds; 70% live within a 30-mile radius; 2% foreign nationals. Admission by interview, assessment and tests; school is fairly selective.

Results Standard Grade: 95% gain at least 5 grades 1-3. Highers: 55% of entries graded A or B.

Destinations Virtually all stay for Highers; 92% remain for a sixth year; 83% of these proceed to higher education (2 or 3 a year to Oxbridge).

Sport Chiefly rugby for the boys, hockey for the girls; both are strong. Athletics, cricket, badminton, fencing also on offer. Facilities include first-rate playing fields, indoor heated pool, large games hall, squash and tennis courts.

Remarks Good all round.

DOUAY MARTYRS

Edinburgh Drive,
Ickenham,
Uxbridge,
Middlesex UB10 8QY
Tel (0895) 635371

Comprehensive (voluntary-aided –
grant-maintained from January 1993) •
Roman Catholic • Co-educational • Ages
11-19 • 1,036 pupils (equal numbers of
girls and boys) • 200 in sixth form
Head: Mrs Marie Stubbs, 52, appointed
1986.

*Outstanding comprehensive; first-class
head; enthusiastic staff; highest all-round
standards.*

Background Founded 1962 on a private
housing estate in suburban Ickenham; dreary
1960s architecture enlivened by imaginative
internal decoration, including a fine mural.
Numbers have steadily increased; 2 junior
years housed a short walk away in workaday
building and huts (cheered by displays of
artwork). Other facilities, including science
labs and language suite (full satellite TV links),
are adequate. Parents voted by a huge majority
for grant-maintained status, which will bring
extra cash.

Atmosphere Vibrant, purposeful, bustling;
an air of confidence and energy. Catholic ethos
is fundamental: full-time chaplain, regular
mass. Good manners strongly encouraged
(children stand up for visitors); discipline,
hard work, punctuality expected; uniform
rigidly adhered to (head will not tolerate
sloppiness – no shirts hanging out here);
truancy virtually non-existent. Permanent reception desk manned by a succession of pupils;
large 'Welcome to Douay' mat; big emphasis
on doing everything with style. Parents receive
'entitlement' statements explaining in detail
what to expect for their child; regular reporting, meetings, advice.

The head Dynamic, bristling with ideas;
clearly the inspiration for much of the school's
recent blossoming (says she found it 'in need
of its 25,000-mile service' when she arrived).

Has more than doubled the size of the sixth
form, appointed an Oxbridge adviser, introduced vocational alternatives to A-levels and
forged a formal link with Eton to help train
teachers. Educated in Glasgow; wide and
varied teaching experience in primary, secondary and special schools in Scotland, England
(including inner London) and the USA. Constantly seeking to raise standards; will not
countenance second best; trains everyone to
be 'brisk' (her favourite word); commands
loyalty and very hard work from her staff.
Evidently revels in her work. Married (to an
educationist), 3 children.

The teaching Formal, structured, challenging; strong emphasis on traditional standards
of accuracy, presentation, grammar, spelling;
some classes positively buzz. Enthusiastic,
highly qualified staff of 70, more than half
appointed by present head (those who did not
like her approach left). Pupils taught in broad
ability bands from the start; additional setting
in English, maths, science, modern languages;
extra help for those with special needs. Broad
curriculum includes drama, home economics,
computing, French *and* Spanish; Latin on
offer from second year. Daily homework,
rigorously monitored; regular grades; full termly subject reports; achievement board on
display to reward good work. All do religious
education for GCSE; options include business
studies, child care, graphic communication,
food and nutrition. Good A-level results in
science, maths, English, languages; vocational
alternatives include well-established BTEC
diploma course in business and finance
(helped by sponsorship from industry). All do
2 weeks' work experience, soon to be extended
into Europe. More than 80 active clubs and
societies; every pupil expected to participate in
something. Very good music: outstanding
chamber choir performs annually at Montreux
(head decreed she wanted 'patrician singing,
no mid-Atlantic droning'); 2 orchestras, numerous smaller ensembles. Annual Shakespeare play. Regular language trips to France
and Spain.

The pupils Busy, motivated, responsive.
From a wide social spread and across the
ability range, mainly from Hillingdon and

Harrow but also Brent and Buckinghamshire. Essential qualification: membership of Roman Catholic church. Heavily over-subscribed; apply to chairman of governors 2 years before starting date (applications already received for 1999); only those for whom the school is first choice are likely to be offered a place.

Results GCSE: 35% gain at least 5 grades A-C (national average). A-level: modest 19% of entries graded A or B (below national average).

Destinations Impressive 80% continue into the sixth form; 80% of these proceed to higher education (2 or 3 a year to Oxbridge).

Sport Not a particular strength, though good range on offer. Matches against other schools in football, rugby, hockey, netball, tennis, athletics. Badminton, basketball, swimming also on offer. Playing fields on adjoining site.

Remarks Highly recommended for children of all abilities.

DOWNE HOUSE
Cold Ash,
Newbury,
Berkshire RG16 9JJ
Tel (0635) 200286

Independent • Girls • Boarding and some day • Ages 11-18 • 468 pupils (94% boarding) • 117 in sixth form • Fees (1992-93), £10,890 boarding; £7,890 day
Head: Miss Susan Cameron, early-50s, appointed 1989.

Lively academic school; first-rate results; plenty of extra-curricular activities.

Background Privately founded in 1907 by Olive Willis, a woman of vision and adventurous spirit, who remained headmistress until 1946; moved from Kent in 1921 to a pine ridge near Newbury, taking over the Spanish-style buildings of the Order of Silence. Miss Willis, who had been unhappy as a girl at Roedean, aimed at 'no labels, no examinations, a school

where each individual would matter, where life would be normal and relations between people would be easy'; daughters of the well-to-do and the forward-thinking flocked to join. The school has had its ups and downs but numbers doubled under the last head and its reputation now is high.

Atmosphere The austere white-washed buildings (no grand rooms or country-house facades) have a Mediterranean feel; rural Berkshire outside the gates seems a world away, shut out by acres of woodland. A terraced cloister runs down the sloping site; girls practise the piano in the cells where the religious used to meditate. The overall impression is gracious; the ethos friendly and un-hierarchical; the girls talk easily but respectfully to those who teach them. This is still a school where an eccentric enthusiast can flourish, but it is no place for the sluggard: the days are long; Saturday morning lessons survive. Boarding accommodation is reassuringly domestic and feminine. Out of the windows are views of 'loads of hills', as one junior put it, and the rooms are full of posters, soft toys, photographs and homely touches. Good home-cooked food.

The head Comes, like Miss Jean Brodie, from Edinburgh, and is in her prime. Educated at Wycombe Abbey and London, where she read history; housemistress at Queenswood and Sherborne Girls'; formerly head of Cobham Hall. Very open, confident style; much liked by staff and pupils; obviously well in control.

The teaching Academic standards have risen over the past 10 years – thanks, apparently, to the solid imparting of information for examinations. Now the emphasis seems to be returning to the original aims of the founder: the girls are to be kindled and excited into enjoying work, becoming intellectually curious, wanting knowledge for its own sake. (They are clever enough to cope but it means a change of technique for some staff.) Science is housed in a spacious new building with 6 good labs and some forceful teaching: chemistry and biology vie with English as the most popular A-level subject. Languages on offer include Russian and Spanish to A-level; all

12-year-olds are sent to a rented chateau in France for a term to be taught in French, partly by native French teachers, and immerse themselves in French life and culture. Computing is well-looked after; technology has recently been introduced; a few girls still do cookery and needlework. There are 2 art studios and many opportunities for drama and music of a high standard. A wide range of extra-curricular activities or 'hobbies' has always been part of the school's philosophy of challenging and extending its pupils. It seems to work: as one said, 'My mother wants me to take a secretarial course when I leave, but I want to go to South America and learn to fly'.

The pupils One would be hard put not to warm to these girls. They are happy, relaxed, friendly, with no fake sophistication or need to impress. Hair is tied back for lessons; uniform is a kilt in winter and a simple dress in summer; sixth-formers wear flowing skirts. Most come from London and the South East; strong contingent from Scotland; foreign nationals can be counted 'on 1 hand'. Main entry at 11 (some join at 12, a few at 13); lists close 2 years beforehand; tests and interview 1 year later ('We throw things at them they can't be crammed for'); the half not weeded out are accepted as Common Entrance candidates; minimum 60% mark required; all girls will be of university calibre. Some assisted places, bursaries, scholarships.

Results GCSE: all gain at least 5 grades A-C. A-level (1992): creditable 58% of entries graded A or B.

Destinations Several leave after GCSE, but 'not the best'; nearly all proceed to higher education (about 6 a year to Oxbridge). Popular careers are law, medicine and the media.

Sport Lacrosse probably the strongest game; tennis (17 courts) also popular. Other activities include rowing (with Pangbourne), clay-pigeon shooting, sub-aqua, sailing. Fine indoor pool; 3 squash courts.

Remarks Girls are encouraged to make decisions, take responsibility, think critically, become poised and confident. Academic stan-dards are rising, and parents who like the idea of hard work, simple surroundings and plenty of activities for their daughters, are beating a path to the door. Highly recommended.

DR CHALLONER'S

Chesham Road,
Amersham,
Buckinghamshire HP6 5HA
Tel (0494) 721685

Grammar (voluntary-controlled) • Boys • Ages 12-18 • 1,031 pupils • 384 in sixth form
Head: John Loarridge, 60, appointed 1972 (retires January 1993).

First-class traditional grammar school; geared to able pupils from largely middle-class homes. Good sport, music, art, drama.

Background Founded 1624; moved to present site 1903. Formerly co-educational; girls moved to separate site 1962 (Dr Challoner's High, *qv*); strong links remain. Overcrowded, complex site. Premises include 2 excellent recent extensions modelled on original Edwardian buildings (to which they are linked by cloisters). Also, shabby late 1950s 5-storey concrete block and some 'temporary' accommodation which has seen better days.

Atmosphere Calm, cultured, civilised. Pupils courteous, self-disciplined; talented staff enjoy working here and give freely of their time and energy.

The head Warm, supportive; appreciated by boys and staff alike. Wedded to the school (and to the traditional values it reflects) but nearing retirement after a long stint.

The teaching High-quality; nice balance of formal and modern methods; practical approach combined with academic rigour. Good modern languages: 3 well-used language laboratories (in which teachers are most reluctant to speak English); all boys do French and

German for first 2 years; many continue to A-level. Most take 3 separate sciences for GCSE (Nuffield Science – learning by doing); many take A-level physics and chemistry. Strong English and maths (7 Oxford Firsts in maths in 3 years). Art, drama and music (choirs, orchestras, wind band, string ensemble) not neglected. Impressive chess (3 team members have played for England); excellent debating; active, popular Christian Union.

The pupils Clever (top 20% of the ability range), self-motivated, determined to make the best of their advantages. Entry at 12+ governed by county's admission procedures but the school is responsible for testing, interviewing and selecting. Over-subscribed (2 applicants per place); pupils drawn from wide catchment area (semi-rural commuter belt).

Results (1991) GCSE: 99% gained at least 5 grades A-C. A-levels: 51% of entries graded A or B.

Destinations Over 90% stay on for A-levels; 90% of them proceed to degree courses (15-25 a year to Oxbridge).

Sport All main games; excellence and wide involvement the twin targets; national reputation for cross-country and athletics; 6 soccer or cricket teams fielded on Saturdays.

Remarks Offers everything day boys receive at the best independent schools without the fees. Her Majesty's Inspectors reported: 'This is a good school which earns, and rightly enjoys, the esteem of the wider community which it serves.'

DR CHALLONER'S HIGH
Little Chalfont,
Amersham,
Buckinghamshire
Tel (0494) 763296

Grammar • Girls • Ages 12-18 • 820 pupils • 272 in sixth form
Head: Dr Sheila Cousens, early-60s, appointed 1987.

First-rate, academic school; high achievement encouraged across a broad range of activities.

Background Formerly part of Dr Challoner's *(qv)*; became a separate school in purpose-built premises on pleasant rural site in 1962 (links with boys' school remain); has more than doubled in size since (with many additional buildings).

Atmosphere Good order, courtesy, concern for others. Dedicated teachers; supportive parents.

The head Nearing retirement. Started as a research chemist; came into teaching after the birth of her 2 sons; here since 1965; became deputy head 1976. Traditional management style but plenty of consultation.

The teaching Geared to the needs of able, competitive, self-motivated girls (who put themselves under considerable pressure). All introduced to French, German, Spanish, classical studies (includes Latin). No streaming (within a fairly narrow ability band); some setting in maths. Most do 8 GCSEs: exam programme deliberately restricted to allow time for a broader curriculum, including creative subjects, technology. Many links with industry; work experience for all after GCSE. Sixth-formers do 3-4 A-levels plus compulsory general studies. Lots of drama and music; 3 choirs, 2 orchestras, wind band. Active Duke of Edinburgh award scheme; sixth-formers undertake much community service – helping the disabled, visiting the elderly etc. Parents expected to pay for participation in wide range of school visits and journeys.

The pupils Hard-working, self-confident. Top

20% of the ability range from Home Counties commuter belt (within a radius of about 12 miles). 20% over-subscribed; entry at 12+ by verbal reasoning test and primary school report.

Results (1992) GCSE: 97% gained at least 5 grades A–C. A-level: creditable 51% of entries graded A or B.

Destinations All but a handful stay on for A-levels; 75% of these proceed to higher education (9 to Oxbridge); some take a 'gap year' and do voluntary service.

Sport Chiefly netball, hockey, tennis, athletics, cross-country; lacrosse, judo, fencing etc also on offer.

Remarks Good all round; highly recommended for able girls.

DOWNSIDE

Stratton-on-the-Fosse,
Bath BA3 4RJ
Tel (0761) 232206

Independent • Roman Catholic • Boys • Boarding • Ages 11-18 • 500 pupils • 176 in sixth form • Fees, £9,918
Head: Dom Aidan Bellenger, 42, appointed 1991.

Famous Catholic boarding school; good teaching; wide range of abilities; strong arts and sport.

Background Founded 1606 at Douai, France by the English Benedictine community of St Gregory; moved to England 1789; established at Downside (12 miles from Bath) 1814. Austere Victorian-Gothic buildings (arched doorways, spiral staircases, stone cloisters) on a secluded 200-acre estate (including a working farm) at the foot of the Mendip Hills. Campus is dominated physically and spiritually by the pinnacles and flying buttresses of the magnificent neo-Gothic abbey church, the largest post-Reformation Catholic church in England; 50-strong community of monks, half involved in the school.

Atmosphere Peaceful, unhurried, benignly tolerant (desperadoes co-exist with the fervent, bohemians with the orthodox). Religious ethos is powerful and all-pervasive (and its effect long-lasting); prominent in every classroom is a crucifix of the suffering Christ; compulsory prayers morning and evening; High Mass (incense and Gregorian chants) on Sundays. The school would rather shrink than lose its essential nature of a self-contained, male, boarding community. Traditional uniform of black jacket and pinstripe trousers re-introduced September 1992. Boarding accommodation (each house run by a monk) is spartan and without privacy: up to 20 to a dormitory; sixth-formers have own rooms. Fagging retained but not, apparently, abused.

The head Calm, reserved, contemplative; a scholar with a distinguished academic record (took a First and a PhD at Cambridge); author of several erudite works on the history of Catholicism and Anglo-French relations; spent a year in Rome studying spirituality. Came here as a lay master in 1978 to teach history; took his solemn vows in 1986. Keen to raise academic standards. Abhors ostentatious and expensive material goods (like stereos); regrets the 'exclusion of silence from so many people's lives' (loud music is banned, TV rooms locked – opened on request).

The teaching Very committed staff. National curriculum-plus; big emphasis on European languages; French, Spanish, German, Russian, Italian, Portugese on offer (most take 2 for GCSE); Latin and Greek retained; English taught as a foreign language to boys from abroad. Streaming by ability introduced September 1992; extra help for those with learning difficulties. Excellent library; 20,000 volumes. Thriving art; lots of drama and music; all first-years can learn an instrument free for a term. Much charitable work; annual pilgrimage to Lourdes. Well-supported cadet force. Regular language exchanges with pupils in France, Germany and Spain.

The pupils Confident, charming, poised; more than 95% Catholic – no place for those not in sympathy with Christian values – from a mix of backgrounds, including a significant European contingent, wealthy landed gentry and successful professionals. (However, the monks are not paid so funds do exist to help deserving and able Catholics.) Admission to junior section by references and tests; at 13+ by Common Entrance; minimum 50% mark required but the school is 'very flexible'.

Results GCSE: 81% gain at least 5 grades A-C. A-level (1992): 53% of entries graded A or B.

Destinations 85% stay on for A-levels; most of these proceed to higher education (10-15 a year to Oxbridge).

Sport Wide choice on offer; good rugby, hockey, cricket (superb square overlooking the school); first-rate fencing.

Remarks Good all round; leaves its mark at a deeper level than consciousness.

DUKE OF YORK'S ROYAL MILITARY
Dover,
Kent CT15 5EQ
Tel (0303) 249541

Independent • Boys • Boarding • Ages 11-18 • 461 pupils • 100 in sixth form • Fees, £1,258 (!)
Head: Lt. Col. Gordon Wilson, 43, appointed September 1992.

Sound, well-run school for Service children.

Background Founded 1801 in Chelsea by Frederick, Duke of York to provide 'an orphanage for the children of soldiers killed in battle and to prepare boys for entry into the Army'. Moved to present 150-acre site on the cliffs above Dover in 1909. Opened to all 3 Services in 1991; girls to be admitted from September 1994. Owned and funded by the Ministry of Defence (but 'executive agency'

status gives it a degree of independence from ministry control).

Atmosphere Well-ordered; good relations between staff and boys and between younger and older boys. Pleasant, well-furnished boarding houses.

The head New appointment. Formerly a senior Army education administrator in Germany. Married, 2 children.

The teaching Generally good; well-qualified staff of 49 (7 women). National curriculum followed; setting by ability in some subjects. Sixth-formers can choose between A-levels (12 subjects on offer) and BTEC (vocational) diploma in business finance or engineering (taken by about 30%). Spacious, well-equipped library. Plenty of music; 80-strong band, chapel choir; all first-years can learn an instrument free. Careers department does not push the armed forces.

The pupils Well-behaved, hard-working; from wide variety of social backgrounds (parents range from privates to colonels). At least 1 parent must have completed 4 years' regular service (but need not still be in the armed forces). Entry by tests in maths, English – waived on compassionate grounds for up to 5 children a year. Fees heavily subsidised.

Results GCSE: 78% gain at least 5 grades A-C. A-level (1992): modest 36% of entries graded A or B.

Destinations About a third leave after GCSE; 60% proceed to higher education.

Sport Chiefly rugby, hockey, cricket; also swimming, water polo, athletics, cross-country, badminton, squash, basketball, sailing, canoeing, horse riding, tennis, fencing.

Remarks Her Majesty's Inspectors concluded (February 1991): 'This is a good school with high standards of work and behaviour, excellent care, sound teaching, generous resources, spacious premises and generally good accommodation.'

DULWICH

College Road,
Dulwich,
·London SE21 7LD
Tel (081) 693 3601

Independent • Boys • Day and some boarding • Ages 8-18 • 1,391 pupils (90% day) • 380 in sixth form • Fees, £5,085-£5,355 day; £10,290-£10,710 boarding
Head: Anthony Verity, 53, appointed 1986.

Distinguished school; high all-round standards; superb facilities.

Background Founded 1619 by Edward Alleyn; moved to present, semi-rural site (only 5 miles from central London) in 1870. Magnificent buildings (designed by the younger Charles Barry) sensitively adapted and modernised; good later additions (school is generously endowed) include separate junior section.

Atmosphere Scholarly, busy. First-rate staff; strongly motivated boys; beautiful, spacious surroundings.

The head Much respected by his peers. Read classics and oriental languages at Cambridge; taught here first then at Manchester Grammar and Bristol Grammar; was head of Leeds Grammar for 10 years. Committed to academic excellence and high standards of discipline. Married, 2 adult sons.

The teaching Leans to the traditional; much formal instruction but also plenty of coursework and investigation. Big emphasis on self-discipline, good study habits, meeting deadlines (failure to complete homework leads to same-day detention). Classes meticulously streamed by ability (3 bands, each further divided into 3 levels). Compulsory French and Latin for first 2 years of senior school; plenty of computing; separate sciences; able boys do 3 languages for GCSE. Most take at least 10 GCSEs and 3-4 A-levels plus non-examined general studies. Extra lessons geared to Oxbridge entrance. Parents kept closely informed of progress. Huge range of extra-curricular activities; particular strengths in music (4 orchestras), drama, art; flourishing cadet force, scout troops; steady flow of outside speakers. Community service an alternative to compulsory games for senior boys.

The pupils Predominantly middle-class but 25% have assisted places, ensuring wide social mix; 20% Asian. Catchment area stretches from north of the Thames to 20 miles south (fleet of buses shared with neighbouring schools, breakfast served from 8 a.m.). Main entry ages 8+, 11+, 13+; tests in English, maths, verbal reasoning plus interview.

Results Nearly all gain at least 5 grades A-C. A-level (1992): creditable 61% of entries graded A or B.

Destinations 94% continue into the sixth form; 90% of these proceed to higher education (30 a year to Oxbridge)

Sport Chiefly rugby (5 teams turn out on Saturday mornings), hockey, cricket, swimming, athletics. Well-equipped sports hall.

Remarks Excellent, well-run school; strongly recommended.

DUNDEE HIGH

Euclid Crescent,
Dundee DD1 9BP
Tel (0382) 202921/5

Independent • Co-educational • Day • Ages 5-18 • 1,125 pupils (52% boys) • 211 in sixth form • Fees, £2,142-£3,168
Head: Robert Nimmo, mid-50s, appointed 1977.

Highly regarded academic school; first-rate results; good sport.

Background Founded 1239; united with 2 others 1829; moved to present city-centre site and imposing purpose-built premises 1834. Austere neo-classical facade conveys an air of authority and permanence (portrayed on TV as the headquarters of both the KGB and the

Gestapo!); more ornate girls' building added 1890. Recent acquisitions include 2 disused churches. Became fully independent in 1985 with the abolition of grant-aided status.

Atmosphere Well-ordered, traditional (girls curtsy to the head, boys salute); strong sense of community; staff and pupils take pride in a revered institution with a long-established academic reputation. High standards expected in and out of the classroom.

The head (Rector) Respected, influential educationist; not as distant as he might seem to his younger pupils; responds benignly to all greetings. Read modern languages at Edinburgh; trained as a Russian interpreter with the Army Intelligence Corps before starting his teaching career at George Heriot's. Keen Rotarian.

The teaching Juniors taught mostly by form teachers; specialist teaching from age 12; streaming by ability from 13; classes average 22-25. Choice of 19 subjects for Standard Grade; most do 7. 94% stay on for Highers; all do English plus at least 4 other subjects; 80% stay for a second year to take additional Highers and/or Certificate of Sixth-Year Studies (CSYS). Lots of drama and music; wide range of extra-curricular activities; literary and debating society particularly strong. Well-supported cadet force, Duke of Edinburgh award scheme, charity fund-raising. Regular language exchanges with schools in France, Germany and Spain.

The pupils Mostly from professional and farming backgrounds within a 30-mile radius. Entry at 4+ by interview and assessment; at 12+ by interview and tests.

Results (1991) Standard Grade: 96% gained at least 5 grades 1-3. Highers: 58% of entries graded A or B. CSYS: 63% of entries graded A or B.

Destinations 85% proceed to higher education (2 or 3 a year to Oxbridge).

Sport Good rugby and girls' hockey; other activities include cricket, athletics, tennis, swimming. 20 acres of playing fields 2 miles away; school has ready access to the excellent indoor sports facilities at Dundee University.

Remarks Very sound school; good all round.

EASINGWOLD
York Road,
Easingwold,
York YO6 3EF
Tel (0347) 21451

Comprehensive • Co-educational • Ages 11-18 • 1,000 pupils (53% girls) • 140 in sixth form
Head: Robert Kirk, 59, appointed 1981.

Attractive, well-run school; good teaching; all abilities catered for.

Background Roots go back to 1784; became a bilateral (grammar/modern) school 1954; went comprehensive in 1971. 1950s buildings on a large, open site fronted by lawns and flowerbeds and surrounded on 3 sides by farmland. Well-lit, spacious, carpeted classrooms; furniture and decor in good order; pupils' work on display (including fine textiles); state-of-the-art facilities for computing, design/technology, languages, science, music. School is the community education centre for surrounding villages.

Atmosphere Friendly, welcoming, well-ordered; high aspirations for all; good pastoral care system. Strong community links; supportive parents.

The head Charismatic leader, strong manager, dedicated teacher (teaches religious education to juniors, general studies to sixth-formers). Has lectured in education and taught in both independent and state schools.

The teaching Good quality; pupils get lots of individual attention; those with individual needs (about 8%) taught separately; some setting by ability for GCSE; most take 10. Particular strengths in languages (regular exchanges with European schools), design/technology, business education (including computing, typewriting, book-keeping). Vocational alternatives to A-levels include BTEC diploma course in business and finance. Good careers advice. Lots of music: orchestras, bands, choirs.

The pupils Many come from beyond the rural catchment area, their parents attracted by the school's reputation for sound teaching and a wholesome ethos.

Results (1991) GCSE: 45% gained at least 5 grades A-C. A-level: 27% of entries graded A or B.

Destinations 85% stay on in full-time education or training after 16, but not necessarily here; 50% of these proceed to higher education.

Sport Good record in cricket, basketball, girls' hockey. Facilities include extensive playing fields, 6 hard tennis courts, heated outdoor pool (but no sports hall).

Remarks Good all round.

EASTBOURNE
The College,
Eastbourne,
East Sussex BN21 4JX
Tel (0323) 37655

Independent • Boys (plus girls in sixth form) • Boarding and day • Ages 13-18 • 540 pupils (60% boarding) • 250 in sixth form (70% boys) • Fees, £9,807 boarding; £7,251 day
Head: Christopher Saunders, appointed 1981.

Friendly, middle-of-the-road school. Good arts and sport.

Background Founded 1867 by 8th Duke of Devonshire. Red-brick buildings (leaded windows, oak doors) and superb cloisters arranged around a cricket square. 10-year building and refurbishment programme just completed at a cost of £6 million (excellent boarding accommodation).

Atmosphere Happy, welcoming, well-disciplined.

The head Insists on high academic and personal standards. Gets on well with pupils, parents and staff. Avid sportsman (cricket and soccer blue), natural flair for PR.

The teaching Wait-and-see policy towards national curriculum. All follow core of English language and literature, maths, French, 3 sciences and choose another 3 subjects out of 14, including German, Spanish, Latin. Good design and technology. 55 staff (6 women), two-thirds appointed by present head. Class sizes average 20 in the lower school, 12 in the sixth form. Excellent facilities for art (pottery workshop), music (choirs, orchestras, wind band) and drama (250-seat theatre, computerised lighting etc). Every boy expected to act in a play in his first term. Extra-curricular activities include fencing, judo, shooting, squash, rowing, water polo. Cadet force compulsory for 1 year. Expanding community programme: helping out in primary schools, visiting the elderly.

The pupils Drawn from more than 80 prep schools in London and the South East. Fairly wide ability range: modest 50% required at Common Entrance.

Results (1991) GCSE: 91% gained at least 5 grades A-C (88% passed 8). A-level: 38% of entries graded A or B (but the proportion is rising).

Destinations 80% continue from GCSE to A-level (most of the rest go to sixth-form colleges); 80% of these proceed to higher education (7 to Oxbridge in 1991) .

Sport Rugby, hockey, cricket for the boys (recent tours to Australia, New Zealand and Barbados); lacrosse, netball, hockey for the girls (tours to Germany, Holland, Belgium). Indoor heated swimming pool.

Remarks Exam results improving steadily. Notably good relations between staff and pupils.

EATON
Eaton Road,
Norwich,
Norfolk NR4 6PP
Tel (0603) 54015

Comprehensive • Co-educational • Ages
12-18 • 1,155 pupils (52 boys) • 310 in
sixth form
Head: Dr Tom Elkins, 52, appointed 1978.

---

*Well-regarded, rather formal
comprehensive; high standards
expected; respectable results; good
music and art.*

Background Founded 1910 as the City of
Norwich School, the result of the local
community's wish to have a grammar school to
match those in other great cities. Magnificent
purpose-built premises (including a fine hall)
were opened by the then headmaster of Eton,
and a tradition of academic excellence was
rapidly established. Became comprehensive
1970. Later additions, including an extensive
range of huts, are rather less impressive.
Facilities generally adequate; those for music
and art are good. School has a unit for the
visually handicapped.

Atmosphere Demanding, purposeful. Traditional grammar-school ethos retained; academic expectations high; discipline firm. Distinct air of formality: not even the head is
allowed to walk on the grass; silence expected
at morning assembly the moment a member of
staff appears on the platform. (Some pupils
have difficulty accommodating themselves to
the regime.) Strong parent-school association;
head produces weekly newsletter.

The head Quietly dignified style; runs a tight
ship. Read English at Queen's, Belfast; PhD in
educational administration. Still teaches; keen
on physical fitness. Married to a teacher; 2
grown-up children.

The teaching Very much in the academic
tradition; experienced, long-serving staff
(nearly half have been here more than 10
years, 5 were here when it was a grammar
school). Main languages French and German;

maths and science results consistently good;
first-rate art (many take it for GCSE). Large
classes – 28 is typical – but smaller in the sixth
form. Choice of more than 20 subjects at
A-level, including Spanish, politics, music;
many take a 1-year vocational alternative; extra
help for Oxbridge candidates. Good music: 2
orchestras, various bands, choir; active drama.
Lots of charity fund-raising. Regular language
exchanges with schools in France and Germany.

The pupils Fairly wide cross-section of abilities and backgrounds; school is popular with
parents and consistently over-subscribed.

Results (1991) GCSE: 48% gained at least 5
grades A-C. A-level: 30% of entries graded A
or B.

Destinations 80% continue into the sixth
form (no minimum entry qualifications); 60%
of these proceed to higher education (2 or 3 a
year to Oxbridge).

Sport 'Unisex': boys and girls play same
games in mixed groups. Strong tennis, hockey;
basketball, cricket also popular. Facilities include extensive playing fields, sports hall,
tennis courts.

Remarks Good school for average and above-
average children; others may struggle to survive.

ECCLESBOURNE

Wirksworth Road,
Duffield,
Derby DE6 4GB
Tel (0332) 840645

Comprehensive (grant-maintained) •
Co-educational • Ages 11-18 • 1,250
pupils (equal numbers of girls and boys) •
250 in sixth form
Head: Dr Robert Dupey, 51, appointed
1976.

First-rate, well-run comprehensive; good teaching and results; all abilities catered for.

Background Opened 1957 as a co-educational grammar school; went comprehensive 1976; opted out of council control 1990. Functional, single-storey buildings on a large, leafy site; many classrooms in temporary huts. Grant-maintained status has brought extra cash; major building programme to be completed by Easter 1993.

Atmosphere Friendly, purposeful, secure; high standards expected and achieved; traditional values retained. Most of the staff send their children here (always a good sign); estate agents quote the catchment area (another good sign). Strongly supportive parents (5 are interviewed every year and asked their opinions about the school). Sixth-formers volunteer to help first-years with reading. Wheelchair access throughout.

The head A tremendous enthusiast for comprehensive education; believes the school should fit round the child, not vice versa. Read zoology at Leicester; steered Ecclesbourne through its transition from grammar to comprehensive. Liked and respected by staff and pupils. Married, 3 children (2 were pupils here, 1 still is); wife teaches children with special needs.

The teaching High-quality; 95 staff (23 part-time), nearly all appointed by present head. Pupils set by ability in maths and modern languages from second year, science and English from third year; extra help for the

gifted ('as resources allow') and those with special needs; progress carefully monitored. Good languages; all do French and – unusually – 1 year each of Spanish and German. Strong religious education; many take it for GCSE and A-level. Choice of 24 subjects at A-level, including law, economics, computing; vocational alternatives include BTEC diplomas in business and finance, information technology. Burgeoning music; orchestra competes successfully at local festival. Regular language trips to France, Germany and Spain; arts visit to Paris; lower-sixth pupils take part in month-long exchange with a school near Philadelphia.

The pupils Articulate, polite (they open doors for adults), confident without being cocky. Most from middle and lower-middle-class homes in a mixed 'urban village' and rural catchment area north of Derby; a few from further afield. Neat uniform (designed by parents); sixth-formers wear suits. Disciplinary problems rare. Over-subscribed; entry is non-selective (priority to the disabled); apply to school by Christmas for the following September.

Results (1991) GCSE: impressive 74% gained at least 5 grades A-C. A-level: 30% of entries graded A or B.

Destinations 60% continue into the sixth form; 85% of these proceed to higher education (5 a year to Oxbridge).

Sport Regular county honours in hockey, football, rugby, cricket, athletics, tennis, netball, swimming. Building programme includes a sports hall.

Remarks A school that will welcome and do its best for any child; highly recommended.

EDINBURGH ACADEMY

42 Henderson Row,
Edinburgh EH3 5BL
Tel (031) 556 4603

Independent • Boys (plus girls in sixth form) • Day and boarding • Ages 10½-18 (plus associated prep school) • 569 pupils (86% day) • 194 in sixth form (80% boys) • Fees (1992-93), £4,635 day; £9,801 boarding
Head: John Rees, 48, appointed September 1992.

Good academic school; fairly wide range of abilities; first-rate art; strong sport.

Background Founded 1824 as 'a school for classical instruction', the major subjects to be Greek and Latin; handsome, purpose-built, neo-classical Georgian premises (including magnificent hall) plus later additions.

Atmosphere Sober respect for scholastic achievement ('Education is the mother of both wisdom and virtue', proclaims the Greek inscription on the Doric portico) allied to patient encouragement for the less academically able (about a third of the pupils would not have passed the old 11+). Boy boarders in 2 purpose-built, late-Victorian houses (linoleum and ageing furniture – but a pleasant, homely feel); girls in more comfortable accommodation.

The head (Rector) New appointment. Energetic leader; had been head of Blundell's since 1980.

The teaching Broad curriculum; specialisation deferred as long as possible. Science taught as 3 separate subjects; all do Latin and 'taster' courses in German and Russian; Greek still on offer. Pupils set by ability in all subjects from second year; maximum class size 24. Most take 9 GCSEs, including at least 2 sciences (60% do 3); business studies, economics on offer. Sixth-formers choose between A-levels and Highers. First-rate art (85 gained grade A at all exam levels); 15% of sixth-form leavers go on to courses in art/ design/architecture. Good music: 35% learn an instrument; 2 orchestras, 150 in choir; regular performances. Cadet force compulsory for 2 years; active Duke of Edinburgh award scheme. School owns a field centre in Angus.

The pupils Confident, courteous, sophisticated; mostly from Edinburgh professional classes. Admission by Common Entrance or tests in English, maths; not severely selective; pupils at the associated prep school transfer automatically.

Results GCSE: 83% gain at least 5 grades A-C. A-level: 55% of entries graded A or B.

Destinations 95% continue into the sixth form; 90% of these proceed to higher education (7 a year to Oxbridge).

Sport Strong. Compulsory rugby for first 3 years (1992 tour of South Africa) and cricket for first year; athletics, cross-country, hockey, fencing also on offer. Facilities include extensive playing fields 2 miles away and courts for squash and tennis (but no sports hall or indoor pool).

Remarks Strongly traditional school but keeping up to date.

EGGBUCKLAND

Westcott Close,
Eggbuckland,
Plymouth PL6 5YB
Tel (0752) 779061

Comprehensive • Co-educational • Ages 11-18 • 1,464 pupils (equal numbers of boys and girls) • 237 in sixth form
Head: Howard Green, 48, appointed September 1992.

Good neighbourhood comprehensive; wide range of abilities; first-rate facilities.

Background Opened 1979 as a purpose-built comprehensive on a greenfield site to serve the new suburbs of north Plymouth. Attractive red-brick buildings too small for present numbers; some classrooms in huts. Separate sixth-form centre has an adult atmosphere much appreciated by pupils.

Atmosphere Warm, caring – with a firm underlying commitment to high standards of behaviour, attitude, effort. Sensible, thoughtful pupils; relations with staff are excellent. Governors fear the school is becoming too popular and that pressure to increase numbers further could change its character.

The head New appointment (following the sudden death of Mike Caddy, who had been head since the school opened). Educated at a Direct Grant school and Cambridge; previously head of a comprehensive in Oxfordshire; has been involved in training new heads. Married, 2 daughters.

The teaching Predominantly practical: children learn through doing; class teaching 'when appropriate'. Enthusiastic staff of 99 (55% women), all committed to the school's philosophy. Mixed-ability classes for first 2 years; setting thereafter in some subjects; great emphasis on each child achieving at his/her own level; strong provision for those with special needs (including a specialist unit for deaf children). Homework thoroughly monitored. Choice of 24 subjects at A-level; 20% of sixth-formers take vocational courses, including BTEC diplomas in business and finance. First-rate facilities, especially for design/technology and music.

The pupils Wide range of abilities (but local grammar schools cream off some of the most able). Nearly all from the surrounding owner-occupied housing estates; substantial minority are the children of Service families. Truancy rate negligible. School is over-subscribed; local authority handles admissions; priority to siblings and those living closest.

Results (1991) GCSE: 35% gained at least 5 grades A-C (close to the national average). A-level: 20% of entries graded A or B (below the national average).

Destinations 60% continue into the sixth form; 58% of these proceed to higher education.

Sport Extensive, well-used facilities. Special-

ist teaching in aerobics, golf, weight-training plus a wide variety of other options.

Remarks Her Majesty's Inspectors commented in a recent report: 'This is an exceptional school which provides a rich, enjoyable and successful educational experience...It is a good school to be a pupil in.'

ELTHAM

Grove Park Road,
Mottingham,
London SE9 4QF
Tel (081) 857 1455

Independent • Boys (plus girls in the sixth form) • Day (and some boarding) • Ages 11-18 (plus associated junior school) • 551 pupils (25 boarding) • 143 in sixth form (70% boys) • Fees, £4,710 (£9,315 boarding)
Head: Malcolm Green, late-40s, appointed 1990.

First-class teaching and results; strong music and sport.

Background Founded 1842 for the sons of missionaries; moved to present 25-acre parkland site in 1912. Imposing early 18th-century mansion; other buildings more functional; fine new performing arts centre. Reverted to full independence with the abolition of Direct Grant status in 1976. Shares governing body with Walthamstow Hall *(qv)*.

Atmosphere Warm, friendly; high degree of mutual consideration and support; good relations between staff and pupils; strong parental involvement; distinct Christian ethos retained. Small, homely boarding house (named after Eric Liddell, Olympic champion and China missionary, who was a pupil here).

The head Read English at Cambridge; formerly head of Warminster. Teaches all first-years. Married, 2 grown-up daughters.

The teaching High-quality. Committed, well-qualified staff of 53 (12 women); particularly good results in maths, chemistry, physics, French, geography, history. Demanding curriculum; most boys take 10 GCSEs; science taught as 3 separate subjects; German, Latin on offer; design/technology still fairly rudimentary. No streaming by ability except in maths; maximum class size 25. Most take 3-4 A-levels (from choice of 21) plus broad general studies programme including life skills, Japanese studies, economic literacy. Lots of drama and music; 25% learn an instrument; 2 orchestras, several smaller ensembles and choir (a very supportive environment for any boy with a musical bent). Flourishing debating society and Christian Union; community service among the elderly and handicapped. Extensive programme of UK and foreign visits; language exchanges with schools in France and Germany.

The pupils 45 of the 75 places available at 11+ go to pupils from the associated junior school; rest take tests in English, maths, verbal reasoning. School over-subscribed and academically quite selective. Assisted places, scholarships (including music) available.

Results GCSE: virtually all gain at least 5 grades A-C. A-level (1992): creditable 64% of entries graded A or B.

Destinations 95% stay on for A-levels; virtually all of these proceed to higher education (10 a year to Oxbridge).

Sport Good record in rugby (recent tour to Canada), cricket and swimming (full-time coach). Facilities include 25 acres of playing fields, large indoor pool.

Remarks Good all round; strongly recommended.

EMANUEL

Battersea Rise,
London SW11 1HS
Tel (081) 870 4171

Independent • Boys • Day • Ages 10-18 • 760 pupils • 147 in sixth form • Fees, £4,200-£4,500
Head: Peter Thomson, 53, appointed 1984.

Sound, traditional school; not unduly selective; heavily over-subscribed. Strong choral music and rowing.

Background Founded 1594; moved to a former Victorian orphanage 1893; imposing, ivy-clad buildings in 13 acres. Later additions include science and technology blocks and a galleried assembly hall big enough to seat the whole school; sixth-form centre under construction. Co-education under consideration.

Atmosphere Committed teachers (some *very* long serving); enthusiastic, hard-working pupils; supportive parents (up to £15,000 raised annually). Pronounced Christian tradition (2 full-time chaplains).

The head Initially rather intimidating but well-respected by staff and boys. Read history at Cambridge; formerly second master at St Paul's. Teaches general studies to the sixth form, history and divinity to younger pupils.

The teaching Traditional academic curriculum; Latin compulsory for first 3 years; all take French; German, Russian, Greek also on offer. Plenty of computing; good maths, chemistry, physics, technology. Average class size 24. Choice of 19 subjects at A-level. Strong drama and music; first-rate chapel choir (annual tours). Extra-curricular activities include well-supported cadet force, flourishing Christian Union, much community service. Regular language exchange with a school in France.

The pupils Considerable social and ethnic mix; more than a third have assisted places. Entry at 10, 11 by interview and tests (much weight attached to the former); 300 apply for 100 places; fairly wide range of abilities admitted.

Results GCSE (1991): 80% gained at least 5 grades A-C. A-level (1992): 35% of entries graded A or B.

Destinations 70% stay on for A-levels (rest seek vocational courses elsewhere); 75% of these proceed to higher education (a few a year to Oxbridge).

Sport Strong cricket and rugby (1991 tour of Australia and New Zealand) but greatest prowess is on the water; crews have rowed on the Thames for 60 years with notable success (boathouse near Barnes bridge). Facilities include athletics track, indoor pool and a further 12 acres of playing fields near Raynes Park.

Remarks Solid school for boys of average and above-average ability.

EMMANUEL
Consett Road,
Lobley Hill,
Gateshead,
Tyne and Wear NE11 0AN
Tel (091) 460 2099

City Technology College • Co-educational • Ages 11-18 • 450 pupils (rising by 150 a year to 900; equal numbers of girls and boys) • Sixth form opens 1995
Head: William Smith, late-50s, appointed September 1992 for 1 year.

Fine modern school; emphasis on maths, science, technology; strongly Christian ethos.

Background Opened September 1990, one of 15 City Technology Colleges set up by the Government and partly funded by business and industry. Solid, red-brick purpose-built premises on the site of a former council school, surrounded by playing fields which until recently the council barred it from using. Spacious, very well-equipped classrooms, lecture theatres, labs; exceptionally good provision for computing; superb dance studio. School open from 8 a.m. to 6 p.m.

Atmosphere Bustling, purposeful; a feeling of space and warmth (more like an industrial plant than a school); ethos is strongly Christian and traditional (which might appear to sit uneasily with the emphasis on technology – but it does not). Neatly uniformed pupils clearly aware of the standards of behaviour and effort expected – and sense they are privileged to be here; sympathetic pastoral care system; exceptionally good parental support. Tasty, well-presented food (served in an atmosphere reminiscent of a motorway service station).

The head (Principal) New appointment; formerly head of a local comprepensive.

The teaching Emphasis is on ensuring a firm grasp of the basic skills but methods are based more on group and individual work than whole-class teaching. Highly qualified staff, noticeably younger than average, collectively willing to go the extra mile. Half the timetable is devoted to maths, science and technology; the rest to the normal range of national curriculum subjects. Pupils set by ability from second year in maths, science, modern languages (French and German); average class size 24, reducing to 18 for maths, science, technology. Special attention paid to information technology; all have their own pass key to the enormous computer network. Full range of GCSE courses is envisaged in due course. Growing range of lunch-time and leisure activities.

The pupils Bright, cheerful, well-adjusted. All carefully selected to cover the full range of ability and social and ethnic backgrounds; intake more perfectly comprehensive than that of any normal comprehensive school. Catchment area covers most of Gateshead, inner-city areas of Newcastle and part of Derwentside. Entry by standardised tests and interviews with parents and children; main purpose is to establish the requisite motivation. School more than 4 times over-subscribed.

Results First pupils will take GCSE in 1994.

Destinations All are expected to stay on into the sixth form.

Sport Thriving rugby, soccer, hockey, netball, cross-country. Facilities include first-rate sports hall (but no swimming pool).

Remarks A nice blend of Christian values and a curriculum which exploits the latest technology unhampered by academic tradition. Highly recommended.

EPSOM
College Road,
Epsom,
Surrey KT17 4JQ
Tel (0372) 723621

Independent • Boys (plus girls in the sixth form) • Boarding and day • Ages 13-18 • 635 pupils (60% boarding) • 309 in sixth form (80% boys) • Fees, £9,255-£9,405 boarding; £6,600 day
Head: Dr John Cook, 51, appointed 1982 (retiring December 1992).

First-rate school; good academic results; strong science. Superbly equipped for a wide range of activities.

Background Founded 1853 for the sons of doctors (opened by Prince Albert); strong medical links remain. 88-acre site; handsome Victorian buildings (extensively refurbished) centred on an Anglican chapel which is a major focus of school life. Later additions include grand sports centre (opened by the Queen).

Atmosphere Tremendously busy, but with a minimum of fuss. Very much a boarding school: 6-day week; keen inter-house rivalry; most staff live on site. School boasts that no other has so many former pupils with medical degrees.

The head Scientist; read physics at King's College, London; awarded a PhD for cancer research at Guy's Hospital; became head of science at Haileybury at 26; formerly head of Christ College, Brecon. Married, 3 grown-up children. Successor from January 1993: Tony Beadles, 52, formerly head of King's, Bruton.

The teaching Methods tend towards the formal; no streaming by general ability but setting in some subjects. Average class size 20. Powerful science department (facilities among the best in the country). All take 10 GCSEs, including 3 sciences; options include German (which all do in their first year), Latin, music. Most take 3 A-levels plus compulsory courses in English, health education, religious studies etc. Extra coaching for Oxbridge entry. Art particularly strong (former pupils include Graham Sutherland, John Piper); many take it as an additional A-level. All lessons in the morning or early evening, leaving afternoons free for music (frequent concerts), drama, cadet force (compulsory for 1 year and among the biggest in the country), Duke of Edinburgh award scheme, hobbies, games.

The pupils Hard-working; top 20% of the ability range; about 15% join from state primary schools. Most boarders live within a 50-mile radius; day boys travel up to 20 miles. Some assisted places, scholarships; special awards for children of doctors; closed scholarships to some medical schools.

Results All gain at least 5 grades A-C. A-level (1992): 57% of entries graded A or B.

Destinations 95% stay for A-levels; 90% of these to higher education (25 to read medicine, 18 to Oxbridge in 1991).

Sport Outstanding (9 internationals in 1991); shooting particularly strong. 25 sports on offer; up to 38 teams turn out on Saturday afternoons. Facilities include 2 sports halls, gym, swimming pool, squash courts, climbing wall, weight training area.

Remarks All-round excellence; highly recommended.

ERMYSTED'S
Gargrave Road,
Skipton,
North Yorkshire BD23 1PL
Tel (0756) 792186

Grammar (voluntary-aided) • Boys • Ages
11-18 • 523 pupils • 138 in sixth form
Head: David Buckroyd, early 50s,
appointed 1982.

*Grammar school tradition at its best; high
standards combined with a lively social
conscience.*

Background Celebrated its 500th anniversary in 1992. (John Wesley applied for the headship but was turned down.) Mostly (19th-century buildings in pleasant grounds; attractive classrooms; spartan gym (sports hall badly needed).

Atmosphere Calm, purposeful (reflecting the 'virtue and discipline' specified in the original charter).

The head Yorkshireman; Rotarian with a passion for choral singing and rugby. Proud of his staff; consults and involves them, tough decisions tactfully implemented. Takes care to ensure pupils are part of the wider community.

The teaching Attractive mix of formal lessons and group work, taking full advantage of the boys' ability and their willingness to work hard. No streaming except in Latin; some setting in maths, English and modern languages. National curriculum implemented without slavish adherence to detail. Particularly good technology and geography (sea temperatures examined by satellite). Most boys take 10 GCSEs, including 3 separate sciences. Homework strictly organised. 35 teachers; low turnover almost too low (only 2 women). Classrooms old, well-worn but welcoming; plenty of work on display. Class sizes average 27 in lower school; smaller for GCSE; sixth-form groups of 6-15. Strong art and music – large orchestra and the high-quality brass band one would expect to find in these parts. Boys encouraged to meet pupils from other schools in competitions and debate.

Formidable array of educational trips at home and abroad .

The pupils Friendly, lively, practically-minded. Drawn from wide, predominantly rural catchment area: parts of Lancashire, Bradford and towns as far away as Keighley, Colne, Shipley and Burnley. Entrance test set by local authority; preference given to local boys on the recommendation of primary school heads.

Results GCSE: 90% gain at least 5 grades A-C (most pass 9). A-level: 52% of entries graded A or B.

Destinations 90% stay on into the sixth form; nearly all of these proceed to higher education.

Sport Team ethic prevails; particularly strong rugby (playing fields two-thirds of a mile away); also orienteering, fly-fishing and golf. Remarkably, half the staff can be found supervising and refereeing most Saturday mornings.

Remarks A grammar school which makes the most of its privileged position. The balance between academic excellence, individual development and extra-curricular activities is hard to fault.

ETON
Windsor,
Berkshire SL4 6DW
Tel (0753) 671000

Independent • Boys • Boarding • Ages
13-18 • 1,270 pupils • 500 in sixth form •
Fees, £10,800
Head: Dr Eric Anderson, 56, appointed
1980.

*Distinguished school, living up to its fine
reputation. First-class teaching; excellent
results; superb facilities.*

Background Founded 1440 by Henry VI to provide free education for 70 King's Scholars (whose successors live in the same buildings);

350 well-tended acres; magnificent chapel; incomparable graffiti. Old Boys include 19 Prime Ministers.

Atmosphere Surprisingly warm despite the outward formality (boys in white ties, black tail coats, striped trousers; 'beaks' in subfusc suits, white ties, gowns); an air of constant activity. 24 boarding houses; boys have their own bed-sitting rooms.

The head Able, scholarly, highly respected; makes no excuses for encouraging and promoting academic excellence. Educated at George Watson's, St Andrews, Oxford; taught at Fettes, Gordonstoun; previously head of Abingdon (at 34) and Shrewsbury. Married, 2 grown-up children.

The teaching Generally outstanding; highly qualified, committed staff of 135. Broad curriculum; all first-years do design/technology, computing, art, drama, music; 3 sciences taught separately. Streaming by ability from second year; all take GCSE maths, French, Latin a year early then go on to do 7-8 more (including, for some, a 1-year 'crash' course in Spanish, German or Russian); design & realisation also on offer (woodwork, metalwork, jewellery-making). Choice of 30 subjects at A-level. All teaching areas spacious, well-equipped (26 science labs served by 14 technicians, language rooms have satellite TV links to Europe). Work and progress closely monitored; internal exams twice a year; full termly reports to parents. Exceptionally strong music; 650 learn an instrument (8 full-time, 42 visiting staff); 3 choirs, 2 orchestras, 2 wind bands. High standards in painting, drawing, sculpture, pottery, print-making (many do A-level history of art); plenty of good drama. 2 excellent libraries; fine manuscript collection. Vast range of extra-curricular activities includes active cadet force, community service. Regular exchanges with schools in France, Germany, Spain, Russia; opportunities to visit US, Japan, India.

The pupils Confident, privileged (if only in the sense that they are here); 37% are the sons of Old Etonians; 20% receive some help with fees. School is less academically selective than St Paul's or Westminster; some boys of marginal grammar-school ability admitted. Registration with a house from age 4; entry test at 11; those who pass (1 out of 3-4) receive a conditional offer and take Common Entrance at 12-13, minimum mark of 60%-65% required (5%-8% fail); non-academic abilities/interests taken into account but places are not offered to those who will have a struggle to keep up. Boys relate closely to their house, housemaster and 'dame' (matron); other points of contact are division master (form teacher) and academic tutor; no one can feel ignored – advice, help readily at hand. Election to 20-member 'Pop' (coloured waistcoats, sponge-bag trousers) the ultimate accolade.

Results (1991) GCSE: all gained at least 5 grades A-C. A-level: impressive 73% of entries graded A or B.

Destinations Nearly all continue into the sixth form; 97% proceed to higher education (65 a year to Oxbridge in 1991); 7-8 a year to the Army (the biggest single career destination).

Sport Standards are high. Main activities: soccer, rugby, rowing (40% participate), cricket, tennis, athletics, swimming. Squash, rackets, fives, judo, fencing also on offer. Facilities include fine playing fields (21 cricket squares), indoor pool, gym, 9-hole golf course.

Remarks Possibly better now than it has ever been. 'Excellence without arrogance' is the aim – and it is very largely achieved.

EXETER
Exeter,
Devon EX2 4NS
Tel (0392) 73679

Independent • Boys (plus girls in sixth form) • Day and some boarding • Ages 11-18 (plus associated prep school) • 772 pupils (92% day) • 263 in sixth form (85% boys) • Fees, £3,282 day; £6,147 boarding
Head: Neil Gamble, 48, appointed September 1992.

Solid school; good all round.

Background Founded 1633; moved to present 25-acre site (1 mile from city centre) and dignified, purpose-built premises 1880; attractive later additions. Former Direct Grant grammar school; reverted to full independence 1976.

Atmosphere Unpretentious, purposeful, orderly; an oasis of tranquility among the urban bustle.

The head New appointment. Educated at Oxford; taught economics and politics at Repton; head of King Edward VI, Aston for 7 years. Ambitions include learning every pupil's first name, sharing a century opening partnership with his son, having a painting accepted for the Royal Academy's summer exhibition.

The teaching Emphasis on learning-by-doing rather than instruction and note-taking; lots of discussion and project work. 66 staff (10 women); most aged 35-45. Class sizes range from 29 for younger pupils to 10 at A-level. National curriculum-plus; all do Latin in second year (but not all take science to GCSE); computers widely used. Science labs spacious, well-equipped; less impressive facilities for art, languages, technology. Choice of more than 30 subjects at A-level; all do at least 1 AS-level to ensure breadth. First-rate art, drama, music (41 peripatetic teachers, 35 concerts a year). Regular exchanges with schools in France, Germany and Moscow School Number 31. Flourishing cadet force, Duke of Edinburgh award scheme.

The pupils Mature, articulate, highly motivated. Many have parents in medicine, teaching, science, engineering; 28% have assisted places. Entry at 11+ by competitive tests in English, maths, verbal reasoning (minimum IQ 120); at 13+ by Common Entrance (minimum 55 mark). 40 enter at 16 for A-levels; at least 5 GCSEs grades A-C required.

Results GCSE: 97% gain at least 5 grades A-C. A-level (1992): 51% of entries graded A or B.

Destinations 95% proceed to higher education (20 a year to Oxbridge).

Sport Chiefly cricket, rugby, hockey, squash; school competes strongly at local and national level. Good facilities.

Remarks Good value for money.

FELSTED
Dunmow,
Essex CM6 3LL
Tel (0371) 820258

Independent • Boys (plus girls in sixth form) • Boarding and some day • Ages 13-18 (plus associated prep school) • 428 pupils (95% boarding) • 208 in sixth form (70% boys) • Fees, £10,170 boarding; £8,025 day
Head: Edward Gould, 49, appointed 1983.

Small rural school; wide range of abilities; respectable results; excellent facilities.

Background Founded 1564; mid-Victorian buildings set in 70 acres of quiet Essex countryside; many later additions. Becoming fully co-educational 1994.

Atmosphere Warm, friendly; effective pastoral care system; good relations between staff and pupils. Pleasant boarding houses.

The head Read geography at Oxford (teaches it to sixth-formers); taught at Harrow for 16 years. Invites all new pupils to breakfast/supper in their first term. Married, 2 daughters. Keen sailor.

The teaching Well-qualified staff of 52 (only 4 women), half appointed by present head. Broad curriculum; Latin, Greek, German, Spanish on offer; most take 7-9 GCSEs, 3-4 A-levels plus general studies. Streaming and setting by ability; remedial help for those who need it. Outstanding computer centre: 160 screens in 18 buildings connected by 7.5 km of cable; technology includes computer-aided design/manufacture. Lots of music (in purpose-built school); 2 orchestras, choirs; more than 20 visiting teachers. Good drama. Regular exchange trips to France, Germany, Spain. Busy extra-curricular programme; more than 40 active clubs and societies; well-supported cadet force (boys and girls); flourishing Duke of Edinburgh award scheme.

The pupils Most from professional/middle-class homes in Essex and neighbouring counties. Wide range of abilities; IQs extend from 105 (sometimes lower) to 125+. 13 assisted places a year plus some scholarships, bursaries.

Results GCSE: all gain at least 5 grades A-C. A-level (1992): 45% of entries graded A or B.

Destinations Most stay on for A-levels; 90% of these proceed to higher education (5 a year to Oxbridge).

Sport High profile; good facilities. Main games: rugby, hockey (particularly strong – many county and national honours), cricket. Regular overseas tours.

Remarks Attractive school; lots on offer.

FETTES

Carrington Road,
Edinburgh EH4 1QX
Tel (031) 332 2281

Independent • Co-educational • Boarding and day • Ages 10-18 • 420 pupils (55% boys; 85% boarding) • 167 in sixth form • Fees, £7,170-£10,290 boarding; £4,470-£6,915 day
Head: Malcolm Thyne, 49, appointed 1988.

Good (and improving) academically; first-rate music and drama.

Background Founded 1870 under the will of an eminent Lord Provost of Edinburgh to provide education for the needy. Site a 100-acre oasis within 1½ miles of the city centre; main building an august Gothic creation of grey stone turrets, lofty spire, 'soaring battlements and leering gargoyles' (architect inspired by 16th-century French chateaux). Later additions include state-of-the-art technology block.

Atmosphere Friendly, happy community – despite the austere building and the weight of tradition it represents; easy informality within a disciplined framework. Victorian boarding houses refurbished at great expense.

The head Has worked tirelessly to restore the school's somewhat faded glory. Puts a big emphasis on academic achievement (and is well-armed with graphs to demonstrate improving standards). His firmness and personal commitment quickly won the staff's respect; delegates more out of necessity than inclination; likes to keep his finger on the pulse. Believes in co-education but looks for a 60-40 split ('boys need numerical superiority to counter more rapidly maturing girls'). Taught at Edinburgh Academy and Oundle; formerly head of St Bees, Cumbria. Married, 2 teenage sons.

The teaching Juniors streamed by ability from the start; all take French, computing, technology; lots of cross-curricular project work; every waking hour time-tabled. Seniors divided into at least 3 ability sets for all subjects (average class size 20). All do 'taster' courses in German, Spanish; bright chidren take GCSE maths, French, RE a year early. More than 90% continue into the sixth form: half take 3 A-levels (choice of 16); half do 5 Scottish Highers (choice of 13); all do general studies and a diploma course in computing. 52 teachers (12 women); substantial 'old guard' (recruitment has favoured experience rather than youth); one of the best classics departments in Scotland. Outstanding drama (7 plays a year, *Oedipus Rex* performed at Edinburgh Fringe) and music; a third learn an instrument; 2 orchestras plus smaller ensembles; several choirs. Enthusiastic cadet force (includes girls) and Duke of Edinburgh award scheme. Trips include skiing in Ecuador, climbing in Norway and Kenya, collecting botanical specimens in Siberia.

The pupils Well-motivated, courteous, smartly turned-out. Generally from professional/executive backgrounds; 50 from Scotland. Entry – not unduly selective – by tests in English, maths (or, at 13+, by Common Entrance). Many scholarships (including music, classics), awards and bursaries available.

Results GCSE: 86% gain at least 5 grades A-C. A-level (1992): impressive 68% of entries graded A or B.

Destinations 95% proceed to higher education (7 a year to Oxbridge).

Sport Games for all 5 afternoons a week; staple diet of rugby, hockey, cricket for the boys; hockey, lacrosse for the girls; much else on offer. Facilities include extensive playing fields, indoor pool, shooting range; courts for fives, squash, tennis.

Remarks A classical tradition made palatable to today's tastes; one of the more cosmopolitan of the Scottish schools.

FOREST

Snaresbrook,
London E17 3PY
Tel (081) 520 1744

Independent • Co-educational (but separate boys' and girls' sections to age 16) • Day (and some boys' boarding) • Ages 11-18 (plus associated junior school) • 1,173 pupils (67% boys; 25% boarding) • 255 in sixth form • Fees, £4,449 (£6,861 boarding)
Head: Andrew Boggis, late-30s, appointed September 1992.

Good school for a wide range of abilities; high academic standards; strong music, drama, sport.

Background Founded 1834 by a group of City businessmen living in then-upmarket Walthamstow; fine Georgian building in beautiful grounds surrounded by Epping Forest; additions range from Victorian-Gothic to distinguished late 20th-century, including £1-million computer centre and fine theatre. Effectively 3 schools – junior, girls', boys' – on 1 campus, coming together in a co-educational sixth form.

Atmosphere Happy, relaxed – but high standards demanded in work, behaviour and dress (uniform worn throughout). No air of élitism; pupils more socially mixed than in many independent schools; individual talents nurtured. Low-key Christian tradition (full-time chaplain); good pastoral care system. Much fund-raising by supportive parents.

The head (Warden) New appointment. Formerly master-in-college at Eton, in charge of the scholars. Quiet, authoritative style. Married, 3 young children.

The teaching Good-quality. Enthusiastic, committed staff of 98 (40 women); average age mid-30s. National curriculum-plus; science taught as 3 separate subjects (first-rate labs); German, Latin on offer; all become computer-literate from an early age; maximum class size 24. Most take 10 GCSEs and at least 3 A-levels (choice of 22 subjects) plus general studies.

Excellent drama and music; more than a third learn an instrument; 3 orchestras plus many smaller ensembles; several choirs (strong tradition in singing). Flourishing debating society and Duke of Edinburgh award scheme. Lots of ambitious foreign trips: Russia, China, India, Ecuador; regular language exchanges with schools in France and Germany. Good careers advice and work experience.

The pupils Fairly broad academic, social and ethnic mix from a wide catchment area. School heavily over-subscribed (in 1992, 250 girls applied for 50 places; 370 boys for 100 places); entry by competitive tests but places offered to non-high-flyers. Assisted places, scholarships (some for music), bursaries; reduced fees for Service and clergy children.

Results GCSE (1991): 86% gained at least 5 grades A-C. A-level (1992): 45% of boys' entries but modest 34% of girls' entries graded A or B.

Destinations 90% stay for A-levels; 80% of these proceed to higher education (12 to Oxbridge in 1991).

Sport Chiefly soccer, cricket, netball, hockey, tennis; golf, riding, rowing also on offer. Regular county honours; busy fixture list. Facilities include sports hall, squash courts, indoor pool.

Remarks Large, well-organised school; single-sex and co-education combined; wide range of talents catered for.

FULNECK

Pudsey,
West Yorkshire LS28 8DT
Tel (0532) 571864 (boys' school),
570235 (girls' school)

Independent • Co-educational (but girls and boys taught separately from 7-16) • Day and some boarding • Ages 7-18 • 652 pupils (equal numbers of girls and boys; 91% day) • 119 in sixth form • Fees, £3,300-£3,750 day; £5,583-£7,773 boarding
Heads: David Cleland (boys' school), 51, appointed 1980; Mrs Bernice Heppell (girls' school), 53, appointed 1991.

Small, caring school; wide range of abilities; creditable GCSE results.

Background Both schools founded 1753 by the Moravian Church to educate the sons and daughters of missionaries; 18th-century buildings (grade-1 listed) plus later additions extending 400 yards along the steep side of a valley on the outskirts of the town. Joint sixth form since 1984; 2 schools formally amalgamated (under separate heads) January 1992. All faiths admitted.

Atmosphere Hard-working, happy; strong sense of community. Boarding accommodation being upgraded.

The heads David Cleland: read history at Leeds; has taught in both state and independent schools; married, 3 children. Bernice Heppell: read biochemistry at Leeds; formerly senior mistress at Tunbridge Wells Girls' Grammar; came here as deputy head 1989; married, 1 son. Both heads are Methodists and fit easily into the non-conformist environment.

The teaching Traditional in style. National curriculum broadly followed. Enthusiastic, long-serving staff; small classes; no streaming by ability but setting in maths, French; special help for those with special needs, including dyslexia. Homework closely monitored. Good music, drama.

The pupils Wide range of abilities; heads estimate about a third are of grammar-school standard. Mainly from the suburbs of Leeds and Bradford, also Keighley, Skipton, Ilkley, Otley; school is becoming increasingly popular with Muslim and Hindu families. Entry by tests at 7, 11, 12, 13.

Results (1991) GCSE: 68% of boys and impressive 83% of girls gained at least 5 grades A-C. A-level (1992): very modest 18% of entries graded A or B.

Destinations 65% of the girls and up to 80% of the boys stay on for A-levels; 65% of these proceed to higher education.

Sport Girls' netball and table tennis are particularly strong; boys do well at rugby. Indoor and outdoor facilities only just adequate.

Remarks Well-run school for children of average ability.

GEORGE HERIOT'S
Lauriston Place,
Edinburgh EH3 9EQ
Tel (031) 229 7263

Independent • Co-educational • Day •
Ages 3-18 • 1,467 pupils (984 in senior school; 57% boys) • 297 in sixth form •
Fees (1992-93), £1,791-£3,420
Head: Keith Pearson, 51, appointed 1983.

Sound academic education for children of a fairly wide range of abilities and social backgrounds; good programme of extra-curricular activities.

Background Founded 1628 under the will of George Heriot, Edinburgh jeweller, banker and goldsmith, who left the bulk of his estate 'for the maintenance, relief, bringing up and education of poor fatherless children, freemen's sons of Edinburgh'. School still occupies its original $8^1/_2$-acre site near the city centre (fine view of Edinburgh Castle from the playground); turreted buildings said to represent 'a climax of Scottish Renaissance architecture'. New nursery opened August 1992.

Atmosphere A large school proud of its history and traditions. The inevitable bustle of a compact campus is cheerful but never unruly.

The head Educated at Cambridge; was head of modern languages at Rossall and George Watson's.

The teaching Emphasis in the prep department on the basic skills of numeracy and language; classroom displays of work testify to much imaginative activity; average class size 25. Standard curriculum in senior school; science taught as 3 separate subjects; Latin, Spanish, German on offer; all do computing and technical studies. Pupils broadly streamed by ability; progress closely monitored; plenty of extra help for those with specific difficulties; average class size 30. All do English, maths and French for Standard Grade plus 4 other subjects from a choice of 19; 90 stay for Highers; 21 on offer. Wide range of courses available in the sixth year, for which 80 stay on. Enthusiastic staff support a wide range of extra-curricular activities. Lots of music: 3 orchestras and various smaller ensembles. Well-supported cadet force and Duke of Edinburgh award scheme.

The pupils Cheerful, unaffected, courteous; well-disciplined without being subdued. Drawn from a wider range of social backgrounds than at most independent schools; all live within a 15-mile radius. Admission by interview and assessment or tests; moderately selective.

Results Standard Grade: 90% gain at least 5 grades 1-3. Highers: 56% of entries graded A or B.

Destinations 90% stay on for Highers; nearly 90% of these proceed to higher education (4 or 5 a year to Oxbridge).

Sport Traditionally strong in rugby and hockey; athletics, cricket, tennis, badminton, fencing, swimming etc also on offer. 25 acres of playing fields 2 miles away.

Remarks Well-run, purposeful school; good value for money.

GEORGE WATSON'S

Colinton Road,
Edinburgh EH10 5EG
Tel (031) 447 7931

Independent • Co-educational • Day (and some boarding) • Ages 3-18 • 2,144 pupils 1,267 in senior school (56% boys; 97% day) • 426 in sixth form • Fees, £975-£3,375 (£6,675 boarding) Head: Frank Gerstenberg, 51, appointed 1985.

Strong academic school; wide range of activities; some facilities stretched.

Background Founded 1741; moved to present purpose-built premises 1932; numerous later additions (some cramped); ambitious development programme under way. Co-educational since 1974; one of the largest schools in Scotland.

Atmosphere Busy, well-ordered but not regimented. 'Teachers' expectations were high,' Her Majesty's Inspectors said in a recent (1990) report, 'and this paid off in the response of generally articulate, well-motivated, achievement-oriented pupils.' Good pastoral care system helps counter the daunting size. 'The school had a pleasant atmosphere,' the inspectors noted. 'Relationships between pupils and teachers were generally good.' Boarding accommodation is friendly and homely, though considerable untidiness is apparently tolerated.

The head (Principal) Genial, quietly spoken. Inspectors said he had won the confidence and esteem of staff and praised his firm leadership. Educated at Glenalmond, Cambridge and London, was head of history at Millfield; formerly head of Oswestry.

The teaching Generally formal in style (core of very experienced teachers). Nursery and first 3 primary years cheerfully housed in separate, semi-open-plan building; average class size 27, big emphasis on language and maths; inspectors mentioned that the more able pupils were 'often insufficiently challenged'. Upper primary pupils more aus-terely accommodated (traditional, high-ceilinged classrooms); curriculum becomes increasingly formal; plenty of extra help for those with learning difficulties, including dyslexia; virtually all transfer to senior school. Science taught as 3 separate subjects; Latin, German, Russian, Spanish on offer; setting by ability in maths, English, French; progress closely monitored. All take 7 Standard Grade subjects but some by-pass the exams to go straight on to Highers (taken by 98%). Sixth-form classes are small, the range of options wide (from robotics to New Testament Greek). Lots of drama and music (in the fine music school): 4 orchestras, many smaller ensembles, several choirs; 'colours' awarded for excellence in the performing arts. Well-supported Duke of Edinburgh award scheme. Regular exchanges with schools in France, Germany, Russia, Spain and USA.

The pupils Solidly middle-class: children of solicitors, chartered accountants, doctors etc; 75% come from within a 15-mile radius. Entry to junior school by assessment and interview; to senior school by tests in English, maths, verbal reasoning. Assisted places, scholarships, bursaries available.

Results Standard Grade results are not meaningful because the more able by-pass the exam. Highers: 60% of entries graded A or B.

Destinations 98% stay on for Highers; 90% of these stay for a sixth year; 85% of these proceed to higher education (6 a year to Oxbridge).

Sport Chiefly rugby for the boys, hockey for the girls; other activities on offer include squash, fencing, rowing, swimming, tennis, badminton, golf, skiing, sailing, curling, cricket etc. Facilities include extensive playing fields, floodlit all-weather hockey pitch, indoor heated pool, tennis and squash courts.

Remarks Well-run school; good all round.

GIGGLESWICK

Settle,
North Yorkshire BD24 0DE
Tel (0729) 823545

Independent • Co-educational • Boarding
and day • Ages 13-18 • 300 pupils (65%
boys; 90% boarding) • 120 in sixth form
(equal numbers of boys and girls) • Fees,
£9,468 boarding, £6,279 day
Head: Peter Hobson, 50s, appointed 1986.

---

*Small, not especially selective school.
Good all round.*

Background Founded 1512; moved to present idyllic Dales site 1869; fully co-educational since 1983. (Associated prep school – Catteral Hall – near by.)

Atmosphere Busy, purposeful; friendly relations between staff and pupils. Solid grey sandstone buildings maintained with pride; magnificent chapel (like a miniature St Paul's) looks down on a cricket field any English village would covet. Pleasant classrooms; attractive, well-equipped boarding house; cheese-and-wine evenings in new sixth-form social centre.

The head Read classics at Oxford; taught at Wellington for 15 years. Pioneered development of links between schools and industry. Has set about modernising a rather old-fashioned institution.

The teaching Full national curriculum; good technology and computing. Pupils divided by ability into 3 streams; top do German, Latin optional; choice between 3 sciences and combined course. Setting for GCSE in English, French, maths, science. Class sizes 24; 10-14 for A-level. Good drama; plenty of music; a third learn an instrument. Regular language exchanges with schools in Bordeaux, Frankfurt.

The pupils Lively, outgoing; mostly in the top half of the ability range (average IQ tending to rise). Largely from Lancashire, Yorkshire, Cumbria but quite a few from overseas. Assisted places; school generously endowed with scholarships and bursaries.

Results GCSE: 82% gain at least 5 grades A-C. A-level (1992): 42% of entries graded A or B.

Destinations Most continue into the sixth form; 85% of these to higher education (a few to Oxbridge).

Sport Good rugby, hockey, cricket, athletics. Also on offer: badminton, basketball, fencing, fives, golf, karate, shooting, swimming, modern dance.

Remarks Happy school; academically sound but with much else to offer.

GLASGOW HIGH

637 Crow Road,
Glasgow G13 1PL
Tel (041) 954 9628

Independent • Co-educational • Day •
Ages 3-18 • 951 pupils (590 in senior
school; roughly equal numbers of boys
and girls) • 165 in sixth form • Fees,
£1,380-£2,595
Head: Robin Easton, 48, appointed 1983.

---

*Strongly academic school; excellent
value for money.*

Background Founded 1124 as Grammar School of Glasgow; became selective, fee-paying local authority school; closed by Glasgow Corporation in 1976. New, independent school arose from the ashes in purpose-built premises on the western outskirts of the city; numbers have grown steadily – and new buildings added – ever since. All areas bright, attractive, well-maintained.

Atmosphere Friendly, purposeful; success has engendered an uncommon degree of pride in staff and pupils alike. High academic expectations allied to good pastoral care.

The head (Rector) Committed Christian; efficient manager; gets on well with staff and pupils. Read modern languages at Cambridge; taught at George Watson's. Glowing report by

Her Majesty's Inspectors (Feb 1990) said he set the tone in a 'happy, ordered and caring community'.

The teaching Good. Well-qualified, hard-working staff of 56 (31 women); mixture of modern and well-proven methods. Juniors transfer to senior school at 11+; mixed-ability classes of 30; setting in maths, languages. Broad curriculum includes French, Latin, 'taster' course in German, introduction to computing; all do music, religious education, PE, games. Choice of 17 subjects at Standard Grade; most take 5 Highers (compulsory English) plus general studies 1 year later; 90 return for Certificate of Sixth Year Studies (CSYS) in up to 3 subjects (Greek, Spanish available). Vocational courses also on offer. Homework burden ranges from 5 to 12½ hours a week. Busy programme of extra-curricular activities includes drama, debating, music (choirs, 70-strong senior orchestra), Duke of Edinburgh award scheme.

The pupils Confident, open, cheerful; mostly from professional/business backgrounds. School over-subscribed; pupils selected for academic ability and potential.

Results Standard Grade: 98% gain grades 1-3 in 5 or more subjects. Highers: 67% of entries graded A or B. CSYS: 62% of entries graded A or B. (Results reflect both the ability of the pupils and the quality of the teaching.)

Destinations 99% stay for Highers; 86% of these proceed to higher education (3 a year to Oxbridge).

Sport 23 acres of playing fields. Major games: rugby, cricket (boys); hockey, athletics (girls). Also on offer: badminton, volleyball, fencing, karate, swimming (in local pool).

Remarks Successful, well-run school; highly recommended.

GLENALMOND

Glenalmond,
Perth PH1 3RY
Tel (0738) 88205/88442

Independent • Boys (plus girls in sixth form) • Boarding • Ages 12-18 • 300 pupils • 154 in sixth form (70% boys) • Fees, £7,425-£9,900
Head: Ian Templeton, 47, appointed September 1992.

Traditional boarding school in glorious rural setting; sound teaching; fairly wide ability range; superb sport.

Background Founded by W E Gladstone in 1841 as a theological college and school for the Scottish Episcopal Church; opened 1847. 250 acres in idyllic surroundings 10 miles north of Perth 'away from the narrowing influences of town life'. Imposing Victorian collegiate-style buildings (plus neo-Tudor towers and turrets). Later additions include music school by Sir Basil Spence and de luxe technology centre.

Atmosphere Cloistered quadrangles, prefects in gowns: a Scottish public school on the English model ('the Eton of the North'). Grim boarding accommodation (echoes of Dickens's Dotheboys Hall) being upgraded (not before time); brand-new house for girls.

The head (Warden) New appointment. Educated at Gordonstoun and Edinburgh; taught at Daniel Stewart's & Melville and Robert Gordon's; formerly head of Oswestry. Married, 2 children.

The teaching Little evidence of any departure from well-tried and proven methods; long-serving staff of 36 men plus 4 part-time women teachers; average class size 16. Setting by ability in maths, Latin; all do technology, art, music, divinity, PE; German, Spanish, Greek on offer. Most take 9 GCSEs; some do maths and French a year early. Most take 3 A-levels (choice of 18); Scottish Highers taken 'en passant'. Lots of drama (350-seat theatre) and music; orchestras, pipe band, 90-strong chapel choir. Strong debating, active cadet force (the oldest in Scotland).

The pupils Polished, sophisticated; 70% Scots, 25% English; most from professional, farming, business backgrounds. Entry from state primary schools at 12 after tests in English, maths, verbal reasoning and a general paper; at 13 by Common Entrance. School is academically selective – but not severely so. Scholarships, bursaries available.

Results GCSE: 97% gain at least 5 grades A-C. A-level (1992): modest 42% of entries graded A or B (tending to support past accusations of complacency).

Destinations 96% per year continue into the sixth form; 87% of these proceed to higher education (7 a year to Oxbridge).

Sport Splendid pitches in parkland setting for rugby (long, proud tradition), hockey and cricket. Excellent facilities include sports hall, heated indoor pool, squash courts, 9 all-weather courts for tennis and netball, well-manicured 9-hole golf course (designed by the architect of Gleneagles), artifical ski slope, private fishing on the River Almond.

Remarks Highly-regarded school; less selective than its reputation might suggest; beginning to pull up its socks.

GODOLPHIN
Milford Hill,
Salisbury,
Wiltshire SP1 2RA
Tel (0722) 333059

Independent • Girls • Boarding and day • Ages 11-18 • 353 pupils (65% boarding) • 81 in sixth form • Fees, £8,985 boarding; £5,250 day
Head: Mrs Hilary Fender, late-40s, appointed 1990.

Sound academic school; good teaching and results; strong music.

Background Founded 1726 under the will of Elizabeth Godolphin; moved to present site on a hill above the city 1891; later additions include new science and technology block.

Atmosphere Happy, purposeful, well-organised; strong Church of England tradition. Younger girls wear royal blue 19th-century pinafores. Pleasant boarding accommodation (dormitories for up to 6); sixth-formers have single or double study-bedrooms (and 'unobtrusively controlled freedom') in self-contained house.

The head Read history at Exeter; came here as deputy head 1987; still teaches extensively. Believes girls gain in self-esteem and confidence in single-sex schools. Married; lives on site.

The teaching Traditional in style; plenty of lively pupil participation. All do technology and computing for first 3 years; science taught as 3 separate subjects; setting by ability in maths, French, English; extra help for dyslexics. All take 9 GCSEs, including at least 1 science; German, Spanish on offer. Choice of 21 subjects at A-level; all sixth-formers continue with a foreign language and do a diploma course in computing. Exceptionally strong music; 50% learn at least 1 instrument; orchestras, choirs etc. Regular language trips to France.

The pupils Two-thirds enter at 11 from prep schools, one-third from primary schools; day girls from Salisbury and district; boarders from

50-60 mile radius. Admission by Common Entrance after preliminary assessment 15 months earlier; candidates must be capable of 9 GCSEs followed by A-levels. Some assisted places.

Results GCSE: virtually all gain at least 5 grades A-C. A-level (1992): 48% of entries graded A or B.

Destinations Almost all stay for A-levels; 85% proceed to higher education.

Sport Choice of 30 activities, including lacrosse, aerobics, yoga, self-defence and trampolining. Facilities include sports hall, ample playing fields, tennis courts, heated outdoor pool.

Remarks Forward-looking school; good all round.

GODOLPHIN & LATYMER
Iffley Road,
Hammersmith,
London W6 0PG
Tel (081) 741 1936

Independent • Girls • Day • Ages 11-18 • 700 pupils • 200 in sixth form • Fees (1992-93), £4,830
Head: Miss Margaret Rudland, 47, appointed 1986.

Outstanding school; excellent results; scope allowed for individuality.

Background Built 1861 to house the Godolphin School for Boys; became a girls' day school in 1905 supported by the Latymer Trust. Fees abolished 1945, when the school became voluntary-aided; returned to independent sector in 1977 to avoid being turned into a comprehensive. Handsome Victorian buildings on 4-acre urban site (space for grass and flower beds); later additions include well-designed block of 10 science labs, art studios etc.

Atmosphere Conspicuously energetic and purposeful but also informal. Grammar school ethos still very much in evidence.

The head Easy, approachable style; makes time to teach and knows the girls well. Taught at St Paul's Girls' for 11 years.

The teaching Variety of (evidently effective) styles employed by impressively well-qualified staff of 76. Demanding curriculum; setting by ability in maths, French. Good modern languages (French, German, Russian, Spanish on offer); excellent facilities for science; less good for computing (outdated network to be replaced). Class sizes 26; smaller for GCSE; 8-10 in sixth form. Fine music and drama (4 plays in 1991 Edinburgh Fringe); pupil exchanges with schools in France, Germany, Italy, United States.

The pupils Articulate, friendly, healthily individual (independence expected). Entry by highly competitive 11+ exam (shared with City of London Girls', North London Collegiate etc) in English and maths; girls need an IQ of at least 125 'to feel comfortable' but admission not based on academic competence alone (head and deputy interview applicants – 4 for every place). Wide range of social backgrounds; up to half come from state primary schools; 25 assisted places a year plus bursaries for those in need.

Results GCSE: 99% gain at least 5 grades A-C. A-level (1992): impressive 71% of entries graded A or B.

Destinations About 10% leave after GCSE to take A-levels elsewhere; more than 90% proceed to higher education (9-10 a year to Oxbridge).

Sport Facilities include 3 all-weather tennis courts, hockey pitch, well-equipped gym and fitness centre (compulsory PE below the sixth form).

Remarks Hard to fault (even the food is described as 'brilliant'). Intelligence essential; perhaps self-confidence too.

GORDONSTOUN
Duffus,
Elgin,
Moray IV30 2RF
Tel (0343) 830445

Independent • Co-educational • Boarding and some day • Ages 13-18 • 465 pupils (53% boys; 93% boarding) • 195 in sixth form • Fees (1992-93), £10,650 (£6,870 day)
Head: Mark Pyper, 44, appointed 1990.

Remote, attractive school; more academic than it used to be. Lots of music and drama; extensive programme of outdoor pursuits.

Background Founded 1934 by Dr Kurt Hahn, the influential educational reformer, after he had been forced to flee from Nazi Germany: his aim was to counteract the 'four social declines' of physical fitness, initiative, care and compassion; regarding puberty as something of a deformity, he prescribed a rigorous regime of morning runs and cold showers. Original 17th-century buildings – including the famous Round Square – plus many later additions (and some rather basic wooden huts) on a pleasant 150-acre estate on the Moray Firth, 6 miles from Elgin. Prince Charles, Prince Andrew and Prince Edward were all pupils here. Co-educational since 1972.

Atmosphere No longer the rugged, spartan place it was but much of Hahn's legacy survives: he was keen on self-reliance, outdoor education, community service. Coastguards, firefighters and mountain rescue are all important features of life here; there is a big emphasis on internationalism (regular exchanges with schools in Australia, New Zealand, Canada, France and Germany); 15% of the pupils come from abroad. Boarding accommodation varies in age and quality; some houses are crowded; others are new and of a high standard.

The head Quiet and modest. Educated at Winchester; has a degree in modern history from London. Formerly deputy head of Sevenoaks, where he taught classics. His father, grandfather and great-grandfather were all heads. Married, 3 young children.

The teaching Broad curriculum; science taught as 3 separate subjects; all do French plus at least 1 from German, Italian, Spanish, Latin; good design/technology. Some streaming by ability; additional setting in maths, French; extra help for those with specific learning difficulties; progress closely monitored. All do at least 8 GCSEs; nearly all take 3 A-levels (from a choice of 18) plus wide-ranging general studies course. Lively interest in the arts: 40 learn a musical instrument; 2 orchestras and several smaller ensembles; 50-strong choir; lots of drama. Big emphasis on expeditions, seamanship (school owns 66-foot yacht) and Duke of Edinburgh award scheme (which Hahn invented).

The pupils Confident, co-operative, contented. Mostly from business/professional backgrounds (45 Scottish). Admission by Common Entrance; school is not unduly selective. Parents may assess themselves above or below the standard fee; those opting below may be offered top-up grants; payments above the standard fee are put into a scholarship and bursary fund.

Results GCSE: most gain at least 5 grades A-C. A-level (1992): 45% of entries graded A or B.

Destinations 90% continue into the sixth form; 85% of these proceed to higher education.

Sport Not dominant (there is so much else going on) but facilities are first-rate: sports hall, indoor heated pool, squash and tennis courts, shooting range, athletics track, extensive playing fields.

Remarks Plenty here to excite and inspire; the aim of stretching every pupil is very largely achieved (motto, *Plus est en vous*).

GRESHAM'S Holt
Holt,
Norfolk NR25 6EA
Tel (0263) 713271

Independent • Co-educational • Boarding and day • Ages 13-18 (plus associated prep school) • 465 pupils (boys outnumber girls 2:1; 73% boarding) • 191 in sixth form • Fees, £9,696 boarding; £6,786 day
Head: John Arkell, 53, appointed 1991.

Solid school; strong all round.

Background Founded 1555 by Sir John Gresham, local merchant and landowner; links with Fishmongers' Company. Beautiful rural setting; mostly 20th-century buildings (including thatched huts) in 50 well-cared-for acres plus 90 acres of woodland. Junior school has doubled in size in past 8 years. Old Boys include Benjamin Britten, W H Auden, Stephen Spender.

Atmosphere Genuinely friendly relations between staff and pupils; fine chapel is a major focal point of school life. Boarding accommodation pleasant, spacious.

The head Open, cheerful, enthusiastic; keen on boats (keeps one in the Mediterranean) and old cars (drives to school in a 1931 Austin). Read English at Cambridge; formerly head of Wrekin. Married, 3 grown-up children.

The teaching Well-qualified, confident, experienced staff; plenty of traditional chalk-and-talk and high expectations; plain classrooms; little glossy apparatus. Pupils set by ability in English, maths, French; largest class size 20. Particular strengths in maths (70% take it at A-level), science (taught as 3 separate subjects), computing, technology; languages are thinner, classics almost gone. Choice of 24 subjects at GCSE, 25 at A-level (including engineering drawing, graphic communication, home economics). Not much help for those with learning difficulties: pupils need to be potentially able and positively willing. Splendid new art/design/technology centre; disappointing library. Good music (strong choral

tradition) and drama (Arcadian open-air theatre in the woods). Well-supported cadet force; first-rate Duke of Edinburgh award scheme.

The pupils Natural, unpretentious; mostly from professional, business backgrounds in East Anglia; small recruitment from overseas. Entry to junior school by informal test and interview (90% proceed to senior school); to senior school by Common Entrance (not excessively selective). Some scholarships, bursaries; assisted places in sixth form only.

Results GCSE: nearly all gain at least 5 grades A-C. A-level (1992): 48% of entries graded A or B.

Destinations Most stay on for A-levels; 90% proceed to higher education (about 7 a year to Oxbridge).

Sport Strong tradition (but the non-athletic are not penalised). Main games: rugby, hockey, cricket; excellent full- and small-bore shooting. Sports centre, indoor pool.

Remarks Geographically remote; good for all-rounders, 'doers' and those who appreciate country life.

GUILDFORD COUNTY
Farnham Road,
Guildford,
Surrey GU2 5LU
Tel (0483) 504089

Comprehensive (grant-maintained) • Co-educational • Ages 12-18 (11-18 from September 1993) • 759 pupils • 159 in sixth form
Head: David Smith, 50s, appointed 1977.

Popular, successful comprehensive; wide range of abilities; good results.

Background Founded in the early 1900s as a girls' grammar school; moved soon afterwards to purpose-built premises on pleasant (though restricted) site 1 mile from the city centre. Later additions include 2 modern 3-storey teaching blocks; other areas in need of refurbishment. Became a co-educational comprehensive in 1977; grant-maintained since 1990. School plans to retain its present character and style; numbers expected to increase to 900.

Atmosphere Purposeful, well-disciplined; high targets set and achieved.

The head Read classics at Oxford. In post 15 years (he managed the transition from single-sex grammar to co-educational comprehensive); proud of what has been achieved; looks forward 'with unabashed enthusiasm' to the opportunities of grant-maintained status, including better accommodation and smaller classes. Wife teaches technology; 1 of their 3 daughters is a pupil.

The teaching Good-quality; less able children perform well. All divided at age 12 into 3 bands by 'ability, attainment and promise for the future'; continuous assessment leads to transfers up and down. All do technology, art, textiles; two-thirds add a second language from 13 (Latin, German, Spanish on offer). Most take at least 8 GCSEs (boys and girls get equally good results). Choice of 20 subjects at A-level (history particularly popular); some sixth-formers do extra GCSEs or vocational courses. Lots of music, drama; popular Duke of Edinburgh award scheme; fund-raising for charity.

The pupils All abilities admitted without selection or discrimination; priority to siblings and those who live nearest (but governors can make exceptions in cases of special need). All social classes represented; some from professional families with parents commuting to London. Demand for places is high.

Results GCSE: the proportion gaining 5 or more grades A-C increased from 51% in 1989 to 65% in 1991. A-level (1992): creditable 43% of entries graded A or B.

Destinations About 65% continue into the sixth form (most of the rest to further education colleges); 25% leave after 1 year; more than half who take A-levels proceed to higher education.

Sport Soccer, rugby, netball, hockey in the winter; athletics, cricket, tennis, rounders in the summer. Indoor games include basketball, badminton, table tennis.

Remarks Well-run, expanding school; model comprehensive.

GUILDFORD HIGH

London Road,
Guildford GU1 1SJ
Tel (0483) 61440

Independent • Girls • Day • Ages 11-18 (plus associated junior school) • 444 pupils • 100 in sixth form • Fees, £4,029 Head: Mrs Sue Singer, 50, appointed 1991.

Highly academic school; first-rate results; good music and sport.

Background Founded 1888; one of 7 independent schools governed by the Church Schools Company providing a sound education based on Christian principles. Red-brick Victorian building added to over the years as the school expanded; now slightly crowded; some classrooms in wooden huts. Ambitious building programme.

Atmosphere Purposeful, hard-working, fairly formal, conformist. Decent behaviour and high standards expected (truancy inconceivable). Striving for excellence is fundamental to the school but overt competitiveness is discouraged; big emphasis on concern for others, responsibility to the community (girls do lots of voluntary work). Christian tradition fundamental, but not pushed. Strong parental support and involvement.

The head Highly intelligent, strong personality, polished appearance. Came to the job by a slightly unorthodox route (finds this useful when talking to girls about careers): educated at St Mary's, Calne; abandoned her original plan to do medicine; married young and acquired a maths degree from the Open University while bringing up small children and running a playgroup; taught briefly in a comprehensive and then at St Paul's Girls', where she became head of maths. Says she has inherited a first-class school and excellent staff and is only gradually initiating changes. Teaches 5 periods a week, principally as a means of getting to know the girls. Much liked by her sixth-formers, who find her approachable and clued-up.

The teaching Thorough, mostly traditional. Academic standards high across the curriculum; children well-grounded; work well-presented. Highly qualified all-graduate staff of 39 (mostly women); some have been here a long time. Broad-based curriculum; choice of combined or 3 separate sciences (extensive labs, excellent teaching); good languages. Mixed-ability classes (average size 20); setting in maths, French from second year. Wide choice of subjects at A-level; imaginative general studies course. Strong musical tradition (both singing and instrumental); drama less developed. Excellent careers provision, including work experience. Regular French and German language exchanges.

The pupils Bright, well-mannered, predominantly middle-class; about 50% of parents are 'first-time buyers' of independent education. Highly competitive entry from age 4 onwards by school's own tests and interview; oversubscribed at 11+ by more than 2 to 1. Some assisted places.

Results GCSE: virtually all gain at least 5 grades A-C. A-level (1992): very creditable 66% of entries graded A or B.

Destinations 80% continue into the sixth form; virtually all of these proceed to higher education (average of 7 a year to Oxbridge).

Sport Strong sporting tradition. Lacrosse played to high standard, some girls reaching county level; also netball, swimming, tennis, rounders, athletics. Facilities include 4 acres of games fields, heated indoor pool, 6 tennis courts, good gym.

Remarks Very good school, run on traditional lines; highly recommended for able girls.

HABERDASHERS' ASKE'S BOYS'

Butterfly Lane,
Elstree,
Borehamwood,
Hertfordshire WD6 3AF
Tel (081) 207 4323

Independent • Boys • Day • Ages 11-18 (plus adjoining prep school) • 1,100 pupils • 300 in sixth form • Fees (1992-93), £4,677 Head: Keith Dawson, early-50s, appointed 1987.

Impressive, highly selective school; excellent results; superb facilities.

Background Founded in Hoxton in 1690 from an estate left in trust to the Haberdashers' Company by Robert Aske; moved to Hampstead in 1898 and to its present 100-acre campus, shared with Haberdashers' Aske's Girls' *(qv)*, in 1961. Queen Anne-style red-brick mansion plus later additions; 1960s buildings showing their age; good sports centre and music block; splendid new classroom complex – first stage of a 20-year development plan.

Atmosphere Cheerful and extremely busy. (School notices are displayed on a BR-type viewdata screen, a high-tech innovation of which the staff are very proud but the boys sceptical: there are so many messages to get on to the screen that they tend to scroll by too quickly to take in.)

The head Started teaching (history) here in 1963; left after 7 years to become head of a comprehensive and then 2 sixth-form colleges, the first in his native Scarborough. Style is low key but high care; he strides round looking busy but friendly. Staff admire his energy; boys warm to his quiet optimism and integrity. School feels secure in his hands. (Idealism tempered by northern practicality.)

The teaching First-rate: hard-working, professional staff of 83 (8 women); wide range of expertise; low turnover. Science and arts subjects attract brightest boys in equal numbers. Art, computing (run by a woman of missionary zeal), design and technology all compulsory for at least 3 years. Staff and boys fizz together. Excellent drama and music (choir has sung at Covent Garden). 42 flourishing societies; cadet force and community service taken seriously. Work experience for all; lots of school trips.

The pupils Out-going, resilient, alert (if somewhat conformist); determined to get the most out of their education; tend to see Oxbridge as their goal. (Head says boys here need stickability, an appetite for learning, and must be 'joiners and givers'; the boys say you are 'thought more of if you do everything'.) Rich North London religious and ethnic mix; faiths flourish in profusion. (On Wednesdays boys can choose between Hindu, Moslem, Jewish and Christian assemblies – and some move between them in the way their parents might choose to eat in different ethnic restaurants.) Heavily over-subscribed; entry at 11 by examination (4 compete for every place); 70 come from state primary schools. More than 300 have assisted places, bursaries, scholarships.

Results GCSE: all gain at least 5 grades A-C. A-level (1992): impressive 75% of entries graded A or B.

Destinations Almost all to higher education (27 a year to Oxbridge).

Sport Important to a lot of boys; keen inter-school rugby, hockey and cricket in particular, plus many others. Facilities include indoor cricket school, squash courts, swimming pool, athletics track, all-weather pitch etc.

Remarks Cosmopolitan school preparing the brightest boys in North London for successful careers in the 21st century – and doing it superbly well.

HABERDASHERS' ASKE'S GIRLS'
Aldenham Road,
Elstree,
Hertfordshire WD6 3BT
Tel (081) 953 4261

Independent • Girls • Day • Ages 5-18 • 1,125 pupils (833 in senior school) • 240 in sixth form • Fees, £2,490-£3,030
Head: Mrs Penelope Penney, 49, appointed 1991.

One of the top 10 girls' schools. Highly academic; excellent results; particularly strong in maths and science.
Country-park setting helps relieve the hot-house atmosphere.

Background Founded in west London 1901, part of the ancient foundation of Robert Aske; moved to present 50-acre site 1974. Linked (by the 'Passion Gates') to Haberdashers' Aske's Boys' *(qv)* next door.

Atmosphere Sensible, minimum of fuss or trouble – everyone is here from choice and knows the school's academic aims. Accommodation strained by rising numbers; some areas looking drab and rather crowded. Grand technology complex just opened.

The head English graduate (Bristol). Gives an appearance of calm competence and guarded friendliness. Her third headship: the first – 7 years at an inner London comprehensive – tested her toughness when the school burned down; the second – 5 years at Putney Girls' High – must have been comparatively plain sailing. She and her husband live in a house in the grounds: in to work by 7.30 a.m. Cares enormously about the school's sense of community; personally takes a photograph of every girl who has achieved something noteworthy, and displays it in the front hall.

The teaching Delivers the goods, to judge by the results. At A-level, 60% take at least 1 science; 40% take maths. Individual work graded but no class rankings at any stage. First-rate staff (a third men); the few who leave do so for family reasons, not because they can think of anywhere else they would rather teach. Strong music (most learn an instrument), art and drama. Girls shine in inter-school debating and quizzes. (Last bus leaves school at 5.30 p.m. so everyone can join in the extra-curricular activities.) Not much done jointly with the boys' school; both sides seem too busy.

The pupils North London social, ethnic and religious mix (Christian Union, Jewish assembly, Muslim society). Girls respect each other; tend to be over-modest about their own capabilities. They observe the rules because they are keen to get things right (deputy head vaguely remembers that a girl was caught smoking about 3 years ago). Some 50 a year enter at 5 after playgroup activity and interview. Most join in 11 after maths, English and IQ-type tests; only 1 in 5 succeeds (equally from state and independent schools). Able girls obviously stand a better chance but head emphasises she is choosing a 'family' and wants a good mix, including a few eccentrics. Half are vegetarians. 20 assisted places a year (not all taken up), bursaries and 1 or 2 scholarships.

Results GCSE: virtually all gain at least 5 grades A-C. A-level (1992): impressive 73% of entries graded A or B.

Destinations All but a handful stay on in the sixth form; 85% of these proceed to higher education (including, in 1991, 17 to Oxbridge).

Sport All do something up to the sixth form. Lacrosse the great success (girls play for junior England team). Also: netball, gym, swimming, fencing, tennis (floodlit courts).

Remarks Well-run by an enthusiastic head; remarkable value for money. Intelligent girls carefully prepared for careers in the modern world.

HABERDASHERS' MONMOUTH GIRLS'

Hereford Road,
Monmouth,
Gwent NP5 3XT
Tel (0600) 714214

Independent • Girls • Day and boarding • Ages 11-18 (plus associated junior school) • 500 pupils (75% day) • 140 in sixth form • Fees, £3,519-£3,831 day; £6,651 boarding
Head: Vacant.

Traditional academic school; good teaching and results; fine facilities.

Background Founded 1892 from the proceeds of the 17th-century bequest made by William Jones, a member of the Haberdashers' Company, to establish Monmouth School *(qv)*, with which it shares a governing body. Imposing, high Victorian building in 25 acres with fine views over the Wye Valley. First-rate facilities, including new art and technology centre; school awash with money (hence reasonably modest fees).

Atmosphere Happy, very traditional (candy-striped frocks, white socks); high expectations all round. Girls made to feel there is nothing they cannot do (but sixth-formers complain about not being treated as adults). Good boarding accommodation (new house); juniors in dormitories (4-6 beds); sixth-formers in double or single study-bedrooms.

The head Previous head – Miss Helen Gichard, in post since 1988 – left 'by mutual agreement' in August 1992, 3 weeks before the start of the new term; Mrs Dorothy Newman, the deputy head, will hold the fort until a new head is appointed.

The teaching Worthy, hard-working, highly qualified staff of 78 (20 men). National curriculum-plus; science taught as 3 separate subjects; all do German, classical studies, technology (in well-equipped workshop), food and textiles, computer studies; Latin on offer from second year. Setting by ability in maths from second year; maximum class size 25. Most take

9 GCSEs and 3 A-levels (some teaching shared with the boys' school; the governors want more, which was a point of disagreement with the departed head). Lots of drama and music; 2 orchestras, 2 choirs; full opera staged every other year.

The pupils From farming/professional/middle-class backgrounds in a wide catchment area. Most join from associated junior school; entry at 11 by school's own tests (not unduly selective). Assisted places, scholarships.

Results GCSE: virtually all gain at least 5 grades A-C. A-level (1992): 52% of entries graded A or B.

Destinations Nearly all stay on for A-levels and proceed to higher education (up to 8 a year to Oxbridge).

Sport Netball, lacrosse, tennis, swimming, athletics. Facilities include spacious playing fields, vast sports hall, huge indoor pool overhanging the slopes above the river.

Remarks Sound, old-fashioned school; good all round.

HAILEYBURY
Hertford SG13 7NU
Tel (0992) 463353

Independent • Boys (girls in the sixth form) • Boarding and day • Ages 11-18 day; 13-18 boarding • 623 pupils (75% boarding) • 300 in sixth form (97 girls) • Fees, £10,545 boarding; £4,994-£7,380 day
Head: David Jewell, 58, appointed 1987.

Fine traditions; good facilities; fairly wide ability range.

Background Founded 1862 in grand, neo-classical college built 50 years earlier for the East India Company (quadrangle 9 sq ft bigger than Trinity Great Court). Spectacular Byzantine-domed chapel added 1877 (promptly burnt down and had to be rebuilt). Merged with Imperial Service College (for the sons of Army officers) 1942.

Atmosphere More than a hint of Victorian triumphalism. Proud imperial and military tradition: 16 VCs; names of 1,100 Haileyburians killed in action recorded in chapel cloisters. Most famous Old Boy, Clement Attlee; school's link with an East End boys' club is credited with converting him to socialism – a fact the present head stresses. Relaxed attitude to uniform but not to discipline: any pupil caught smoking a second time likely to be expelled. Vast dormitories divided by chest-high partitions.

The head Devout Christian; jovial, larger-than-life; fine singer; embodies the school motto *Sursum Corda* (Lift up your hearts). Studied chemistry at Oxford; first headship at 35 (Bristol Cathedral), then Repton. Puts big emphasis on moral values; believes schools like his have a duty to 'encourage young people to repay their advantages through service'. Recently called in a firm of management consultants, who reported Haileybury was weathering the recession better than most boarding schools.

The teaching Well-qualified staff; low turnover; men outnumber women 12-1. Particular strengths in (combined) sciences (two-thirds of GCSE pupils gain A grades), maths and French. Excellent art; business-like technology and computing; compulsory Latin for first 2 years. Lessons on Saturday mornings; 1½ hour prep every evening. Well-equipped classrooms; average class size 18. Good music, drama. Resident doctor. Plenty of community work, visiting speakers, European exchanges.

The pupils Good-humoured, poised, articulate. Fairly broad ability range: head estimates top 35%. (A-level results not spectacular but school claims to do as much for the high-fliers as for the less academic). Most come at 13 after Common Entrance but some day boys admitted from local primary schools at 11. Variety of scholarships (some for music and art), bursaries and assisted places. Relationships between boys and girls kept within the bounds of propriety and good manners.

Results (1991) GCSE: 93% gained at least 5 grades A-C. A-level: 45% of entries graded A or B.

Destinations Nearly all continue into the sixth form and go on to higher education.

Sport Good rugby and cricket. Superb facilities: vast sports hall, all-weather pitches, heated indoor pool, 10 squash courts, 8 tennis courts. Games not compulsory but some form of physical exercise is.

Remarks Traditional public school becoming less selective; facing the future with confidence.

HAMPTON
Hanworth Road,
Hampton,
Middlesex TW12 3HDP
Tel (081) 979 5526

Independent • Boys • Day • Ages 11-18 • 889 pupils • 246 in sixth form • Fees, £3,690 (plus £240 for lunch)
Head: Graham Able, 44, appointed 1988.

High academic reputation; good sport; lots of extra-curricular activities.

Background Endowed 1557 by Robert Hammond, local merchant; re-established 1612, since when its history is unbroken. Fully independent since 1975. Main buildings on 25-acre site date from late 1930s with subsequent additions (drama studio, music rooms, technology centre etc).

Atmosphere Strong sense of purposefulness and involvement; inquiring minds encouraged to inquire further. At a time when many schools are reducing their lunch hours because of difficulties of supervision and control, Hampton's lasts 1½ hours: boys do everything from drama, art, music and technology to debating, chess, bridge and war games.

The head Cambridge-educated; committed to securing widest possible social intake (keen supporter of assisted places scheme).

The teaching Varied methods, all aimed at securing pupils' fullest possible participation. 76 staff, predominantly male; minimal turnover. Traditional curriculum; 3 separate sciences; compulsory Latin for first 2 years, optional Greek; modern languages include German, Russian, Spanish. Technology optional but facilities excellent; high standards achieved. Most take 10 GCSEs; brightest do maths and French a year early. Choice of 20 subjects at A-level (compulsory general studies); extra tuition for Oxbridge entrance. Homework regular and demanding; full reports to parents twice a year. Lots of drama (from Shakespeare to the avant-garde) and music: over 20% learn an instrument; regular choral, orchestral and wind band concerts and recitals. Large cadet force (voluntary); lots of community service run in conjunction with neighbouring girls' school (Lady Eleanor Holles, *qv*).

The pupils Courteous, friendly, confident. Helpful to visitors; supportive of each other; appreciative of staff; quick to applaud success in all fields (including the academic). Sixthformers offered plenty of opportunities to develop leadership and self-discipline. Mostly from middle-class homes (few ethnic minorities); outer London and Surrey-Berkshire commuter belt. Demanding entry standards; intake limited to top 20% of the ability range. 27 assisted places a year, music and choral scholarships, some bursaries. Entry at 11 from state primary schools by examination, at 13 from prep schools via Common Entrance (early application essential – list for 1995 entry closed in January 1992).

Results GCSE: Nearly all gain at least 5 grades A-C. A-level: 51% of entries graded A or B.

Destinations Virtually all stay on into the sixth form (despite presence next door of a popular and free tertiary college) and proceed to higher education (roughly 10 a year to Oxbridge).

Sport Emphasis on involvement (200

represent the school on Saturdays); all main games taught (rowing a special strength); well-equipped sports hall.

Remarks Popular school; good all round; strong *esprit de corps*.

HARROGATE GRAMMAR
Arthur's Avenue,
Harrogate,
North Yorkshire HG2 0DZ
Tel (0423) 531127

Comprehensive • Co-educational • Ages 11-18 • 1,608 pupils (roughly equal numbers of girls and boys) • 400 in sixth form
Head: Kevin McAleese, 45, appointed January 1992.

Impressive, well-run school; very good results.

Background Founded as a grammar school 1903; moved to present site in a pleasant residential area on the outskirts of the town 1936; became comprehensive 1973. Imposing older buildings being refurbished; good quality additions.

Atmosphere Pleasant, well-ordered; code of conduct emphasises self-discipline, courtesy (pupils stand when adults enter the room). Grammar-school ethos retained. Well-supported parents' association.

The head Recent appointment (only the fifth in the school's history). Formerly head of a comprehensive in Essex. Married, 2 children.

The teaching High-quality. Broad curriculum; science taught as 3 separate subjects; all do French from first year, half add German from second year; Spanish and Latin also on offer. First-rate facilities for design/technology and computing. Average class size 30. Homework closely monitored. Extra help for those with special needs. Lots of drama and music: nearly 20% learn an instrument; 2 orchestras,

2 choirs. Popular Duke of Edinburgh award scheme.

The pupils Self-confident, polite, proud of their school; truancy not a problem. Fair range of abilities from a relatively affluent catchment area. School over-subscribed: 350 apply for 245 places; local education authority handles admissions at 11+.

Results (1991) GCSE: 84% of girls and 79% of boys gained at least 5 grades A-C. A-level: 44% of entries graded A or B. Impressive, even by grammar school standards.

Destinations Up to 90% continue into the sixth form; 80% of these proceed to higher education (11 to Oxbridge in 1991).

Sport Compulsory for first 5 years. Main games rugby, hockey, cricket. Badminton, netball, tennis also on offer. Facilities include sports hall, all-weather hockey pitch, tennis and netball courts.

Remarks Very good all round; effectively a grammar school.

HARROGATE LADIES'
Clarence Drive,
Harrogate,
North Yorkshire HG1 2QG
Tel (0423) 504543

Independent • Girls • Boarding and day • Ages 10-18 • 400 pupils (75% boarding) • 90 in sixth form • Fees, £7,485 boarding; £5,025 day
Head: Mrs Cynthia Lawrance, late-50s, appointed 1974 (retiring August 1993).

Boarding education at its best. Graceful surroundings; caring, dedicated staff; high-quality curriculum.

Background Celebrates centenary (under only 4 heads) in 1993. Purpose-built premises (Edwardian mock-Tudor) in spacious grounds. Surrounding homes of 19th-century elegance converted into intimate boarding houses (offering better accommodation than many girls will find at university).

Atmosphere Relaxed, friendly; discipline unobtrusive and unstuffy; girls allowed to express their individuality.

The head Oxford-educated; married with grown-up family. School has flourished under her leadership.

The teaching Outstanding staff; warm, informal relations with pupils; exceptionally broad curriculum, including first-rate technology and computing. All take 2 modern languages (out of French, Spanish, German). Choice of 20 subjects at A-level. Class sizes average 18-20; 6-8 in sixth form. Excellent music centre (350 instrumental lessons a week); good art. Amateur radio station makes contact with astronauts. Staff place due weight on both academic success and wider accomplishments.

The pupils Good mix of local day girls, northern boarders and those based overseas (foreign national and Service/diplomatic families). Almost any girl could find her feet here. Ability range above average but fairly broad. Assisted places and some scholarships.

Results GCSE: 88% gain at least 5 grades A-C. A-level: 50% of entries graded A or B.

Destinations Proportion continuing into the sixth form varies: up to 20% go elsewhere. Virtually all proceed to higher education.

Sport Excellent facilities (including second-largest sports hall in Yorkshire). Good lacrosse and athletics. Gentler pursuits – dance, horse riding, golf – also on offer.

Remarks A school with everything. Rounded individuals nurtured in secure, friendly environment.

HARROW
Harrow-on-the-Hill,
Middlesex HA1 3HW
Tel (081) 422 2196

Independent ● Boys ● Boarding ● Ages 13-18 ● 775 pupils ● 300 in sixth form ● Fees, £11,175
Head: Nick Bomford, mid-50s, appointed 1991.

Solid school; fine traditions; good results; strong sport.

Background Founded 1572 by John Lyon, yeoman; more than 300 acres (including a farm) on the slopes of the Hill. 'Old Schools' date from 17th century. Fine chapel; 800-seat Speech Room for concerts, plays, Harrow Songs. Later additions include grand technology centre. Sir Winston Churchill 1 of 7 Old Harrovian Prime Ministers.

Atmosphere Happy, well-behaved; traditions cherished (waistcoat and tails on Sundays, 'monitors' wear top hats). 11 boarding houses; 1 new, 8 extensively modernised. All staff accommodated on the Hill.

The head Recent appointment. Read history at Oxford; taught at Wellington; head of Monmouth (1976-82) and Uppingham (1982-91). Married, 2 grown-up daughters.

The teaching Broad curriculum includes technology, computing, art, music; German, Greek, Spanish on offer. Setting by ability in maths, French. All take at least 9 GCSEs (including double science). Choice of 21 subjects at A-level; maths, physics, chemistry popular; also history, economics, geography. First-rate teaching in well-equipped and, mostly, spacious rooms. Lots of drama (annual Shakespeare in replica of the Globe Theatre); good sculpture, pottery, painting (artist-in-residence); lively, high-quality music. 90 extra-curricular activities on offer; active cadet force (85% join). Regular exchanges with France, Germany; many opportunities for travel. Sixth-formers join girls from neighbouring schools for 'Way of Life' course in drugs, AIDS etc.

The pupils 25% are sons of Old Harrovians (and many are grandsons); nationwide catchment area plus 100 from Europe and overseas (wide racial and religious mix). Powerful house loyalties (applications for admission to either housemaster or head); boys live in single or shared rooms. Entry via Common Entrance; minimum mark a modest 50% (school not as academically selective as its famous name might imply); 20 scholarships a year.

Results GCSE (1991): nearly all gained at least 5 grades A-C. A-level (1992): creditable 63% of entries graded A or B.

Destinations Nearly all continue into the sixth form: 80% to higher education (20 to Oxbridge); many of the rest join the Army.

Sport Fine rugby, soccer, cricket; much inter-house competitiveness. Facilities include sports complex; courts for rackets, fives, squash; 9-hole golf course.

Remarks Good all round; keeping up to date. (Harrovians are a favourite butt of public school jokes. Sample: *A lady wants a chair: the Wykehamist fetches it, the Etonian offers it, the Harrovian sits on it...*)

HAYDON
Wiltshire Lane,
Eastcote,
Pinner HA5 2LX
Tel (081) 429 0005

Comprehensive (grant-maintained) •
Co-educational • Ages 11-18 • 1,158
pupils (equal numbers of girls and boys) •
227 in sixth form
Head: David Dobson, early-50s,
appointed 1980.

Successful comprehensive school; good results; strong music.

Background 1977 merger of 2 neighbouring single-sex grammar schools; 1950s buildings plus extensive additions. Under-funding by Hillingdon council led to the premises becoming drab and run-down; grant-maintained status has brought significant improvements. Site now clean and well-kept; classrooms being carpeted.

Atmosphere Hard-working, well-ordered; big emphasis on individual care and the comprehensive ethos; sixth-formers volunteer to help younger children with their work. Relations between staff and pupils marked by mutual respect; good home-school links; active parents' association (£10,000 raised in 1991).

The head Enthusiastic; modest about his achievements. Has taught widely in the state system (maths and physics); strongly committed to comprehensive education and equal opportunities (says he would resign if selection were re-introduced here). Married, 5 grown-up children.

The teaching Able staff of 67, 90% appointed by present head. Mixed-ability classes of 27-30 in first year; setting in maths, science, languages (French, German or Spanish) thereafter; lots of help for those with special needs. Good computing across the curriculum; large, well-organised library. Sixth-formers choose between A-levels (25 subjects on offer) and vocational alternatives; all take general studies. Exceptionally good music: 17 learn an instrument; 2 orchestras, 3 choirs, etc; regular recitals and concerts. Extra-curricular activities include Duke of Edinburgh award scheme, charity fund-raising, community service. Regular trips abroad.

The pupils Mostly from middle-class/professional homes in the immediate neighbourhood. School heavily over-subscribed (460 applied for 210 places in 1992); applications to head by early November in the year preceding entry; priority to siblings, those living nearest. Sixth form is popular and expanding.

Results (1991) GCSE: 53% gained at least 5 grades A-C. A-level (1992): 35% of entries graded A or B.

Destinations Most stay on either for A-levels or vocational courses; 60% proceed to higher education.

Sport Wide choice includes aerobics,

athletics, badminton, basketball, cricket, cross-country, golf, gymnastics, hockey, netball, rounders, rugby, sailing, soccer, squash, swimming, tennis, weight training. Ample playing fields; 2 gymnasia.

Remarks Happy, well-run school; all abilities catered for.

HEADINGTON
Headington,
Oxford OX3 7DT
Tel (0865) 62711

Independent • Girls • Day and boarding • Ages 4-18 • 722 pupils (567 in senior school; 60% day) • 130 in sixth form • Fees (seniors), £3,648 day; £7,146 boarding Head: Miss Elizabeth Tucker, 56, appointed 1982.

Selective, cosmopolitan school; first-rate teaching; good results.

Background Founded 1915; attractive site 2 miles from city centre; main building opened 1930; extensive additions blend in seamlessly. Spacious classrooms; older boarding houses homely, later ones less so (tatty carpets, rickety furniture).

Atmosphere Lively (even boisterous); girls encouraged to formulate, express, argue for their opinions; good relations with staff and each other.

The head Read classics at Cambridge; formerly head of Christ's Hospital. Firm on discipline (woe betide any girl who walks on the wrong side of a corridor or wears jewellery before the sixth form); very little happens without her knowing about it. Well-liked by staff and pupils.

The teaching Good. Interesting, well-prepared, orderly lessons; teachers have high expectations. Well-qualified staff of 37 (only 2 men); 10 have been here more than 20 years. 'Careful attention' paid to national curriculum; 3 sciences taught separately (well-equipped labs); all do at least 2 years' Latin; compulsory technology, religious education, computing (all expected to be fully literate), home economics (includes fashion, fabrics, needlework); German, Spanish on offer. Setting by ability in maths, French; regular testing; lots of homework. Class sizes vary widely from 30 to 10. All take 9-10 GCSEs; most do 3 A-levels (or 2 and 2 AS-levels) plus wide programme of general studies. Strong music. Popular Duke of Edinburgh award scheme.

The pupils Mainly from middle-class/professional homes; many from overseas, particularly Malaysia, Hong Kong; girls enthusiastic about the mix. Entry to junior school (traditional teaching – much emphasis on tables, spelling, handwriting) by tests and interview; at 11+ by Common Entrance and interview with head, who looks for personality, well-roundedness, ability to hold a conversation. Early registration advised. Assisted places, scholarships, bursaries.

Results GCSE (1991): nearly all gained at least 5 grades A-C. A-level (1992): creditable 57% of entries graded A or B.

Destinations Two-thirds stay on for A-levels; nearly all of these proceed to higher education.

Sport Respectable match record but not a sporty school. Main activities: hockey, netball (national finals for past 4 years), swimming (large outdoor pool), athletics, tennis.

Remarks Every girl challenged to make full use of her abilities.

HEATHFIELD

London Road,
Ascot,
Berkshire SL5 8BQ
Tel (0344) 882955

Independent • Girls • Boarding • Ages
11-18 • 220 pupils • 46 in sixth form • Fees
(1992-93), £10,770
Head: Mrs Julia Benammar, 38, appointed
September 1992.

---

*Small, friendly, well-equipped school;
good results; flourishing art and drama.*

Background Founded 1880 by Eleanor Beatrice Wyatt, one of a formidable band of 19th-century pioneers of girls' education; moved to present site on the outskirts of Ascot 1899. Gracious, white-painted Georgian house surrounded by well-tended lawns and lofty trees; later additions include first-rate science block, art studios, sixth-form centre.

Atmosphere Cosy, friendly, extremely supportive; good manners *de rigueur* (badges awarded for 'bearing'); girls seem relaxed and happy. Very good pastoral care system; any difficulties picked up quickly. School has particular success with those who have not fitted in to a less flexible mould. Strong Church of England tradition; daily worship in period-piece Victorian chapel. Pleasant boarding accommodation: juniors in cheerful dormitories (up to 8 beds); older girls have own bedrooms; sixth-formers live independently in custom-built bungalows.

The head New appointment. Grammar school educated, has a First in modern languages from Leeds, PhD from Lille; formerly a housemistress at Wellington (where her husband is head of modern languages). Keen to preserve the school's ethos and character and build up the sixth form.

The teaching Lively, traditional in style; emphasis on sound foundations – grammar, accuracy, presentation; well-qualified, predominantly female staff. Girls taught in mixed-ability classes of 12-15; setting in maths, French; remedial help where necessary (including full-time dyslexia expert). Broad curriculum; all do drama, word processing, Spanish from second year; GCSE options include computer studies, law, almost any language (including Japanese). Good science, taught as 3 separate subjects; 4 well-equipped labs; computing used across the curriculum. A-level choice includes media studies, ceramics, business studies. Regular grades for academic achievement and effort; full termly reports to parents. First-rate art (artist-in-residence) and drama; strong music tradition.

The pupils Fairly wide range of abilities, predominantly from moneyed middle-class backgrounds. Admission by Common Entrance and school's own assessment; applications at age 9. Some scholarships.

Results GCSE: all gain at least 5 grades A-C. A-level (1992): 52% of entries graded A or B.

Destinations Two-thirds stay on for A-levels (most of the rest go to co-educational sixth forms); nearly all of these proceed to higher education.

Sport Chiefly lacrosse, netball, rounders, tennis; other activities include badminton, basketball, volleyball, athletics, fencing, squash (2 courts). Excellent new sports hall, small outdoor pool.

Remarks Happy, supportive school; new head expected to strengthen the sixth form.

HEATHFIELD HIGH

Box Lane,
Congleton,
Cheshire CW12 4NS
Tel (0260) 273013

Comprehensive • Co-educational • Ages 11-18 • 827 pupils (equal numbers of girls and boys) • 119 in sixth form
Head: Keith Whitby, mid-40s, appointed 1989.

Successful comprehensive; high expectations of work and conduct.

Background Opened as a comprehensive in 1964. Numbers have grown recently and space is very tight; some classrooms in dilapidated huts; attractive new science labs; further buildings urgently needed.

Atmosphere Polite, well-behaved children; enthusiastic staff.

The head Spends much time outside his study talking and listening; enjoys warm relations with pupils and staff. Has a degree in music; plays piano, cello, saxophone; teaches German, sociology. Married, 2 children.

The teaching Experienced, highly qualified staff. Pupils divided into 2 ability bands; setting in some subjects; extra help for those with learning difficulties (but 'labelling' carefully avoided). Plenty of computing; successful motor-vehicle technology course and workshop for boys with less of an academic bent. Sixth-form provision shared with 2 other high schools, ensuring wide choice of courses. Adventurous drama and music; lots of extra-curricular activities (pupils help at a toddlers' playgroup in the grounds). Merit system rewards evidence of commitment, motivation, success in all aspects of school life.

The pupils Impressively self-confident and articulate; proud of their achievements. From wide range of backgrounds (but predominantly middle-class) in south Cheshire and beyond.

Results (1991) GCSE: 44% gained at least 5

grades A-C. A-level: 40% of entries graded A or B.

Destinations About half proceed to higher education.

Sport Inter-school matches in athletics, cricket, hockey, netball, rounders, tennis (skills tuition in each). Excellent playing fields; some netball and tennis courts.

Remarks All abilities catered for in a successful, happy school.

HELSTON

Church Hill,
Helston,
Cornwall TR13 8NR
Tel (0326) 572685

Comprehensive • Co-educational • Ages 11-18 • 1,450 pupils • 260 in sixth form (more girls than boys)
Head: Dennis Johnson, late-40s, appointed 1989.

Well-run, purposeful school; good music and sport.

Background Opened September 1972; 26-acre site on the outskirts of the town. Lower school (ages 11-13) occupies the 1939 premises of former Helston Grammar School; upper school 500 yards away; buildings on both sites are functional. School recently won a £250,000 technology grant from the Department for Education.

Atmosphere Supportive, happy; good rapport between staff and pupils. Emphasis on good manners, sense of duty; code of behaviour understood and accepted. Highly competitive house system; points awarded for work and conduct. Parents' evenings well attended; weekly newspaper keeps all in touch.

The head Determined, businesslike; strong leader; keen to inject vigour into all aspects of academic work. Read French at London; worked in inner London comprehensives for

15 years (deputy head of one, head of another) before returning to his West Country roots. Happier now in a more firmly disciplined environment where pupils want to succeed and make the most of their opportunities. Teaches French and Spanish for nearly a third of the timetable. Available to parents for an hour before school each morning.

The teaching Efficient, well-structured. Lower school self-contained with largely its own staff; mixed-ability classes; setting in maths; all do French; computers used across the curriculum. Spanish, Latin available in senior school; good science; technology promises to be outstanding. Most take 8 GCSEs. Sixth-form options include BTEC (vocational) courses; good A-level teaching in sciences, modern languages, art, English. Pupils' progress closely monitored; special needs well catered for. Excellent library; good careers advice. Music is a strong feature: choirs, orchestras, many learn an instrument. Wide range of extra-curricular activities, including community service and well-supported Duke of Edinburgh award scheme. Regular language trips to France and Spain. School runs adult education courses for 2,500 students and benefits from the equipment provided.

The pupils Hard-working, responsive; truancy negligible; 35% qualify for free school meals. Catchment area has a radius of 7-8 miles; most pupils drawn from 6 feeder primaries. About 40-50 enter at age 16.

Results (1991) GCSE: 39% gained at least 5 grades A-C. A-level: very modest 19% of entries graded A or B (has been much higher). Good results in vocational courses.

Destinations 70% continue into the sixth form; of those who take A-levels, 90% proceed to higher education (a few to Oxbridge).

Sport First-rate tuition, high standards, good facilities (including use of on-site Helston Sports Centre), spacious grounds.

Remarks Well-regarded school with a bright future.

HENDON

Golders Rise,
London NW4 2HP
Tel (081) 202 9004

Comprehensive (grant-maintained) •
Co-educational • Ages 11-18 • 892 pupils
(54% boys) • 123 in sixth form
Head: Bob Lloyd, 45, appointed 1987.

First-rate comprehensive; wide social and ethnic mix; good teaching and results; strong music.

Background Opened 1914; became a grammar school after the 1944 Education Act; went comprehensive 1978; opted out of council control 1989 (to avoid the threat of closure), the first London school to do so. Functional 1970s brick and glass buildings on a pleasant (but restricted) site in congested north London suburbia. Specially equipped unit for the hearing-impaired.

Atmosphere Well-ordered community with a strong sense of purpose and pride. Full advantage taken of the managerial and financial freedom grant-maintained status brings: staff morale has been boosted; parents' commitment strengthened (they spend their weekends redecorating classrooms and offices); pupils seem properly appreciative. Comprehensive ethos retained: academic high-fliers challenged and extended; less able benefit from a thorough programme of extra support.

The head Widely experienced; formerly deputy head of 2 London schools; has made a notable success of his new responsibilities.

The teaching Lively: pupil participation encouraged. Mix of young and long-serving teachers (some here more than 25 years), nearly half appointed by present head. Pupils set by ability in all subjects from second year; average class size 25, reducing to 12 in the sixth form. Most do at least 9 GCSEs; sixth-formers choose between A-levels (16 on offer) and vocational courses, including BTEC diploma in business and finance. Very good music: strong choral tradition; orchestra, wind band, smaller ensembles. Regular language trips to France and Germany.

The pupils Wide social and racial mix from Barnet, Camden, Brent, Harrow; 50% ethnic minorities. School heavily over-subscribed; 440 applied in 1992 for 200 places; priority to siblings and those living nearest.

Results (1991) GCSE: 46% gained at least 5 grades A-C. A-level: 38% of entries graded A or B.

Destinations (1991) 38% stayed for A-levels, 25% for vocational courses; 70% of those who take A-levels proceed to higher education.

Sport Chiefly football, cricket, netball, tennis, athletics; sailing, golf, badminton also on offer. Some playing fields on site, others 1 mile away.

Remarks Well-run, popular school.

HENRIETTA BARNETT
Central Square,
Hampstead Garden Suburb,
London NW11 7BN
Tel (081) 458 8999

Grammar (voluntary-aided) • Girls • Ages 11-18 • 615 pupils • 155 in sixth form
Head: Mrs Jane de Sweit, late-40s, appointed 1989.

Impressive, highly academic school; outstanding results; acutely short of money.

Background Founded 1911 by Dame Henrietta Barnett, tireless crusader for social and educational betterment, particularly for women; she also helped found Hampstead Garden Suburb, in the middle of which the school is sited. Splendidly imposing Lutyens building (shared with adult education institute); 'temporary' huts behind.

Atmosphere Space – and money – at a premium; premises over-used, ageing and in urgent need of redecoration (bare plaster, peeling paintwork); desks in some classrooms packed closely together. Head and staff make heroic efforts to cope; girls seem quite unfussed. Grant-maintained status under consideration.

The head Nerve-centre of the school: good administrator; brisk, alert; holds decided (doctrinaire?) views. Read classics at Cambridge; formerly at City of London Girls'. Keen to keep abreast of educational developments; great advocate of the ideals of state education; on good terms with Barnet council, who are extremely proud of the school.

The teaching First-rate. Keen, loyal staff (nearly all women) doing their best to teach to a high level, cope with the ever-growing volume of paper-work and attend endless meetings. National curriculum-plus; all girls learn French and German; Latin, Greek offered up to A-level. Large classes: average size 31. Impressive science labs; adequate provision for art; poor facilities for music and drama. Well-used field studies centre near Shaftesbury – to introduce city girls to country life.

The pupils Bright, ambitious, high-flying; under strong pressure from parents and peers to do well. Some from moneyed homes, others from disadvantaged backgrounds; large Jewish element, Asian numbers growing; 25 are bilingual. Entry by interview and highly competitive tests in English, maths. (682 took the exams in 1991, 250 chosen for interview, 93 finally admitted.)

Results (1992) GCSE: 99% gained at least 5 grades A-C. A-level: impressive 59% of entries graded A or B (one of the best state-school results in England and Wales).

Destinations Virtually all proceed to higher education (14 to Oxbridge in 1991).

Sport All take some sort of physical exercise; options include netball, tennis, hockey, rounders; also weight-lifting, rugby.

Remarks High-quality school; popular choice with parents who might otherwise consider going private. 'We don't have glamorous facilities,' says the head. 'We don't have the polish, but what comes out is very good.'

HEREFORD CATHEDRAL SCHOOL

Old College,
29 Castle Street,
Hereford HR1 2NN
Tel (0432) 273757

Independent • Co-educational • Day and boarding • Ages 11-18 (plus associated junior school) • 600 pupils (equal numbers of girls and boys; 85% day) • 160 in sixth form • Fees, £3,675 day; £6,330 boarding Head: Dr Howard Tomlinson, 44, appointed 1987.

Good academic school; fairly wide range of abilities; fine music and drama.

Background Records go back to 1384 but foundation probably coincides with the cathedral's in the 7th century; variety of charming Georgian and Victorian buildings with later additions beside the cathedral close. Co-educational since 1970. Became fully independent with the abolition of Direct Grant status in 1976.

Atmosphere Busy, friendly; strong Christian ethos (daily assembly in the cathedral). Pleasant boarding accommodation; 8 to a dormitory.

The head Reserved, scholarly; committed Christian with high personal standards and expectations; has tightened up on discipline and dress. Formerly head of history at Wellington College. Teaches the first-years in order to get to know them.

The teaching Enthusiastic staff, more than half appointed by present head. Standard national curriculum; particularly good results in religious studies. First-rate drama and music; more than a third play an instrument; 2 orchestras, 3 choirs; regular music scholarships to Oxbridge. Strong debating. Well-supported cadet force. Head keen to develop more links with Europe; regular language exchanges with pupils in France.

The pupils Happy, confident. Broad social mix: half receive help with fees (more than a third have assisted places); two-thirds drawn from local primary schools; many from Services backgrounds (big SAS presence in Hereford). Admission at 7+ and 11+ by interview and tests in English, maths, non-verbal reasoning; minimum IQ of 110 required and good report from previous head; voice trials for 18 boy choristers (no girls as yet).

Results GCSE: 83% gain at least 5 grades A-C. A-level (1992): 48% of entries graded A or B.

Destinations 80% stay on for A-levels; 75% of these proceed to higher education (about 8 a year to Oxbridge).

Sport Hockey, netball for the girls; rugby, cricket for the boys. Good facilities include playing fields by the River Wye.

Remarks Pleasant, well-run school.

HEWETT

Cecil Road,
Norwich,
Norfolk NR1 2PL
Tel (0603) 628181

Comprehensive • Co-educational • Ages 12-18 • 1,870 pupils (equal numbers of girls and boys) • 600 in sixth form Head: Christopher Wade, 48, appointed 1990.

Huge comprehensive; progressive philosophy; good teaching and results; strong in sport and the arts.

Background 1970 amalgamation of 3 neighbouring schools – 1 grammar, 2 secondary moderns; functional 1950s purpose-built premises plus soulless concrete tower block on a sprawling 50-acre site on the outskirts of the city. School is fairly well resourced and maintained; no plans to opt out of council control.

Atmosphere Calm, purposeful and – given the size of the place – remarkably friendly. Good pastoral care system; pleasant relations between staff and pupils, who seem proud to be here; no signs of vandalism or rowdiness. Parents' queries answered at weekly 'clinic'; 80% attendance at parents' evenings.

The head Enthusiastic, ambitious; likes to be 'out there doing'. Read natural sciences at Cambridge; has taught in both independent and state schools; formerly head of a comprehensive in Essex. Married (to a teacher), 2 grown-up daughters.

The teaching Good-quality. Liberal approach; extra help for those with special needs. Choice of 25 subjects for GCSE, ranging from theatre studies to motor-vehicle maintenance; French, German, Spanish, Latin on offer; good results in English, sciences, design/ technology, music. A-level options (choice of 30) include accounting, psychology, sociology, classical civilisation, history of art; good results in sciences, history, geography, German, economics, art & design; 1-year vocational alternative includes courses in child development, infant care, travel and tourism, typing, law. First-rate art, drama and music; orchestras, bands, jazz groups, choirs; annual Shakespeare production tours Germany. Regular study trips to Hungary, Russia, France and Austria.

The pupils Vast catchment area in and around Norwich; no entry tests but all applicants interviewed.

Results GCSE: 33% gain at least 5 grades A-C (national average). A-level: 27% of entries graded A or B (national average).

Destinations 60% continue into the sixth form (no minimum qualifications required – pupils must undertake to complete the course), of whom 70% take A-levels; 60% of these proceed to higher education (4 a year to Oxbridge).

Sport Wide range on offer. Facilities include extensive playing fields, athletics track, numerous tennis courts, fine sports pavilion, indoor heated pool.

Remarks Effective, well-run school but some will find its size daunting.

HIGHGATE
North Road,
London N6 4AY
Tel (081) 340 1524

Independent • Boys • Day and some weekly boarding • Ages 13-18 (plus associated junior school) • 600 pupils (92% day) • 200 in sixth form • Fees, £6,285 day; £9,126 weekly boarding Head: Richard Kennedy, 43, appointed 1989.

Traditional academic school; fairly wide range of abilities; sound teaching and results; wide range of extra-curricular activities.

Background Founded 1565; Victorian-Gothic buildings plus later additions; well-equipped, carpeted classrooms; 20 acres of playing fields and fine sports centre near by.

Atmosphere Despite the recent sharp fall in the number of boarders, the atmosphere is still that of a boarding school: firm discipline; unusually powerful house system based on where boys live; well-organised pastoral care; strong community feeling (half the staff live in school accommodation). Pleasant boarding house on a leafy site.

The head Able, enthusiastic, approachable. Educated at Charterhouse and Oxford; taught at Shrewsbury and Westminster; formerly deputy head of Bishop's Stortford. Ran for Britain; now sings semi-professionally for the Academy of St Martin in the Fields. Married, 2 young sons; wife is an engineer.

The teaching Traditional subjects taught with traditional thoroughness but innovation is encouraged. Well-qualified staff (a third are Oxbridge graduates), ranging from longserving veterans to recent graduates. Science taught as a combined subject; choice of French, German, Spanish; all become computer-literate. Setting by ability in some subjects; average class size 25, reducing to 15 for GCSE, 8 for A-levels. Most do at least 8 GCSEs and 3 A-levels. Big emphasis on extra-curricular activities: lots of drama, music (joint orchestra with girls at Channing *(qv)*; well-supported Duke of Edinburgh award scheme, cadet force. School owns a field centre in Snowdonia.

The pupils Keen, appreciative. Wide variety of races and nationalities, mainly from Barnet, Hampstead, Islington. Selective entry at every level; head says 'bottom line' is the ability to cope with 3 A-levels and university; range of ability is wider than at the top academic schools. Admission to junior school by exam and interview at age 7 (130 apply annually for 30 places) and 11 (150 apply for 26 places); to senior school by interview and/or Common Entrance. Junior school provides half the senior school's intake. Assisted places.

Results GCSE: 90% gain at least 5 grades A-C. A-level (1992): creditable 52% of entries graded A or B.

Destinations 90% stay on for A-levels; 90% of these proceed to higher education (14 to Oxbridge in 1992).

Sport Strong soccer, cricket, fives, athletics, fencing, swimming, basketball. First-rate facilities (including Hampstead Heath for cross-country runs).

Remarks Well-run school; academic reputation is rising.

HOWARD OF EFFINGHAM

Lower Road,
Effingham,
Surrey KT24 5JR
Tel (0372) 453694

Comprehensive • Co-educational • Ages 12-18 (11-18 from September 1993) • 1,021 pupils (equal numbers of boys and girls) • 211 in sixth form
Head: Michael Marchant, early 40s, appointed 1989.

Effective school; good results; strong sport.

Background Founded 1940 as a secondary modern; became a neighbourhood comprehensive in the 1970s. Spacious buildings; delightful rural setting.

Atmosphere Civilised, hard-working; strong emphasis on good manners and courteous behaviour; friendly relations between staff and pupils.

The head Capable, approachable, firmly committed to academic standards. Read geography at Cambridge (and still finds time to teach it).

The teaching Highly competent (county inspector praised standards of pupils' written work and the thorough marking); particularly good results in maths, science, design/technology. Setting by ability in most subjects; Latin on offer from second year. Extra help for those with special needs, including dyslexia. Sixth-formers choose between A-levels (24 subjects on offer) and vocational courses, including business education. Lots of drama; small, well-equipped music school; orchestra, jazz band, 30-strong choir. Regular exchanges with France and Germany.

The pupils Cheerful, well-behaved, highly motivated; largely from middle-class families. Parents contribute £5,000 a year to school funds; friends raise another £10,000.

Results (1991) GCSE: 55% gained at least 5 grades A-C. A-level (1992): creditable 43% of entries graded A or B.

Destinations About 30% leave at 16 and go into jobs; 70% of sixth-formers proceed to higher education (5 a year to Oxbridge).

Sport Good, rugby, soccer, cricket, netball, cross-country. Squash, tennis (7 courts), table tennis, fencing also on offer; swimming at nearby leisure centre.

Remarks Well-run, successful comprehensive.

HULME GRAMMAR
Chamber Road,
Oldham OL8 4BX
Tel (061) 624 4497

Independent • Boys • Day • Ages 7-18 • 855 pupils (735 in senior school) • 185 in sixth form • Fees, £1,990-£2,985
Head: Geoffrey Dunkin, 50s, appointed 1986.

Vigorous, well-established school; flourishing in the face of stiff competition. Good academic record; almost as many make music as play football.

Background Founded 1606; reconstituted 1887, Direct Grant until 1976, when it became fully independent. Original buildings (in pleasant residential area) date from 1895; Victorian riches intact. Many additions since late 1950s; further major extensions under way (classrooms, laboratories, sixth-form centre etc – all financed from school's own resources).

Atmosphere Masculine without being macho. Nice balance between self-expression and discipline (murmur of conversation before morning worship ends the instant a senior teacher stands up). Boys encouraged to understand that the privilege of a first-class education must be balanced against a practical sense of concern for others: prep school recently raised £2,000 for the Save the Children Fund; senior form raised a quarter of the town's total contribution to the NSPCC.

The head Quiet, shrewd, pragmatic. Grammar school boy, read history at Cambridge after National Service. Previous teaching career in state sector; now guiding the school through the biggest physical changes in its history. Married with 2 sons (one in the sixth form before going to Cambridge).

The teaching Designed to produce results: a range of classroom methods but no fear of formality; realistic acceptance that progress depends on a firm acquisition of the basics – even in creative subjects. Standard curriculum; no streaming. Class sizes range from 30 in first-year of senior school to 8-9 in the sixth form. Strong musical tradition: all boys entered for GCSE in history and appreciation of music (a year early); choir, orchestra, brass and wind ensembles plus very successful dance band (revealing hitherto unsuspected talents). Committed staff run a huge range of extra-curricular activities.

The pupils Lively, vigorous; respond well to the diverse opportunities offered them. Wide social spread (a third on assisted places); refreshing absence of snobbery. Few significant discipline problems (detention once a week). Entry to prep school at 7 + after tests in English, maths. Senior school admission depends on performance in English, maths, verbal reasoning (no minimum IQ specified).

Results GCSE: 95% gain at least 5 grades A-C (in 1991, 3 boys obtained 11 As). A-level: 45% of entries graded A or B.

Destinations About 85% proceed from GCSE to A level, virtually all of these go on to degree courses (12 a year to Oxbridge)

Sport Soccer pre-eminent (many regional and national players); also strong in swimming, squash, table tennis. Hockey, basketball, volleyball, badminton, golf, cross-country all pursued with enthusiasm. Superb sports hall but modest playing fields. (Despite the absence of squash courts, the under-14s won a place in the national finals – other schools please note.)

Remarks First-class reputation successfully maintained; a tradition of high expectations.

HULME GRAMMAR (GIRLS)
Chamber Road,
Oldham OL8 4BX
Tel (061) 624 2523

Independent • Girls • Day • Ages 7-18 • 640 pupils (525 in senior school) • 110 in sixth form • Fees, £2,985
Head: Miss Marlena Smolensky, 44, appointed September 1992.

Traditional academic school; good teaching and results; strong sport.

Background Founded 1895 on a site shared with Hulme Grammar *(qv)*; purpose-built Victorian-Gothic premises plus later additions in a quiet residential area close to the town centre; returned to full independence with the abolition of Direct Grant status in 1975.

Atmosphere Businesslike, purposeful; big emphasis on the traditional grammar-school values of good manners, a sense of duty, academic dedication.

The head New appointment. Read science at Manchester; formerly deputy head of Leicester High.

The teaching Traditional in style (rows of desks facing the blackboard); long-serving staff. All do Latin for first 2 years and add German to French from second year. Some setting by ability in maths only; classes of up to 30. Nearly all take 8 or 9 GCSEs and 4 A-levels (from a choice of 18) plus a course in computing. Lots of drama and music; 2 orchestras, choirs. Flourishing Duke of Edinburgh award scheme.

The pupils Confident, responsive; from a fairly wide cross-section of backgrounds, including Hindus, Muslims, Jews; more than 200 have assisted places. Admission at 7 and 11 by interview and school's own tests in English, maths, verbal reasoning; girls expected to be capable of university entry. School over-subscribed; 3 apply for each place.

Results GCSE: nearly all gain at least 5 grades A-C. A-level (1992): 40% of entries graded A or B.

Destinations Nearly all stay on for A-levels; 80% proceed to higher education (6-8 a year to Oxbridge).

Sport Good record, particularly in hockey, tennis, netball, swimming. Facilities include sports hall and indoor pool shared with boys' school.

Remarks Well-regarded, old-fashioned school for able, hard-working girls.

HUNTINGTON
Huntington Road,
York YO3 9PX
Tel (0904) 760167

Comprehensive • Co-educational • Ages 11-18 • 1,300 pupils (equal numbers of girls and boys) • 200 in sixth form
Head: Dr Keith Wragg, 50, appointed 1981.

Successful, well-run comprehensive; wide range of abilities; first-class teaching and results.

Background Opened 1966 as a secondary modern; became a comprehensive in 1973; sixth form added 1979. Complex of buildings with numerous extensions (and 'temporary' huts) on a pleasant 22-acre site on the outskirts of the city. Good provision for science, technology, modern languages and business studies; other areas need improving and updating.

Atmosphere Bustling, friendly; school sets high standards in achievement and behaviour without being in the least stuffy or traditional. The accent is on common purpose rather than academic or social distinctions: to be less able here is no more a disadvantage than being really bright. Good food, attractively served.

The head Full of ideas: the school owes much of its success to him. Read science at Oxford; formerly deputy head of a comprehensive in Leeds.

The teaching The best of modern methods:

emphasis on group and individual learning backed by a sound approach to basic skills; self-evidently effective with the whole range of pupils, including the less able. Standard national curriculum; greatest strengths in English, maths, science and technology; more able take a second foreign language and science as 3 separate subjects. Mostly mixed-ability classes with some setting in English, maths and science; average class size 28, reducing to 21 for GCSE. Sixth-formers choose between 15 A-level subjects and a BTEC vocational course in business and finance. Wide range of extra-curricular activities.

The pupils Full range of social backgrounds and academic abilities; more than half come from outside the official catchment area.

Results GCSE: 59% gain at least 5 grades A-C. A-level (1992): impressive 50% of entries graded A or B.

Destinations 70% continue into the sixth form (some for only 1 year); 75% of those who take A-levels proceed to higher education.

Sport Strong netball and rugby; soccer on the up; all first-years learn to swim. Facilities include sports hall, gymnasia, good on-site playing fields.

Remarks Very good all round; highly recommended.

HUTCHESONS'

21 Beaton Road,
Glasgow G41 4NW
Tel (041) 423 2933

Independent • Co-educational • Day • Ages 5-18 • 1,693 pupils (1,078 in senior school; roughly equal numbers of girls and boys) • 325 in sixth form • Fees, £2,520-£2,916
Head: David Ward, 56, appointed 1987.

Distinguished academic school; good teaching and results; wide range of extra-curricular activities.

Background Founded 1641 by the brothers George and Thomas Hutcheson; moved to present, rather uninspiring, purpose-built premises 1959; later additions include splendid new science block. Juniors in elegant, neo-classical buildings 1 mile away. Co-educational since 1976.

Atmosphere Well-organised and well-ordered (necessarily so given the large numbers); cheerful enough but above all hard working and purposeful.

The head (Rector) Educated at Sedbergh and Cambridge; taught history at Winchester, Wellington, City of London, Portsmouth Grammar; formerly head of Hulme Grammar. A man of authority, but by no means the authoritarian his imposing stature might suggest; although inevitably a remote figure for most pupils, he is a keen advocate of the corporate spirit. Sees the advantages of a large school as 'variety, richness of choice – academic and extra-curricular – and opportunities for distinction in a number of areas at the same time'.

The teaching Mixed-ability classes in junior school; average size 25. Broad curriculum in senior school; science taught as 3 separate subjects; all do Latin, computer studies. Pupils streamed by ability; average class size 30, reducing to 20 in the sixth form. Demanding homework programme. Most study 7 Standard Grade subjects (from choice of 16) but by-pass the exams; virtually all do 5 Highers (from choice of 17). Lively music: a third learn an instrument; 70-strong orchestra; frequent concerts. Abundance of clubs and societies. Regular exchanges with schools in France and Germany.

The pupils Courteous, well-behaved and, for the most part, proud of the school; some 'small-boy' untidiness but generally smart (all in uniform). Backgrounds primarily in the professions, industry and commerce; 80% from within a 15-mile radius. Entry to junior school by assessment, to senior school by exam and interview; regularly over-subscribed. Assisted places, scholarships available.

Results Standard Grade results are not meaningful because so many by-pass the exam. Highers: 65% of entries graded A or B.

Destinations All stay on for Highers; two-thirds stay on for a sixth year and proceed to higher education (6 a year to Oxbridge).

Sport Strong; wide participation. Chiefly rugby, athletics, cricket for the boys; hockey, athletics, tennis for the girls. Also on offer: swimming, soccer, netball, cross-country, badminton, squash, golf, curling, rowing. Playing fields 2 miles away.

Remarks Good all round; a stimulating atmosphere for bright pupils.

ILKLEY GRAMMAR
Cowpasture Road,
Ilkley,
West Yorkshire LS29 8TR
Tel (0943) 608424

Comprehensive (voluntary-controlled) •
Co-educational • Ages 13-18 • 1,000
pupils (equal numbers of girls and boys) •
300 in sixth form
Head: Peter Wood, 50, appointed 1979.

Well-run comprehensive; good teaching and results.

Background Founded 1607; moved to its present site between the moor and the town in 1893; merged with a secondary modern school to become a comprehensive in 1970. Solid, grey sandstone buildings plus 1970s additions; 12 classrooms in 'temporary' huts; overall impression is of a well-used rabbit warren. Facilities are generally good. Grant-maintained status under consideration.

Atmosphere A conscious blend of the traditional and modern: the school is proud of its history but the teaching and the friendly relationships between staff and pupils are thoroughly contemporary.

The head Appointed at the age of 36 (since when he has appointed most of the staff).

The teaching Methods range from the traditional to the most imaginative and up-to-date. National curriculum-plus; science on offer as 3 separate subjects; all do either German or Spanish in addition to French; big emphasis on coursework and computing. Setting by ability in most subjects; extra help for those with special needs; average class size 30 (smaller for slow-learner groups). Sixth-formers choose between A-levels and BTEC vocational courses in business studies and health studies. Good careers advice. Lots of trips abroad.

The pupils Friendly and well-behaved. Intake is genuinely comprehensive but predominantly middle-class; 20% come from outside the catchment area.

Results (1992) GCSE: 57% gained at least 5 grades A-C. A-level: 44% of entries graded A or B. BTEC results are good.

Destinations 60% continue into the sixth form; 60% of these proceed to higher education.

Sport Chiefly soccer, cricket and tennis for the boys; hockey, volleyball and tennis for the girls. On-site facilities include sports hall, gymnasia and refurbished Victorian swimming pool; playing fields 2 miles away.

Remarks Attractive school; all abilities catered for.

INGATESTONE

Willow Green,
Ingatestone,
Essex CM4 0DJ
Tel (0277) 354018

Comprehensive • Co-educational • Ages
11-18 • 1,148 pupils (equal numbers of
boys and girls) • 246 in sixth form
Head: Bob Reed, 44, appointed 1990.

*Sound comprehensive with a strong
European ethos; good languages;
International Baccalaureate offered as an
alternative to A-levels.*

Background Originally a 1950s secondary
modern; re-opened 1972 as an Anglo-Euro-
pean comprehensive. Conglomeration of over-
crowded, mostly shabby buildings, including
11 wooden huts (not untypical of Essex
schools); sixth-formers work in corridors.

Atmosphere Hard-working staff, courteous
pupils, supportive parents.

The head Formerly deputy head of a Cambridgeshire community college. Strongly committed to the school's European ethos.

The teaching Enthusiastic, first-rate staff; aim
is to help pupils become independent, self-
motivated learners. National curriculum-plus;
first-years take a crash-course in European
culture; all do French, adding German in the
second year; Russian available in third year
(foreign language programmes received by
satellite). Choice between 3 separate sciences
and 'balanced' course; facilities for technology
urgently need improving. Setting by ability in
most subjects; extra help for those with learning difficulties (6 pupils have statements of
special needs); average class size 28, reducing
to 12 in sixth form. Top 25%-30% of sixth-formers take the International Baccalaureate
(balanced, challenging mixture of 6 subjects)
in preference to A-levels. Impresssive art; good
music (more than 10% learn an instrument).
Regular study/exchange visits to Belgium,
France, Germany, Russia, Austria, Norway;
750 pupils participate each year; in return,
school plays host to 450.

The pupils From wide range of social backgrounds but most are middle-class. Those
living within the catchment area have right of
admission; in September 1992, 325 applied
(from more than 70 primary schools) for the
remaining 144 places. Priority to those wanting an education with an emphasis on European studies (current pupils speak 21 languages) or who have links with Europe (major
local employers include Ford of Europe and
Marconi). Substantial numbers join the sixth
form from other schools to take the IB
(minimum of 6 GCSE passes required, 3 at
grade B).

Results GCSE: 59% gain at least 5 grades
A-C. A-level and IB: 36% of entries graded A
or B or equivalent.

Destinations 65% continue into the sixth-
form; 75 % of these proceed to higher education (a few to Oxbridge).

Sport Football, rugby, cricket, hockey, tennis,
netball, badminton, gymnastics, athletics,
swimming.

Remarks Thriving, innovative school; deserves to be better-resourced.

IPSWICH

Henley Road,
Ipswich,
Suffolk IP1 3SG
Tel (0473) 255313

Independent • Boys (plus girls in sixth
form) • Day (and some boarding) • Ages
11-18 • 615 pupils (37 boarders) • 200 in
sixth form (83% boys) • Fees,
£3,810-£4,020 (£5,955-£6,840 boarding)
Head: Dr John Blatchly, 59, appointed
1972 (retires August 1993).

*Solid school; good results; first-rate
music and drama.*

Background Founded *circa* 1390 by the Merchant Guild of Corpus Christi. Moved to

present fine premises 1852; many later additions. Separate prep school on adjoining site.

Atmosphere Friendly, open, hard-working. Strong boarding-school ethos remains (lessons on Saturday mornings).

The head Retiring after 21 years in post. PhD in chemistry from Cambridge; keen musician (runs baroque chamber music group); writes on East Anglian history and archaeology. Married, 2 grown-up children. His successor is Ian Galbraith, 43, currently head of the sixth form at Dulwich, where he was a pupil. Read geography at Cambridge (starred First); taught at Dulwich for 12 years and at Kingston Grammar. Married, no children.

The teaching Good; traditional grammar-school approach; well-qualified, long-serving staff of 50+ (a quarter here even longer than the head). All boys streamed by general ability from second year; further setting thereafter. Broad curriculum; choice of 17 subjects at GCSE; Latin, Greek, German, Russian on offer. All take 3 A-levels (choice of 19) plus general studies; most popular are maths, history, chemistry, English, economics. Fine drama (in well-appointed performing arts complex) and music (classical to jazz); more than a quarter play at least 1 instrument. Extra-curricular activities include chess, film-making, art, photography, printing, bird-watching, mountaineering etc. Flourishing cadet force; keen interest in Duke of Edinburgh award scheme.

The pupils Mostly from middle and upper-middle-class families; catchment area covers east Suffolk, north Essex. Entry tests to ensure boys can cope with 8-9 GCSEs; half join from associated prep school. Keen competition among girls for sixth-form places (6 GCSE grades A-C required). Boarding available in case of need – but not actively promoted. Assisted places, scholarships.

Results GCSE (1991): 98% gained at least 5 grades A-C. A-level (1992): 48% of entries graded A or B.

Destinations 90% continue into the sixth form; 80% of these proceed to higher education (10 a year to Oxbridge).

Sport Up to 10 teams fielded regularly for rugby, hockey, cricket. Good facilities; heated indoor pool; new sports hall scheduled for September 1993; courts for tennis, squash, fives; 30 acres of playing fields 10 minutes' walk away.

Remarks All-round strengths; long-serving, dedicated staff.

IPSWICH HIGH
Woolverstone Hall,
Woolverstone,
Ipswich,
Suffolk IP9 1AZ
Tel (0473) 780201

Independent ● Girls ● Day ● Ages 5-18 ●
590 pupils (415 in senior school) ● 90 in
sixth form ● Fees, £3,156
Head: Miss Pamela Hayworth, 62,
appointed 1971 (retires April 1993).

First-rate school; good results; superb location and facilities.

Background Founded 1878 by the Girls' Public Day School Trust; became fully independent in 1976 with the abolition of Direct Grant status. Moved in September 1992 to Woolverstone Hall, 18th-century, grade-1 listed mansion with spacious later additions (including 400-seat theatre); 80 acres of gracious parkland 4 miles south-west of Ipswich. Gradually expanding to take 800 pupils.

Atmosphere Strong sense of family togetherness and loyalty; long-serving staff have close rapport with (and high expectations of) their pupils.

The head Warm, quietly purposeful. Would have retired at 60 but stayed on to oversee the move to Woolverstone Hall – fitting end to a successful career. Spends summers painting in the Dordogne. Successor: Miss Valerie MacCuish, formerly head of Tunbridge Wells Girls' Grammar *(qv)*.

The teaching Traditional grammar school-style (6 teachers have been here longer than the head). Wide choice of subjects, including 3 sciences; national curriculum regarded as a bare minimum; lots of computing (excellent facilities). Setting by ability in maths, French; maximum class size 24. Sixth-fomers take non-examination course in general studies. Excellent music (compulsory for first 5 years); most learn an instrument; flourishing orchestra, wind band; 3 choirs. Lots of drama. Annual exchanges with schools in France, Germany. Extra-curricular activities include chess, debating, Duke of Edinburgh award scheme.

The pupils Confident, articulate, well-mannered; few disciplinary problems. Modest fees and assisted places help ensure fairly wide social mix. School heavily over-subscribed; catchment area mainly east Suffolk, north Essex. Entry at 11+ by tests in English, maths plus previous school reports; interview for borderline cases; nearly all juniors proceed to senior school.

Results GCSE: all gain at least 5 grades A-C. A-level (1992): 50% of entries graded A or B (has been higher).

Destinations 75% stay on for A-levels (most of the rest transfer to co-educational sixth forms); nearly all of these proceed to higher education (3 a year to Oxbridge).

Sport Good hockey, netball, tennis, fencing (county and national honours). Facilities include extensive playing fields, large sports hall. Indoor heated pool planned.

Remarks Successful school poised for even greater things; highly recommended for able girls.

ISLEWORTH & SYON

Ridgeway Road,
Isleworth,
Middlesex TW7 5LJ
Tel (081) 568 5791

Comprehensive (voluntary-controlled) •
Boys • Ages 11-18 • 870 pupils • 127 in sixth form.
Head: Tony Phillips, 49, appointed 1984.

Successful comprehensive in mixed social and ethnic area; brings out the best of pupils of all abilities. Grammar school roots carefully preserved.

Background Result of 1979 merger of grammar school and comprehensive; links with a charity school founded 1630. Main buildings (1930s red brick with 1970s additions) crowded; showing signs of wear and tear and limited maintenance; science labs are museum pieces; some classrooms in wooden huts. Immaculate grounds; gleaming art deco entrance hall; walls lined with honours boards (celebrating success in sport, drama, chess, Oxbridge entry, Duke of Edinburgh award scheme).

Atmosphere Warm, friendly, rather noisy; strong community spirit (older boys voluntarily help the younger ones). Excellent relationships between staff and pupils; discipline based on praise and reward. Supportive parents: £8,000 raised 1991-92.

The head Warm, jolly; describes himself as a benevolent despot; more likely to be seen talking to pupils around the school (knows all their first names) than dealing with paper work at his desk. High expectations: 'I make sure every boy knows success is possible.' A man for whom being a head is a way of life. Wife on the staff: teaches pupils with special needs.

The teaching Formal (nucleus of long-serving staff) but geared to the needs of a wide range of abilities. All boys prepared for 10 GCSEs but some eventually allowed to follow a reduced programme – and given additional teaching. Mixed-ability classes (average size 27); some setting in languages and maths.

Homework set regularly, closely monitored. Sixth-form courses include vocational studies. Music and drama with neighbouring girls' school.

The pupils Drawn equally from private and council housing estates; a third Asian. Most boys rise to the challenge of high expectations and trust (sixth-formers sign themselves in and out and are required on site only for timetabled commitments). Full uniform insisted upon (below the sixth form): transgressions lead to a letter home suggesting parents 'may feel another school would be more appropriate'. Truancy rate negligible. Heavily oversubscribed; school has no control over admissions, which are handled by Hounslow council. (Priority to: siblings, those with medical or social needs, preference for single-sex education, proximity to school.)

Results (1991) GCSE: 40% gained 5 or more GCSEs grades A-C. A-level: impressive 52% of entries graded A or B.

Destinations 59% stay on into the sixth form, 66% to do A-levels; most proceed to higher education.

Sport Full programme of fixtures on Saturdays: rugby in the autumn, soccer in spring, cricket in summer.

Remarks Well-disciplined, high-achieving school. Traditional values merged with a caring philosophy.

JAMES ALLEN'S GIRLS'
East Dulwich Grove,
London SE22 8TE
Tel (081) 693 1181

Independent • Girls • Day • Ages 11-18 • 720 pupils • 180 in sixth form • Fees, £4,635-£4,770
Head: Mrs Brigid Davies, 50, appointed 1984.

First-rate, selective school; excellent results; wider education not neglected.

Background Founded 1741 (in 2 rooms of the Bricklayer's Arms) by James Allen, Master of Dulwich College *(qv)*, with which it retains close links; moved to present 22-acre site 1886. Extensive later additions include new classrooms and labs.

Atmosphere Happy environment; girls encouraged to give of their best without feeling under undue pressure.

The head Came here as head of history in 1976; deputy head 1981. Attaches greatest importance to concern for others, independence of mind, pursuit of excellence in all things. Married, 3 daughters.

The teaching Challenging: problem-solving, open-ended approach; classroom discussion encouraged. All do Latin, 2 modern languages (from French, German, Italian, Spanish, Russian) and drama; setting by ability in maths, languages, physics, chemistry. Technology has more to do with wood, metal and plastics than cookery or needlework. Most take 10 GCSEs; choice of 24 subjects at A-level; all take at least 3 plus general studies, language 'taster' course (Russian, Spanish, Japanese or Arabic) and weekly public speaking lesson. Good art and music (Gustav Holst taught here); 55 learn an instrument; orchestras, choirs. Exchanges with schools in France, Germany, Italy, Russia; work experience in Algeria. Long-established botanical garden is an ecologist's dream.

The pupils Mostly from middle-class homes but the intake (from a radius of 15 miles) covers the whole social and ethnic spectrum; 20% have assisted places; up to 20 scholarships a year. Entry at 11+ by (searching) tests in English, maths, verbal reasoning plus interview and previous school report.

Results All gain at least 5 grades A-C (average tally is 9.4). A-level (1992): impressive 69% of entries graded A or B.

Destinations 85%-90% stay on for A-levels; nearly all of these proceed to higher education (25 a year to Oxbridge), many after taking a 'gap year'.

Sport Traditional team games have their place but emphasis is on individual sports, including fencing, self-defence, weight training, canoeing, climbing, skiing, pot-holing.

Remarks Highly recommended for able girls.

JOHN LYON
Middle Road,
Harrow,
Middlesex HA2 0HN
Tel (081) 422 2046

Independent • Boys • Day • Ages 11-18 • 504 pupils • 137 in sixth form • Fees, £4,155
Head: Rev Tim Wright, early-50s, appointed 1986.

Sound, grammar school-type education; modest facilities.

Background Founded 1876 under the management of a committee appointed by the governors of Harrow (which overshadows it); expanded in the 1930s. Later additions include fine assembly hall/theatre. Attractive village setting at the bottom of Harrow Hill.

Atmosphere Not posh; reminiscent of a grammar school. Good relations between staff and boys.

The head Formerly a parish priest in Oxford; spent 15 years at Malvern as chaplain and housemaster. A 'hands-on' head: always around, knows what is going on. Wife a theologian and teacher; 2 grown-up children.

The teaching Competent, dedicated staff. Boys take 8-10 GCSEs, including separate sciences; nearly all do French; Latin, German on offer. Good results in history, economics. Average class size 24 (some classrooms rather cramped). Facilities for science, computing, technology are poor and need upgrading. Good music; a third learn an instrument; choir regularly tours abroad. Popular Duke of Edinburgh award scheme.

The pupils Hard-working, well-behaved, tidily dressed. Wide social and religious mix. Most enter from state primary schools after competitive tests in English, maths; 3-4 apply for each place. 20 assisted places; a few scholarships.

Results GCSE (1991): all gained at least 5 grades A-C. A-level (1992): 49% of entries graded A or B.

Destinations Nearly all continue into the sixth form; 80% of these proceed to higher education (10 a year to Oxbridge).

Sport School overlooks Harrow's playing fields but its own are 10-15 minutes away (changing rooms and pavilion in poor condition). Main games: football, cricket; championship-standard archery; swimming and golf at Harrow.

Remarks Workmanlike school handicapped by lack of funds (although supportive parents do their best).

JUDD

Brook Street,
Tonbridge,
Kent TN9 2PN
Tel (0732) 770880

Grammar (voluntary-aided) • Boys • Ages
11-18 • 730 pupils • 210 in sixth form
Head: Keith Starling, 47, appointed 1985.

Well-earned reputation for academic and sporting achievement. Dedicated staff working in poor conditions (head wages constant battle for funding).

Background Established 1888 by the Skinners' Company out of funds provided by the Sir Andrew Judd Foundation; moved to present site 1896. New classroom and technology block completed September 1992; 2 new science labs opening January 1993 (total cost nearly £2 million, of which the school had to raise 15%).

Atmosphere Old-fashioned, disciplined grammar school. Quiet and well-ordered: even at break times there are no boys racing noisily around the (dark) corridors.

The head Has worked in both state and independent schools; admits to being frustrated by the lack of resources. Teaches general studies to first years. Very supportive of staff; proud of the boys' achievements (his office is decorated with their artistic efforts). Married, 2 sons both of whom have been through the school.

The teaching Dark, gloomy classrooms with rows of ageing wooden desks and little evidence of modern facilities. This is constantly mentioned by both staff and pupils, but clearly has no effect on the high quality of the teaching or the application of the boys: seems to be a uniting force. All take 10 GCSEs, including 3 sciences. Computing across the curriculum. No streaming but setting in French and maths (top 2 sets take maths a year early and then embark on an A-level modular course). Maximum class size 28. Hard-working staff of 50; half appointed by present head (10% women); nearly all involved in weekend sport. Good music (15% participate in choir or orchestra), art, drama (joint productions with local girls' school). Community service, Duke of Edinburgh award scheme, Combined Cadet Force plus a host of clubs and societies keep everyone occupied during the lunch break and after school.

The pupils Studious, well-motivated, very aware they are expected to do well. Mainly from middle-class commuter belt. Discipline not an issue; uniform worn throughout the school without too many complaints (sixth-formers' main gripe is lack of car parking). 90 boys admitted a year via Kent Selection Procedure (11+); 20 more join at 13+ on basis of prep school reports; a few governors' places for those who live outside the residential qualification area of Kent and Sussex.

Results GCSE: nearly all gain at least 5 grades A-C. A-level (1991): 53% of entries graded A or B.

Destinations 99% stay on into the sixth form; around 80% of these proceed to higher education (about 12 a year to Oxbridge).

Sport Outstanding record, especially in rugby, cricket and cross-country; packed weekend programme.

Remarks Strongly traditional boys' school doing a fine job.

KATHARINE LADY BERKELEY'S

Wotton-under-Edge,
Gloucestershire GL12 8RB
Tel (0453) 842227

Comprehensive (grant-maintained from September 1992) • Co-educational • Ages 11-18 • 1,061 pupils (52% boys) • 170 in sixth form
Head: John Law, 50s, appointed 1982.

Well-run comprehensive; grammar-school ethos retained; respectable results.

Background Founded 1384 by Katharine, wife of Thomas, Lord Berkeley, as a free grammar school; moved to present purpose-built premises in an attractive setting on edge of the town 1963; went comprehensive 1973. Grant-maintained status expected to boost ambitious expansion plans.

Atmosphere Orderly, purposeful; big emphasis on traditional values of discipline, politeness, importance of hard work; crystal-clear expectation that all pupils will aim for the highest possible all-round standards. School takes pride in its grammar-school ethos; many staff send their own children here.

The head Direct, forceful, leads from the front. Educated at Oxford; teaches GCSE and A-level law (in his study) for a quarter of the timetable. Keen to introduce the International Baccalaureate and vocational courses as an alternative to A-levels. Runs a tight ship ('We act rather than chat').

The teaching Fairly formal in style; desks in rows. Committed, long-serving staff, half appointed by present head. Pupils streamed by ability; extra help for those with learning difficulties. Science taught as 3 separate subjects; good design/technology; computing used across the curriculum; Russian on offer. Choice of 25 subjects at GCSE, 18 at A-level (most take 3). Busy extra-curricular programme, including Duke of Edinburgh award scheme. Regular language exchanges with schools in France and Germany.

The pupils Fairly wide social mix from rural/small-town catchment area of south Gloucestershire and north Avon; up to 8% have some degree of special need but most are in the upper half of the ability range.

Results (1991) GCSE: 46% gained at least 5 grades A-C. A-level: 29% of entries graded A or B (has been higher).

Destinations 50% stay on for A-levels; 53% of these proceed to higher education (2 or 3 a year to Oxbridge).

Sport Boys' hockey and football are particularly strong; girls' hockey catching up.

Remarks Expanding, forward-looking school.

KIMBOLTON

Kimbolton,
Huntingdon,
Cambridgeshire PE18 0EA
Tel (0480) 860505

Independent • Co-educational • Day and some boarding • Ages 7-18 • 720 pupils (556 in senior school; 55% boys; 90% day) • 148 in sixth form • Fees, £4,230 day; £7,290 boarding
Head: Roger Peel, 46, appointed 1987.

Solid, traditional school; good results; first-rate music.

Background Founded 1600; previously a county grammar school; became fully independent in 1976 with the abolition of Direct Grant status. Main premises in Kimbolton Park and Castle (once the home of Katharine of Aragon). Latest additions include computer centre, fine new sports hall.

Atmosphere Family feel; good relations between staff and pupils; strong pastoral care system. Saturday morning lessons retained. Pleasant boarding houses in Kimbolton High Street.

The head Read chemistry at Nottingham; formerly a housemaster at Trent College;

strongly committed to boarding – and would like to boost numbers. Keeps his finger firmly on the pulse; teaches all first-years; keen on rugby; plays guitar in school's jazz band. Says he is looking for 'joiners in' not 'opters out'. Married, 3 children (all pupils here).

The teaching Largely traditional in style. Long-serving, predominantly male staff (a recent appointment to the chemistry department was the first there for 30 years). Fairly broad curriculum; setting by ability in most subjects from age 13. Choice of 17 subjects at A-level; most do 3 plus general studies. Strong music: half learn at least 1 instrument; 19 musical groups. Busy extra-curricular programme includes well-supported cadet force, Duke of Edinburgh award scheme; active community service unit helps the homeless in London. Regular language trips to France and Spain.

The pupils Mostly from professional/business backgrounds in a predominantly rural catchment area including Kettering, St Ives, St Neots; many mothers work to pay the fees. Fairly wide ability range; minimum IQ of 110 required (but relaxed for siblings). 75 enter the senior school at 11+ (two-thirds from the prep department), 20 at 13+ via Common Entrance. Assisted places, scholarships, bursaries available.

Results GCSE (1991): 94% gained at least 5 grades A-C. A-level (1992): disappointing 38% of entries graded A or B (has been higher).

Destinations 85% stay on for A-levels; 85% of these proceed to higher education (6 to Oxbridge in 1991).

Sport Chiefly soccer, hockey, cricket for the boys; hockey, netball, tennis for the girls. Strong shooting, canoeing. Facilities include 20 acres of playing fields, all-weather pitch, grass tennis courts, fine new sports hall, outdoor heated pool.

Remarks Good all round. (John Major sent his children here.)

KING DAVID HIGH
Childwell Road,
Liverpool L15 6UZ
Tel (051) 722 7496

Comprehensive (Jewish voluntary-aided)
• Co-educational • Ages 11-18 • 521 pupils (55% girls) • 117 in sixth form
Head: Miss Vivienne Canter, 41, appointed September 1992.

Hard-working comprehensive; high academic standards; strong music.

Background Founded as a Jewish elementary school 1854; became a secondary school on its present site 1957; campus shared with primary school, Jewish youth centre, synagogue. Starkly unattractive flat-roofed buildings.

Atmosphere Happy, relaxed, well-ordered; pupils are well looked after and clearly have a high regard for their teachers. Corporate life essentially Jewish but non-Jewish children very welcome (separate provision made for religious education).

The head New appointment. Studied music and French at college, took an Open University degree in humanities and then a master's degree in media studies and education at Bristol. Has taught in Roman Catholic and Jewish schools. Young, open, enthusiastic.

The teaching Formal, traditional style – but in a non-threatening atmosphere; dedicated professional staff of 37. National curriculum followed; choice between 3 separate sciences and 'balanced' course; French, German plus modern Hebrew on offer (supported by regular exchange trips to France, Germany, Israel). Special needs taken seriously. First-rate music; full symphony orchestra; regular concerts.

The pupils Lively, co-operative; keenly interested in the world and its ways. Wide catchment area covers Liverpool, the Wirral, Southport; school is over-subscribed (number of Jewish pupils declining); priority to pupils from associated primary school, all other Jewish applicants, siblings, children of proven musical ability, those living locally.

Results (1992) GCSE: 86% gained at least 5 grades A-C. A-level: creditable 50% of entries graded A or B.

Destinations 60% stay on for A-levels; 75% of these proceed to higher education (3 to Oxbridge in 1991) often after taking a 'gap year' in Israel.

Sport Not particularly strong (limited games fields); netball, hockey, rounders, football, basketball, badminton, swimming on offer.

Remarks Committed Jewish philosophy and ethos; children of all faiths will benefit.

KING EDWARD'S Bath
North Road,
Bath BA2 6HU
Tel (0225) 464313

Independent • Boys (plus girls in sixth form) • Day • Ages 11-18 (plus associated junior school) • 680 pupils • 225 in sixth form (80% boys) • Fees, £2,256-£3,321 Head: Dr John Wroughton, late-50s, appointed 1982 (retires August 1993).

Good all-round; strong art, drama, sport.

Background Founded 1552; moved to present 14-acre hill site (magnificent views of the city) 1961; junior school followed 1990. Formerly a Direct Grant grammar school; reverted to full independence in 1976.

Atmosphere Lively, friendly, good-humoured; strong sense of community; a school that clearly knows what it is about.

The head Read history at Oxford; here since 1965; became second master in 1974. Leads from the front. Strongly committed to the grammar school tradition (and lowest possible fees).

The teaching Varied, challenging styles. High-quality staff of 52 (8 women); half appointed by present head. Pupils set by ability in maths, French; up to half take a second modern language (choice of German, Span-

ish). Average class size 27, reducing to 24 for GCSE. Choice of 18 subjects at A-level. Particular strengths in art (an acknowledged centre of excellence), drama, music. Few links with industry; little work experience.

The pupils Confident, enthusiastic; from a fairly wide range of social backgrounds in Bath, north Bristol, Somerset, Wiltshire. Entry at 11+ and 13+ by tests and interview (half enter from the junior school); 2 applications for every place; not excessively selective. Assisted places, scholarships, bursaries.

Results GCSE: 92% gain at least 5 grades A-C. A-level (1992): very creditable 62% of entries graded A or B.

Destinations 90% continue into the sixth form; up to 80% of these proceed to higher education (10 a year to Oxbridge).

Sport Principally rugby (1992 tour of Canada), hockey, cricket, athletics, tennis. Volleyball, basketball, badminton etc also on offer. Facilities include sports hall, all-weather pitch.

Remarks Successful school; hard-working staff and pupils.

KING EDWARD'S Birmingham
Edgbaston Park Road,
Edgbaston,
Birmingham B15 2UA
Tel (021) 472 1672

Independent • Boys • Day • Ages 11-18 • 850 pupils • 220 in sixth form • Fees, £3,690 Head: Hugh Wright, early 50s, appointed 1991.

Outstanding school; consistently one of the top 3 but far from narrowly academic; firmly committed to developing all-round talents. Facilities exceptional.

Background Founded 1552 by King Edward VI; one of 7 schools (2 independent, 5 grammar) in the King Edward's Foundation.

Moved to its present 42-acre site – shared with King Edward VI High School for Girls *(qv)* – 1936. Imposing red-brick building; spacious classrooms; wide, uncrowded corridors; elegant 440-seat hall (scene of the climax to John Cleese's film *Clockwise*). Attractive additions include first-rate technology centre, music centre and chapel.

Atmosphere Sense of cheerful earnestness prevails; emphasis on responsibility, self-discipline, respect for learning – and it shows.

The head (Chief Master) Charismatic, personable, widely experienced (previously head of Stockport Grammar and Gresham's). Oxford classicist; still finds time to teach. Deeply committed to twin goals of academic excellence and developing individual talent. Married, 3 children.

The teaching Ranges from formal to pupil-centred: lively, challenging and unquestionably outstanding. 65 teachers (10 women); all well-qualified graduates; 100% match of specialist teachers to subject taught. All boys do 13 subjects for first 3 years (including 3 separate sciences, Latin) plus music for first 2 years and introductory courses in computer studies and electronics: awesome but no apparent signs of overload. All take 10 GCSEs, usually followed by 3 A-levels plus general studies and 'extra studies' (3 lessons a week from long lists of options). Some setting in maths and science; average class size 15-25 up to GCSE; 5-15 in sixth form. Music central to the life of the school (2 orchestras, several bands, choral society, chapel choir). Enrichment activities are legion (all spend 2 weeks on the Continent); Saturday morning gifted children project, cadet force, community service etc.

The pupils Bright-eyed, bushy-tailed; all have the potential to cope with the academic rigour and broad-based personal development which the school expects (a third have IQs of 140+). From across the social spectrum; 20% ethnic minorities; scholarships and 50 assisted places a year. No problems of discipline or attendance (school rules formally accepted by parents); excellent relations with staff. Admission at 11 and 13 by (stiffly competitive) exams.

Results 99% gain at least 5 grades A-C. A-level: astounding 81% of entries graded A or B.

Destinations Virtually all continue into the sixth form; 90% of these proceed to university (40 a year to Oxbridge).

Sport Particular strengths: rugby, basketball, cricket, hockey; long list of others. 4 members of sports staff are international players or trainers. Superb facilities: sports hall, 2 gymnasia, indoor swimming pool, all-weather running track, plus extensive playing fields.

Remarks Successful, well-run, prestigious school; enviable standards achieved on all fronts.

KING EDWARD VI CAMP HILL BOYS'

Vicarage Road,
King's Heath,
Birmingham B14 7QJ
Tel (021) 444 3188

Grammar (voluntary-aided) • Boys • Ages 11-18 • 637 pupils • 179 in sixth form
Head: Roger Dancy, mid-40s, appointed 1986.

Widely respected grammar school. Impressive exam results; strong parental support.

Background Founded 1883 (part of the King Edward's Foundation); moved to its present spacious campus – shared with King Edward VI Camp Hill Girls' *(qv)* – 1956. Usual 1950s glass and brick, parts in need of redecoration.

Atmosphere Welcoming, purposeful. School large enough to be diverse and interesting but small enough for all to know one another.

The head Enthusiastic, innovative, full of ideas for future development. Relaxed, warm relations with staff and pupils. Economics graduate (Exeter); main interests cricket and theatre (Christopher Hampton dedicated *Les*

Liaisons Dangereuses to him – they were at Lancing together). Married, 2 children.

The teaching High-quality, challenging; sensible balance of formal and pupil-centred. 40 staff (7 women); all graduates; average age mid to late-30s. Mixed-ability classes (within narrow ability band); some setting in maths and French. National curriculum for first 3 years; all take 9 GCSEs. Class sizes 30, reducing to 22 for GCSE, 15 in sixth form. Strict homework policy. Library stock needs expanding and updating. Extensive programme of field trips, language exchanges and expeditions; much music and drama with girls' school. Admirable termly newsletter to parents.

The pupils Academically able, from wide social spectrum; 20% ethnic minorities; 5% qualify for free school meals. No problems of discipline or attendance; rules few in number and well-observed; school uniform worn throughout. Admission by 11+ tests (maths, verbal and non-verbal reasoning) administered by Birmingham City Council.

Results GCSE: 95% gain at least 5 grades A-C. A-level (1991): 57% of entries graded A or B.

Destinations 85% continue into sixth form; 85% of these proceed to university (8 a year to Oxbridge).

Sport Rugby, cricket, hockey played to a high standard; swimming and athletics also strong. Swimming pool shared with girls' school; gymnasium, tennis courts, sports hall.

Remarks Happy, well-run, high-achieving school.

KING EDWARD VI CAMP HILL GIRLS'
Vicarage Road,
King's Heath,
Birmingham B14 7QJ
Tel (021) 444 2150

Grammar (grant-maintained from April 1993) • Girls • Ages 11-18 • 624 pupils • 161 in sixth form
Head: Mrs Joan Fisher, appointed September 1992.

Highly selective, business-like school; good results.

Background One of the King Edward VI Foundation's 2 independent and 5 grammar schools. Founded 1883; moved to present, spacious parkland site (next to King Edward VI Camp Hill Boys' *qv*) in 1958. Pleasant, low-profile, '50s building (plenty of glass and light); later additions include science labs, design/technology centre. Parents voted overwhelmingly for grant-maintained status.

Atmosphere Friendly, low-key. Secure, well-ordered environment; high standards of behaviour.

The head New appointment. Modern linguist; previously deputy head of girls' grammar school in Essex. Married, 4 daughters (including triplets).

The teaching High-quality, challenging; varied (but mostly traditional) styles; big emphasis on mastering skills, techniques. National curriculum-plus; all do Latin in first year, add second modern language (from German, French, Spanish, Russian) in second year. GCSE options include Greek; all take non-examined course in design/technology. Choice of 17 subjects at A-level; most do 3, plus general studies, religious education and PE. All-graduate staff of 41 (9 men). Bright, cheerful classrooms, some rather cramped; maximum class size 31, reducing to 24 for GCSE. Homework increases progressively from $1^1/_4$ hours nightly; thoroughly marked and corrected. Good drama and music (often in conjunction with boys' school). Regular

French, German, Spanish exchanges. Community service for older girls in local schools, nurseries, hospitals.

The pupils Confident, articulate, responsible; all academically able (top 5% of the ability range) from varied social backgrounds (13% ethnic minority). No problems of attendance, discipline or timekeeping. Compulsory uniform (girls had a hand in its choice); sixth-formers expected to look 'neat and well-groomed'. Entry at 11+ by (highly competitive) tests in maths, verbal and non-verbal reasoning administered by Birmingham City Council; 10 applicants for every place (apply by mid-October for following September). Admission to sixth form requires average of at least grade B in 8-9 GCSEs.

Results (1992) GCSE: 99% gained at least 5 grades A-C. A-level: disappointing 40% of entries graded A or B (has been higher).

Destinations 80% continue into the sixth form; 85% of these proceed to higher education (6 a year to Oxbridge).

Sport Chiefly hockey (county honours), netball, athletics. Facilities include tennis courts, indoor pool, gymnasium.

Remarks Successful, well-regarded grammar school.

KING EDWARD VI Chelmsford
Broomfield Road,
Chelmsford,
Essex CM1 3SX
Tel (0245) 353510

Grammar (grant-maintained) • Boys (plus girls in sixth form) • Ages 11-18 • 700 pupils • 200 in sixth form (85% boys)
Head: Tony Tuckwell, late 40s, appointed 1984.

Popular, highly selective school drawing from 400 square miles around Chelmsford.

Background Founded 1551; moved to present forbidding Victorian premises (cloisters, quadrangles) 1892. Overcrowded; seriously underfunded (flaking paintwork, peeling plaster – some classes in dilapidated wooden huts). Parents have raised £80,000 in recent years; grant-maintained status should bring extra cash.

Atmosphere Warm, supportive – far from forbidding. School hums with purposeful activity and relaxed good humour.

The head Oxford graduate; historian; taught in state schools for 20 years. Runs a happy and effective team (consults exhaustively). Aims to 'give pupils wings'. Firm believer in single-sex education; admission of girls to the sixth form 'reflects parental choice'.

The teaching Triumphs over adverse circumstances (cramped, poorly-equipped, box-like classrooms; iron-framed desks with fixed seats). Hard-working, experienced staff of 46 (14 women); average age 41. Standard grammar school curriculum (3 sciences, Latin); mediocre technology. No streaming but some setting in maths (which half take 1 year early). Pupils generally well-prepared to achieve good academic results but development of original thought takes an even higher priority – no mere exam factory. Lots of music and drama; numerous extra-curricular activities despite extensive commuting.

The pupils Alert, confident, courteous; eager to learn, participate, contribute. Overwhelmingly from middle-class homes; top 5% of the ability range in Essex. Truancy negligible; uniform worn throughout.

Results (1991) GCSE: 99% gained at least 5 grades A-C. A-level: 52% of entries graded A or B.

Destinations Virtually all go into the sixth form and proceed to higher education (12 a year to Oxbridge).

Sport Limited on-site facilities but 31-acre playing fields (gift of a former pupil) 3 miles away. Good cricket and rugby (national and county honours).

Remarks Well-run, friendly school producing first-rate results.

KING EDWARD VI Handsworth
Rose Hill Road,
Handsworth,
Birmingham B21 9AR
Tel (021) 554 2342

Grammar (voluntary-aided) • Girls • Ages 11-18 • 844 pupils • 226 in sixth form
Head: Miss Elspeth Insch, early-40s, appointed 1989.

Successful academic school; flourishing under an exceptional head.

Background: Founded 1883 (part of the King Edward's Foundation); moved to present site (inner-city oasis) 1911. Stately, well-proportioned buildings in need of redecoration; lofty rooms, wide corridors, ornate staircases, large hall with graceful arched ceiling.

Atmosphere Friendly, reassuring despite the grand buildings, not at all intimidating. Emphasis on good behaviour and respect for others. Whole school assembles daily for act of worship.

The head Dynamic leader; inexhaustibly enthusiastic, actively involved in every aspect of school life (personally preparing 70 girls for Duke of Edinburgh bronze award). Geogra-

phy graduate (London and Edinburgh); won a Churchill Fellowship to lead expedition to Iceland. Involves the whole staff in running the school; claims to be 'an autocrat trying to be a democrat'. Recreation: Scottish culture.

The teaching Conscientious, challenging; full range of styles (formal when required). 55 staff (4 men), all graduates (average age 40); 100% match of qualifications to subject taught. Rigorous academic diet: compulsory Latin; all girls do at least 9 GCSEs (2 modern languages). No streaming (within narrow ability band) but some setting in maths and French. Strict homework policy. Class sizes: 32 in first year, reducing to 20-25; 10-20 in sixth form. Attractive library but fiction stock dated. Strong musical tradition; more than half learn an instrument. Nearly 50 extra-curricular activities offered (mainly in the lunch break); extensive programme of exchanges, foreign visits.

The pupils Bright (top 10% of the ability range) and eagerly responsive. Wide social spectrum (from whole of Birmingham conurbation); 25% ethnic minorities. Good relations with staff and each other; no problems of discipline or attendance. Inexpensive uniform, chosen by pupils. Entry at 11+ (6 applicants for every place) by tests in maths, verbal and non-verbal reasoning; becoming even more selective.

Results (1991) GCSE: 91% gained at least 5 grades A-C. A-level: 47% of entries graded A or B.

Destinations 80% continue into sixth form; 98% of these proceed to higher education (9 a year to Oxbridge) .

Sport First-rate hockey, netball, tennis. Gymnastics, trampolining, dance, swimming also on offer. Limited grounds but new gym and sports hall.

Remarks Happy, vibrant, high-achieving school, efficiently preparing girls for higher education.

KING EDWARD VI HIGH

Edgbaston Park Road,
Birmingham B15 2UB
Tel (021) 472 1834

Independent • Girls • Day • Ages 11-18 •
550 pupils • 160 in sixth form • Fees,
£3,381
Head: Miss Ena Evans, mid-50s,
appointed 1977.

Distinguished school; very good results; excellent facilities.

Background Founded 1883; one of 7 schools in the King Edward's Foundation. Moved to present 35-acre park-like site adjoining King Edward's *(qv)* 1940. Spacious, well-proportioned 1930s red-brick buildings with seamless additions. Elegant, wood-panelled entrance hall; wide, uncluttered corridors; everything impeccably decorated and maintained.

Atmosphere Cheerful, purposeful, orderly; rules few in number and well-observed; emphasis on individual responsibility, self-discipline. School small enough for each girl to be known by most staff; relations admirably cordial.

The head Highly regarded by staff and pupils; approachable, experienced, refreshingly direct; shows no signs of flagging after a long stint. Read maths at London; confesses to strictly non-athletic interests, particularly music, singing (but an unswerving supporter of all school activities).

The teaching Universally challenging, lively, inter-active. 'By teaching, we learn', reads the Latin engraving in the staff room; 'Excellence is sought in aesthetic, practical and physical activities as well as in academic study', adds the handbook; no empty phrases here. National curriculum acknowledged – but not to the exclusion of other areas of study. Separate sciences, Latin introduced in second year; computing from third year; fourth-year options include Greek, German. All take 9-10 GCSEs (Italian, Spanish, Russian on offer) followed, usually, by at least 3 A-levels plus general studies – a formidable diet on which

the girls evidently thrive. Setting by ability in some subjects (no form positions); average class size 26, reducing to maximum of 15 for A-level; all-graduate staff of 48, two-thirds appointed by present head. Lots of (meticulously marked) homework. Extensive music (orchestras, band, choral society) and drama, much of it shared with King Edward's. Clubs of all kinds; regular exchanges with France, Germany; community service actively encouraged.

The pupils Confident, responsive, fluent; most come from professional families but mix of social backgrounds is wide (up to a third receive some form of help with fees); girls 'of all faiths or of none' equally welcome. Entry at 11+ by highly competitive tests in English, maths; around 20 of applicants succeed; school in contact with 290 primary schools. Scholarships, bursaries, assisted places.

Results GCSE: all gain at least 5 grades A-C. A-level (1992): relatively disappointing 64% of entries graded A or B (has been *much* higher).

Destinations 90% continue into the sixth form; virtually all proceed to higher education (25 a year to Oxbridge).

Sport Chiefly hockey (usually county champions or runners-up), netball, tennis, swimming; fencing, golf also on offer. First-rate facilities include sports hall, 25-metre heated indoor pool, 9 hard tennis courts.

Remarks One of the best.

KING EDWARD VI Southampton
Kellett Road,
Southampton S09 3FP
Tel (0703) 704561

Independent • Boys (plus girls in sixth form) • Day • Ages 11-18 • 955 pupils • 280 in sixth form (80% boys) • Fees, £3,762
Head: Tommy Cookson, late-40s, appointed 1990.

First-rate, selective school; strong academic record (especially in science); excellent facilities; good sport.

Background Founded 1553 by Edward VI (original royal charter preserved); moved 1938 to present site 1½ miles from city centre. Imposing buildings with central clock tower; excellent later additions include fine sports centre and theatre. Formerly a voluntary-aided grammar school; returned to full independence 1979. Girls admitted to sixth form 1983; no plans to become fully co-educational.

Atmosphere Lively, hard-working. Clear rules govern dress, conduct, discipline; good pastoral care system.

The head Educated at Winchester and Oxford; taught English at Winchester for 20 years (where he was a housemaster). Married, 3 daughters.

The teaching Strongly academic curriculum: all do design/technology, Latin for first 2 years; choice of German or Spanish in third year; 3 separate sciences (compulsory physics, chemistry); GCSE options include Greek, economics, theatre studies. Setting by ability in maths only; lots of homework. 20 of staff are women. Choice of 19 subjects at A-level plus a variety of non-examined courses. Good music; 3 orchestras, jazz band, chamber choir (tours abroad). Wide range of clubs and societies include Conversationalists and Junior Heretics; popular Duke of Edinburgh award scheme.

The pupils Mainly from middle-class families, parents in the professions or business; catchment area extends from Bournemouth to Portsmouth. Entry at 11+ and 13+ by highly competitive exam (several applicants for each place); up to 35 assisted places a year (not all taken up) plus academic and music scholarships.

Results GCSE: 99% gain at least 5 grades A-C. A-level (1992): creditable 57% of entries graded A or B.

Destinations All expected to stay on into the sixth form; 85% of these proceed to higher education (10-20 a year to Oxbridge).

Sport Chiefly rugby, hockey, cricket; 17 other activities available, including sailing. Some playing fields are 4 miles away.

Remarks Good all round; highly recommended for able boys (and sixth-form girls).

KING EDWARD VI Stratford
Church Street,
Stratford-upon-Avon,
Warwickshire CV37 6HB
Tel (0789) 293351

Grammar (voluntary-aided) • Boys • Ages 11-18 • 411 pupils • 114 in sixth form
Head: Neville Mellon, 55, appointed 1981.

Old-fashioned, academic school; good results; strong sport.

Background Founded 1553 but its history goes back to the 13th century. Shakespeare ('creeping like a snail'?) was probably a pupil in the 1570s (staff and pupils lead annual birthday procession through the town). 15th- and 16th-century timbered buildings supplemented by well-maintained 1960s additions; major building programme planned (financed by substantial annual revenue from medieval Guild of the Holy Cross).

Atmosphere Scholarly, traditional; well-behaved boys in neat uniforms; morning worship in guild chapel.

The head Formal, polite, keen sense of

humour. Read modern languages at Oxford. Married, 2 children (and 2 grandchildren).

The teaching Didactic style geared to the needs of able boys; well-qualified staff (few women). Setting by ability in some subjects; extra help for Oxbridge entrants. Technology and computing introduced recently; separate sciences replaced by 'balanced' course. Class sizes 30, reducing to 25 for GCSE, 16 in sixth form. Nearly all do 3 A-levels plus general studies. Good facilities in most areas but art, music, drama await new buildings.

The pupils Bright, responsive; top 15 of the ability range (IQs 115-140+); mainly from professional/managerial homes. Entry by local authority 11+ exam plus essay and verbal reasoning test (no interview). Half from Stratford and environs; rest commute from further afield (no formal catchment area).

Results GCSE: virtually all gain at least 5 grades A-C. A-level (1992): 43% of entries graded A or B (has been higher).

Destinations More than 90% continue into the sixth form; 85% of these proceed to higher education (a few to Oxbridge).

Sport Major games are rugby (national champions 1990-91) and cricket; rowing and fencing also strong. Fine indoor pool; playing fields some distance away.

Remarks Her Majesty's Inspectors reported (May 1989) that the atmosphere was excessively formal, the teaching narrowly academic and the school was failing to prepare pupils well either for employment or higher education. Head replied tartly that the inspectors bore much of the blame for declining standards.

KING HENRY VIII
Warwick Road,
Coventry CV3 6AQ
Tel (0203) 673442

Independent ● Co-educational ● Day ●
Ages 11-18 ● 822 pupils (55% boys) ● 218
in sixth form ● Fees, £2,883
Head: Rhidian James, 60, appointed 1977.

Selective, high-achieving school; fine sporting record. Lots of help with fees.

Background Founded 1545; part of the Coventry Foundation (shares governing body with Bablake, *qv*); moved to suburban 4-acre site 1885 (playing fields 2 miles away). Handsome Victorian red-brick buildings (grade-2 listed) in need of redecoration; impressive (£1-million) science block; some classes in wooden huts.

Atmosphere Well-ordered, friendly; big emphasis on appearance and behaviour in and out of school.

The head Still youthful, spirited and ready for challenge despite 27 years at the school (15 as head). Effective leader; good communicator (daily bulletin to staff and pupils). Economist (Swansea and Leeds); trustee of a shelter for victims of child abuse. Married, 2 children. Recreations: golf, armchair politics.

The teaching Traditional classroom layouts but varied and innovative styles; staff of 60 experienced graduates (20 women) nearly all appointed by present head. Rigorous curriculum: 3 sciences, compulsory Latin, computer studies. All take 9 carefully balanced GCSEs; 3 A-levels plus general studies. Mixed-ability classes for first 2 years; setting in maths and French thereafter. Average class size 25, reducing to 22 for GCSE, 9-12 in sixth form. (Hutted accommodation for modern languages does not appear to affect GCSE results: 99% grades A-C in French, 98% in German.) 3 thoroughly marked homeworks set nightly; elaborate and efficient reporting to parents. Lots of music (choir, orchestra etc) and drama (everything from Shakespeare and Ibsen to contemporary musicals). 30 thriving clubs and societies; exchange and other foreign visits actively encouraged; school owns residential centres in mid-Wales and Normandy.

The pupils Deliberately broad social mix (600 of 1,660 pupils at the 2 Coventry Foundation schools qualify for some financial help – assisted places, governors' scholarships, bursaries). Excellent staff-pupil relations; no problems of discipline or attendance; rules formally adopted by parents. Entry by tests in English, maths, verbal reasoning. (Pupils joining at 11 + are drawn equally from school's own junior department and state primaries.)

Results GCSE: 99% gain at least 5 grades A-C. A-level: 50% of entries graded A or B.

Destinations 85% continue into the sixth form; 85% of these proceed to higher education (10% to Oxbridge).

Sport Strong in rugby, hockey, cricket, tennis, athletics. 28 acres of playing fields; indoor swimming pool and 2 all-weather, floodlit hockey pitches shared with Bablake.

Remarks Successful, business-like school.

KING'S Canterbury
Canterbury,
Kent CT1 2ES
Tel (0227) 475501

Independent • Co-educational • Boarding and day • Ages 13-18 (plus associated pre-prep and junior school) • 724 pupils (70% boys; 70% boarding) • 344 in sixth form • Fees, £10,350 boarding; £7,245 day Head: Canon Anthony Phillips, 56, appointed 1986.

Distinguished academic school; good results; fine music; beautiful setting.

Background Founded 1541 by Henry VIII after the dissolution of the monasteries but roots go back to the 6th century. Medieval, 16th- and 17th-century buildings plus later additions in the cathedral precincts (tourists have right of way through grounds) and at nearby St Augustine's Abbey. Fully co-educational since 1990.

Atmosphere Appears formal, scholarly – but less daunting in reality. Traditions strictly adhered to: boys *and* girls in 19th-century 'Canterbury dress' of black jacket, striped trousers, stiff wing collar; King's Scholars and monitors wear gowns. Boarders well-looked after; accommodation benefits from rolling programme of refurbishment.

The head Extrovert; firm disciplinarian; makes a great effort to get to know the pupils. Trained as a lawyer, was a don at Cambridge, then chaplain of St John's College, Oxford (teaches the Old Testament to the sixth form). Initially sceptical of co-education, now convinced of its value to both sexes. Says this is not a 'macho' school – it does not concentrate solely on bright children. Married, 3 children.

The teaching Good all round (though head would like more younger and women teachers). Sciences now almost as strong as the arts; lots of computing (all learn to do their prep on word processors). Pupils streamed by ability from the start; setting in all subjects from second year. Small classes: 15 for GCSE, 12 at A-level. Most take 10 GCSEs (maths, French a year early), 13 are possible; choice of 20 subjects at A-level; most take 3 (some 4) plus compulsory general studies. Excellent art (in converted 13th-century priory), drama, music; 70-strong symphony orchestra, chamber orchestra, 3 choirs. Extra-curricular activities include cadet force, Duke of Edinburgh award scheme, community service.

The pupils Confident, well-motivated, ambitious (few rebels here); mostly from professional families (an increasing number from Europe); girls feel welcome – no question of tokenism. Highly competitive entry; minimum 60% mark required at Common Entrance. Numerous scholarships: 15 academic, 12 music, 2 art.

Results GCSE (1991): 92% gained at least 8 grades A-C. A-level (1992): impressive 66% of entries graded A or B.

Destinations Almost all continue into sixth

form; 90% of these proceed to higher education (about 40 a year to Oxbridge).

Sport Usual team games plus squash, badminton, swimming, fencing, sculling, sailing etc. Facilities include 2 all-weather pitches and new £2.5-million recreation centre (shared with the public).

Remarks Very successful, well-run school.

KING'S Chester
Chester CH4 7QL
Tel (0244) 680026

Independent • Boys • Day • Ages 8-18 •
600 pupils • 120 in sixth form • Fees,
£2,790-£3,615
Head: Roger Wickson, early 50s,
appointed 1981.

Outstanding school for able boys (one of the top 10); famed for its rowing.

Background Founded 1541 by Henry VIII in association with Chester Cathedral for the education of '24 poor and friendless boys'. Moved 1960 (after 400 years within the city walls) to 32-acre site on the Wrexham Road. Extensive 1980s additions. Further expansion planned.

Atmosphere Tremendously committed: staff, pupils, parents united in a common endeavour. Much fund-raising by Mother's Guild (Father's Association contributes, too).

The head Cambridge graduate previously head of grammar school in Dorset. Knows every boy (teaches first- and second-years); tempers powerful academic ethos with an emphasis on the need for pupils to be sensitive, considerate, compassionate. Enthusiasms include medieval history, canals, Gilbert and Sullivan (directs and sings).

The teaching Formal, traditional, challenging. Unstreamed classes (of 24) for first 3 years; some setting thereafter and groups are smaller. Crowded timetable (Latin at 8.20

a.m. Nearly all take 3 A-levels plus general studies (maths, chemistry, economics the most popular subjects). First-rate staff (half appointed by present head). Remarkable range of extra-curricular activities. Several choirs, orchestras, swing band; biennial Gilbert and Sullivan (in collaboration with Queen's School, *qv*).

The pupils Hard-working, bright boys (IQs 120+) from wide catchment area: Whitchurch, Nantwich, Wrexham, North Wales coast. (Good public transport: many stay late.) Admission to junior school at 8-9 by entrance exam; at 11+ by tests in maths, comprehension and composition. Assisted places and bursaries.

Results GCSE: 99% gain at least 5 grades A-C (and most a good deal more). A-level: impressive 64% of entries graded A or B.

Destinations 95% stay on into the sixth form and proceed to higher education (15 a year to Oxbridge).

Sport Superb facilities for rowing (on River Dee): 50 boats, 10 coaches; more than 100 participate.

Remarks: Busy, thriving school; boys have plenty to be enthusiastic about.

KING'S COLLEGE SCHOOL
Wimbledon Common,
London SW19 4TT
Tel (081) 947 9311

Independent • Boys • Day • Ages 13-18
(plus associated junior school) • 667
pupils • 260 in sixth form • Fees, £5,070
Head: Robin Reeve, 57, appointed 1980.

First-class academic school; excellent teaching and results; wide range of cultural and sporting activities.

Background Founded 1829 as the junior department of King's College to 'provide in the most effectual manner for the two great objects of education – the communication of general knowledge, and specific preparation for particular professions'. Moved from the college's premises in the Strand to a 17-acre site on the south side of Wimbledon Common 1897; continual building since 1945; recent additions include fine science block and sixth-form centre.

Atmosphere Well-ordered, purposeful; rules understood rather than visibly enforced. Excellent relations between long-serving staff and able, self-confident boys. Strong Anglican tradition; full-time chaplain.

The head Distinguished educationist; warm, shrewd, firmly committed to highest academic standards. Took a First in history at Cambridge; taught here from 1958-62 and then spent 18 years at Lancing, where he became director of studies. Married, 3 grown-up children.

The teaching High-quality. All boys streamed by ability from first year; setting thereafter. National curriculum-plus; top sets take Latin or classical civilisation plus either German, Greek or Spanish; choice of science as 3 separate subjects or 'dual award'. All take 10-13 GCSEs (some a year early) and at least 3 A-levels plus non-examined general studies course. Progress closely monitored throughout. Big emphasis on extra-curricular activities: 2 afternoons a week set aside. Strong music: 60 learn an instrument; 4 orchestras, 3 choirs; lots of drama in fine studio-theatre; annual arts festival. Frequent trips abroad.

The pupils Top 15 of the ability range from business/professional homes in Wandsworth, Merton, Kingston, Richmond, north Surrey; assisted places and scholarships help widen the social range. Entry to junior school at 8, 9, 10, 11 by tests in English, maths, reasoning; 90 a year proceed to senior school; 50+ join at 13 via Common Entrance or scholarship exams.

Results GCSE: all gain at least 5 grades A-C. A-level (1992): impressive 71% of entries graded A or B.

Destinations 96% stay on for A-levels; nearly all of these proceed to higher education (25 to Oxbridge in 1991).

Sport Very strong. Main games rugby (1992 tour of New Zealand and Fiji), hockey, cricket; first-class rowing; soccer, tennis, squash, badminton, fencing also on offer. Up to a third of the school turns out on Saturday mornings. Facilities include on-site playing fields plus 15 acres at Barnes, sports hall, indoor heated pool.

Remarks Exceptionally good, well-run school; highly recommended.

KING'S Macclesfield
Macclesfield,
Cheshire SK10 1DA
Tel (0625) 618586

Independent • Boys (plus girls in sixth form – co-educational from 1993) • Day • Ages 7-18 • 1,008 pupils (800 in senior school) • 282 in sixth form (70% boys) • Fees, £2,715-£3,465 Head: Adrian Silcock, early-50s, appointed 1990.

Traditional, well-regarded school; broad curriculum.

Background Founded 1502; moved to present (cramped) town-centre site 1855. Junior school transfers to premises of a former girls' school in September 1993 (when it will become co-educational); girls aged 11-16 will then be admitted to a separate section of the senior school.

Atmosphere Grammar-school ethos: hard work, high standards.

The head Energetic, dedicated; teaches French, German; previously senior master at King Edward VI, Southampton.

The teaching Broad curriculum includes compulsory computing, divinity, PE; all do second language (choice of Latin or German); all take at least 8 GCSEs. Well-qualified, long-serving staff; friendly relations with pupils; average class size 22. Spacious library includes video-learning area. Good music, art, drama. Regular French and German exchanges.

The pupils Courteous; well-behaved; take pride in their work. Wide catchment area (coach service organised by parents and friends of the school). Entry to junior and senior school by examination (juniors promoted automatically – and make up 50% of the senior school's intake); minimum of 55% required at Common Entrance (approximate IQ of 110) – but many admitted with lower scores. Lots of assisted places, bursaries and scholarships (school is keen to remove financial barriers to admission).

Results GCSE (1991): 93% gained at least 5 grades A-C. A-level (1992): 44% of entries graded A or B.

Destinations 90% stay on for A-levels; nearly all of these proceed to higher education (14 to Oxbridge in 1991).

Sport Rugby (tours to Argentina, Australia), cricket, netball, hockey, athletics, cross-country, swimming, squash; many county and national honours. Facilities include indoor pool, gymnasium, all-weather pitch, 20 acres of playing fields.

Remarks Effective school; planning to expand.

KING'S Peterborough
Park Road,
Peterborough PE1 2UE
Tel (0733) 64938

Comprehensive (grant-maintained) •
Co-educational • Day and boarding •
Ages 11-18 • 786 pupils (56% boys; 90% day) • 160 in sixth form • Boarding fees, £4,875
Head: Michael Barcroft, 53, appointed 1974.

Middle-class comprehensive with strong cathedral links. Good exam results; excellent music.

Background Founded as a cathedral school in 1541 by Henry VIII. Changed from boys' grammar to co-educational comprehensive 1976. Main building 19th-century; 1960s and 1970s additions; reasonable facilities but cramped premises (new technology block for September 1993). Parents, who contribute an impressive £80,000 a year to school funds, voted for grant-maintained status.

Atmosphere Friendly, open; church-school ethos; prefects wear gowns. Pleasant boarding house (principally for cathedral choristers).

The head Read history at Cambridge (and taught it to Prince Charles at Gordonstoun). Keen musician (plays the piano, composes); teaches history and general studies 11 periods a week (so knows the pupils well). Plans to stay until he retires. Wife teaches at a school for children with special needs.

The teaching Well-structured, lively, enthusiastic; mixture of traditional methods and investigative group work. Nearly all staff appointed by present head. Pupils set by ability in most subjects; class size 30, reducing to 20. Regular exchange with grammar school in Germany. Lots of drama; excellent music (concerts, recitals); wide range of extra-curricular activities (chess a speciality).

The pupils Most of above-average ability from middle-class homes; strong tradition of sons following fathers. School heavily over-subscribed; admission procedures give priority to children of worshipping members of the cathedral congregation, siblings, children of practising members of the Church of England, choristers and those of outstanding musical ability.

Results (1992) GCSE: creditable 80% gained at least 5 grades A-C. A-level: 40% of entries graded A or B.

Destinations 50% stay on to take 3 A-levels (rest to further education or sixth-form colleges); nearly all proceed to higher education (2 to Oxbridge in 1991).

Sport Chiefly rugby, hockey, cricket, athletics, but many other activities available. Playing fields 1 mile away.

Remarks Successful comprehensive; high expectations all round.

KING'S Rochester
Satis House,
Boley Hill,
Rochester ME1 1TE
Tel (0634) 843913

Independent • Boys (plus girls in sixth form) • Day and some boarding • Ages 4-18 • 652 pupils (337 in senior school; 90% day) • 150 in sixth form (80% boys) • Fees, £5,001-£5,517 day; £8,196-£8,712 boarding
Head: Dr Ian Walker, 40, appointed 1986.

Strongly traditional school meeting modern needs with innovation and flair; not especially selective; respectable results.

Background Founded 604 by Benedictine monks; re-founded 1541 (with 6 other King's schools) by Henry VIII. Fine site in the precincts of the cathedral (for which it is the choir school); 1950s purpose-built additions; some neighbouring houses bought up and developed. Boarding being phased out from September 1993, when the school will become fully co-educational.

Atmosphere Strong Christian ethic; day usually starts with a service in the cathedral. Stark motto – 'Learn or leave' – belies caring, sympathetic approach. Big emphasis on commitment and involvement.

The head Forceful, no-nonsense style; fierce critic of 1960s educational theories; claims the British education system is becoming incapable of producing either brain surgeons or plumbers. Born in Australia, left school at 14, trained as an accountant, switched to theology and became an unordained chaplain. Came to Britain to do a PhD (at Swansea), appointed head of divinity at Dulwich. Martial arts black belt (and was an accomplished rugby player). Keen on language teaching; introduced German for 4-year-olds; wants every pupil fluent by 13 and studying some subjects in German. Brought in a teacher appraisal scheme which led to the departure of a third of the staff. Married, 2 children.

The teaching Traditional emphasis in the junior school on basic skills (regular spelling and tables tests) plus computing and German. Broad curriculum in the senior school; all start Latin, half continue it to GCSE; Greek also available; modern languages include Italian, Russian. Most take 8-9 GCSEs plus computer studies; choice of 15 subjects at A-level. Remedial help for those who need it. Nightly homework; twice-termly reports for parents record effort and achievement. Head insists on art, drama, music being taught properly, not treated as 'Mickey Mouse' subjects: artist-in-residence; 3 major drama productions a year; 3 orchestras, jazz band, annual choir tour; new music school planned.

The pupils All well-mannered, bright, articulate; mostly from local middle-class families. Smart uniform strictly adhered to (blazers and boaters in summer). Admission by tests (even for 3-year-olds) and interviews with parents: head says he is looking for a partnership; those wanting to hand over all responsibility are not encouraged. No automatic entry from junior to senior school but admission requirements are below grammar-school standard. Girls entering the sixth form (with 6 GCSE grades A-C) have to work hard to catch up but finish doing marginally better than the boys. Voice tests for cathedral choristers (at 8 or 9); successful applicants then tested academically. Generous range of scholarships, bursaries, exhibitions.

Results GCSE (1991): 80% gained at least 5 grades A-C. A-level (1992): rather modest 35% of entries graded A or B.

Destinations Most continue into the sixth form; 90% of these proceed to higher education (10-15 to Oxbridge).

Sport Excellent facilities; successful rugby, cricket, hockey, fencing, rowing, cross-country (and netball for the girls).

Remarks Impressive school; combines traditional values with best of new ideas; individual talents fostered and appreciated. Highly recommended.

KING'S Taunton
Taunton,
Somerset TA1 3DX
Tel (0823) 272708

Independent • Co-educational • Boarding and day • Ages 13-18 • 463 pupils (85% boys; 88% boarding) • 213 in sixth form (75% boys) • Fees, £9,630 boarding; £7,020 day
Head: Simon Funnell, mid-50s, appointed 1988.

Solid school; not especially selective; respectable results.

Background Roots go back to the 13th century; present foundation dates from 1880 when the school was bought by Nathaniel Woodard, a Victorian Anglo-Catholic cleric who set out to blanket the country with Christian public schools for the irreligious middle classes. Belongs to the Woodard Coporation and is still run on distinctly Christian lines. 100 acres (with fine views of the Quantocks); earliest buildings 19th-century Gothic. Becoming fully co-educational.

Atmosphere Purposeful, friendly; strong sense of a joint enterprise between (youthful) staff and pupils. Victorian boarding houses being pleasantly converted.

The head Read English at Cambridge. Experienced; good manager.

The teaching High-quality; emphasis on active learning and problem solving. Streaming by ability throughout; national curriculum being phased in; all take 7-9 GCSEs (depending on their stream). Basic computing for all (but a shortage of equipment); average class size 19. Choice of 17 subjects at A-level; all take extra courses to broaden outlook. First-class facilities for drama and music; choir, orchestra, wind band etc.

The pupils Lively, articulate; largely from middle-class backgrounds; mostly from the south-west; a few from overseas. Admission by Common Entrance or school's own tests; entry not unduly selective. Some scholarships.

Results GCSE: 86% gain at least 5 grades A-C. A-level (1992): 42% of entries graded A or B.

Destinations Most stay on for A-levels; 90% of these proceed to higher education (6 a year to Oxbridge).

Sport Wide range of activities; excellent facilities, including extensive playing fields, sports hall, squash courts, indoor pool. Shooting and mountaineering on offer.

Remarks Hard-working school; good all round.

KING'S Worcester
Worcester WR1 2LH
Tel (0905) 23016

Independent • Co-educational • Day and boarding • Ages 11-18 (plus adjacent junior school) • 750 pupils (80% boys; 85% day) • 275 in sixth form (70% boys) • Fees, £7,284 boarding; £4,440 day
Head: Dr John Moore, 56, appointed 1983.

Successful, expanding school; becoming fully co-educational.

Background 7th-century foundation, refounded by Henry VIII in 1541 after the suppression of the priory (14th-century refectory is the main hall). Superb setting in cathedral precincts overlooking the Severn; main buildings 17th- and 18th-century with later additions; extensive development programme under way (science labs, technology centre, theatre complex etc – all financed out of income). 11-year-old girls first admitted September 1991.

Atmosphere Strong Christian and musical traditions maintained. Boarding houses fully refurbished (carpeted and curtained).

The head Enthusiastic, friendly. Educated at Rugby and Cambridge; doctorate in classics; taught at Winchester and Radley. Author of 6 books; part-time magistrate. Married, 1 son.

The teaching Highly qualified staff of 66 (nearly a third women); half appointed by present head. National curriculum-plus; 3 separate sciences available to GCSE; good design/technology; more than 100 computers. No streaming (within a fairly narrow ability band); setting in maths, languages. Average class size 24; smaller for GCSE; 8-12 in sixth form. Excellent drama and music (regular organ/choral scholarships to Oxbridge); 6 orchestral and choral concerts a year. Popular cadet force and Duke of Edinburgh award scheme; residential centre in the Black Mountains.

The pupils Well-mannered, responsive; mostly from professional, business and Service backgrounds. Boarders include foreign nationals from Malaysia, Hong Kong; day pupils from 20-mile radius. Admission at 11+ and 13+ by tests in English, maths, verbal reasoning plus interview and previous school report; half annual intake of 100 come from adjacent junior school. Assisted places, scholarships, bursaries.

Results GCSE (1991): 95% gained at least 5 grades A-C. A-level (1992): 46% of entries graded A or B (has been higher).

Destinations Nearly all stay for A-levels; 90% of these go on to higher education (10 a year to Oxbridge).

Sports Strong rugby, rowing, hockey, netball. Fencing, sailing, canoeing, judo also on offer. 25 acres of playing fields across the river; new indoor pool.

Remarks Well-run school; high all-round standards.

KINGSTON GRAMMAR
70-72 London Road,
Kingston upon Thames,
Surrey KT2 6PY
Tel (081) 546 5875

Independent • Co-educational • Day • Ages 10-18 • 585 pupils • 150 in sixth form • Fees, £4,080-£4,290
Head: Duncan Baxter, 39, appointed 1991.

Strong all round; good results; excellent sport.

Background Founded 1561. Victorian and early 20th-century buildings plus many later additions and improvements on cramped town-centre site.

Atmosphere Friendly, well-ordered. Committed staff; supportive parents; pupils take pride in the school.

The head Educated at Oxford (scholarships in English and music); taught at Gresham's and Wycliffe. Sums up his educational philosophy in 2 words – excellence, respect: excellence in every aspect of school life; respect by pupils for themselves, others and the environment. Married, 2 boys at prep school.

The teaching Emphasis on practical work, investigation; lessons require active involvement rather than passive listening. Compulsory Latin from the start; optional Greek; all do computing, music, French and at least 1 year's German; 3 sciences taught separately. All take 8-9 GCSEs (options include business studies, economics, ancient history); most do 3 A-levels plus non-examined general studies (life skills, currrent affairs, computing). Some streaming by ability; setting in maths, languages. Spacious, well-equipped library. Busy extra-curricular programme (all pupils expected to arrive early, leave late) includes drama, music (a quarter learn an instrument), cadet force, Duke of Edinburgh award scheme, Christian Union, chess, debating.

The pupils Many from fairly prosperous homes, but scholarships, bursaries and assisted places ensure the full social spread of the traditional grammar school. Entry at 10+, 11+ by tests in English, arithmetic, verbal reasoning plus interview and school report; at 13+ by Common Entrance. Over-subscribed; ability range wider than in most state grammar schools.

Results GCSE: virtually all gain at least 5 grades A-C. A-level (1992): 41% of entries graded A or B (has been higher).

Destinations 85% stay on for A-levels; 80% of these proceed to higher education (10 a year to Oxbridge).

Sport International reputation for hockey; rowing prowess highly regarded. Cricket, tennis, cross-country, athletics all pursued to a high standard. First-class facilities on beautiful 22-acre site by the Thames opposite Hampton Court Palace.

Remarks Successful school; thriving in the face of strong local competition.

KNUTSFORD HIGH
Bexton Road,
Knutsford,
Cheshire WA16 0EA
Tel (0565) 632277

Comprehensive • Co-educational • Ages 11-19 • 1,439 pupils (52% boys) • 258 in sixth form
Head: Michael Valleley, 51, appointed 1981.

Fine, well-run comprehensive; good GCSE results; first-rate music, art, sport.

Background 1973 merger of 2 single-sex schools on 2 sites half a mile apart; solid, well-maintained 1950s and 1960s brick premises in attractive grounds with views across the Cheshire plain. Growth in numbers is putting pressure on space.

Atmosphere Orderly, relaxed, friendly; a nice balance between tolerance and discipline; committed staff and hard-working pupils engaged in a common purpose. Good pastoral care system. Highly supportive parents covenant £10,000 a year.

The head Quietly spoken, humorous, down-to-earth. Went to art school and trained as a potter before reading English and history at Manchester; formerly deputy head of a Cheshire comprehensive. Good manager; innovative without being trendy; gets on well with staff and pupils. Francophile (cottage in the Loire valley) and wine buff. Married to an educationist.

The teaching Wide variety of styles: tradiional chalk-and-talk, group discussions, imaginative problem solving. Youthful staff of 93 (52 women), two-thirds appointed by present head. Full national curriculum; French, German, Spanish on offer; science taught as an 'integrated' subject; mixed-ability classes with some setting from second year; average class size 30, reducing to 25 for GCSE, 12-15 in sixth form. Homework strictly monitored. Vocational alternatives to A-level include BTEC diploma in business and finance. 42 children have formal statements of special needs: department is a model of practical compassion. Strong music tradition: 10% learn an instrument; full orchestra, steel band, 2 choirs. Good drama and some impressively spirited, confident artwork. First-rate careers advice; frequent field trips, foreign visits, language exchanges with French and German schools.

The pupils Confident, courteous. Wide variety of backgrounds from Manchester overspill and Trafford; intake skewed towards the upper end of the ability range. School always over-subscribed; no selection tests; priority to those living in the catchment area, siblings, geographical proximity.

Results (1992) GCSE: creditable 54% gained at least 5 grades A-C. A-level: 33% of entries graded A or B.

Destinations 70% continue on into the sixth form; 90% of these proceed to higher education (up to 5 a year to Oxbridge).

Sport All major games; strong hockey. Excellent facilities include extensive playing fields, floodlit all-weather pitch, huge sports hall and swimming pool, squash courts.

Remarks Attractive, effective school.

KYLE ACADEMY
Overmills Road,
Ayr KA7 3LR
Tel (0292) 262234

Comprehensive • Co-educational • Ages 12-18 • 778 pupils (56% boys) • 93 in sixth year
Head: John Cooke, mid-50s, appointed 1984.

Good, well-run comprehensive; first-rate results.

Background Established 1979 to cope with the expanding population of Ayr; pleasant site on the outskirts of the town; undistinguished, poorly maintained buildings (but no signs of graffiti or vandalism); facilities generally good.

Atmosphere Children and staff are friendly, happy and approachable. Discipline unobtrusive; behaviour impeccable.

The head Quietly spoken, modest (but the essential steel is there). He is constantly around the school; seems to know every pupil. Formerly deputy head of a local comprehensive.

The teaching Emphasis on individual learning and coursework; staff intent on ensuring all receive a sound grounding in the basics. Broad curriculum; particular strengths in maths, sciences (especially chemistry) and computing. Mostly mixed-ability teaching with a minimum of setting; extra help for the less able; average class size 27. Most take 8 subjects at Standard Grade (from a choice of more than 20); 26 Highers on offer in addition to vocational modules. Strong drama and debating; good links with industry.

The pupils Largely from middle-class families with high aspirations; nearly a third come from outside the catchment area.

Results Highers: 29% gain at least 5 grades A-C.

Destinations 90% stay on for the fifth and sixth years; 30% of those who enter the school go on to higher education.

Sport Strong soccer but swimming has declined with local authority spending cuts, as have Saturday morning games. First-rate facilities include fine sports hall and gymnasia.

Remarks Good all round, with an enviable reputation for academic success.

LADY ELEANOR HOLLES
102 Hanworth Road,
Hampton,
Middlesex TW12 3HF
Tel (081) 979 1601

Independent • Girls • Day • Ages 7-18 •
812 pupils (625 in senior school) • 160 in
sixth form • Fees, £4,335 (seniors)
Head: Miss Elizabeth Candy, 49,
appointed 1981.

*Strong academic school; first-rate
teaching and results; good art and sport.*

Background Founded 1711 under the will of
Lady Eleanor Holles; moved to present purpose-built premises 1936; charmless, factory-
style buildings on a flat 33-acre site. Later
additions include fine new art and design
centre. Facilities generally good; light, airy
classrooms.

Atmosphere Vigorous, professional; a big
school – and feels like it, but certainly not
unfriendly. (Its name helped give it a rather
snobbish reputation, which the head has done
her best to dispel.) High standards all round;
impressive artwork displayed to full advantage
down the long corridors.

The head Able, humorous, enthusiastic
('Miss Candy joins in'); enjoys organising and
being in charge. Read chemistry at London;
formerly second mistress at Putney High.

The teaching Some very traditional – and
none the worse for that – but there is no sense
of the school being behind the times. Well-
qualified staff; 85% appointed by present head.
National curriculum-plus; languages on offer
include German, Spanish and Russian (the
first girls' school to teach it); 3 separate
sciences are being replaced by a combined
course (despite the head's misgivings); all
become computer-literate. Average class size
24, reducing to 10 in the sixth form. A-level
options include home economics, human biology, textiles, theatre studies; good results in
maths, sciences, modern languages. First-rate
art; good drama and music (a quarter learn an
instrument).

The pupils Confident, outgoing; mostly from
professional homes in a wide catchment area –
Weybridge, Maidenhead, Richmond etc.
Entry by interview and tests in English, maths,
verbal reasoning; 6 or 7 apply for each place;
promotion from junior school is not automatic. Scholarships, bursaries, 10 assisted
places a year.

Results GCSE: all gain at least 5 grades A-C.
A-level (1992): 57% of entries graded A or B.

Destinations Up to 90% stay on for A-levels;
90% of these proceed to higher education (10
a year to Oxbridge).

Sport Strong in lacrosse, netball, tennis, athletics, rowing, gymnastics; swimming, badminton, hockey, fencing also on offer. Facilities include spacious playing fields, tennis
courts, indoor heated pool.

Remarks Well-run school: they do everything
properly here.

LADY MANNERS
Bakewell,
Derbyshire DE4 1JA
Tel (0629) 812671

Comprehensive (voluntary-controlled) •
Co-educational • Day and some boarding
• Ages 11-18 • 1,356 pupils (equal
numbers of boys and girls; 45 boarders) •
288 in sixth form • Boarding fees,
£3,825-£4,250
Head: John Morris, late-40s, appointed
1978.

*Highly regarded comprehensive; good
results; strong sporting record.*

Background Founded 1636 by Grace, Lady
Manners 'for the better instructinge of the
male children' of Bakewell; re-established
1896 as the first co-educational grammar
school; became comprehensive 1972. Rather
grim 1930s premises; worn-looking classrooms, labs, corridors.

Atmosphere Busy, convivial; grammar-school traditions retained (speech day, commemoration service, badges, blazers). Boarders live in comfortable listed mansion on the other side of town.

The head Derbyshire-born; read geography at Liverpool. Teaches religious education to first-years, general studies to sixth-formers. Emphasises importance of self-discipline; keen to develop pupils' hidden talents.

The teaching Styles vary 'from the domineering to the humane', according to a sixth-former. Generally a problem-solving approach; lots of discussion and debate. Mixed-ability classes in first year; setting in most subjects thereafter. All do French and German for first 2 years; separate sciences now giving way to combined course; compulsory religious education up to GCSE. Extra help for those with special needs. Impressive choice of 25 subjects at A-level (but no vocational courses). Active music; 2 huge choirs; many instrumental groups. Well-organised work experience.

The pupils Enthusiastic, appreciative ('We're not regarded as faceless kids in blazers'). All abilities; drawn from wide rural catchment area, mostly in Derbyshire. School controls admission of boarders (and advertises places).

Results (1991) GCSE: 59% gained at least 5 grades A-C. A-level: 37% of entries graded A or B.

Destinations 45% continue into the sixth form (most of the rest transfer to further education colleges); majority proceed to higher education (between 6 and 10 a year to Oxbridge).

Sport Strong all round (rarely beaten); high participation rate; good facilities.

Remarks Successful school: offers broad, balanced education for all abilities and plays a strong community role.

LANCING

Lancing,
West Sussex BN15 0RW
Tel (0273) 452213

Independent ● Boys (plus girls in sixth form) ● Boarding and some day ● Ages 13-18 ● 545 pupils (90% boarding) ● 250 in sixth form (70% boys) ● Fees (1992-93), £10,770 boarding; £8,085 day
Head: Jim Woodhouse, 59, appointed 1981 (retiring August 1993).

Very sound school; strong religious ethos; respectable results; fine setting and facilities.

Background Founded 1848 by Rev Nathaniel Woodard as an Anglo-Catholic boarding school for the (irreligious) middle classes, the corner-stone of what he hoped would grow to be an empire. Stunning Victorian-Gothic chapel plus imposing collection of flint and sandstone buildings arranged around 2 cloistered quadrangles on 550-acre site high on the South Downs; recent additions include fine design/technology centre.

Atmosphere Friendly, warm, civilised (panelled halls echo Oxbridge); discipline firm but not oppressive; compulsory chapel (regular Eucharist) and religious studies. Genuine tolerance of individuality, though not perhaps to extremes; radical and spiky intellectuals might look for a more abrasive atmosphere (and some might resent the central position of the chapel); sixth-form girls, provided they have some spirit, feel accepted, unthreatened and involved. Boys' boarding accommodation somewhat spartan; 2 recent girls' houses have every amenity. Good food; vegetarians catered for.

The head Very able; has had a distinguished career. Read English at Cambridge, taught at Westminster, became head of Rugby aged 34 and remained for 14 years. Has raised academic standards here and expanded horizons. Married, 4 grown-up children.

The teaching Clear, informal; well-qualified staff of 65 (10 women); aim is to encourage co-operation rather than score intellectul points. National curriculum-plus; choice of science as 3 separate subjects or combined; German, Spanish, Russian, Latin, Greek on offer. Setting by ability from first year; some take GCSE maths, French a year early; maximum class size 22, reducing to 15 in sixth form. Wide choice of subjects at A-level, including economics, ancient history; all do general studies, which includes English, art and religious studies. Good music (strong choral and organ tradition); drama not timetabled but taken seriously; numerous productions in well-equipped theatre (and long reviews in school magazine). 1 afternoon a week devoted to extra-curricular activities ranging from astronomy to ballroom dancing; second-years and upwards choose between cadet force, community service and practical courses in first aid/car maintenance/life-saving. Other options include Duke of Edinburgh award scheme, cookery and working on the college farm. Lots of adventurous expeditions; links with schools in Russia, Malawi; regular French exchanges.

The pupils Natural, polite, generally at ease with themselves and their surroundings. Nearly all come from professional or business families in the South East; two-thirds go home every other weekend; handful from Hong Kong and Korea. Admission by Common Entrance; boarders require minimum 55% mark; day boys 65%; entrants from state sector or overseas take school's own exams. Entry to sixth form with 5 GCSE grade Cs or above. Music and academic scholarships; bursaries for clergy and Service children.

Results GCSE: 95% gain at least 5 or more grades A-C. A-level (1992): 43% of entries graded A or B (has been higher).

Destinations Virtually all stay for A-levels; 90% proceed to higher education (about 15 a year to Oxbridge).

Sport Strong soccer, rugby and girls' hockey. Fine facilities include ample playing fields, sports hall, squash courts, fives courts, 10 hard and 6 grass tennis courts, indoor pool.

Remarks Attractive, well-run school; good all round.

LATYMER
Haselbury Road,
Edmonton,
London N9 9TN
Tel (081) 807 4037

Grammar (voluntary-aided) •
Co-educational • Ages 11-18 • 1,242 pupils (equal numbers of boys and girls) • 341 in sixth form
Head: Geoffrey Mills, mid-50s, appointed 1983.

High-powered, selective school; outstanding music; strong sport.

Background Founded 1624; became co-educational and moved to present sombre premises (behind high railings in a drab residential street) in 1910; many later additions. Vast, arched assembly hall can seat the whole school; science labs urgently need refurbishing.

Atmosphere Very traditional and extremely busy (can seem rather overwhelming at first – 'Reception is the 12th door on your left'); staff and pupils work, practise, rehearse on the premises from 7.30 a.m. to 6.00 p.m. daily.

The head Effective manager of a complex institution (don't be misled by his self-effacing manner). Read modern languages at Cambridge; formerly head of a comprehensive in West Sussex. Married, 2 children (1 a pupil at the school).

The teaching Styles vary from formal whole-class teaching to less didactic group work. Enthusiastic, hard-working staff of 73 (average age mid-30s); 85% appointed by present head. Strongly academic curriculum; good science (many go on to do medicine) but weak technology; all take 2 languages for at least the first 3 years; most do 9-10 GCSEs. Impressive choice of 25 subjects at A-level, including

Russian, German (particularly strong), business studies (increasingly popular), theatre and media studies; most take 3 or 4. First-rate library; nearly 20,000 volumes plus wide selection of periodicals. Outstanding music (despite lack of a purpose-built centre): 40% learn an instrument (28 visiting teachers); 3 full symphony orchestras plus a variety of smaller ensembles; 2 choirs (involving more than 300 pupils); 12 major musical events a year and regular foreign tours (all too much, complain some non-musicians). Good art and drama. Regular (and well-supported) exchanges with schools in France, Germany, Russia. Much community service; charity fund-raising taken seriously. Residential centre in Snowdonia.

The pupils Lively, articulate, demanding; big social and ethnic mix from all over Enfield and beyond. School *very* heavily over-subscribed; governors control admissions on basis of aptitude and ability. All applicants take a non-verbal reasoning test; previous school reports requested on the 500 who score highest; parents invited to complete a questionnaire on their children's special interests; places offered to the 180 judged likely to respond best to what the school has to offer. Special consideration for those of exceptional musical ability.

Results (1992) GCSE: 98% gained at least 5 grades A-C. A-level: 45% of entries graded A or B.

Destinations 85% continue into the sixth form; up to 90% of these proceed to higher education, some after taking a 'gap year' (at least 12 a year to Oxbridge).

Sport First-rate; policy is to encourage widest participation in recreational sport and competitiveness at the highest level. Soccer, rugby, basketball, hockey, netball, volleyball, tennis, athletics, cross-country, gymnastics all on offer; consistent success in borough, county, national competitions. Canoeing, sailing, swimming, golf, squash also available. Facilities include 2 gymnasia, full-size athletics track.

Remarks Exceptional school; highly recommended.

LATYMER UPPER
King Street,
Hammersmith,
London W6 9LR
Tel (081) 741 1851

Independent • Boys • Day • Ages 9-18 • 1,060 pupils (972 in senior school) • 275 in sixth form • Fees, £3,750-£4,860
Head: Colin Diggory, 37, appointed 1991.

Sound, grammar-school education; wide cross-section of pupils.

Background Founded 1624 for the education of '8 poor boys from the town of Hammersmith'; became one of London's leading Direct Grant grammar schools; present governors say the aim is to offer 'an opportunity for able boys from all walks of life to develop their talents to the full'. Moved to present Thames-side site 1895; institutional red-brick plus functional modern additions.

Atmosphere Busy, crowded, lively (every inch of space put to effective use). Less academically and socially exclusive than some of its rivals.

The head Capable, vigorous. Educated at Durham; taught maths at Manchester Grammar, St Paul's, Merchant Taylors'; formerly deputy head here. Wife teaches aerobics.

The teaching Good. Staff of 85 (12 women). No streaming by ability; setting in maths from third year. All do drama for first 2 years; languages include German, Russian, Spanish. Class sizes start at 25, smaller for GCSE, 12 at A-level. First-rate music; quarter learn an instrument; 3 orchestras, smaller ensembles, choirs. Regular exchanges with France, Germany. Popular Duke of Edinburgh award scheme.

The pupils Street-wise, friendly, reasonably unscruffy; enthusiastic about what is on offer.

Up to 70 come from state primaries (admission at 11 is out of sync with prep schools). Competitive entry (350 apply for 140 places); 50 assisted places a year plus scholarships, bursaries ('No gifted boy should be denied a place through lack of parental means,' say governors).

Results GCSE (1991): 85% gained at least 5 grades A-C. A-level (1992): 47% of entries graded A or B.

Destinations Up to 10% leave to take A-levels elsewhere; 90% proceed to higher education (15 a year to Oxbridge).

Sport Strong rowing; soccer, rugby, cricket, athletics also on offer. Swimming pool, large sports hall; playing fields 1½ miles away. All have to do PE and 1 afternoon of games.

Remarks Stimulating, unpretentious school.

LEEDS GIRLS' HIGH
Headingly Lane,
Leeds LS6 1BN
Tel (0532) 744000

Independent • Girls • Day • Ages 3-18 •
949 pupils (589 in senior school) • 140 in
sixth form • Fees, £3,831
Head: Miss Philippa Randall, 50,
appointed 1977.

Outstanding academic school; first-class results; good facilities.

Background Founded 1876 as part of a contemporary movement to provide secondary education for the daughters of the middle and upper classes. Elegant 3-storey Victorian red-brick buildings on 10 acres, 2 miles from city centre.

Atmosphere Scholarly. Skilled staff; bright pupils; big emphasis on pursuit of excellence.

The head Read history at London School of Economics; took a master's degree in education at Sussex. Abroad until September 1992

on 1 year's sabbatical (studying provision for gifted pupils).

The teaching Challenging. No streaming (within a narrow ability band); setting in maths, French. Strong science (many go on to medical/scientific careers); good computing; up to half do 2 modern languages for GCSE. Average class size 25. Choice of 20 subjects at A-level; most do 4. Superb facilities for music (more than a third learn an instrument) and drama (in converted church). Regular exchanges to France, Germany.

The pupils Very able. Half 11+ entry come from junior school (promotion not automatic); rest by tests and interview (130 apply for 45 places). Assisted places, bursaries, scholarships.

Results GCSE: 99% gain at least 5 grades A-C. A-level: impressive 66% of entries graded A or B.

Destinations Nearly all stay for A-levels; 80% proceed to higher education (17 to Oxbridge in 1991), some after taking a 'gap year'.

Sport Good netball, hockey. Facilities include sports hall, handsome indoor pool, floodlit tennis courts.

Remarks Highly recommended for very able girls.

LEEDS GRAMMAR
Moorland Road,
Leeds LS6 1AN
Tel (0532) 433417

Independent • Boys • Day • Ages 7-18 •
1,150 pupils • 270 in sixth form • Fees,
£3,834
Head: Bryan Collins, 54, appointed 1986.

Solid, highly selective school; good results.

Background Founded 1552; moved to its present site 1 mile from the city centre 1859. Victorian-Gothic buildings of a rather sombre, ecclesiastical appearance; many later additions, including £2-million science block. Reverted to full independence in 1976 with the abolition of Direct Grant status; remains the city's grammar school.

Atmosphere Lively, busy; 'serious in purpose but light in spirit', according to the head. Boys' relations with staff are respectful but relaxed.

The head Biologist; degrees from London and Bristol. Has taught widely in the state sector; formerly head of a comprehensive. Keen Rotarian; sings. Married, 2 young children.

The teaching Challenging, rigorous. Long-serving staff of 90 (16 women); most leave only for promotion. Good languages, including French, German, Russian, Spanish; all do Latin in first year; Greek available from fourth year. 3 sciences taught separately; splendid new labs; lots of computing (popular at GCSE); technology ranges from computer-aided design to work in wood, metal, plastics. Most take at least 9 GCSEs and 3 A-levels plus general studies. Strong music: more than a quarter learn an instrument; several orchestras, bands, choirs. New 300-seat drama theatre equipped to professional standards. Regular foreign exchanges. Lots of fundraising for charity; sixth-formers spend half a day a week doing community service. Well-used residential centre in Teesdale.

The pupils Very able; wide social, ethnic, religious mix; 20 Jewish; nearly 25 on assisted places. Highly competitive entry at 11+ by school's own tests; 3-4 apply for each place; juniors required to meet senior school standards.

Results GCSE (1991): 97% gained at least 5 grades A-C. A-level (1992): 56% of entries graded A or B.

Destinations 80% proceed to higher education (31 to Oxbridge in 1991).

Sport Generally strong, particularly rugby, tennis, swimming, rowing; squash; basketball etc also on offer. Facilities include indoor pool, new sports hall; playing fields some distance away.

Remarks Stimulating school; good all round.

LEICESTER GRAMMAR
8 Peacock Lane,
Leicester LE1 5PX
Tel (0533) 621221

Independent • Co-educational • Day • Ages 10-18 (plus associated junior school) • 570 pupils (equal numbers of girls and boys) • 125 in sixth form • Fees (1992-93), £3,225
Head: John Sugden, 55, appointed 1989.

Strong academic school; good teaching and results; lots of music; modest fees.

Background Founded 1981 (with 90 pupils) after the local education authority decided to abolish the city's grammar schools; 2 attractive Victorian buildings adjacent to the cathedral – with which there are strong links; impressive extension opened by Lady Thatcher in 1987.

Atmosphere A young school with a strong pioneering spirit; relatively youthful staff (nearly all under 40), full of infectious enthusiasm. Emphasis on hard work, good discipline; prefects wear gowns. Active parent-teacher association.

The head Energetic, stimulating; insists education should be enjoyable. Formerly deputy head of Newcastle-under-Lyme.

The teaching Broadly national curriculum; half take 2 modern languages to GCSE; Latin, Greek, classical civilisation feature strongly. No streaming by ability but setting in maths, French from age 13; average class size 26, reducing to 14 for GCSE. All do at least 8 GCSEs and 3 A-levels (from a choice of 18); 3 sciences popular; particularly good results in maths, history. First-rate music; more than a third learn an instrument; many play in county orchestras.

The pupils Bright, lively, smartly turned-out in sensible grey uniform. Entry at 10 by tests in English, maths (sample papers sent to parents with the prospectus) and verbal reasoning; 120 apply for 40 places; another 40 admitted at 11+; grammar-school standard required.

Results GCSE: all gain at least 5 grades A-C (92% achieved at least 8 in 1991). A-level (1992): 54% of entries graded A or B.

Destinations 85% stay on for A-levels; 80% of these proceed to higher education (4 to Oxbridge in 1991).

Sport Lack of on-site facilities has not prevented the school from producing performers of county standard in rugby, cricket, hockey, athletics, tennis, netball and swimming (splendid off-site facilities at local polytechnic and community centre).

Remarks Vigorous, relatively new school offering a modern, grammar-school education.

LEICESTER HIGH

454 London Road,
Leicester LE2 2PP
Tel (0533) 705338

Independent • Girls • Day • Ages 3-18 • 435 pupils (310 in senior school) • 45 in sixth form • Fees (1992-93), £2,070-£3,510 Head: Mrs Patricia Watson, 46, appointed September 1992.

Sound academic school; good teaching and results.

Background Founded 1906 as Portland House (teaching flower arranging to young ladies in white gloves); Victorian country house in 3 pleasant acres, 3 miles south of the city centre; every nook and cranny adapted for teaching; good science labs. Assumed present name 1985.

Atmosphere Friendly, relaxed – with a residual trace of hauteur from days gone by. Christian emphasis; strong commitment to community service (including working at a centre for battered wives and a hostel for drop-outs); being top regarded as less impor-

tant than being tolerant. Supportive parents raise funds for new facilities.

The head New appointment; formerly deputy head of South Hampstead *(qv)*. Grammar-school educated; read maths at Reading and has taught it for 24 years, 14 at Godolphin & Latymer. Will find a wider range of abilities here than she is used to – and is likely to make changes (predecessor was here 17 years).

The teaching Long-serving staff (mostly married women); small classes (maximum size 20); setting by ability in maths, French. Good languages but little teaching of the classics; all take at least 1 science for GCSE; twice as many take home economics as English literature (!) Choice of 14 subjects at A-level; twice as many take sociology as English or maths; all sixth-formers computer-literate and able to use a word processor. First-rate art, especially pottery, textile design. Lots of drama and music; 2 orchestras, 2 choirs.

The pupils Happy – with each other and their teachers. Entry to junior school (in separate premises on same site) by interview and assessment; at 11+ by tests; grammar-school standard required. 2 scholarships a year.

Results GCSE: virtually all gain at least 5 grades A-C (70% achieved at least 8 in 1991). A-level (1992): 51% of entries graded A or B.

Destinations Up to 65% stay on for A-levels (many of the rest go to local sixth-form colleges); virtually all of these proceed to higher education.

Sport Good netball, gymnastics. Own sports hall, tennis courts and use of facilities at nearby Leicester University.

Remarks Small, safe school ready to move forward under a new head.

THE LEYS
Trumpington Road,
Cambridge CB2 2AD
Tel (0223) 355327

Independent • Boys (plus girls in sixth form) • Boarding and day • Ages 13-18 (plus associated prep school) • 373 pupils (75% boarding) • 195 in sixth form (two-thirds boys) • Fees, £10,035 boarding; £7,425 day
Head: Revd John Barrett, 49, appointed 1990.

Small, friendly school; fairly wide ability range.

Background Founded 1875 by a group of leading Methodists; much-modernised late-Victorian buildings on attractive 50-acre site not far from the city centre; many later additions, including fine technology centre. Sixth-form girls admitted since 1984; school going fully co-educational from 1994.

Atmosphere Friendly, relaxed, well-disciplined; not overly academic; emphasis on concern for the individual; strong sense of community.

The head Read economics at Durham, theology at Cambridge; trained for the ministry. Prominent Rotarian; British secretary of the World Methodist Church. Formerly head of Kent College. Married.

The teaching Mix of traditional and less formal styles; enthusiastic, dedicated staff. National curriculum-plus; German, Spanish, Greek, Latin on offer; good science (well-equipped labs), computing (all learn word processing). Setting by ability in main subjects; academic progress carefully monitored; class sizes range from 15-20 to 8-12 in sixth form. All do at least 8 GCSEs; most take 3 A-levels plus general studies. Lots of music: orchestras, bands, choirs; regular concerts (including rock concerts for charity). Good drama in well-equipped theatre (many do theatre studies for A-level). Technology centre heavily used throughout the day and late into the evening – houses a magnificent printing press. Extra-curricular activities include cadet force, Duke of Edinburgh award scheme, community service.

The pupils Confident, articulate; mostly from middle and upper-middle-class homes. Entry not unduly selective; 20 join from St Faith's prep school. 12 assisted places a year.

Results GCSE (1991): 88% gained at least 5 grades A-C. A-level (1992): 44% of entries graded A or B.

Destinations Most stay on for A-levels; 90% of these proceed to higher education (half after taking a 'gap year').

Sport Good coaching in rugby, hockey, cricket; school holds its own against bigger competitors. Regular overseas tours. Clay-pigeon shooting a speciality.

Remarks Attractive school; good all round.

LLANDOVERY
Llandovery,
Dyfed SA20 0EE
Tel (0550) 20314

Independent • Co-educational • Boarding and day • Ages 11-18 • 236 pupils (70% boys; 78% boarding) • 79 in sixth form • Fees (1992-93), £6,813-£8,061 boarding; £4,680-£5,259 day
Head: Dr Claude Evans, 50s, appointed 1988.

Small school; fairly wide range of abilities; good sport; fine rural setting; lots of outdoor pursuits.

Background Founded 1847, an outpost of the English public school tradition in rural South Wales; purpose-built Victorian-Gothic premises (gables and battlemented tower with gargoyles coming loose); recent additions include Tesco-style sports hall. Facilities being improved.

Atmosphere Small, intimate, caring; good relations between staff and pupils. Daily morning service in chapel. Pleasant boarding accommodation, some new; seniors have study-bedrooms. Undistinguished food.

The head (Warden) Read chemistry at Aberystwyth; taught it at Westminister for 18 years. Wants to give the school 'a more European dimension'. Unmarried.

The teaching Generally good; strong in English, chemistry, biology. Welsh taught as a first and second language (compulsory for first 2 years); Latin and Greek offered to A-level (but no Spanish or German). Popular new sport science course; business studies on offer; computer literacy for all. All take at least 8 GCSEs and 3 A-levels (from choice of 22). Small classes (average size 12); pupils set by ability. Lots of drama and music; a third learn an instrument; small orchestra. Well-supported cadet force and Duke of Edinburgh award scheme.

The pupils Largely middle-class, mostly local, drawn from prep schools in Cardiff, Porthcawl, Swansea; some boarders from Hong Kong and Malaysia (English taught as a foreign language). Admission by Common Entrance or school's own tests; not unduly selective. Assisted places, scholarships.

Results GCSE: 70% gain at least 5 grades A-C. A-level (1992): 32% of entries graded A or B.

Destinations 70% stay on for A-levels; 80% of these proceed to higher education (1 or 2 a year to Oxbridge).

Sport Famed for its rugby; cricket and girls' hockey also strong; cross-country, tennis, badminton, golf on offer. Facilities include 50 acres of playing fields in glorious valley bottom beside the River Towey.

Remarks Pleasant school; quite good all round.

LLANDRINDOD HIGH
Dyffryn Road,
Llandrindod Wells,
Powys LD1 6AW
Tel (0597) 822992

Comprehensive • Co-educational • Ages 11-18 • 750 pupils (roughly equal numbers of girls and boys) • 100 in sixth form
Head: Brian Heard, 47, appointed 1982.

Well-run, lively, rural comprehensive; respectable results.

Background Opened 1954; became comprehensive 1972. Bleak, factory-like, flat-roof buildings.

Atmosphere Lively, industrious, no-nonsense: 'The emphasis is firmly on measurable and reportable achievement through hard work and a sense of purpose', says the prospectus. All – staff and pupils – know what goals they are aiming for; there is a marked sense of pride in the school. Sixth-formers help teach the younger ones.

The head Welsh-born; read physics at Birmingham; taught in grammar and comprehensive schools. Found the school 'pleasant, old-fashioned, bumbling along – I bumbled along too for a time'. Then in 1987 Her Majesty's Inspectors descended: 'That really shook me. They said the school was not half as good as it should be. So I took it by the scruff of the neck.' Decided management was the key: did a course with Marks and Spencer in Cardiff. 'The intensity and force with which they ran things impressed me tremendously.'

The teaching Standard national curriculum; all do Welsh (as a first or second language) for first 3 years; German, Spanish on offer from third year; history, geography, religious education offered in Welsh medium. Pupils set by ability in Welsh and French from start and in other subjects thereafter; progress carefully monitored; lots of extra help for those with special needs. Sixth-formers take compulsory courses in a foreign language, general studies and computing. Lots of music; orchestra, 2 bands, 2 choirs (trips to Vienna). All do 2 weeks' work experience in fourth year; sixth-formers spend 2 weeks in France.

The pupils Wide range of abilities drawn from a large rural catchment area. Attendance averages 94.

Results GCSE: 50% gain at least 5 grades A-C. A-level: 40% of entries graded A or B.

Destinations 38% stay on for A-levels; most of these proceed to higher education.

Sport Usual games on offer; facilities include new sports hall and swimming pool.

Remarks Up and running – thanks to rigorous organisation and teamwork.

LONDON ORATORY
Seagrave Road,
London SW6 1RX
Tel (071) 385 0102

Comprehensive (grant-maintained) •
Roman Catholic • Boys (plus girls in sixth form) • Ages 11-19 • 1,200 pupils • 300 in sixth form (85% boys)
Head: John McIntosh, 47, appointed 1975.

Exceptional, mixed-ability school; very high all-round standards; traditional academic, cultural and spiritual values.

Background Founded 1863 by the Fathers of the London Oratory. Formerly co-educational and fee-paying; became a boys' grammar school 1963; went comprehensive (in purpose-built premises) 1970. Grant-maintained since 1989. Extensive building programme in progress, including £2.2-million arts centre (inaugurated by John Major). Premises carefully maintained; free of inner-city litter and graffiti.

Atmosphere Highly disciplined; an oasis of cultured calm in the shadow of Chelsea's Stamford Bridge stadium. 'Boys are here to learn and teachers to teach,' head says firmly. 'The school aims to assist parents in fulfilling their obligation to educate their children in accordance with the principles and teachings of the Church,' adds the prospectus.

The head Bachelor; devotes his life to the school (begins the day with a swim in the pool and rarely leaves before 8 p.m. Started his teaching career here; appointed head at 30. Firmly believes grammar-school standards can and should be upheld in a comprehensive. Influential member of the Government's National Curriculum Council.

The teaching Mixture of modern and traditional methods but all fairly formal. Computing prominent in otherwise conventional curriculum (Latin, 3 sciences). 2 ability streams with a top set in each; brightest boys take 4 GCSEs a year early. Most do at least 3 A-levels plus AS-level general studies; rest take 6-subject course of additional GCSEs. Full homework programme. Great importance attached to art, drama, music (orchestra and choir have recently visited US, Austria, Italy). Active Army Cadet Company; lots of overseas trips and foreign exchanges.

The pupils All from practising Catholic families; varied social backgrounds (a third are bilingual); catchment area extends from Richmond to Watford. Parents required to commit their sons to a full 7-year course and to 'support the school in maintaining high standards of discipline'. Immaculate and carefully prescribed uniform for all ('trousers – mid-grey worsted flannel, parallel not flared or tapered'). Heavily over-subscribed: 380 apply for 180 first-year places; more than 200 inquiries for 40 additional sixth-form places; all applicants interviewed. Pupils take full advantage of everything on offer (many arrive early, leave late) and clearly enjoy being members of a successful school. Parents expected to contribute £36 a year to school funds.

Results (1991) GCSE: 59% gained at least 5 grades A-C. A-level: 35% of entries graded A or B.

Destinations 95% stay on into the sixth form; 65% of these proceed to university (7 a year to Oxbridge).

Sport Strong rugby (10 teams turn out on

Saturday mornings); recent tours to US, Canada, Australia. Also, soccer, badminton, basketball, tennis, swimming (indoor pool). Playing fields in Barnes.

Remarks First-rate school: clear evidence that boys thrive in a disciplined society backed by caring staff who demand high standards.

LORD WILLIAMS'S
Oxford Road,
Thame,
Oxfordshire OX9 2AQ
Tel (0844) 213681

Comprehensive (voluntary-controlled) •
Co-educational • Ages 11-18 • 1,850
pupils (equal numbers of boys and girls) •
300 in the sixth form
Head: David Kenningham, 56, appointed
1985.

True comprehensive; broad curriculum; good teaching.

Background Founded 1559 by John, Baron Williams of Thame, sheriff of Oxfordshire; moved to present site 1875; changed from boys' grammar to co-educational comprehensive 1971. 3 self-contained sections on 2 sites 10 minutes apart; teachers have to commute. 16 classrooms in temporary huts.

Atmosphere Strong sense of community, despite the size. Pupils feel they and their opinions count; nearly every wall covered with displays of work, much of it excellent. Good pastoral care system (even the dinner ladies are trained to give help with emotional matters); regular newsletters keep everyone in touch.

The head Read physics at Oxford after National Service; spent 3 years doing research in electronics before starting teaching at Marlborough. Formerly head of Cheney comprehensive, Oxford; strongly committed to comprehensive education. Teaches science to the seniors for nearly 6 hours a week (and 'usually can't wait to get into the classroom').

The teaching Well-qualified staff of 110 (60 women), 70% appointed by present head; 5 have PhDs. Most lessons last 70 minutes; few signs of boredom; teachers maintain friendly control, but noise levels are high. Mixed-ability classes (maximum size 30); setting in maths, modern languages from 13+. Good learning support for those who need help (everyone tested on entry – 1 in 3 found to have a 'spelling deficit' of 2 years or more). Most take 9 GCSEs from choice of 17, including child development, dance, drama, computing, business studies. Vocational qualifications offered as alternative to A-levels. Homework averages 1 hour a night (some days none). All gain work experience. Busy extra-curricular programme includes community service, Duke of Edinburgh award scheme; music and drama at local arts centre.

The pupils Pleasant, willing, articulate. Genuine cross-section – parents range from rural workers to Oxford dons; wide spread of abilities, slightly skewed towards the top. School heavily over-subscribed.

Results (1991) GCSE: 52% gained at least 5 grades A-C (65% of girls but only 43% of boys – *why?*). A-level (1992): 37% of entries graded A or B.

Destinations 65% continue into the sixth form (most of the rest go to further education colleges); 70% of those who take A-levels proceed to higher education (10 a year to Oxbridge), often after a 'gap year'.

Sport Extensive playing fields; high participation rate; good match record in netball, football, rugby, hockey, cricket, athletics, tennis, squash. Indoor games (at local sports centre) include badminton, volleyball, basketball, trampolining. No swimming pool.

Remarks Successful, well-run comprehensive.

LORETTO
Musselburgh,
East Lothian EH21 7RE
Tel (031) 665 5003

Independent • Boys (plus girls in sixth form) • Boarding (and and a few day) • Ages 13-18 (plus associated prep school) • 300 pupils (87% boys) • 140 in sixth form (70% boys) • Fees, £9,645 (£6,429 day) Head: Rev Norman Drummond, 40, appointed 1984.

Small school; lots of individual attention; fairly wide range of abilities; good facilities; strong rugby.

Background Founded 1827 (one of the first boarding schools in Scotland); pleasant 80-acre campus on the outskirts of the town, 6 miles from Edinburgh; buildings – dating from late 14th century to late 20th century – include spacious labs, well-equipped business centre, fine chapel, first-rate theatre and music school. No plans to become fully co-educational. Associated prep school is one of only 2 in Scotland catering exclusively for boys (no frills but not spartan either).

Atmosphere Small, close-knit community; civilised, family feel; strong boarding ethos; lessons on Saturday mornings. Some boarding accommodation dates from 17th century and is scarcely homely; other houses being up-graded (battered furniture, few pictures or posters); sixth-form girls have pleasant single or double rooms.

The head Appointed at 32. Read law at Cambridge (rugby Blue) and divinity at Edinburgh; ordained 1976; Army chaplain to the Parachute Regiment and the Black Watch; formerly chaplain of Fettes. Publicises his school with missionary zeal. Married, 4 children.

The teaching Well-qualified staff of 31 (5 women); standard national curriculum; pupils set by ability; average class size 17. Most do 8-10 GCSEs (some only 6) and 2-3 A-levels from a limited choice of 14 (Highers may be taken *en passant*). Good drama and music; orchestra and smaller ensembles, choir; regu-

lar public performances. Cadet force compulsory for 2 years; well-supported Duke of Edinburgh award scheme.

The pupils Friendly, confident, smartly dressed. Mostly from professional, business, landowning, Services background; many are the children of former pupils; 65% from Scotland. Admission at 13+ by Common Entrance; not unduly selective. Strong competition for sixth-form places, particularly from girls.

Results GCSE: 94% gain at least 5 grades A-C. A-level: modest 38% of entries graded A or B.

Destinations Virtually all continue into the sixth form and proceed to higher education (5 a year to Oxbridge).

Sport Wide choice; very strong rugby (1993 tour of South Africa); girls play hockey, lacrosse; all do athletics. Fine facilities include extensive playing fields (8 rugby pitches), sports hall, indoor heated pool and courts for fives, squash, tennis.

Remarks Popular school for children of a wide range of abilities; good all round.

LOUGHBOROUGH GRAMMAR
Burton Walks,
Loughborough LE11 2DU
Tel (0509) 233233

Independent • Boys • Day (and some boarding) • Ages 10-18 (plus associated junior school) • 925 pupils (95% day) • 260 in sixth form • Fees (1992-93), £3,780-£4,032 (£6,246-£7,488 boarding) Head: Neville Island, late-50s, appointed 1983.

Strong academic school; good teaching and results.

Background Founded 1495; moved to present purpose-built premises 1852; fine Victorian-Gothic buildings in 27 acres; later additions include science labs, art and design centre. Became fully independent with the abolition of Direct Grant status in 1976. Shares governing body with neighbouring Loughborough High *(qv)*.

Atmosphere Firm discipline and genuine caring go hand in hand; good relations between staff and pupils. Smart school uniform. First-rate food.

The head Forthright, combative; gives the impression he would stop at nothing to promote his pupils' interests. Formerly director of studies at University College School.

The teaching Long-serving, well-qualified staff of 70 (nearly a third are Oxbridge graduates). National curriculum-plus; science taught as 3 separate subjects (all take at least 2 to GCSE); Latin, Greek on offer. Pupils streamed by ability; average class size 27. Choice of 18 subjects at A-level; good results in maths, geography, history; all do general studies. Lots of music and drama in conjunction with the girls' school. Well-supported cadet force, Duke of Edinburgh award scheme.

The pupils Relaxed, confident. Entry at 10, 11 by tests in English, maths, verbal reasoning; at 13 by Common Entrance. Assisted places, scholarships, bursaries.

Results GCSE: all gain at least 5 grades A-C (94% achieved at least 8 in 1991). A-level (1992): 52% of entries graded A or B.

Destinations Nearly all stay on for A-levels and proceed to higher education (23 to Oxbridge in 1991).

Sport Strong rugby, cricket, athletics, badminton. Facilities include county-standard cricket square, sports hall, 70 acres of playing fields 10 minutes' walk away.

Remarks Well-run school; good all round.

LOUGHBOROUGH HIGH
Burton Walks,
Loughborough LU11 2DU
Tel (0509) 212348

Independent • Girls • Day (and some weekly boarding) • Ages 11-18 (plus associated junior school) • 528 pupils (22 boarding) • 140 in sixth form • Fees (1992-93), £3,471 (£5,506 boarding) Head: Miss Julien Harvatt, 49, appointed 1977.

Strong academic school; good teaching and results.

Background Founded 1849, the first girls' grammar-school in England; moved to present site (shared with Loughborough Grammar, *qv*) 1879; late-Victorian buildings in spacious, pleasant grounds; many later additions, including modern science block. Became fully independent with the abolition of Direct Grant status in 1976.

Atmosphere Close, caring community; traditional, hard-working grammar-school ethos; strong Christian spirit (morning assembly in fine, panelled hall). Bright, pleasant boarding house. Supportive parents' association.

The head Able, energetic, humorous; has virtually re-built the school in her 15 years here. Read languages at London; formerly deputy head of Bolton Girls'.

The teaching Long-serving staff (mostly married women, many of whom send their own children here). National curriculum-plus; science taught as 3 separate subjects (all take at least 2 for GCSE); all do computing; many take 2 modern languages for GCSE (from French, German, Spanish); Latin, Greek on offer. Setting by ability in English, French, maths, science from second year; average class size 26. Choice of 18 subjects at A-level; French the most popular; good results in history, geography, biology; all do general studies (in conjunction with boys' school). First-rate art and design; flourishing music.

The pupils Confident, happy. Entry at 11 by tests in English, maths, verbal reasoning;

grammar-school standard required. Some scholarships, bursaries.

Results GCSE: virtually all gain at least 5 grades A-C (83% achieved at least 8 in 1991). A-level (1992): impressive 67% of entries graded A or B.

Destinations Nearly all stay on for A-levels and proceed to higher education (6 to Oxbridge in 1991).

Sport Strong hockey, netball, tennis, athletics, swimming. On-site playing field, modern gym.

Remarks Attractive, well-run school.

MAGDALEN COLLEGE SCHOOL
Oxford OX4 1DZ
Tel (0865) 242191

Independent • Boys • Day (plus a handful of boarders) • Ages 11-18 • 500 pupils • 150 in sixth form • Fees, £3,825 (£7,260 boarding)
Head: Peter Tinniswood, early-40s, appointed 1991.

Strong academic school; good teaching and results.

Background Founded 1478 by William of Waynflete as part of Magdalen College (and still educates the college choristers). Unimpressive conglomeration of buildings on a fairly cramped site plus 11 splendid acres of playing fields moated on 2 sides by the Cherwell and overlooking Christ Church Meadows. Cardinal Wolsey taught here; William Tyndale was a pupil.

Atmosphere Informal but business-like (and very masculine – only 1 female teacher). Good relations between staff and pupils (who feel they are taken seriously); effective pastoral care system. School professes to have only 1 rule – 'all boys must at all times behave

sensibly and well' – but the rule's sub-sections run to 3 pages.

The head Able, enthusiastic, ambitious. Taught at Marlborough for 12 years and then did an MBA at Insead, Paris. Married, no children.

The teaching Highly professional; well-prepared, well-managed lessons; all-graduate staff of 38. Broad curriculum; all take 3 sciences, computing, 2 languages (but no design/technology). Third-years choose between third language and art (65% take art). Setting by ability in maths, Latin, French. Nearly all take 11 GCSEs, some a year early. Big choice at A-level (including Russian, Italian shared with girls at Oxford High); all do 3 in addition to 2 non-examined subjects. Lessons on Saturday mornings (until 12.30); class sizes vary from 9 to 27; end-of-term tests plus 3-weekly assessments. Excellent library; strong careers guidance. All expected to participate in extracurricular activities; 60% join the cadet force, 40% do community service; many other clubs and societies.

The pupils Mainly from professional backgrounds (15% are the sons of academics) but 25% have assisted places, ensuring a social mix. Catchment area has a radius of about 20 miles. Entry at 11 by searching tests in English (attention paid to presentation, spelling, punctuation, handwriting), maths (calculator-free competence required), verbal reasoning; at 13 either by tests or Common Entrance – minimum mark of at least 60%. Aspirant choristers should apply to the Dean of Divinity at Magdalen College.

Results GCSE: all gain at least 5 grades A-C. A-level (1992): creditable 63% of entries graded A or B.

Destinations Nearly all continue into the sixth form; 80%-85% of these proceed to higher education (18 to Oxbridge in 1991).

Sport Chiefly rugby, hockey, rowing, cricket, lawn tennis; canoeing, sailing, shooting, cross-country also on offer. Some playing fields 3 miles away.

Remarks Good all round.

MALVERN

College Road,
Malvern,
Worcestershire WR14 3DF
Tel (0684) 892333

Independent • Co-educational (from
September 1992) • Boarding and day •
Ages 13-18 (plus associated prep school)
• 700 pupils (78% boys; 90% boarding) •
300 in sixth form • Fees (1992-93),
£10,980 boarding; £7,995 day
Head: Roy Chapman, 56, appointed 1983.

---

*Academically sound, traditional school
undergoing a major transformation; good
art, drama, music.*

Background Founded 1865; imposing stone
buildings in 100 acres on the slopes of the
Malvern Hills with impressive views across the
Severn Vale. Boys' school merged with
Ellerslie Girls' and Hillstone Prep September
1992.

Atmosphere Stimulating, purposeful; high
expectations all round. Good pastoral-care
system; sixth-formers choose own tutors. 11
pleasant, boarding houses (formerly private
houses).

The head Read modern languages at St Andrews; taught at Glenalmond and Marlborough before becoming head of Glasgow Academy. Forceful, direct style; strong believer in
self-discipline, firm moral values. Married, 3
grown-up children.

The teaching Good. Well-qualified, experienced, committed staff of 80 (20 women);
more than half appointed by present head.
Setting by ability from first year; extra help for
those in difficulty. Choice of 23 subjects at
GCSE, including Greek, German, Spanish;
healthy balance at A-level between arts and
sciences; International Baccalaureate on offer
from September 1992. First-rate art (as a
subject and a leisure activity), drama (lots of
school, house plays), music (more than half
learn at least 1 instrument). Good work-
experience scheme; head keen to ensure all are
'fully aware of the exciting challenges of

industry'. Extra-curricular activities include
cadet force, Duke of Edinburgh award
scheme, voluntary service.

The pupils Mostly from professional/busi-
ness backgrounds, some from the Services.
Entry at 13+ by Common Entrance (minimum
mark of 50% required in main papers) and
interview.

Results GCSE (1991): 94% gained at least 5
grades A-C. A-level (1992): 51% of entries
graded A or B (has been higher).

Destinations 90% stay on for A-levels; 90%
of these proceed to higher education (20-30 a
year to Oxbridge).

Sport Wide choice: soccer, rugby, cricket plus
lacrosse, netball, tennis, rackets, badminton,
squash, shooting, fencing, judo, canoeing,
sailing etc. Facilities include fine playing fields,
sports hall, indoor pool.

Remarks Respected rural boarding school
facing up to the challenges of the '90s.

MALVERN GIRLS'

15 Avenue Road,
Great Malvern,
Worcestershire WR14 3BA
Tel (0684) 892288

Independent • Girls • Boarding and day •
Ages 11-18 • 500 pupils (90% boarding) •
170 in sixth form • Fees, £9,468 boarding;
£6,312 day
Head: Dr Valerie Payne, 50s, appointed
1986.

---

*Sound academic school; good results;
strong sport.*

Background Founded 1893; moved to its
present imposing premises – formerly the
Imperial Hotel – in 1919. Attractive setting at
foot of the Malvern Hills.

Atmosphere Friendly, purposeful; strong
commitment to academic excellence.

Boarders pleasantly housed in converted Victorian and Edwardian residences.

The head Read physics at Imperial College; came here in 1969; promoted deputy head 1985. Married (to a physicist), 1 daughter.

The teaching Varied styles; generally challenging. Long-serving, enthusiastic staff of 85 (few men). National curriculum-plus; all do Latin for first 3 years; science taught as 3 separate subjects; language options include German, Spanish, classical Greek. Most take 9 GCSEs, including at least 1 science. Maximum class size 20. Choice of 20 subjects at A-level. Strong music: 90% learn at least 1 instrument; orchestras, choirs etc. Lots of community service. Regular language trips to France and other European countries.

The pupils Bright, lively, articulate. Mainly from professional, managerial, farming backgrounds; wide catchment area; 20% from overseas.

Results GCSE: virtually all gain at least 5 grades A-C. A-level (1992): very impressive 73% of entries graded A or B (an unusually good year).

Destinations Most stay on for A-levels; 75%-80% proceed to higher education (about 10 a year to Oxbridge).

Sport Strong record in lacrosse, hockey, tennis, athletics, swimming, rounders, gymnastics; squash, volleyball, badminton, fencing, aerobics, riding also on offer. Facilities include all-weather pitch and (hotel's original) heated indoor pool.

Remarks High standards all round.

MANCHESTER GRAMMAR

Rusholme,
Manchester M13 0XT
Tel (061) 224 7201

Independent ● Boys ● Day ● Ages 11-18 ● 1,440 pupils ● 400 in sixth form ● Fees, £3,366
Head: Geoffrey Parker, 59, appointed 1985.

Distinguished academic school (one of the top 10); outstanding teaching and results; strong sport.

Background Founded 1515 by Bishop Hugh Oldham to ensure that 'grace, virtue and wisdom should grow, flower and take root in youths during their boyhood'. Moved 1931 to present 28-acre site at Fallowfield on the south side of the city; solid, rather drab red-brick buildings plus extensive additions; appeal launched recently for £5.8 million. Formerly Direct Grant; now the biggest independent senior school in the country and one of the best-known day schools in the world.

Atmosphere Animated, self-confident, no-nonsense. ('We're not an up-market school and we're certainly not in the business of gentrifying people,' observes the head.) Strong sense of staff and boys engaged in common, high-minded (but far from solemn) endeavour. ('Ensuring they achieve outstanding exam results is one of our functions: we don't harp on about it.')

The head (High Master) The 40th in the school's history. Shrewd, low-key, widely respected. Read history at Cambridge; taught at Bedford Modern and Tonbridge; previously head of Wakefield Grammar for 10 years. Keen to stress the importance of boys' physical, moral and spiritual development and to inject a measure of softness and compassion into the school's busy life. Married, 2 grown-up daughters.

The teaching Mostly formal, always challenging. Hard-working, gifted, highly qualified staff of 106 (6 women); 12% have PhDs. Standard grammar school curriculum; Latin compulsory for first 4 years; classical Greek, German, Russian also on offer; all do combined science for first 2 years, 3 separate sciences thereafter; religious education taken seriously. All take 9 GCSEs; most do maths, French a year early. Average class size 30, reducing to 18-25 for GCSE, 10-12 in sixth form. Most sixth-formers restricted to 3 A-levels to allow maximum time for a general studies course offering 109 options; each boy chooses 12. First-rate art (superb ceramics), flourishing music, 6 drama productions annually. Wide range of extra-curricular activities; 50 clubs and societies; active community action programme. Strong tradition of camping and trekking.

The pupils Top 5% of the ability range: some are brilliant, all are clever, none is dull. Entry at 11 by searching, two-stage examination in English and maths lasting more than 4 hours; only the brightest are advised to try; two-thirds fail to make the grade. Vast catchment area stretching from Buxton to Blackpool and as far south as Stoke-on-Trent; 60% come from state schools; a third receive some help with fees through assisted places or bursaries (which cost the school more than £100,000 a year); no boy refused entry on financial grounds.

Results GCSE: all gain *at least* 5 grades A-C. A-level (1992): very impressive 78% of entries graded A or B.

Destinations Virtually all stay on for A-levels and proceed to higher education (60 a year to Oxbridge).

Sport Very strong – particularly soccer, rugby, cricket, cross-country, swimming, water polo, squash, hockey, tennis. Large playing fields, indoor pool; sports centre planned as part of current appeal.

Remarks Marvellous school for able boys.

MANCHESTER HIGH

Grangethorpe Road,
Manchester M14 6HS
Tel (061) 224 0447

Independent ● Girls ● Day ● Ages 11-18 (plus associated prep school) ● 730 pupils ● 190 in sixth form ● Fees, £3,480
Head: Miss Mary Moon, late-50s, appointed 1983.

Good, academic school; first-rate teaching.

Background Founded 1874 'to provide for Manchester's daughters what has been provided without stint for Manchester's sons'; from the start, girls were actively encouraged to seek careers. Direct Grant 1944-76, when it reverted to full independence. Pleasant, wooded 11½-acre site; much recent building includes science labs, music school.

Atmosphere Relaxed yet ordered; relationships manifestly good; hard work not something teachers impose on children but something all accept as essential to success.

The head Read English at Manchester; formerly at Bolton Girls' and head (for 12 years) of Pate's Grammar. Everyone's ideal headmistress: warm, welcoming, white-haired; knows exactly what makes girls tick; rules with a light, diplomatic touch. Sketches, paints; active church-goer.

The teaching First-rate. Well-qualified, dedicated staff (average age mid-30s); well-prepared, orderly lessons. No streaming (within narrow ability band); some setting in maths, French. Standard grammar-school curriculum; all do Latin, computing for first 3 years; combined science in first year, separate sciences thereafter; options include Greek, Spanish, Russian. Choice of 22 subjects at A-level. Homework compulsory, carefully monitored. Class sizes 29, reducing to 20-25 for GCSE, 6-7 in sixth form. Good, much-used library; full-time professional librarian. Very strong music: more than a quarter learn an instrument; 2 choirs. Lots of extra-curricular activities, including community service, Duke of Edinburgh award scheme.

The pupils Eager, hard-working, socially aware. Many from professional, academic, business homes but others from very modest backgrounds (nearly half join from state primary schools). Extensive catchment area – Greater Manchester, parts of Cheshire, Derbyshire, Lancashire; some travel 30 miles to school. Entry at 4 (to delightful junior school) by informal assessment; at 7 by tests in English, arithmetic plus interview; to senior school by tests in English, maths and general paper (which aims to spot potential and eliminate the effect of coaching). Nearly all junior pupils proceed to senior school.

Results GCSE: virtually all gain at least 5 grades A-C. A-level (1992): very creditable 64% of entries graded A or B.

Destinations 90% stay for A-level; 95% proceed to higher education (8 or 9 a year to Oxbridge).

Sport Gymnastics, hockey, netball, athletics, cross-country running on offer; swimming taken particularly seriously – water polo, synchronised swimming, life saving.

Remarks Happy, well-run school; individuals valued.

MARLBOROUGH

Marlborough,
Wiltshire SN8 1PA
Tel (0672) 515511

Independent • Co-educational • Boarding
• Ages 13-18 • 873 pupils (70% boys) •
521 in sixth form (55% boys) • Fees,
£10,500-£11,550
Head: David Cope, 58, appointed 1986
(leaving August 1993).

Fine school; first-rate teaching; exceptionally good art, music, drama; strong sport.

Background Founded 1843 for the sons of Anglican clergymen; elegant 18th-century and Victorian red-brick buildings ranged round a vast quadrangle at the top of the High Street; later additions include fine art school and 3 modern, motel-like boarding houses. Pioneered the admission of girls into the sixth form in 1968; now fully co-educational.

Atmosphere Was extremely male (mainly bachelor staff, heavy emphasis on rugby) and frankly loutish; now gentler (thanks to the girls) and better-disciplined. First-rate art, music and drama underpins the traditionally liberal, slightly long-haired image (Old Boys include William Morris and Sir John Betjeman). High Church religious ethos (2 full-time chaplains) but pupils can choose between a Sunday service (in enormous Victorian-Gothic chapel) and a humanitarian lecture. Recent £7-million building programme (financed by the sale of 800 acres of farmland) has produced some splendid boarding accommodation; other houses (designed by the architect of Wormwood Scrubs – and they look it) still to be upgraded. Juniors in dormitories; third-years and above in study-bedrooms. Well-organised pastoral care system.

The head Hides a shy warmth behind a rather austere, distant manner; plays second violin in the school orchestra. Scholar at Winchester, gained a First in history at Cambridge; taught at Eton and Bryanston; became head of Dover at 28 ('I was arrogantly ambitious'), followed by the headship of the British School in Paris. Married, 3 children. Has had a difficult time here: found when he came that numbers and academic standards were in decline ('the rugby prize was more highly regarded than the Latin'); the boys ran the school and the staff were nervous of them; powerful housemasters opposed his plans to reassert control; his determination to introduce full co-education met fierce resistance; drugs had become a major problem. Many staff have since left; academic standards are rising ('but this is a busy school, not a cramming one'); co-education (despite some severe hiccups) has been a success; it is now a condition of entry that parents agree to their child taking a urine test if there is reason to suspect drug-taking. Numbers, however, remain a worry: school is currently 27 below capacity but determined not to lower admission standards.

The teaching Lively, challenging, high-quality. First-rate staff of 106 (some here more than 30 years), 20% women. National curriculum-plus; strong classics (30 do Latin for GCSE, 12 take Greek at A-level); science taught as 3 separate subjects; good design/technology (25% do it for GCSE); lots of computers ('but they don't leave as computer-literate as they should'); 10 languages on offer, including German, Russian, Spanish, Arabic, Japanese, Chinese. Pupils set by ability from the start in maths, science, French; largest class 25 (17 in the sixth form); progress closely monitored. All do 10-11 GCSEs and 3-4 A-levels plus non-examined general studies course; extra coaching for Oxbridge entry. Outstanding art – one of the jewels in Marlborough's crown; 6 full-time teachers; up to 40 pupils take it for A-level. Vigorous music (more than a third learn an instrument; 7 full-time teachers, 450 lessons a week) and drama (30 productions a year, A-level theatre studies burgeoning). Good careers advice (but very little work experience). Choice of cadet force or social service. School owns an outdoor centre in Snowdonia. Regular language exchanges with France, Germany and Spain.

The pupils Friendly, articulate (but it is important to be 'laid back' here); sons and daughters of doctors, lawyers, officers, clergy, accountants, bankers and business people. Admission (from more than 100 prep schools) by Common Entrance; average 60% mark required in English, maths, French, science; having family connections or being good at games still helps ('We don't want duds – but we do want to fill our places'). Entry to sixth form requires 6 GCSEs grades A-C. No assisted places but 20 receive some help with fees through scholarships, bursaries and an emergency fund for parents who 'experience a sudden down-turn' (a growing number).

Results GCSE: virtually all gain at least 5 grades A-C. A-level (1992): 53% of entries graded A or B.

Destinations Nearly all continue into the sixth form; 90% proceed to higher education (30 a year to Oxbridge), 70% after taking a 'gap year'.

Sport Traditionally strong, especially in rugby; boys field 17 hockey teams, girls 8 netball teams; first-rate gymnastics. Lacrosse, basketball, athletics, cross-country, swimming, squash, rackets, fives also on offer. Fine facilities include sports hall, fencing *salle*, cinder athletics track, 2 all-weather pitches, 30 tennis courts and 'a mile of playing fields'. Schools owns a beagle pack and a pretty stretch of the Kennet.

Remarks Emerging strongly from a difficult period: now good all round; highly recommended.

MASCALLS
Maidstone Road,
Paddock Wood,
Kent TN12 6LT
Tel (0892) 835366

Comprehensive • Co-educational • Ages
11-18 • 1,335 pupils (equal numbers of
boys and girls) • 156 in sixth form
Head: Fredric Gale, 44, appointed 1989.

---

*Happy, orderly school; well-regarded
locally.*

Background Early-1970s amalgamation of 2
small single-sex schools. Scattered buildings,
including atractive sixth-form block, in 20
immaculately kept acres. Relatively well-
funded; regarded as Kent's 'showpiece
comprehensive'.

Atmosphere Friendly, well-organised; smart,
well-mannered children moving between lessons in purposeful fashion. School very much
part of the local community.

The head Likeable, down-to-earth. Came as
deputy head in 1985: his promotion was
popular with staff, parents and pupils. Grammar-school boy; read classics and English at
Oxford; always wanted to be a teacher – and
still teaches A-level English. Wants children to
be themselves 'without being cowed or over-
familiar'. Consults staff freely and issues a
daily bulletin to keep them informed. Married,
2 children (1 a pupil here).

The teaching Lively. 'Active-learning' methods favoured; emphasis on problem-solving
approach. All pupils set by ability from the
start (parents talk of a 'grammar school
stream' but head resents this); only geography
is taught in mixed-ability classes (and results
are excellent). All take French and German for
first 2 years; most take 6 GCSEs, many 9 or 10.
Class sizes up to 30. Extra help for those who
need it (including dyslexia). Plenty of music,
drama, art; dance particularly popular with
girls. Well-supported community service,
Duke of Edinburgh award scheme.

The pupils Bright, happy, responsive. Broad
social mix from small towns, villages, rural

communities of West Kent. Discipline seldom
a problem; truancy rate almost nil; introduction of anonymous 'bully box', though seldom
used, has worked well; uniform worn by all (by
choice in the sixth form); no sign of make-up,
jewellery or outrageous hairstyles.

Results (1991) GCSE: 31% gained 5 or more
grades A-C (national average – but usually
higher). A-level: 30% of entries graded A or B.
School has to compete for able pupils against
local grammars.

Destinations Only 40% carry on into the
sixth form; most of these proceed to higher
education.

Sport All usual games played; reasonable
facilities.

Remarks Sound neighbourhood comprehensive; becoming over-subscribed.

MERCHANT TAYLORS' Crosby
Crosby,
Liverpool L23 0QP
Tel (051) 928 3308

Independent • Boys • Day • Ages 7-18 •
832 pupils (720 in senior school) • 193 in
sixth form • Fees, £2,250-£3,330
Head: Simon Dawkins, 46, appointed
1986.

---

*Strongly traditional school: Christian,
academic, disciplined. Makes no excuse
for pursuing scholastic excellence;
achieves first-class results.*

Background Founded 1620; moved to present site on Liverpool-Southport road 1878.
Main building a splendid pile – looks like a
miniature Victorian town hall (chandeliers in
the board room); many extensions and additions. Shares governing body with Merchant
Taylors' Girls' *(qv)* with which there are
strong links.

Atmosphere Ordered, civilised; all staff
aware of the need to inculcate virtuous

behaviour (without being repressive). Prefects ('monitors') wear badges and undergraduate gowns. Honours boards and old photographs emphasise the school's history and traditions; boys seem genuinely proud of the place. No hint of disorder in classrooms or corridors; work ethic obviously respected.

The head Courteous, gentle; educated at Solihull School and Nottingham University (economics, philosophy and politics). Formerly head of economics at Dulwich. Married, 2 children (1 at the school). Plays tennis and golf; retreats (infrequently) to cottage in Cornwall.

The teaching Purposeful; clear academic aims; pupils challenged to think, spot prejudice, respect facts. Dedicated staff of 58 (8 women). Balanced core curriculum (3 sciences) plus plenty of options, including Latin, Greek, philosophy, theatre studies. All expected to take 9-10 GCSEs and 4 A-levels (including general studies); compulsory sixth-form course in computing. Design and technology available but less highly valued than academic subjects. Class sizes up to 29, reducing to 22 for GCSE, 8-9 in sixth form. Daily (and increasing) homework. Flourishing music (nearly a quarter learn an instrument) and drama, both shared with girls' school. Outstanding cadet force; lots of clubs and societies (everthing from pottery to railways); trips and expeditions abroad.

The pupils Lively, vigorous; they work and play hard; respond well to high expectations; co-operative without being creepy. Some very bright but spread of ability is fairly wide; social range even wider (a good smattering of Scouse accents); 280 on assisted places. Mature sixth-formers set fine example to younger pupils. Few serious discipline problems (no drugs – despite proximity to a dubious area – head takes a very hard line). Entry at 7+ by informal tests of potential in English and maths; at 11 + and 13+ by exams in English, maths, verbal reasoning. No minimum IQ level specified but only able boys will thrive. Admission to the sixth form requires an average of at least 5 GCSEs grade B.

Results GCSE: 99% gain at least 5 grades A-C. A-level: creditable 58% of entries graded A or B.

Destinations Almost all junior school pupils obtain places in the senior school at 11+ (others come from 70 primary schools). 95% proceed from GCSE to A-level; 90% of these go on to higher education (12-20 a year to Oxbridge).

Sport Major games: rugby, hockey (particularly strong), cricket, athletics, tennis. (Boys who win sporting honours wear blazers edged with yellow piping.) Fine playing fields, attractive pavilions; indoor swimming pool.

Remarks Academically strong, no-nonsense school; successfully achieving its admirable aims.

MERCHANT TAYLORS' GIRLS' Crosby
Crosby,
Liverpool L23 5SP
Tel (051) 924 3140

Independent • Girls • Day • Ages 4-18 •
900 pupils (630 in senior school) • 160 in
sixth form • Fees, £2,070-£3,168
Head: Miss Jane Panton, 44, appointed
1988.

Fine, traditional academic school; very good sporting record.

Background Founded 1888; occupies site formerly belonging to neighbouring Merchant Taylors' Boys' school *(qv)* with which it shares a governing body. Original 1620 stone building is now the library. Many recent additions, including a fine hall.

Atmosphere Outside – busy, urban maelstrom; inside – oasis of civilised calm. Tradition and high expectations are the key. Everyone beautifully turned out; big emphasis on self-discipline and good manners.

The head Grammar-school educated plus 1 year in this school's sixth form; read history at

Oxford. Warm, candid; keen on equal opportunities but no feminist radical. Delegates cheerfully to very able deputies (1 has a double First from Cambridge). School expanding under her influence: she is anxious to maintain its diverse social mix.

The teaching Variety of styles but no one afraid of traditional chalk-and-talk and textbooks. Class teaching and group work both take place in an ordered, committed atmosphere. Broad curriculum; Latin, Russian, Spanish on offer; maths and science popular (excellent results achieved). No streaming; class sizes 25, reducing to 20 for GCSE, 13-14 in sixth form. Hard-working staff: lessons carefully prepared, work systematically marked. Wide range of extra-curricular activities; joint music, drama, debating etc with boys' school.

The pupils Delightful: younger ones keen, co-operative; sixth-formers articulate, mature, well-informed. (All interested in careers – but also very aware of the family option.) Relations with staff are relaxed and friendly; serious discipline problems very rare (1 girl asked to leave by mutual consent in 4 years). No prefects but every sixth-former has to participate in one of a series of committees concerned with school life – and it works. Selective entry by tests in English, maths, verbal reasoning. Minimum IQ not specified but girls have to be bright to get in and thrive. Wide range of backgrounds; assisted places, scholarships, bursaries.

Results GCSE: 97% gain at least 5 grades A-C. A-level: 50% of entries graded A or B.

Destinations About 90% continue from GCSE to A-level; 85% of these go on to degree courses (10 a year to Oxbridge).

Sport Main games: hockey (PE teacher is a former English international), netball, athletics, swimming, and cross-country; also squash, lacrosse and aerobics.

Remarks Civilised, welcoming, happy school; excellent all-round education.

MERCHANT TAYLORS' Northwood

Sandy Lodge,
Northwood,
Middlesex HA6 2MT
Tel (0923) 821850

Independent • Boys • Day and boarding • Ages 11-18 • 725 pupils (90% day) • 235 in sixth form • Fees, £5,500 day; £8,850 boarding
Head: Jon Gabitass, late-40s, appointed 1991.

Efficient, workmanlike school; good results; impressive facilities; strong sport.

Background Founded 1561 by Worshipful Company of Merchant Taylors (original building destroyed in the Great Fire of London); moved to present purpose-built premises 1933; 250 acres of magnificent grounds in green belt 2 miles from M25.

Atmosphere Quietly industrious; spacious buildings, carpeted classrooms, everything tidy, well-maintained. Most staff address boys by their first names. Large, comfortable boarding house. Lessons on Saturday mornings.

The head Read English at Oxford (rugby Blue); taught at Clifton, Abingdon (deputy head). Married, 2 daughters at university.

The teaching Competent, thorough; particular strengths in maths, science, English (head anxious to increase the number doing languages). All do French to GCSE; German, Russian, Greek also on offer; Latin compulsory for first 2 years (a handful continue it to A-level); all do computing for first 3 years (but not for GCSE). Pleasant, spacious classrooms; tables arranged formally; largest class 24, average 18-19. Excellent facilities for art, design/technology but take-up is low. Choice of 21 subjects at A-level; economics increasingly popular. All work closely monitored; homework plentiful. Abundant drama, music; more than a quarter learn an instrument; orchestras, choirs etc. Good careers advice; well-organised work experience. Regular exchanges with schools in France, Germany, Russia; cultural visits to Poland, Italy.

The pupils Many have parents who are doctors, lawyers, business people; 25% Asian, 12% Jewish (but all attend same daily assembly). 1 in 3 benefits from financial help (assisted places, bursaries, scholarships). Entry at 11 by tests in maths, English, verbal reasoning; 5-6 apply for each place; minimum of 50% required at Common Entrance (but 60% in maths).

Results GCSE: virtually all gain at least 5 grades A-C. A-level (1992): creditable 61% of entries graded A or B.

Destinations 90% stay on for A-levels; 90% of these proceed to higher education (20 a year to Oxbridge).

Sport Plays a big part in school life. Splendid facilities: extensive playing fields (12 cricket squares), sports hall, fine 25-metre indoor pool, courts for squash, fives. Main games: rugby (17 teams fielded), hockey, cricket; also athletics, tennis, sailing, squash, fencing, soccer, judo, cross-country, shooting; windsurfing on lake in the grounds.

Remarks Sound (but not particularly exciting).

MERCHISTON CASTLE

Colinton,
Edinburgh EH13 0PU
Tel (031) 441 1567

Independent • Boys • Boarding and day •
Ages 11-18 • 377 pupils (81% boarding) •
126 in sixth form • Fees, £9,480 boarding;
£6,120 day
Head: David Spawforth, 54, appointed
1981.

Traditional academic school; fairly wide range of abilities; good results; strong music and sport.

Background Founded 1833; moved in 1930 to present purpose-built premises on a magnificent 96-acre estate 4 miles south-west of the city; many later additions. The last major all-boys' boarding school in Scotland.

Atmosphere Happy, purposeful; traditional values upheld; no frills; proudly Scottish (kilts on Sundays and formal occasions). First-rate boarding accommodation for juniors (cosy dormitories with up to 6 beds); 2 senior houses being extensively refurbished; sixth-formers have study-bedrooms. Day boys stay for prep and evening prayers.

The head Energetic, determined. Educated at Oxford; taught at Winchester and Wellington, where he was a housemaster for 12 years. A 'hands-on' head, fully involved in the day-to-day running of the school.

The teaching Mostly traditional in style ('the value of chalk, talk and hard work is not overlooked'). Well-qualified staff of 46 (5 women), most resident on campus. Fairly broad curriculum; Latin, German, Spanish on offer; science taught as 3 separate subjects. Setting by ability in all academic subjects; class sizes 17-20, reducing to 6-12 in sixth form; progress closely monitored. All take 8-10 GCSEs from a choice of 17. Sixth-formers choose between A-levels (taken by 60%) and Highers; all do general studies. Lots of music: more than a third involved; orchestra, 2 choirs. Cadet force compulsory for 2 years; active Duke of Edinburgh award scheme.

The pupils Not excessively polished or sophisticated: better characterised by their open honesty, quiet confidence and sense of purpose; most from professional, business backgrounds; 60 from Scotland. Admission by interview and tests in English, maths; at 13+ by Common Entrance; only moderately selective. Scholarships available.

Results GCSE: 92% gain at least 5 grades A-C. A-level: 54% of entries graded A or B. Highers: 48% of entries graded A or B.

Destinations 93% continue into the sixth form; up to 75% of these proceed to higher education (4 or 5 a year to Oxbridge).

Sport Outstanding rugby (1st XV has dominated Scottish schools rugby for the past 7 years) and cricket (1992 tour to Barbados); hockey, swimming, athletics, cross-country, fencing, fives, squash, curling also on offer. Good facilities include extensive playing fields, sports hall, indoor heated pool, 3 all-weather tennis courts.

Remarks Very good all round.

MILLFIELD
Street,
Somerset BA16 0YD
Tel (0458) 42291

Independent • Co-educational • Boarding and day • Ages 13-18 • 1,211 pupils (63% boys; 75% boarding) • 503 in sixth form • Fees (1992-93), £11,820 boarding; £7,155 day (stabling of horses extra)
Head: Christopher Martin, 54, appointed 1990.

Distinctive school. Wide range of abilities; small classes; fine facilities; first-rate sport.

Background Founded 1935 by Jack ('Boss') Meyer – son of a plantation owner in India – as a crammer for the sons of wealthy Indians. Aims were philanthropic from the start: the school's substantial income was used to pay for the education of less well-off children; today 40% receive bursaries. Vast 67-acre campus (plus 97 acres of playing fields, 40-acre nature reserve) in semi-rural surroundings. First-class facilities for study and sport.

Atmosphere Friendly, business-like, hums with activity ('existentialist', says the head – 'people expect the school to be different tomorrow from today'). 28 boarding houses varying in size (from 55 beds to 4), nature (from purpose-built to adapted country house) and character (reflecting the personalities of their 'houseparents').

The head Read modern languages at St Andrews; taught at Westminster for 15 years; formerly head of Bristol Cathedral School.

The teaching Stimulating. Varied styles; remarkably small classes (average size 12); close contact between teachers and pupils (full-time staff of 160, 49 women). National curriculum-plus; impressive choice of 39 subjects at GCSE, 35 at A-level (including 9 languages) plus some vocational courses (more planned). First-rate facilities for computing, physics, technology, business studies – all taught to a high standard. Specialist help for those with learning difficulties; 180 attend dyslexia unit; speech therapist on hand. Plenty of art (one of the best-equipped schools in the country), music (36 ensembles rehearse weekly), drama; wide range of extra-curricular activities includes 55 clubs, societies; community service with the elderly and emotionally disturbed youngsters.

The pupils From across the spectrum, including many children of the wealthy and the famous (and some who are very gifted). Entry is selective, but not entirely on academic grounds; pupils need to show potential for something; nearly half transfer from Edgarley Hall *(qv)*, associated junior school. 50 a year join the sixth form from state schools. Generous scholarships, bursaries.

Results GCSE: 73% gain at least 5 grades A-C. A-level (1992): 50% of entries graded A or B.

Destinations Up to 25% leave after GCSE; 80% proceed to higher education (about 17 a year to Oxbridge).

Sport Very strong (this is the school others aspire to beat). Choice of 40 activities (no lacrosse or rowing); first-class coaching. Facilities include 2 sports halls, 25 tennis courts, squash courts, floodlit all-weather pitch, athletics track, 9-hole golf course, fencing *salle*, polo pitch (and stabling for 30 horses).

Remarks Something for everyone; individuals valued.

MILL HILL
The Ridgeway,
Mill Hill,
London NW7 1QS
Tel (081) 959 1176

Independent • Boys (plus girls in sixth form) • Day and boarding • Ages 13-19 • 565 pupils (57% day) • 247 in sixth form (75% boys) • Fees (1992-93), £6,645 day; £10,050 boarding
Head: Euan MacAlpine, 50s, appointed September 1992.

Solid school; wide range of abilities; fine facilities.

Background Founded 1807 (the first non-sectarian public school); went into decline in the 1970s when the local authority stopped funding pupils; now back in business. Elegant, listed buildings in 120 acres of parkland (only 12 miles from central London).

Atmosphere Happy, busy, cosmopolitan; strong emphasis on development of the individual. Boarding accommodation adequate, some being modernised.

The head New appointment; previously head of Bedales *(qv)* for 10 years, where he was highly regarded.

The teaching Sound; enthusiastic staff; predominantly modern approach (tables in groups rather than desks in rows, overhead projectors rather than blackboards). Setting by ability in most subjects; curriculum offers high-quality alternatives to traditional academic diet. All do computing, music, pottery to GCSE; half take design/technology; business studies the most popular A-level course (classics also on offer). English teaching attracts particular praise from pupils; English as a foreign language offered to 12 and 13-year-olds from abroad. Average class size 18, reducing to 10 in sixth form. Strong drama; improving music (2 music scholarships offered). Wide programme of extra-curricular activities: active cadet force (180 take part), community service, chess, photography, war games etc. Annual exchanges to France, Germany, Spain.

The pupils Articulate, responsive, appreciative of what the school has to offer (but critical of the homework burden). Big mix of ability, race, nationality; significant minorities of Muslims, Hindus; up to 15% live abroad. Not unduly selective but children need to be self-motivated to prosper. Half transfer at 13+ from Belmont, associated junior school. Assisted places, scholarships.

Results GCSE (1991): 90% gained at least 5 grades A-C. A-level (1992): 42% of entries graded A or B.

Destinations 90% stay on for A-levels; 80% of these proceed to higher education (a few to Oxbridge).

Sport Excellent facilities include outdoor and indoor pools, sports hall, indoor shooting range. All main games plus golf, fives, riding, sailing, wind-surfing.

Remarks Competent school; interesting new head; likely to become fully co-educational.

MILTON ABBEY
Blandford Forum,
Dorset DT11 0BZ
Tel (0258) 880484

Independent • Boys • Boarding and day • Ages 13-18 • 270 pupils • 85 in sixth form • Fees, £9,450 boarding; £6,615 day
Head: Robert Hardy, 59, appointed 1987.

Wide range of abilities; small classes; superb setting.

Background Opened 1954; Georgian mansion in beautiful grounds adjoining medieval Benedictine abbey.

Atmosphere Exceptionally friendly; high level of personal care; school capitalises on its intimate size. Enthusiastic participation at morning chapel; more than 50 boys confirmed in 1992.

The head Scholar at Winchester, read classics at Oxford; housemaster at Eton for 15 years. Teaches English and classical civilisation to GCSE.

The teaching Small classes, plenty of individual attention; hard work expected. First-years divided by ability into 4 sets in main subjects. GCSE options include technology, history of art; choice of 14 subjects at A-level plus variety of non-A-level courses (science in society, French for business studies, understanding industrial society etc); all take AS-level in general studies. Specialist help for dyslexic pupils at all levels; remedial teaching available in maths. Long-serving staff of 32, mostly men. Extra-curricular activities include music (plainsong choir), drama, strong cadet force, community service.

The pupils Mostly upper-middle-class, professional, Service backgrounds from all parts of the country; a few from abroad. Wide spread of abilities (IQs range from 90 to 120+); target of 50% at Common Entrance but in practice lower; 15% diagnosed dyslexic.

Results GCSE (1991): 77% gained at least 5 grades A-C. A-level (1992): only 18% of entries graded A or B.

Destinations Nearly all enter the sixth form; up to half proceed to higher education (5 a year to Sandhurst).

Sport All main games plus sailing, canoeing, golf (9-hole course). Indoor pool.

Remarks Attractive school, especially for less academically able boys.

MONKTON COMBE

Monkton Combe,
Bath BA2 7HG
Tel (0225) 721102

Independent • Co-educational (from September 1992) • Boarding and day • Ages 11-18 • 410 pupils (85% boarding) • 170 in sixth form (65% boys) • Fees, £9,720 boarding; £7,170 day Head: Michael Cuthbertson, 40s, appointed 1990.

Attractive school; fairly wide ability range; respectable results.

Background Founded 1868 for the sons of Anglican clergy and overseas missionaries (lively evangelical Christian spirit retained). Beautiful setting 2½ miles from Bath; premises – some in Cotswold stone, others purpose-built – interwoven with the village. Going co-educational by stages (following collapse of plans to merge with a girls' school).

Atmosphere Exceptionally friendly; warm relations between staff and pupils; a genuinely caring community. Pleasantly refurbished boarding accommodation; even the classrooms are carpeted and curtained.

The head Read history at Cambridge; formerly head of the sixth form at Radley. Wants young people to go out into the world with a moral framework and sense of service.

The teaching Long-serving, dedicated staff of 38 (few women); wide range of styles; careful balance between pressure and encouragement. Broad curriculum; good computing, design/technology; choice of 18 subjects for GCSE. Maximum class size 20, reducing to 12 for A-level. Extra help for those with learning difficulties, including dyslexia. Lots of art, music, drama; emphasis on involvement and enjoyment. Extra-curricular activities include debating, photography, chess, bridge etc.

The pupils Thoughtful, well-mannered, unaffected. Backgrounds include clergy, Services, farming, business, professional; 15% from overseas. Fairly wide spread of abilities; entry at 11+ by tests in English, maths, verbal reasoning; at 13+ by Common Entrance; pupils need the potential to achieve grade Cs at GCSE. 11-year-old girls first admitted September 1992.

Results GCSE (1991): 87% gained 5 or more grades A-C. A-level (1992): 37% of entries graded A or B.

Destinations Most stay on for A-levels; 60% of these proceed to higher education (a few to Oxbridge).

Sport Wide participation encouraged; up to half the school involved in matches on Saturday afternoons. Particular strengths in rowing (boathouse on the Avon), rugby, hockey, cricket. Also available: tennis, netball, swimming, cross-country, fencing, squash, judo, shooting. Facilities include heated outoor pool, all-weather pitch, extensive playing fields.

Remarks Sound, supportive school; all-round development nurtured.

MONMOUTH
Almshouse Street,
Monmouth,
Gwent NP5 3XP
Tel (0600) 713143

Independent • Boys • Day and boarding • Ages 11-18 (plus associated junior school) • 550 pupils (66% day) • 164 in sixth form • Fees (1992-93), £4,428 day; £7,374 boarding
Head: Rupert Lane, 48, appointed 1982.

Traditional academic school; good results; strong sport.

Background Founded (and generously endowed) in 1614 by William Jones, a member of the Haberdashers' Company, with which close links remain. Victorian buildings plus some bleakly functional additions sandwiched between the main street and the motorway (which cuts the school off from its playing fields).

Atmosphere Formal, old-fashioned: a traditional town grammar school. Some spartan boarding houses – for sleeping in rather than living in. Lessons on Saturday mornings.

The head Pleasant, reassuring, much liked by parents. Read natural science at Trinity College, Dublin; taught physics at Marlborough and was a housemaster there for 14 years. Married, 3 sons.

The teaching National curriculum-plus; all do Latin for at least 1 year; Greek, German, Spanish on offer. Good facilities, including modern science block with specialist labs and new design/technology department. Pupils set by ability from the start; average class size 22, reducing to 12 in the sixth form. Most take 8 GCSEs and 3 A-levels (from choice of 18) plus non-examined general studies course. Strong music; everyone learns the theory, whether musical or not; orchestra, choir. Compulsory cadet force; well-supported Duke of Edinburgh award scheme; school owns field centre in North Wales.

The pupils Fairly wide mix of abilities and backgrounds (25% have assisted places). Entry at 11 by interview and tests in maths, English, verbal reasoning; at 13 by Common Entrance (modest 50% mark required); to sixth form with at least 5 GCSEs grades A or B. Academic and music scholarships.

Results GCSE: nearly all gain at least 5 grades A-C. A-level (1992): creditable 61% of entries graded A or B.

Destinations Nearly all stay on for A-levels; 85% proceed to higher education (12 a year to Oxbridge).

Sport Wide choice: rugby, cricket, squash, tennis, cross-country, soccer; canoeing and rowing particularly popular. Facilities include 23 acres of playing fields, sports hall, indoor pool, 3 squash courts, boathouse on the Wye.

Remarks Solid school; good all round.

NEWCASTLE-UNDER-LYME
Mount Pleasant,
Newcastle-under-Lyme,
Staffordshire ST5 1DB
Tel (0782) 613345

Independent • Co-educational • Day •
Ages 11-18 (plus associated junior
school) • 1,220 pupils (equal numbers of
boys and girls) • 330 in sixth form • Fees,
£2,547-£2,931
Head: Dr Ray Reynolds, 49, appointed
1990.

*Traditional, academic school; good
results; strong sport.*

Background 1984 amalgamation of 2 single-
sex schools on adjoining sites; girls' premises
drab, utilitarian; boys more grandly accommodated (boys and girls taught separately from
11-16).

Atmosphere Bustling, cheerful, friendly;
good relations between staff and pupils.

The head Scientist; PhD (in atomic colli-
sions) from Belfast; previously head of science
at Millfield. Teaches general studies to sixth-
formers. Married, 1 daughter.

The teaching Skilled, long-serving staff;
plain, old-fashioned classrooms, desks in rows.
National curriculum plus Latin for first 3
years; German from second year; all do
computing and a course based on metalwork,
woodwork, needlework, home economics.
Choice of 21 subjects at A-level including
Russian, Greek, fashion and fabric; all do
general studies. Good drama and music: 45%
learn an instrument; 3 orchestras, choir. Extra-
curricular activities include popular cadet
force and Scout troop.

The pupils Lively, articulate; most from professional, managerial, academic backgrounds.
School uniform worn throughout; merit in
sport earns a red blazer, in art a green (green
blazers rather less in evidence than red);
competitive house system recently revived;
cups and regalia purchased. Entry to senior
school by 11+ tests in English, maths, verbal
reasoning (A-level potential required); no
automatic promotion from junior school; half
join from 50 state primary schools. Wide
catchment area; heavy demand for places. 73
assisted places a year.

Results GCSE: nearly all gain at least 5 grades
A-C. A-level (1992): 52% of entries graded A
or B.

Destinations 90% proceed to higher education (about 12 a year to Oxbridge).

Sport Strong cricket, rugby, hockey, tennis,
netball, athletics; golf, water polo, synchronised swimming also on offer. Good
playing fields and sports hall.

Remarks Sound school; highly regarded locally.

NEWENT
Watery Lane,
Newent,
Gloucestershire GL18 1QF
Tel (0531) 820550

Comprehensive (grant-maintained) •
Co-educational • Ages 11- 18 • 1,150
pupils (equal number of girls and boys) •
204 in sixth form (slightly more girls)
Head: Peter Landau, 53, appointed 1977.

*Successful rural comprehensive; good
music and art; first-rate sport.*

Background Established 1965 on pleasant
40-acre site bordering open countryside; large
rural catchment area west of Gloucester.
Original flat-roof, panel-clad building is
deteriorating (damp stains, missing tiles);
1970s additions functional but uninspiring.
Inside: some badly worn carpets, bleak corridors and no proper dining area. Parents voted
2:1 for grant-maintained status, which should
bring extra cash.

Atmosphere Well-ordered, relaxed; air of
mutual respect between staff and pupils.
Lingering grammar school tradition (head
wears gown at assembly).

The head Tough, no-nonsense approach. Committed to comprehensive schools and genuine community involvement. Educated at Monmouth School and University of Wales. Married, 2 children (1 at an independent school).

The teaching Sound; mixture of child-centred and more formal methods. Mixed-ability classes in first year (maximum size 30); setting by subject thereafter; support for slow learners and dyslexics. Particularly good maths, science (bright children can succeed here). Staff of 68 includes some exceptionally talented teachers. Art department positively leaps with life; excellent creative work covers the walls and hangs from the ceiling. More than 10% of pupils learn a musical instrument; regular concerts enjoy huge parental support. Well-developed home-school links; impressive 90% attendance at parents' evenings. Community and charity work encouraged (pupils help at a centre for the homeless in Gloucester); Duke of Edinburgh award scheme well supported. Ski trips to Austria; frequent exchanges with France, Germany; school keen to enlarge pupils' experience of the world.

The pupils Happy, confident, generally well-disciplined. (Excellent pastoral system ensures every child stays with the same house tutor for 5 years, developing a sense of belonging to a family group.) Uniform worn throughout; extremes of hairstyle etc not tolerated.

Results GCSE: 43% gain at least 5 grades A-C. A-level: 32% of entries graded A or B.

Destinations About 80% stay in full-time education after 16, though not necessarily here. 60% of A-level pupils proceed to higher education (1-2 a year to Oxbridge).

Sport A great strength thanks to teachers' enthusiasm. Prime aim is to encourage participation and enjoyment. Numerous county players in rugby, soccer, cricket, basketball, hockey, netball. Excellent facilities (of which the community makes full use) include extensive playing fields, indoor swimming pool, squash courts, well-equipped sports hall.

Remarks A community school since 1989: 90 day-time adult students; 900 take evening classes; on-site creche and base for Help the Aged. Ensures the whole family is involved.

NEWSTEAD WOOD

Avebury Road,
Orpington,
Kent BR6 9SA
Tel (0689) 853626

Grammar (grant-maintained) • Girls • Ages 11-18 • 704 pupils • 205 in sixth form
Head: Mrs Valerie Smith, 53, appointed 1978.

Strong, traditional grammar school; good teaching and results.

Background Opened as a grammar school 1954; purpose-built premises on a large site with ample playing fields on the edge of the town. Opted out of council control April 1992.

Atmosphere Happy, purposeful: responsive, well-behaved pupils; well-qualified, committed staff. 'Girls aim confidently and successfully for demanding careers,' says the prospectus. 'No goal is considered unattainable.' Supportive parents contribute £14,000 a year to school funds.

The head Read physics at university; taught widely in the state sector. Originally appointed to turn the school into a comprehensive (the plan fell with the last Labour Government); decided to stay on. Keen to encourage girls to study science. Married with grandchildren.

The teaching Generally sound, though Her Majesty's Inspectors noted in a recent report (November 1991) that some work was too simple and the pace too slow; they said pupils should be given more opportunities to have their views and opinions heard. National curriculum-plus; science taught as 3 separate subjects; all add German or Spanish to French (half take 2 languages for GCSE); all do at least 1 year's Latin; good design/technology and drama. Setting by ability in maths only; average class size 25, reducing to 10 in the sixth form. Most take at least 10 GCSEs (including religious studies) and 3 A-levels (half add a fourth, usually general studies) from a choice of 23; maths the most popular subject. Lots of music: 60% learn an instrument; 2 orchestras, 2 choirs. All fourth-years do work experience.

The pupils Bright, confident; from a wide range of backgrounds but mainly from middle-class, professional homes within a 9-mile radius. Entry by school's own tests in English, maths, verbal reasoning; top 25%-30% of the ability range. School heavily over-subscribed: up to 500 apply for 112 places.

Results (1992) GCSE: all gained at least 5 grades A-C (most achieve 10). A-level: creditable 51% of entries graded A or B.

Destinations Nearly all stay on for A-levels and proceed to higher education (up to 8 a year to Oxbridge).

Sport Wide choice, including hockey, netball, tennis, athletics, badminton, fencing.

Remarks 'A good school,' reported Her Majesty's Inspectors, 'which could be even better.'

NORTH BERWICK HIGH

Grange Road,
North Berwick,
East Lothian EH39 4QS
Tel (0620) 4661

Comprehensive • Co-educational • Ages 12-18 • 586 pupils (roughly equal numbers of boys and girls) • 75 in sixth year
Head: George Smuga, 44, appointed 1990.

Well-run comprehensive; high academic standards.

Background Founded 1893 but roots go back to 1661. Moved in 1940 to present fine site overlooking Berwick and the Forth estuary; undistinguished premises, including 14

'temporary' huts; school urgently needs new buildings and general refurbishment (no hint of vandalism or misuse); classrooms spacious but spartan; some good labs.

Atmosphere Friendly and lively. Effective pastoral care system based on a nice blend of sympathy, support and firmness. Staff and pupils have done all they can to humanise the surroundings, to upgrade rooms and to provide warmth through pictures and plants. Food (provided by a contract caterer) is of poor quality.

The head (Rector) Good manager; open style ('the wider the views the better') but there is little doubt who has the last say. Formerly deputy head of a comprehensive in Lothian; keen sportsman.

The teaching Style is moving away from the purely formal to a balance of class teaching, group work and individual learning; standards continue to rise. Broad, balanced curriculum; science taught as 3 separate subjects; little setting by ability (extra help for the less able); class sizes vary between 20 and 30. Good range of subjects at Standard Grade: most do 7 or 8. Fifth-years choose between Highers (20 on offer) and vocational modules.

The pupils Biddable but lively; almost all drawn from 5 local primary schools in a well-heeled catchment area; average ability level is high. Sixth-year common room is a model of self-imposed decorum.

Results Highers: 31% gain at least 5 grades A-C.

Destinations Nearly all stay on for Highers; 70% proceed to higher education (1 or 2 a year to Oxbridge).

Sport High profile: regular successes in rugby, hockey, badminton and golf. Good sports fields but the gymnasia are positively Victorian.

Remarks Good all round (apart from the buildings).

NORTH BROMSGROVE HIGH
School Drive,
Stratford Road,
Bromsgrove,
Worcestershire B60 1BA
Tel (0527) 72375

Comprehensive • Co-educational • Ages
13-18 • 717 pupils (53% girls) • 150 in
sixth form
Head: Kevin Peck, mid-30s, appointed
1991.

---

*Sound school; good teaching;
respectable results.*

Background Became a comprehensive in
1970; functional 1950s and 1960s buildings on
a large, well-maintained campus (shared with
a further education college); recent additions
include sixth-form centre and music suite.

Atmosphere Hard-working, well-ordered;
relaxed, friendly relations between staff and
pupils; emphasis on high standards of work
and discipline. ('This school is a community in
which we care for one another, not in a weak
or indulgent way but with firmness and
discipline,' says the prospectus.) Supportive
parents, ambitious for their children.

The head Youthful, enthusiastic, approachable; gets on well with staff, pupils and parents.
Read English at Cambridge; has taught in a
variety of state schools; came here as deputy
head in 1989. Teaches a quarter of the
timetable; keen sportsman.

The teaching Lively, competent; pupils encouraged to accept responsiblity for their own
learning. All grouped by ability into upper and
lower bands; setting in some subjects. Strong
languages; many take French and German to
GCSE; Spanish also on offer; computing
across the curriculum; design/technology gaining ground. Technical and vocational alternatives to A-level planned. Good music, art,
drama. Thriving Duke of Edinburgh award
scheme. Regular language exchanges with
schools in France and Germany. Work experience for all.

The pupils Friendly, forthcoming; from a
predominantly middle-class catchment area.

Results (1991) GCSE: 45% gain at least 5
grades A-C. A-level: 35% of entries graded A
or B.

Destinations 40% stay on for A-levels; 90%
of these proceed to higher education (2 to
Oxbridge in 1991).

Sport Chiefly soccer, cricket, hockey. Extensive playing fields, netball and tennis courts.

Remarks Lively, well-run comprehensive.

NORTH LONDON COLLEGIATE
Canons,
Edgware,
Middlesex HA8 7RJ
Tel (081) 952 0912

Independent • Girls • Day • Ages 11-18
(plus associated junior school) • 711
pupils • 210 in sixth form • Fees, £3,942
Head: Mrs Joan Clanchy, 53, appointed
1986.

---

*Distinguished school (one of the top 5 for
girls); excellent results; turns out civilised
career women.*

Background Founded 1850 by Frances Mary
Buss; its girls became the first to sit public
examinations and the first women to graduate
from Cambridge. Moved 1929 to Canons,
elegant 18th-century mansion in 30 acres of
parkland; has expanded and built steadily
since.

Atmosphere Lively girls everywhere: chattering under cedar trees, balancing on garden
walls and pillars, hurrying down the broad
staircase on to the Persian rugs in the polished
hall. Oil paintings and sepia group photographs of strong-faced Victorian women gaze
down, mutely exhorting the young ladies of
today to noble endeavour. Adults are treated
as amusing additions to a conversational
group; relaxed informality is the tone. Music

and art departments overlook pond and ducks; delightful rock garden tended 1 morning a week by a retired teacher.

The head Very able. Only the seventh in the school's history; all but 1 have served more than 20 years. Educated at Oxford; formerly head of St George's, Edinburgh. Member of the Government's National Curriculum Council. Girls respond well to her cheerful, straightforward manner. Married, 2 children.

The teaching High-quality, challenging; enthusiastic staff of 60 (5 men); exceptionally warm relationships with pupils. Strong modern languages; 70% of 12-year-olds add German to their French, 30% add Latin; all take 9-10 GCSEs. Science and maths as important at A-level as arts subjects; increasing number of sixth-formers do a mixture; all computer literate. Music is a real strength; lots of instrumental teaching; 2 orchestras, 2 choirs. Lively drawing school staffed by practising artists teaches pottery, silkscreen, painting etc in 4 large studios. Career choices taken seriously; overseas work experience. Regular exchanges with France, Germany.

The pupils Bright, responsive, articulate; 20% are Asian; Jews, Greeks, Christians, Chinese all fit in amicably. No pressure to conform; 'performers' are looked up to – and many make successful careers in the media. Sensible uniform, but hair styles are gloriously varied. Entry at 11 by highly competitive exams; 45% come from the junior school, 25% from other private schools, 30% from state primaries. Assisted places, bursaries.

Results GCSE: virtually all gain at least 5 grades A-C. A-level (1992): impressive 76% of entries graded A or B.

Destinations Nearly all stay on for A-levels; all proceed to higher education (27 a year to Oxbridge).

Sport Does not come very high on the list of things to shout about, but there are good tennis courts; netball, athletics and cross-country are on offer, and there is an outdoor pool. Treadmill in the gym for those who feel the tempo is not fast enough.

Remarks First-rate, well-run school; hectic academic pace mitigated by a feeling of spacious style.

NORTON HILL
Charlton Road,
Midsomer Norton,
Bath,
Avon BA3 4AD
Tel (0761) 412557

Comprehensive • Co-educational • Ages 11-18 • 1,120 pupils (equal numbers of boys and girls) • 152 in sixth form
Head: Richard Wherry, mid-50s, appointed 1977.

Sound school; respectable results; good music.

Background Formerly a grammar school; went comprehensive in 1970. Unattractive mixture of over-crowded, functional buildings and ageing huts in 29 acres surrounded by new 'executive' housing.

Atmosphere Supportive, caring ethos; high standards of behaviour expected and achieved. Internal maintenance impeccable; pupils' work well displayed.

The head Only the fifth head in 80 years. Came as deputy in 1973; has built a strong team of long-serving, committed teachers. His youngest daughter is a pupil here.

The teaching Wide range of styles, all challenging and effective. Setting by ability in most subjects from second year; average class size 26. Particular strengths in modern languages (regular exchanges with French and German schools), economics and business studies (good links with local firms), computing. Choice of 16 subjects at A-level. Extra help for those with special needs. Good music: orchestras, bands, choirs; residential summer school for instrumentalists. Busy programme of extra-curricular activities at lunch-time and after school.

The pupils Most from business, farming backgrounds; 20% in council housing. Truancy rate virtually nil (thanks to strong parental support). School is slightly over-subscribed; numbers have risen 15% since 1985.

Results (1991) GCSE: 42% gained at least 5 grades A-C. A-level: 40% of entries graded A or B.

Destinations About 50% stay on into the sixth form; 70% of these proceed to higher education.

Sport Good rugby, hockey (county honours); facilities include tennis courts, outdoor pool.

Remarks Solid, well-run comprehensive.

NORWICH HIGH
Eaton Grove,
95 Newmarket Road,
Norwich,
Norfolk NR2 2HU
Tel (0603) 53265

Independent • Girls • Day • Ages 11-18
(plus associated junior school) • 620
pupils • 160 in sixth form • Fees, £3,156
Head: Mrs Valerie Bidwell, 40s, appointed
1985.

Traditional grammar-school education; first-rate music.

Background Founded 1875 (member of Girls' Public Day School Trust). Moved to present premises 1933; 3 handsome, spacious 19th-century houses in attractive grounds; extensive later additions (including new labs, technology workshop).

Atmosphere Lively: highly motivated pupils; academically sharp staff to match. Self-regulating society; minimum of rules and regulations; strong sense of mutual care and support.

The head Imposing, authoritative personality, with a lively sense of humour. Read modern languages at Newcastle and London.

The teaching Traditional, formal approach; high academic expectations (girls respond well). No streaming (within a narrow ability band); average class size 24, reducing to 15 for A-level. Particular strengths in maths, science (first-rate labs), classics, French, German. Choice of 16 subjects at GCSE, 17 at A-level (including economics, sociology); all do general studies. Sixth-formers in separate block (where there is a feeling of equality between teachers and taught). Splendid, well-used library (full-time librarian). Good art, drama; outstanding music (Verdi's Requiem performed in Norwich Cathedral with only 4 outside players). Professional careers advice; strong links with local industry and commerce, including work experience. Well-supported Duke of Edinburgh award scheme.

The pupils From Norwich and up to 20 miles away (school is heavily over-subscribed). Entry by tests in English, maths, verbal reasoning plus previous school reports and interview; nearly all junior school pupils promoted. Assisted places, scholarships, bursaries.

Results GCSE: nearly all gain at least 5 grades A-C. A-level (1992): 49% of entries graded A or B.

Destinations Most proceed to higher education (8 a year to Oxbridge).

Sport Good lacrosse, netball; plenty of tennis, swimming (fine indoor pool). Fencing, rowing also on offer.

Remarks Highly regarded locally; not the school for a girl who needs to be brought out of her shell.

NOTRE DAME HIGH
Surrey Street,
Norwich,
Norfolk NR1 3PB
Tel (0603) 611431

Comprehensive (voluntary-aided) •
Roman Catholic • Co-educational • Ages
11-18 • 1,065 pupils (54% girls) • 255 in
sixth form
Head: Sister Mary Cluderay, 61,
appointed 1968.

*First-rate comprehensive; good teaching
and results; strong religious ethos.*

Background Founded as a girls' convent
school 1864; buildings of varying ages, styles
and standards (some classrooms in huts) on a
confused, restricted city-centre site (limited
play areas); major refurbishment required but
money is tight; grant-maintained status contemplated. Well-equipped science/techno-
logy/business studies centre; large sports hall
in converted bus station. Became a co-
educational comprehensive in 1979; the only
Catholic secondary school in Norfolk.

Atmosphere Successful, happy, caring
school; staff and pupils pleased to be here. Not
smart or grand (in some respects, inescapably
scruffy); relaxed attitude to clothing. Strongly
Christian; regular mass and visiting chaplains;
not all staff are believers or Catholics, but all
must subscribe to the ethos.

The head Dynamic, inspirational leader; exercises enormous influence (no one would
wish to upset Sister Mary!). Daughter of a
Liverpool doctor (two of her 7 brothers
became heads); read French at Liverpool;
entered the sisterhood as a teacher. Has
postponed her retirement to campaign against
a road scheme that would slice off part of the
school. Keen ornithologist.

The teaching Fairly traditional, formal
(though a lively independence of spirit is
evident); big emphasis on academic achievement. Pupils set by ability in main subjects;
extra help for those with special needs (but no
specialist unit). Broad syllabus; first-rate (and

liberal) religious education; strong languages
(3 plus Latin on offer); good science, geography, design/technology, art. Choice of 25
subjects at A-level, including textiles, theatre
studies, sociology. Lots of music; 2 orchestras,
2 choirs.

The pupils Wide range of abilities and social
backgrounds, largely (but not exclusively)
from Catholic families; pupils of all faiths and
none welcome but expected to support the
religious ethos. Expanding and over-subscribed; priority to Catholics and siblings.
Catchment area has a 20-mile radius.

Results (1991) GCSE: creditable 57% gained
at least 5 grades A-C. A-level: 27% of entries
graded A or B (national average).

Destinations 70% continue into the sixth
form (60% take A-levels); 50% of these
proceed to higher education (3 a year to
Oxbridge).

Sport Good results in soccer, netball, athletics; 6 tennis courts on site; use of playing fields
5 minutes' bus ride away.

Remarks Well-run, highly regarded school.

NOTTINGHAM HIGH
Waverley Mount,
Nottingham NG7 4ED
Tel (0607) 786056

Independent • Boys • Day • Ages 11-18
(plus associated prep school) • 810 pupils
• 230 in sixth form • Fees (1992-93),
£3,960-£4,140
Head: Dr Dennis Witcombe, early-60s,
appointed 1970 (retires 1995).

*First-rate, traditional, academic school;
very strong science; good music; fine
facilities.*

Background Founded 1513; moved to present pleasant urban site 1868; Victorian-Gothic
buildings and excellent later additions, includ-

ing science block, sports hall and design/technology centre.

Atmosphere Well-ordered, highly competitive; every boy expected to participate with might and main inside the classroom and out.

The head Respected elder statesman; courteous, humorous; a traditionalist (hands out silver groats to scholars on founder's day) who has kept up to date. Read history at Oxford; PhD from Manchester; formerly head of history at Manchester Grammar. Insists on highest academic standards.

The teaching Experienced staff of 78 (some have been here decades); a quarter teach science. National curriculum-plus; science taught as 3 separate subjects (most take all 3 to GCSE); pupils set by ability from second year; average class size 30, reducing to 24 for GCSE. Majority take maths and 2 sciences for A-level (but less than 20% take English). Very good music: a quarter learn an instrument; 2 orchestras, 2 choirs. Lots of drama in conjunction with Nottingham Girls' High *(qv)*. Compulsory choice from fourth year of cadet force, Scout troop or community service. Strong chess. Regular language exchanges with schools in France and Germany.

The pupils Hard-working, civilised, smartly dressed. Admission at 11 by interview and tests in English, maths, verbal reasoning; half join from associated prep school (but no automatic right of entry); 3 apply for each of the 60 remaining places. Wide catchment area (hired coaches shared with girls' school). Scholarships and 40 assisted places a year.

Results GCSE: all gain at least 5 grades A–C (93% achieved at least 9 in 1991). A-level (1992): 58% of entries graded A or B (has been higher).

Destinations Virtually all stay for A-levels and proceed to higher education (20 to Oxbridge in 1991).

Sport Fine reputation for cricket and rugby; regular county and national honours. Facilities include magnificent sports hall, indoor pool, rifle range; 20-acre playing fields $1\frac{1}{2}$ miles away.

Remarks Fine school for able boys; a splendid mixture of the traditional and the forward looking.

NOTTINGHAM GIRLS' HIGH
9 Arboretum Street,
Nottingham NG1 4JB
Tel (0607) 417663

Independent • Girls • Day • Ages 11-18 (plus associated junior school) • 805 pupils • 240 in sixth form • Fees, £3,156
Head: Mrs Christine Bowering, mid-50s, appointed 1984.

Fine school for able girls; first-class results; good art, drama, music.

Background Founded 1875 (member of Girls' Public Day School Trust); conglomeration of Victorian and newer buildings not far from the city centre. Supportive parents raise up to £10,000 a year.

Atmosphere Bubbling, busy; pupils on good terms with their teachers (and teachers say the girls are kind to one another).

The head Approachable, humorous; insists that learning should be exciting. Has degrees in science and law; formerly senior mistress at Sheffield High. Married to a Yorkshire vicar, 2 grown-up children.

The teaching Lively. Experienced, well-qualified staff of 60 (12 men). National curriculum followed; setting by ability from second year in maths, French; class size 26 in first year, reducing to 20. All take at least 9 GCSEs. Choice of 23 subjects at A-level (ranging from Greek to design/technology); best results in English, maths, chemistry, biology, economics, general studies. Plenty of evidence of creativity, including some stunning art and sculpture; lots of music (3 orchestras, choirs, etc); impressive drama (in splendid new hall). Effective, well-organised careers guidance.

The pupils Confident, responsible (they are given a good deal of freedom and have been trained to use it wisely). School heavily over-subscribed; entry to junior school at age 4 (2 apply for each place) by informal intelligence tests and observation; at 7 and 11 (3 apply for each place) by school's own tests in English, maths (past papers closely guarded to discourage cramming) and verbal reasoning. Automatic entry from junior to senior school.

Results (1991) GCSE: all gained at least 5 grades A-C (87% gained at least 9). A-level (1992): 54% of entries graded A or B (has been higher).

Destinations Nearly all go on to higher education (14 girls to Oxbridge in 1991).

Sport County honours in hockey, netball, athletics. (In 1991, a girl was selected for the England women's cricket team.) Good facilities include large gym, all-weather pitch.

Remarks Attractive school (but no place for the academically faint of heart). Highly recommended.

NOTTING HILL & EALING HIGH

2 Cleveland Road,
London W13 8AX
Tel (081) 997 5744

Independent • Girls • Day • Ages 5-18 • 837 pupils (565 in senior school) • 147 in sixth form • Fees, £3,108-£4,020
Head: Mrs Susan Whitfield, 45, appointed 1991.

Sound academic school; good teaching and results.

Background Founded 1873 by the Girls' Public Day School Trust; moved to present site 1931; mixture of converted private houses and more recent additions in quiet residential area; some classrooms in need of upgrading; little space to spare.

Atmosphere Friendly, happy, unpretentious; strong family feel. First-rate pastoral care system.

The head Read science at Cambridge; taught biology at St Paul's Girls' for 12 years. Has an easy, unruffled manner; gets on well with staff and parents. Married, 5 children.

The teaching Sound. Core of long-serving staff. National curriculum-plus; good languages; all take German or Spanish in addition to French for at least 1 year. Choice of 17 subjects at A-level, including theatre studies. Strong music: more than half learn an instrument; 3 orchestras, choirs. Regular language exchanges with school in France, Germany and Spain.

The pupils Mostly from Ealing but the catchment area is wide. Admission at 5 by interview and assessment; at 7 and 11 by interview and tests. Half the intake at 11 comes from the junior school; 180 apply for the remaining 40 places. Assisted places, scholarships, bursaries.

Results GCSE: virtually all gain at least 5 grades A-C. A-level (1992): impressive 66% of entries graded A or B.

Destinations 80% stay on for A-levels; 90% of these proceed to higher education (7 or 8 a year to Oxbridge).

Sport Strong netball; hockey, tennis, athletics also on offer. Main playing fields 10-minute bus ride away.

Remarks Good, safe school.

OAKHAM

Chapel Close,
Oakham,
Rutland LE15 6DT
Tel (0572) 722487

Independent • Co-educational • Boarding and day • Ages 10-18 • 1,000 pupils (equal numbers of boys and girls; 58% boarding) • 289 in sixth form • Fees, £9,510 boarding; £5,265 day
Head: Graham Smallbone, late-50s, appointed 1985.

Not unduly selective; respectable results; wide choice of activities; fine facilities.

Background Founded (like Uppingham, *qv*) 1584 by Robert Johnson, Archdeacon of Leicester; original school room survives. Attractive campus embracing much of the town; recent extensive additions spacious and well designed. Fully co-educational since 1971.

Atmosphere Friendly, well-ordered; rules based on common sense and courtesy. Strong Anglican tradition; brisk services most mornings; 2 resident chaplains. Homely, comfortably furnished boarding houses; most pupils in double rooms. Good food in splendid dining hall.

The head Oxford music scholar; formerly director of music at Eton for 14 years; still teaches. Constantly accessible to staff and pupils. Married, 4 children.

The teaching Good. Diverse styles, all challenging; experienced, well-qualified staff of 100 (30 women), half appointed by present head; pupils set by ability in all subjects at all levels. Broad curriculum: French from age 10, Latin from 11, choice of German, Spanish or Russian from 13; creative arts options include painting, pottery, textiles; all do computing and micro-electronics. Theatre studies, social science, food & nutrition on offer for GCSE. Choice of 20 subjects at A-level; most do 3, plus general studies. Special educational needs taken seriously; appropriate help provided at both ends of the spectrum; extra coaching for Oxbridge entry. Maximum class size 24, re-

ducing to 15 in the sixth form. Vast range of extra-curricular activities; strong drama, music; well-supported Duke of Edinburgh award scheme; big emphasis on community service. Lots of language exchanges and foreign expeditions (Madagascar 1992).

The pupils Self-assured, responsive; from wide variety of backgrounds (diplomats to shopkeepers); nearly half have or have had siblings here. Entry at 10, 11 by tests designed to identify those capable of proceeding to A-levels and higher education. School is not unduly selective; minimum 50% mark required at Common Entrance; slightly oversubscribed. Scholarships, bursaries available.

Results GCSE: 94% gain at least 5 grades A-C. A-levels (1992): 50% of entries graded A or B.

Destinations 90% stay on for A-levels; 95% of these proceed to higher education (20 a year to Oxbridge).

Sport Lots on offer; high standards; good facilities. Main games: rugby, hockey, cricket for the boys; hockey, netball, tennis for the girls; others include fencing, golf, riding, sailing.

Remarks Well-resourced school; good all round.

OLD PALACE

Old Palace Road,
Croydon CR0 1AX
Tel (081) 688 2027

Independent • Girls • Day • Ages 6-18 • 760 pupils (600 in senior school) • 154 in sixth form • Fees, £2,295-£3,222
Head: Miss Kathleen Hilton, late 50s, appointed 1974.

Popular, highly selective school; good exam results.

Background Founded 1889 by the (Anglican) Sisters of the Church: they withdrew in

1975 with the loss of Direct Grant status, and the school became fully independent. Buildings (behind a high wall) include the 15th-century Old Palace, former residence of the Archbishops of Canterbury (open to the public at weekends).

Atmosphere Compulsory prayers in the banqueting hall; lunch in the vaulted dungeons; lessons in a room where Elizabeth I once slept. Sense of dignified calm prevails.

The head Historian; direct, meticulous. Determined to keep up to date.

The teaching Challenging. Broad curriculum, plenty of choice. All do 3 sciences, Latin, technology, computing; more than a third take 2 modern languages at GCSE. 22 subjects on offer at A-level: all do 3 or 4 plus general studies and are expected to attend lessons in maths and French. Large classes; average size 30, reducing to 10 in the sixth form. Experienced, well-qualified staff of 57 (3 men). Preparatory department crowded, due for renewal. Very strong music: 40% learn an instrument at school and another 25% at home; 3 choirs (performances at Llangollen, Festival Hall, St John's, Smith Square), 2 orchestras, wind band, chamber ensembles.

The pupils Mostly from middle-class, professional homes. Entry by (highly) competitive examination; places at 7+ and 11 + oversubscribed several times over. Nearly all juniors proceed to the senior school; 60% of the intake at 11 + come from the state sector. (All need the potential to achieve 3 or 4 good A-levels.) 40 assisted places plus scholarships and bursaries.

Results GCSE: all gain at least 5 grades A-C (in 1991 13 obtained 9 or more As). A-level: creditable 58% of entries graded A or B.

Destinations 80% stay on into the sixth form; 90% of these proceed to higher education (10 or more a year to Oxbridge).

Sport Netball, swimming, tennis, squash, badminton, cross-country.

Remarks Solid, hard-working school; strong Anglican ethos.

OLD SWINFORD
Stourbridge,
West Midlands DY8 1QX
Tel (0384) 370025

Comprehensive (grant-maintained) •
Boys • Day and boarding • Ages 11-18 •
550 pupils (two-thirds boarding) • 170 in
sixth form • Boarding fees, £2,820
Head: Chris Potter, 52, appointed 1978.

State boarding school competing strongly with the independent sector; good results; strong sport.

Background Founded 1667 (on the model of Christ's Hospital, *qv*) by Thomas Foley, who richly endowed it with land (600 acres remain) and money, which is still controlled by his descendants. Formerly voluntary-aided; became one of the first to opt out of council control (in September 1989). Lofty, red-brick 17th-century buildings plus extensive later additions on a hill overlooking Stourbridge. Facilities as good as those of many independent boarding schools. Department of Education helped pay for 3 new science labs.

Atmosphere Firmly traditional; big emphasis on high achievement, good manners. Some excellent boarding accommodation; first-class food.

The head Able, vigorous; a great enthusiast. Read classics and archaeology at Cambridge; both his father and grandfather were heads. Married, 5 children.

The teaching Methods generally formal; well-qualified staff of 42 (5 women); pupils set by ability in most subjects; extra help for those who need it. Small classes; average 22-23, reducing to 20 for GCSE, 12 for A-level. National curriculum-plus; GCSE options include classics, geology, electronics; archaeology, business studies available at A-level; all sixth-formers take a course in modern languages. First-rate computing (150 machines). Lots of drama, music; brass band accompanies morning assembly. Extra-curricular activities include cadet force, Duke of Edinburgh award scheme, amateur radio station.

The pupils Well turned-out (sixth-formers in grey suits) and proud of their school. Growing number of day boys elect to be 'day boarders': they remain at school until after prep and supper. Good social mix from Midland shire counties, Birmingham conurbation; backgrounds mainly professional (including teaching), farming, middle management, Services, skilled craftsmen; 8% ethnic minority (mainly Asian). Most in the top 20 of the ability range (IQ 120+). School heavily over-subscribed (recruitment almost entirely by word of mouth); 300+ apply for 70 boarding places a year; some places booked for 2002; applicants for up to 25 day places need to live within 400 yards (!) Entry at 11, 12, 13 from primary and prep schools by interview and reports (no written tests). Head is looking for all-rounders, ability to do A-levels, strong parental support, likelihood of benefiting from boarding. Scholarships, bursaries available.

Results (1992) GCSE: 96% gained at least 5 grades A-C. A-level: 37% of entries graded A or B.

Destinations More than 90% stay for A-levels; 95% of these proceed to higher education (3-4 a year to Oxbridge).

Sport Strong rugby (1st XV beats Malvern, Shrewsbury, King Edward's, Birmingham); also soccer, athletics, squash, fencing, judo, archery, golf (18-hole course), fly-fishing. Good facilities, including extensive playing fields, large gym, climbing wall, indoor shooting gallery; indoor pool planned.

Remarks Strong, well-run school; remarkably good value for money. Recommended.

THE ORATORY
Woodcote,
Near Reading,
Berkshire RG8 OPJ
Tel (0491) 680207

Independent ● Roman Catholic ● Boys ● Boarding and day ● Ages 11-18 (plus associated prep school) ● 400 pupils (62% boarding) ● 140 in sixth form ● Fees, £7,584-£9,633 boarding; £5,463-£6,735 day
Head: Simon Barrow, 50, appointed January 1992.

Small, first-rate school; fairly wide ability range; very good results; Catholic values emphasised.

Background Founded 1859 by Cardinal Newman to meet the needs of the Catholic laity; moved during World War II to a fine 150-acre site on a spur of the Chilterns; premises mostly modern and purpose-built.

Atmosphere Relaxed, closely knit community in the liberal Catholic tradition; lay teachers and married housemasters help create a strong sense of family. Boys encouraged, not pressured, to develop their full potential; discipline unobtrusive. Boarding accommodation recently refurbished.

The head Here 23 years and steeped in the school's traditions. Educated at Stonyhurst and Reading; came to teach history and stayed. Married, 2 young children.

The teaching Long-serving staff; emphasis on individual attention in small classes with maximum pupil involvement. National curriculum-plus; science taught as 3 separate subjects; all do computing; Latin, Greek, Spanish, Italian, German on offer. All do 7-11 GCSEs and 3 A-levels. Progress closely monitored; fortnightly check on effort and attainment. First-rate art; many take it for GCSE and A-level and achieve high grades. Strong music; 55% learn an instrument; 2 orchestras, chapel choir, frequent public performances. Cadet force compulsory for 2 years. School owns a farmhouse in Normandy.

The pupils Largely from middle-class Catholic homes in London and the South East; day boys live within 15-mile radius; many fathers are past pupils. Ability range wider than a grammar school's; IQs from 105 to 140. Entry at 11+ by tests in English, maths, non-verbal reasoning, school report and interview; at 13+ by Common Entrance. Scholarships, bursaries but no assisted places.

Results GCSE (1991): 93% gained at least 5 grades A-C. A-level (1992): 49% of entries graded A or B (has been higher).

Destinations 90% stay on for A-levels; 85% of these proceed to higher education (6 or 7 a year to Oxbridge).

Sport Chiefly rugby, soccer, cricket; other activities, all of a high standard, include athletics, cross-country, hockey, rowing, sailing, shooting, swimming, tennis. Boys expected to participate 5 times a week. Sports hall, indoor pool, squash courts, real tennis court, boathouse on the Thames.

Remarks Attractive, well-run school. Good all round; highly recommended.

OUNDLE

New Street,
Oundle,
Peterborough PE8 4EN
Tel (0832) 273536

Independent • Co-educational • Boarding (plus associated day school) • Ages 11-18 (plus associated junior school) • 840 pupils (85% boys) • 340 in sixth form • Fees (1992-93), £8,910-£11,670
Head: David McMurray, 55, appointed 1984.

Fine school; very good teaching and results; superb facilities; first-rate music, art, drama and sport.

Background Founded 1556 by Sir William Laxton, Lord Mayor of London and Master of the Grocers' Company (who are still the governors); school split into 2 in 1876, separating the sons of the landed gentry (who were prepared for entry to Oxbridge) from the sons of local tradesman (who were not). Pupils from both schools – Oundle and Laxton – are now taught together but (oddly) lead separate social lives and wear different uniforms. 17th-, 18th- and 19th-century buildings scattered around the town; many excellent later additions. Co-educational since 1990.

Atmosphere Busy, well-ordered, unpretentious (but undeniably upper-class); good pastoral care system. Dedicated staff; bright-eyed, confident pupils. Arrival of girls (whose numbers are being increased) has helped smooth the rougher edges.

The head Very able. Informal, relaxed, humorous; leads from the front; regarded by his peers as the 'complete schoolmaster'. Educated at Loretto and Cambridge (read English); taught at Stowe and Fettes; formerly head of Loretto. Introduced co-education here out of conviction, not economic necessity (believes that attempting to inculcate sensible attitudes to the opposite sex while keeping the sexes separate is 'like teaching people to swim without allowing them to get wet'). Formally appraises half his 100+ staff every year; interviews all prospective parents; keen sportsman; still finds time to teach general studies. Married, 3 daughters; wife much involved in school life.

The teaching Fairly traditional in style; experienced, well-qualified staff, half appointed by present head; average age 40. Pupils streamed by ability; further setting in maths, French, Latin. National curriculum-plus; science taught as 3 separate subjects; German, Greek, Spanish on offer; good design/technology (in exceptionally well-equipped workshops). Most take 10 GCSEs (many do maths, French a year early) and 3 A-levels; 25% of sixth-form timetable devoted to a wide range of non-specialist courses, including geology, Russian, Japanese studies, philosophy, computing, woodwork. Very strong music; 65% learn at least 1 instrument; 3 orchestras, numerous smaller ensembles, good choir; art and drama similarly impressive. 450-member cadet force is one of the biggest in the country. Numerous overseas study trips and expeditions.

The pupils Nearly all from privileged backgrounds – monied families with a tradition of boarding; catchment area stretches from Scotland to London. Entry at 11+ by school's own tests, at 13+ by Common Entrance; minimum IQ 110. Many scholarships but no assisted places.

Results GCSE: virtually all gain at least 5 grades A-C. A-level (1992): creditable 64% of entries graded A or B.

Destinations Nearly all stay on for A-levels and proceed to higher education, half after taking a 'gap year' (20 a year to Oxbridge).

Sport Compulsory but the choice is wide. Rugby is exceptionally strong; cricket, rowing, fencing, tennis not far behind; hockey, netball, cross-country, athletics, shooting, golf, fives, squash also on offer. Excellent facilities include extensive playing fields, sports hall, indoor pool.

Remarks Exceptionally good all round; highly recommended.

OXFORD HIGH
Belbroughton Road,
Oxford OX2 6XA
Tel (0865) 59888

Independent • Girls • Day • Ages 9-18
650 pupils (550 in senior school • 155 in sixth form • Fees, £2,424-£3,156
Head: Mrs Joan Townsend, late-50s, appointed 1982.

Outstanding school for bright, middle-class girls; splendid all-round education.

Background Founded 1875; member of the Girls' Public Day School Trust – which accounts for the modest fees. Utilitarian, unpretentious 1960s buildings in leafy North Oxford.

Atmosphere Vibrant; high-achieving daughters of dons, doctors, lawyers (but the school is not, the head insists, a hot-house).

The head Shrewd, witty, unassuming. Oxford graduate (maths). Writes long, chatty newsletters to parents; clearly loves her job.

The teaching First-class staff (including a fair proportion of dons' wives); bristling with talent. Traditional curriculum for juniors (they can all recite the names of Henry VIII's wives and make beautiful earthenware mugs). Seniors do 3 sciences (physics and chemistry compulsory for GCSE); Latin compulsory for first 2 years. Strong maths and modern languages (much to-ing and fro-ing with twinned schools in Germany, France, Spain and Russia). Class sizes average 26-27 (2 girls to a computer – but they all have their own at home). Effective mechanisms for spotting anyone struggling. Good library, computerised and user-friendly. Excellent art and music – nearly half learn an instrument; choirs, 2 orchestras, wind band.

The pupils Charming, ready to laugh at themselves, but appear to know their own worth. The youngest, according to the head, are eager and biddable; by the time they reach the sixth form they are balanced and responsible; in the middle years they tend to be rebellious and intractable. (Resentments aired in school council run by sixth-formers, but it must not be supposed OHS is a hotbed of revolution.) Elaborate entry procedures (by examination and assessment); school heavily oversubscribed but claims not to be 'abnormally' choosy. 25 assisted places a year plus up to 6 scholarships.

Results GCSE: All gain at least 5 grades A-C. A-level: impressive 67% of entries graded A or B.

Destinations 85% go on to higher education (20 a year to Oxbridge).

Sport Good netball, hockey, tennis, badminton, swimming.

Remarks Invites an avalanche of superlatives; record speaks for itself.

OXTED
Bluehouse Lane,
Oxted,
Surrey RH8 0AB
Tel (0883) 712425

Comprehensive • Co-educational • Ages 12-18 (11-18 in 1993) • 1,536 pupils (rising to 1,836 in 1993; equal numbers of boys and girls) • 306 in sixth form
Head: Roger Coles, 50, appointed 1981.

First-rate comprehensive; good results; strong in music and sport.

Background Opened 1929 as a co-educational grammar school; went comprehensive 1977. Buildings of every shape, size and condition (including ageing huts, soon to be removed) in spacious grounds between Oxted and the North Downs (straddling the Greewich meridian). New science block under construction.

Atmosphere Happy, purposeful, well-ordered (despite the school's size and the complexity of its buildings); strong house system; good staff-pupil relationships clearly evident; parents' evenings well attended (PTA raises £15,000 a year). No smoking on the premises – by anyone.

The head Enthusiastic, charismatic, leads from the front (and knows everything that is going on). Was deputy head here from 1971-79 before taking up a headship in Cumbria. Teaches geography. Has 2 daughters, 1 doing a PhD at Cambridge.

The teaching Competent, professional staff of 98; high standards expected and achieved. All first-years do French, German; 20% add Latin. Setting by ability in most subjects; extra help both for gifted and those in difficulties (some pupils partially sighted). Good science, computing, design/technology (including pot-

tery, photography). Choice of 21 subjects at A-levels; sixth-form options include vocational courses. Homework starts at $1^1/_2$ hours a night and increases; internal exams in all subjects; twice-yearly reports to parents. Strong music department (one of the best in Surrey); good drama; some exciting art. Excellent careers advice; work experience for all. Annual camps; regular exchanges with France, Germany; popular Duke of Edinburgh award scheme.

The pupils Broad social mix (but few ethnic minority). Annual intake of 300, most from 6 feeder primaries.

Results (1992) GCSE: 58% gained at least 5 grades A-C. A-level: creditable 44% of entries graded A or B.

Destinations Impressive 70% continue into the sixth form; most of those who take A-levels proceed to higher education (2 a year to Oxbridge).

Sport Strong rugby, soccer, cricket, netball, cross-country. Facilities include fine sports hall, heated outdoor pool, 8 tennis courts.

Remarks Well-run, effective school.

PANGBOURNE
Pangbourne,
Reading,
Berkshire RG8 8LA
Tel (0734) 842101

Independent • Boys • Boarding and day • Ages 11-18 • 457 pupils (86% boarding) • 132 in sixth form • Fees, £6,825-£9,300 boarding; £4,740-£6,525 day
Head: Anthony Hudson, 53, appointed 1988.

Solid, traditional school; wide range of abilities; strong naval ethos; good sport.

Background Founded as a nautical college in 1917 to train boys for the merchant and royal navies; dropped 'nautical' from its title in 1969 and is now a conventional independent school (but naval traditions are proudly retained). Purpose-built functional premises on an attractive 250-acre site; recent additions include fine peforming arts centre, sports hall, design/technology block. Disused 19th-century chapel being re-built as a Falklands war memorial.

Atmosphere Emphasis on discipline, smartness, teamwork, sharing in the necessary chores. Day begins with the raising of the ensign and ends with the ceremony of sunset; boys wear midshipman's uniform for Sunday chapel; prefects still called 'chiefs', dining rooms are 'messes' and kitchens 'galleys'. However, the atmosphere is neither militaristic or harsh; relationships are supportive and friendly. Boarding accommodation being upgraded.

The head Educated at Tonbridge and Oxford; formerly deputy head of Radley, where he taught for 24 years. Francophile, amateur magician, interested in water colours and antiques; married, 3 grown-up children.

The teaching Mixture of traditional and modern styles. National curriculum-plus; choice of science as 3 separate subjects or 'dual award'; German, Latin on offer. Setting by ability in most subjects; extra help for those with dyslexia or whose first language is not English; average class size 17. Most do 10 or 11 GCSEs; top set takes maths, Latin a year early. Most do 3 A-levels plus AS-level general studies; extra coaching for Oxbridge candidates. Lots of music; orchestra, marching band, large chapel choir. Full-scale film production unit wins commercial contracts. Well-supported cadet force.

The pupils Self-reliant, courteous, well-behaved. Most from London and the South East but a growing proportion from abroad; wide range of abilities; IQs from 105-140. Entry to junior school at 11+ and by Common Entrance at 13+. Scholarships, bursaries.

Results GCSE (1991): 88% gained at least 5 grades A-C. A-level (1992): very modest 25% of entries graded A or B.

Destinations 90% stay on for A-levels; 95% of these proceed to higher education (6 a year to Oxbridge).

Sport Big emphasis on team games, particularly rugby (14 teams fielded on Saturdays), hockey, cricket, rowing. Badminton, sailing, shooting, squash, tennis also on offer. Facilities include magnificent sports hall; boathouse on the Thames.

Remarks Good school for all-rounders.

PARRS WOOD
Wilmslow Road,
East Didsbury,
Manchester M20 0PG
Tel (061) 445 8786

Comprehensive • Co-educational • Ages 11-18 • 1,550 pupils (slightly more boys than girls) • 240 in sixth form
Head: Iain Hall, 49, appointed 1991.

First-rate, lively comprehensive.

Background Founded 1967 as a purpose-built comprehensive in a leafy suburb of south Manchester. Buildings were meant to last 25 years and it shows: some are falling apart.

Atmosphere Exceptionally happy; staff morale sky-high; children enthusiastic, courteous, well-behaved. Good pastoral care system, including careful induction of first-years. School's ethos is to emphasise the positive; everything, from good work to regular attendance, is rewarded with merit points resulting in letters of congratulation from head or governors. Big emphasis on negotiation and consultation through committees and councils. (One boy complained the cost of removing graffiti was not something he needed to know about, and then added, 'It does make you think though'.) Parents are asked to sign a contract spelling out their educational rights and duties.

The head Very able; showman, energiser, superb manager (has reorganised the school along the lines of a successful commercial enterprise – staff are given performance targets, reviewed at the end of each term). Makes everyone feel valued and is highly regarded in return (to the point of adulation) by staff and pupils. ('It's got loads better since he's been here,' remarked a 13-year-old). Read maths, statistics, physics at Liverpool; has taught in a grammar school and a succession of difficult comprehensives; his second headship. Takes 4 assemblies a week and classes throughout the school for teachers who are absent.

The teaching Well-qualified staff of 96 (55 women), most over the age of 40. Lessons well-prepared, delivered in a firm but friendly way; pupils encouraged to participate. Farily large classes (up to 30). Setting by ability in maths, science, modern languages; all do German as a second modern language from age 14; compulsory courses in life skills, economic and social awareness. All take up to 10 GCSEs; options include Urdu, dance, business studies, computing (but facilities are poor), media studies, child development. A-level options include psychology, electronics, theatre studies; vocational alternatives available, including BTEC courses. Extra help available for the bright and the not-so-bright. Good careers advice; work experience for all. Busy extra-curricular programme; frequent exchange visits to European schools.

The pupils Varied backgrounds; 18% entitled to free school meals; 20% Asian. No selection on any basis other than living in the catchment area of East and West Didsbury (those outside have little hope of admission, except into the sixth form). Ability range 'skewed to the top end'.

Results GCSE: 37% gain at least 5 grades A-C. A-level (1992): 36% of entries graded A or B.

Destinations 70% of those who take A-levels proceed to higher education (3-5 a year to Oxbridge).

Sport Facilities 'absolutely hopeless' (according to head of sports); no sports hall, no swimming pool and nowhere near enough staff. However, participation rates in a reasonably wide range of activities are high.

Remarks Exceptionally well-run school.

THE PERSE

Hills Road,
Cambridge CB2 2QF
Tel (0223) 247008

Independent • Boys • Day (boarding ceases September 1993) • Ages 11-18 (plus associated prep school) • 495 pupils • 140 in sixth form • Fees, £3,678 Head: Dr Martin Stephen, 43, appointed 1987.

First-rate school; impressive results; good music and sport.

Background Founded 1615 under the will of Dr Stephen Perse, a fellow of Gonville and Caius College; reverted to full independence 1976 with the abolition of Direct Grant status. Moved to its present purpose-built premises 1960; pleasant 28-acre site on the edge of the city.

Atmosphere Ability, enthusiasm, commitment in abundance. Friendly relationships all round; effective pastoral care system (head believes parents want their children to be 'loved a little bit').

The head Vigorous, articulate, multi-talented. Educated at Uppingham (took his A-levels at 16), Leeds (English and history), Sheffield (PhD). Has worked in remand homes; taught at Uppingham; housemaster at Haileybury; deputy head of Sedbergh. Prolific author (13 books on English literature, naval history); draws, paints; teaches religious education 10 periods a week. Knows all his pupils (operates 'small claims court' after assembly when any boy can approach him about anything); runs a tight ship. His wife is head of a girls' school in Bedford. 3 sons, 1 a pupil here.

The teaching Traditional grammar-school approach; first-rate, highly qualified staff of 35 (few women); a third appointed by present head. National curriculum-plus; most take

French and German for GCSE; good arts-science balance; plenty of computing. Setting by ability in maths only. Strong music; half learn an instrument; joint orchestra and smaller ensembles with Perse Girls' *(qv)*. Good drama (in new 180-seat theatre) and art. Well-developed links with business, industry. Active cadet force (more than 200 members). Lots of overseas trips, exchanges.

The pupils Confident, mature, articulate. Top 25% of the ability range; half from Cambridge (large university element); remainder travel up to 30 miles. Entry by aptitude tests and interview at 11 from associated prep school (two-thirds of the intake) and state primaries – and at 13. Assisted places (not all taken up). School keen not to be seen as economically or socially élitist.

Results GCSE: all gain at least 5 grades A-C. A-level (1992): impressive 70% of entries graded A or B.

Destinations All but a handful stay for A-levels (despite the challenge of local – free – sixth-form colleges); virtually all of these proceed to higher education (a third to Oxbridge).

Sport Not an obsession but good, nonetheless. Chiefly rugby (county honours), hockey, cricket, tennis; squash, judo, fencing, cross-country also on offer. New sports hall, swimming pool planned.

Remarks Well-run school; strong all round.

PERSE GIRLS'
Union Road,
Cambridge CB2 1HF
Tel (0223) 359589

Independent • Girls • Day • Ages 11-18 (plus associated junior school) • 550 pupils • 150 in sixth form • Fees, £3,570 Head: Miss Helen Smith, 50, appointed 1989.

Strong academic school; good results; first-rate music and drama.

Background Founded 1881; formerly Direct Grant. Surprisingly spacious site near the city centre (entered through a small black door); recent additions include fine labs, attractive music wing, drama studio.

Atmosphere Lively. Dedicated staff; enthusiastic, highly motivated pupils.

The head Read maths at Oxford; taught at Cheltenham Ladies' and International School, Brussels. Came here to teach maths in 1971; promoted to deputy 1988. Quiet, firm leadership style; totally committed to single-sex education. Plays the clarinet.

The teaching Generally traditional in style; long-serving staff of 51 (7 men); particular strengths in science (taught as 3 separate subjects), languages; computing, design/technology not neglected. Second language chosen at end of first year from German, Italian, Russian, Spanish; all do 8-11 GCSEs. Setting by ability in maths, languages; average class size 27. Choice of 24 subjects at A-level (nearly half the subject entries are in maths and science). Arts feature prominently; standards are high, particularly in music (24 visiting teachers) and drama (excellent facilities); some joint activities with Perse Boys' *(qv)*. Busy lunch-time programme of extra-curricular activities includes Christian Union, debating, charity fund-raising, Duke of Edinburgh award scheme. Regular language exchanges; classics trips to Italy, Greece.

The pupils Confident, articulate; from a variety of social backgrounds (current roll includes the daughters of a lorry driver, a viscount and many academics) in a wide catchment area. All of above-average ability – and under strong pressure from peers, parents and staff to succeed. Entry by school's own tests; junior school provides most of the intake. Lots of assisted places but currently only 70 of 115 taken up; 23 receive help from bursaries.

Results GCSE (1991): 97% gained at least 5 grades A-C. A-level (1992): creditable 64% of entries graded A or B.

Destinations Most stay for A-levels and proceed to higher education (up to 20 a year to Oxbridge), many after taking a 'gap year'.

Sport Chiefly hockey, netball, tennis, rounders; cross-country, gymnastics also on offer. Limited on-site facilities; playing fields 10 minutes away.

Remarks Successful, hard-working, friendly school.

PIMLICO
Lupus Street,
London SW1V 3AT
Tel (071) 828 0881

Comprehensive • Co-educational • Ages 11-19 • 1,213 (55% boys) pupils • 180 in sixth form
Head: Miss Kathleen Wood, 44, appointed 1990.

Successful progressive comprehensive; wide ability range; respectable results; excellent music.

Background Opened 1970 as a purpose-built, showpiece comprehensive; looks like a giant greenhouse; 5 levels, 2 of them subterranean, surrounded by a concrete concourse. The architecture (and the school's reputation) attracts visitors from around the world. Remarkable music centre in neighbouring Victorian mansion (intensive musical education offered to 15 pupils a year selected by audition). Adult education and youth centre on same site.

Atmosphere Very welcoming; staff and pupils take evident pride in the school. (Staff turnover is low: accommodation provided for 20 in neighbouring houses.) Big emphasis on music and the creative arts; individualism encouraged. No uniform; rules kept to a minimum.

The head Grammar-school educated; has a degree from the Open University and a diploma in management. Taught mostly in the London area; formerly head of a comprehensive in Hertfordshire. Strongly committed to the school's progressive ethos.

The teaching Mixture of styles (individual learning, group work, whole-class teaching); mixed-ability classes throughout; average size 27, reducing to 12-15 for A-level. National curriculum; Spanish or German may be added to French in second year. Choice of 23 subjects at GCSE; most do 8. Sixth-form consortium with 2 other schools permits wide choice of A-levels and vocational options, including BTEC. Lots of art, dance, drama and – particularly – music (choirs, orchestras, ensembles, composer-in-residence). First-rate school newspaper (*Pimlico Matters*): wide-ranging views freely and forcefully expressed.

The pupils Multi-lingual (up to 40 languages spoken) and multi-ethnic; from council estates and Georgian terraces; wide range of abilities. School is currently 30% over-subscribed; priority to siblings and those living nearest, but many come from other London boroughs.

Results (1991) GCSE: 33% gained at least 5 grades A-C (just above the national average). A-level: respectable 39% of entries graded A or B.

Destinations 70% continue into the sixth form; 85% of these proceed to higher education.

Sport Limited on-site facilities include 2 gymnasia, swimming pool, 2 all-weather pitches.

Remarks Attractive, effective comprehensive (unusual for London).

PORTSMOUTH GRAMMAR
High Street,
Portsmouth PO1 2LN
Tel (0705) 819125

Independent • Co-educational (since 1991) • Day • Ages 5-18 • 1,087 pupils (768 in senior school; 88% boys) • 215 in sixth form • Fees, £2,190-£3,480
Head: Tony Evans, 50s, appointed 1982.

Traditional academic boys' school now going fully co-educational; good teaching and results.

Background Founded 1732; became fully independent 1976 with the abolition of Direct Grant status. Spacious city-centre site close to the cathedral; main buildings date from 1920s; later additions include theatre, music school, sports centre. Girls admitted at all ages; school aims to be fully co-educational by 1995.

Atmosphere Energetic, enthusiastic; pupils kept busy.

The head Read modern languages at Oxford and London; taught at Winchester for 10 years; formerly head of the sixth form at Dulwich. Was the first teacher to be appointed to the Government's National Curriculum Council. Married; his 2 sons were both educated here.

The teaching Aims to offer the best of 'old' and 'new': small classes, broad curriculum, a sense of competition. Senior school timetable emphasises English literature and science at the expense of art, music and technology – but parents seem to approve. Particularly good teaching (and results) in maths, science, history, modern languages (French, German, Spanish), computing (good facilities). Choice of 19 subjects at A-level; maths, economics, 3 sciences are popular. 20% of the staff are women (and the proportion is rising). Extra-curricular activities include music, cadet force (boys and girls), Duke of Edinburgh award scheme. Well-organised careers advice and work experience.

The pupils Drawn from a wide catchment area (some travel 2 hours a day); many have parents in business, education, the Services. Entry at 5 by assessment; at 8 and 11 by interview and tests in English, maths, verbal reasoning; at 13 by Common Entrance. Competition can be stiff; nearly all are from the top 20% of the ability range. Up to 30 assisted places a year.

Results GCSE: all gain at least 5 grades A-C. A-level (1992): 51% of entries graded A or B.

Destinations 90% proceed to higher education (16 to Oxbridge in 1991); 25% take a 'gap year'.

Sport Wide choice; impressive results in rugby; playing fields 4 miles away.

Remarks Effective, well-run school.

PORTSMOUTH HIGH
Kent Road,
Southsea,
Hampshire PO5 3EQ
Tel (0705) 826714

Independent • Girls • Day • Ages 4-18 • 709 pupils (520 in senior school) • 107 in sixth form • Fees, £2,424-£3,156
Head: Mrs Judith Dawtrey, mid-40s, appointed 1984.

Strong academic school; first-rate teaching and results (top of The Daily Telegraph*'s A-level league table in 1991).*

Background Founded 1882; one of 26 schools belonging to the estimable Girls' Public Day School Trust which aims to offer an academic education at a reasonable cost to girls of ability and talent. Modest Victorian buildings near the Esplanade; recent additions include sports hall and art centre.

Atmosphere Kindly but firm – and very hard-working (girls never seem to feel they have quite done enough). Staff and pupils take great pride in the school; prominent honours boards record scholarships and university successes.

The head Read modern languages at London; formerly senior mistress at Rickmansworth Masonic Girls'. Claimed to be 'surprised and overwhelmed' by school's league-table performance: 'We knew we were good but not that good'.

The teaching Excellent. Long-serving, well-qualified staff; challenging, encouraging approach. National curriculum-plus; up to half take 2 modern languages for GCSE (from French, German, Spanish); Latin, Greek on offer; science taught to seniors as 3 separate subjects. Setting by ability in maths, languages. Heavy homework load from the start of senior school. Good music (small orchestra, choir) and art. Regular exchanges with France, Germany, Spain.

The pupils Confident, articulate, highly motivated. Most are from middle-class homes but 29 assisted places a year ensures some social mix; wide catchment area. Entry to junior school at 4, 7, 8; to senior school at 11 by competitive entrance exam (more than 2 contenders for each place); nearly all are in top 20% of the ability range.

Results GCSE: 95% gain at least 5 grades A-C. A-level (1992): relatively disappointing 60% of entries graded A or B (has been *much* higher).

Destinations A significant minority leave at 16 for co-educational sixth-form colleges; nearly all who stay proceed to higher education.

Sport 'Idiosyncratic', according to the head. Lacrosse, netball, tennis are popular.

Remarks Fine school for bright girls.

POYNTON HIGH
Yew Tree Lane,
Poynton,
Stockport,
Cheshire SK12 1PU
Tel (0625) 871811

Comprehensive • Co-educational • Ages 11-19 • 1,693 pupils (equal numbers of boys and girls) • 310 in sixth form
Head: John Jones, 47, appointed 1979.

Outstanding comprehensive; good results; strong sport; all abilities catered for.

Background Established as a comprehensive 1972; pleasant, well-maintained 23-acre site in a largely affluent area of Macclesfield; functional, rather drab buildings, bursting at the seams. School enjoys strong support from parents and the community.

Atmosphere Calm, well-ordered (despite the school's size); rules clearly stated and well understood; no feeling of coercion but a definite sense of authority and high expectations. Corridors adorned with pupils' work; display cabinet groans with sporting silverware. Well-organised pastoral care system (staff get to know the children well).

The head Open, courteous, thoughtful; has a high regard for the traditional virtues (uniform, homework, regular examinations, pupils standing up when he enters the room). Grammar-school educated; read history at Cambridge. Skilled manager, liked and respected by all; teaches for a quarter of the timetable. Writes history textbooks in his spare (!) time; plays cricket, squash. Married, 3 children.

The teaching Hard-working, professional, manifestly contented staff of 100 (55 women), 80 appointed by present head; full range of teaching methods used. Wide, varied curriculum; 5 languages on offer, including Russian and Italian (but no classics); sciences taught as 3 separate subjects. Pupils take 7-10 GCSEs; options include childcare, computing, office technology, graphic communication, home economics. No streaming by ability; setting from third year in maths, sciences, languages; extra help for those with special needs. Choice of 23 subjects at A-level plus vocational alternatives, including BTEC; all do general studies. Largest classes 30, reducing to 12-15 in sixth form. Homework strictly monitored by teachers and parents. Good drama and music; 3 choirs, orchestra, swing band; instrumental lessons from visiting teachers. Extra-curricular activities include outstanding community services programme covering the elderly, the young, the handicapped, and the environment (school has won a Rotary Club award for 'wholehearted service to the community'). Regular exchanges with schools in Germany, France, Spain.

The pupils From a variety of backgrounds but most are from middle-class homes; many parents move house to be sure of a place (and many teachers send their children here – always a good sign). No entry tests of any kind; applications for admission dealt with by Cheshire County Council, not the school; basic criterion is that a child must have attended 1 of 8 primary schools in Poynton, Adlington and Disley. 273 places available a year, over-subscribed by 50-100 (despite strong competition from excellent independent schools). Truancy rate virtually nil; serious disciplinary problems rare.

Results (1992) GCSE: 68% gained at least 5 grades A-C (more than twice the national average). A-level: 35% of entries graded A or B.

Destinations About 50% continue into the sixth form; 65% of these proceed to higher education (5-6 a year to Oxbridge).

Sport Facilities include fully equipped leisure centre (shared with the public after school hours), indoor pool, extensive on-site playing fields. All the usual games are played to a high level; tennis, rounders, squash, badminton also on offer.

Remarks Happy, well-run school; highly recommended.

PRINCE HENRY'S GRAMMAR

Farnley Road,
Otley,
West Yorkshire LS21 2BB
Tel (0943) 463524

Comprehensive • Co-educational • Ages 11-18 • 1,120 pupils (equal numbers of girls and boys) • 200 in the sixth form
Head: Michael Franklin, 52, appointed 1985.

Effective, well-run comprehensive; high standards of work and behaviour.

Background Founded 1611 with the motto 'Fear God and Mind Thy Book'; moved to present sturdy, stone-built premises 1927; merged with a secondary modern to become a comprehensive in 1968. 1960s flat-roofed additions in urgent need of refurbishment; fine modern languages centre opened 1990.

Atmosphere Well-motivated, well-behaved children; enthusiastic, committed staff. Deserved reputation for good teaching and high standards of achievement but no hint of élitism – school fully aware of its responsibility to all pupils. Close co-operation with parents expected and achieved.

The head Popular with staff and pupils. Read physics at Bradford; formerly head of a comprehensive in Leeds. Married, 2 grown-up children.

The teaching Traditional classrooms – tables and desks face the blackboard – but the atmosphere is relaxed and the pupils responsive. 66 staff (slightly more women than men), half appointed by present head. Mixed-ability classes; setting from age 13 in maths, modern languages; all do 9 GCSEs; big emphasis on personal and social education. Usual choice of subjects at A-level plus vocational alternatives, including BTEC course in business and finance. Good music and drama; regular public performances.

The pupils Mostly from middle-class professional homes. Pupils drawn principally from 5 feeder primaries but the catchment area is expanding and the pressure for places growing.

Results GCSE: 50% gain at least 5 grades A-C (20% achieve 9). A-level: 38% of entries graded A or B.

Destinations Half continue into the sixth form; up to 70% of these proceed to higher education.

Sport Good facilities for both indoor and outdoor activities; boys' rugby and girls' gymnastics are particularly successful.

Remarks Good all round; living up to its reputation.

PUTNEY HIGH
35 Putney Hill,
London SW15 6BH
Tel (081) 788 4886

Independent • Girls • Day • Ages 11-18 (plus associated junior school) • 600 pupils • 150 in sixth form • Fees, £3,384 Head: Mrs Eileen Merchant, 48, appointed 1991.

Sound academic school; good teaching and results; strong music.

Background Founded 1893; member of Girls' Public Day School Trust. 2 Victorian mansions (plus a third housing the junior department) surrounded by spacious and beautiful gardens; recent additions include design/technology centre, 3-storey classroom block; some temporary huts awaiting replacement.

Atmosphere Friendly, supportive; tradition of older girls helping younger ones; emphasis on praise and encouragement rather than criticism. Girls expected to work hard (and they do) but no undue pressure; good relations between staff and pupils.

The head Educated at a convent school and Sheffield (degree in chemistry); has taught in state and independent schools; formerly deputy head of Latymer. Hopes girls will leave 'with the courage and integrity to support a minority view in which they believe'. Married, 2 grown-up sons.

The teaching Challenging; designed to develop independent thinking and investigative skills. National curriculum from first year; choice of Latin, German from second year; all do combined science; compulsory modular course in computing, design/technology, textiles; setting by ability in maths, modern languages. All take 9 GCSEs and 3 A-levels (from a choice of 18) plus general studies. Strong music: all but a handful learn an instrument in first year; many orchestral and choral groups. Much fund-raising for charity.

The pupils Most from middle-class homes with parents in the media, arts, professions, City; scholarships and up to 30 assisted places a year help ensure some social mix. Entry at 11+ by interview and tests in English, maths; minimum IQ of 115.

Results GCSE (1991): 97% gained at least 5 grades A-C. A-level (1992): 51% of entries graded A or B.

Destinations 80% stay on for A-levels; 75% of these proceed to higher education (8 to Oxbridge in 1991).

Sport Netball and tennis are the main team games, but the emphasis is on individual activities; dance and gymnastics are prominent; swimming, aerobics, golf, trampolining, volleyball, badminton, fencing also on offer.

Remarks Good all round.

QUEEN ANNE'S
Henley Road,
Caversham,
Reading,
Berkshire RG4 0DX
Tel (0734) 471582

Independent • Girls • Boarding and day •
Ages 11-18 • 400 pupils (75% boarding) •
130 in sixth form • Fees, £9,180 boarding;
£5,745 day
Head: Miss Audrey Scott, 58, appointed
1977.

*First-rate school; good all round; strong
music and sport.*

Background Founded 1894; fine red-brick
buildings on attractive 46-acre site; substantial
later acquisitions and additions.

Atmosphere Friendly, well-ordered. Hard-
working, committed staff; girls feel obliged not
to let them down. Christian values central to
everyday life; good pastoral care system. Day
girls stay until 7 p.m.; lessons on Saturday
mornings.

The head Read modern languages at Reading; previously head of Peterborough High and
a school in Kenya. Keen that girls should be
fully involved in sport and creative activities as
well as academic work; believes all have the
potential to excel at something.

The teaching Broad curriculum in first 3
years includes computing, design/technology,
drama, dress-making, class singing; all take
Latin plus German or Spanish from second
year; Greek also on offer. Setting by ability in
maths, modern languages; average class size
20, reducing to 16 for GCSE. All take 8-10
GCSEs and 2-4 A-levels plus compulsory
general studies and general English. Progress
closely monitored. Good music: all expected
to learn an instrument; 2 orchestras, large
choir.

The pupils Lively, articulate, self-assured.
Most have parents in business and the professions; minority from abroad. Entry at 11, 12, 13
by Common Entrance; school says it requires
a minimum mark of 65% but internal evidence
suggests it accepts rather less; minimum IQ
probably 115. 6 scholarships a year.

Results GCSE: all gain at least 5 grades A-C.
A-level (1992): 49% of entries graded A or B.

Destinations 70%-80% stay on for A-levels;
90% of these proceed to higher education (6 a
year to Oxbridge).

Sport Outstanding lacrosse (school has been
national champion for 7 of the past 10 years);
netball, tennis, squash, swimming, athletics all
of a high standard; golf, badminton, rowing
also on offer. Facilities include 24 tennis
courts, 9 lacrosse pitches, 3 squash courts,
heated indoor pool.

Remarks General atmosphere of peace, calm
and contentment conceals a high level of
commitment to work and extra-curricular
activities.

QUEEN ELIZABETH'S BOYS' Barnet
Queen's Road,
Barnet,
Hertfordshire EN5 4DQ
Tel (081) 441 4646

Comprehensive (grant-maintained) • Boys
• Ages 11-18 • 1,060 pupils • 183 in sixth
form
Head: Eamonn Harris, 58, appointed 1984.

*Rigorously run comprehensive;
respectable results; strong music and
sport.*

Background Founded 1573 by Elizabeth I as
a grammar school for 'the training of boys in
manners and learning' ('and this remains our
purpose to this day'); moved to present
purpose-built premises 1930; solid, spacious
buildings in 23 acres. Went comprehensive
1971; opted out of council control 1989;
annual funding equivalent to £2,700 a pupil.

Atmosphere Sternly traditional: uncompro-
mising dedication to hard work, hard play;

highest standards of behaviour and dress insisted upon; big emphasis on service to the community. 'Mission' is to produce boys who are 'confident, able and responsible'. 'The impact and effect of the school on your son through his formative years will be profound and permanent,' says the prospectus – and it is not difficult to believe. Not all can take the pressure; expulsions not uncommon. Highly supportive parents; loyal, committed staff; commercial sponsors fund 100 bursaries for those whose 'work and motivation is consistently excellent'.

The head Leads from the front. Formerly a Dominican friar; started his teaching career lecturing on the Old Testament at Liverpool College of Education; has extensive experience of comprehensive schools. 'We are aware of developments around us,' he told parents recently. 'The anxiety to perpetuate moral confusion leads some schools to wish to foist on children accounts and descriptions of all manner of marginal human experiences. I am deeply concerned that amorality has assumed for these people the proportions of dogma.' Warmer, more affable than that might imply. Married, 1 daughter.

The teaching Generally formal; all pupils streamed by ability; classes of 28-30. Science taught as 3 separate subjects; good results in maths, English, Russian; French less impressive. All work carefully checked (and rewarded with house points); homework rigorously monitored. Big emphasis on technology, vocational education, links with industry, work experience, careers advice. Very strong music: half learn an instrument; orchestra, bands, ensembles; 5 concerts a term. Extra-curricular activities include chess, debating, cadet force, charity fund-raising. Regular language trips to France, Germany and Russia.

The pupils 180 a year carefully selected from the 600 who apply; no tests but parents – from a relatively affluent catchment area – required to demonstrate that their expectations and 'pattern of life' are in harmony with the school's expectations. Fairly wide range of abilities.

Results GCSE: 53% gain at least 5 grades

A-C. A-level (1991): 34% of entries graded A or B.

Destinations Most stay on for A-levels and proceed to higher education (3 to Oxbridge in 1991).

Sport Very strong, particularly rugby and cricket; also athletics, cross-country, swimming, water polo, tennis; all expected to participate. Facilities include fine indoor pool.

Remarks Old-fashioned public school without the fees.

QUEEN ELIZABETH'S GRAMMAR Blackburn
Blackburn BB2 6DF
Tel (0254) 59911

Independent • Boys (plus girls in sixth form) • Day • Ages 8-18 • 1,224 pupils (1098 in senior school) • 365 in sixth form (72% boys) • Fees, £2,499-£3,180 Head: Philip Johnston, 56, appointed 1978.

First-rate academic school; good teaching and results; strong sport.

Background Founded 1509 as a chantry school by the second Lord Derby (the present Lord Derby is the school's Visitor); re-established as a grammar school 1567 (continuous records of governors' meetings from 1590); Direct Grant from 1944 to 1976, when it reverted to full independence. Moved to present 6-acre site and dignified purpose-built premises 1882; extensive later additions; everything immaculately maintained.

Atmosphere Traditional values, high expectations, dedicated teaching. Discipline strict but humane; civilised (if slightly formal) relations between staff and pupils; work ethic clearly respected. Assemblies genuinely Christian, with a real sense of reverence. Evidence everywhere of the school's long history (portraits of former heads, photographs of sports teams, a cupboard full of silver trophies fit for the Tower of London).

The head Immensely energetic, totally dedicated, very professional: would be awe-inspiring if it were not for his sense of humour and frequent self-deprecation. Strides about the place, gown billowing in the wind, exchanging pleasantries, administering admonishments. Scholar at Manchester Grammar; read history and theology at Cambridge and did a research degree at Oxford (half Blue in lacrosse); appointed head of a grammar school at 33. Both a traditionalist and a visionary; constantly pondering ways of improving the school (whose flourishing reputation owes much to him). Committed Christian. Married, 2 grown-up children; wife teaches maths here part time.

The teaching Hard-working, highly qualified staff of 96 (22 women – 2 with PhDs in science); good mixture of didactic teaching and pupil involvement; well-ordered classrooms. Standard grammar-school curriculum; choice of 3 separate sciences or dual award; Latin, Greek on offer to A-level; Italian, Spanish, Russian available as alternatives to French and German; good computing (but the school does not make a fetish of it). A-level choice of 22 subjects, including design/technology, economics, politics, drama. No streaming by ability; setting in most subjects from second year of senior school. Average class size 30, reducing to 18-20 for GCSE, 12-14 in sixth form. Fine music (strong links with neighbouring cathedral): 10% learn an instrument; large orchestra, brass ensemble, string quartet, jazz group. Well-supported Duke of Edinburgh award scheme and Scout group. Regular exchanges with schools in France, Germany.

The pupils Keen, courteous, smartly uniformed. Drawn from a wide variety of backgrounds from all over north-east Lancashire and beyond (coach service has 74 pick-up points); more than 200 on assisted places; nearly 25 Asian (school is more socially representative than most inner-city comprehensives). Virtually all aiming for degree courses and the professions. School is over-subscribed;

entry by tests in English, maths, intelligence; no interviews for fear of favouring those from privileged homes and pushy schools.

Results GCSE: 96% gain at least 5 grades A-C. A-level (1992): 55% of entries graded A or B.

Destinations 95% stay for A-levels; 95% of these proceed to higher education (about 25 a year to Oxbridge).

Sport Very strong, particularly in soccer and swimming. Athletics, golf, croquet, tennis etc also on offer. Facilities include 16 acres of playing fields (near by), sports hall, superb indoor pool.

Remarks Fine, well-run school; highly recommended.

QUEEN ELIZABETH GRAMMAR
Wakefield
Northgate,
Wakefield,
West Yorkshire WF1 3QY
Tel (0924) 373943

Independent • Boys • Day • Ages 11-18 (plus junior school on same site) • 750 pupils • 180 in sixth form • Fees, £3,339 Head: Robert Mardling, 48, appointed 1985.

Traditional grammar school-type education. Good results; strong sport. Highly regarded locally.

Background Charter dates from 1591. Main buildings 1854; handsome Victorian Gothic (stone staircases, wood panelling). Untidy additions in mixture of styles on rather cramped inner-city site. Strong links with Wakefield Cathedral, for which it is the choir school.

Atmosphere Unpretentious, well-ordered; everyone seriously engaged but without stress.

The head Humane, kindly; takes great pride in school's reputation.

The teaching Sound; high standards of work and conduct expected; bright boys excel. Choice of 19 subjects at A-level (courses run jointly with neighbouring girls' school); half take sciences; all do general studies. Maximum class size 28, reducing to 22-24 for GCSE. Homework strictly monitored with parents' co-operation. Good music; more than 40% play an instrument; choir, orchestra, wind band, swing band (much in demand for functions outside school). Duke of Edinburgh's award scheme popular. Much charity work.

The pupils Fairly wide ability range (IQs 105+); admission to both junior and senior school by tests in English, maths, verbal reasoning. Largely from middle-class, professional homes but a quarter pay less than full fees – assisted places, bursaries, scholarships (including choral). Most from 20-mile radius.

Results GCSE: All gain at least 5 grades A-C. A-level (1992): creditable 63% of entries graded A or B.

Destinations 80% to higher education (approximately 12 a year to Oxbridge).

Sport Voluntary but more than half take part. Strong rugby, hockey, cricket, athletics (all produce county players). Playing fields a short walk away.

Remarks High-quality rounded education in a caring atmosphere.

QUEEN ELIZABETH'S HOSPITAL
Berkeley Place,
Bristol BS8 1JX
Tel (0272) 291856

Independent • Boys • Day and boarding • Ages 11-18 • 482 pupils (83% day) • 110 in sixth form • Fees, £3,324 day; £5,835 boarding
Head: Dr Richard Gliddon, 52, appointed 1985.

Very traditional academic school; good results; generous help with fees; enthusiastic music and sport.

Background Founded 1590 as a 'shelter for the children of the poor' on the model of Christ's Hospital *(qv)*; generous endowment enables the school to offer places to able and worthy boys irrespective of financial considerations (more than half receive help with fees). Moved 1847 to present city-centre site; austere Victorian-Gothic buildings (known as Colditz) plus 1970s additions arranged around a large, paved quadrangle (excellent for lunch-time soccer); fine new theatre and technology centre. Formerly Direct Grant; reverted to full independence 1976.

Atmosphere Formal but friendly; school small enough for every child to be known well; high standards of conduct and appearance expected (boarders wear Tudor Bluecoat uniform of clerical bands and saffron socks). Full daily assemblies; 'marshall' announces head's entrance to lunch; Saturday morning lessons retained. Good boarding accommodation for seniors but cramped for juniors (up to 6 sharing a limited space).

The head A conservative rather than an innovator; sees himself as a 'custodian of timeless values'. Read zoology at London; PhD from Bristol; taught at Winchester and, for 17 years, Clifton. Gets on well with staff; children respond to his friendly manner (and ability to recall important facts about their lives).

The teaching Generally traditional in style; academic success high on the agenda (governors set A-level performance targets in each subject). Long-serving staff of 36, nearly all men. Mixed-ability classes (sizes range from 22-28); some setting in maths, French. Lively English (making good use of superbly equipped 250-seat theatre); first-rate results in maths, physics, German. Enthusiastic music and art. Regular language exchanges with schools in Bordeaux and Hanover.

The pupils Polite, respectful; from diverse backgrounds, some quite under-privileged (more than a third have assisted places). Admission by entry exam shared with Bristol Grammar and Bristol Cathedral (old 11+ standard); parents state first choice; 2 or 3 apply for each place.

Results GCSE: virtually all gain at least 5 grades A-C. A-level (1992): 41% of entries graded A or B (has been higher).

Destinations 80% stay for A-levels; nearly all of these proceed to higher education (a few a year to Oxbridge).

Sport Good rugby and cricket (county honours); athletics, sailing, rowing etc also on offer. 14 acres of playing fields plus well-appointed modern pavilion a 10-minute bus ride away.

Remarks Successful, old-fashioned school.

QUEEN ELIZABETH'S
Wimborne
Wimborne Minster,
Dorset BH21 4DT
Tel (0202) 885233

Comprehensive (voluntary-controlled) •
Co-educational • Ages 13-18 • 1,381
pupils (roughly equal numbers of girls and
boys) • 378 in sixth form
Head: Simon Tong, 49, appointed 1987.

*Good, forward-looking comprehensive;
respectable results; strong music.*

Background 1971 merger of 15th-century

grammar school and 2 secondary moderns; functional post-war buildings on a lofty site on the northern edge of the town. Recent additions include design/ technology block, European business centre.

Atmosphere Mature, well-ordered: a school at ease with itself. Strong Anglican ethos; serious-minded, responsible pupils (no sign of graffiti or vandalism); supportive parents.

The head Read English at Cambridge; has taught extensively in the state sector. Keen on Renaissance Italy and old cars.

The teaching Broad curriculum; pupils set by ability in most subjects; extra help for those who need it, including the gifted. Staff of 94, half appointed by present head. Choice of 20 subjects at A-level; all do general studies; a third take 1- or 2-year vocational courses. First-rate music; orchestra, wind band etc. Regular language exchanges with schools in France and Germany; some sixth-formers do work experience in Dusseldorf.

The pupils Drawn from a large, semi-rural catchment area; most from 4 middle schools (ages 9-13) in Wimborne, Cranborne, Verwood and Colehill.

Results GCSE: 42% gain at least 5 grades A-C. A-level: 33% of entries graded A or B.

Destinations 65% continue into the sixth form; 60% of these proceed to higher education (a few a year to Oxbridge).

Sport Emphasis on sport for all; particular strengths in swimming, athletics, hockey. Extensive playing fields; school has day-time use of on-site council leisure centre.

Remarks Well-run, effective school.

QUEEN MARY'S GRAMMAR
Sutton Road,
Walsall WS1 2PG
Tel (0922) 720696

Grammar (voluntary-aided) • Boys (plus a few girls in sixth form) • Ages 11-18 • 672 pupils • 190 in sixth form (8 girls)
Head: Keith Howard, late-50s, appointed 1979.

First-rate, traditional grammar school; very good results; strong sport.

Background Founded 1554 by Mary Tudor; moved to present 12-acre campus in leafy south Walsall 1966; functional 1960s brick and glass buildings plus later additions, all scrupulously clean, tidy, well decorated.

Atmosphere Civilised, purposeful, secure; high morale; proudly traditional ethos. Eager, quick-witted pupils; no problems of attendance, time-keeping or discipline; relations with staff formal but friendly. Supportive parents raised £35,000 in 1991.

The head Decisive leader; direct, uncomplicated style; communicates well with staff and parents. Read modern languages at Cambridge. Lives over the shop and teaches French for 20% of the timetable; coaches rugby, sings in Lichfield Cathedral. Married, 4 children.

The teaching Wide range of styles; challenging, well-prepared lessons; plenty of pupil participation. Well-qualified staff of 42 (2 women), half appointed by present head. National curriculum-plus; science taught as 3 separate subjects; all do Latin; Greek on offer; top sets do German as well as French. Particularly good results in maths, science, design/technology, modern languages; first-rate facilities for computing. Pupils set by ability in French, maths, Latin; largest class size 32, reducing to 26 for GCSE, 15 in sixth form. All take 3 or 4 A-levels plus general studies. Homework meticulously set and marked. Good library: 18,000 volumes; full-time librarian. Plenty of music and drama; strong debating and chess; well-supported

cadet force. All first-years spend a week at school's field centre in North Wales.

The pupils Top 15% of the ability range drawn from 40 primary schools; 16% from ethnic minorities. Entry at 11+ by tests in English, maths, verbal and non-verbal reasoning; 5 apply for each place. Admission to sixth form requires at least 6 GCSEs grades A-C.

Results (1992) GCSE: 99% gained at least 5 grades A-C. A-level: creditable 52% of entries graded A or B.

Destinations 95% stay on for A-levels; 90% of these proceed to higher education (about 10 a year to Oxbridge).

Sport Chiefly rugby (county, regional, national honours), cricket (1992 tour of South Africa), hockey. Others include badminton, swimming, shooting. First-rate facilities.

Remarks Effective, well-run school.

QUEENS' Bushey
Aldenham Road,
Bushey,
Hertfordshire WD2 3TY
Tel (0923) 224465

Comprehensive •Co-educational • Ages 11-18 • 1,188 pupils (60% boys) • 154 in sixth form
Head: Mrs Mary Marsh, mid-40s, appointed 1990.

Widely respected school; hard-working, well-disciplined.

Background 1969 merger of 1930s red-brick grammar with 1960s flat-roofed secondary modern: they lie on opposite sides of a busy suburban road and are linked by a subway.

Atmosphere Relaxed, friendly – but with unusually high standards of discipline and courtesy. Pupils address staff as 'Sir' or 'Ma'am'. Saturday morning detention for persistent or serious offenders.

The head Geography graduate; has an MBA from London Business School; formerly deputy head of a progressive independent school. Wants to break down the boundaries between subjects, keen to build up industrial contacts. Mother of 4 boys.

The teaching Style is changing: more 'discovery learning', less traditional chalk-and-talk. Pupils streamed by ability after diagnostic screening; progress carefully monitored. Lots of computers (all receive a thorough grounding in first year); electronic mail links with schools abroad (including Russia). Choice of 24 subjects at A-level plus wide range of vocational courses, especially business studies. First-rate careers guidance (contacts with 140 local employers) Good music: over 50% learn an instrument; regular orchestral concerts Community service for sixth-formers: helping in school for mentally handicapped, gardening for the elderly etc.

The pupils Mixed social backgrounds but mostly from middle-income homes all over Watford. Heavily over-subscribed (25 apply for each place – priority to siblings, geographical proximity etc). Strong house-based pastoral system (house badges and ties) ensures no one gets lost.

Results GCSE: 37% gain at least 5 grades A-C. A-level: 22% of entries graded A or B (below the national average).

Destinations Just under half stay on into the sixth form (rest to further education colleges or jobs) .

Sport Football, hockey, cricket, netball tennis, athletics. 25 acres of playing fields.

Remarks Popular school now in transition under energetic new head.

QUEEN'S Chester
City Walls Road,
Chester CH1 2NN
Tel (0244) 312078

Independent • Girls • Day • Ages 4-18 • 580 pupils (420 in senior school – planned to rise to 500) • 120 in sixth form • Fees, £1,872-£3,264
Head: Miss Diana Skilbeck, 50s, appointed 1989.

Outstanding school; excellent results.

Background Founded 1878; became Direct Grant in the late 1940s; independent since 1976. Original Victorian building (within city walls) much modernised and extended; pleasant classrooms. Prep and junior departments 5 minutes away by car.

Atmosphere Hard-working but not frenetic; high standards achieved without evident stress; friendly staff-pupil relations.

The head Patient, warm, good humoured. Gets on well with staff, pupils and parents; ensures all pulling in the same direction. Was deputy head of a comprehensive, then head of another independent girls' school. Proud of her exam results but emphasises importance of 'educating the whole person'.

The teaching Extremes of academic competitiveness discouraged; girls urged to make the most of their own potential (no class rankings). No streaming, very little setting (within narrow ability band). All take 8-9 GCSEs; Latin and Greek on offer, also French, German, Spanish, Italian. Lots of computers but technology introduced only recently and science labs are outdated. Choice of 17 subjects at A-level; most do 3 plus general studies. Well-qualified staff of 46 (5 men). Average class size 24; 12 or fewer at A-level. Lots of music ('mainly for pleasure'); choir, 2 orchestras etc. Drama, opera, debating with neighbouring King's School *(qv)*. Extensive links with local hospitals, old people's homes, school for disabled children; much fund-raising for charity.

The pupils Cheerful, self-confident. Mainly from business, professional, farming backgrounds; wide catchment area (radius 40 miles). Strict uniform, relaxed for the sixth form (but no sartorial extremes). Admission at 4 by assessment interview; at 8 and 11 by tests in English, maths, general knowledge (designed to probe intellectual promise and 'willingness to have a go'). All 11-plus entrants (140 apply for 72 places) expected to continue to A-level. Assisted places, some scholarships.

Results GCSE: all gain at least 5 grades A-C. A-level (1992): impressive 70% of entries graded A or B (demonstrating both the quality of the teaching and the accuracy of the selection procedure).

Destinations Nearly all continue into the sixth form; 85% of these proceed to higher education (7-8 a year to Oxbridge).

Sport Hockey, lacrosse, tennis, athletics. Playing fields over the road; swimming pool at the junior department.

Remarks Busy, successful school; deservedly held in high regard.

QUEEN'S Taunton

Taunton,
Somerset TA1 4QS
Tel (0823) 272559

Independent • Co-educational • Day and boarding • Ages 12-18 (plus associated junior school) • 466 pupils (60% boys; 65% day) • 147 in sixth form • Fees, £4,980 day; £7,620 boarding
Head: Christopher Bradnock, 49, appointed 1991.

Good academic school; strong music and sport.

Background Founded 1843; run by the Board of Methodist Colleges and Schools. Moved to present semi-rural site on southwestern outskirts of the town 1846; grounds shared with pre-prep and junior school. Gloomy Victorian premises plus later additions (including fine hall and science block), some rather cramped.

Atmosphere Purposeful, busy; girls and boys served equally well. Comfortable, well-run boarding houses.

The head Cambridge-educated; formerly deputy head of a Methodist independent school in Harrogate. Keen musician and sportsman. Married, 3 children.

The teaching Generally sound; variety of styles; pupil participation encouraged. Broad curriculum; emphasis on English, maths, French; good design/technology. Pupils streamed by ability up to age 14, setting thereafter; extra help for those with special needs, including dyslexia; class sizes vary from 10-26. Choice of 18 subjects at A-level, including business studies, politics, Latin, Spanish; vocational alternatives under consideration. Enthusiastic music: nearly half learn an instrument. Well-supported Duke of Edinburgh award scheme.

The pupils Cheerful, polite, well-disciplined; mostly from middle-class/professional/Service families. Admission to junior school at 8 by tests, after which entry to senior school is automatic; admission to senior school by Common Entrance and interview; school is not unduly selective. 70 assisted places, some scholarships.

Results GCSE: 86% gain at least 5 grades A-C. A-level (1992): 45% of entries graded A or B (has been higher).

Destinations Nearly all stay on for A-levels; 82% proceed to higher education (4 a year to Oxbridge).

Sport Good record in rugby, cricket, tennis, netball, hockey, fencing. Facilities include 40 acres of playing fields, sports hall, squash courts, indoor pool.

Remarks Good all round.

QUEENSWOOD

Shepherd's Way,
Brookmans Park,
Hatfield,
Hertfordshire AL9 6NS
Tel (0707) 52262

Independent • Girls • Boarding (a few day)
• Ages 11-18 • 400 pupils • 110 in sixth
form • Fees, £9,210-£9,600 (£6,075 day)
Head: Mrs Audrey Butler, mid-50s,
appointed 1981.

---

*Small, lavishly equipped school. Fairly
wide ability range; respectable results;
everything on offer.*

Background Founded 1894; moved to stunning Green Belt site 1925. Elegant, mostly purpose-built premises in 420 acres of rural seclusion close to London.

Atmosphere Idyllic, quintessentially English.

The head Combines realism and vision, humour and dedication. Keeps staff on fairly tight rein. Believes there will always be a market for the best in single-sex education.

The teaching Unashamedly traditional; each year-group divided into 3 streams graded by ability. French, German, Spanish taught largely by native speakers (and lacking nothing in gadgetry). Elaborate facilities, also, for science: state-of-the-art lab/classrooms can switch smoothly from didactic to experimental mode. (Good GCSE results in languages and combined science: nearly all get As or Bs). Wide range of options at GCSE and A-level – despite school's relatively small size. Computer network reaches into every corner; lots of electronics. 50 highly qualified staff (12 men); normal class size 18-20. Very high standard of coursework (perhaps too high, given the time that must go into it?) Impressive art department (proper teaching, no sign of self-indulgence). Music can justly claim to be 'a vital force': 6 full-time members of staff, 17 visiting teachers, 24 sound-proof practice rooms. More than half learn at least 1 instrument; 2 orchestras, various ensembles, 3 choirs (Queenswood Singers have performed in Ba-

varia and Moscow). Head very keen on international contacts: European exchanges, delegation to Model UN Assembly in The Hague, expedition to Ecuador etc.

The pupils Lively, articulate; appear to appreciate how lucky they are and to make the most of it. Entry at 11, 12, 13. Fairly wide ability range: school says 'no special skills required except motivation to make good use of opportunities offered'. Stiff competition for 5 academic, 2 music, 2 tennis scholarships. Small number of 'day boarders'; planned increase to 80. Upper sixth have own study-bedrooms.

Results GCSE (1991): 99% gained at least 5 grades A-C. A-level (1992): 40% of entries graded A or B.

Destinations 80% continue into the sixth form; 90% of these proceed to higher education (5-6 a year to Oxbridge).

Sport Superb facilities (even aerobics has its own room); 16 tennis courts, immense sports hall, heated indoor pool, splendid gym (regarded as outdated and about to be gutted and re-designed). Hockey and tennis particularly good.

Remarks No one here lacks for anything.

RADLEY

Abingdon,
Oxford OX14 2HR
Tel (0235) 520294

Independent • Boys • Boarding • Ages
13-18 • 600 pupils • 120 in sixth form •
Fees, £10,350
Head: Richard Morgan, 52, appointed
1991.

---

*Fine, traditional boarding school;
first-rate teaching; superb facilities.*

Background Founded 1847; beautiful buildings in 800 idyllic acres (some laid out by 'Capability' Brown) 5 miles south of Oxford.

Atmosphere Very traditional; elaborate rules and customs; first-years ('shells') take 2 weeks to learn a whole new vocabulary. All boys wear short hair and academical gowns; any tempted to be different are reminded of a previous head's dictum, 'Suede shoes lead to drug abuse' (10 expelled recently for cannabis). Seniors complain it is like a very large prep school. Compulsory chapel 5 times a week; all given a pocket Bible when they join. Eight boarding houses ('socials'); older boys have own bedsits. Good food in oak-panelled dining hall (complete with high table and portraits).

The head (Warden) Relentlessly enthusiastic; firm disciplinarian ('If there is no discipline there are no standards'). Read economics and law at Cambridge; taught here for 15 years and then became head of Cheltenham, where he stayed 12 years. Keen to 'pioneer change', in particular: raise academic standards, put technology at the centre of the curriculum, 'forge links with Europe' (teachers encouraged to spend 3 hours a week studying French) and make all boys do 2 weeks' community service in the summer holidays (a cause of some resentment). Describes himself as a 'strong churchman' and would like to make chapel compulsory for the staff. Married, 3 daughters.

The teaching Every department has its own suite of rooms and specialist library; most have built-in audio-visual equipment; many have computer rooms attached (with dedicated software). The teachers, however, are exceptionally able and keen and quite capable of capturing the interest of a class of potentially rather rebellious boys with nothing more than a blackboard and a piece of chalk (which is not to say that they do not make imaginative use of the glittering array of aids at their disposal). The classrooms are also conducive to learning; carpeted and full of natural light. National curriculum-plus; science on offer as 3 separate subjects; setting by ability in maths, languages. Work marked with grades and copious comments; detailed reports to parents. All take 10 or 11 GCSEs and 3 A-levels plus general studies and religious education; non-linguists must do an AS-level in a modern language.

Facilities for technology, art and music are outstanding. Compulsory cadet force.

The pupils Most are of average intelligence and come from upper and upper-middle-class homes 'where parents have traditional values'; many are sons of Old Radleians; catchment area stretches from Scotland to Cornwall. Early registration advised; waiting list currently for 2004. Admission by Common Entrance; average mark 55%-60%. Some scholarships.

Results GCSE: all gain at least 5 grades A-C. A-level (1992): very creditable 67% of entries graded A or B.

Destinations Nearly all stay on for A-levels; 90% proceed to higher education (18 a year to Oxbridge).

Sport Magnificent facilities include indoor sports complex (used by local schools and the community), heated pool (with a very deep end for sub-aqua diving), all-weather hockey pitch, 9-hole golf course, 20 hard tennis courts, athletics track, boathouse (130 boats) on the college's 4-mile stretch of river below Nuneham Courtenay; Beagle pack hunts twice a week during winter. Main activities: rugby (up to 20 teams fielded), rowing, cricket, tennis, athletics. Basketball, cross-country, judo, fencing, squash, fives, rackets also on offer.

Remarks Very good all round.

RANNOCH

Rannoch,
By Pitlochry,
Perthshire PH17 2QQ
Tel (0882) 632332

Independent • Co-educational • Boarding (and some day) • Ages 10-18 • 295 pupils (77% boys; 97% boarding) • 88 in sixth form • Fees, £7,725-£8,385 (£4,950 day) Head: Michael Barratt, 51, appointed 1982.

Fine outdoor school; magnificent setting; wide range of abilities; small classes.

Background Founded 1959 by 3 teachers from Gordonstoun *(qv)* on the character-building principles expounded by Kurt Hahn; splendidly isolated 120-acre Highland estate on the south shore of Loch Rannoch, 25 miles from the nearest town (surrounding countryside used as an adventure playground). Main building is an eye-catching mid-Victorian Scottish baronial mansion recently restored and redecorated; later additions include classroom and science blocks. Co-educational since 1983.

Atmosphere Happy, close-knit community. Regime still fairly robust but less rugged and spartan than it was: not, however, for the unadventurous or comfort-loving. Staff-pupil relations are excellent without being over-familiar (teachers get to know the children well out of the classroom). Some boys' boarding houses showing distinct signs of wear and tear; juniors enjoy few creature comforts; girls better provided for in new purpose-built accommodation. Good food.

The head Educated at St Andrews and Oxford; taught English at Epsom; formerly a housemaster at Strathallan. Committed to the Kurt Hahn traditions of service, self-reliance, character development. Married; wife much involved in the school (as are all staff spouses).

The teaching Younger pupils follow standard primary curriculum with emphasis on good grounding in English, maths, French plus computer studies, design/technology, drama, home economics, current affairs. Science taught as 3 separate subjects from age 13; German on offer in addition to French. Small classes (average size 14); pupils set by ability; extra help for those with special needs; progress carefully monitored. Nearly all take 7 Standard Grades from choice of 15 (English and maths compulsory); 85% stay on for an average of 35 Highers; a few take A-levels; class sizes vary from 5-12. Nearly half learn a musical instrument; regular informal concerts. Pupil-run services (in the Hahn tradition) include ambulance, fire, loch patrol, mountain rescue; well-supported Duke of Edinburgh award scheme (inspired by Hahn); impressive total of 400 gold awards achieved by 1991. Outdoor expeditions a regular feature of school life.

The pupils Confident, cheerful, refreshingly natural; varied backgrounds, including business, industry, farming, professions; 55% from Scotland, 10% foreign nationals. Entry from $10^1/_2$-12 by test and interview, at 13+ by Common Entrance. School is selective but not severely so; prepared to accept those with learning difficulties. Some scholarships.

Results Standard Grade: 48% gain at least 5 grades A-C. Highers: 32% of entries graded A or B. (A-level entry too small to be significant.)

Destinations 85% continue into the sixth form; 55% of these proceed to higher education (1 or 2 a year to Oxbridge).

Sport Chiefly rugby, netball, hockey, skiing, athletics. Soccer, cricket, sailing, canoeing, basketball, badminton also on offer. Facilities include extensive playing fields, sports hall, 3 all-weather tennis courts, 6-hole golf course, rifle range, heated pool.

Remarks A challenging but unstressful regime which breeds self-reliance. Good choice for less academically able children who enjoy the outdoor life.

READING
Erleigh Road,
Reading RG1 5LW
Tel (0734) 261406

Grammar (grant-maintained) • Boys • Day
and boarding • Ages 11-18 • 670 pupils
(85% day) • 181 in sixth form • Boarding
fees, £2,790
Head: Dr Peter Mason, 42, appointed
1990.

---

*Strong academic school; good teaching
and results; inadequate buildings and
facilities; strong sport.*

Background Founded 1486 (but roots go
back even further); refounded 1560 by Elizabeth I, who made its upkeep the reponsibility
of the borough of Reading. Moved to present
imposing premises 1871; later additions rather
less impressive; some classrooms in huts;
facilities limited. Opted out of council control
1991.

Atmosphere Civilised, purposeful. First-rate
teachers give freely of their time; pleasant,
courteous boys (in neat grey suits) recognise
their privileges and opportunities. Lessons on
Saturday mornings, games on Saturday afternoons. Supportive parents and Old Boys.

The head Grammar-school educated; took a
BSc and PhD in chemistry at Newcastle;
formerly head of department at Royal Grammar, Newcastle. Married, 2 children (1 a pupil
here).

The teaching National curriculum-plus; 3
sciences taught separately; all do Latin or
classical studies; German on offer. All take 10
GCSEs and at least 3 A-levels (from a choice
of 16) plus non-examined general studies
course. Setting by ability introduced from
third year; progress closely monitored. High-
quality art and design (despite limited facilities); lots of drama; up to 25% learn a musical
instrument; 2 orchestras, large chapel choir.
Well-supported cadet force; sixth-formers do
community service in local primary schools,
old people's homes. Regular overseas trips.

The pupils Very able; IQs range from 120-

140+. Day boys from up to 40 miles away;
boarders nationwide; full spectrum of social
backgrounds and parental occupations.
School heavily over-subscribed; 93 admitted
annually at 11+ and 10 at 13+ by tests in
English, maths, reasoning.

Results (1992) GCSE: 98% gained at least 5
grades A-C. A-level: disappointing 39% of
entries graded A or B (has been much higher).

Destinations 92% stay on for A-levels; 80%
of these proceed to higher education (average
of 7 a year to Oxbridge).

Sport Plays an important part in the life of the
school; up to 14 teams fielded on Saturday
afternoons. Main games rugby, hockey,
cricket; tennis, squash, badminton, cross-
country, athletics, swimming, basketball, sailing, rowing also on offer. Restricted playing
fields; indoor pool.

Remarks Good school for able boys; grant-
maintained status will bring much-needed
improvements.

REDLAND HIGH
Redland Court,
Bristol BS6 7EF
Tel (0272) 245796

Independent • Girls • Day • Ages 4-18 •
655 pupils (475 in senior school) • 88 in
sixth form • Fees, £2,055-£3,165
Head: Mrs Carole Lear, 51, appointed
1989.

---

*Solid, traditional school; good teaching
and results; first-rate art.*

Background Founded 1882; handsome Georgian mansion plus later additions on a sprawling site; junior school across a busy main road.
Formerly Direct Grant; independent since
1982.

Atmosphere Calm, friendly, non-authoritarian (self-discipline rather than enforced rules);
a certain timeless quality.

The head Well-liked and respected. Appointed after 18 years here as head of classics and deputy head.

The teaching Fairly formal in style. Hardworking, largely female staff 'going along' with the national curriculum; computing and technology still in their infancy. Strong languages: French, German, Spanish; Latin on offer to A-levels; science taught as 3 separate subjects; chemistry particularly popular. First-rate art and craft department led by a husband and wife team; nearly all take art for GCSE. Good music: 40% learn an instrument; orchestra, 2 choirs. Well-supported Duke of Edinburgh award scheme. Regular language exchanges with pupils in France and Germany.

The pupils Happy, unpretentious; mostly from middle-class/professional families. All juniors proceed to senior school; joint entry exam (11+ standard) with Red Maids' and Colston's. Assisted places, scholarships available.

Results GCSE: 96% gain at least 5 grades A-C. A-level (1992): 44% of entries graded A or B.

Destinations Nearly all stay on for A-levels and proceed to higher education (3 or 4 a year to Oxbridge).

Sport All the usual games; good hockey, netball, cricket, cross-country; growing interest in rugby. Facilities include fine gym; playing fields a few minutes' walk away.

Remarks Unadorned, honest, hard-working.

RED MAIDS'
Westbury-on-Trym,
Bristol BS9 3AW
Tel (0272) 622641

Independent • Girls • Day and boarding • Ages 11-18 • 500 pupils (78% day) • 116 in sixth form • Fees, £3,420 day; £6,780 boarding
Head: Miss Susan Hampton, 50s, appointed 1987.

Solid school; good results; strong music.

Background Founded 1634 by John Whitson, merchant, for 'forty poor women children, daughters of Burgesses deceased or decayed', who were to 'go apparelled in Red Cloth' and be taught to read, do fine needlework and be trained in some useful trade. Moved to its present delightful 12-acre suburban site and purpose-built premises 1910; later additions include 7 well-equipped labs, well-stocked library, first-rate facilities for art, design/technology. Became fully independent with the abolition of Direct Grant status in 1976.

Atmosphere Friendly, civilised, well-ordered; hard-working girls anxious not to disappoint their teachers. 4 pleasant boarding houses; upper sixth have study-bedrooms.

The head Read maths at London; formerly deputy head of a Bristol comprehensive. Has introduced the national curriculum; teaches ancient history and general studies in the sixth form.

The teaching Range of styles. Well-qualified, long-serving staff (35 full-time, 18 part-time). Good languages; Spanish, Russian, Latin on offer from second year; choice of science as 3 separate subjects or integrated. No streaming by ability; setting in maths from third year; average class size 25. Most do 10 GCSEs (from choice of 20) and 3 A-levels (from 17). Strong music: two-thirds learn at least 1 instrument; good singing (choirs tour the Continent). Regular language trips to Bordeaux, Barcelona.

The pupils Competitive, articulate, unaffected;

most of average ability, some high-fliers. Catchment area covers Bristol, north Avon, south Gloucestershire, north Somerset; three-quarters join from primary schools. Entry by tests (shared with 5 other Bristol schools) in maths, verbal reasoning. Some scholarships, bursaries; 25 assisted places.

Results GCSE: virtually all gain at least 5 grades A-C. A-level (1992): creditable 62% of entries graded A or B.

Destinations 70% stay on for A-levels; 85% of these proceed to higher education (3 or 4 a year to Oxbridge).

Sport Girls encouraged to take part in hockey, netball, squash, badminton, tennis, athletics, gymnastics, fencing, swimming, cross-country. All facilities on site.

Remarks Pleasant, unpretentious school.

REPTON
The Hall,
Repton,
Derby DE6 6FH
Tel (0283) 702375

Independent • Co-educational (from 1992) • Boarding and day • Ages 13-18 • 583 pupils (86% boys; 80% boarding) • 260 in sixth form • Fees (1992-93) £10,440 boarding; £7,830 day
Head: Graham Jones, 47, appointed 1987.

Strong academic school; good teaching and results; first-rate art; outstanding sport.

Background Founded 1557 on the site of an Augustinian priory dissolved by Henry VIII. Fine village location, historic buildings, spacious grounds, excellent facilities. School has become fully co-educational to stave off falling numbers (and hopes to expand to 650 pupils); £3-million building programme includes 2 girls' boarding houses.

Atmosphere Strong sense of tradition and

purpose; all aware that great things are expected of them. Powerful house system; housemasters are key figures and have considerable autonomy. Recent appeal to parents and former pupils raised £1 million.

The head Read economics at Cambridge; formerly a housemaster at Charterhouse. Exudes a fine combination of traditional courtesy and modern pragmatism.

The teaching Hard-working, well-qualified staff of 70 (26 Oxbridge graduates), all expected to play a full part in the life of the school. National curriculum-plus; science taught as 3 separate subjects; all take 9/10 GCSEs. Average class size 20. Choice of 22 subjects at A-level, including Latin, Greek; all take at least 3, plus general studies; best results in maths, economics. First-rate art (2 artists-in-residence) and music; 25 learn an instrument; orchestra, choir. Well-supported cadet force and Duke of Edinburgh award scheme.

The pupils Very sure of themselves (and aware of being at a first-class school). Admission by Common Entrance; average 50% mark required. Assisted places; 20% hold academic, music or art awards.

Results GCSE: virtually all gain at least 5 grades A-C. A-level (1992): 49% of entries graded A or B.

Destinations Nearly all stay on for A-levels and proceed to higher education (10 to Oxbridge in 1991).

Sport Outstanding tennis; good record in cricket, football, hockey. Fine facilities include splendid new sports hall, 2 indoor tennis courts.

Remarks Produces both scholars and rounded individuals.

RICHMOND
Darlington Road,
Richmond,
North Yorkshire DL10 7BQ
Tel (0748) 850111

Comprehensive • Co-educational • Ages 11-19 • 1,168 pupils (roughly equal numbers of boys and girls) • 200 in sixth form
Head: James Jack, 45, appointed 1992.

First-rate comprehensive: does an outstanding job for pupils of all abilities.

Background Result of 1971 merger of grammar and secondary modern schools; roots go back to 14th century. Split site: juniors in former grammar school buildings by the River Swale (Lewis Carroll carved his initials on a desk). Main school on pleasant campus; buildings range from award-winning 1939 block to better-than-average 1960s and 1970s architecture. School expanding as catchment area grows.

Atmosphere Throbs with energy and enthusiasm. Strong sense of purpose; healthy emphasis on achievement, balanced by outward-looking community conscience. Everything spick-and-span: flowers in the reception area, bright classrooms, corridors full of pupils' work (there is pride here). Catering would put many a restaurant to shame.

The head Arrived May 1992 after successful headship in Cumbria. Intends to continue the tradition of excellence and expand the vocational side.

The teaching Sound methods adapted to individual needs; stimulus and challenge for every pupil. Good foreign languages; strong classics (60 do GCSE Latin). Well-qualified, dedicated staff. Class sizes average 25-30 to GCSE; 12 thereafter. Discipline firm but unobtrusive; homework carefully monitored. Lots of help for those with special needs. Business and technology courses offered as an alternative to A-level. Good music. Wide range of extra-curricular activities; accent on

service to the community (some prodigious feats of fund-raising).

The pupils Drawn from the whole community of Richmond and its hinterland; many from middle-class and farming backgrounds. Children are happy here – not because they have an easy life but because they succeed.

Results GCSE: 45% gain at least 5 grades A-C. A-level (1992): creditable 43% of entries graded A or B.

Destinations 45% stay on to do A-levels; 80% of them continue to higher education.

Sport Good soccer, rugby, netball, hockey. Excellent sports hall.

Remarks Successful, happy school; gets results, instils confidence. Competes strongly with the independent sector.

RIPON GRAMMAR
Clotherholme Road,
Ripon,
North Yorkshire HG4 2DG
Tel (0765) 602647

Grammar • Co-educational • Day and boarding • Ages 11-18 • 640 pupils (60% girls; 88% day) • 160 in sixth form • Boarding fees, £1,950-£2,700
Head: Alan Jones, 45, appointed January 1992.

Strong, traditional grammar school; good teaching and results.

Background Founded 1556 (but roots go back further – claims to be the oldest grammar school in England); moved to its present wooded site on the edge of the city in the 19th century. Mixture of Victorian buildings and functional later additions, many in need of refurbishment; old-fashioned labs; ageing furniture; some classrooms in huts. Became co-educational in 1962; now one of the few state schools to provide boarding for both boys and girls. Parents voted against opting out of council control.

Atmosphere Civilised, well-disciplined; a proud school conscious of its traditions; big emphasis on hard work and high academic standards; staff and prefects wear gowns. Modern boarding accommodation for girls (8-bed dormitories, seniors in single rooms); boys' house older, more spartan (but recently upgraded). Appetising meals served by friendly staff.

The head Pragmatic, purposeful. Has taught in both independent and state schools; formerly deputy head of a comprehensive in Berkshire. Keen to modernise the school (his predecessor was here 18 years) and widen the range of teaching methods. Married.

The teaching Academic, formal; largely traditional chalk-and-talk, but more up-to-date methods are being introduced. Able, long-serving staff (some here more than 20 years). National curriculum-plus; science taught as 3 separate subjects; all do 2 years' Latin (many take it for GCSE); Greek and German on offer. Most do 9 or 10 GCSEs from a fairly limited range; choice of 18 subjects at A-level, including good general studies course. Good library; professional librarian. Lots of music.

The pupils Friendly, articulate; from a fairly wide range of social backgrounds. Top 25% of the ability range; entry by county council's 11+ test and previous school reports; wide catchment area. Many boarders from Service families; some scholarships.

Results GCSE: virtually all gain at least 5 grades A-C. A-level (1992): 37% of entries graded A or B (has been higher).

Destinations 85% stay for A-levels; 75% of these proceed to higher education (a few to Oxbridge).

Sport Strong, particularly in rugby, hockey, athletics, cross-country. Facilities include extensive playing fields, first-class cricket pitch, good indoor pool, all-weather tennis courts (but no sports hall).

Remarks Old-fashioned grammar school; boarding is a 'best buy'

ROBERT GORDON'S

Schoolhill,
Aberdeen AB9 2PA
Tel (0224) 646346

Independent • Co-educational • Day (and some boarding) • Ages 5-18 • 1,205 pupils (895 in senior school; 80% boys; 98% day) • 258 in sixth form • Fees, £1,980-£3,050 (plus £3,600 for boarding) Head: George Allan, 56, appointed 1978.

Traditional school; fairly wide range of abilities; good teaching and results.

Background Founded 1732 by Robert Gordon, successful Aberdonian merchant, for the 'maintenance, aliment, entertainment and education of young boys'; classical 18th-century building plus many later additions on crowded city-centre site; new 5-storey block nearing completion. School is still expanding and recently acquired a 50-acre site 3 miles away. Became fully independent with the abolition of Direct Grant status in 1985; girls first admitted 1989.

Atmosphere Busy, well-ordered. Small boarding house 1 mile away; genuinely homely feel.

The head Came here as deputy head in 1973; previously taught classics at Glasgow Academy and Daniel Stewart's & Melville.

The teaching Well-qualified staff of 76 (22 women); senior school pupils streamed by ability; average class size 25. Broad curriculum; emphasis on maths, English; all do Latin, French. Most take 7 subjects at Standard Grade from a choice of 18, including accounting, German, Greek, graphic communication; 95% stay on to take 5 Highers (choice of 17); vocational alternative available; 86 return for a sixth year to do a variety of modular courses, repeat Highers or take the Certificate of Sixth Year Studies (CSYS); A-levels offered in accounting, biology, business studies, economics. Lots of drama and music; choir, orchestra and a variety of smaller ensembles, including thriving drum and pipes band.

Well-supported cadet force and Duke of Edinburgh award scheme.

The pupils Cheerful, friendly, well-turned-out (uniform for all). Most from professions and oil industry-related backgrounds. Entry at 5, 10, 12 by assessment or tests and interview. Fairly wide range of abilities.

Results Standard Grade: 93% gain at least 5 grades 1-3. Highers: 53% of entries graded A or B. CSYS: 40% of entries graded A or B.

Destinations 90% of those who take Highers proceed to higher education (2 or 3 a year to Oxbridge).

Sport Chiefly: rugby, hockey, cricket, athletics, tennis for the boys; hockey, netball, tennis, athletics for the girls. Facilities include 2 gyms, heated indoor pool on site; good playing fields and floodlit all-weather hockey pitch/tennis courts 3 miles away.

Remarks Highly regarded school; expanding with confidence.

ROEDEAN
Brighton,
East Sussex BN2 5RQ
Tel (0273) 603181

Independent • Girls • Boarding (some day girls in sixth form from September 1992) • Ages 11-18 • 475 pupils • 152 in sixth form • Fees (1992-93), £11,655 (£7,740 day) Head: Mrs Ann Longley, 50, appointed 1984.

First-rate boarding school for confident, able girls; strong community life; good teaching and results; fine facilities.

Background Founded 1885 by the 3 Lawrence sisters in strict imitation of a boys' public school: emphasis on games, competitive houses, fresh air, plain food, cold baths (corsets strictly forbidden). Moved 1899 to present Jacobean-style fortress in a commanding but exposed position on the Downs above Rottingdean; premises clean, functional, well-equipped but not luxurious. Former attics converted into modern teaching suites; recent additions include sports hall, design/technology workshops; theatre under construction.

Atmosphere Confident, dignified, unpretentious; clear expectations well understood by all (rules run to 50 pages). Traditionally rigorous regime has been softened and liberalised; more emphasis on individual care; but this is still no place for idlers. Staff-pupils relationships respectful but easy (in spite of the quaintly formal use of 'Madam' for female staff). Powerful house system creates fierce loyalties ('blood sisters'). Junior boarders in partitioned cubicles in long, light dormitories; 3 or 4 share at 13+; rest in double or single study-bedrooms. Choice of well-cooked hot food or salads.

The head Shrewd, warm, elegant, approachable. Educated at Walthamstow Hall and Edinburgh; formerly a head in the USA. Tremendously efficient; has done much to make the school more outward-looking and progressive. Widowed; grown-up children.

The teaching Quite formal; very professional. High-calibre, long-serving staff of 76 (15 men). Girls taught in house groups of 18-20 for first 3 years; setting by ability in maths, French, science (taught as 3 separate subjects). All do Latin for first 2 years; choice of German or Spanish. Big emphasis on hands-on experience: everyone tries out a stringed instrument, works in wood and plastics (girls have built a hovercraft and an electric car) and can take a certificate in computing. Most do 9 or 10 GCSEs and 3 A-levels; options include design/technology, ancient history, economics, theatre studies. Lots of drama, dance (nearly half take extra lessons) and music; orchestras, prestigious choir (Cecilian Singers) performs locally. Regular language exchanges with school in Paris.

The pupils Friendly, self-contained, serious-minded; perhaps less worldly-wise than some of their contemporaries but more intensely loyal to their friends. Living in a tight community fosters tolerance and mutual support, discourages loners and show-offs. Most come from fairly well-to-do professional or expatriate backgrounds; 20% from overseas. School is full – but only just. Admission by Common Entrance at 11, 12, 13; minimum 55% mark required (but sisters rarely refused entry). Admission from other schools to the sixth form (day girls being recruited for the first time) by interview and 6 GCSEs grade C or above. Academic, music, art scholarships.

Results GCSE: all gain at least 5 grades A-C. A-level (1992): creditable 59% of entries graded A or B.

Destinations All stay for A-levels; 80% proceed to higher education (a few to Oxbridge).

Sport Still taken seriously; compulsory grounding in tennis, lacrosse, hockey, rounders, netball; fencing, squash, badminton, cricket (county honours) also on offer. Splendid facilities include sports hall, indoor pool, 15 tennis courts

Remarks Fine school, not resting on its laurels. Solitary or off-beat individuals, or those with very strong home ties, might not settle easily.

ROYAL GRAMMAR Colchester
Lexden Road,
Colchester,
Essex CO3 3ND
Tel (0206) 577971

Grammar • Boys • Day (and a few boarding) • Ages 11-18 • 655 pupils (17 boarding) • 187 in sixth form • Boarding fees, £3,012
Head: Stewart Francis, 54, appointed 1985.

First-rate traditional grammar school; good teaching and results; strong sport.

Background Founded 1540; moved to present attractive site on the outskirts of the town 1853; Victorian buildings and later additions; much refurbishment and self-help redecoration.

Atmosphere Purposeful, calm, well-ordered. Strong grammar-school ethos; mutual respect between staff and pupils; smart uniform; no litter. Recently refurbished boarding house will accommodate 40 but demand is not strong, despite intensive marketing: B & B offered at £8.20 a night.

The head Insists on high standards from staff and pupils. Read classics at Cambridge; taught in both independent and state schools; formerly head of Chenderit, Banbury. Teaches Latin to first-years, English to second-years. Keen sportsman (cricket, hockey, Buckinghamshire County squash champion). Married, 2 grown-up children; wife teaches at local comprehensive.

The teaching Traditional in style. Well-qualified staff of 47 (8 women), nearly half appointed by present head; classes are mixed-ability (within a fairly narrow range). National curriculum-plus; Latin, Greek on offer; choice of French or German; most take 8-10 GCSEs. Some sixth-form teaching shared with Colchester County High School for Girls *(qv)*; choice of 21 subjects at A-level. Good drama and music. Well-supported Duke of Edinburgh award scheme. Extra-curricular activities include strong chess, bridge, debating. Regular language exchanges with pupils in France and Germany.

The pupils Happy and proud to be here. Top 10% of the ability range from a wide and diverse catchment area in north-east Essex. Entry by county council's 11+ test.

Results (1992) GCSE: 98% gained at least 5 grades A-C. A-level: creditable 53% of entries graded A or B.

Destinations Virtually all stay on for A-levels; 70% proceed to higher education (at least 8 a year to Oxbridge).

Sport High profile. Rugby, hockey, cricket played to a very high standard (mainly against independent schools); squash, badminton, golf, croquet also on offer. Facilities include extensive playing fields half a mile away, tennis courts, indoor cricket school, outdoor heated pool.

Remarks Well-run school; good all round.

ROYAL GRAMMAR Guildford
High Street,
Guildford GU1 3BB
Tel (0483) 502424

Independent • Boys • Day • Ages 11-18
(plus associated junior school) • 807
pupils • 240 in sixth form • Fees, £4,785
Head: Tim Young, 40, appointed
September 1992.

---

*First-rate academic school; very good
teaching and results; strong sport.*

Background Founded 1552 by Edward VI
'for the education, institution and instruction
of boys and youths in grammar at all future
times for ever to endure'; fine purpose-built
Tudor buildings in the High Street (in continuous use for 440 years); main teaching block
built 1965 now being extended and refurbished. Formerly maintained by the local
education authority, the school reluctantly
decided to become independent in 1977 but
aims to remain 'accessible to boys from all
backgrounds'.

Atmosphere Traditional, academic, purposeful; Oxbridge is the aim. High standards
of dress and behaviour (prefects held in
esteem); compulsory religious education and
Christian assemblies; competitive house system. Good pastoral care: trained counsellor on
hand to give confidential advice.

The head New appointment. Has spent
much of his life at Eton: was a pupil there;
returned to teach after reading history at
Cambridge (soccer Blue); became a
housemaster. Has also taught in California and
New Zealand. Married, 1 child.

The teaching Good quality. National curriculum-plus; all do Latin and German; Greek on
offer; science can be taken as 3 separate
subjects. Some setting by ability; progress
closely monitored. All do at least 9 GCSEs and

3 A-levels (from a choice of 21); maths,
economics, physics particularly popular; wide
programme of non-examined courses shared
with 2 neighbouring girls' schools. Lots of
drama and music; orchestra, several smaller
ensembles, choir. Well-supported cadet force
and Duke of Edinburgh award scheme.

The pupils Top 10% of the ability range;
mostly from middle-class families in a catchment area that extends to Ascot and
Petersfield. Entry at 11 by tests in numeracy,
literacy and IQ; at 13 by Common Entrance
(minimum 65% mark required); to sixth form
with 6 higher grade GCSEs; all candidates
interviewed. Scholarships and 20 assisted
places a year (not all taken up).

Results GCSE: virtually all gain at least 5
grades A-C. A-level (1992): creditable 65% of
entries graded A or B (has been even higher).

Destinations 90% stay on for A-levels; 95%
of these proceed to higher education (20-30 a
year to Oxbridge).

Sport Good record in rugby, hockey, cricket;
sailing 'almost embarrassingly successful', according to the head. Facilities include 20 acres
of playing fields 2 miles away; splendid modern pavilion.

Remarks Very good all round; highly recommended.

ROYAL GRAMMAR High Wycombe

Amersham Road,
High Wycombe,
Buckinghamshire HP13 6QT
Tel (0494) 524955

Grammar (voluntary-controlled –
grant-maintained from April 1993) • Boys •
Day and some boarding • Ages 12-18 •
1,125 pupils (95% day) • 370 in sixth form
• Boarding fees, £3,426-£4,560
Head: Rowland Brown, late-50s,
appointed 1975.

First-class academic school; good teaching and results; strong music and sport.

Background Founded 1562; moved to present 22-acre hill-top site and imposing purpose-built premises 1914; later additions opened by the Queen and the Princess of Wales.

Atmosphere Competitive, hard-working, well-ordered. Able boys; committed teachers; fairly formal staff-pupil relations. Supportive parents raise £20,000 a year for school funds; they voted in July 1992 to opt out of council control.

The head Very able. Read modern languages at Oxford; called to the Bar; taught at Hampton and Tudor Grange, Solihull; formerly head of King Edward VI, Nuneaton.

The teaching First-rate. Lively, challenging lessons; intelligent boys expected to assimilate information in their own time. National curriculum-plus; science taught as 3 separate subjects; all do Latin for at least 1 year; German or Spanish may be added to French. All do at least 9 GCSEs, including 2 sciences; sixth-formers take 3 or 4 A-levels from a choice of 23; extra coaching for Oxbridge entry. Wide range of extra-curricular activities (everyone finds something to shine at); lots of music (2 orchestras, jazz band, large choral society); well-supported cadet force; strong debating society. Regular exchanges with schools in France, Germany, Spain and USA.

The pupils Top 20% of the ability range, predominantly from middle-class homes in south Buckinghamshire commuter belt. Admission by tests, interview and previous school report; 2,000 apply annually for 180 places.

Results GCSE: virtually all gain at least 5 grades A-C (most achieve 9). A-level: impressive 53% of entries graded A or B (one of the top state schools in 1992).

Destinations 94% stay on for A-levels; 90% of these proceed to higher education (impressive 35 a year to Oxbridge).

Sport Chiefly: rugby (tours to France, Portugal, USA), hockey (tours to Holland, Germany), cricket, rowing, athletics, cross-country; other activities include tennis, fives, swimming, basketball, badminton, squash, golf, fencing, sailing, shooting. Facilities include superb sports hall, first-class cricket ground.

Remarks Everything a good independent school has to offer at no cost except for boarding.

ROYAL GRAMMAR Lancaster

East Road,
Lancaster LA1 3EF
Tel (0524) 381458

Grammar (grant-maintained) • Boys • Day and boarding • Ages 11-18 • 900 pupils (80% day) • 250 in sixth form • Boarding fees, £3,165
Head: Peter Mawby, 50, appointed 1983.

First-rate, selective school; good results; outstanding sport.

Background Founded 1472; one of the oldest and best-known schools in the north-west; opted out of council control 1990. Awkward site divided by crossroads on a hill overlooking the city. 19th-century buildings with later additions, many in need of upgrading; spartan classrooms (some in temporary huts); ageing furniture; no social areas. Recent appeal raised 650,000; substantial improvements under way; parents voted to opt out of local authority control in 1990.

Atmosphere Staff and pupils share a strong sense of pride in the school. Boarding element adds a public-school overtone to the grammar-school ethos. Accommodation cheerful, clean; single rooms for fifth and sixth-formers.

The head Consults widely (elected pupils allowed to grill staff, make recommendations); believes education is 'all about giving opportunities'. Has taught in independent schools on both sides of the Border; keen on rugby; plays squash to county standard.

The teaching Emphasis on high academic standards. National curriculum-plus; 3 separate sciences on offer (good labs); compulsory Latin in second year (40% continue it to GCSE); all sample Spanish, German or Greek in third year. Imaginative design/technology; excellent facilities. No streaming (within a narrow ability band) but setting in some subjects. Sixth-fomers encouraged to mix arts and sciences; 70% do so; good general studies course. Class sizes 30, reducing to 24 for GCSE, 12 for A-levels. Relations between staff and pupils relaxed but purposeful. Strong music and drama; active cadet force.

The pupils Open, friendly, well-behaved. Most (but not all) from middle-class backgrounds. Entry at 11+ by highly competitive tests (minimum IQ of about 118), school reports and recommendations. Most drawn from primary schools in Lancaster and Lune valley; boarders from Cumbria, parts of Lancashire.

Results (1992) GCSE: 98% gained at least 5 grades A-C (average tally 9.25). A-level: 45% of entries graded A or B.

Destinations 12-15 leave after GCSE; nearly all the rest proceed to higher education (about 12 a year to Oxbridge).

Sport Taken very seriously. Among the top dozen schools for swimming, athletics, cricket; not far behind in rugby. Sailing, rowing, indoor tennis also on offer; all boys (and most staff) take part in cross-country. Facilities include large sports hall; swimming pool built in 1886 (!)

Remarks Impressive school; strong roots in the local community; boarding an attractive option for those in the north-west without a grammar school on the doorstep.

ROYAL GRAMMAR Newcastle
Eskdale Terrace,
Newcastle-upon-Tyne NE2 4DX
Tel (091) 281 5711

Independent • Boys • Day • Ages 11-18 (plus associated junior school) • 950 pupils • 300 in sixth form • Fees (1992-93), £3,180
Head: Alister Cox, late-50s, appointed 1972.

Distinguished academic school; first-rate teaching and results; civilised environment; modest fees.

Background Founded 1525; moved to purpose-built neo-Georgian premises on a spacious site close to the city centre in 1906. Well-equipped buildings constantly up-graded and refurbished; grand assembly hall doubles as the school's main thoroughfare – and resembles a Roman forum at break-times.

Atmosphere A relaxed liberal establishment; confidence bred by academic success. Happy, hard-working staff and pupils; discipline based on mutual respect. Food (home-baked bread) is unusually good.

The head Relaxed, un-stuffy; says he 'approaches the middle ground of education from the liberal flank'. Still patently enjoying the job after 20 years in post; supported by a strong management team.

The teaching Full range of styles from traditional chalk-and-talk to group work: common thread is the involvement of pupils in discussion and debate. Well-qualified staff of 72 (12 women). National curriculum-plus; science taught as 3 separate subjects; all do Latin for at least 2 years; German, Greek on offer from third year. All do 10 GCSEs, including at least 2 sciences. Some setting by ability in English, maths, science; average class size 24, reducing to 15 for GCSE, 10 in the sixth form. Choice of 24 subjects at A-level, including computing, classical civilisation, design/technology, economics; all do at least 3. Lots of music; 3 orchestras, choirs. Wide range of extra-curricular activities, including flourishing cadet force.

The pupils Predominantly from middle-class homes all over the North East; 250 have assisted places, ensuring some social mix. Entry at 11 and 13 by interview and tests; school heavily over-subscribed and competition is keen.

Results GCSE: virtually all gain at least 5 grades A-C. A-level (1992): creditable 64% of entries graded A or B.

Destinations Nearly all stay on for A-levels; 85% proceed to higher education (up to 30 a year to Oxbridge).

Sport Wide range of activities on offer; regular county honours; rugby holds pride of place. Facilities include excellent on-site sports fields, swimming pool, gymnasia.

Remarks First-class school for able boys; highly recommended.

ROYAL GRAMMAR Worcester

Upper Tything,
Worcester WR1 1HP
Tel (0905) 613391

Independent • Boys • Day and a few weekly boarders • Ages 11-18 (plus associated prep school) • 765 pupils (15 boarding) • 182 in sixth form • Fees, £3,654 (£6,147 boarding)
Head: Tom Savage, mid-50s, appointed 1978.

Good academic school; strong sport.

Background Founded 1291; moved to present, cramped, city-centre site 1868; Victorian red-brick buildings plus later additions grouped round a quadrangle. Became a voluntary-aided grammar school in 1950; reverted to independent status in 1983 to avoid becoming a comprehensive.

Atmosphere Friendly, well-ordered. Boarding facilities basic but adequate.

The head Read modern languages at Cambridge. Teaches Russian and general studies; keen to foster European ties. Married, 2 children (1 was a pupil here).

The teaching Styles vary from traditional to modern ('from gowns to shirt sleeves'). Well-qualified staff of 64 (25% Oxbridge graduates), 80% appointed by present head. National curriculum-plus; science taught as 3 separate subjects (40% take all 3 to GCSE); languages on offer include German, Russian, Latin; strong maths (65% achieve grade A at GCSE); good facilities for computing, technology, art and design. Boys set by ability in maths, French, English; maximum class size 24. Wide choice of subjects at A-level, including business studies, design/technology, politics, geology. Lots of drama and music (often in conjunction with girls at neighbouring Alice Ottley, *qv*); well-supported cadet force, Duke of Edinburgh award scheme. Extensive programme of exchanges with schools in the USA, France, Germany, Russia.

The pupils Most from professional home backgrounds in a catchment area that includes

Hereford and the outskirts of Birmingham. Entry at 11+ by tests in English, maths, verbal reasoning; minimum IQ 110. Half join from associated prep school. Assisted places, scholarships, bursaries.

Results GCSE: virtually all gain at least 5 grades A-C. A-level (1992): 50% of entries graded A or B.

Destinations 90% stay for A-level; 90% of these proceed to higher education (8-10 a year to Oxbridge).

Sport First-rate, especially cricket (Imran Khan was a sixth-former here), rowing, cross-country; rugby, soccer, hockey also popular.

Remarks Good all round.

RUGBY
Rugby,
Warwickshire CV22 5EH
Tel (0788) 537035

Independent • Boys (plus girls in sixth form – becoming fully co-educational from September 1993) • Boarding and day • Ages 13-18 • 652 pupils (85% boys; 85% boarding) • 330 in sixth form (70% boys) • Fees, £10,725 boarding; £6,300 day
Head: Michael Mavor, 45, appointed 1990.

Distinguished school; good teaching and results; first-rate facilities; strong music and sport.

Background Founded 1567; moved to present site on the outskirts of the town 1750; early 19th-century battlemented buildings and many later additions – including, most recently, a fine sports hall and design centre – on 150-acre campus. Girls admitted to sixth form since 1976; when fully co-educational (in 1995), school aims to have 475 boys, 250 girls. (The change has not been universally welcomed – senior boys greeted the news with black armbands.)

Atmosphere Pervasive, compelling sense of history: the great Dr Arnold, immortalised in *Tom Brown's Schooldays*, is credited with inventing the modern public school here; William Webb Ellis first picked up the ball and ran with it, so inventing the game that bears the school's name. Air of calm, well-ordered, purposeful activity; emphasis on good manners, consideration for others (it has not always been so); adult relationships between staff and pupils. Boarding houses being up-graded (traditionally, they command strong loyalties but the head is keen to emphasise that Rugby is a school rather than a collection of houses).

The head Vigorous leader and innovator. Read English at Cambridge; taught at Tonbridge; formerly head of Gordonstoun. Strongly committed to co-education ('It shows boys and girls they can be friends'); emphasises the importance of 'having a go' and seeing things through. Likes fishing, playing the bagpipes. Married, 2 children.

The teaching Wide variety of styles, all lively, challenging; highly qualified staff of 77 (8 women), average age mid-40s. National curriculum-plus; science taught as 3 separate subjects; Greek, Latin, German, Spanish, Russian on offer; good design/technology; lots of computing. Meticulous attention paid to both oral and written work; pupils set by ability throughout; notable provision for special needs at both ends of the ability range; average class size 10-12. Most take 10 GCSEs and 3 or 4 A-levels; options include economics, business studies, ancient history, philosophy, politics, history of art. Music features strongly: 300 instrumental lessons a week; 2 orchestras, brass and swing bands. Lots of drama; plays taken to Edinburgh Festival. Well-supported cadet force and Duke of Edinburgh award scheme. Careers education taken seriously. Many language exchanges, visits, expeditions abroad.

The pupils Responsive, articulate, self-assured. Most from professional families; 15% ethnic minorities. Entry at 13+ by Common Entrance (minimum 55% mark required); to sixth form with 6 GCSEs grades A-C including As or Bs in A-level options. Academic, music, art, design scholarships.

Results GCSE: 95% gain at least 5 grades A-C. A-level (1992): 53% of entries graded A or B.

Destinations Nearly all stay for A-levels; 90% proceed to higher education (up to 25 a year to Oxbridge).

Sport Choice of 20 activities, coached and played to a high level. First-rate facilities include 80 acres of playing fields, all-weather pitch, sports hall, indoor heated pool.

Remarks Well-run school; very good all round.

RUGBY HIGH
Longrood Road,
Bilton,
Rugby,
Warwickshire CV22 7RE
Tel (0788) 810518

Grammar (grant-maintained from 1993) • Girls • Ages 12-18 • 560 pupils • 160 in sixth form
Head: Mrs Margaret Thornton, early-50s, appointed 1988.

Strong academic school; good teaching and results; lots of music.

Background Founded 1903; functional 1960s premises on a fairly restricted site on the outskirts of Rugby; later additions include fine music centre. Money is tight (the school deserves a better library); grant-maintained status should help. Meanwhile, there is a healthy air of make-do.

Atmosphere Well-ordered, purposeful, admirably earnest; school magazine reveals that the girls are concerned about pollution, deforestation, Third World poverty, homelessness, discrimination and 'what is the difference between eating animals and eating people?' Prize-winning wildlife garden ('vivarium') in the grounds underlines a strong practical interest in conservation. Some sixth-form teaching shared with neighbouring Lawrence Sheriff boys' school; the occasional youth strolling down the corridor is not seen as an invader from an alien planet.

The head Read maths at Oxford; has taught extensively in the state system; still teaches A-level maths for a third of the timetable. Sees her girls as future leaders, top managers and artistic creators; bridles at any suggestion that they might settle for subordinate roles. Married, 2 daughters (1 a pupil here).

The teaching High academic standards expected and achieved. National curriculum-plus; all do Latin for at least the first 2 years; German on offer from second year in addition to French; science taught as a 'combined' subject to make room for other priorities; good design/technology and computing. Some setting by ability for GCSE; average class size 30. Choice of 18 subjects at A-level; best results in maths. Strict homework policy; parental co-operation expected. Lots of music: 2 orchestras, 2 choirs; regular performances. Art taken seriously. Good work experience programme. Much fund-rasing for charity. Annual language exchanges with schools in France and Germany.

The pupils Entry at 12+ by county council-administered tests; top 20% of the ability range from a largely middle-class catchment area.

Results (1992) GCSE: 93% gained at least 5 grades A-C. A-level: 47% of entries graded A or B.

Destinations 75% stay on for A-levels; virtually all of these proceed to higher education.

Sport Not compulsory but nearly all participate. Regular county honours in hockey, netball, tennis, athletics. Facilities include on-site playing fields, heated outdoor pool.

Remarks Well-run traditional grammar school; highly regarded by parents.

SADDLEWORTH
High Street,
Uppermill,
Oldham OL3 6BU
Tel (0457) 872072

Comprehensive • Co-educational • Ages
11-18 (11-16 from 1993) • 1,301 pupils
(roughly equal numbers of girls and boys)
• 128 in sixth form
Head: John Hodgkinson, 40s, appointed
1989.

*Good, well-run school; wide range of
abilities; strong music and sport.*

Background Opened 1911; became a secondary modern in 1974 and a comprehensive in
1980. Will lose its sixth form through council
re-organisation in 1993 (to the sorrow of many
staff). Bleak, functional buildings (enlivened
by pupils' artwork) on a pleasant hilly site;
school is poorly resourced.

Atmosphere Welcoming, stimulating; pupils
take pride in the school (they helped to draw
up the code of conduct and clearly respect it);
high standards expected at all times; attendance averages 94%. Strong local feel; many
teachers send their own children here; supportive parents; good links with the community.

The head Modern manager; go-ahead without being trendy. Read geology at Sheffield;
formerly head of a comprehensive in Colchester. Married, 2 sons.

The teaching Dedicated, enthusiastic staff
get the best out of a genuinely comprehensive
intake. National curriculum with a European
flavour: French, German, Spanish all on offer;
regular language exchanges with European
schools. Good facilities for design/technology,
computing; GCSE options include new course
in business information studies. Extra help for
those with special needs, including some who
are severely disabled. Strong music tradition: 3
choirs; brass band voted the best in Oldham in
1991 (no mean achievement in this area).
Ambitious extra-curricular programme includes first-rate Duke of Edinburgh award
scheme.

The pupils Wide range of abilities and social
backgrounds from a 5-mile radius. School
heavily over-subscribed; no entry tests of any
kind; priority to siblings and those living
nearest.

Results GCSE: 42% gain at least 5 grades
A-C. A-level: 34% of entries graded A or B.

Destinations Only 26% stay on into the sixth
form; 75% of these proceed to higher education (3 a year to Oxbridge).

Sport Plenty on offer: soccer, rugby, netball,
basketball, hockey, swimming, tennis, athletics, cross-country; regular county honours.
School has a sports hall but no swimming pool;
playing fields are inadequate.

Remarks Genuine comprehensive: every
child valued (and challenged).

SAWSTON
New Road,
Sawston,
Cambridge CB2 4BP
Tel (0223) 832217

Comprehensive • Co-educational • Ages
11-16 • 1,220 pupils (roughly equal
numbers of boys and girls)
Head: John Marven, 59, appointed 1970.

*Successful, happy school; good
teaching and results; lots of music and
sport.*

Background Opened 1930, the first of the
Cambridgeshire village colleges; serves as an
adult education centre for the area (choice of
150 evening activities); fully comprehensive
since 1974. Mostly single-storey functional
buildings scattered over a 30-acre semi-rural
site. Wheelchair access; unit for children with
partial hearing difficulties.

Atmosphere Hard-working, well-ordered,
supportive; strong sense of community; active

parent-teacher association. Size made less daunting by a good pastoral care system. Madrigal practices in the lunch break.

The head (Warden) Warm, low-key, avuncular; treats the pupils as responsible adults and counts on them to rise to the challenge; trusts the staff to get on with the job (the school is very much his creation). Read physics at London. Married, 3 grown-up children (2 were pupils here). Has a wait-and-see attitude towards opting out of council control: school functions well as it is.

The teaching Good. Long-serving staff, nearly all appointed by present head (half have been here more than 10 years); pupils sit in rows facing the blackboard (maximum class size 32); written work corrected promptly and helpfully; strict homework policy. National curriculum-plus; science taught as 3 separate subjects; all do 2 languages (from French, German, Spanish) for at least 2 years. All set by ability in maths, science from first year and in English, languages, geography, history from second year; top 2 sets take GCSEs a year early. Particular strengths in science and languages; good technology and computing. GCSE options include motor-vehicle studies, child development; further vocational courses planned. Strong learning support department for those with special needs, including slow readers. Well-equipped library. Music is a prevailing passion; vast number of choirs, orchestras, bands and smaller ensembles; regular public performances. Good careers advice; all do 2 weeks' work experience. Frequent foreign visits and language exchanges.

The pupils Full range of abilities: head reckons top 3 sets (out of 8) in each year group are grammar school standard; on the other hand, many in the 2 bottom sets gain no GCSEs grades A-C. Catchment area covers south Cambridgeshire as far as the Essex border; many university lecturers send their children here.

Results (1991) GCSE: 52% gained at least 5 grades A-C.

Destinations 60% go on to take A-levels; rest into training or jobs.

Sport Chiefly: rugby, soccer for the boys; netball, hockey for the girls; cricket, athletics, swimming, basketball, badminton, squash also on offer. First-rate facilities, including indoor pool.

Remarks Attractive, well-run school.

SEDBERGH
Sedbergh,
Cumbria LA10 5HG
Tel (05396) 20535

Independent • Boys • Boarding • Ages 11-18 • 470 pupils • 150 in sixth form • Fees (1992-93), £10,560
Head: Dr Roger Baxter, 50s, appointed 1982.

Good all round (losing its 'rugby and running' image); fairly wide ability range; beautiful setting.

Background Founded 1525; saved from dissolution by Thomas Lever, Master of St John's College, Cambridge, who persuaded Edward VI that the school was desperately needed 'in the North Country amongst the people rude in knowledge'; reconstituted 1874, from when many of the buildings date; 1960s additions. Vast campus encircling the town; marvellous views over the Cumbrian hills. Teaching facilities lack for nothing; first-rate library; graceful assembly hall; lovely chapel.

Atmosphere A robust, manly sort of place; regime now more humane than it was but echoes remain of a rigorous tradition of cold baths, 10-mile runs, tough rugby, firm discipline (motto, *Dura Virum Nutrex* – 'a hard nurse of men'). Powerful house system (prefects and fairly strict rules); 7 pleasant houses; juniors in dormitories of up to 12; seniors have small bed-sits. Adequate food.

The head Scientist; lectured at Sheffield University until the age of 30, then switched careers by going to Winchester, where he became Second Master (deputy head). Quiet, charming, determined style; has toned down the school's traditional image; liked and respected by the staff. Married; wife plays double-bass in the school orchestra.

The teaching Mainly formal in style; experienced, long-serving staff. National curriculum-plus; science taught as 3 separate subjects from third year (all 3 compulsory to GCSE); most do French and German, a few Greek; good computing. Pupils streamed by ability; additional setting in some subjects; maximum class size 24, reducing to 16 for GCSE, 10-12 in sixth form. All do 10 GCSEs and 3 or 4 A-levels (from a choice of 16) in addition to a general cultural course; 25%-30% take sciences; best results in classics, maths, geography. Good music in well-equipped centre; numerous choirs, orchestras and a dashing marching band.

The pupils Mostly from the North and Scotland. 25 a year enter at 11 from state primaries after tests and interview; 60 join at 13 from prep schools via Common Entrance; school is not unduly selective. Numerous scholarships, bursaries, assisted places.

Results GCSE: 97% gain at least 5 grades A-C. A-level (1992): modest 35% of entries graded A or B (has been higher).

Destinations Nearly all stay on for A-levels; 85% proceed to higher education (up to 10 a year to Oxbridge).

Sport Very strong (many international coaches on the staff); first-rate rugby and cricket; annual 10-mile cross-country. Fine facilities include sports hall, indoor pool, tennis and squash courts.

Remarks Suits active, gregarious boys with academic potential.

SEVENOAKS
Sevenoaks,
Kent TN13 1HU
Tel (0732) 455133/4

Independent • Co-educational • Day and boarding • Ages 11-18 • 910 pupils (60% boys; 65% day) • 400 in sixth form (equal numbers of girls and boys) • Fees (1992-93), £6,264 day; £10,305 boarding Head: Richard Barker, early-50s, appointed 1981.

Attractive academic school; strong international flavour (International Baccalaureate offered as an alternative to A-levels); good music, art, drama; enviable facilities.

Background Founded 1418; mainly 20th-century buildings on fine 100-acre campus bordering Knole Park. The International Centre (opened 1962) attracts 50 nationalities; girls first admitted 1978; school now fully co-educational. First-rate facilities include observatory, theatre, recording studio.

Atmosphere Lively, purposeful, well-ordered (rules strictly enforced); head claims school runs on adrenalin. Strong academic emphasis; good pastoral care system. Pleasant boarding houses (one dating from 1718).

The head Charming, astute. Read economics at Cambridge; taught at Marlborough for 17 years (pioneered business studies courses). Keen on staff appraisal; likes to keep teachers on their toes ('It's the teachers' job to develop the children, mine to develop the staff'). Married, 3 grown-up children; wife teaches here part-time and helps on the pastoral side.

The teaching Modern approach; emphasis on getting pupils to think about concepts and how to apply them rather than on learning by rote. Committed, hard-working staff of 130. National curriculum-plus; many take 3 languages (from French, German, Spanish, Russian, Latin, Greek – others can be provided); good facilities for electronics, computing. Pupils streamed by ability; most able take GCSE maths, French a year early; all do 9-10 GCSEs;

plenty of term-time trips and exchanges to break up the school routine. Sixth-formers choose between A-levels and the more academically demanding International Baccalaureate (head keen to encourage European and international awareness). Strong music; more than a third learn an instrument; choirs, orchestras, smaller ensembles; regular concerts. Good art (annual summer festival) and drama; frequent productions. Well-supported cadet force (girls and boys), Duke of Edinburgh award scheme, voluntary service.

The pupils Bright, confident, articulate. Seniors, who have some involvement in decision-making, complain the school is 'too public-relations oriented'. Entry at 11 by tests, interview and previous school reports (minimum IQ 115 – grammar-school standard – required); at 13 by Common Entrance, reasoning test and interview; at 16 by GCSE, tests and interview. Assisted places and generous 60 scholarships a year.

Results GCSE: virtually all gain at least 5 grades A-C. A-level and International Baccalaureate (1992): very creditable 59% of entries graded A or B.

Destinations Nearly all continue into the sixth form and proceed to higher education (25-30 a year to Oxbridge).

Sport Wide range on offer; good record in cricket, rugby; girls play mainly hockey and netball. School is among the top 5 in tennis, shooting and sailing. Also on offer: golf, athletics, squash etc. Good facilities, including sports centre, all-weather track.

Remarks Successful, innovative school for bright, capable children. (The more average may feel neglected.)

SEXEY'S
Cole Road,
Bruton,
Somerset BA10 0DF
Tel (0749) 813393

Comprehensive (grant-maintained) •
Co-educational • Boarding and day •
Ages 11-18 • 398 pupils (equal numbers of girls and boys; 75% boarding) • 197 in sixth form • Boarding fees, £3,150
Head: David Charman, 49, appointed 1989.

Unusual boarding comprehensive; wide range of abilities; good teaching and GCSE results.

Background Founded 1638 by Sir Hugh Sexey, chancellor to Elizabeth I; moved to present attractive site 1891; pleasant, mellow buildings plus well-designed later additions; some huts. Girls admitted 1977; went comprehensive 1978; opted out of local authority control 1991. All pupils board between ages of 11 and 16.

Atmosphere Friendly, hard-working (sixth form constitutes half the school). High standards of effort and behaviour expected and achieved; good pastoral care system. Boarding accommodation varies from ancient ('Oh, God – they didn't show you Cliff House, did they!') to modern; small dormitories, some partitioned; sixth-formers have study-bedrooms; seniors do their own laundry and ironing. Good food served cafeteria-style in central dining hall.

The head Relaxed, informal. Educated at Oxford; worked for the British Council; taught in Australia; formerly head of geography at Eastbourne. Married; wife much involved in school life.

The teaching Good quality. Thoughtful, committed staff (60% men), one third appointed by present head. Broad curriculum; all do French, Latin; German also on offer; science taught as 3 separate subjects. Choice of 23 subjects at A-level; strong business studies; first-rate modular maths course. Reports home every 4 weeks; grades for effort. Extra help for dyslexics. Strong choral tradition.

The pupils Wide range of abilities and social backgrounds; 30% of boarders from Service families. Admission at 11 by previous school reports; school over-subscribed; priority to those likely to benefit from boarding education. No minimum qualifications for entry to sixth form – which acts as a centre for neighbouring secondaries – but those taking A-levels need 4 GCSEs grades A-C. Financial help available for Somerset residents.

Results GCSE (1992): creditable 78% gained at least 5 grades A-C. A-level (1991): modest 18% of entries graded A or B.

Destinations 80% continue into the sixth form; many proceed to higher education.

Sport Good; wide variety of activities on offer; emphasis on participation.

Remarks Sound, sensible school; boarding is a bargain.

SHEFFIELD HIGH
10 Rutland Park,
Sheffield S10 2PE
Tel (0742) 660324

Independent • Girls • Day • Ages 11-18
(plus associated junior school) • 520
pupils • 120 in sixth form • Fees, £3156
Head: Mrs Margaret Houston, 40s,
appointed 1988.

Sound school; respectable results.

Background Founded 1878; member of Girls' Public Day School Trust; moved to present purpose-built Victorian premises in quiet, residential setting 1884; later additions include science labs, art and music centre; junior school on same site. Gracious collection of well-maintained buildings.

Atmosphere Busy, composed; friendly relations between staff and pupils. Separate as-

semblies for Christians, Jews and Muslims. Strongly supportive parents.

The head Calm, cordial, determined. Read English at Leeds; previously deputy head of a comprehensive in Harrogate.

The teaching National curriculum-plus; all do Latin; science taught as 3 separate subjects; German added to French from second year; Spanish, Russian, Greek on offer. Most take at least 8 GCSEs; choice of 23 subjects at A-level; all do general studies.

The pupils Largely from professional/managerial families in a wide catchment area, including Barnsley, Chesterfield, Retford, Doncaster. Juniors progress automatically to senior school; others take tests in English, maths, verbal reasoning; potential to gain good GCSEs required. Assisted places, bursaries.

Results GCSE: most gain at least 5 grades A-C. A-level (1992): 44% of entries graded A or B.

Destinations Most stay on for A-levels; 65% proceed to higher education.

Sport Chiefly netball, hockey, tennis. Facilities include all-weather games pitch.

Remarks Safe, traditional girls' school.

SHERBORNE
Abbey Road,
Sherborne,
Dorset DT9 3AP
Tel (0935) 812646

Independent • Boys • Boarding (and some day) • Ages 13-18 • 650 pupils (96% boarding) • 260 in sixth form • Fees, £10,545 (£8,025 day)
Head: Peter Lapping, 51, appointed 1988.

Old-fashioned school; good results; strong music and sport.

Background Origins date back to 8th century (links with Benedictine Abbey); re-founded

1550 by Edward VI. Venerable buildings grouped around a vast gravel quadrangle; later additions include good modern languages and computing block; art/technology centre planned.

Atmosphere Extremely traditional. High standards of behaviour expected; boys required to adapt to school's routines, to 'roll up their sleeves and get on with it'. 'We establish ground rules and parameters which do not shift easily with the latest fashion,' the prospectus proclaims. 'Most Old Boys are decent, hard-working, unpretentious men who take nothing for granted.' Current pupils take this philosophically; enthusiasm is out of fashion here. Strong religious ethos (Abbey links retained); compulsory chapel. Lessons on Saturday mornings. 10 boarding houses scattered round the town, some in need of refurbishment: each has its own strong identity; housemasters are powerful figures; careful choice advised. Chaplain acts as independent, confidential adviser. Juniors in dormitories (up to 7 beds); most sixth-formers have study-bedrooms (but personal privacy can be hard to find). Cafeteria service in central dining hall; reasonably good food.

The head Rather dry; pleasant but remote. Educated in South Africa and at Oxford; taught history at Loretto; formerly head of Shiplake. Married, 2 children.

The teaching Formal, very academic; few signs of new ideas. Best GCSE results in maths, English literature, languages (choice of French, German, Spanish) history, geography; good facilities for computing but little enthusiasm for it among many staff. Boys streamed by ability; additional setting in some subjects; average class size 22; regular grades for attitude and achievement. All do 8 or 9 GCSEs and 3 A-levels (some teaching shared with Sherborne Girls', *qv*); extra coaching for Oxbridge entry. Art good but narrow; lots of drama but it is not offered for GCSE or A-level. Strong music: more than half learn an instrument; 2 orchestras; large chapel choir. First-rate careers advice. Well-supported cadet force (90% choose it in preference to community service).

The pupils Hard-working, civilised. Most from the South West – an arc from Bristol to Portsmouth; rest from South East; mainly professional and Service backgrounds. Admission by Common Entrance – minimum 50% mark required – or school's own tests. Some scholarships; closed awards for sons of serving or former officers.

Results GCSE: all gain at least 5 grades A-C. A-level (1992): 55% of entries graded A or B.

Destinations Most stay on for A-levels and proceed to higher education (20-25 a year to Oxbridge).

Sport Wide range. Good cricket, rugby (1992 tour of South Africa), hockey, athletics, cross-country; regular county honours. Facilities include 50 acres of playing fields, all-weather hockey pitch, 20 tennis courts, sports hall, indoor pool.

Remarks Solid school, one of the last of a dying breed: no girls, no weekly boarders, very few day boys. Has a curious sense of being 'on hold'.

SHERBORNE GIRLS'

Sherborne,
Dorset DT9 3QN
Tel (0935) 812245

Independent • Girls • Boarding (and some day) • Ages 12-18 • 450 pupils (98% boarding) • 150 in sixth form • Fees, £9,225 boarding (£6,150 day)
Head: Miss June Taylor, 49, appointed 1985.

First-rate academic school; very good teaching and results; strong sport.

Background Founded 1899; imposing Victorian buildings plus elegant modern additions on 40-acre site on the outskirts of the town; strong links with Sherborne Abbey and Sherborne Boys' *(qv)*.

Atmosphere Purposeful, pleasant – but not

overly welcoming: a school you need to settle into; good manners and self-discipline taken for granted; girls and staff share high expectations. Religion is important; daily prayers and Sunday service compulsory. 8 large, civilised boarding houses; comfortable dormitories, most with single cubicles. Good food; vegetarians catered for.

The head Quiet, dignified; previously a pupil here ('I arrived with the furniture'). Read maths at Sussex then came back to teach in 1966.

The teaching Relaxed in style but challenging; lively, hard-working staff (60% women); girls here to learn – and they intend to. Art, English, French, home economics, physics particularly well-taught; religious education compulsory throughout. Class sizes flexible: sometimes a large group of 20-30, sometimes much smaller, according to the demands of the subject. Facilities generous and up-to-date: satellite reception of foreign broadcasts keeps modern language teaching relevant and lively; outstanding provision for art, design/technology. Choice of more than 20 subjects at A-level. Termly reports on progress; 4 parents' meetings a year. Lots of drama and music; most learn an instrument. First-rate careers advice gets the girls thinking. Active community service; visits to the elderly and sick.

The pupils They work hard, play hard and clearly enjoy the school. Fairly narrow social mix, mainly the Services and professions. Admission by Common Entrance and previous head's report; girls must have sufficient academic potential for 3 A-levels – and enjoy boarding. Some scholarships.

Results GCSE: all gain at least 5 grades A-C. A-level (1992): impressive 66% of entries graded A or B.

Destinations Most stay on for A-levels; up to 90% proceed to higher education.

Sport Very important, and greatly enjoyed. Main activities: hockey, lacrosse, tennis, athletics; basketball, archery, fencing etc also on offer.

Remarks Hard-working, traditional school; highly recommended.

SHREWSBURY

The Schools,
Shrewsbury SY3 7BA
Tel (0743) 344537

Independent • Boys • Boarding and day • Ages 13-18 • 650 pupils (80% boarding) • 255 in sixth form • Fees, £10,125 boarding; £7,140 day
Head: Ted Maidment, 49, appointed 1988.

Distinguished school; steadily improving results; fine location.

Background Founded 1552 (like so many others) by Edward VI. *(When Edward the Sixth was a stripling/And Warwick believed him a fool,/The Severn went placidly rippling/Past Shrewsbury, lacking a school...)* Original town-centre building now the county library; moved 1882 to stunning 105-acre site on a bluff ('the greenest grass in England') overlooking an elegant bend in the Severn. Identified by the Victorians as one of the 9 'great' public schools (having come close to extinction in the 18th century under a succession of incompetent heads). Most famous Old Boy: Charles Darwin (who recalled his education there as 'simply a blank').

Atmosphere Warm, friendly – despite the Victorian austerity of some of the classrooms and many of the boarding houses.

The head Previously head of Ellesmere. Keen on European awareness and links with industry. Sings bass solo in Haydn's *Creation*.

The teaching 'The well-tried, traditional methods of teaching work best,' says the prospectus: results bear it out. Setting by ability from the start. All do 3 sciences (and achieve a useful level of computer literacy); religious studies compulsory to GCSE. Strong emphasis on practical work in technology and art. Choice of 20 subjects at A-level (including business studies rather than 'less practical' economics); computing and 1 foreign language compulsory for sixth-formers; optional courses range from public speaking to palaeontology. Lots of music: all instruments taught; 2 orchestras, jazz band, madrigal choir etc. Fine Jacobean library (with medieval manuscripts). Boys raise money for charity and help to run a community centre in the Everton district of Liverpool (consideration for others, within and beyond the school, is much encouraged).

The pupils Most (but not all) come from prep schools; minimum 55% mark required at Common Entrance. Up to 25 scholarships and bursaries a year (some for music and art). Catchment area nationwide but particularly the North-West, Midlands, Wales, Yorkshire. Powerful and competitive house system; careful choice advised.

Results GCSE: 95% gain at least 5 grades A-C. A-level (1992): creditable 61% of entries graded A or B.

Destinations 90% go on to higher education (25-30 a year to Oxbridge). Most popular career choices: law, medicine, industry, engineering.

Sport Long-standing reputation for soccer and rowing: well-equipped boat house; 300 row regularly; seniors spend up to 10 hours a week on the river. Spectacular cross-country event – the Hunt – is Shrewsbury's answer to Eton's Wall Game.

Remarks Busy, friendly, successful school; pupils encouraged to aim high.

SHREWSBURY HIGH
32 Town Walls,
Shrewsbury,
Shropshire SY1 1TN
Tel (0743) 362872

Independent ● Girls ● Day ● Ages 4-18 ● 611 pupils (395 in senior school) ● 73 in sixth form ● Fees, £2,424-£3,156
Head: Miss Susan Gardner, mid-40s, appointed 1990.

Small, happy school; popular with parents.

Background Founded 1885 by the estimable Girls' Public Day School Trust; moved to present site overlooking the Severn in 1897 (junior school across the river); many additions (labs, gym) to original Victorian buildings (largest classroom formerly a billiards room, technology housed above the stables). Became fully independent when Direct Grant status was abolished in 1975.

Atmosphere Domestic, self-contained, almost cosy.

The head Energetic; strong leader. Formerly deputy head of a London comprehensive. Teaches politics to the sixth form plus personal and social education.

The teaching Takes place in a relaxed and friendly atmosphere. All do Latin, French and German; technology less firmly established. 17 subjects on offer at A-level (bias towards arts and humanities); most taught in groups of 8 or fewer. Lots of music and drama. Lunch times busy with aerobics, singing, bread making, computing etc.

The pupils Bright, self-assured. Most start in the junior school; entry at 11 by tests in English and maths (lively, inquiring minds required). County-wide catchment area; many travel long distances. Assisted places, some scholarships and bursaries.

Results GCSE: 98% gain at least 5 grades A-C. A-level (1992): 59% of entries graded A or B.

Destinations The few who leave at 16 usually

continue full-time education elsewhere. Virtually all sixth-formers go on to higher education.

Sport Hockey, netball, athletics and, unusually, rowing (some in conjunction with Shrewsbury, *qv*).

Remarks Safe single-sex choice.

SIBFORD

Sibford Ferris,
Banbury,
Oxfordshire OX15 5QL
Tel (0295) 78441

Independent • Co-educational • Boarding and day • Ages 7-18 • 307 pupils (282 in senior school; 65% boys; 73% boarding) • 50 in sixth form • Fees, £6,000-£10,218 boarding; £2,625-£6,057 day
Head: John Dunston, 39, appointed 1990.

Attractive mixed-ability school specialising in dyslexic and less academically able children; first-rate vocational courses.

Background Founded 1842 by Society of Friends as a self-sufficient community growing its own food (horticultural tradition continues – rows of beautifully tended vegetables in tranquil walled garden). Cotswold stone manor house in delightful 70-acre estate plus slightly battered 1930s addition (institutional appearance relieved by colourful artwork). School was one of the first to recognise fully the needs of dyslexics and provide first-class support. Co-educational from the start; junior school opened 1989.

Atmosphere Gentle, informal, very relaxed; Quaker ethos fundamental (though only 10% are the children of Quakers). Individual achievement recognised and delighted in; pupils thrive in the supportive, encouraging atmosphere; no one here feels second best. Daily meeting based, in Quaker tradition, on silence; individuals encouraged to take responsibility for their own behaviour instead of having standards enforced by rigid rules; no prefects but sixth-formers expected to set an example. Girls board in original manor house (spacious, comfortable dormitories); boys in 3 functional 1960s buildings (juniors in 8-bed dormitories gradually progress to shared rooms); sixth-formers housed separately (boys at one end, girls at the other, dividing door locked at night). Meals served cafeteria-style in main dining room. Relaxed attitude to parents visiting.

The head Radiates enthusiasm and delight in his job; Jewish but totally in sympathy with the Quaker philosophy. Read French and German at Cambridge; formerly head of modern languages at Bancroft's. Believes strongly in the importance of building up confidence, in helping children who may have been thought 'failures' to recognise their strengths and value. Insists the school is not about easy options: children gain self-esteem through achieving appropriately challenging targets (hence the high-quality vocational education programme). Teaches French to the juniors and European studies to sixth-formers. Married, 2 young children.

The teaching Highly committed staff; variety of styles and approach; emphasis throughout on the needs of each child. Outstanding support for dyslexics (up to a third of any class) and those in need of extra help (no stigma here); dyslexia unit (a cosy suite of rooms in the heart of the school) has 5 full-time teachers (4 women); several other members of staff have attended dyslexia courses; pupils taught in small mixed-ability groups; setting in maths. Curriculum embraces usual academic subjects (including a foreign language) in addition to a wide range of practical courses (all equally valued and respected). For first 3 years all do textiles (boys learn to sew and iron), drama, music, design/technology, art, home economics, word processing (25% use laptop computers); most take 7 or 8 GCSEs; business studies on offer. The real departure comes after GCSE, when the more academic leave to do A-levels elsewhere. Here all take the 2-year City and Guilds diploma in vocational education, specialising in 1 of 5 vocational areas:

catering, retailing, care, horticulture, business; they may add an A- or AS-level (e.g. in English, textiles, design/technology), take an exam course in drama or sports studies and opt for extra studies in computing, conservation or word processing. All gain real 'hands-on' experience: in retailing, pupils buy for the shop, plan new lines etc; in catering, they lay on 'restaurant meals' several times a term. Regular reporting to parents; grades for effort every half term, full profile once a year. Thriving drama in small memorial theatre (links with Oxford Playhouse); fast-developing music; nearly a third learn an instrument, 3 choirs, ensembles. Usual range of extra-curricular activities, including Duke of Edinburgh award scheme.

The pupils Wide range of backgrounds and abilities; a third are dyslexic; for some, a few GCSEs at grade D will be an enormous achievement; others will gain a whole clutch of As. School does not take those who are both dyslexic and of low ability. Day pupils come from as far afield as Stratford and Oxford; some boarders from the Far East (English taught as a foreign language). Some children have official statements of special need and are paid for by local education authorities. Academic and music scholarships, bursaries.

Results Improving; more than 50% GCSE entries graded A-C.

Destinations About half continue into the sixth form; many of these proceed to agricultural, nursing or art college; a few go on to degree courses.

Sport Reasonable range on offer, including soccer, rugby, athletics, cricket for the boys; hockey, netball, tennis for the girls. Extensive, well-tended pitches; first-rate sports hall; heated indoor pool.

Remarks Extremely happy school which does wonders for many children who might not shine elsewhere. Highly recommended.

SILVERDALE
Bents Crescent,
Sheffield S11 9RT
Tel (0742) 369991

Comprehensive • Co-educational • Ages 11-18 • 1077 pupils (roughly equal numbers of boys and girls) • 200 in sixth form
Head: Mike Smith, 40s, appointed 1987.

Well-run but poorly funded. Enjoys strong parental and community support.

Background 1950s secondary modern; became a comprehensive and acquired a sixth form in the 1970s; last redecorated by Sheffield council in 1975. (Parents, however, voted against applying for grant-maintained status.)

Atmosphere Calm, well-ordered; teachers busy and cheerful.

The head Workaholic; strong leader; promoted from deputy head. Has published a tourist guide to Derbyshire.

The teaching Mixed-ability in the first year; streaming thereafter. Plenty of help for those with learning difficulties; no stigma in asking for help. Classes of 28, smaller for GCSE. Space at a premium; furniture ageing. Special unit for 12 profoundly deaf pupils, who spend half their time in mainstream classes (first-year pupils are instructed in 'deafness awareness'). Firm homework policy; strong links with parents, including home visits by teachers. Good contacts with local industry; work experience for all.

The pupils Co-operative, well behaved. No uniform but 'standard dress'. Catchment area predominantly middle-class/skilled artisan; places allocated by Sheffield council (100+ apply for 13 places available to applicants outside the catchment area).

Results (1991) GCSE: 65% gained at least 5 grades A-C (impressive for a non-selective school). A-level: 35% of entries graded A or B.

Destinations 65% stay on after 16; most of these proceed to higher education (4 to Oxbridge in 1991).

Sport Plays a big part in school life; all main games plus basketball, badminton etc.

Remarks Good school; deserves to be better accommodated and equipped.

SIMON LANGTON BOYS'
Langton Lane,
Nackington Road,
Canterbury CT4 7AS
Tel (0227) 463567

Grammar (grant-maintained) • Boys •
Ages 11-18 • 645 pupils • 150 in sixth form
Head: John Harris, 57, appointed 1977.

Popular, thoroughly traditional grammar school; good teaching and results; strong sport.

Background Opened (like its sister school, Simon Langton Girls' *qv*) in 1878 but foundation dates back to 13th century. Moved to present purpose-built premises (now battered and dingy) 1959; some classrooms in huts. Grant-maintained status (achieved January 1992) should lead to improvements.

Atmosphere Traditional, businesslike. Emphasis on good behaviour and manners; older boys take responsibility for younger ones. Many staff send their sons here (always a good sign). Supportive parents.

The head Educated at Cambridge; teaches English, Russian, French; coaches hockey, soccer; regrets that recent education reforms have driven heads into business management. Introduced the first annual exchange with a Russian school in 1988. Married, 3 grown-up children (1 was a pupil here)

The teaching Range of styles. Long-serving, hard-working staff of 44; no streaming by ability for first 3 years; some setting thereafter; maximum class size 32. All do French (and take it a year early for GCSE); Spanish, German, Russian also on offer; good design/technology; compulsory computing; strong science; half take GCSE maths a year early. All do 8-10 GCSEs and at least 3 A-levels (some courses shared with girls' school). More than a quarter learn a musical instrument; orchestra, brass band. All 13-year-olds spend a period in France. School owns a field studies centre in North Wales.

The pupils Wide social mix (some qualify for free school meals) from Canterbury and surrounding towns. Admission via 11+; grammar school standard required. School is popular with parents and fully subscribed.

Results (1991) GCSE: 87% gained at least 5 grades A-C. A-level: 43% of entries graded A or B.

Destinations 85% stay for A-levels; 80% of these proceed to higher education (6-8 a year to Oxbridge).

Sport Wide range; everyone receives basic coaching. Cricket and hockey particularly strong.

Remarks Good academic school.

SIMON LANGTON GIRLS'
Old Dover Road,
Canterbury,
Kent CT1 3EW
Tel (0227) 463711

Grammar (voluntary-controlled) • Girls •
Ages 11-18 • 850 pupils • 220 in the sixth form
Head: Trevor Conway, 59, appointed 1975 (retiring December 1992).

Hard-working, happy, well-regarded school; good academic record, especially in maths and science.

Background Founded 1881. Moved to present site (and ugly premises) 1950. Has had only 5 heads in 110 years.

Atmosphere Busy, friendly – despite tatty, cramped accommodation. Enthusiastic staff; strong team spirit. Pupils well behaved, responsible.

The head Appointed amid much local controversy (male head of an all-girls' school) at a time when it seemed the school would be forced to go comprehensive (1979 general election changed that). Softly spoken, self-deprecating; won the respect of his staff.

The teaching First-rate. No setting (within narrow ability band) except in maths, which enables cleverest girls to do GCSE a year early and then continue with AS-level; half of sixth form take A-level maths and nearly all get grade A. All do Nuffield combined science; A-level science popular. Good languages: French, German, Spanish, Italian, Russian; several teachers are foreign nationals. Small classics department kept ticking over. Nearly 70 staff, including part-timers (20% men – head likes the idea of strong female role models for girls). Homework timetabled and parents informed. Good music: half learn an instrument; orchestras, ensembles, jazz band, choirs. Lots of art, drama. $1\frac{1}{2}$-hour lunch break to allow time for clubs and societies; community service and Duke of Edinburgh award scheme popular. School was the first to arrange a pupil exchange with Russia – a regular feature ever since.

The pupils Well-motivated, outgoing; largely from middle-class families – daughters of doctors, local businessmen, university staff. Entry via Kent Selection Procedure (11+); heavily over-subscribed. Not the best-dressed school in town; sixth-formers excused uniform, anything goes (*en masse*, the effect is scruffy rather than outrageous). Some academic and social contact with Simon Langton Boys' *(qv)*.

Results (1992) GCSE: 98% gained at least 5 grades A-C. A-level: 43% of entries graded A or B (has been higher).

Destinations Nearly all proceed to higher education (10-12 a year to Oxbridge); some go straight into banking, insurance, retail management.

Sport Efforts being made to offer more than traditional games so as to involve more girls. Netball flourishes; growing demand for dance. No sports hall.

Remarks Well-run school doing a good job for able girls.

SIR WILLIAM PERKINS'S
Guildford Road,
Chertsey,
Surrey KT16 9BN
Tel (0932) 562161

Independent • Girls • Day • Ages 11-18 • 504 pupils • 100 in sixth form • Fees, £3,085
Head: Mrs Anne Darlow, late-50s, appointed 1982.

Strong academic school; good teaching and results; modern facilities.

Background Founded and endowed by Sir William Perkins in 1725; moved to present delightful 12-acre site 1828; Victorian building plus good modern additions; fully independent since 1978.

Atmosphere Friendly, business-like, down-to-earth. Good relations between staff and pupils.

The head Read history at London; formerly deputy head of Surbiton High. School has doubled in size under her leadership. Teaches civics to first-years, advises fifth-years on careers, discusses politics with the lower-sixth; knows her pupils well – and is tolerant with the more difficult ones.

The teaching Good quality. Pupils set by ability in maths, French from second year and in science – taught as 3 separate subjects – from third year. Three-quarters take German as second modern language; Latin also on offer; all do home economics, technology, computing for first 2 years. Compulsory GCSE core of English, maths, 3 sciences, religious education and PE plus 4 options. Maximum class size 20; all teaching areas spacious and well-equipped. Sixth-form options include Spanish, Russian; most popular A-levels are French, biology, chemistry, art (gifted teaching and good work in drawing, painting, sculpture). Lots of music (in substandard accommodation – new music school planned); 25% learn an instrument; 2 orchestras, 4 choirs. Well-supported Duke of Edinburgh award scheme, community service, charity fund-raising. Regular language exchanges with schools in France and Germany; work experience in Spain.

The pupils Wide social mix from a big catchment area. Entry by competitive tests at 11+ in English, maths; 200 apply for 88 places. Assisted places, some scholarships.

Results GCSE (1991): 96% gained at least 5 grades A-C. A-level (1992): very impressive 69% of entries graded A or B.

Destinations 80% stay on for A-levels (nearly all the rest to sixth-form colleges); 90% of these proceed to higher education (1 or 2 a year to Oxbridge).

Sport Chiefly hockey, tennis, athletics; badminton, netball, 5-a-side football also on offer. Facilities include modern sports hall, 6 tennis courts, large playing field (but no swimming pool).

Remarks Delightful, well-run school; good value for money.

SOLIHULL
Warwick Road,
Solihull,
West Midlands B91 3DJ
Tel (021) 705 4273

Independent • Boys (plus girls in sixth form) • Day • Ages 7-18 • 1,000 pupils • 269 in sixth form (75% boys) • Fees, £2,400-£3,400
Head: Alan Lee, mid-50s, appointed 1983.

Strong academic school; good teaching and results; flourishing music and sport.

Background Founded 1560; moved to present 50-acre parkland site 1882; later additions include elegant chapel, design/technology centre, £1-million junior school. All accommodation spacious, well designed, impeccably maintained. School gives away £300,000 annually in bursaries.

Atmosphere Hard-working, purposeful, well-behaved. Only 1 (all-embracing) rule: 'Members of the school shall in all circumstances conduct themselves in a proper and sensible manner'. 100% attendance at parents' evenings.

The head Effective leader; approachable, low-key, unobtrusive; inspires confidence. (The 35th head in the school's history; Dr Johnson's application in 1736 was rejected, the trustees being put off by his facial twitches.) History scholar at Cambridge; formerly second master at Rugby. Still teaches for a quarter of the timetable. Married, 3 sons; wife regularly listens to junior boys reading aloud.

The teaching Mixture of methods, all challenging, lively and admirably attuned to the needs of highly able pupils. National curriculum-plus; French from age 10, at least 1 year of Latin from 11, 1 year of German from 12; science taught as 3 separate subjects; all take 10 GCSEs (7 core, 3 options); timetable wizardry accommodates virtually all choice patterns. Little streaming by ability (within a fairly narrow band); average class size 24, reducing to 20 for GCSE, 12-15 in sixth form. Most do 3 A-levels plus general studies; 3 hours' homework required 5 nights a week. Impressive range of extra-curricular activities; strong drama, flourishing music: 3 orchestras, ensembles galore, chapel choir, choral society; frequent choral/organ scholarships to Oxbridge. Long tradition of community service.

The pupils Bright, responsive, confident, largely from professional families. Entry at ages 7-11 by tests in English, maths, verbal reasoning; minimum IQ 115. Half 11+ entry comes from junior school.

Results GCSE: virtually all gain at least 5 grades A-C. A-level (1992): 47% of entries graded A or B.

Destinations 85% stay on for A-levels; 90%

of these proceed to higher education (12 a year to Oxbridge).

Sport Wide choice, high standards (particularly in rugby), good facilities.

Remarks Well-run school; good all round.

SOUTH HAMPSTEAD
3 Maresfield Gardens,
London NW3 5SS
Tel (071) 435 2899

Independent • Girls • Day • Ages 11-18 (plus associated junior school) • 575 pupils • 150 in sixth form • Fees (1992-93), £4,020
Head: Mrs Averil Burgess, 54, appointed 1975 (retiring April 1993).

Distinguished, unashamedly academic school; fine teaching; very good results.

Background Founded 1876; flagship of the Girls' Public Day School Trust whose 26 members are renowned for offering a sound, no-nonsense, academic education to able girls (and for charging remarkably modest fees). Moved to present 'compact' site (as the prospectus calls it) in 1882; a mish-mash of buildings, cleverly slotted into a small area with no obvious rhyme or reason. Recent additions include science block with good-sized labs and a sports hall. Adjacent Victorian mansion houses sixth-form cafeteria and staff creche.

Atmosphere 'A scruffy little place' the head calls it, affectionately and almost proudly. True, it would never win a Keep Britain Tidy award: books are not usually in piles nor waste paper always in baskets, but girls cheerfully lug around black sacks full of cans for recycling, and adorn the walls and boards with posters and paintings in striking profusion. They clatter up and down stairs, round corners, through basements, with an occasional breath of air between buildings; there is no grass or open space to speak of, but the cramped conditions help foster the close network of relationships, the relaxed informality between pupils and teachers. Staff clatter up and down too, and no-one holds back for anyone else; everyone smiles and forges full speed ahead.

The head 'I've been here for nearly a third of my life and I'm clapped out,' was how she announced her decision to take early retirement after 18 distinguished years here. An institution, greatly respected and admired by staff, girls and Hampstead's notoriously awkward parents. Successor: Mrs Jean Scott, 51; formerly head of St George's, Edinburgh *(qv)*. Widowed, 2 grown-up children.

The teaching Exceptionally good. Hard-working, endlessly self-critical staff, desperate to do their best whilst having the intellectual self-confidence to cope with these bright girls and adapt to new ideas. The timetable is crammed full for the first 3 years; main complaint is shortage of time. All do computing; design/technology has a place (fighting for room with everything else instead of having a pleasure-dome built for it); classics still holding their corner; modern languages strong (German becoming more popular). All take 9-10 GCSEs, including dual award science. Good take-up of maths and science in the sixth form. Art is well taught and made available to all as a fourth A-level; it is fine-art orientated, and girls are encouraged to develop their own style. Music is also important; more than a third learn instruments ('cox and box', said the head of music, looking for somewhere for a group to practise). No streaming by ability; no form places or prizes except in the sixth form. Classrooms are pretty tight for space and there are not many up-to-date teaching aids like satellite TV, videos or language labs.

The pupils Tough, clever, competitive; they enjoy quick-fire verbal combat, yet are sensitive to each other's troubles. They perform well in national competitions – musical, dramatic, debating – and have a great deal of 'up-front' self confidence. Mainly from professional and academic homes in north and north-west London. School is heavily oversubscribed; entry by searching tests and interview. (Head says: 'Our intake is comparable with that of the old grammar schools; it ranges from the slightly above average to the well above average and the ability range in any class will in fact be quite wide.') Some assisted places, scholarships, bursaries.

Results GCSE: virtually all gain at least 5 grades A-C. A-level (1992): disappointing 58% of entries graded A or B (an unusually bad year – has been *much* higher).

Destinations 88% stay for A-levels; nearly all of these proceed to higher education (21 to Oxbridge in 1991).

Sport Does not have a very high profile (so little is available on site) but a wide variety of activities – particularly netball and tennis – are enjoyed at all levels.

Remarks An outstanding school with a proud tradition of liberal, non-denominational education; remarkable for its driving energy and freedom of spirit. Girls with brains and stamina will enjoy the ceaseless round of activity and striving.

ST AIDAN'S

Oatlands Drive,
Harrogate,
North Yorkshire HG2 8JR
Tel (0423) 885814

Comprehensive (voluntary-aided) •
Co-educational • Ages 11-18 • 1,350 pupils (slightly more boys than girls) • 460 in sixth form
Head: Dennis Richards, 47, appointed 1989.

Successful comprehensive; first-rate staff; strong sixth form.

Background 1968 merger of two Church of England secondary modern schools; became comprehensive in 1973; huge, ecumenical sixth form shared with a neighbouring Roman Catholic school. 1960s buildings plus 'temporary' huts on a spacious, wooded campus (sprinkled with picnic tables); particularly

good facilities for science, technology and drama; good library; everything meticulously clean and well cared for.

Atmosphere Strong Christian ethos; caring, family approach; new head has added an air of academic rigour and purposefulness. Friendly but not over-familiar relations between staff and well-behaved pupils.

The head Has degrees in modern languages and theology; formerly deputy head of a church school in Northamptonshire. Married; youngest daughter is a pupil here (as are the children of many members of staff).

The teaching Styles range from traditional 'chalk and talk' to group and individual learning. Academic standards are high but the staff, who have just the right blend of youth and experience, seem equally at ease with the middle-of-the-road and the less able. Standard national curriculum; particularly good work in technology, English and modern languages (all introduced to French and German); first-rate science taught as 3 separate subjects; computers used across the curriculum. Setting by ability in all subjects except religious studies (which all do for GCSE) and design; average class size 27. Choice of 21 subjects at A-level; half do at least 1 science; vocational alternatives include BTEC diploma in business and finance. Strong music and drama.

The pupils Clearly proud to be here. Intake is predominantly middle-class (from a wide catchment area) but genuinely comprehensive; many parents choose the school because of its success with the less able.

Results GCSE: 66% gain at least 5 grades A-C. A-level: 30% of entries graded A or B.

Destinations 70% continue into the sixth form; 90% of those who take A-levels proceed to higher education (about 6 a year to Oxbridge).

Sport Wide choice; strong soccer, cricket, basketball, athletics. Facilities include good on-site playing fields, all-weather track, sports hall, tennis courts.

Remarks Attractive school; all abilities catered for.

ST ALBANS HIGH
Townsend Avenue,
St Albans,
Hertfordshire AL1 3SJ
Tel (0727) 53800

Independent • Girls • Day • Ages 11-18
(plus associated junior school) • 510
pupils • 117 in sixth form • Fees, £3,777
Head: Miss Elizabeth Diggory, 46,
appointed 1983.

Sound, traditional academic school;
good teaching and results.

Background Founded 1889 by the Church
Schools Company (first pupils were the 8
daughters of local clergymen). Pleasant, purpose-built, red-brick premises and good-
quality later additions in a residential area near
the town centre; delightful junior school across
the road.

Atmosphere Happy, well-disciplined ('If the
rules weren't strict, people wouldn't be so
nice,' observed a second-year); friendly relations between staff and pupils. Not an academic hot-house but the girls are naturally
competitive. 'Christian teaching, based on the
doctrine of the Church of England, is fundamental to the life of the school, but we are by
no means exclusively Anglican,' says the prospectus. Traditional uniform strictly enforced
(no shirts out in summer).

The head Able, charming, forthright; consults widely with senior staff but is very much
in charge. Read history at London and taught
it for nearly 15 years at King Edward VI High,
Birmingham. Active Christian; decided to
become a teacher because she had 'got such a
big kick' out of being head girl (of Shrewsbury
High). President for 1992 of the Girls' School
Association (which represents most of the
independent girls' schools in this guide);
believes many – but not all – girls 'feel more
confident and grow into successful young
women when they are not subject to the
pressure of competition from boys during the
vulnerable years of adolescence'.

The teaching Generally traditional in style:
whole-class teaching but plenty of discussion
and investigative work, too. Well-qualified
staff of 40 (only 3 men), half appointed by
present head (who laments the fact that men
do not apply). National curriculum-plus; science taught as 3 separate subjects from third
year; all do Latin for at least 2 years and add
German or Spanish to French from third year
(more than half do 2 modern languages for
GCSE); all take art, music, computing for 3
years. Setting by ability in maths, French; class
sizes 26, reducing to 20 for GCSE, 10-12 in
sixth form. Most do 9 GCSEs and at least 3
A-levels (from a choice of 20) plus non-
examined courses in maths, computing, a
language and English. Maths and science are
particularly strong. Good drama and music;
joint orchestra with boys at St Albans School,
various smaller ensembles, 4 choirs. Regular
exchange with St Albans School, Vermont.

The pupils Lively, polite (they open doors for
adults, stand up in class); nearly all from
middle-class homes in an extensive
Hertfordshire/north London catchment area.
Half of 11+ entry comes from the junior
school; rest take tests in English, maths, verbal
reasoning and are discreetly observed ('to see
how they apply themselves') during a trial day;
minimum IQ 110 but head will go to 105 if a
girl seems well motivated and her parents
supportive. School is over-subscribed (by
about 20-30 a year) but is not as severely
selective as some of those it competes with
(such as North London Collegiate and
Haberdashers' Aske's Girls'). 10 assisted
places a year (not all taken up), some scholarships and bursaries.

Results GCSE: all gain at least 5 grades A-C.
A-level (1992): creditable 64% of entries
graded A or B.

Destinations 75% stay on for A-levels (rest
tend to move to co-educational sixth forms at
Haileybury, Oundle etc); nearly all of these
proceed to higher education (5 or 6 a year to
Oxbridge).

Sport Compulsory lacrosse; netball, tennis,
athletics, swimming, gymnastics, fencing also
on offer. Facilities include smart new sports

hall, outdoor pool; games field 10 minutes' walk away.

Remarks Attractive, well-run school.

ST AMBROSE
Hale Barns,
Altrincham,
Cheshire WA15 0HF
Tel (061) 980 2711

Independent • Roman Catholic • Boys • Day • Ages 5-18 • 800 pupils (650 in senior school) • 150 in sixth form • Fees, £1,599-£2,517
Head: Eric Hester, 50s, appointed 1991.

Catholic ethos; traditional grammar school-type education; generally good results. Remarkable value for money.

Background Founded 1946 by the Christian Brothers; has grown steadily in response to parental demand. Set in 27 acres of attractive parkland in Cheshire stockbroker belt; most buildings date from 1960s; recent additions include new prep school building, science labs, excellent music suite.

Atmosphere Quiet, courteous, civilised; but no sign of draconian discipline. Strong emphasis on moral and spiritual development; tradition of service to the sick and needy (annual trip to Lourdes). Marvellous choir sings Magnificat at morning worship.

The head Committed, traditional Roman Catholic; makes no excuse for pursuing excellence in all things; in favour of healthy competition and rewarding effort and achievement. Shrewd, very experienced (was head of Catholic comprehensive for 16 years). School's first lay head; clearly respected by staff; teaches A-level English. Married, 4 children, 2 grandchildren.

The teaching Methods vary – but no problems getting heads down for concentrated work. Pupils have freedom within well-understood limits: the teacher is in charge. No

streaming in first 2 years; setting by ability thereafter. Broad, demanding curriculum: nearly all take 11 GCSEs, none less than 10. Sciences taught as 3 separate subjects. Hard-working staff prepare lessons well, mark conscientiously. Maximum class size 30 in first 2 years; roughly 20 thereafter; smaller groups in sixth form. Daily homework. Strong emphasis on religious education: Catholic faith taught systematically and authentically.

The pupils Well behaved, responsible (sixth-form common room run by the boys is immaculate); refreshingly free of fashionable cynicism. Varied backgrounds: some from moneyed families, but two-thirds paid for by Trafford council after passing 11+; many assisted places. Attractive, expanding prep school filled with scrubbed, uniformed juniors. Entry at 4+ and 7+ by interview and assessment; at 11+ by tests in English, maths, verbal reasoning. No minimum IQ specified but roughly top 30% of the ability range.

Results GCSE: 85% gain at least 5 grades A-C. A-level (1992): disappointing 29% of entries graded A or B (has been higher).

Destinations Almost all prep school boys enter the senior school. 80% continue from GCSE to A-level; 85% of these proceed to higher education (about 10 a year to Oxbridge).

Sport All usual games; first-class facilities, including splendid, on-site playing fields, heated swimming pool. Good cross-country record.

Remarks Respected school, ambitious to do better; immune to fads and fashions.

ST BEDE'S
The Dicker,
Hailsham,
East Sussex BN27 3QH
Tel (0323) 843252

Independent • Co-educational • Boarding
and day • Ages 13-19 • 350 pupils (60%
boys, 70% boarding) • 130 in sixth form •
Fees, £9,150 boarding; £5,745 day
Head: Roger Perrin, 51, appointed 1978.

---

*Wide range of academic and
extra-curricular choices offered to pupils
of all abilities.*

Background Founded 1978 and grew rapidly; moved 1979 to Horatio Bottomley's Edwardian country home in Upper Dicker. School owns houses and 65 acres in the village. Some boarding houses and most classrooms in wooden huts – built on site by resident carpenters.

Atmosphere Polite, orderly, cosmopolitan (94 pupils from abroad). Pleasant dormitories and study-bedrooms; carpeted, curtained. Excellent food (choice of 5 main courses).

The head Has been here since the school opened (it is very much his creation). Teaches Latin and general studies for a quarter of the timetable. His wife, Angela, looks after the domestic side.

The teaching Large staff of 47 offer an impressive 29 subjects at GCSE, 25 at A-level. All introduced to 3 sciences, 2 languages (out of French, German, Spanish), computing, technology, home economics, religious, ethical and philosophical studies etc. GCSE policy is to 'prepare students for a useful number of subjects rather than a superfluous number'. Streaming by ability from the start; setting in English and maths. Average class size 15 but many taught in smaller groups. Extra help for dyslexics. High-quality art (abstract and life painting, pottery); expanding music (more than a third learning an instrument); well-equipped drama studio (pupils take Shakespeare to neighbouring prep schools). Choice of more than 80 extra-curricular activities a

week: fly-fishing, riding, jewellery making, vehicle maintenance, yoga, mountain biking etc.

The pupils Wide range of abilities, diverse backgrounds; admission on first-come basis. Up to 20 scholarships and bursaries a year. Boys in tweed jackets, girls in kilts.

Results GCSE: 49% gain at least 5 grades A-C. A-level (1992): modest 20% of entries graded A or B.

Destinations Two-thirds go on to higher education.

Sport 30 games to choose from (the school believes success in one of them could hold the key to a child's self-confidence). Good tennis (3 all-weather courts), swimming, athletics, judo. School uses the village soccer and cricket pitches in return for maintaining them.

Remarks Something for everyone; particularly recommended for less academically able.

ST BEDE'S COLLEGE
Alexandra Park,
Manchester M16 8HX
Tel (061) 226 3323

Independent • Roman Catholic •
Co-educational • Day • Ages 11-18 (prep
school on same site) • 940 pupils (60%
boys) • 300 in sixth form (65% boys) •
Fees, £3,198 (£2,019 in prep school)
Head: John Byrne, 45, appointed 1983.

---

*Serious, hard-working school;
academically selective, socially mixed.
Big emphasis on service to others.*

Background Founded 1876 by Bishop, later Cardinal, Vaughan. The only school to retain its independence when the Catholic secondary sector in Manchester was re-organised in 1976; now the second-largest of its type. Became fully co-educational 1986. Main building an impressive Victorian pile, originally designed as a museum: high, moulded ceilings; oak banisters; splendid, wide corridors. Many new additions, including science labs and well-equipped technology centre.

Atmosphere Everywhere a sense of quiet, purposeful endeavour and concern for the individual child. Catholic commitment pervasive but not obtrusive: the iconography of the faith, to be seen in the hall, corridors, and some classrooms, impresses rather than overwhelms. High expectations of personal behaviour and self-discipline; good manners the norm (children *always* hold doors open for adults).

The head Constantly about the place, begowned and eager to be involved. Grammar-school boy; read history at London, took master's degree at Birmingham. Committed, clear-sighted Catholic; determined to maintain the school's reputation in an increasingly secular and cynical world; insists pupils' outlooks should include a 'vision of eternity'. Married, with 4 children under 7.

The teaching Wide range of styles and approaches, underpinned by strong work ethic: 'no work, no progress' is the message. Mixed-ability classes for first 2 years; streaming thereafter. Class sizes 30, reducing to 25 for GCSE, maximum of 15 in sixth form. 70 staff (30 women); two-thirds appointed by present head. All give up free time to help any child struggling. Broad curriculum; 20 subjects on offer at A-level, including Latin, Greek, geology, politics. Good drama and music; 100 learn an instrument; orchestra and early-music ensemble. Regular trips to the Continent; exchanges with schools in France and Spain. Annual camping in the Lake District and pilgrimages to Lourdes. Much charitable work: Third World Group raises £6,000 a year.

The pupils Bright, courteous, serious; eager to talk about themselves and their work. Some have wealthy parents but most come from very modest backgrounds; 70% receive some help with fees, including 280 on assisted places. Heavily over-subscribed at 11+ (4 applicants for each place); entry tests (in English, maths, verbal reasoning) plus careful interviewing to identify potential. (Most from the prep school

admitted to the senior school.) All current pupils Catholics but other faiths admitted.

Results GCSE: 95% gain at least 5 grades A-C. A-level (1992): modest 37% of entries graded A or B.

Destinations 95% proceed from GCSE to A level; 90% of these go on to degree courses (usually 10 a year to Oxbridge but 16 in 1991).

Sport Soccer and cross-country particularly strong; other games include badminton, basketball, netball, hockey, tennis, cricket, athletics, rugby, orienteering. 13 acres of playing fields near by; new netball and tennis courts, 3 all-weather pitches. On a typical Saturday up to 250 pupils and teachers involved, supported by large numbers of parents.

Remarks School which lives its faith; doing a fine job.

ST BEDE'S GRAMMAR
Highgate,
Heaton,
Bradford,
West Yorkshire BD9 4BQ
Tel (0274) 541221

Comprehensive (voluntary-aided) •
Roman Catholic • Boys • Ages 13-18 • 600
pupils • 160 in sixth form
Head: Dr James Hagerty, 49, appointed
1987.

Good academic record; strong religious ethos; genuinely comprehensive.

Background Founded 1900 to serve the Roman Catholic community of Bradford. Main bulding 1930s: forbidding, square-set, grey stone; surrounded by 16 acres of well-kept gardens and playing fields. School has tentative plans to become co-educational in 1994.

Atmosphere Warm, friendly; a close, supportive community with a strong sense of purpose. Spacious, pleasantly decorated rooms and corridors; modernisation still in progress.

The head A former pupil (as are 8 other teachers); the first lay head. Teaches history, religious studies for 9 out of 25 periods a week.

The teaching Experienced, well-qualified staff of 41. Boys streamed by ability from the start (based on previous reports and school's own tests). Average class size 23. Impressive GCSE choice of 28 subjects (in consortium with other north Bradford schools); includes 3 sciences, 9 languages. 'Enhanced learning' built into the timetable for gifted children and those with learning difficulties. Good technology, art, music (active brass band). Annual visits to Spain and France (pilgrimages to Lourdes); residential field trips to Cumbria.

The pupils From wide social backgrounds; school will take any Roman Catholic boy who applies; 15% of places offered annually to non-Catholics (70 apply for 20 places – criterion for acceptance is parents' sympathy with Catholic ethos).

Results (1991) GCSE: 73% gained at least 5 grades A-C (impressive for a non-selective school). A-level (1992): 40% of entries graded A or B.

Destinations 60% continue into the sixth form (rest into jobs or training); 75% of these proceed to higher education (2-3 a year to Oxbridge).

Sport All main games; good record. Facilities include 3 all-weather pitches, indoor swimming pool.

Remarks Well-run school; deservedly proud of its achievements.

ST BERNARD'S
Langley Road,
Slough,
Berkshire SL3 7AF
Tel (0753) 527020

Grammar (voluntary-aided) • Roman Catholic • Co-educational • Ages 11-18 • 732 pupils (85% girls) • 194 in sixth form
Head: Sister Mary Stephen Bell, late-50s, appointed 1982.

Good academic school; strong Christian ethos.

Background Founded 1897 by the Cistercian Bernardine Order of Nuns; Victorian mansion (built by Baroness Coutts) plus later additions on attractive 38-acre site; facilities include 9 well-equipped labs, first-rate design/technology centre. Co-educational since 1989; all faiths welcome.

Atmosphere Profoundly Christian. Strong family spirit; lots of mutual support. Dedicated staff; orderly, considerate pupils; supportive parents.

The head Quiet, undemonstrative; held in the highest regard by all. Has spent most of her career in the Order's schools; formerly head of St Bernard's, Southend.

The teaching Fairly traditional in style (but modified by the 'active-learning' demands of GCSE). Well-qualified, long-serving staff of 38 (8 men), 4 of whom are members of the Order. Strongly academic curriculum; all take 2 foreign languages (good language-awareness course in second year); choice of French, German, Spanish, Latin, Japanese (close links and exchanges with a Bernardine school in Japan); good results in maths, science (many go on to do medicine and dentistry). Most take 9 GCSEs (including religious studies) and 3 A-levels (from a choice of 20 – half do English literature). Maximum class size 30, much smaller in the sixth form. Lots of drama and music; orchestra, 2 choirs. Big emphasis on public speaking (timetabled lessons). Wide-ranging charitable interests and generous giving. Regular language exchanges with pupils in France and Germany; classics tours to Sicily.

The pupils Top 25% of the ability range from a wide catchment area; 10% Asian. Entry at 11+ and 12+ by Berkshire County Council tests; school heavily over-subscribed; governors give priority to siblings and those making St Bernard's their first choice. Non-Catholic parents must state their willingness to have their children educated in a Catholic atmosphere.

Results (1991) GCSE: 96% gained at least 5 grades A-C. A-level (1992): 47% of entries graded A or B.

Destinations 90% stay on for A-levels; 80% of these proceed to higher education.

Sport Netball, hockey, football, rugby, cricket, tennis, badminton all played regularly; teams compete locally and at county level. Facilities include extensive playing fields, 10 tennis courts, small outdoor pool.

Remarks Attractive school; good all round.

ST CATHERINE'S
Bramley,
Guildford GU5 0DF
Tel (0483) 893363

Independent • Girls • Day and boarding •
Ages 5-18 • 585 pupils (439 in senior
school; 73% day) • 103 in sixth form •
Fees, £4,170-£4,875 day; £7,470-£7,980
boarding
Head: John Palmer, mid-40s, appointed
1982.

---

*Good, traditional school; solid grounding;
strong in science, art, music, dance.*

Background Founded 1885 (close links with Cranleigh, *qv*); well-equipped, purpose-built red-brick premises set in beautiful countryside 3 miles south of Guildford; exquisite Victorian chapel; junior school in 2 converted houses across the road.

Atmosphere Happy, busy, strongly traditional; pupils well-mannered and well-groomed. Cosy boarding accommodation; powerful house loyalties.

The head Read chemistry at Southampton; formerly girls' housemaster at Wellington. Clearly respected in a school with strong female traditions and long-serving female staff. Married, 3 teenage children; wife much involved in school life and teaches the flute.

The teaching Junior girls learn to read and write well at an early age; word processing from age 5; French from 8; lots of singing, dance and music (all 8-year-olds learn the violin); small classes. National curriculum-plus in senior school; science on offer as 3 separate subjects; Latin from 11; German or Spanish from 12; setting by ability in maths, French. Good art, especially painting and drawing; good PE, especially gymnastics. Choice of 20 subjects at A-level, including sociology, ancient history, and even Chinese. Lots of music: 4 choirs, madrigal group, orchestra, wind band; tap dancing starts in the junior school; jazz club thrives in the senior school. Well-supported Duke of Edinburgh award scheme; active Christian Union. Regular language exchanges with pupils in France.

The pupils Day girls from up to 20 miles away in Surrey, West Sussex and Hampshire; 75% of boarders live within an hour's drive; 15%-20% from abroad, some expatriates, some Chinese. Entry to junior school at 5, 8, 9 by tests in maths, English, verbal and numerical reasoning; at 11 by Common Entrance (minimum 55% mark required). About half the entrants at 11 come from the junior school; most girls have IQs of 115+. Assisted places, scholarships.

Results GCSE: all gain at least 5 grades A-C. A-level (1992): creditable 60% of entries graded A or B. Good results also in music, speech, drama and ballet exams.

Destinations 65% stay for A-levels (some transfer to Cranleigh's sixth form, others go to sixth-form colleges); 80% of these proceed to higher education (a few every year to Oxbridge).

Sport Lacrosse, netball, tennis, squash; fine indoor heated pool.

Remarks Well-regarded school; good all round.

ST DAVID'S
Gloddaeth Hall,
Llandudno,
Gwynedd LL30 1RD
Tel (0492) 875974

Independent • Boys • Boarding and day •
Ages 11-18 • 210 pupils (74% boarding) •
62 in sixth form • Fees, £8,130 boarding;
£5,250 day
Head: Will Seymour, mid-40s, appointed
1991.

Small school specialising in boys with dyslexia and other learning difficulties; good all-round education; big emphasis on outdoor pursuits.

Background Founded 1965 as a 'venture of faith' by John Mayor, a former prep school head who wanted to provide an education for boys likely to sink in a conventional school; began with 38 pupils and has grown steadily. Fine Tudor mansion surrounded by woodlands on the edge of Snowdonia.

Atmosphere Relaxed, friendly. Good relations between staff and pupils; boys constantly encouraged to achieve their potential ('Success leads to confidence, and confidence in one area leads to success in others'). Strong Christian ethos. Boarding accommodation comfortable; has a family feel.

The head Read biology at Cambridge; came here in 1969 (one of John Mayor's early appointments); formerly joint deputy head. Keen that the school should cater for all abilities, including academic high-fliers.

The teaching Pupils divided by ability into 2 streams; half are dyslexic or have other learning difficulties and receive specialist help (close links with Bangor University's educa-tion department); class sizes 10-15 up to GCSE, maximum of 12 for A-level. Big emphasis on information technology for those who have difficulty with the printed word; art and design/technology are popular subjects at GCSE and A-level. All do French; German, Spanish on offer; Welsh, Urdu, Portuguese and Italian can be provided. Progress closely monitored; monthly grades for effort and achievement. Wide range of extra-curricular activities to help boys whose self-esteem may have been damaged by previous school experiences to become more self-confident: music, rock-climbing, caving, canoeing, white-water rafting, community service etc.

The pupils Most come from the Cheshire-Wirral area but intake is nationwide and the school is beginning to attract pupils from abroad. Some enter at 11 or 12 but most at 13. Some scholarships available.

Results GCSE (1991): creditable 60% gained at least 5 grades A-C. A-level (1992): very low 14% of entries graded A or B (has been higher).

Destinations 80% continue into the sixth form; many of these proceed to higher education.

Sport Good record in rugby, athletics, cross-country; cricket, tennis, hockey, football, squash also on offer. Facilities include 23 acres of playing fields.

Remarks Good school for children who might not thrive elsewhere.

ST EDWARD'S
Oxford OX2 7NN
Tel (0865) 515241

Independent • Boys (plus girls in sixth form) • Boarding and day • Ages 13-18 • 581 pupils (80% boarding) • 250 in sixth form (75% boys) • Fees, £10,350 boarding; £7,770 day
Head: David Christie, 50, appointed 1988.

First-rate academic school; good teaching and results; fine facilities.

Background Founded 1863; moved 1873 to present 2 sites (connected by a subway) in salubrious North Oxford. Attractive red-brick buildings around an immaculate quadrangle; many good-quality later additions (not even the most modern looks like an afterthought); school has a spacious feel. Fine library: stained-glass windows, vaulted ceiling, 12,000 volumes. Kitchen ('not adapted to the 20th-century') due for replacement, as is the draughty, noisy dining hall.

Atmosphere Purposeful, relaxed, friendly; strong sense of community; good pastoral care system. Hard-working, unpretentious pupils; girls made to feel an integral part of the school; spirited inter-house rivalry. Boarding accommodation – varying in age from 1870 to 1991 – is of a uniformly high standard (though none of the houses is carpeted). Food reasonably good. Day pupils required to stay until 9 p.m.

The head A Scot whose soft accent and manner belies a steeliness of purpose ('If he wants something done, it's done'). Eager to emphasise that the school, traditionally seen as 'hearty but not top-notch academically', now has a first-class academic record. Read economics at Strathclyde; trained teachers (but felt much of what they were being taught was 'unhelpful'); taught at the European School in Luxembourg (keen on Europe but thinks 'a lot of nonsense is talked about a European spirit'); formerly at Winchester. Teaches general studies to the sixth form, and wishes he had time to do more. Describes himself as 'not very sociable' but is charming and gets on well with parents. Married, 3 children.

The teaching High quality; mainly front-of-class; pupils clearly expected to think for themselves. Enthusiastic, well-qualified staff of 63 (8 women); some here more than 20 years. National curriculum-plus; science taught as 3 separate subjects; all do Latin; Greek, German, Spanish on offer in addition to French. Pupils streamed by ability after first term; additional setting in maths, modern languages; class sizes vary widely but tend to get smaller as the pupils get older; 2 hours' prep a night ($1^1/_2$ hours on Saturdays). Most do 10 GCSEs and 3 A-levels plus general studies and religious education. Strong music; numerous concerts and recitals. Compulsory cadet force; well-supported Duke of Edinburgh award scheme; lots of community service.

The pupils Nearly all from prep schools (Caldicott, The Dragon, Horris Hill etc) and professional home backgrounds in Berkshire, Buckinghamshire and Oxfordshire. Admission at 13 by interview, previous school report and Common Entrance (alternative tests available); minimum 55% mark required; registration advised on entry to prep school. No assisted places but a significant number of scholarships, for which boys compete (in the May before September entry) by sitting an 8-paper examination during a 5-day stay at the school. Entry to sixth form with at least 5 GCSEs grade A or B plus school's own tests (including IQ) and 3 separate interviews.

Results GCSE: 90% gain at least 5 grades A-C. A level (1992): 48% of entries graded A or B (has been higher).

Destinations Nearly all stay on for A-levels; 90% proceed to higher education (up to 18 a year to Oxbridge).

Sport Wide variety; superb facilities, including 90 acres of playing fields, 11 tennis courts, 2 swimming pools, 9-hole golf course, boat house on the Thames and a sports centre shared with the community. Match record is good but school is more proud of the participation rates.

Remarks Very good all round; highly recommended.

ST FELIX
Southwold,
Suffolk IP18 6SD
Tel (0502) 722175

Independent • Girls • Boarding and day •
Ages 11-18 (plus associated
co-educational junior school) • 290 pupils
(74% boarding) • 80 in sixth form • Fees,
£9,195 boarding; £5,895 day
Head: Mrs Susan Campion, 40s,
appointed 1991.

*Remote rural school; distinctive ethos;
fairly wide range of abilities; lots of
outdoor activities.*

Background Founded 1897 by Margaret
Isabella Gardiner, an educational pioneer who
set out to create a school 'where girls can be
treated as sensible beings': it was to be an
undenominational, self-governing community
with no gates, no rules, no marks or prizes
('Achievement is its own reward'). Handsome,
purpose-built, red-brick buildings on attractive 75-acre estate overlooking the estuary of
the River Blyth; extensive later additions, most
of which blend in. Good facilities for art,
design, computing, science, music; fine
chapel.

Atmosphere Civilised surroundings; a sense
of harmony and style; founder's ideals still very
much in evidence; strong feminist flavour.
Quietly self-assured girls work and play hard.
Pleasant boarding houses; some dormitories a
bit cramped; sixth-formers in first-class study-
bedrooms.

The head Enthusiastic, decisive; has an open-
door style of consultative leadership. Read
modern languages at Cambridge; formerly
head of a girls' comprehensive. Married, 2
sons.

The teaching Traditional academic approach; new emphasis on science (taught as 3
separate subjects) and technology; strong English, drama and music (orchestras, choir);
accelerated teaching for gifted pupils. National
curriculum-plus; Latin and Greek on offer in
addition to 4 modern languages; choice of 21

subjects at A-level, including business studies,
theatre studies, history of art. Many take a
vocational qualification in computing. Enter-
prising, well-supported Duke of Edinburgh
award scheme (5 golds a year); lots of outdoor
pursuits (life-saving particularly popular).

The pupils From East Anglia and corridor to
London; many have family connections; few
from abroad. Admission by Common Entrance at 11, 12, 13; numbers have declined but
school is careful to restrict entry to those able
enough to cope and benefit. Assisted places,
scholarships.

Results GCSE: 95% gain at least 5 grades
A-C. A-level (1992): 49% of entries graded A
or B.

Destinations Most stay for A-levels; 70%
proceed to higher education.

Sport Strong tradition, particularly in hockey
(regular county honours), tennis, athletics.
Good access to sailing, riding and other
outdoor pursuits. Facilities include extensive
playing fields, adequate gym (no sports hall),
squash and tennis courts, 2 outdoor pools.

Remarks Attractive, well-run school; surviv-
ing against the odds.

ST GEORGE'S GIRLS'
Garscube Terrace,
Edinburgh EH12 6BG
Tel (031) 332 1947

Independent • Girls • Day and boarding •
Ages 5-18 • 859 pupils (568 in senior
school; 80% day) • 156 in sixth form •
Fees, £1,845-£3,525 day; £5,895-£6,915
boarding
Head: Mrs Jean Scott, 51, appointed 1986
(leaving April 1993).

*Traditionally strong; impressive exam
results; first-rate music.*

Background Founded 1888 to 'prepare
young women to play a full and equal role in

society' – and still does. Moved to present 11-acre, hill-crest site 1912; imposing buildings with many later additions including art block, sports hall, splendid music centre.

Atmosphere The world of Angela Brazil: wooden desks and blackboards; stone-floored corridors lined with portraits of founders and former headmistresses; large hall with honours boards and high wainscoting; few concessions made to comfort. Scattered, pleasant boarding houses (but communal areas are rather bleak).

The head Skilled manager; competent, business-like; very aware of her importance as a role model for career-oriented girls. 'The leadership provided by the headmistress was a determining factor in the performance of the school,' Her Majesty's Inspectors noted in a recent (May 1992), highly complimentary report. Leaves April 1993 to beome head of South Hampstead.

The teaching Well-qualified, dedicated, predominantly female staff; highly motivated, responsive pupils; pervasive work ethos. Broad curriculum; choice of 17 subjects at GCSE; most do 8 or 9. Computer literacy for all but limited technology. Class sizes 20-24 in some subjects but smaller in the sixth form. Two-thirds take 1-year Scottish Highers; rest (the more able) do A-levels. Very strong music: 70% have instrumental or vocal lessons; 3 orchestras, several ensembles. Lots of drama; numerous lunch-time clubs and societies; 60 working for Duke of Edinburgh gold award.

The pupils Disciplined, co-operative; from the cream of the Edinburgh professional classes. Entry by test and interview; most join at 5; others at 9 and 11. Head eager to dispel the view that only the brightest thrive; average girl will do well if she works hard. Assisted places and bursaries available.

Results GCSE: 97% gain at least 5 grades A-C. A-level: impressive 78% of entries graded A or B. Highers: 70% A or B.

Destinations 83% continue into the sixth form; 87% of them proceed to higher education (approximately 7 a year to Oxbridge).

Sport Varied programme; outstanding lacrosse.

Remarks Much sought-after – but less academically able girls may struggle.

ST HELEN & ST KATHARINE
7 Faringdon Road,
Abingdon,
Oxfordshire OX14 1BE
Tel (0235) 520173

Independent • Girls • Day (and some weekly boarding) • Ages 11-18 • 500 pupils • 140 in sixth form • Fees, £3,150 (£6,075 weekly boarding)
Head: Miss Yolande Paterson, 50s, appointed 1975.

Disciplined, traditional school; academic achievement expected; home economics and needlework not neglected.

Background St Helen's, founded 1903 by the Anglican community of St Mary the Virgin, amalgamated with its sister school, St Katharine's in 1938. Staff no longer members of the community but strong links maintained. Unattractive, purpose-built, late-Victorian premises: acoustics discourage noise, scruffy wooden floors, windows set high enough to make looking out impossible. Some later additions more congenial, but 7 classrooms in tatty huts. Pleasant, well-kept grounds

Atmosphere Slightly oppressive; honours boards somehow manage to convey the message that lack of achievement is bad.

The head Read geography at Oxford (and teaches it to the sixth form). School's first lay head; has appointed 90% of the staff; rules by consensus; door always open. Lives in a bungalow in the grounds; dines with the boarders on Wednesdays.

The teaching Mainly from the front (desks in pairs facing the blackboard). No streaming (within fairly narrow ability band) but some girls complain of being pushed and others of being spoon-fed; some setting in maths and French. Wide range of options, especially at A-level; some courses shared with boys from Radley and Abingdon. Compulsory divinity ('Stifling,' according to one sixth-former, 'we're not even allowed to question it'); lots of computing – all taught basic keyboard and programming skills; thriving home economics (including 'bed-sit survival'). Good library; computerised index system (which all know how to use). Very strong music: half learn an instrument (including the harp); joint productions with Radley and Abingdon. Big emphasis on service to the community: regular 'famine lunch' of soup and roll; money saved donated to charity.

The pupils Well-behaved, articulate, responsive; mainly from middle-class, professional homes – but assisted places scheme (15 a year) helps ensure social mix. Half enter from prep schools, half from state primaries. Wide catchment area means long travelling times (and cuts down after-school activities). Sixth-form boarders have attractive study bedrooms and can invite boys to tea. No written rules (head anxious to avoid the impression that anything not expressly forbidden is permitted). Entry by tests in English, maths and observation during a lesson to guage 'level of involvement' and academic ability; girls need to be able to shine in at least 1 area and be competent in most others. Head discourages applications before age of 8.

Results GCSE: all gain at least 5 grades A-C. A-level (1992): 53% of entries graded A or B.

Destinations Nearly all go on to university (many to Oxbridge).

Sport Strong, especially lacrosse (county and national players). Also: netball, aerobics, athletics, tennis. Large swimming pool (life saving encouraged).

Remarks Girls expected to achieve academically, imbibe traditional Christian values and develop a strong sense of duty to the community.

ST HELEN'S
Northwood,
Middlesex HA6 3AS
Tel (0923) 828511

Independent • Girls • Day and some boarding • Ages 4-18 • 920 pupils (572 in senior school; 90% day) • 147 in sixth form • Fees, £2,142-£3,900 day; £7,356 boarding
Head: Dr Yvonne Burne, mid-40s, appointed 1987.

Strong academic school; sound teaching; good results; first-rate music.

Background Founded 1899 by local businessmen; converted Victorian houses and later additions on delightful 24-acre site.

Atmosphere Happy, friendly; emphasis on courtesy and good manners; sensible behaviour everywhere apparent. Traditional Christian assemblies; good pastoral care system (no one should feel overwhelmed). Pleasant, comfortable boarding houses; older girls in single or double rooms.

The head Quiet, competent, maternal. PhD in modern languages from London; has taught in state schools and worked in educational publishing. Married.

The teaching Very professional. Traditional approach; emphasis on high standards in all areas of the curriculum; poor work must be repeated. Long-serving staff of 80 (8 men). Strong languages; all do Latin from age 11; choice of Latin, German or Spanish at 12 to be taken with French up to GCSE; science taught as 3 separate subjects. Computers used across the curriculum (from age 4). Pupils set by ability in maths, French; average class size 20; homework from age 5. Choice of 25 subjects at A-level; most take 3; English, history, maths, languages are popular. Fine library, drama studio; superbly equipped kitchens for home economics; first-rate art (several a year go on to art college). Very good music: half learn an instrument (26 visiting teachers); 2 orchestras, 2 choirs. Senior girls share a 'way of life' course with Harrow boys; joint cadet force with

Merchant Taylors'; well-supported Duke of Edinburgh award scheme. Work experience in France. Regular language exchanges with pupils in France, Germany and Spain.

The pupils Mostly from professional families. Entry competitive from the earliest age; school heavily over-subscribed (4 or 5 apply for each place). Assisted places, scholarships available.

Results GCSE (1991): 96% gained at least 5 grades A-C. A-level (1992): 55% of entries graded A or B.

Destinations Nearly all stay on for A-levels and proceed to higher education (6 a year to Oxbridge).

Sport Particularly strong lacrosse and swimming; badminton, netball, tennis, fencing also on offer (but no hockey or athletics). Facilities include 2 lacrosse pitches, 9 tennis courts, 1 squash court, covered heated pool.

Remarks Good all round.

ST JAMES

61 Eccleston Square,
London SW1V 1PH
Tel (071) 834 0471

Independent • Co-educational (but boys and girls taught separately) • Day • Ages 4$^1/_2$-18 • 626 pupils (55% boys) • 42 in sixth form • Fees, £2,865-£4,140
Joint heads: Nicholas Debenham, 59; Sheila Caldwell, 60s; both appointed 1975.

Distinctive, idealistic school; wide range of abilities; good teaching and results.

Background Founded 1975 by parents and teachers from the School of Economic Science (itself founded in 1937 'to study and teach economics and the natural laws which govern men in society'); links between the 2 are strong (nearly all the staff and a third of the parents are students of philosophy at the SEC); idealistic – but without 'isms' or 'ologies' (philosophical sources range from Socrates to the Upanishads). Juniors elegantly housed in Queen's Gate; senior boys in Eccleston Square (former premises of Westminster Under School); senior girls in 2 converted houses in Pembridge Villas.

Atmosphere Junior school is unusually happy and purposeful; discipline old-fashioned – instant scraping back of chairs and a chorus of 'Good morning, Mr Debenham' when the head enters, but reassuringly noisy and natural at other times. Boys' senior school is cramped and short of facilities; girls' senior school has a friendly, homely feel (mistresses in long skirts). At all 3, there is an insistence on good manners, particularly at meal-times when staff and pupils eat together: grace is said; pupils wait on each other (and must offer food to their neighbours before eating themselves). These niceties, however, are not inhibiting: pupils enjoy both their food (vegetarian) and plenty of talk. Corporal punishment retained 'for serious offences'.

The heads Debenham read economics at Cambridge and then spent many years in industry; became a teacher owing to lack of fulfilment. A kindly authoritarian; gravely courteous but with a definite sense of humour. Caldwell was deputy head of a grammar school in Harrow. Reserved, rather austere; determined to ensure girls are properly equipped for any career they might choose. Both are entirely sincere about their distinctive education philosophy, with its emphasis on mind, body and spirit.

The teaching Dedicated, appropriately qualified staff who believe that what the school offers is of real and unusual value. (The wide ability range means the teaching has to be inventive, and it is remarkable how well the children cope with material and ideas that would be thought beyond them in more conventional schools.) Big emphasis in the junior school on handwriting, reading (taught by the traditional 'sounding-out' method) and maths (taught with old-fashioned thoroughness). Extra help for those with dyslexia or who are learning English as a second language. Philosophy – Christian, Hindu, Greek – introduced at an early age; also Sanskrit and Greek.

Myths and epics from East and West take up a significant part of the timetable, as does singing (Mozart rather than nursery rhymes); high standards achieved. Curriculum becomes more conventional in the senior schools; science taught as 3 separate subjects. Art, drama (lots of Shakespeare) and music are all outstanding. Meditation taught from the age of 10 to those who want it, and whose parents agree.

The pupils Individual, thoughtful, articulate. A third are Indians, attracted by the school's culture and firm discipline (parents are asked to ensure that children do not listen to pop music, watch too much television or read bad literature). Catchment area includes Chiswick, Dulwich, Croydon, Wimbledon. Entry is non-selective at 4$^1/_2$; interview and test thereafter. A few bursaries available.

Results GCSE: 80% gain at least 5 grades A-C. A-level: 47% of entries graded A or B.

Destinations 75% stay on for A-levels; 90% of these proceed to higher education.

Sport All have to take some form of exercise daily; rugby, cricket, swimming, cross-country for the boys; lacrosse, gymnastics, athletics, swimming, riding for the girls. No sports facilities on any of the 3 sites.

Remarks School offers an unusual and interesting education; the children are happy and achieve sound standards.

ST LEONARDS
St Andrews,
Fife KY16 9QU
Tel (0334) 72126

Independent • Girls • Boarding and day • Ages 12-18 (plus associated junior school) • 303 pupils (81% boarding) • 112 in sixth form • Fees, £9,930 boarding; £5,220 day
Head: Mrs Mary James, late 40s, appointed 1988.

Highly regarded school; good teaching and results; strong music and sport.

Background Founded 1877; Victorian baronial buildings (some rather dismal) plus later additions on a 30-acre site in an idyllic setting on the edge of the town.

Atmosphere Calm, civilised, well-ordered; the well-tended gardens and tree-lined walks help diminish the gravity of the imposing grey stone buildings. According to the head, the St Leonards girl can be distinguished by 'the easy way in which she is able to combine feminism, in the sense of being independent and well qualified, with the femininity in which pride and pleasure in being female are represented'. Pleasant boarding accommodation: juniors in small, cosy dormitories (4-6 beds); seniors have study-bedrooms; new, well-appointed house for sixth-formers.

The head Dynamic, determined; believes passionately in the value of single-sex education for girls. Was a pupil here; took a First in history at York; did post-graduate research at Oxford; taught at Sedbergh and Casterton; formerly head of Queen Ethelburga's, Harrogate. Strongly opposed to the 'finishing-school philosophy'; wants her girls to be ambitious, independent, assertive. Married, 2 sons.

The teaching Broad curriculum; first-language choice between French, German and Spanish; classical civilisation on offer as an alternative to Latin; science taught as 3 separate subjects; all do design/technology, art and design, and computing (first-rate facilities). Pupils set by ability; average class size 16;

progress closely monitored. Most take at least 8 GCSEs and either 3 A-levels or 5 Highers plus general studies; vocational courses in word-processing, office skills, home economics also available. Strong music: a third learn an instrument (numerous practice rooms); 3 orchestras, 2 choirs. Other extra-curricular activities include good drama and art, photography, cookery, bridge, chess, yoga etc (daily 'aesthetic and reflective hour'). Well-supported Duke of Edinburgh award scheme (14 gold medals a year). Regular language exchanges with schools in France, Germany and Spain.

The pupils Friendly, open, smartly dressed (cloaks or Barbours in inclement weather); most from farming or professional backgrounds; 60% Scottish, 10% foreign nationals. Admission by Common Entrance or school's own tests; not severely selective (girls from associated prep school promoted automatically).

Results GCSE: 94% gain at least 5 grades A-C. A-level: 52% of entries graded A or B. Highers: 57% of entries graded A or B.

Destinations 85% continue into the sixth form; 88% of these proceed to higher education (6 a year to Oxbridge).

Sport Proud tradition (the first British girls' school to play lacrosse, back in 1890); all play games 4 afternoons a week plus matches on Saturdays. Major activities: hockey, lacrosse (county and national honours), athletics, tennis (numerous courts); skiing, sailing, squash, fencing, golf, cross-country also on offer. Facilities include extensive playing fields, indoor heated pool, gym.

Remarks High standards all round.

ST LEONARDS-MAYFIELD

The Old Palace,
Mayfield,
East Sussex TN20 6PH
Tel (0435) 873383

Independent ● Roman Catholic ● Girls ● Boarding and day ● Ages 11-18 ● 525 pupils (64% boarding) ● 160 in sixth form ● Fees (1992-93), £8,400 boarding; £5,595 day
Head: Sister Jean Sinclair, 57, appointed 1980.

First-rate school. High academic standards; strong musical tradition; fairly wide range of abilities; delightful atmosphere.

Background Founded 1872 by Cornelia Connelly, foundress of the Society of the Holy Child Jesus, in the grounds of the former residence of the pre-Reformation Archbishops of Canterbury; merged 1976 with an earlier foundation at St Leonards on Sea. Peaceful, rural setting; new buildings blend harmoniously with the medieval; chapel – said to have the widest unsupported arches in Europe – is exceptionally fine. Appeal launched for new music and science blocks.

Atmosphere Informal, tolerant, gentle; no dogmatic attitudes or rigid structures; school run on a system of trust. Christian values fundamental; emphasis on kindliness and concern for others; older girls given responsibility for younger ones. A general sense of quiet purpose and underlying self-discipline. No prizes until sixth form; commendation cards ensure everyone is congratulated and encouraged for something. Mass on Sundays (after 10 a.m. breakfast) but no compulsory daily chapel. Dormitories functional rather than cosy; sixth-formers have study-bedrooms. Outstandingly good food (dedicated and very popular chef). Strong links with parents; flexible attitude to 'dropping in'.

The head Very able; dedicated, devout, forgiving (with a humorous light in her eyes). Called to join the Society of the Holy Child Jesus after reading maths at London (her brother is Sir Clive Sinclair, computer wizard); has taught Greek, Latin and maths at the society's schools in London, Birmingham and Preston; came here 1971 as director of studies; deputy head 1972. Commands enormous respect from pupils, staff and parents; constantly assessing how the school is living up to the high-minded ideals of its founder.

The teaching High standards encouraged in all areas; girls expected to work seriously – but through individual commitment rather than competitive pressure. Long-serving staff, including several men. Broad curriculum; all do computing and word processing (good facilities); science taught as 3 separate subjects from third year (very good results – many go on to do medicine, veterinary science, engineering); strong maths and languages; all do drama for first 3 years. Pupils set by ability in English, French, science, maths; average class size 20, reducing to 8 in the sixth form. Wide choice of subjects at A-level; lower-sixth do general studies course. Good pottery in modern, well-equipped art block; strong music tradition; excellent singing, 5 choirs, orchestra.

The pupils Friendly, articulate; mainly from the South East; large expatriate contingent (Services, diplomatic, business, medical); boarders all Roman Catholic. Admission by Common Entrance at 11+ and 13+; wide ability range (from 2 Es to 4 As at A-level); borderline children accepted for special reasons. Means-tested scholarships, some bursaries.

Results GCSE: 98% gain at least 5 grades A-C. A-level (1992): 55% of entries graded A or B.

Destinations 90% stay on for A-levels; 85% of these proceed to higher education (6 or 7 a year to Oxbridge).

Sport Chiefly: hockey, netball, tennis, volleyball, athletics, swimming. Facilities include superb indoor pool, 2 gyms, all-weather pitch.

Remarks Nurturing Christian school with high all-round standards. Highly recommended.

ST MARTIN'S
Hanging Hill Lane,
Hutton, Brentwood,
Essex CM13 2HG
Tel (0277) 227650

Comprehensive • Co-educational • Ages 11-18 • 1,057 pupils (53% boys) • 165 in sixth form
Head: Jack Telling, early 50s, appointed 1986.

Popular, over-subscribed; wide ability range; good results.

Background Built in the late 1950s as 2 single-sex schools; merged 1971. Became severely run down; now in the middle of £2.5-million refurbishment. Attractive, well-kept 25-acre site. Steadily expanding sixth form.

Atmosphere Busy, well-ordered, well-behaved.

The head Has taught in Essex since 1965 (after 3 years in industry). Leads from the front; insists on highest academic standards but lays equal emphasis on arts and sport.

The teaching Hard-working, stable staff; expect much of their pupils. National curriculum-plus; strong links with industry (industrialist 'in residence'); all senior pupils do 3 weeks' work experience. Plenty of music (choir, orchestra, wind band) and drama; exchange visits to France and Germany.

The pupils Majority from middle-class homes, half from outside the official catchment area – Billericay, Basildon etc. 400 apply for 190 places. Strict uniform; negligible truancy (keen competition between classes to maintain highest attendance rate).

Results (1991) GCSE: 51% gained at least 5 grades A-C. A-level: creditable 46% of entries graded A or B.

Destinations 55% stay on to take A-levels; 71% of these go on to higher education .

Sport Chiefly football, rugby, hockey. Extensive playing fields; heated outdoor pool; fine new gymnasium. Teachers supervise Saturday games.

Remarks Good all-round comprehensive.

ST MARY'S Ascot

Ascot,
Berkshire SL5 9JF
Tel (0344) 27788

Independent • Roman Catholic • Girls • Boarding (and a handful of day pupils) • Ages 10-18 • 330 pupils (10 day) • 84 in sixth form •Fees, £9,834 (£5,901 day) Head: Sister Mark Orchard, 47, appointed 1982.

Good academic school; strong Catholic ethos; first-rate teaching and results.

Background Founded 1885; owned by the Institute of the Blessed Virgin Mary (but the school is run by its own governing body). Purpose-built premises (no gloomy Gothicism here) on pleasant 55-acre site; many recent improvements and additions (funded by appeals); everything well cared for and sensibly used, without being in any way lavish. Governors have decided not to expand numbers, despite demand.

Atmosphere Sunny, welcoming; strong sense of shared purpose and Catholic tradition. Girls encouraged to be competitive – which gives a cutting edge to a caring community. There is an easy relationship between teacher and pupil based on trust and respect yet with a fair degree of informality and shared jokes. Sisters of the Order live in a house in the grounds, their presence a silent reminder of the faith behind the school. Pleasant boarding accommodation; juniors in dormitories; sixth-formers have single rooms.

The head Inspires great confidence. Her mind is keen, her speech direct, her bearing a mixture of the caring and the downright practical. Was a pupil here; joined the Order; read history at Royal Holloway College; taught

at St Mary's, Cambridge for 10 years; returned as head, taking over from her sister. Greatly respected by staff and pupils; parents praise her for raising academic standards. Works and plans tirelessly; school is flourishing under her strong lead.

The teaching Hard-working staff (many non-Catholics, a few men). Strong languages: choice of French, German, Italian, Spanish, Portuguese – up to half take 2 modern languages for GCSE. Science, previously neglected, is improving; technology and computing taught as tools but not for GCSE, good art and design (including dress-making, ceramics, photography); all do religious studies. Choice of 16 subjects at A-level; history of art popular; nearly a quarter take Latin. Flourishing drama and music; more than two-thirds learn at least 1 instrument; chapel choir sings Sunday masses. Well-supported Duke of Edinburgh award scheme.

The pupils Although their homes are geographically scattered, the common bond of Catholicism and the size of the school (45 in each year-group) creates a close family atmosphere in which the girls feel secure and relaxed. They are immediately friendly, making adults feel at ease. Most enter at 11, from a very wide range of schools including all the main London prep schools; applicants must come from Catholic families and state where they were baptised. Admission by interview and tests in maths, English; fairly high academic standard required. Some scholarships, bursaries. Head wants girls to leave with a sense that since their lives so far have been privileged they owe service to those less fortunate; she encourages them to use their 'gap year' to help others.

Results GCSE: virtually all gain at least 5 grades A-C. A-level (1992): creditable 59% of entries graded A or B.

Destinations 85% stay on for A-levels; nearly all of these proceed to higher education (5 a year to Oxbridge).

Sport Tennis and hockey are the main strengths; netball and rounders also played. Large gym, superb new swimming pool.

Remarks Secure, well-run school for bright Catholic girls.

ST MARY'S Calne
Calne,
Wiltshire SN11 ODF
Tel: (0249) 815899

Independent • Girls • Boarding and some day • Ages 11-18 • 315 pupils (90% boarding) • 80 in sixth form • Fees, £9,225 boarding; £5,484 day
Head: Miss Delscey Burns, early-40s, appointed 1985.

Old-fashioned, highly academic school; excellent results.

Background Founded 1873 by the Vicar of Calne; relatively modern premises (behind a high wall) on a pleasant 25-acre site on the outskirts of the town.

Atmosphere Very traditional. Purposeful, formal, strongly academic – slightly forbidding. Stark entrance hall; bare, functional classrooms. Boarding accommodation, however, is warm and civilised; sixth-formers in attractive study-bedrooms.

The head Enthusiastic, forthright, incisive. Read English at York; research degree from Oxford; formerly head of English at St George's, Ascot. Appointed in her early-30s.

The teaching Long-serving staff; formal, didactic style; big emphasis on academic achievement; pace of work is brisk. 'In step' with the national curriculum; very strong languages; all do French and Latin; choice of German, Spanish, Greek from third year; good science. No streaming by ability ('We don't cater for those with learning difficulties'); average class size 15. Choice of 16 subjects at GCSE, 17 at A-level. First-rate music: three-quarters learn at least 1 instrument; sparkling choir. Lots of art and drama. Busy extra-curricular programme; nearly all involved in exceptionally well-organised Duke of Edin-

burgh award scheme; all do community service. Regular language exchanges with schools in France and Germany; cultural trips to Italy, Greece and Russia.

The pupils Confident, able, well-motivated ('but they're not geniuses'); mostly from professional and Services backgrounds; a third from London and the Home Counties. Two-thirds join at 11+, rest at 12+; admission by interview and Common Entrance; minimum 60% mark required.

Results GCSE: virtually all gain at least 5 grades A-C. A-level (1992): creditable 63% of entries graded A or B (has been even higher).

Destinations Nearly all stay on for A-levels and proceed to higher education (5 or 6 a year to Oxbridge).

Sport Strong lacrosse (2 international players on the staff) and tennis; hockey, netball, cross-country, swimming, athletics also on offer. No indoor pool.

Remarks Very strong school; but not all will warm to it.

ST MARY'S Cambridge
Bateman Street,
Cambridge CB2 1LY
Tel (0223) 353253

Independent • Roman Catholic • Girls • Day and weekly boarding • Ages 11-18 • 600 pupils (87% day) • 115 in sixth form • Fees (1992-93), £3,300 day; £5,910 weekly boarding
Head: Miss Michele Conway, 42, appointed 1989.

Traditional grammar-school education; strong religious ethos; good teaching and results.

Background Founded 1898 by the Institute of the Blessed Virgin Mary; Victorian buildings and many later additions close to the city centre; good facilities, including pleasant classrooms, labs, libraries, specialist suites. 50% of pupils are non-Catholic.

Atmosphere Happy, purposeful; hard work taken for granted.. Strong Christian ethos. Good boarding accommodation; sixth-formers have study-bedrooms.

The head First lay head (practising Catholic); leads from the front; has an excellent rapport with staff and pupils. Educated at a convent school; read maths at Oxford; taught in an Oxfordshire comprehensive and at Dulwich; formerly head of maths at St Leonards-Mayfield. Teaches maths to first-years, religious education to sixth-formers. Owns 8 cats; accomplished silversmith; keen on synchronised swimming.

The teaching Long-serving, largely female staff (including 3 nuns); some have been here more than 20 years. National curriculum-plus; science taught as 3 separate subjects; Latin on offer from second year; Greek, German, Spanish, Italian from third year; all do religious education for GCSE; plenty of computing. All take 8-10 GCSEs. Choice of 23 subjects at A-level, including 6 languages, sociology, theatre studies; all do general and religious studies. Good drama and music; 2 orchestras, several smaller ensembles, choirs. Well-supported Duke of Edinburgh award scheme; lots of charity fund-raising. Regular language exchange with school in Paris.

The pupils Wide range of social backgrounds: 140 on assisted places. Day girls from within 25-30 mile radius; weekly boarders (heavy demand for places) from north London and north Norfolk. Entry at 11 + by school's own tests; top 25% of the ability range; minimum IQ 110 (but may be less for siblings).

Results GCSE: virtually all gain at least 5 grades A-C. A-level (1992): 44% of entries graded A or B.

Destinations Nearly all stay on for A-levels and proceed to higher education (6 a year to Oxbridge).

Sport All play hockey, netball, tennis, rounders; gymnastics, swimming, athletics, squash, tennis, badminton, archery also on offer.

Facilities include large sports hall, netball/tennis courts; 5 acres of playing fields some distance away.

Remarks Good all round.

ST PAUL'S

Lonsdale Road,
Barnes,
London SW13 9JT
Tel (081) 748 9162

Independent • Boys • Day and boarding • Ages 13-18 • 750 pupils (88% day) • 300 in sixth form • Fees, £6,450 day; £10,200 boarding
Head: Stephen Baldock, 47, appointed September 1992.

Distinguished academic powerhouse (one of the top 10); broad range of sports and other activities; achieves great things with tough, committed boys.

Background Founded 1509 by John Colet, Dean of St Paul's, who rooted it in the secular world of the City of London by making the Mercers' Company trustees of the foundation. Moved 1884 to west Kensington (where it grew and became academically pre-eminent) and in 1968 to a riverside site in Barnes (drab, featureless buildings but plenty of space). Attractive Milton building (John Milton was a Pauline) added 1991, adding vastly to the facilities for art and technology. Ethos is still that of Colet's original foundation: hard work and scholarship, leading to worldly success.

Atmosphere Efficient yet warm: this is a highly motivated, highly organised school (though some might think it has a touch of the well-run academic factory as bells ring and people move with measured speed and purpose from place to place). Instead of assembly (for which there is no hall), notices and announcements are relayed to classrooms by intercom. Utilitarian image somewhat softened during the 2-hour lunch break, when a great array of extra-curricular activities take place.

The head (High Master) New appointment. A Pauline born and bred; read classics and theology at Cambridge; returned here to teach Greek; surmaster (deputy head) since 1984. Efficient, reliable administrator; devoted to the school. Married, 3 daughters, 1 (Pauline) son.

The teaching At its best, absolutely outstanding. Knowledge imparted at a fast pace by lively, friendly teachers (70 men, 7 women). No acceleration for extra-bright boys, but all classes streamed, with setting as needed. Some do 3 sciences, others take Nuffield co-ordinated course. Sixth form has equal numbers of science and arts specialists; choice of more than 20 AS-levels allows boys to broaden their studies. A-level languages are French, German, Italian; classics still draw some. Well-equipped science labs; good facilities for computing and technology. No Saturday morning school, which explains the hectic school day; 2 hours' homework on weekdays, 3 at weekends. A third learn a musical instrument (joint concerts with St Paul's Girls' *qv*); enthusiastic art department; 300-seat theatre. Daily communion in school chapel, which doubles as a concert hall.

The pupils Londoners, public school streetboys; ambitious, intellectually demanding. A good lesson is an earnest dialogue between teacher and taught; note-taking is studious; no time for posturing or airs and graces. (This is no school for the shrinking violet or the unmotivated: some few boys in each year are unable to cope, despite the firm pastoral structure and a school counsellor.) Many boys travel long distances to school, so life is also physically tough. Boarders can choose each week whether to stay for the weekend; some have parents abroad, but others live as near as Kensington and still prefer to board. (The facilities do not compare with those in a well-run boarding school.) Discipline not really an issue, but the authorities are strict on smoking and drugs, and there is a tight absence-note system. Entry highly competitive; minimum 65% at Common Entrance;

compulsory Latin. Some assisted places plus, at any one time, 153 foundation scholars (as many as the Biblical miraculous draught of fishes).

Results Ought to be good and are outstandingly so. GCSE: virtually all gain at least 5 grades A-C (it takes a strong-minded young man to fail here). A-level (1992): remarkable 84% of entries graded A or B.

Destinations 94% continue into the sixth form; 90% of these proceed to university (40 a year to Oxbridge).

Sport All expected to take some part in sport. Large range of activities on offer, including golf, sailing, fencing. The rugby is impressive, and sometimes the rowing equally so; athletics taken seriously (naturally). Big sports centre; swimming pool.

Remarks If you have an intelligent, self-motivated, capable boy, ambitious but without pretensions, enter him for St Paul's and watch them make a success of him. It may be, as some say, an assembly line, but the final product is unmistakeably first-rate.

ST PAUL'S GIRLS'
Brook Green,
London W6 7BS
Tel (071) 603 2288

Independent • Girls • Day • Ages 11-18 • 618 pupils • 210 in sixth form • Fees, £5,070
Head (acting): Miss Janet Gough, late-50s, appointed September 1992.

Excellent academic school (one of the top 5 for girls); fine teaching and results; first-rate music; strong sport.

Background Founded 1904 by the John Colet Foundation; administered (like St Paul's, *qv*) by the Mercers' Company. Handsome Edwardian buildings and many later additions, including fine theatre, on a fairly restricted site in a pleasant part of Hammersmith.

Atmosphere Marble entrance hall, polished wood, honours boards, well-planned, modern facilities in every direction. A secure, highly motivated community; girls respect each others' abilities, seem totally at ease in a single-sex environment. Staff and pupils appear to run the school jointly, with mutual respect; in class, the atmosphere is informal but disciplined; there is little need for punishment, and no uniform.

The head (High Mistress) Appointed as a stop-gap after Mrs Helen Williams, in post for only 3 years, was forced to resign in August 1992: she had fallen out with parents and governors, partly over her decision to restrict the girls to 7 GCSEs to save them from being 'overloaded with boring, mechanistic exam work' and leave more time for a broader education. Miss Gough, formerly the deputy head, is regarded as a safe pair of hands; she has taught English here since 1965.

The teaching Totally professional: this is a demanding, stimulating place to teach; women are still largely in control – and *very* competent; methods are on the whole traditional. Most classrooms are adequate, but several are overcrowded, with no space at all between the desks; school badly needs a projected new building, which will include classrooms, science labs and more space for design/technology. Good languages (several native-speakers); lots of computing; setting by ability in maths, Latin, French; no competitive grading or form orders. Art flourishes happily up near the roof; drama and speaking are taken seriously in the new theatre. The high standard of music is legendary (Gustav Holst taught here); 4 choirs, 3 orchestras and various other groups and ensembles; every girl expected to learn an instrument. Well-stocked libraries (school subscribes to 67 periodicals). First-rate careers advice. Well-supported Duke of Edinburgh award scheme.

The pupils Very able: 360 compete by examination for 78 places a year; the successful ones (only 10% to 15% come from state primaries) are high-fliers, self-motivated, needing emotional, intellectual and physical stamina to cope; many come from meritocratic or privileged backgrounds (Mrs Williams found them 'chic, slick, socially conscious and arrogant'). Some assisted places; means-tested bursaries, scholarships.

Results GCSE: virtually all gain at least 5 grades A-C. A-level: remarkable 80% of entries graded A or B (the top girls' school in 1992).

Destinations Nearly all stay on for A-levels; 95% proceed to higher education (up to 40 a year to Oxbridge).

Sport Compulsory up to the end of the fifth year: most carry on. Unbeaten in 1991 at lacrosse, the girls also shine in athletics, play tennis, netball, squash and row. Old-style gym but no sports hall; fine indoor pool, 300-metre running track.

Remarks Unbeatable all-round education for able, confident girls.

ST PETER'S
York YO3 6AB
Tel (0904) 623213

Independent • Co-educational • Boarding and day • Ages 13-18 • 480 pupils (two-thirds boys, two-thirds boarding) • 180 in sixth form • Fees, £8,505-£8,745 boarding; £4,953-£5,205 day
Head: Robin Pittman, 55, appointed 1985.

School in transition; not unduly selective; good results.

Background Founded 627 (one of the oldest in Europe). Attractive 27-acre site by the River Ouse; main buildings date from 1830s. Went co-educational 1987 to stave off decline in demand for boys' boarding. Most famous Old Boy: Guy Fawkes.

Atmosphere Was a sternly traditional school with a take-it-or-leave-it attitude; now gradually being brought up to date. Arrival of girls has improved the quality of life for all, not least in the boarding houses, which are becoming less spartan. Lessons still cover 6 full days (8.30 a.m. to 5.30 p.m., but only to 4.30 p.m. on Wednesdays and Saturdays); day pupils required to conform. Compulsory chapel 3 mornings a week.

The head Formerly head of an independent school in Bristol. Likes a professional challenge – and has found one here.

The teaching Enthusiastic staff of 43 (6 women); half appointed by present head. Curriculum being broadened: technology, computing, business studies etc. Good facilities: 3 fully equipped labs for chemistry, physics, biology; satellite dish to record French and German TV; pleasant classrooms, most carpeted. Pupils falling behind are offered extra help at lunchtime. Compulsory general studies at A-level. Good music: choir, orchestra, a third learn an instrument.

The pupils Business, professional, farming backgrounds. 75% come from St Olave's, a prep school on the same site from which entry is automatic. Entry for the rest by school's own exam, similar to Common Entrance; modest 50% mark required. Assisted places (not all taken up).

Results Improving. GCSE (1991): 92% gained at least 5 grades A-C. A-level (1992): 51% of entries graded A or B.

Destinations All stay on into the sixth form; 90% proceed to higher education (up to 10 a year to Oxbridge).

Sport Mainly rugby, hockey, cricket. Rowing went into decline but has been revived; fencing re-introduced. Sports hall, indoor swimming pool, squash courts.

Remarks Solid school; on the way up.

ST SWITHUN'S
Winchester SO21 1HA
Tel (0962) 861316

Independent • Girls • Boarding and day • Ages 11-18 • 441 pupils (55% boarding) • 100 in sixth form • Fees, £9,210 boarding; £5,565 day
Head: Miss Joan Jefferson, 46, appointed 1986.

Solid, Anglican girls' school on the outskirts of Winchester. Good results (among the top 20); excellent accommodation, particularly for boarders.

Background Founded 1884 through public subscription by Anna Bramston, daughter of the Dean of Winchester; moved to its present hill-top site 1931; purpose-built, Queen Anne style with matching later additions. Unusually, it still serves the purpose for which it was founded: a Church of England girls' boarding and day school.

Atmosphere Warm, welcoming; fine classrooms and boarding houses.

The head Historian; formerly head of a Methodist boarding school in Yorkshire. Has a strong Christian faith and educational philosophy.

The teaching Some is outstanding; high standards evident throughout; staff and girls working towards common goals. French or German from 11 (the second language added at 13); Latin from 12; 3 sciences. Classics, drama, music, technology (teacher was an industrial designer) all taken far beyond examination requirements. Choice of more than 20 subjects at A-level (Latin, French, history of art, chemistry especially popular), plus compulsory general studies. Plenty of good drama and music (most play an instrument, many more than one); visits to theatres, concerts; joint productions with Winchester College. Good library always open; computerised self-service.

The pupils Energetic, competitive, self-confident, take pride in each other's achievements. Upper-sixth girls live in a separate house and are expected to take adult responsibilities for their lives; free to go into the city; some have their own cars. Admission mostly through Common Entrance at 11, 12, 13 (many coming from adjacent junior school); lists often over-subscribed but casual vacancies do occur; early registration advised. Assisted places; a few scholarships and bursaries, including music.

Results GCSE: virtually all gain at least 9 grades A-C. A-level (1992): very impressive 73% of entries graded A or B. Good results also in music and Guildhall drama exams.

Destinations Most stay on for A-levels but some go to boys' schools or a neighbouring sixth-form college. Majority proceed to higher education (recently to do classics, medicine, English, French).

Sport Notable for lacrosse (1992 Junior England captain). Other games range from compulsory netball and tennis to voluntary archery and scuba diving.

Remarks Good, Christian school; much praised by parents.

ST URSULA'S CONVENT

Crooms Hill,
Greenwich,
London SE10 8HN
Tel (081) 858 4613

Comprehensive (voluntary-aided) •
Roman Catholic • Girls • Ages 11-16 • 604 pupils
Head: Sister Elizabeth Campbell, 60s, appointed 1977.

Popular comprehensive; wide ability range; good GCSE results. Priority to girls from committed Catholic families.

Background Run by the Ursuline Sisters. Founded 1877 as a grammar school; became comprehensive 1977; lost its sixth form (to a new Catholic sixth-form college) 1991. Attractive site near Greenwich Park; Georgian (grade-2 listed) and Jacobean (grade-1 listed) buildings. Oak staircases, endless corridors, lots of nooks and crannies. £1.5-million programme of repairs and refurbishment just completed.

Atmosphere Well-mannered, serious, purposeful; no vandalism, litter or graffiti.

The head Firm, astute; committed to comprehensive education; widely respected by both staff and pupils. History graduate; teaches 8 periods a week (general studies and local government); approaching retirement.

The teaching Fairly formal (lines of wooden desks facing the blackboard). Setting by ability from the start (after entry tests in reading and maths); all expected to take 9 GCSEs; plenty of extra help for those in difficulty. English, geography, RE, art particularly strong; good facilities for computing and technology. Average class size 24. Staff of 36 (5 men) including 5 Ursuline Sisters; some expected to transfer to the new sixth-form centre. Pleasant, well-stocked library (with fine views over the Thames and the City). Music improving and expanding: 2 choirs, orchestra, clarinet group etc. Extra-curricular activities mainly at lunchtime. Lots of foreign visits (connections with schools in Normandy and Spain).

The pupils Polite, well-motivated; many from working-class backgrounds; 25% ethnic minority; wide catchment area (Bexley, Bromley, Catford, Forest Hill etc). Entry procedures partly dictated by Greenwich council, which requires 10% of the intake to be drawn from the lowest ability band. All applicants (and their parents) interviewed by Sister Elizabeth or her deputy; priority to girls from committed Catholic families.

Results (1992) GCSE: creditable 64% gained at least 5 grades A-C.

Destinations 96% stay on in full-time education after 16: half to sixth-form college, half to vocational courses.

Sport Tennis and rounders in Greenwich Park; swimming, squash, badminton at local leisure centre. New sports hall planned.

Remarks An all-round quality of education hard to better in the state sector.

STAMFORD
St Paul's Street,
Stamford,
Lincolnshire PE9 2BS
Tel (0780) 62171

Independent • Boys • Day and boarding • Ages 13-18 (plus associated junior school) • 571 pupils (72% day) • 202 in sixth form • Fees, £3,300 day; £6,600 boarding
Head: Geoffrey Timm, 52, appointed 1978.

Solid school; respectable results; lots of music, drama, sport.

Background Founded 1532; shares board of governors with Stamford High *(qv)*. Main buildings date from 1870s; 34 acres of attractive grounds and playing fields on the edge of the town. Formerly Direct Grant; reverted to full independence 1976 and has grown steadily.

Atmosphere Strong sense of community and commitment. Academically selective but socially comprehensive; no airs and graces. Boarding school ethos retained (including fagging); Saturday morning lessons; thriving chapel on Sundays.

The head Warm, friendly; a strong leader. Lincolnshire-born; read modern languages at Cambridge. Taught Spanish at Fettes for 9 years; formerly head of modern languages at Bishop's Stortford. Keen on cricket. Married, 2 grown-up children. Likely to remain here until he retires.

The teaching Predominantly traditional in style. Enthusiastic, long-serving staff; most (but not all) appointed by present head. National curriculum-plus; German, Spanish, Russian, Latin on offer. Some take GCSE maths and French a year early; extra help for those with learning difficulties, including dys-

lexia. Choice of 20 subjects at A-level. Vigorous drama and music (much of it in conjunction with the girls' school); numerous concerts; chapel choir sings in local cathedrals and churches. Well-supported cadet force and Duke of Edinburgh award scheme (community service an alternative); wide range of other extra-curricular activities. Regular language exchanges and overseas study visits.

The pupils Well-balanced, down-to-earth; from a wide spread of social backgrounds. Vast majority of boarders are from Service families (NCO to Air Vice-Marshall); day boys from a 20-mile radius. Top 25% of the ability range; minimum IQ about 110. Assisted places and 25 scholarships from Lincolnshire County Council.

Results GCSE (1991): 98% gained at least 5 grades A-C. A-level (1992): 51% of entries graded A or B.

Destinations 80% stay on for A-levels; 65% of these proceed to higher education (3 to Oxbridge in 1991).

Sport Features prominently. Major games: rugby, hockey (1991 tour of Russia), cricket, tennis, athletics. Shooting, swimming, squash, badminton, golf, canoeing (1992 British schools' champions) also on offer. Good facilities include extensive playing fields, all-weather pitch, tennis courts, sports hall.

Remarks Good all round.

STAMFORD HIGH

St Martin's,
Stamford,
Lincolnshire PE9 2LJ
Tel (0780) 62330

Independent • Girls • Day and boarding •
Ages 4-18 • 1,000 pupils (736 in senior
school) • 171 in sixth form • Fees,
£2,640-£3,300 day; £5,940-£6,600
boarders
Head: Miss Gladys Bland, 54, appointed
1978.

*Traditional, grammar-school type
education; highly regarded locally.*

Background Founded 1877; shares governing body with Stamford School *(qv)*, with
which it has close links. Purpose-built Victorian premises on Stamford High Street resemble a row of prosperous town houses. Formerly
Direct Grant (ethos carefully preserved).

Atmosphere Comfortable, warm, friendly.
Pleasant boarding houses; dormitories named
Laura Ashley, Marks & Spencer, Debenham's
etc.

The head History graduate (London); was
senior mistress at Malvern Girls'. Open, accessible, good listener but well aware she is in
charge. Great traveller: Albania, Outer Mon-
golia etc.

The teaching No streaming in first year but
setting thereafter in maths, English, French, 3
sciences. National curriculum-plus: all girls
introduced to 4 languages (some do 3 for
GCSE); 2 years' compulsory Latin; additional
courses in computing, general studies, arts
appreciation etc. Mostly traditional, whole-
class teaching: wooden desks in rows; blackboards fixed to the walls. Average class size 28,
reducing to 20 for GCSE. 75 staff (16 men);
nearly all graduates; most appointed by present head. Strong drama and music (shared
with Stamford School); 40% learning an
instrument. Popular Duke of Edinburgh
award scheme (24 golds in 1991).

The pupils Confident, well-behaved; friendly
without being subservient. Top 25% of the

ability range; mostly middle-class backgrounds. Day girls from up to 20 miles away;
most boarders from Service families. Entry at
11 + by tests in English, maths, verbal reasoning. Some assisted places; others paid for by
Lincolnshire County Council; music and art
scholarships.

Results GCSE: nearly all gain at least 5 grades
A-C. A-level: 42% of entries graded A or B.

Destinations 75% continue into the sixth
form; most of these proceed to higher education.

Sport Strong in hockey, netball, tennis, athletics, cross-country, gymnastics. Also on
offer: badminton, canoeing, fencing, golf,
ice-skating etc. Large sports hall; heated
indoor pool; playing fields at nearby junior
school.

Remarks Solid school; good all round.

STOCKPORT GRAMMAR

Buxton Road,
Stockport,
Cheshire SK2 7AF
Tel (061) 456 9000

Independent • Co-educational • Day •
Ages 11-18 (plus associated junior
school) • 998 pupils (roughly equal
numbers of boys and girls) • 260 in sixth
form • Fees, £3,258
Head: David Bird, 56, appointed 1985.

*Very sound school; good results; strong
music.*

Background Founded 1487 by Sir Edmond
Shaa, goldsmith; in continuous existence since
then under the patronage of the Goldsmiths'
Company. Mock-Tudor main buildings date
from 1916; substantial later acquisitions and
additions. Reverted to full independence with
the abolition of Direct Grant status in 1976;
girls first admitted 1980, since when numbers
have increased substantially.

Atmosphere Happy, go-ahead. Strong sense of tradition (oak-panelled corridors adorned with photographs of the assembled school going back 60 years) and order, but no hint of coercion. Relationships between teachers and pupils civilised without being familiar. Separate morning assembly for Jewish pupils.

The head Energetic, shrewd; has a flair for balancing traditional values with necessary innovation and development. Educated at St Paul's and Cambridge (read geography); has taught in both state and independent schools; formerly head of a grammar school in Kent. Insists on all-round excellence; school has flourished under his leadership. Married, 3 children.

The teaching Challenging. Plenty of modern teaching aids – but used as adjuncts to, not replacements for, traditional chalk, talk and text book. Broadly grammar-school curriculum; science taught as 3 separate subjects after first year; religious education taken seriously. Mixed-ability classes; setting in maths from third year. All take at least 3 A-levels plus general studies (including courses in Greek, Italian, Spanish). Systematic homework, carefully monitored (3 hours a night in sixth form). Very strong music: 3 string orchestras, 2 wind bands, 3 choirs; concert tours to the US. Busy extra-curricular programme. Regular visits, language exchanges, expeditions abroad.

The pupils Lively, courteous, eager to participate (and all beautifully turned-out); relationships between the sexes is relaxed and unselfconscious. Many from business, farming and professional backgrounds – doctors and teachers especially well represented – but others from modest homes; 200 have assisted places. Catchment area covers south Manchester, north Cheshire, parts of Derbyshire; school very heavily over-subscribed. Entry at 4 through observed play and conversation; at 7 by tests in English, maths; at 11+ by tests in English, maths, verbal reasoning. No minimum IQ specified but a third of those who apply for the junior school and 80% of those who apply for the senior school are turned away.

Results GCSE: virtually all gain at least 5 grades A-C (98% gain at least 6). A-level (1992): 58% of entries graded A or B. Good results, too, in Associated Music Board exams.

Destinations More than 90% stay for A-levels; 90% of these proceed to higher education (about 20 a year to Oxbridge).

Sport Major games: rugby, lacrosse, cricket, netball, hockey; up to 400 play on Saturdays. Facilities include extensive playing fields, all-weather pitch, squash courts (but no sports hall).

Remarks Well-run, attractive school – and getting even better.

STONAR
Cottles Park,
Atworth,
Near Melksham,
Wiltshire SN12 8NT
Tel (0225) 702309

Independent • Girls • Boarding and day • Ages 5-18 • 553 pupils (445 in senior school; 59% boarding) • 114 in sixth form • Fees, £7,242-£7,908 boarding; £2,331-£4,380 day
Head: Mrs Sue Hopkinson, early 50s, appointed September 1985.

Attractive school; wide range of abilities; outstanding riding.

Background Founded 1895; moved to present 80-acre parkland setting 1939; handsome 19th-century listed mansion surrounded by converted 17th-century cottages and barns plus substantial later additions; a village-like feel.

Atmosphere Cheerful, warm, welcoming; pupils and staff clearly feel at ease in this low-key, caring, unstuffy environment. Attractively furnished boarding houses (dormitories for up to 6); sixth-formers in high-quality single or double study-bedrooms.

The head Open, enthusiastic. Read history at

Oxford; has taught in both state and independent schools; formerly deputy head of Queen Ethelburga's, Harrogate. Happiest when walking a long way from home (Canadian Rockies, Nepal) with a small group of people. Married, 2 grown-up children; husband teaches history and politics here.

The teaching Fairly formal, didactic; desks in rows. Long-serving staff (75 women): average age 42. Pupils set by ability in English, maths, French, science; extra help for those who need it, including dyslexics; class sizes in low-20s. A-level options include business studies, theatre studies, geology; alternatives include 1-year vocational course and, unusually, a diploma in horse studies (internationally renowned equestrian centre has 4 full-time instructors, 55 horses). Good art, drama, music; more than half learn an instrument.

The pupils Lively, confident, unaffected; day girls from local farming and business families; boarders from London, Home Counties, west of England and Wales; 12% Service families; 12% from abroad, particularly Hong Kong, Zambia. School is non-selective; range of abilities fairly wide.

Results GCSE (1991): 67% gained at least 5 grades A-C. A-level (1992): modest 32% of entries graded A or B.

Destinations About a third proceed to higher education (1 or 2 a year to Oxbridge).

Sport Good hockey (regular county honours), swimming and cross-country; netball, tennis, athletics, badminton, squash, canoeing also on offer. 200 girls ride; many bring their own horses.

Remarks Lots of unobtrusive support for girls of average academic ability; good value for money.

STONYHURST
Stonyhurst,
Lancashire BB6 9PZ
Tel (0254) 826345

Independent • Roman Catholic • Boys (plus a handful of girls in the sixth form) • Boarding and day • Ages 13-18 • 440 pupils (90% boarding) • 185 in sixth form • Fees, £9,465 boarding; £5,136 day
Head: Dr Giles Mercer, 43, appointed 1985.

Distinguished school; an education reflecting the ideals of the Society of Jesus. Good teaching; superb facilities; strong sporting record.

Background Founded in St Omer 1593; moved here (after many vicissitudes) 1794; one of the oldest Jesuit colleges in continuous existence. Elizabethan house with grand 19th-century additions in beautiful Ribble Valley.

Atmosphere Immensely dignified – a palpable sense of history and living tradition. Lots of fine art on walls and ceilings; oak staircases; long, wide corridors. A true community; emphasis on self-respect, self-reliance, respect for others. Numbers martyrs and saints among its Old Boys, and 7 holders of the Victoria Cross.

The head Highly qualified historian (Cambridge MA, Oxford DPhil); committed Roman Catholic; first lay head. Makes no apology for the central place of Christian worship in the life of the school. Family man; lives on campus (and stresses the value of boarding education).

The teaching Outstanding: varied styles; skilful questioning; sixth-form lessons resemble university tutorials. Mature, civilised pupil-teacher relations; boys' commitment to hard work taken for granted; serious discipline problems almost unheard of. Broad curriculum, including Latin, Greek, 2 modern languages, ancient history, astronomy. Compulsory religious doctrine in sixth form; impressive computer-aided design (used by local industry). Small classes (pupil-teacher ratio

8:1); setting by ability in maths, Latin, French. Lots of community service (boys help in psychiatric hospital, school for handicapped children) and fund-raising for charity; annual visit to Lourdes; popular cadet force and Duke of Edinburgh award scheme.

The pupils Articulate, courteous. Youthful vigour combined with a basically thoughtful outlook. Most from professional families (small number of bursaries and assisted places) from all over UK and abroad. Fairly wide ability range (school proud of its success with the less academically able). Half start at one of 2 prep schools: St Mary's Hall (on site) and St John's, Windsor.

Results GCSE: virtually all gain at least 5 grades A-C. A-level (1992): 46% of entries graded A or B.

Destinations 90% proceed to higher education (10 a year to Oxbridge).

Sport Superb facilities, including swimming pool, squash courts, 9-hole golf course. Main sports: rugby (recent tours to Portugal, Australia, Fiji, Belgium), cricket, athletics. Also available: soccer, squash, tennis, badminton, basketball, water polo, clay-pigeon shooting; first-class fishing on nearby River Hodder.

Remarks Well-run school with clear, consistent ideals, offering a wide range of activities in and out of the classroom.

STOWE

Stowe,
Buckingham MK18 5EH
Tel (0280) 813164

Independent • Boys (plus girls in sixth form) • Boarding and some day • Ages 13-18 • 587 pupils (90% boarding) • 198 in sixth form (55% boys) • Fees, £10,860 boarding; £7,599 day
Head: Jeremy Nichols, 48, appointed 1989.

Wide range of abilities; fine setting; plenty of art, drama, music, sport.

Background Founded 1923 to pioneer new principles in boarding education – courtesy, tolerance, freedom to develop individual talents of mind and body – in response to contemporary criticisms of the harsh and repressive regimes of many public schools. Magnificent 17th-century mansion (former home of the Dukes of Buckingham and Chandos) extensively enhanced by Vanbrugh; 750 acres laid out by 'Capability' Brown (much of the grounds is the responsibility of the National Trust). Many sympathetic later extensions and improvements.

Atmosphere Sheer magnificence of the buildings and grounds creates a strong impression. Friendly, supportive relations between staff and pupils; individualism encouraged; big emphasis on participation and involvement. (New boys put on a play in their first fortnight; helps them to get to know each other – and leaves less time to be homesick.) Most staff live on site and play a full part in the extra-curricular activities. Boarding accommodation has been upgraded.

The head Educated at Lancing and Cambridge; taught at Rugby; formerly a housemaster at Eton. Married, 4 children. Keen to encourage initiative, resourcefulness, confidence, self-discipline.

The teaching Emphasis is on practical work and an investigative approach. Pupils streamed by ability; additional setting in English, maths, French. All do computing; choice of 'integrated' or 3 separate sciences; 2 top forms take Latin plus Greek, German or Spanish. Maximum class size 20. All do 8-9 GCSEs; most take 3 A-levels plus life skills course. Checks on progress every 3 weeks; school examinations twice a year; termly reports to parents. Lots of drama and music; a third learn an instrument; weekly concerts. Good art. Choice between cadet force, Duke of Edinburgh award scheme and community service.

The pupils Most from fairly prosperous homes in London and the South East; 10% from abroad (a cosmopolitan dimension). IQs range from under 100 to 140+. Scholarships, bursaries available.

Results GCSE (1991): 85% gained at least 5 grades A-C. A-level (1992): modest 38% of entries graded A or B.

Destinations 90% stay on for A-levels; 65% of these proceed to higher education (8 to Oxbridge in 1991).

Sport All play at least 2 afternoons a week. Major activities: rugby, hockey, cricket, tennis, athletics, swimming for the boys; lacrosse, hockey, netball, tennis, swimming for the girls. Many minor sports also played to a high level. Facilities include sports hall, outdoor pool, all-weather pitch.

Remarks Attractive school, particularly for less academically able children.

STRATHALLAN
Forgandenny,
Perth PH2 9EG
Tel (0738) 812546

Independent • Co-educational • Boarding (and some day) • Ages 10-18 • 530 pupils (68% boys; 98% boarding) • 165 in sixth form (72% boys) • Fees, £7,560-£9,360 (a third less for day pupils)
Head: David Pighills, late-50s, appointed 1975 (retires August 1993).

Stimulating, successful school; wide range of abilities catered for; big emphasis on sport and outdoor pursuits.

Background Founded 1912; moved 1920 to present 150-acre, richly wooded site 7 miles south of Perth. Main building an early 19th-century mock-Tudor reconstruction of an 18th-century house; later additions in the same style plus a complex of serviceable but unattractive classrooms; good new design/technology centre. Fully co-educational since 1982.

Atmosphere Busy, robust community that will not suit the slouch: unsophisticated, down-to-earth (but less rugged since the introduction of girls). Outstanding boarding accommodation for seniors in 6 new houses; 14-year-olds and above have own well-appointed study-bedrooms; junior house comfortable but rather basic by comparison.

The head Energy undiminished despite a long stint. Prospective parents struggle to keep up with the pace of his conducted tours unless he stops to pick up litter, chivvy a pupil with an undone shirt button or remove an illicit drawing-pin from the wall of a new study-bedroom. Firm believer in the constructive use of leisure; does not look kindly on couch potatoes. Cambridge-educated; previously a housemaster at Fettes. Bachelor; devotes all his time to the school; knows every pupil by name; gives frequent dinner parties for staff.

The teaching Sound; particularly good design/technology, business studies and computing. Emphasis in the first 2 years on the '3 Rs';

French introduced, plus foundation courses in design/ technology and computing. German on offer from third year. Pupils all streamed by ability; additional setting in maths, French; class sizes 12-15. All do at least 8 GCSEs, including English, maths, 1 science, 1 foreign language and history or geography. Sixth-form choice of A-levels, Highers or a combination; 20 take Highers only (in 5 subjects). Lots of drama and music; a third learn an instrument; 2 orchestras, several choirs; 91 play the bagpipes (!) Big emphasis on outdoor pursuits: cadet force, Duke of Edinburgh award scheme, adventure expeditions.

The pupils Not the tidiest nor the most polished – but happy and self-confident; girls are equal citizens, unabashed by numerical inequality. Primarily Scots or expats from engineering or financial backgrounds. Wide academic range accepted; entry sometimes limited by number of places available. Some scholarships.

Results GCSE: 80% gain at least 5 grades A-C. A-level: modest 35% of entries graded A or B (but creditable for the range of abilities).

Destinations 85% continue into the sixth form; 65% of these proceed to higher education (about 4 a year to Oxbridge).

Sport Mainly rugby (South American tour 1991), hockey, cricket for the boys; hockey, athletics for the girls. Also on offer: squash, fives, tennis, swimming, shooting, angling, sailing, skiing.

Remarks Well-run school. Spacious grounds in splendid rural setting: will best suit those who enjoy the outdoor life.

STREATHAM HILL & CLAPHAM HIGH
Wavertree Road,
London SW2 3SR
Tel (081) 674 6912

Independent • Girls • Day • Ages 11-18 (plus associated junior school) • 397 pupils • 57 in sixth form • Fees, £3,864
Head: Miss Gillian Ellis, late-40s, appointed 1979.

Successful academic school; good teaching and results; lots of music.

Background Founded in Brixton 1887 (member of Girls' Public Day School Trust); moved to present site – in a warren of narrow suburban streets – 1894; main premises partly rebuilt 1952 after war damage; slightly forbidding appearance. Neighbouring houses acquired for classrooms.

Atmosphere Busy, friendly community. Highly motivated, articulate pupils; hardworking, enthusiastic staff.

The head Read chemistry at Glasgow. Has rescued the school from declining numbers and growing debt; her leadership and influence apparent throughout. Pays great attention to recruiting top-quality staff (all but 4 are her appointments); short-listed candidates required to teach a lesson under observation (other heads please note).

The teaching Undoubtedly traditional in style but modified by the 'active learning' requirements of GCSE and the national curriculum. Strongly academic curriculum; all do French in first year, add Latin in second year; choice of German or Spanish in third year. Science – taught as 3 separate subjects – is particularly strong; in 1992 a pupil became the first British girl to win a gold medal at the International Mathematical Olympiad. Most take 9 GCSEs (choice of 18). No streaming by ability (within a fairly narrow range); classes of 22 or fewer. A-levels complemented by ambitious general studies programme: all continue with a foreign language; Spanish, Russian, Japanese on offer; emphasis on oral skills. All take a course in self-defence. Lots of drama and music, timetabled and otherwise; a third learn an instrument; 2 orchestras, many smaller ensembles, 2 choirs. Busy extra-curricular programme, including much fund-raising for charity. Regular language exchanges with schools in France, Spain, Germany.

The pupils Wide social and racial mix from across south London; nearly a third have assisted places. School heavily over-subscribed; 250 apply for 65 places. Girls from associated junior school are guaranteed a place; rest enter by interview and tests in English, maths, verbal reasoning. At least half have IQs of 120+.

Results GCSE (1991): 83% gained at least 5 grades A-C. A-level: disappointing 42% of entries graded A or B (has been much higher).

Destinations 65% stay for A-levels; 85% of these proceed to higher education (4 to Oxbridge in 1991).

Sport Particularly good netball, Olympic gymnastics, sports acrobatics. Fully equipped sports hall.

Remarks Strong, well-run school.

SURBITON HIGH
Surbiton Crescent,
Kingston upon Thames,
Surrey KT1 2JT
Tel (081) 546 5245

Independent • Girls (and 99 junior boys in separate premises) • Day • Ages 5-18 • 704 pupils (438 in senior school) • 80 in sixth form • Fees, £2,319-£3,870
Head: Mrs Rosemary Thynne, late-50s, appointed 1979 (retires July 1993).

Lively, effective school; good exam results; lots of art.

Background Founded 1884 by group of Anglican clergy to provide 'superior education for girls in accordance with the principles of the Church of England'. (Education still superior but all faiths now admitted.) One of 7 schools administered by the Church Schools Company, which sets the fees. 3-storey Victorian houses with many later additions on a cramped site. Junior girls' department moving in 1993 and doubling in size; senior school will then expand.

Atmosphere Enthusiastic, well-mannered girls. Stylish decor (grey carpets, stripped wooden doors); lots of art on the walls.

The head Long-serving; clearly the force behind the school's emphasis on high academic standards and self-discipline.

The teaching Varied, challenging styles. All girls take at least 9 GCSEs; a third do 2 languages; 3 sciences on offer; computing has a toe-hold. Most sixth-formers take 3 A-levels (out of 21) plus wide choice of general studies. Maximum class size 24; smaller for GCSE and A-level. Good art; two-thirds learn a musical instrument – orchestra, chamber groups, choirs.

The pupils Top 15 of the ability range. Huge catchment area (Leatherhead, Weybridge, Twickenham, Teddington). Half enter at 11 from state primary schools; admission by tests in English, maths and interview. Heavily over-subscribed (but many parents apply to more than 1 school). 5 assisted places a year; 3 scholarships.

Results GCSE: all gain at least 5 grades A-C. A-level (1992): 49% of entries graded A or B.

Destinations 75% continue into the sixth form (remainder to further education and sixth-form colleges); nearly all of these proceed to higher education (2-5 a year to Oxbridge).

Sport Good hockey, tennis, netball, athletics; rowing on the Thames for sixth-formers. Floodlit netball court on site; playing fields 1 mile away.

Remarks Well-run school; doing a sound job.

SUTTON HIGH
55 Cheam Road,
Sutton,
Surrey SM1 2AX
Tel (081) 642 0594

Independent • Girls • Day • Ages 4-18 •
803 pupils (547 in senior school) • 123 in
sixth form • Fees, £2,844-£3,684
Head: Miss Alison Cavendish, 50s,
appointed 1980.

*High academic standards; good results;
strong sport.*

Background Founded 1884; member of the
Girls' Public Day School Trust. 5-acre site in
the centre of Sutton; Victorian houses with
many later additions surrounding pleasant
garden and playing field.

Atmosphere Calm, friendly.

The head Formerly head of an inner-London
comprehensive; began working life as a librarian (new school library named after her).

The teaching Most take 9-10 GCSEs (3 sciences or Nuffield co-ordinated course); choice
of 20 subjects at A-level – most do 3, plus
compulsory extras. Lots of computing and
technology. Classes of 28; smaller for GCSE
and A-level. Good art (no tiny, restricted
drawings here) and music (more than a
quarter learn an instrument).

The pupils Hard to miss in their bright
mauve and navy uniform. Under-7s admitted
after observation of group activities and conversation; 7-year-olds by tests in reading and
maths; 11-year-olds by exam and interview
(45% come from state primary schools); 'good
academic ability' looked for. Over-subscribed,
from a wide catchment area (Reigate,
Leatherhead, Dorking, Epsom). 25 assisted
places a year. Much concern for the less
privileged: girls help in school for mentally
handicapped.

Results All gain at least 5 grades A-C. A-level
(1992): 51% of entries graded A or B.

Destinations 80% continue into the sixth

form; nearly all of these proceed to higher
education (12 to Oxbridge in 1991).

Sport Netball, hockey, badminton, gymnastics, tennis all strong; many county players.
Sports hall; heated indoor pool (donated by
parents).

Remarks Solid school; good all round.

SUTTON VALENCE
Sutton Valence,
Maidstone,
Kent ME17 3HL
Tel (0622) 842281

Independent • Co-educational • Day and
boarding • Ages 11-18 • 387 pupils (60%
boys; 60% day) • 132 in sixth form • Fees,
£6,039 day; £9,426 boarding
Head: Michael Haywood, 50, appointed
1980.

*Small school specialising in children of
average academic ability; good music
and sport.*

Background Founded 1576; main buildings
date from 1910; numerous later additions.
Attractive 100-acre site (including 30 acres of
playing fields) with spectacular views over the
Weald of Kent. Co-educational since 1983.

Atmosphere Friendly. Christian ethos;
strong sense of community; parental involvement encouraged.

The head Passionate advocate of the merits of
small co-educational boarding schools. Educated at Edinburgh and Cambridge; taught
history at Dulwich; formerly deputy head of
Dollar Academy. Married, 4 children (all of
whom have been pupils here); wife teaches
English full time and runs girls' games.

The teaching Good science and maths; languages include German, Spanish, Russian.
Pupils streamed by ability; additional setting in
English, maths, French. Small classes: 12-15
for first 2 years, 17-18 for GCSE, 8 in the sixth

form; extra help for mild dyslexia. Two-thirds of staff appointed by present head; two-thirds men. Choice of 18 subjects at A-level; all take diploma course in information technology. Strong music: orchestra, wind band, 4 choirs. Lots of art and drama. Active community service unit visits London centre for homeless, local hospitals etc; popular Duke of Edinburgh award scheme and cadet force.

The pupils Mostly from business, professional, farming backgrounds; minority from Hong Kong, Africa, Europe. No serious disciplinary problems (head believes in 'minimum number of rules, maximum number of conventions'). Entry at 11 by tests and interview; at 13 by Common Entrance – modest 50% mark required. 10 assisted places a year.

Results GCSE (1991): 85% gained 5 or more grades A-C. A-level (1992): very modest 25% of entries graded A or B (has been higher).

Destinations 85% stay on for A-levels; 75% of these proceed to higher education (1-2 a year to Oxbridge).

Sport Good record for a small school, particularly in rugby, cricket, netball, tennis, hockey, shooting.

Remarks Caring community; suits all-rounders.

TAUNTON
Taunton,
Somerset TA2 6AD
Tel (0823) 284596

Independent • Co-educational • Day and boarding • Ages 13-18 (plus associated junior schools) • 539 pupils (equal numbers of girls and boys; 52% day) • 200 in sixth form • Fees, £6,300 day; £9,825 boarding
Head: Barry Sutton, late-50s, appointed 1987.

Good all round; not unduly selective.

Background Founded 1847 for the sons of dissenters; moved to present 50-acre site 1870; mid-Victorian Gothic buildings plus large, austere chapel (donated by a member of the Wills tobacco family) and many later additions. Good facilities for science, art, design/technology.

Atmosphere In the non-conformist tradition: sober, hard-working, no-nonsense. Compulsory chapel; lots of rules; co-educational ethos not strong, despite the balanced numbers. Boarding accommodation clean, comfortable; maximum of 6 per room; sixth-formers have own study-bedrooms.

The head Formerly head of Hereford Cathedral School for 17 years. Married, 3 grown-up children; wife teaches maths here.

The teaching Wide variety of styles. Pupils streamed by ability into 2 broad bands; additional setting in maths, French; average class size 20. All take 9 GCSEs (5 core, 4 optional subjects). Good science – including radio astronomy – computing, art, design/technology. Most do 3 A-levels; vocational alternatives include BTEC diploma in business and finance. Lots of music; a third learn an instrument; strong chapel choir. Successful debating society; popular Duke of Edinburgh award scheme. Regular language exchanges with France and Germany.

The pupils Smartly dressed; slightly solemn. Mostly from professional, business, Service backgrounds in the South West; 15% from abroad. Fairly wide ability range; minimum 50% mark required at Common Entrance; 70% join from the associated boys' and girls' junior schools (soon to be merged). A few scholarships and assisted places.

Results GCSE: 80% gain at least 5 grades A-C. A-level (1992): 43% of entries graded A or B.

Destinations Most stay on for A-levels; nearly 90% proceed to higher education (5 or 6 a year to Oxbridge).

Sport Chiefly rugby, hockey, cricket, netball, tennis. Good facilities include sports hall, heated pool, all-weather pitch.

Remarks Sound school.

TIFFIN BOYS'
Queen Elizabeth Road,
Kingston upon Thames,
Surrey KT2 6RL
Tel (081) 546 4638

Grammar (grant-maintained from January 1993) • Boys • Ages 11-18 • 894 pupils • 260 in sixth form
Head: Dr Tony Dempsey, 48, appointed 1988.

First-rate academic school with all-round strengths, not least in music.

Background Founded 1638; moved to its present cramped 1½-acre urban site 1929; previously independent, became voluntary-controlled after the 1944 Education Act; parents voted in 1992 to opt out of council control. Buildings of various ages and condition include 18th-century listed library, wooden huts and fine new creative studies block.

Atmosphere First impression is of a rigorously traditional institution: strict uniform (blazers of many stripes and colours), prefects in gowns, a clear hierarchy among pupils, an almost puritanical acceptance of hardship as the basis for sound education. The reality is a lively, friendly, supportive school with mature, self-confident boys. Enthusiastic staff give freely of their time; parents fully involved.

The head A former pupil here; took a BSc and PhD in chemistry at Bristol; has taught extensively in both state and independent schools (formerly deputy head of a comprehensive); seeks to bring together the best of the 2 systems. Married, 1 son (at King's College School, Wimbledon).

The teaching Traditionally strong in maths and science (taught as 3 separate subjects) but art, drama, music and technology – taught to all in the first 2 years – are becoming increasingly important. National curriculum-plus; all do at least 2 years of Latin; GCSE options include Greek, second modern language, computing; all take 10 GCSEs. No streaming by ability (within a narrow range); average class size 24. Wide choice of subjects at A-level, including business studies, geology, government and politics; all do at least 3, plus non-examined course in general studies (with Tiffin Girls', *qv*). Very strong music; 40 learn an instrument; orchestra, bands, choirs; annual European tour; numerous ambitious drama productions; superb facilities. Wide range of extra-curricular activities; well-supported Scouts, Venture Scouts. Regular language trips to France and Germany.

The pupils Top 15% of the ability range; mostly, but not exclusively, from middle-class homes in an extensive catchment area. Entry by severely competitive 11+ tests of verbal and spatial reasoning.

Results (1992) GCSE: 96% gained at least 5 grades A-C – and most a good deal more. A-level: 43% of entries graded A or B.

Destinations More than 90% stay on for A-levels and proceed to higher education (about 12 a year to Oxbridge).

Sport Team games play an important role in the life of the school; 12 rugby or cricket teams turn out on Saturdays; boat club has a full programme of regattas; athletics, cross-country, tennis, basketball also on offer. Space on site is limited but there are excellent facilities near Hampton Court.

Remarks Long under-funded, now looking forward to a secure future; highly recommended.

TIFFIN GIRLS'
Richmond Road,
Kingston upon Thames,
Surrey KT2 5PL
Tel (081) 546 0773

Grammar • Girls • Ages 11-18 • 834 pupils • 195 in sixth form
Head: Mrs Sandra Buchanan, 44, appointed 1989.

Successful academic school; good results; wide range of extra-curricular activities.

Background Founded 1880; moved to present site 1987, taking over the 1950s premises of a former secondary modern school; pleasant setting but buildings beginning to show signs of age. No current plans to join Tiffin Boys' *(qv)* in opting out of council control.

Atmosphere Serious, hard-working, well-disciplined – regularly enlivened by 'fun days' when lessons are abandoned and staff and pupils join in charity fund-raising and other activities.

The head Read English at Lancaster; taught in Sicily for a year; formerly deputy head of a comprehensive in Lowestoft. Keen that girls should learn to project themselves, be confident and self-assured. Married, no children.

The teaching Emphasis on high academic standards; school has a good reputation for curriculum development and innovation. All do national curriculum for first 3 years plus classical studies and Latin; all take at least 9 GCSEs plus non-examined course in aesthetic education. Some setting by ability in maths, French. Most take 3 A-levels plus general studies. Lots of speech and drama, music; 2

orchestras, 2 choirs. Good library. Regular language trips to France, Germany.

The pupils Top 15% of the ability range from Surrey commuter belt. Entry by council's 11+; school heavily over-subscribed.

Results (1992) GCSE: 99% gained at least 5 grades A-C. A-level: creditable 53% of entries graded A or B.

Destinations 70% stay on for A-levels; nearly 80% of these proceed to higher education (6 to Oxbridge in 1991).

Sport Chiefly hockey, netball, tennis, athletics; other options include basketball, volleyball, badminton. On-site playing fields and 2 large gymnasia.

Remarks Strong all round.

TONBRIDGE
Tonbridge,
Kent TN9 1JP
Tel (0732) 365555

Independent • Boys • Boarding and day • Ages 13-18 • 650 pupils (68% boarding) • 260 in sixth form • Fees, £10,425 boarding; £7,350 day
Head: Martin Hammond, 47, appointed 1990.

First-class academic and sporting record; one of the top 3 or 4 boys' boarding schools.

Background Founded (and generously endowed) 1553 by Sir Andrew Judde, Master of the Skinners' Company (who are still the governors). Main buildings early-Victorian Gothic plus substantial later additions; set in 150 acres on the northern edge of the town. Cricket ground – the Head – regarded as one of the best in the country (Sir Colin Cowdrey is an Old Boy). Fine Edwardian Gothic chapel burnt down in 1988; being re-built at a cost of £7 million.

Atmosphere Traditional standards and values maintained. Emphasis on academic and sporting excellence, good manners, sense of duty and responsibility. All gather for daily chapel ('Christian witness and worship are at the heart of the school's life').

The head Modest, quietly-spoken. Oxford classicist; taught at St Paul's, Harrow, Eton; formerly head of City of London Boys'. Has published a translation of the *Iliad* and is working 'in a leisurely way' on the *Odyssey*; travelled round Greece with a donkey in the footsteps of R L Stevenson. Teaches all boys in their first year 'so that they can get to know me'. Married to a teacher; 2 children.

The teaching Long-serving, hard-working staff who give freely of their time (two-thirds live in school accommodation). Boys streamed by ability from the start; setting in all subjects thereafter. Class sizes 21-22, reducing to 17 for GCSE, 8 for A-level. All take at least 10 GCSEs; most do 2 modern languages (native-speaking assistants in French, German, Spanish, Russian – Japanese recently introduced) and 3 sciences. Choice of 23 subjects at A-level; all do at least 3, 40 take 4. First-rate music and drama; half a day each week for cadet force, community service, Duke of Edinburgh award scheme. Extensive programme of foreign exchanges and trips.

The pupils Serious, highly motivated; discipline not seen as a problem but school takes a hard line on drugs. Admission at 13 by Common Entrance; minimum 60% mark required. 25 scholarships a year; school gives away £1.5 million annually in financial assistance. Head notes proudly that the drive is not full of Range Rovers.

Results GCSE (1991): 95% gained at least 5 grades A-C. A-level (1992): impressive 70% of entries graded A or B.

Destinations Virtually all stay for A-levels and proceed to higher education (30 a year to Oxbridge). Law, medicine, engineering the most popular careers.

Sport Very strong; coaching in 20 sports; emphasis on providing something for everyone. Excellent facilities include fine playing fields, heated indoor pool, all-weather courts and athletics track.

Remarks Fine school: high-pressure but caring.

TONBRIDGE GRAMMAR
Deakin Leas,
Tonbridge,
Kent TN9 2JR
Tel (0732) 365125

Grammar • Girls • Ages 11-18 • 863 pupils • 232 in sixth form
Head: Mrs Wendy Carey, 46, appointed 1990.

Solid grammar school; good exam results; popular with parents.

Background Founded 1905. 19 acres in the middle of residential Tonbridge on a hill overlooking the Kentish Weald. Functional buildings much added-to over the years. Grant-mantained status under consideration.

Atmosphere Busy school; lots going on at lunchtime when most girls are involved in a wide range of activities. Sixth-formers given plenty of responsibility; active school council taken seriously.

The head Australian-born. Forceful, determined; prepared to fight hard for her school in a famously low-spending county. Has made many changes in a short time and promises more. Teaches English to the older girls; door always open. Strong believer in the 'enabling' virtues of single-sex education. Married to a teacher, 4 children.

The teaching Broad curriculum: all first-years do Latin, technology, computing; second language from second year; combined or separate sciences for GCSE. Mixed-ability teaching at first; setting in maths and French thereafter. Impressive choice of 24 subjects at A-level; most do 3. Average class size 30; 20 for GCSE; 15 at A-level. Regular homework carefully monitored. 60 staff (14 men); head has made a number of young appointments 'to bring in new ideas and vitality'. Exceptionally good library. A quarter learn a musical instrument; orchestras, jazz band, choirs. Drama popular throughout the school (keen sixth-formers supervise younger girls).

The pupils Enthusiastic, hard-working; discipline not a problem. Fashionable new uniform chosen by head (but sixth-formers can wear what they like, including jeans). Admission by Kent Selection Procedure at 11; over-subscribed; expanding catchment area (Tonbridge, Tunbridge Wells, Sevenoaks).

Results (1992) GCSE: 98% gained at least 5 grades A-C. A-level: 43% of entries graded A or B.

Destinations Most stay on for A-levels and continue into higher education (10-12 a year to Oxbridge).

Sport Good hockey, netball, cross-country, athletics, tennis; gymnastics popular (PE compulsory throughout the school). Also badminton, squash, dry-skiing, self-defence. Good facilities, being steadily improved.

Remarks Prepares bright, capable girls to make their way in the modern world.

TRINITY
Shirley Park,
Croydon CR9 7AT
Tel (081) 656 9541

Independent • Boys • Day • Ages 10-18 • 834 pupils • 200 in sixth form • Fees, £4,233
Head: Robin Wilson, late-50s, appointed 1972.

Solid school; good facilities; generous bursaries; first-rate music.

Background Founded 1596 by John Whitgift, Archbishop of Canterbury; moved to present 27-acre site and spacious, purpose-built premises 1965. Later additions include 1,250-seat drama and music hall.

Atmosphere Everything neat and orderly (uniformed porter at reception); well-furnished classrooms and labs; no expense spared on equipment.

The head Cambridge-educated; formerly head of English at Nottingham High. 1993 chairman of the Headmasters' Conference (representing the 230 leading boys' and co-educational independent schools). Retires August 1994.

The teaching Broad curriculum; more than half take 2 languages for GCSE (from French, German, Spanish); choice of 3 separate sciences or dual award; strong design/technology. Maximum class size 25. Choice of 21 subjects at A-level; most take 3, plus non-examined general studies course (occupies 20% of the timetable). Strong music, including renowned Trinity Boys' Choir. Popular cadet force; thriving Duke of Edinburgh award scheme.

The pupils More than half benefit from generous Whitgift Foundation bursary scheme; assisted places, music scholarships also available. Entry at 10, 11, 13 by interview and tests in English, maths.

Results GCSE: all gain at least 5 grades A-C. A-level (1992): 47% of entries graded A or B (has been higher).

Destinations 90% stay on for A-levels and proceed to higher education (10 to Oxbridge in 1991).

Sport Very strong, particularly rugby, cricket, water polo. Good facilities, including 10 acres of playing fields, heated indoor pool.

Remarks Good all round.

TRURO

Trennick Lane,
Truro,
Cornwall TR1 1TH
Tel (0872) 72763

Independent • Co-educational • Day and boarding • Ages 11-18 (plus associated junior school) • 932 pupils (79% boys; 75% day) • 300 in sixth form • Fees (1992-93), £4,110 day; £7,650 boarding
Head (acting): Brian Jackson, late-50s, appointed September 1992.

Solid school; fairly wide range of abilities; respectable results.

Background Founded 1880; became fully independent 1977 with the abolition of Direct Grant status; governors apppointed by the Methodist Conference. Victorian-Gothic buildings plus many later additions in a magnificent setting overlooking the city. Fully co-educational since 1990; proportion of girls increasing.

Atmosphere Friendly, unpretentious; a Christian school teaching Christian values. Committed staff; keen, responsive pupils. Boarding houses (some a distance away in the city) vary in size and comfort.

The head Stepped into the breach when Barry Hobbs, appointed in 1986, was forced to take early retirement through ill health. Formerly deputy head; has been here 35 years. New appointment imminent.

The teaching Broad curriculum; all do French to GCSE; German, Latin on offer from second year; science taught as 3 separate subjects. Setting by ability from second year in French, maths; progress closely monitored. First-rate facilities for science (16 labs), computing, design/technology, languages. Choice of 20 subjects at A-level; strong maths, science and a distinct bias towards engineering. Lots of music; 20% learn an instrument; orchestra, bands, choir. Busy extra-curricular programme; 106 activities on offer (!) including thriving Christian Union, exceptionally strong chess, well-supported Duke of Edinburgh award scheme.

The pupils Mostly from middle-class Cornish backgrounds; many parents in farming, Services; some boarders from the Far East. Entry at 11 by tests in English, maths; up to 300 apply for 125 places but school is not unduly selective. 70 join the sixth form, mostly from comprehensives. Some assisted places, scholarships, bursaries.

Results GCSE (1991): 80% gained 5 or more grades A-C. A-level (1992): 41% of entries graded A or B.

Destinations 75% stay on for A-levels; 70% of these proceed to higher education (up to 12 a year to Oxbridge).

Sport An important aspect of the school's life. Main games: rugby, soccer, hockey, cricket, netball, volleyball. First-rate facilities include 40 acres of playing fields, all-weather pitch, running track, outdoor pool, fine sports hall.

Remarks Well-regarded local school.

TUDOR GRANGE

Dingle Lane,
Solihull B91 3PD
Tel (021) 705 5100

Comprehensive • Co-educational • Ages 11-16 • 1,203 pupils (roughly equal numbers of girls and boys)
Head: John Evans, mid-40s, appointed 1990.

Highly regarded comprehensive; good GCSE results; strong sport.

Background 1974 amalgamation of 2 single-sex grammar schools; drab 1950s brick buildings on spacious 20-acre campus; later additions include fine library ('learning resource centre'), music block and some 'temporary' huts. Parents rejected 1991 move to opt out of council control.

Atmosphere Orderly, purposeful; high standards set; grammar-school ethos largely retained (honours boards celebrate Oxbridge successes, Latin far from dead).

The head Formerly deputy head of a comprehensive in Pembrokeshire. Married, 2 children (both pupils here).

The teaching Progressive rather than didactic in style (known as 'active learning') but girls still take home economics while boys do design/technology. Main language French; Russian, German on offer. Most do 9-10 GCSEs; best results in science and business studies. Setting by ability in some subjects, including maths. Lots of drama and music (a third learn an instrument). Popular Duke of Edinburgh award scheme. Regular exchanges with France and Germany.

The pupils Lively, responsive; largely from middle-class homes. School is over-subscribed (competes strongly with the independent sector). Truancy rate negligible.

Results (1991) GCSE: creditable 61% gained at least 5 grades A-C.

Destinations 80% continue in full-time education at sixth-form or further education colleges.

Sport Strong – particularly rugby, hockey, netball, tennis, athletics; Saturday fixtures flourish. Good playing fields but no sports hall.

Remarks Middle-class comprehensive doing a sound job.

TUDOR HALL
Wykham Park,
Banbury,
Oxfordshire OX16 9UR
Tel (0295) 263434

Independent • Girls • Boarding and some day • Ages 11-18 • 250 pupils (93% boarding) • 70 in sixth form • Fees, £8,790 boarding; £5,610 day
Head: Miss Nanette Godfrey, late-40s, appointed 1984.

Small, friendly school of charm and character; good results; first-rate facilities.

Background Founded 1850; moved to present premises 1945; elegant 17th-century manor house in 35 acres of parkland (stately drive and splendid views across rolling countryside). Well-designed later additions include fine music school.

Atmosphere More like a gracious country house than a school (morning assembly in the ballroom). Teacher-pupil relationships friendly, with a degree of formality in the classroom. Superbly furnished boarding houses (based on age groups): 3-5 beds in pleasant rooms; sixth-formers have own study-bedrooms. Good food; choice of menu.

The head Read English at London; started her teaching career at the Royal Ballet School. Keen to sustain the school's friendly, family atmosphere; held in high esteem by staff and girls. Serves as a part-time magistrate.

The teaching Well-qualified staff of 24 (2 men). Broad, academic curriculum; choice of 5 modern languages; 'integrated' rather than separate sciences; good facilities for art, technology. Setting by ability in maths, science, languages; largest classes 20, smaller for GCSE, 2-14 for A-level. Good music; lots of drama.

The pupils Confident, outgoing, responsive. Largely from professional backgrounds (particularly the City) in the shire counties and London. Recruitment mostly by word of mouth; many have strong family ties. Entry at

11+ and 12+ by Common Entrance; IQs range from 110-140; school is over-subscribed.

Results GCSE: virtually all gain at least 5 grades A-C. A-level: modest 41% of entries graded A or B (has been higher).

Destinations 75% stay on for A-levels; 70% of these proceed to higher education (1-2 a year to Oxbridge).

Sport All major games on offer; good netball, cross-country; professional coaching available for tennis, riding, fencing. Facilities include large sports hall, squash court, outdoor pool.

Remarks Delightful school; high all-round standards.

TUNBRIDGE WELLS GIRLS'
Southfield Road,
Tunbridge Wells,
Kent TN4 9UJ
Tel (0892) 520902

Grammar • Girls • Ages 11-18 • 824 pupils
• 214 in sixth form
Head: Miss Valerie MacCuish, 46,
appointed 1988 (leaving March 1993).

First-class, rounded education for bright girls; very good results. School is poorly resourced.

Background Founded 1905; extensive grounds close to town centre. Main building solid Victorian but a third of classrooms in dilapidated wooden huts and mobile prefabs.

Atmosphere Happy, purposeful, business-like.

The head Has made big changes – including giving proper emphasis to science and technology – to what was a rather cosy school with unremarkable results. Popular with the girls (regards giving praise as an important part of her job); makes a point of dealing personally with parents' problems and complaints; has appointed some well-qualified, enthusiastic

young teachers. Leaving March 1993 to become head of Ipswich High *(qv)*.

The teaching Moving away from traditional chalk-and-talk to a more child-centred model; small groups working quietly on their own. Mixed-ability classes but setting in maths and French from second year. All do 9 GCSEs; more than 20 subjects offered at A-level. Classes of 30, reducing further up the school. Exceptionally good drama and music: 75% learn an instrument; several orchestras and choirs. Long-standing French and German exchanges. Popular Duke of Edinburgh award scheme.

The pupils Bright, confident, highly motivated; discipline not a problem; mainly (but not exclusively) from middle-class backgrounds. Uniform worn below sixth form, when own smart clothes are allowed (no jeans). Entry at 11+ by (complicated) Kent Selection Procedure; 150 apply for 124 places; mostly from Tunbridge Wells but also Tonbridge, Sevenoaks and East Sussex.

Results Have steadily improved over the past 3 years. GCSE: nearly all gain at least 5 grades A-C. A-level (1992): impressive 54% of entries graded A or B.

Destinations Nearly all continue into the sixth form and proceed to higher education (10 a year to Oxbridge).

Sport Good netball, hockey, trampolining. Recent popular additions include cricket, dance, self-defence. Outdoor swimming pool.

Remarks Combines the best of the grammar school tradition with good modern opportunities. Kent County Council acknowledges an ambitious building programme is necessary but has yet to agree funding.

UNIVERSITY COLLEGE SCHOOL

Frognal,
Hampstead,
London NW3 6XH
Tel (071) 435 2215

Independent • Boys • Day • Ages 13-18
(plus associated junior school) • 520
pupils • 151 in sixth form • Fees, £5,925
Head: Giles Slaughter, 54, appointed
1983.

*First-rate academic school; very good
results; liberal ethos.*

Background Founded 1830 as part of University College, London ('the godless institution in Gower Street') very much in the radical Benthamite tradition of tolerance and non-sectarianism: corporal punishment was rejected, religion was not taught and as much importance was attached to science as the classics. By 1907, when the school moved to its present premises in Hampstead, the revolutionary principles on which it was founded had become widely accepted: the opening ceremony was attended by King Edward VII and the Archbishop of Canterbury. Handsome red-brick buildings (William and Mary style) embellished with ornamental stonework; major building programme under way. Close links with associated junior school (boys taught about Jeremy Bentham from an early age).

Atmosphere Hard-working, high-spirited. Liberal, non-authoritarian ethos ('The tradition of UCS is to have no tradition'); relaxed but not disrespectful relations between staff and pupils. Emphasis on encouragement rather than competitiveness; not an academic sausage machine. 'Boys are taught to think for themselves but not to regard originality as a substitute for accuracy,' observes the prospectus. Religion still regarded as a matter for the family and the individual.

The head Able, decisive, personable; embodies the spirit of the school. Read history at Cambridge. Married, 3 daughters.

The teaching Challenging, orthodox (though younger teachers have widened the range of styles). National curriculum-plus; science taught as 3 separate subjects; strong French and German (but no other modern languages); good results in Latin. GCSE options include art and design, theatre arts; choice of 17 subjects at A-level; nearly all do at least 3; best results in maths, physics, chemistry, design/technology. Busy extra-curricular programme; lots of music (weekly jazz concerts); lively drama; good art.

The pupils Big mixture of races and creeds; 45% Jewish; mostly from professional backgrounds. Most join from the junior school (which admits 1 applicant in 6); 30-40 enter at 13 by school's own tests in maths, English, French or by Common Entrance. High academic standard required. Assisted places.

Results GCSE: virtually all gain at least 5 grades A-C. A-level (1992): very impressive 71% of entries graded A or B.

Destinations 95% continue into the sixth form; 90% of these proceed to higher education (many to Oxbridge).

Sport Plenty on offer, including rugby, hockey, cricket, fencing, sailing, golf, cross-country. Facilities include good playing fields near by; courts for tennis, squash, fives.

Remarks Highly recommended for able boys.

UPLANDS
Wadhurst,
East Sussex TN5 6BA
Tel (0892) 782135

Comprehensive • Co-educational • Ages 11-18 • 797 pupils (roughly equal numbers of girls and boys) • 155 in sixth form
Head: David James, 47, appointed 1976.

Sound, well-run comprehensive; good teaching; improving facilities.

Background Opened 1973 as a secondary modern; became comprehensive (under present head, who fought successfully for a sixth form) 1979. Functional over-crowded premises (built for a school half the size) and many huts; parents do the decorating. Much-needed building programme under way.

Atmosphere Happy, lively; plenty going on. Excellent relations between staff and pupils; good pastoral care system. Facilities open to the community (local farmers use the computers). Many teachers send their children here.

The head Quietly spoken, very able; popular with staff and pupils alike. Read history at Cambridge; has taught in both the independent and state sectors. School's academic reputation and popularity have grown steadily under his leadership. Teaches religious education to the younger children so that he can get to know them. Married to a teacher; 2 sons (both were pupils here).

The teaching Good. High-quality, dedicated staff, nearly all appointed by present head; most leave only for promotion. Wide range of methods: this is not a traditional 'chalk-and-talk' school. Pupils streamed by ability; additional setting in maths; extra help for those with special needs; average class size 25, reducing to 19 for GCSE, 10 in the sixth form; homework set regularly and marked. All do 8 or 9 GCSEs; sixth-form options include BTEC vocational courses. First-rate art; thriving music; orchestras, bands and choirs; regular drama productions in new studio. Lots of

charity fund-raising. Regular foreign visits and language exchanges.

The pupils Bright, cheerful, responsive; truancy rate virtually nil. Most from middle-class/rural backgrounds; sizeable contingent from affluent Tunbridge Wells. Not the best-dressed school, but uniform regulations are being tightened after complaints from both parents and teachers. School is over-subscribed; 2 apply for every place; priority to those living nearest.

Results (1991) GCSE: modest 34% gained at least 5 grades A-C (a bad year – usually 45%-50%). A-level: 28% of entries graded A or B (national average).

Destinations 70% continue into the sixth form; up to 80% of these proceed to higher education (3 a year to Oxbridge).

Sport Good record despite poor facilities. Regular county honours in cricket, football, rugby, athletics.

Remarks Effective school; popular with parents.

UPPINGHAM
Uppingham,
Rutland LE15 9QE
Tel (0572) 822216

Independent • Boys (plus girls in sixth form) • Boarding • Ages 13-18 • 634 pupils (86% boys) • 311 in sixth form (72% boys) • Fees, £10,710
Head: Dr Stephen Winkley, 48, appointed 1991.

Fine school for children of a fairly wide range of abilities; good results; excellent facilities; strong music and sport.

Background Founded 1584; made famous by Edward Thring, head from 1853-87, who modernised the curriculum and pioneered the development of music and sport in public schools. Gracious, well-maintained Victorian buildings (some listed) and many later additions interwoven with the town.

Atmosphere Warm, civilised, hard-working (lessons on Saturday mornings); strong sense of order and tradition (black ties worn since the death of Queen Victoria have only just been replaced by royal blue and white striped ones); friendly staff-pupil relations. 14 pleasant, homely boarding houses (2 for girls); each has a degree of autonomy (and engenders strong loyalties).

The head Charming, very able; came late to headship and loves it. Educated at Oxford; previously second master at Winchester (in charge of the scholars). Teaches ancient history. Highly musical; paints water colours. Married, 3 children.

The teaching Good quality. Long-serving staff of 75; all play a full part in extra-curricular activities. National curriculum-plus; science taught as 3 separate subjects; Latin, Greek, German, Spanish on offer. All pupils streamed by ability; additional setting in some subjects; largest classes 22 (and may be as small as 4-5); specialist help for dyslexics. All take 10-12 GCSEs. Choice of 23 subjects at A-level; most take 3 in addition to non-examined general studies course; extra coaching for Oxbridge entrance. Spacious classrooms; well-equipped science and language labs; workshops for metalwork, woodwork, motor-vehicle maintenance; design/technology centre (housed in 16th-century manor) now celebrating its 25th anniversary. Excellent music (regular Oxbridge choral awards and scholarships); two-thirds learn at least 1 instrument; 3 orchestras; fine chapel choir and swing band toured South-East Asia in summer 1992. Lots of drama (first-rate theatre). Choice of cadet force or community service. Regular expeditions abroad.

The pupils Confident, unpretentious; fairly wide spread of social backgrounds. Mainly from prep schools in North Yorkshire, Midlands, East Anglia, Lancashire, Cheshire. Entry at 13+ by Common Entrance; minimum mark of 50% required. Most apply to houses chosen for their family or prep school links. Academic, music and art scholarships available. 45 girls a year admitted to sixth form; minimum of 5 GCSEs at grades A-C required.

Results GCSE (1991): 95% gained at least 5 grades A-C. A-level (1992): 41% of entries graded A or B.

Destinations 90% proceed to higher education (impressive 44 to Oxbridge in 1991).

Sport Important in the life of the school and played to a high level (but not compulsory). Vast choice: rugby, soccer, hockey, cricket, athletics, cross-country, fives, badminton, fencing, golf, shooting etc. Superb facilities include 56 acres of playing fields, fine sports hall, tennis and squash courts, swimming and diving pools.

Remarks Highly recommended, especially for all-rounders.

WAKEFIELD GIRLS' HIGH
Wentworth Street,
Wakefield WF1 2QS
Tel (0924) 372490

Independent • Girls • Day • Ages 11-18
(plus associated junior school) • 800
pupils • 200 in sixth form • Fees (1992-93),
£3,663
Head: Mrs Patricia Langham, 41,
appointed 1987.

Traditional grammar-school education; respectable results; good music.

Background Founded 1878 by the governors of Queen Elizabeth Grammar *(qv)*; Georgian house plus later acquisitions and additions on a fairly restricted site (playing fields half a mile away).

Atmosphere Well-ordered; strong sense of courtesy and decorum (girls gather in total silence for morning assembly).

The head Energetic, approachable. Read English and Russian at Leeds; taught in the state sector for 16 years; previously deputy head of a neighbouring comprehensive. Hands-on management style.

The teaching Long-serving staff of 71 (10 men). Standard grammar-school curriculum; Latin and Greek on offer; choice of French, German, Italian, Russian, Spanish. All do computing for first 3 years; technology includes wood-turning and needlework. Largest classes 28; GCSE groups of 15. Some A-level courses shared with neighbouring boys' school. Good music; nearly all learn an instrument. Regular exchanges with schools in France, Germany.

The pupils From fairly varied social backgrounds; 150 have assisted places; significant Asian minority. Half from Wakefield; rest travel in up to 20 miles (parents organise coaches). Entry at 11, 13 by tests (including intelligence); most are in the top 25% of the ability range (grammar-school standard); head says no bright girl ever refused entry on financial grounds.

Results GCSE (1991): 97% gained at least 5 grades A-C. A-level (1992): 47% of entries graded A or B.

Destinations Most stay for A-levels and proceed to higher education (a few a year to Oxbridge).

Sport Good hockey, cricket, netball.

Remarks Sound learning; good manners.

WALTHAMSTOW HALL

Hollybush Lane,
Sevenoaks,
Kent TN13 3UL
Tel (0732) 451334

Independent • Girls • Day and some boarding • Ages 3-18 • 630 pupils (420 in senior school; 90% day) • 111 in sixth form • Fees, £3,075-£4,665 day; £6,804-£8,610 boarding
Head: Mrs Jackie Lang, 48, appointed 1983.

Sound academic school; not unduly selective; good drama, art and music.

Background Founded 1838 in East London as both a home and a school for the daughters of Christian missionaries serving abroad; moved to present site (views of the North Downs and Knole Park) in 1882. Became a Direct Grant grammar school in 1944; reverted to full independence in 1976.

Atmosphere Happy, hard-working, down-to-earth (delights in not being 'posh'); strong sense of community; big emphasis on good manners, service, responsibility. Staff-pupil relations are first-rate. Supportive parents raise £12,000 a year.

The head Was a pupil here ('an inspiring education'); took a First in modern languages at Oxford; did research into medieval French literature. Teaches French to 11-year-olds and general studies to the sixth form. Very popular with staff and girls. Married (to a teacher); 2 teenage daughters.

The teaching Mix of modern and traditional methods with emphasis on the acquisition of basic skills. National curriculum-plus; science taught as 3 separate subjects; all become computer-literate (excellent facilities). Setting by ability in maths, French and English; largest class size 20 (but most are taught in much smaller groups). All do 9 GCSEs plus religious education (taken a year early); most take 3 A-levels from a choice of 25. Good art, drama and music: more than two-thirds learn an instrument; 5 choirs, 2 orchestras and various smaller ensembles. Well-supported Duke of Edinburgh award scheme and community service programme. Regular exchanges with schools in France and Germany.

The pupils Confident, responsive; mainly from professional and farming backgrounds; a few from abroad. Admission at 11 and 13 by interview and tests in English and maths; not unduly selective. Assisted places available.

Results GCSE: 90% gain at least 5 grades A-C. A-level (1992): 44% of entries graded A or B.

Destinations Most stay on into the sixth form and proceed to higher education.

Sport Strong, particularly lacrosse (regular county players); netball and tennis also on offer. Facilities include indoor pool and squash courts.

Remarks Attractive, well-run school.

WARWICK
Myton Road,
Warwick CV34 6PP
Tel (0926) 492484

Independent • Boys • Day (and some boarding) • Ages 7-19 • 1,000 pupils (95% day) • 200 in sixth form • Fees (1992-93), £3,561-£4,038 (£8,041-£8,688 boarding) Head: Dr Philip Cheshire, 49, appointed 1988.

Strong, traditional school; good teaching and results.

Background Probably founded in 914; moved to present 50-acre site on the banks of the Avon 1879; rococo Tudor-style Victorian buildings plus many later additions; assembly hall seats the whole school.

Atmosphere High standards all round (not least in dress and behaviour); boys face a challenging day's work and play. Strong emphasis on religion; compulsory chapel. Attractive boarding accommodation.

The head Physicist; worked in industry before taking up teaching. Completely immersed in his job, and expects everyone else to be the same. Runs an extremely tight ship.

The teaching High quality. Traditional emphasis in the junior school on 'the pursuit of oracy, literacy and numeracy' (good standards of reading and writing); all learn computing. Mixed-ability classes of 30; extra help for dyslexics. At 11+ all start Latin (some continue it to GCSE) and begin to learn a musical instrument. Science taught as 3 separate subjects; all take GCSE maths a year early (and pass it). 48% achieve grade A in English; 80% achieve grade A in design/technology (can the exam possibly be hard enough?). Choice of 19 subjects at A-level; economics the most popular; all do general studies. Helpful, informative reports to parents twice a term. Flourishing art and music. After-school choice of cadet force, Duke of Edinburgh award scheme, community service. No work experience arranged (head insists he is offering education not training).

The pupils Top 10%-20% of the ability range. Entry to junior school at 7 or 8; to senior school at 11 or 12 by tests in English, maths, verbal reasoning and at 13 by Common Entrance. Assisted places, bursaries, scholarships available. No plans to admit girls.

Results GCSE (1991): 94% gained at least 5 grades A-C. A-level (1992): 41% of entries graded A or B (has been higher).

Destinations 80% stay for A-levels; most of these proceed to higher education (some to Oxbridge).

Sport Good rugby, cricket, hockey, swimming, tennis, athletics; wide range of other activities on offer. Facilities include new indoor pool (full-time, qualified instructor) and 9-hole golf course.

Remarks Good all round.

WATFORD BOYS' GRAMMAR

Rickmansworth Road,
Watford,
Hertfordshire WD1 7JF
Tel (0923) 224950

Comprehensive (grant-maintained) •
Boys • Ages 11-18 • 1,062 pupils • 248 in
sixth form
Head: Robert Evans, 48, appointed 1991.

---

*Highly academic school; first-class
results; good sport, drama, music.
Heavily over-subscribed.*

Background Founded with Watford Girls'
Grammar *(qv)* in 1704 as a charity school with
separate divisions for boys and girls; moved to
present site 1912. Became nominally comprehensive in the late 1960s (retaining its grammar school title); intake has remained predominantly grammar school standard. Opted out
of council control in 1990 having assured
parents it would not revert to formal academic
selection. Imposing Edwardian building plus
some shabby 1960s additions. Annual budget
of £2.6 million.

Atmosphere Strong sense of history and
tradition (feels more like an independent than
a state school). Exceptionally good relations
between staff and pupils.

The head Has taught in both comprehensive
and independent schools; formerly deputy
head of Colfe's. Keen not to become an
office-bound administrator; committed to
maintaining, and even raising, the school's
academic standards (no resting on laurels).
Sports enthusiast, coaches cricket; part-time
magistrate. Married, 2 sons (at Dulwich College).

The teaching Traditionally didactic in style
but not oppressively so; hard-working, well-
qualified staff; strongly academic curriculum.
All do French or German from first year, Latin
from second year; Spanish, Italian, Greek
available at lunchtimes. Most take 10 GCSEs
(including dual award science); more able do
maths and French a year early. Mixed-ability
classes, maximum size 27; setting in maths,
modern languages. Science department is
particularly strong; chemistry and physics each
taken by 40% of A-level candidates (a third of
university entrants in 1991 were reading science or engineering. Outstanding drama – 5
major productions a year – and strong music;
more than 10% learn an instrument (French
horn a speciality); 2 orchestras, 2 choirs.
Active and successful debating society. Regular exchanges with schools in France, Germany; classics trips to Rome; history visits to
World War I battlefields. Successful annual
exchange of teachers with a school in Melbourne.

The pupils Wide social and ethnic mix (15%
Asian) from a catchment area that extends via
the Metropolitan line to Wembley and Harrow. School heavily over-subscribed (463 applied for 162 places in 1992); all candidates
and their parents interviewed after applying by
letter (no written tests). Priority to siblings and
'those likely to benefit from the kind of
education the school provides' – i.e. the
academically able. (However, head insists,
'The fact that a pupil is willing to take an
energetic part in the life of the school is far
more important than his academic record'.)

Results (1992) GCSE: 83% gained at least 5
grades A-C. A-level: 48% of entries graded A
or B. Impressive, even by grammar school
standards.

Destinations 80% stay on for A-levels; 90%
of these proceed to higher education (9 to
Oxbridge in 1991).

Sport Strong rugby, hockey, cricket (played
mostly against independent schools). On-site
facilities include sports hall, tennis courts,
outdoor pool and 10 acres of playing fields;
another 14 acres half a mile away.

Remarks Very good all round; highly recommended – but hard to get into.

WATFORD GIRLS' GRAMMAR

Lady's Close,
Watford,
Hertfordshire WD1 8AW
Tel (0923) 223403

Comprehensive (grant-maintained) • Girls
• Ages 11-18 • 1,016 pupils • 224 in sixth
form
Head: Mrs Helen Hyde, mid-40s,
appointed 1987.

Heavily over-subscribed school in the centre of Watford. Excellent results; wide variety of extra-curricular activities; good industrial links.

Background Origins lie in a charity school founded 1704; moved to present 8-acre site 1907 (purpose-built premises with many later additions). Became a grammar school after the 1944 Education Act; went comprehensive in the late 1960s – retaining the word 'grammar' in its title. Opted out of council control 1991; extra cash should lead to improvements in maintenance, decoration and the state of the grounds. More classrooms and science labs also urgently needed.

Atmosphere Comprehensive in theory but effectively a grammar school. All applicants interviewed; priority to those deemed likely to benefit from the academic education offered.

The head Taught for 18 years in 2 tough London comprehensives; insists that achievements of the less able (in and out of the class) should be as highly valued as those of high-fliers. Good relations with staff but she is plainly in charge; knows more than many heads do about what is going on in her school. Younger daughter a pupil here.

The teaching Traditional in style; constant pressure on girls to achieve. Curriculum includes Latin (available up to A-level) and classical civilisation; past neglect of technology now being reversed (with the help of a £400,000 capital grant from the Government); computing also needs more investment. Maximum class size 30. Choice of 20 subjects at A-level (emphasis on the academic

– 16-year-olds wanting vocational courses transfer to further education colleges). Strong links with business and industry (particularly Rolls-Royce); courses on women in management and engineering. Good music; 30% learn an instrument; 2 orchestras, jazz band, 2 choirs; regular concerts. Drama very popular. Regular pupil exchanges with schools in France and Germany. Lots of community service: girls visit hospital patients and the elderly; raise funds for charity.

The pupils Very wide (and well-integrated) social mix; about 20% ethnic minority. All abilities admitted but majority are academically able. Heavily over-subscribed (430 apply for 180 places); wide catchment area. Up to 50% of places reserved at governors' discretion for those living outside the borough of Watford; open evenings for prospective parents attract more than 2,000.

Results (1992) GCSE: 80% gained 5 or more grades A-C. A-level: 50% of entries graded A or B – impressive even by grammar school standards.

Destinations 72% stay on to do A-levels (remainder to full-time education elsewhere); 60% of these proceed to higher education (4 to Oxbridge in 1991).

Sport Strong netball, hockey. Adequate facilities, including indoor swimming pool.

Remarks First-rate school for able girls; offers more than academic success.

WELLINGBOROUGH

Wellingborough,
Northamptonshire NN8 2BX
Tel (0933) 222427

Independent • Co-educational • Day and
boarding • Ages 13-18 (plus associated
junior school) • 435 pupils (65% boys;
85% day) • 160 in sixth form • Fees
(1992-93), £4,785 day; £7,965 boarding
Head: Graham Garrett, 59, appointed
1973 (retiring August 1993).

*Solid academic school; respectable
results; good sport.*

Background Founded 1595; moved in 1881
to present purpose-built premises on attractive
50-acre site; many later additions.

Atmosphere Warm, friendly; excellent rapport between staff and pupils. Pleasant boarding accommodation.

The head Coming to the end of a long stint
during which numbers have increased and
academic standards risen. Read maths at
Cambridge; taught at Radley; formerly a
housemaster at Shrewsbury. Plays the organ in
chapel; leads walking tours to the Himalayas.
Married, 3 grown-up children.

The teaching Long-serving staff of 50 (9
women), nearly all appointed by present head.
Pupils set by ability in English, French, maths,
science; extra help for those with special needs.
Lively art and design. Most take 10 GCSEs
and 3 A-levels (some do 4) plus non-examined
general studies course. Lots of music and
drama; thriving cadet force and Duke of
Edinburgh award scheme.

The pupils Nearly all from East Midlands
professional, business, farming families; most
boarders live within a 40-mile radius; some
from East Africa and Hong Kong. Admission
by Common Entrance; modest 50% mark
required (IQ of 110), may be lower for those
joining from the junior school. Assisted places,
scholarships, bursaries.

Results GCSE (1991): 86% gained at least 5
grades A-C. A-level (1992): disappointing 35%
of entries graded A or B (has been higher).

Destinations 80% stay on for A-levels; 80%
of these proceed to higher education (5 to
Oxbridge in 1992).

Sport Strong cricket, girls' hockey, netball;
soccer, rugby, squash, tennis, swimming,
cross-country also on offer. First-rate facilities
include 40 acres of playing fields, sports hall,
heated outdoor pool, 9-hole golf course.

Remarks Good all round.

WELLINGTON COLLEGE

Crowthorne,
Berkshire RG11 7PU
Tel (0344) 771588

Independent • Boys (plus girls in sixth
form) • Boarding and day • Ages 13-18 •
818 pupils (84% boarding) • 360 in sixth
form (86% boys) • Fees, £10,395
boarding; £7,590 day
Head: Jonty Driver, 53, appointed 1989.

*Good, well-run school, rapidly losing its
somewhat Philistine image; decent
results; very strong sport.*

Background Founded 1853 as a monument
to the Iron Duke to provide a free education
for the 'orphan children of indigent and
meritorious' Army officers (*Heroum filii* – the
sons of the brave); paid for by a compulsory
levy of a day's pay imposed on the entire army.
1,200 Old Boys gave their lives in 2 World
Wars; 15 have won the VC. Splendid buildings
('Victorian version of French Grand Rococo')
plus fine chapel by Sir Gilbert Scott in a
magnificent 400-acre estate (including 80
acres of playing fields); later additions include
good design/technology centre and vast sports
hall.

Atmosphere Relaxed, happy; courteous
staff-pupil relations. Big emphasis on independence and leadership; sixth-form girls need to
be thoroughly competent to cope. Good

boarding accommodation (8 in-college houses, 6 others within easy walking distance); all pupils have own study-bedrooms after first year. Compulsory chapel; lessons on Saturday mornings.

The head Imposing, very able; Victorian-liberal in style. South-African born; educated at Cape Town (president of National Union of South African Students, imprisoned without trial) and Oxford. Taught at Sevenoaks and a comprehensive in Humberside before becoming head of Island School, Hong Kong; formerly head of Berkhamsted. Has written 4 novels (including *Send War in Our Time, O Lord*), 3 books of poetry and a biography (of a South African liberal). Takes a tough line on discipline in general and drugs in particular (recent mass expulsions); determined to raise academic standards and soften the school's military image. Fanatical about rugby; jogs daily. Married, 3 grown-up children (1 teaching at Harrow).

The teaching Well-organised curriculum; clear-cut choices. Science taught as 3 separate subjects (20 labs); more able do Latin and Greek; rest add German or Spanish to French; all do some design/technology and computing. All take 10-12 GCSEs, including physics and chemistry. Choice of 24 subjects at A-level; equal numbers do arts and sciences and many mix the two. Maximum class size 24, reducing to 16 in the sixth form. Extra coaching for Oxbridge entry. Lots of art (good painting, pottery), drama (300-seat theatre) and music (all learn an instrument in first year, many continue). First-rate library (full-time librarian); more books borrowed in a day now than in a week 3 years ago. Compulsory cadet force. Regular language exchanges with schools in France, Germany and Spain.

The pupils Largely from middle-class/professional backgrounds; 12% of fathers are Army officers. Entry at 13 by Common Entrance (minimum 55% mark required) and previous school reports; at 16 with at least GCSE grade B in proposed A-level subjects. Some scholarships; means-tested foundation bursaries for the children of deceased Service officers.

School owns adjoining prep school, Eagle House.

Results GCSE: nearly all gain at least 5 grades A-C. A-level (1992): 54% of entries graded A or B.

Destinations 90% proceed to higher education (22 to Oxbridge in 1991), most after taking a 'gap year'.

Sport Very strong, particularly rugby (21 XVs), hockey (16 XIs), cricket (14 XIs). Girls play netball, hockey, lacrosse, cricket. Fine facilities include all-weather pitch, athletics track, indoor and outdoor pools, courts for tennis, squash, fives, rackets.

Remarks Good school – particularly for all-rounders – and getting better. Elegant, informative prospectus.

WELLS CATHEDRAL SCHOOL
Wells,
Somerset BA5 2ST
Tel (0749) 672117

Independent • Co-educational • Boarding and day • Ages 5-18 • 815 pupils (equal numbers of girls and boys, boarding and day pupils) • 158 in sixth form • Fees, £6,891-£7,887 boarding; £2,211-£4,635 day
Head: John Baxter, 53, appointed 1986.

Unusual school combining a mainstream curriculum with specialist teaching for musically gifted children.

Background 12th-century foundation; original grammar and choristers' schools merged 1546; specialist music department for gifted children opened 1970. Fine collection of medieval and 18th-century buildings (plus some that are less distinguished) in beautiful conservation area close to the cathedral.

Atmosphere Calm, friendly; strong Christian ethos. Excellent relationships between staff and pupils; good manners, mutual respect taken for granted. Most boarding houses comfortable – dormitories for up to 8 – but some drab and in need of upgrading. Good food, plenty of choice.

The head Approachable, sensitive; not a musician but has a great love of music; formerly head of history at Westminster. Married, 2 sons.

The teaching Lively junior school; broad curriculum; all learn French from age 10; some setting by ability. National curriculum followed in senior school 'but we're not slaves to it'; most take 8 or 9 GCSEs and 3 A-levels; choristers and music specialists withdrawn from many lessons. Youthful, hard-working staff of 75, 60% appointed by present head.

The pupils From a fairly wide range of social backgrounds including Services, clergy, professions; musicians drawn from London, the South, Wales and the South West. Some have had difficulty settling into other schools; a few have profound physical disabilities. Entry by interview, tests, voice trails, auditions. Scholarships, bursaries, assisted places.

Results GCSE: 90% gain at least 5 grades A-C. A-level (1992): creditable 48% of entries graded A or B.

Destinations Nearly all continue into the sixth form and proceed to higher education.

Sport Wide choice; no pressure to take part but important in the life of the school.

Remarks Her Majesty's Inspectors commented recently: 'The general ambience of the cathedral and its surroundings combine with high standards of music-making throughout the day and often well into the evening to provide a level of aesthetic experience of unusual intensity...The school has a justifiably high reputation.'

WEST HEATH

Sevenoaks,
Kent TN13 1SR
Tel (0732) 452541

Independent • Girls • Boarding and day •
Ages 11-18 • 175 pupils (90% boarding) •
45 in sixth form • Fees, £9,240 boarding;
£6,480 day
Head: Mrs Lavinia Cohn-Sherbok, 39,
appointed 1987 (leaving March 1993).

Small, family school in an idyllic setting; offers the widest possible opportunities to girls from privileged backgrounds.

Background Founded 1865; one of the oldest of the small boarding schools for girls. Moved to its present site in the middle of Sevenoaks Common (32 acres of beautiful grounds) in 1932. Princess of Wales is best-known Old Girl, but the academic emphasis has changed markedly since her day; girls now prepared for careers rather than marriage and home-making.

Atmosphere School feels rather like a large family. Strong emphasis on good manners and an awareness that duty and responsibility go hand-in-hand with privilege. Older girls are encouraged to help and care for the younger ones.

The head Warm, welcoming, extremely competent; describes West Heath as a 'magic school – a bright light in a naughty world'. Educated at Benenden and Cambridge; has taught in state schools; formerly head of general studies at King's, Canterbury. Hobby is taking Open University courses (most recently a diploma in management studies); now working for a PhD at Kent (where her husband, an American rabbi, lectures in theology). 'Education', she observes, 'is a life-long process.'

The teaching Numbers are so small that each girl has an individual timetable. Maximum class size 15, generally smaller. All do 8 or 9 GCSEs; combined science compulsory. Head undertakes to provide any A-level course requested, even if only by 1 pupil; most groups

4-6. Staff of 26 (men as well as women); mix of highly qualified young teachers and the more experienced. Long school day – 8.45 a.m. to 7 p.m. (including prep) – and Saturday mornings. Good music; 2 choirs (madrigals a speciality), orchestra, chamber groups. All expected to take part in drama; excellent dance studio for ballet, tap and modern dancing. Strong spirit of service: most join local Voluntary Services Unit and many take part in Duke of Edinburgh award scheme.

The pupils Polite, articulate, self-assured; daughters of landowners, bankers etc (the fourth generation of some families); always some from Scotland. Admission by Common Entrance or school's own exam. Minimum IQ 105-110 but the ultimate test is whether the head feels a girl will fit in: the highly competitive might not, but for those who need encouragement and respond well to adult attention, this is the ideal environment. Some scholarships, bursaries, assisted places.

Results (1991) GCSE: more than 80% gained at least 5 grades A-C. A-level: 50% of entries graded A or B.

Destinations Most continue into the sixth form and go on to higher education. All expect to have careers.

Sport Everyone encouraged to take part. Main games: netball, lacrosse, tennis (excellent facilities and coaching). Well-equipped sports hall; superb heated indoor pool.

Remarks A delightful school which sets out to encourage and nurture less confident girls and does it extremely well.

WESTMINSTER
17 Dean's Yard,
London SW1P 3PB
Tel (071) 222 5516

Independent • Boys (plus girls in sixth form) • Day and boarding • Ages 13-18 (plus associated junior school) • 610 pupils (60% day) • 284 in sixth form (70% boys) • Fees, £6,900-£7,875 day; £10,425-£11,550 boarding
Head: David Summerscale, 55, appointed 1986.

Distinguished school; unique both in its historic setting and in the unfettered individualism of its highly intelligent pupils.

Background Founded 1542 by Henry VIII from a small Benedictine monastery school; re-founded 1560 by Elizabeth I for boys to be 'liberally instructed in good books to the greater honour of the state'; pre-eminent by the early 18th-century. Historic buildings adjoining Westminister Abbey (many of them owned by the Church – Dean is chairman of the governors); science taught in large office block near by. Numbers now at saturation point.

Atmosphere All is hurly-burly, ebb and flow; a stimulating, surging, constricting, uplifting setting quite unlike any other. A tourist could wander into the green, domestic calm of Dean's Yard without guessing the school was there; its heart lies through a low vaulted arch into Little Dean's Yard, a spacious paved courtyard, off which boarding houses, classrooms and libraries open in haphazard profusion. Hidden behind is an enclosed 10th-century garden, with 3 modern fives courts, defying all preservation orders and planners by forming one wall of the cloister. Boys eat in what was once the Abbot's state dining room, passing the doughnuts and chips down ancient tables (never stopping to think of the past in their haste towards tomorrow). Compulsory morning service in the Abbey 3 times a week.

The head Considerate, unassuming, shuns publicity; has none of the breezy jollity of many heads, but his authority, humanity and integrity are beyond doubt. Educated at Sherborne and Cambridge; taught English at Charterhouse for 12 years; head of Haileybury for 10 years. Married, 2 young children.

The teaching Staff are rigorous in their demands on the pupils and equally hard on themselves. Those who teach here have to be able to deliver the goods 6 days a week (Saturday morning school survives) preferably with humour; the pupils are no respecters of persons when it comes to bad or boring teaching, and the faint-hearted or pretentious 'usher' is lost. Academic subjects are strong right across the board; classics still popular. History of art is easy when the galleries are a short walk away; languages have no terrors for the 50% who have 1 or more parents from abroad; history and politics come alive at Westminster (Queen's scholars have the privilege of queue-jumping for Commons debates). Design/technology is not a major subject but Chinese is available on demand. This has always been a liberal school, and there is still a genuine tolerance, an enjoyment of intellectual differences and a keen cultural life, with music, art and drama all rated as important. Outside the classroom, the boys' time is not nearly as structured and overseen as it is in most boarding schools.

The pupils This is no place for a boy straight from nanny's knee: after making his way here in the rush hour, he has to hurry through the streets between lessons, cross London to play his sport, use his initiative, hang on to his belongings and regulate his activities. Most love the freedom, and soon become poised and independent. The life of the city flows around, and boys are allowed into the thick of it; a prey to fashion and youth culture if they are not strong-minded, but civilised and well-informed if they use their chances properly. The sixth-form girls are tough, confident and clever; after 3 days of mutual incomprehension in September, both sides enjoy the challenge of classroom competition and get on well together. The girls insist this is still a boys' school and it is no use taking a feminist stand. Parents mostly cosmopolitan, managerial, media or executive. Pupils come from a 50-mile radius;

weekly boarding is popular. Entry either by scholarship examination in May (known as The Challenge) or by Common Entrance in June (minimum of 65% required – there is a great crush for places). No guaranteed entry from the Under School but most boys transfer.

Results GCSE: all gain at least 5 grades A-C. A-level: remarkable 85% of entries graded A or B (the top school in 1992).

Destinations Virtually all proceed to higher education (up to 50% to Oxbridge).

Sport All try something, and those who want to play seriously can. Rowing and fencing are particularly strong; soccer, cricket, tennis in Vincent Square; squash, swimming also popular.

Remarks Fine school, adapting and living on its not inconsiderable wits.

WHITGIFT
Haling Park,
Croydon CR2 6YT
Tel (081) 688 9222

Independent • Boys • Day • Ages 10-18 • 839 pupils • 239 in sixth form • Fees, £4,440
Head: Dr Christopher Barnett, 39, appointed 1991.

Solid school; respectable results; excellent facilities; strong music and sport.

Background Founded 1596 by John Whitgift, Archbishop of Canterbury; moved to present purpose-built premises 1931; attractive red-brick collegiate-style buildings set in 45 acres of wooded parkland (peacocks add a gracious touch); luxurious £10-million art/science/technology extension opened 1990.

Atmosphere Open, friendly; mutual respect between teachers and pupils. Strong sense of history and tradition (honours boards, silver cups, paintings of the founder and other benefactors).

The head Read modern history at Oxford; taught at Bradfield and Dauntsey's (deputy head). Married, 4 children (the eldest a pupil here). Keen to develop links with Europe; would like all pupils to spend up to a term in Continental schools.

The teaching Varied, challenging styles. Long-serving, well-qualified staff of 79 (14 women); hard-working pupils; demanding curriculum. All take 9-11 GCSEs, including 3 separate sciences and 2 modern languages (or 1 plus Latin); Greek available from third year (classics well supported throughout). Most take 3-4 A-levels (from choice of 20) plus broad general studies course. Maths and sciences are particularly strong. Superb facilities include 15 science labs, large art studios, fine library, comprehensive provision for computing, first-rate workshops for engineering, electronics, metalwork, silversmithing etc. Lots of music: 2 orchestras, 2 choirs, corps of drums; purpose-built music school has concert hall and drama studio. Frequent language exchanges to France and Germany; classics visits to Italy and Greece; history tours of World War I battlefields. Extra-curricular activities include successful debating society, flourishing Christian Union, well-attended science society, regular community service.

The pupils Wide social mix (lots of assisted places, bursaries). Entry at 10, 11 by tests in English, maths, verbal reasoning; at least 4 apply for each place. Catchment area extends from Chelsea to Brighton.

Results GCSE (1991): 88% gained 5 or more grades A-C. A-level (1992): 50% of entries graded A or B.

Destinations Nearly all continue into the sixth form; 75% of these proceed to higher education (19 to Oxbridge in 1991).

Sport Strong rugby, hockey, cricket, fencing, table tennis (many county and national honours); extensive fixture list. Good facilities include ample playing fields, sports hall, fencing *salle*, shooting range, heated indoor pool and courts for squash, fives, tennis.

Remarks Good all round; enthusiastic new head.

WILLIAM HULME'S GRAMMAR
Spring Bridge Road,
Manchester M16 8PR
Tel (061) 226 2054

Independent • Co-educational • Day •
Ages 11-18 • 791 pupils (78% boys) • 193
in sixth form • Fees, £3,075
Head: Patrick Briggs, 51, appointed 1987.

Sound grammar-school education; respectable results; strong sport.

Background Founded 1887; ageing Victorian buildings (splendid hall and organ) plus a conglomeration of later additions in 20 acres on the southern outskirts of the city. Number of girls gradually increasing.

Atmosphere Lively, bustling; a sense of high-minded seriousness. Pupils challenged and cared for.

The head Warm, gentle, quietly spoken. Read English at Cambridge; taught at Bedford for 22 years. Keen sportsman: plays cricket, manages national students' rugby team. Married, 3 children.

The teaching Wide variety of styles; versatile, hard-working staff (a third women). Standard grammar school curriculum; science taught as 3 separate subjects; most do 8-9 GCSEs. Pupils streamed by ability from third year; average class size 30, reducing to 20 for GCSE, 10 in sixth form. Choice of 17 subjects at A-level, including classics. Big range of extra-curricular activities: lots of music and drama, successful cadet force, active community service programme.

The pupils Well-disciplined, smartly dressed (prefects wear gowns). Wide variety of social backgrounds; some parents struggle to make ends meet; 35 assisted places a year; nearly 40% receive some help with fees. Competitive entry at 11+ by interview and tests in English, maths, verbal reasoning; 60% join from state primaries. Extensive catchment area (some travel 35 miles to school).

Results GCSE: 95% gain at least 5 grades A-C. A-level (1992): modest 39% of entries graded A or B (has been higher).

Destinations 90% stay on for A-levels; 85% of these proceed to higher education (6 a year to Oxbridge).

Sport Strong rugby, cricket, lacrosse, swimming; regular national and county honours. Athletics, tennis, hockey, netball also on offer.

Remarks Traditional school; good all round.

WIMBLEDON HIGH
Mansell Road,
Wimbledon,
London SW19 4AB
Tel (081) 946 1756

Independent • Girls • Day • Ages 11-18 (plus associated junior school) • 507 pupils • 115 in sixth form • Fees, £2,844-£3,684
Head: Mrs Elizabeth Baker, 46, appointed September 1992.

First-rate academic school; fine teaching; excellent results; good music and drama.

Background Founded 1880; member of the Girls' Public Day School Trust. 2 large Victorian houses plus numerous extensions and adaptations on a cramped town-centre site.

Atmosphere Friendly, calm, peaceful (despite the eccentricities of the premises – narrow corridors, steep staircases); girls show care and concern for each other and the staff. Strong Christian ethos does not exclude significant minorities of Muslims and Jews. Parents fully involved in the life of the school.

The head New appointment; previously head of Ellerslie, a girls' boarding school now merged with Malvern College.

The teaching High quality, rigorous, geared to the needs of able girls; creativity, imagination, independent investigation not neglected. National curriculum for first 3 years plus second modern language (French or German) and Latin; science on offer as 3 separate subjects; Spanish, Greek available in 'twilight hours'. All take 9 or 10 GCSEs; little setting by ability (within a narrow range); average class size 28. Wide choice of subjects at A-level, including business studies, economics, geology, history of art; most take 3, some 4, plus non-examined liberal studies course. Progress carefully monitored. All do music for first 4 years; most learn at least 1 instrument; orchestras, jazz band, madrigal group, 2 choirs. Extra-curricular activities include lots of drama, debating. Language trips to Paris, classics visits to Greece.

The pupils Bright, attentive, courteous; top 15% of the ability range from a wide catchment area; most parents in professions, business, City. Entry to junior school at age 5 by interview, at 7 by observation during normal lessons, at 11+ by tests in English, maths, study skills. School heavily over-subscribed; 3 apply for each place at 11+. Scholarships, assisted places.

Results GCSE: virtually all gain at least 5 grades A-C. A-level (1992): impressive 65% of entries graded A or B.

Destinations Up to 90% stay on for A-levels; virtually all of these proceed to higher education (7 to Oxbridge in 1991).

Sport An integral part of the curriculum up to the lower-sixth. Main games: hockey, netball, tennis; others include athletics, swimming. Playing fields 10 minutes' walk away; indoor pool opened September 1992; sports hall planned.

Remarks Fine school; highly recommended.

WINCHESTER

Winchester,
Hampshire SO23 9NA
Tel (0962) 854328

Independent • Boys • Boarding (and some day) • Ages 13-18 • 651 pupils (97% boarding) • 253 in sixth form • Fees, £10,800 (£8,100 day)
Head: James Sabben-Clare, 51, appointed 1985.

Distinguished school. Academically outstanding (one of the top 3); fine music; strong sport; excellence regarded as the norm.

Background The longest unbroken history of any school in Britain. Founded 1382 by William of Wykeham, Bishop of Winchester, so that 'scholars to the number of 60 and 10' might be instructed in Latin – 'without doubt the foundation, gateway and mainspring of all the liberal arts'. Beautifully situated (water meadows were the inspiration for Keats's *Ode to Autumn*), richly endowed (owns 9,000 acres of southern England). Fine collection of buildings, including 14th-century chapel and hall, 17th-century schoolroom (possibly designed by Wren); memorial cloisters by Sir Herbert Baker.

Atmosphere Friendly, busy, stimulating; no evidence of the arrogance or arid intellectualism of which Wykehamists ('desiccated calculating machines') are conventionally accused. Steeped in tradition (the 70 scholars wear gowns and live in the same spartan surroundings as their medieval predecessors). 'Commoners' in 10 pleasant boarding houses: potent communities, varying in character (careful choice advised).

The head Very able; low key but decisive; the 55th in the school's history. A scholar here (like his father); gained a First in classics from Oxford; taught at Marlborough; became head of classics here at 28; deputy head 10 years later. Has written a history of the school. Wife a barrister, teaches law in the sixth form; 2 grown-up children.

The teaching Outstanding. Highly qualified staff (a quarter have PhDs); curriculum extends far beyond the requirements of public exams; boys encouraged to go at their own (daunting) pace. (Many move on to A-level courses before taking GCSE; others are doing university work well before A-levels.) Compulsory Latin; many do 3 languages, including Russian; superb maths and science; vibrant design/technology (fine facilities). All take at least 3-4 A-levels (from a choice of 22): maths the most popular, followed by economics and English. Marvellous music (two-thirds learn an instrument); lots of drama; dazzling array of clubs and societies (everything on offer – take it or leave it).

The pupils Exceptionally bright: 90% are in the top 10% of the ability range; 25% are in the top 1% (IQs of 140+). Applications (usually to a house) after 8th birthday; housemasters interview and test boys (in verbal reasoning and numeracy) at 10½-11; offer of a place is subject to candidate's passing the 3-day Winchester entry exam at 13 (similar syllabus to Common Entrance but more searching questions). Those admitted need to have the potential to excel at something – if only to keep their end up in a high-pressure, competitive environment. Few assisted places. No plans to go co-educational.

Results GCSE: all gain at least 5 grades A-C. A-level (1992): remarkable 79% of entries graded A or B.

Destinations 95% proceed to higher education (about a third to Oxbridge), half after taking a 'gap year'.

Sport All games voluntary; wide choice; high standards.

Remarks Excellent school for able, competitive boys; others likely to sink.

WITHINGTON GIRLS'
Wellington Road,
Fallowfield,
Manchester M14 6BL
Tel (061) 224 1077

Independent • Girls • Day • Ages 11-18
(plus associated junior school) • 470
pupils • 120 in sixth form • Fees, £3,075
Head: Mrs Margaret Kenyon, late-40s,
appointed 1986.

---

*First-rate school; excellent teaching and
results, particularly in science.*

Background Founded 1890 by a group of
Manchester businessmen to provide for girls
what was already available for boys; moved to
present 9-acre urban site 1903; buildings have
been substantially modernised and extended.
Reverted to full independence with the abolition of Direct Grant status in 1976.

Atmosphere Business-like, civilised, assured:
a school that knows where it is going and is at
peace with itself. Size kept small to ensure each
girl receives the maximum amount of support
and recognition (in keeping with the founders'
wishes). Relations between staff and pupils are
excellent (strong sense of shared purpose).

The head Very able; derives greatest pleasure
from helping to transform hesitant girls into
confident, mature young women. Read modern languages at Oxford; taught at Cheadle
Hulme; appointed head of French here in
1983. Married, 2 children.

The teaching High quality. Committed, hard-
working staff of 40 (1 man); broad curriculum.
All take Latin, home economics, design/tech-
nology for first 3 years; excellent maths and
science (available as 3 separate subjects or dual
award). Choice of 16 subjects at A-level,
including Latin and Greek; most take 3
(general studies optional). Some setting by
ability from fourth year; average class size 25,
reducing to 10-12 in sixth form. Homework
carefully monitored. Attractive, well-stocked
library run by professional librarian. Fine
music tradition: nearly half learn an instrument; 2 orchestras, wind ensemble, jazz band,
3 large choirs. Good art in well-lit, lively
studio. Regular overseas visits and exchanges.

The pupils Bright, serious, hard-working –
and exceptionally cheerful; they appear to
relish the challenge set by the school's high
expectations. Most from professional, business families; some from more humble backgrounds (15 assisted places a year). Wide
catchment area; school heavily over-
subscribed (3 apply for each place). Entry at
11+ by interview and tests in English and
maths (to spot potential as well as measure
achievement).

Results GCSE: all gain at least 5 grades A-C.
A-level (1992): 62% of entries graded A or B
(has been even higher).

Destinations 95% stay for A-levels; virtually
all of these proceed to higher education (9-10
a year to Oxbridge); a third do maths, science,
medicine, engineering.

Sport Very strong record, particularly in lacrosse. Other main games: tennis, rounders,
hockey, netball (cricket on the wane). Extensive on-site playing fields. Sports hall planned.

Remarks A school of real distinction; highly
recommended.

WOLDINGHAM
Marden Park,
Woldingham,
Surrey CR3 7YA
Tel (0883) 349431

Independent • Roman Catholic • Girls •
Boarding and day • Ages 11-18 • 462
pupils (85% boarding) • 112 in sixth form •
Fees, £9,045 boarding; £5,472 day
Head: Dr Phil Dineen, mid-50s, appointed
1985.

---

*Well-run, delightful school; good
teaching and results; fine facilities.*

Background Founded as a convent school in
1842 by the Society of the Sacred Heart;

moved to present premises 1946; beautifully restored late 17th-century mansion in gracious grounds surrounded by 200 acres of secluded farmland. Under lay management since 1985; the society remains the trustee (nuns no longer teach but 3 live here). Roman Catholic in the ecumenical tradition: other Christian denominations welcomed.

Atmosphere Happy yet purposeful; a real sense of community; friendly, respectful relations between staff and pupils. High standards of work and behaviour expected and achieved. Individuals encouraged to aim for their personal best, take responsibility for their own lives, contribute to the community. Excellent pastoral care system; any difficulties soon picked up. Juniors (ages 11-12) housed in functional, slightly featureless premises set a little apart; seniors in main building have own study-bedrooms; palatial upper-sixth house opened September 1992. Strong parental support; close liaison encouraged.

The head Formidably energetic; sets high standards, knows exactly what she wants (and will not tolerate incompetent teaching). Born in Ireland, educated at a convent in South Wales, read English literature at Cardiff followed by a PhD (on teaching English). Has taught extensively in the state sector; formerly head of an ecumenical comprehensive in Surrey. Came in here 'like a tornado'; greatly admired by her pupils. Married.

The teaching Lively, high quality. Traditional emphasis on solid grounding, accuracy and presentation, combined with the latest equipment and up-to-the minute thinking. Well-qualified, dedicated staff (three-quarters appointed by present head). Girls taught in mixed-ability classes (of about 18); setting in some subjects; remedial help available. Broad curriculum; most take 9-10 GCSEs, including 2 languages (a particular strength); science on offer as 3 separate subjects; good facilities for computing and technology. All taught study skills and use of library (superb facilities, sophisticated computer network). Wide choice of A and AS-levels, including business studies. Good art: specialist rooms for sculpture, pottery, photography. Strong music tra-

dition (department currently housed in wooden huts); lively singing. First-rate careers advice: starts in third year and constantly available. Lots of extra-curricular activities; many girls involved in voluntary work of various kinds.

The pupils Responsive, confident, polite; seem to love the school and its well-ordered, almost family atmosphere (many come back to get married). Strong international element but most parents live within an hour's travel; many are 'first-time buyers' of independent education and tend to want their children home as often as possible at weekends. Entry at 11+ by Common Entrance; not unduly selective; most have IQs of 110-120. Some scholarships and bursaries.

Results GCSE (1991): 93% gained at least 5 grades A-C. A-level (1992): 46% of entries graded A or B.

Destinations 75% stay on for A-levels; 90% of these proceed to higher education (5 or 6 a year to Oxbridge).

Sport An important part of the curriculum: daily participation, high standards, reasonable record against other schools. Main activities: hockey, netball, cross-country, orienteering, swimming, athletics, tennis. Facilities include 2 gyms, indoor pool, 14 tennis courts, well-equipped (and very popular) fitness studio.

Remarks Exceptionally happy, successful school; highly recommended.

WOLVERHAMPTON GRAMMAR

Compton Road,
Wolverhampton WV3 9RB
Tel (0902) 21326

Independent • Co-educational • Day •
Ages 11-18 • 650 pupils • 180 in sixth form
• Fees, £3,828
Head: Bernard Trafford, mid-30s,
appointed 1990.

Good music and sport; improving academically.

Background Founded 1512 'for the instruction of youth in good manners and learning'; moved to present suburban site 1875; became fully independent 1979 (because left-wing council wanted to shut it). Main building ('Big School') imposing Victorian-Gothic; many later additions. Girls admitted to sixth form 1984; became fully co-educational September 1992 (not least to improve the quality of the intake); plans to expand to 900.

Atmosphere Old-fashioned town grammar (seen as as 'snob school' by some, 'below the salt' by others). Air of order and benevolent authoritarianism.

The head Gifted musician; organ scholar at St Edmund Hall, Oxford; came here as director of music 1981. Strongly committed to co-education – and to independence: he and his wife took their 2 young daughters out of school and are teaching them at home. Believes independent schools are, 'by and large, autocratic and paternalistic and, often, very authoritarian too'; aims to 'encourage the growth of democracy' throughout WGS.

The teaching Was rather formal (chalk-and-talk) but becoming more inter-active and challenging. Fairly rigorous academic curriculum; all do 3 sciences up to GCSE. Sixth-formers encouraged to take extra courses in computer studies, electronics, languages etc; nearly all do general studies. Class sizes 25, reducing to 20 for GCSE. Good music (especially choral); lively art department; abundance of well-supported lunch-time clubs and societies.

The pupils Enthusiastic, hard-working. 80% from state primary schools; 40 have assisted places. Wide catchment area covers parts of Staffordshire, Shropshire, Worcestershire (lots of coaches). Entry tests designed to identify those with IQs of 115+.

Results GCSE (1991): 97% gained at least 5 grades A-C. A-level (1992): 51% of entries graded A or B.

Destinations Nearly all stay for A-levels; 90% of them proceed to higher education (a few to Oxbridge). Popular careers: accountancy, banking, dentistry.

Sport Famed for soccer; rugby, hockey, fives (fixtures with Shrewsbury, Repton, Harrow) also on offer; keen on PE. New sports hall.

Remarks Traditional school in transition under an enthusiastic young head: one to watch.

WOODHOUSE GROVE

Apperley Bridge,
Bradford,
West Yorkshire BD10 0NR
Tel (0532) 502477

Independent • Methodist • Co-educational •
Day and boarding • Ages 11-18 (plus
associated prep school) • 575 pupils
(62% boys; 77% day;) • 160 in sixth form •
Fees (1992-93), £4,575 day; £7,650
boarding
Head: David Welsh, 46, appointed 1991.

Solid school; fairly wide ability range.

Background Founded 1812 by the Methodist Conference for the sons of Wesleyan ministers; now accepts pupils of all faiths but Methodist religious worship is compulsory. Spacious buildings, including well-equipped new business management school, on 65-acre semi-rural site overlooking the Aire Valley. Direct Grant until 1976; co-educational since 1985. Lessons on Saturday mornings.

Atmosphere Busy, friendly. Generally pleasant boarding accommodation but some awaiting upgrading (boys say the arrival of girls has led to an improvement in the quality of life).

The head Modern linguist; formerly at Dollar Academy. Keen to raise academic standards.

The teaching Long-serving staff of 43 (12 women). Basic curriculum; emphasis on English, maths, science; choice of French, German, Spanish; sixth-form options include business studies, economics, marketing, graphic communication, computing, metalwork, motor-vehicle maintenance. Extra help for those with special needs, including dyslexia. Lots of music; nearly half learn an instrument. School owns a field centre in North Wales.

The pupils Fairly wide ability range; mainly from Service, business, professional backgrounds; one quarter have assisted places. Half the intake at 11+ is from the associated prep school; remainder take tests in English, maths.

Results GCSE (1991): 80% gained at least 5 grades A-C. A-level (1992): modest 28% of entries graded A or B.

Destinations 85% stay on for A-levels; 78% of these proceed to higher education (3 to Oxbridge in 1991).

Sport Chiefly rugby (tour of Canada in 1991), squash, cricket. Facilities include extensive playing fields, heated indoor pool, squash courts. Sports hall planned.

Remarks Particularly worth considering for less academically able children.

WOODROFFE

Uplyme Road,
Lyme Regis,
Dorset DT7 3LS
Tel (0297) 442232

Comprehensive (grant-maintained) •
Co-educational • Day and boarding •
Ages 11-19 • 826 pupils (approximately
equal numbers of boys and girls; 88%
day) • 127 in sixth form • Boarding fees,
£1,200-£3,750
Head: Paul Vittle, 48, appointed 1985
(suspended September 1992 during a
dispute over funding and redundancies).

Effective comprehensive; all abilities catered for; good boarding facilities.

Background Opened as a grammar school 1932; boarding houses added for the benefit of Service parents 1950; went comprehensive 1965; opted out of local authority control 1991. Main building on 7 levels has spectacular views of Lyme Regis bay.

Atmosphere Well-disciplined: dress, obedience, good manners are priorities. Strong sense of family; all genuinely concerned for the success and welfare of others; achievement in every aspect of school life recognised and rewarded. An open community which welcomes and shares its activities with parents, visitors and neighbours. Very pleasant boarding accommodation.

The head Educated at a Bristol comprehensive and Bristol University. Taught religious education at state schools in Leicestershire, Avon and Somerset. Married (to a teacher), 3 grown-up children. Experienced marriage-guidance counsellor.

The teaching Calm, purposeful classrooms; lots of group working; easy access to computers; good design/technology. Pupils set by ability in maths, modern languages (choice of French or German); extra help for those with learning difficulties and for the particularly able. GCSE options include 3 separate sciences, creative and media studies, textiles, personal community service. Large simulated office for business studies. Sixth-formers can choose between A-levels and vocational courses. Good art, drama; successful madrigal group. New cadet force.

The pupils Treated as 'learner adults' – children of all abilities given a sense of confidence, a feeling that their activities and goals are worthwhile. 44 come from outside the catchment area; neighbouring Devon grammar schools cream off many of the most able. Entry for boarding by interview; trust funds and bursaries available in cases of hardship.

Results (1991) GCSE: 36% gained at least 5 grades A-C (national average). A-level: 20% of entries graded A or B (below average).

Destinations More than half stay on in the sixth form; 80% of those who take A-levels proceed to higher education (2 to Oxbridge in 1991).

Sport National success in cross-country, sailing, motor racing on grass; county success in team sports, athletics, golf. Fine open air pool.

Remarks Attractive school; traditional flavour retained.

WORTH
Paddockhurst Road,
Turners Hill,
Crawley,
West Sussex RH10 4SD
Tel (0342) 715207

Independent • Roman Catholic • Boys • Boarding (plus a handful of 'day boarders') • Ages 9-18 • 420 pupils (320 in senior school) • 120 in sixth form • Fees, £7,170-£9,600 (£5,376-£7,200 day). Head: Father Stephen Ortiger, mid-50s, appointed 1983.

Wide range of abilities; high academic standards; plenty of sport. Rich opportunities for serving the community.

Background Founded by the Benedictines in 1933 as a prep school for Downside; senior school opened 1959. Glorious 500-acre site; late 19th-century mansion (in continuous need of repair) with many later additions; adjoining monastery and abbey church.

Atmosphere Dignified, spacious. Religion taken seriously. Dormitories cramped, shabby (refurbishment in progress).

The head Story-book monk: jovial, urbane. Was a pupil here; went on to Downside and then read history at Cambridge. Joined the monastery in 1961; started teaching in 1967.

The teaching Juniors prepared for Common Entrance at 13 (national curriculum followed). Seniors offered Greek and Latin – but German and Italian available only by private tuition; choice of 3 separate sciences or combined course. 19 subjects offered at A-level; most do 3, plus general studies and RE. Teaching staff includes 8 monks; maximum class size 20; many groups smaller. Last lessons end 7 p.m. Plenty of drama and music; more than a quarter learn an instrument; orchestra, bands, church choir. Regular exchanges with Benedictine school in Belgium. Extensive voluntary work; 150 boys involved in 17 activities, including soup kitchen in Brighton, shelter for homeless in London, school for handicapped, shopping for the housebound etc. Well-supported Duke of Edinburgh award scheme.

The pupils Wide range of abilities; more than 20% from overseas. Juniors admitted after interview and tests in reading, spelling, maths. Common Entrance requirements may be waived in case of social need. Non-Catholics admitted.

Results GCSE: nearly all gain at least 5 grades A-C. A-level (1992): 47% of entries graded A or B.

Destinations Nearly all stay on in the sixth form; 70% of them proceed to higher education (9 to Oxbridge in 1991); many go into the Army.

Sport Plenty on offer, including soccer, rugby, athletics, tennis, basketball, badminton, fencing, swimming, sailing. 14 pitches, 7-hole golf course, new sports hall.

Remarks School with much to offer: strong emphasis on serving God and one's fellow man.

WYCOMBE ABBEY

High Wycombe,
Buckinghamshire HP11 1PE
Tel (0494) 520381

Independent • Girls • Boarding • Ages
11-18 • 503 pupils • 174 in sixth form •
Fees (1992-93), £11,088
Head: Mrs Judith Goodland, 54,
appointed 1989.

The top girls' boarding school: an academic powerhouse. Excellent teaching and results; very good music, drama and sport; first-rate facilities.

Background Founded 1896 by Dame Frances Dove, one of the pioneers of women's education. Magnificent Gothic mansion (rebuilt 1798) set in 150 serene, wooded acres (requisitioned during World War II by the Air Ministry, who were *very* reluctant to give it back). Later additions include fine science labs, computer rooms, 4 libraries, creative arts centre, fully equipped theatre. Chapel accommodates the whole school.

Atmosphere Highly competitive. Able, hardworking girls; lively, committed staff; strong boarding school ethos; good pastoral care system. All participate in a wide range of cultural and sporting activities. Nine modern, purpose-built boarding houses maintained to a high standard (but they vary considerably in character – careful choice advised).

The head Read modern languages at Bristol; has taught widely in both state and independent schools; formerly head of St George's, Ascot. Divorced, 3 children.

The teaching First-rate: intellectually demanding; aim is to produce independence of thought. National curriculum-plus; all do Latin; most add Greek, German, Spanish or Russian to French; science taught as 3 separate subjects; big emphasis on computer literacy. All do 9-11 GCSEs; many take maths, French a year early. Small classes (all pupils set by ability); lots of individual attention; progress carefully monitored. Most do 3 A-levels plus non-examined general studies course; extra coaching for Oxbridge entry. Very busy extracurricular programme: nearly all learn a musical instrument, sing, act in house plays. Well-supported Duke of Edinburgh award scheme; lots of community service and charity fund-raising.

The pupils Nearly all from prosperous families; nationwide catchment area. Admission by Common Entrance at 11, 12, 13; minimum 55% mark required (in practice, rather higher). Generous scholarships; daughters of 'seniors' (former pupils) may be eligible for a means-tested bursary.

Results GCSE: virtually all gain at least 5 grades A-C. A-level (1992): creditable 66% of entries graded A or B (has been even higher).

Destinations More than 90% stay for A-levels; nearly all of these proceed to higher education (20-25 a year to Oxbridge); 40% read medicine, science or engineering.

Sport Wide range of activities on offer; very strong lacrosse; good tennis, squash. Facilities include extensive playing fields, gym, indoor pool.

Remarks Fine school for able girls; highly recommended.

WYCOMBE HIGH
Marlow Hill,
High Wycombe,
Buckinghamshire HP11 1TB
Tel (0494) 23961

Grammar (voluntary-controlled) • Girls •
Day • Ages 12-18 • 988 pupils • 316 in
sixth form
Head: Mrs Muriel Pilkington, late-40s,
appointed 1985.

Successful academic school; good music and sport.

Background Founded 1901; moved to present 27-acre site in 1956; pleasant grounds (including an open-air theatre); good, self-contained sixth-form block; some areas in need of redecoration.

Atmosphere Orderly, industrious. Lively, well-motivated pupils; hard-working, committed staff. Sixth-formers treated as college students.

The head Business-like; able manager. Oxford graduate. Married, 3 grown-up children.

The teaching Long-serving staff of 52 (10 men); styles vary from strongly traditional to innovative; big emphasis on academic pace and achievement. Most pupils take 9-10 GCSEs; maths and science (taught as 3 separate subjects) are particularly strong. All do French; German, Spanish, Latin also available; good computing; restricted facilities for design/technology. Choice of 24 subjects at A-level, including economics, geology, computing, practical music (performance and composition); about a third take maths (and half gain grade As). First-rate music: nearly a third learn an instrument; 2 orchestras, jazz and wind bands, flute ensemble, 3 choirs. Annual Shakespeare production. Good work experience and links with local business community. Well-supported Duke of Edinburgh award scheme; £10,000 raised annually for charity. Lots of exchanges with schools in France, Germany, Spain.

The pupils Predominantly from middle-class/professional homes; parents move house to be within the catchment area. Entry by tests administered by Buckinghamshire County Council, which is responsible for admissions. Nearly all in top 25% of the ability range.

Results (1992) GCSE: 99% gained at least 5 grades A-C. A-level: 46% of entries graded A or B (has been higher).

Destinations 85% stay for A-levels; 83% of these proceed to higher education (12 to Oxbridge in 1991).

Sport Very strong: good facilities, long fixture list, regular success at local and county level. Main activities: hockey (under-18 champions), netball, gymnastics, dance, tennis, athletics, swimming, basketball; badminton, volleyball, aerobics, squash, trampolining also on offer. Facilities include athletics track, outdoor pool, 13 tennis and netball courts.

Remarks High-powered, well-run school.

WYMONDHAM
Golf Links Road,
Wymondham,
Norfolk NR18 9SZ
Tel (0953) 605566

Comprehensive (grant-maintained) •
Co-educational • Boarding and day •
Ages 11-18 • 878 pupils (56% boys; 67% boarding) • 315 in sixth form • Boarding fees (1992-93), £3,726
Head: John Haden, 50, appointed September 1992.

Unusual state boarding school; bizarre accommodation; strongly traditional ethos.

Background Opened 1951 as a dual school – grammar and technical – under a single head. Astonishing collection of shabby Nissen huts (formerly a World War II military hospital) linked by roofed walkways on an 80-acre campus 12 miles south of Norwich. (School is reluctant to abandon the tin huts, which are pleasant inside and spacious.) Later additions include modern science block and handsome library. Went comprehensive 1981; achieved grant-maintained status in 1991 after fiercely resisting repeated threats of closure; now Europe's largest state boarding school. Planned expansion will increase numbers to 1,200 by 1996.

Atmosphere Traditional grammar-school ethos retained; emphasis on academic standards, self-discipline, strict uniform, no litter. Staff and pupils take great pride in the school's unusual qualities. Strong commitment to boarding; copious after-school activities; 'day boarders' can arrive at 7.30 a.m. and stay until 9 p.m. Boarding accommodation cosy, clean, well-decorated. Parents welcome to visit (best in summer – not when northerly gales are blowing).

The head New appointment; previously head (for 10 years) of King Edward VI, Louth, also a grant-maintained comprehensive. Read chemistry at Oxford; comes from a family of teachers (father was a head); first headship at 27 – of a mission school in Uganda during Idi Amin's coup (so not bothered by the challenges he faces here). Married, 2 sons.

The teaching Conventional academic approach (many long-serving, dedicated staff). Pupils set by ability in major subjects; extra help for slow learners; class sizes 25 for more able children, 15 for others. Strong maths, science, languages (French, German, Spanish – but little classics); lots of computing. Facilities generally good but design/technology, for example, is housed in a World War II mortuary. Choice of 25 subjects at A-level. Good drama and music; bands, orchestras, choirs. First-rate art; excellent computer/video/animation facilities. Extra-curricular programme includes car maintenance, aircraft restoration, cadet force and Duke of Edinburgh award scheme.

The pupils Wide range of abilities and social backgrounds, mostly from Norfolk; 35% of boarders are from Service families (mainly RAF). No admission tests; entry by previous school reports and interview to determine suitability for boarding (boarding 'need' strictly defined as being for domestic *not* behavioural or emotional reasons). More than 100 a year enter the sixth form from other schools; minimum of 5 GCSE grades A-C required.

Results (1992) GCSE: creditable 63% gained at least 5 grades A-C. A-level: 26% of entries graded A or B.

Destinations 65% continue into the sixth form; 60% of these proceed to higher education (1 or 2 a year to Oxbridge).

Sport Main games hockey, rugby, football, tennis, netball. Lavish sports centre, indoor pool, plenty of playing fields.

Remarks Most of the values and facilities (if not the buildings) associated with grander, more ancient (and more costly) establishments.

YARM

The Friarage,
Yarm,
Cleveland TS15 9EJ
Tel (0642) 786023

Independent • Boys (plus girls in sixth form) • Day • Ages 7-18 • 550 pupils (430 in senior school) • 145 in sixth form (85% boys) • Fees, £2,365-£3,950
Head: Neville Tate, 54, appointed 1978.

Broad ability range; respectable results; strong family atmosphere.

Background Founded by parents in 1978 after the council shut down the local grammar school. 18th-century mansion set in 14 wooded acres beside the River Tees. New buildings include music school, sports hall, 400-seat theatre. Ageing labs and technology block; some temporary huts.

Atmosphere Intimate, welcoming (not a stuffy school). Discipline good but unobtrusive; effective, house-based pastoral system.

The head Started as an engineer then read history at Durham; previous experience mostly in boarding schools. Shrewd judge of staff (has appointed them all). Leads school expeditions to Peru and Argentina. Unmarried.

The teaching High quality; successful blend of traditional and modern methods based on good relations between staff and pupils. Setting from the start in maths; later in modern languages, Latin, science. Strong French and German (3 staff are native speakers); all take an excellent technology course up to 14 and many continue to GCSE; computers everywhere. Long school day (9 a.m. to 4.30 p.m.); class sizes average 17 in junior school, 20 in senior school, 12-14 in sixth form. Strong art and drama; well-supported Duke of Edinburgh award scheme.

The pupils Display a natural respect for authority which can make staff almost pine for a few 'rebels'. All wear uniform (house epaulettes) but no caps – school has been careful not to invent too much tradition. Mostly from highly motivated business and professional homes; catchment area extends to North Yorkshire and Durham; buses to and from main towns from Northallerton to Middlesborough. Entry by examination at 7, 11, 13; minimum IQ 105 – roughly top 30% of the ability range. Assisted places and scholarships (including music).

Results GCSE: nearly all gain at least 5 grades A-C. A-level (1992): 42% of entries graded A or B.

Destinations Almost all continue into the sixth form; 90% of these proceed to higher education.

Sport Main games: rugby, hockey, cricket, athletics. Rowing, squash, tennis, cross-country also available. Playing fields some distance away; 4 delightful tennis courts in former walled garden.

Remarks Based on sound grammar school lines – but not hidebound by them. Well-respected locally.

Area Maps

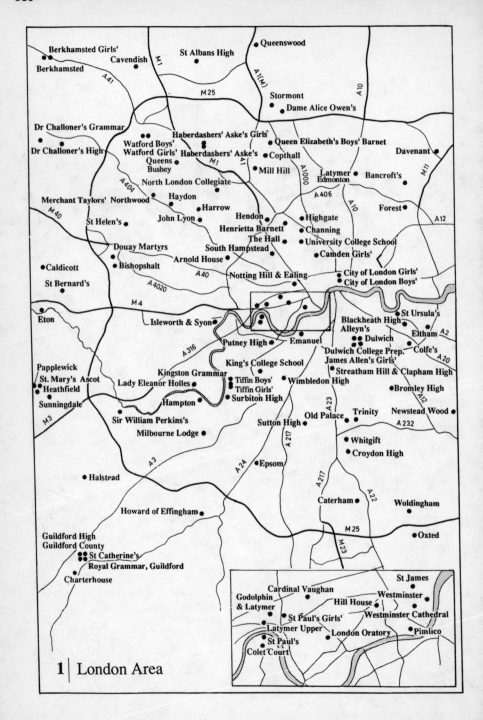

1 | London Area

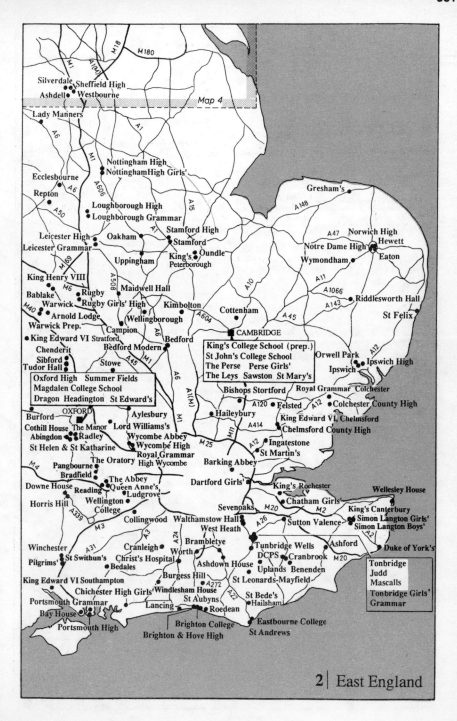

Map 4

2 | East England

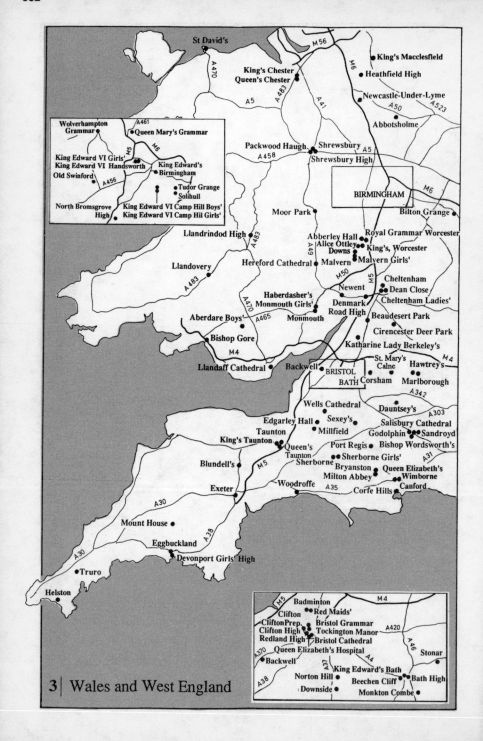

St David's

M56

King's Macclesfield
Heathfield High
M6
King's Chester
Queen's Chester
A470
A483
Newcastle-Under-Lyme
A50
A523
A5
A41
A650
Abbotsholme
Wolverhampton
Grammar
A461
Queen Mary's Grammar
Packwood Haugh
Shrewsbury
A5
Shrewsbury High
A458
King Edward VI Girls'
King Edward VI Handsworth
Old Swinford
M6
M5
A456
King Edward's
Birmingham
BIRMINGHAM
M6
Tudor Grange
Solihull
North Bromsgrove
High
King Edward VI Camp Hill Boys'
King Edward VI Camp Hil Girls'
Moor Park
Bilton Grange
Llandrindod High
A483
Abberley Hall
Alice Ottley
Downs
Royal Grammar Worcester
King's, Worcester
A49
Llandovery
Hereford Cathedral
Malvern
Malvern Girls'
A483
M50
M5
Cheltenham
Dean Close
Cheltenham Ladies'
Newent
Haberdasher's
Monmouth Girls'
A410
A465
Denmark
Road High
Beaudesert Park
Aberdare Boys'
Monmouth
Cirencester Deer Park
Bishop Gore
Katharine Lady Berkeley's
M4
St. Mary's
Calne
Hawtrey's
M4
Llandaff Cathedral
Backwell
BRISTOL
BATH
Corsham
Marlborough
A342
Wells Cathedral
Dauntsey's
A303
Edgarley Hall
Taunton
Sexey's
Millfield
Salisbury Cathedral
Godolphin
Sandroyd
King's Taunton
Port Regis
Bishop Wordsworth's
Queen's
Taunton
A37
Blundell's
M5
Sherborne
Sherborne Girls'
Bryanston
Queen Elizabeth's
Wimborne
Milton Abbey
Canford
Exeter
Woodroffe
A35
Corfe Hills
A30
Mount House
A38
Eggbuckland
Devonport Girls' High
A30
Truro
Helston

Badminton
M5
M4
Clifton
Red Maids'
CliftonPrep.
Bristol Grammar
A420
Clifton High
Tockington Manor
Redland High
Bristol Cathedral
A370
Queen Elizabeth's Hospital
A4
A46
Stonar
Backwell
A37
King Edward's Bath
Bath High
A38
Norton Hill
Beechen Cliff
Downside
Monkton Combe

3 Wales and West England

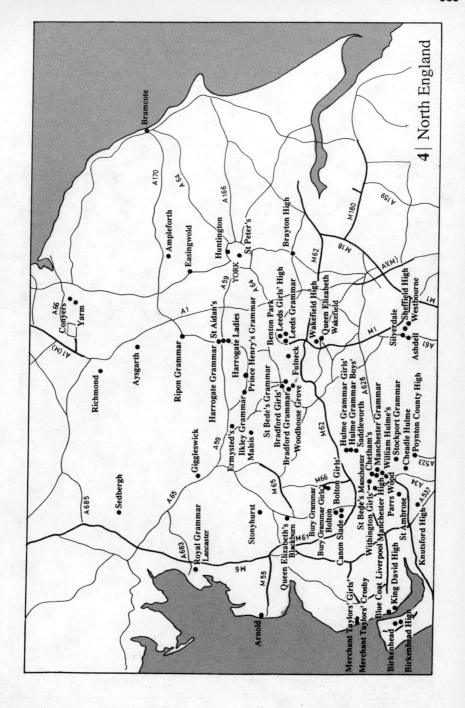

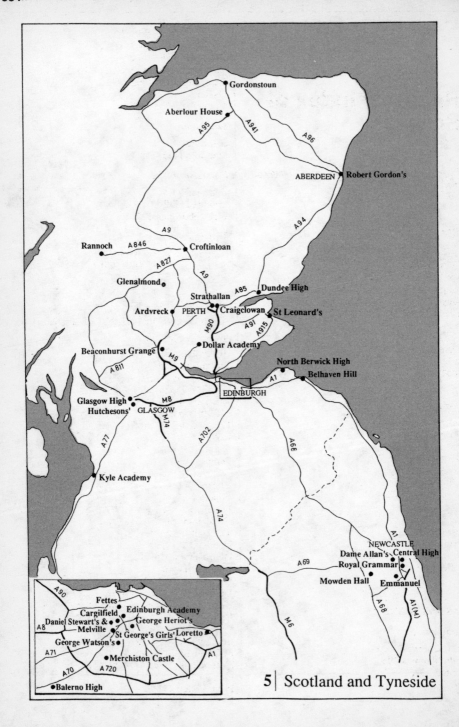

5 | Scotland and Tyneside

Regional Index of Schools

Preparatory schools are indicated by (P); map references are in bold type

Woldingham 349-50, **1**

Sussex (East and West)

Ashdown House (P) 5-6, **2**
Brambletye (P) 10, **2**
Brighton & Hove High 86-7, **2**
Brighton College 85-6, **2**
Burgess Hill 91, **2**
Chichester Girls' High 108-9, **2**
Christ's Hospital 109-10, **2**
Eastbourne 138, **2**
Lancing 207-8, **2**
Roedean 272-3, **2**
St Andrew's (P) 40, **2**
St Aubyns (P) 41, **2**
St Bede's Hailsham 297, **2**
St Leonards-Mayfield 308-9, **2**
Uplands 335, **2**
Windlesham House (P) 49-50, **2**
Worth 353-4, **2**

SOUTH WEST

Avon

Backwell 60-1, **3**
Badminton 61-2, **3**
Bath High 64-5, **3**
Beechen Cliff 69-70, **3**
Bristol Cathedral 87, **3**
Bristol Grammar 88, **3**
Clifton 112-13, **3**
Clifton (P) 13-14, **3**
Clifton High 113, **3**
Downside 134-5, **3**
King Edward's Bath 189, **3**
Monkton Combe 231-2, **3**
Norton Hill 237-8, **3**
Queen Elizabeth's Hospital 259-60, **3**
Red Maids' 268-9, **3**
Redland High 267-8, **3**
Tockington Manor (P) 46, **3**

Cornwall

Helston 171-2, **3**
Truro 331, **3**

Devon

Blundell's 80, **3**
Devonport Girls' High 128-9, **3**
Eggbuckland 141-2, **3**
Exeter 148, **3**
Mount House (P) 31-2, **3**

Dorset

Bryanston 89-90, **3**
Canford 95, **3**
Corfe Hills 118, **3**
Milton Abbey 230-1, **3**
Port Regis (P) 36-7, **3**
Queen Elizabeth's Wimborne 260, **3**
Sherborne 284-5, **3**
Sherborne Girls' 285-6, **3**
Woodroffe 352-3, **3**

Gloucestershire

Beaudesert Park (P) 7, **3**
Cheltenham 104-5, **3**
Cheltenham Ladies' 105-6, **3**
Cirencester Deer Park 110, **3**
Dean Close 127, **3**
Denmark Road High 127-8, **3**
Katharine Lady Berkeley's 187, **3**
Newent 233-4, **3**

Somerset

Edgarley Hall (P) 20, **3**
King's Taunton 202, **3**
Millfield 229, **3**
Queen's Taunton 263, **3**
Sexey's 283-4, **3**
Taunton 326-7, **3**
Wells Cathedral School 342-3, **3**

Wiltshire

Bishop Wordsworth's 77-8, **3**
Corsham 118-19, **3**
Dauntsey's 125-6, **3**
Godolphin 156-7, **3**
Hawtreys (P) 22-3, **3**
Marlborough 223-4, **3**
St Mary's Calne 311, **3**
Salisbury Cathedral School (P) 38-9, **3**
Sandroyd (P) 39, **3**
Stonar 319-20, **3**

WEST MIDLANDS

Herefordshire and Worcestershire

Abberley Hall (P) 1, **3**
Alice Ottley 54-5, **3**
The Downs (P) 17, **3**
Hereford Cathedral School 174, **3**
King's Worcester 203, **3**
Malvern 220, **3**
Malvern Girls' 220-1, **3**
North Bromsgrove High 236, **3**
Old Swinford 243-4, **3**

Index of Schools

Preparatory schools are indicated by (P); map references are in bold type